Study Guide

Principles of Economics

FOURTH EDITION

N. Gregory Mankiw

Harvard University

Prepared by

David R. Hakes

University of Northern Iowa

THOMSON

SOUTH-WESTERN

Australia · Brazil · Canada · Mexico · Singapore · Spain · United Kingdom · United States

THOMSON
™
SOUTH-WESTERN

Study Guide
Principles of Economics, 4ᵗʰ Edition

N. Gregory Mankiw
Prepared by David R. Hakes

VP/Editorial Director:
Jack W. Calhoun

Editor-in-Chief:
Alex von Rosenberg

Publisher:
Steve Momper

Sr. Acquisitions Editor:
Mike Worls

Developmental Editor:
Jane Tufts

Contributing Editors:
Sarah K. Dorger
Jennifer E. Baker

Sr. Marketing Manager:
Brian Joyner

Assoc. Marketing Communications Manager:
Sarah Greber

Sr. Production Project Manager:
Emily S. Gross

Manager of Technology, Editorial:
Vicky True

Technology Project Editor:
Dana Cowden

Web Coordinator:
Karen Schaffer

Sr. Manufacturing Coordinator:
Sandee Milewski

Production House:
OffCenter Concept House

Printer:
Darby Printing
Atlanta, GA

Assistant Editor:
Erin Berger

Ancillary Coordinator:
Erin M. Donohoe

Art Director:
Michelle Kunkler

Production Artist:
Patti Hudepohl

Internal and Cover Designer:
Stratton Design

Cover Illustration:
Tate Gallery, London/Art Resource, NY

Internal Illustrator:
William Low/Cobalt Illustration Services

For more information about our products,
contact us at:

Thomson Learning Academic Resource
Center

1-800-423-0563

Thomson Higher Education
5191 Natorp Boulevard
Mason, OH 45040
USA

One must learn by doing the thing;
For though you think you know it
You have no certainty, until you try.

Sophocles, c. 496–406 B.C.
Greek playwright
Trachiniae

Preface

This *Study Guide* accompanies N. Gregory Mankiw's *Principles of Economics*, Fourth Edition. It was written with only one audience in mind—you, the student.

Your time is scarce. To help you use it efficiently, this *Study Guide* focuses strictly on the material presented in Mankiw's *Principles of Economics*, Fourth Edition. It does not introduce extraneous material.

Objectives of the Study Guide

There are three broad objectives to the *Study Guide*. First, the *Study Guide* reinforces the text and improves your understanding of the material presented in the text. Second, it provides you with experience in using economic theories and tools to solve actual economic problems. That is, this *Study Guide* bridges the gap between economic concepts and economic problem solving. This may be the most important objective of the *Study Guide* because those students who find economics inherently logical often think that they are prepared for exams just by reading the text or attending lectures. However, it is one thing to watch an economist solve a problem in class and another thing altogether to solve a problem alone. There is simply no substitute for hands-on experience. Third, the *Study Guide* includes a self-test to validate areas of successful learning and to highlight areas needing improvement.

It is unlikely that you will truly enjoy any area of study if you fail to understand the material or if you lack confidence when taking tests over the material. It is my hope that this *Study Guide* improves your understanding of economics and improves your test performance so that you are able to enjoy economics as much as I do.

Organization of the Study Guide

Each chapter in the *Study Guide* corresponds to a chapter in Mankiw's *Principles of Economics*. Each chapter is divided into the following sections:

- The Chapter Overview begins with a description of the purpose of the chapter and how it fits into the larger framework of the text. Following this context and purpose section are learning objectives, a section-by-section Chapter Review, and some helpful hints for understanding the material. The Chapter Overview ends with terms and definitions. This part is particularly important because it is impossible for the text to communicate information to you or for you to communicate information to your instructor on your exams without the use of a common economic vocabulary.

- Problems and Short-Answer Questions provide hands-on experience with problems based on the material presented in the text. The practice problems are generally multiple-step problems while the short-answer questions are generally based on a single issue.

- The Self-Test is composed of 15 True/False questions and 20 Multiple-Choice questions.

- The Advanced Critical Thinking section is a real-world problem that employs the economic reasoning and tools developed in the chapter. It is an applied story problem.

- Solutions are provided for all questions in the *Study Guide*. Explanations are also provided for false responses to True/False questions in the Self-Test.

Use of the Study Guide

I hesitate to suggest a method for using this *Study Guide* because how one best uses a study guide is largely a personal matter. It depends on your preferences and talents and on your instructor's approach to the material. I will, however, discuss a few possible approaches, and trial and error may help you sort out an approach that best suits you.

Some students prefer to read an entire chapter in the text prior to reading the *Study Guide*. Others prefer to read a section in the text and then read the corresponding section in the Chapter Overview portion of the *Study Guide*. This second method may help you focus your attention on the most important aspects of each section in the text. Some students who feel particularly confident after reading the text may choose to take the Self-Test immediately. I do not generally support this approach. I suggest that you complete all of the Practice Problems and Short-Answer Questions before you attempt the Self-Test. You will receive more accurate feedback from the Self-Test if you are well prepared prior to taking it.

A study guide is not a substitute for a text any more than *Cliff Notes* is a substitute for a classic novel. Use this *Study Guide* in conjunction with Mankiw's *Principles of Economics*, not in place of it.

Final Thoughts

All of the problems and questions in this *Study Guide* have been checked by a number of accuracy reviewers. However, if you find a mistake, or if you have comments or suggestions for future editions, please feel free to contact me via e-mail at hakes@uni.edu.

Acknowledgments

I would like to thank Greg Mankiw for having written such a well thought-out text that it made writing the *Study Guide* a truly enjoyable task. I thank Erin Berger, the Developmental Editor, for keeping things on schedule. I thank Sheryl Nelson, the Project Editor, for designing the layout and preparing the manuscript. Sandy Mann copyedited the manuscript and Carolyn Crabtree proofread the manuscript. Ken McCormick, a friend and colleague, provided constructive counsel throughout the project.

Finally, I would like to thank my family for being patient and understanding during the time I spent working on this *Study Guide*.

David R. Hakes
University of Northern Iowa
February 2006

COMPARATIVE TABLE OF CONTENTS

Contents

1

Ten Principles of Economics

CHAPTER OVERVIEW

Context and Purpose

Chapter 1 is the first chapter in a three-chapter section that serves as the introduction to the text. Chapter 1 introduces ten fundamental principles on which the study of economics is based. In a broad sense, the rest of the text is an elaboration on these ten principles. Chapter 2 will develop how economists approach problems, while Chapter 3 will explain how individuals and countries gain from trade.

The purpose of Chapter 1 is to lay out ten economic principles that will serve as building blocks for the rest of the text. The ten principles can be grouped into three categories: how people make decisions, how people interact, and how the economy works as a whole. Throughout the text, references will be made repeatedly to these ten principles.

Chapter Review

Introduction Households and society face decisions about how to allocate scarce resources. Resources are scarce in that we have fewer resources than we wish. **Economics** is the study of how society manages its scarce resources. Economists study how people make decisions about buying and selling and saving and investing. We study how people interact with one another in markets where prices are determined and quantities are exchanged. We also study the economy as a whole when we concern ourselves with total income, unemployment, and inflation.

This chapter addresses ten principles of economics. The text will refer to these principles throughout. The ten principles are grouped into three categories: how people make decisions, how people interact, and how the economy works as a whole.

How People Make Decisions

- **People face trade-offs:** Economists often say, "There is no such thing as a free lunch." This means that there are always trade-offs—to get more of something we like, we have to give up something else that we like. For example, if you spend money on dinner and a movie, you won't be able to spend it on new clothes. Socially, we face trade-offs as a group. For example, there is the classic trade-off between "guns and butter." That is, if we decide to spend more on national defense (guns), then we will have less to spend on social programs (butter). There is also a social trade-off between **efficiency** (getting the most from our scarce resources) and **equity** (benefits being distributed fairly across society). Policies such as taxes and welfare make incomes more equal, but these policies reduce returns to hard work, and thus, the economy doesn't produce as much. As a result, when the government tries to cut the pie into more equal pieces, the pie gets smaller.

- **The cost of something is what you give up to get it:** The **opportunity cost** of an item is what you give up to get that item. It is the true cost of the item. The opportunity cost of going to college obviously includes your tuition payment. It also includes the value of your time that you could have spent working, valued at your potential wage. It would exclude your room and board payment because you have to eat and sleep whether you are in school or not.

- **Rational people think at the margin:** **Rational people** systematically do the best they can to achieve their objectives. **Marginal changes** are incremental changes to an existing plan. Rational decision makers only proceed with an action if the marginal benefit exceeds the marginal cost. For example, you should only attend school for another year if the benefits from that year of schooling exceed the cost of attending that year. A farmer should produce another bushel of corn only if the benefit (price received) exceeds the cost of producing it.

- **People respond to incentives:** An **incentive** is something that induces a person to act. Since rational people weigh marginal costs and marginal benefits of activities, they will respond when these costs or benefits change. For example, when the price of automobiles rises, buyers have an incentive to buy fewer cars while automobile producers have an incentive to hire more workers and produce more autos. Public policy can alter the costs or benefits of activities. For example, a luxury tax on expensive boats raises the price and discourages purchases. Some policies have unintended consequences because they alter behavior in a manner that was not predicted.

How People Interact

- **Trade can make everyone better off:** Trade is not a contest where one wins and one loses. Trade can make each trader better off. Trade allows each trader to specialize in what they do best, whether it be farming, building, or manufacturing, and trade their output for the output of other efficient producers. This is as true for countries as it is for individuals.

- **Markets are usually a good way to organize economic activity:** In a **market economy,** the decisions about what goods and services to produce, how much to produce, and who gets to consume them are made by millions of firms and households. Firms and households, guided by self-interest, interact in the marketplace where prices and quantities are determined. While this may appear like chaos, Adam Smith made the famous observation in the *Wealth of Nations* in 1776 that self-interested households and firms interact in markets and generate desirable social outcomes as if guided by an "invisible hand." These optimal social outcomes were not their original intent. The prices generated by their competitive activity signal the value of costs and benefits to producers and consumers, whose activities usually maximize the welfare of society. Alternatively, the prices dictated by central planners contain no information on costs and benefits, and therefore, these prices fail to efficiently guide economic activity. Prices also fail to efficiently guide economic activity when governments distort prices with taxes or restrict price movements with price controls.

- **Governments can sometimes improve market outcomes:** Government must first protect **property rights** in order for markets to work. In addition, government can sometimes intervene in the market to improve efficiency or equity. When markets fail to allocate resources efficiently, there has been **market failure.** There are many different sources of market failure. An **externality** is when the actions of one person affect the well-being of a bystander. Pollution is a standard example. **Market power** is when a single person or group can influence the price. In these cases, the government may be able to intervene and improve economic efficiency. The government may also intervene to improve equity with income taxes and welfare. Sometimes well-intentioned policy intervention has unintended consequences.

How the Economy as a Whole Works

- **A country's standard of living depends on its ability to produce goods and services:** There is great variation in average incomes across countries at a point in time and within the same country over time. These differences in incomes and standards of living are largely attributable to differences in productivity. **Productivity** is the amount of goods and services produced by each hour of a worker's time. As a result, public policy intended to improve standards of living should improve education, generate more and better tools, and improve access to current technology.

- **Prices rise when the government prints too much money: Inflation** is an increase in the overall level of prices in the economy. High inflation is costly to the economy. Large and persistent inflation is caused by rapid growth in the quantity of money. Policymakers wishing to keep inflation low should maintain slow growth in the quantity of money.

- **Society faces a short-run trade-off between inflation and unemployment:** In the short run, an increase in the quantity of money stimulates spending, which raises both prices and production. The increase in production requires more hiring, which reduces unemployment. Thus, in the short run, an increase in inflation tends to reduce unemployment, causing a trade-off between inflation and unemployment. The trade-off is temporary but can last for several years. Understanding this trade-off is important for understanding the fluctuations in economic activity known as the **business cycle.** In the short run, policymakers may be able to affect the mix of inflation and unemployment by changing government spending, taxes, and the quantity of money.

Helpful Hints

1. Place yourself in the story. Throughout the text, most economic situations will be composed of economic actors—buyers and sellers, borrowers and lenders, firms and workers, and so on. When you are asked to address how any economic actor would respond to economic incentives, place yourself in the story as the buyer or the seller, the borrower or the lender, the producer or the consumer. Don't think of yourself always as the buyer (a natural tendency) or always as the seller. You will find that your role-playing will usually produce the right response once you learn to think like an economist—which is the topic of the next chapter.

2. Trade is not a zero-sum game. Some people see an exchange in terms of winners and losers. Their reaction to trade is that, after the sale, if the seller is happy, the buyer must be sad because the seller must have taken something from the buyer. That is, they view trade as a zero-sum game where what one gains the other must have lost. They fail to see that both parties to a voluntary transaction gain because each party is allowed to specialize in what it can produce most efficiently and then trade for items that are produced more efficiently by others. Nobody loses, because trade is voluntary. Therefore, a government policy that limits trade reduces the potential gains from trade.

3. An externality can be positive. Because the classic example of an externality is pollution, it is easy to think of an externality as a cost that lands on a bystander. However, an externality can be positive in that it can be a benefit that lands on a bystander. For example, education is often cited as a product that emits a positive externality because when your neighbor educates herself, she is likely to be more reasonable, responsible, productive, and politically astute. In short, she is a better neighbor. Positive externalities, just as much as negative externalities, may be a reason for the government to intervene to promote efficiency.

Terms and Definitions

Choose a definition for each key term.

Key Terms

_____ Scarcity

_____ Economics

_____ Efficiency

_____ Equity

_____ Rational

_____ Opportunity cost

_____ Marginal changes

_____ Incentive

_____ Market economy

_____ Property rights

_____ "Invisible hand"

_____ Market failure

_____ Externality

_____ Market power

_____ Monopoly

_____ Productivity

_____ Inflation

_____ Business cycle

Definitions

1. The property of distributing economic prosperity fairly among society's members

2. A situation in which the market fails to allocate resources efficiently

3. Limited resources and unlimited wants

4. The amount of goods and services produced per hour by a worker

5. The case in which there is only one seller in the market

6. The principle that self-interested market participants may unknowingly maximize the welfare of society as a whole

7. The property of society getting the most from its scarce resources

8. An economic system where interaction of households and firms in markets determines the allocation of resources

9. Fluctuations in economic activity

10. When one person's actions have an impact on a bystander

11. An increase in the overall level of prices

12. Incremental adjustments to an existing plan

13. Study of how society manages its scarce resources

14. Whatever is given up to get something else

15. The ability of an individual or group to substantially influence market prices

16. Something that induces a person to act

17. The ability of an individual to own and exercise control over scarce resources

18. Systematically and purposefully doing the best you can to achieve your objectives

PROBLEMS AND SHORT-ANSWER QUESTIONS

Practice Problems

1. People respond to incentives. Governments can alter incentives and, hence, be-havior with public policy. However, sometimes public policy generates unin-tended consequences by producing results that were not anticipated. For each of the following public policies, determine which result was likely the intended result and which was the unintended consequence.

    a. The government raises the minimum wage to $10 per hour. Some workers find jobs at the higher wage making these workers better off. Some workers find no job at all because few firms want to hire low-productivity workers at this high wage.

    _____

    _____

    _____

    b. The government places rent controls on apartments restricting rent to $300 per month. Few landlords are willing to produce an apartment at this price causing more homelessness. Some low-income renters are able to rent an apartment more cheaply.

    _____

    _____

    _____

    c. The government raises the tax on gasoline by $2 per gallon. The deficit is reduced, and people economize on their use of gasoline. There is a boom in bicycle sales.

    _____

    _____

    _____

    d. The government declares marijuana and cocaine illegal. The price of illegal drugs increases, creating more gangs and gang warfare. Due to the high price of illegal drugs, fewer street drugs are consumed.

    _____

    _____

    _____

    e. The government prohibits the killing of wolves. The wolf population increas-es. Sheep and cattle herds suffer losses.

    _____

    _____

    f. The government bans imports of sugar from South America. South American sugar beet growers can't repay their loans to U.S. banks and turn to more profitable crops such as coca leaves and marijuana. U.S. sugar beet growers avoid a financial crisis.

_____

_____

_____

2. Opportunity cost is what you give up to get an item. Since there is no such thing as a free lunch, what would likely be given up to obtain each of the items listed below?

a. Susan can work full time or go to college. She chooses college.

_____

_____

b. Susan can work full time or go to college. She chooses work.

_____

_____

c. Farmer Jones has 100 acres of land. He can plant corn, which yields 100 bushels per acre, or he can plant beans, which yield 40 bushels per acre. He chooses to plant corn.

_____

_____

d. Farmer Jones has 100 acres of land. He can plant corn, which yields 100 bushels per acre, or he can plant beans, which yield 40 bushels per acre. He chooses to plant beans.

_____

_____

e. In *a* and *b* above and *c* and *d* above, which is the opportunity cost of which—college for work or work for college? corn for beans or beans for corn?

_____

_____

Short-Answer Questions

1. Is air scarce? Is clean air scarce?

_____

_____

2. What is the opportunity cost of saving some of your paycheck?

_____

_____

3. Why is there a trade-off between equity and efficiency?

    _____

    _____

    _____

4. Water is necessary for life. Diamonds are not. Is the marginal benefit of an additional glass of water greater or lesser than an additional one-carat diamond? Why?

    _____

    _____

    _____

5. Your car needs to be repaired. You have already paid $500 to have the transmission fixed, but it still doesn't work properly. You can sell your car "as is" for $2,000. If your car were fixed, you could sell it for $2,500. Your car can be fixed with a guarantee for another $300. Should you repair your car? Why?

    _____

    _____

6. Why do you think air bags have reduced deaths from auto crashes less than we had hoped?

    _____

    _____

7. Suppose one country is better at producing agricultural products (because they have more fertile land), while another country is better at producing manufactured goods (because they have a better educational system and more engineers). If each country produced their specialty and traded, would there be more or less total output than if each country produced all of their agricultural and manufacturing needs? Why?

    _____

    _____

    _____

8. In the _Wealth of Nations_, Adam Smith said, "It is not from the benevolence of the butcher, the brewer, or the baker that we expect our dinner, but from their regard to their own interest." What do you think he meant?

    _____

    _____

    _____

9. If we save more and use it to build more physical capital, productivity will rise and we will have rising standards of living in the future. What is the opportunity cost of future growth?

_____

_____ _

10. If the government printed twice as much money, what do you think would happen to prices and output if the economy were already producing at maximum capacity?

_____

_____

_____

11. A goal for a society is to distribute resources equitably or fairly. How would you distribute resources if everyone were equally talented and worked equally hard? What if people had different talents and some people worked hard, while others did not?

_____

_____

12. Who is more self-interested, the buyer or the seller?

_____

_____

SELF-TEST

True/False Questions

_____   1. When the government redistributes income with taxes and welfare, the economy becomes more efficient.

_____   2. When economists say, "There is no such thing as a free lunch," they mean that all economic decisions involve trade-offs.

_____   3. Adam Smith's "invisible hand" concept describes how corporate business reaches into the pockets of consumers like an "invisible hand."

_____   4. Rational people act only when the marginal benefit of the action exceeds the marginal cost.

_____   5. The United States will benefit economically if we eliminate trade with Asian countries because we will be forced to produce more of our own cars and clothes.

_____   6. When a jet flies overhead, the noise it generates is an externality.

_____   7. A tax on liquor raises the price of liquor and provides an incentive for consumers to drink more.

_____ 8.   An unintended consequence of public support for higher education is that low tuition provides an incentive for many people to attend state universities even if they have no desire to learn anything.

_____ 9.   Sue is better at cleaning, and Bob is better at cooking. It will take fewer hours to eat and clean if Bob specializes in cooking and Sue specializes in cleaning than if they share the household duties evenly.

_____ 10. High and persistent inflation is caused by excessive growth in the quantity of money in the economy.

_____ 11. In the short run, a reduction in inflation tends to cause a reduction in unemployment.

_____ 12. An auto manufacturer should continue to produce additional autos as long as the firm is profitable, even if the cost of the additional units exceeds the price received.

_____ 13. An individual farmer is likely to have market power in the market for wheat.

_____ 14. To a student, the opportunity cost of going to a basketball game would include the price of the ticket and the value of the time that could have been spent studying.

_____ 15. Workers in the United States have a relatively high standard of living because the United States has a relatively high minimum wage.

Multiple-Choice Questions

1. Which of the following involve a trade-off?
    a. buying a new car
    b. going to college
    c. watching a football game on Saturday afternoon
    d. taking a nap
    e. All of the above involve trade-offs.

2. Trade-offs are required because wants are unlimited and resources are
    a. efficient.
    b. economical.
    c. scarce.
    d. unlimited.
    e. marginal.

3. Economics is the study of how
    a. to fully satisfy our unlimited wants.
    b. society manages its scarce resources.
    c. to reduce our wants until we are satisfied.
    d. to avoid having to make trade-offs.
    e. society manages its unlimited resources.

4. A rational person does not act unless
    a. the action makes money for the person.
    b. the action is ethical.
    c. the action produces marginal costs that exceed marginal benefits.
    d. the action produces marginal benefits that exceed marginal costs.
    e. None of the above is true.

5. Raising taxes and increasing welfare payments
    a. proves that there is such a thing as a free lunch.
    b. reduces market power.
    c. improves efficiency at the expense of equity.
    d. improves equity at the expense of efficiency.
    e. does none of the above.

6. Suppose you find $20. If you choose to use the $20 to go to the football game, your opportunity cost of going to the game is
   a. nothing, because you found the money.
   b. $20 (because you could have used the $20 to buy other things).
   c. $20 (because you could have used the $20 to buy other things) plus the value of your time spent at the game.
   d. $20 (because you could have used the $20 to buy other things) plus the value of your time spent at the game, plus the cost of the dinner you purchased at the game.
   e. none of the above.

7. Foreign trade
   a. allows a country to have a greater variety of products at a lower cost than if it tried to produce everything at home.
   b. allows a country to avoid trade-offs.
   c. makes a country more equitable.
   d. increases the scarcity of resources.
   e. is none of the above.

8. Since people respond to incentives, we would expect that if the average salary of accountants increases by 50 percent while the average salary of teachers increases by 20 percent,
   a. students will shift majors from education to accounting.
   b. students will shift majors from accounting to education.
   c. fewer students will attend college.
   d. None of the above is true.

9. Which of the following activities is most likely to produce an externality?
   a. A student sits at home and watches television.
   b. A student has a party in her dorm room.
   c. A student reads a novel for pleasure.
   d. A student eats a hamburger in the student union.

10. Which of the following products would be least capable of producing an externality?
    a. cigarettes
    b. stereo equipment
    c. inoculations against disease
    d. education
    e. food

11. Which of the following situations describes the greatest market power?
    a. a farmer's impact on the price of corn
    b. Volvo's impact on the price of autos
    c. Microsoft's impact on the price of desktop operating systems
    d. a student's impact on college tuition

12. Which of the following statements is true about a market economy?
    a. Market participants act as if guided by an "invisible hand" to produce outcomes that maximize social welfare.
    b. Taxes help prices communicate costs and benefits to producers and consumers.
    c. With a large enough computer, central planners could guide production more efficiently than markets.
    d. The strength of a market system is that it tends to distribute resources evenly across consumers.

13. Workers in the United States enjoy a high standard of living because
    a. unions in the United States keep the wage high.
    b. we have protected our industry from foreign competition.
    c. the United States has a high minimum wage.
    d. workers in the United States are highly productive.
    e. None of the above is true.

14. High and persistent inflation is caused by
    a. unions increasing wages too much.
    b. OPEC raising the price of oil too much.
    c. governments increasing the quantity of money too much.
    d. regulations raising the cost of production too much.

15. In the short run,
    a. an increase in inflation temporarily increases unemployment.
    b. a decrease in inflation temporarily increases unemployment.
    c. inflation and unemployment are unrelated.
    d. the business cycle has been eliminated.
    e. None of the above is true.

16. An increase in the price of beef provides
    a. information that tells consumers to buy more beef.
    b. information that tells consumers to buy less pork.
    c. information that tells producers to produce more beef.
    d. no information because prices in a market system are managed by planning boards.

17. You have spent $1,000 building a hot-dog stand based on estimates of sales of $2,000. The hot-dog stand is nearly completed, but now you estimate total sales to be only $800. You can complete the hot-dog stand for another $300. Should you complete the hot-dog stand? (Assume that the hot dogs are costless to you.)
    a. Yes.
    b. No.
    c. There is not enough information to answer this question.

18. Referring to question 17, your decision rule should be to complete the hot-dog stand as long as the cost to complete the stand is less than
    a. $100.
    b. $300.
    c. $500.
    d. $800.
    e. none of the above.

19. Which of the following is not part of the opportunity cost of going on vacation?
    a. the money you could have made if you had stayed home and worked
    b. the money you spent on food
    c. the money you spent on airline tickets
    d. the money you spent on a Broadway show

20. Productivity can be increased by
    a. raising minimum wages.
    b. raising union wages.
    c. improving the education of workers.
    d. restricting trade with foreign countries.

ADVANCED CRITICAL THINKING

Suppose your university decides to lower the cost of parking on campus by reducing the price of a parking permit from $200 per semester to $5 per semester.

1. What do you think would happen to the number of students desiring to park their cars on campus?

    _____

    _____

2. What do you think would happen to the amount of time it would take to find a parking place?

    _____

    _____

3. Thinking in terms of opportunity cost, would the lower price of a parking permit necessarily lower the true cost of parking?

    _____

    _____

4. Would the opportunity cost of parking be the same for students with no outside employment and students with jobs earning $15 per hour?

    _____

    _____

    _____

SOLUTIONS

Terms and Definitions

_3_ Scarcity

_13_ Economics

_7_ Efficiency

_1_ Equity

_18_ Rational

_14_ Opportunity cost

_12_ Marginal changes

_16_ Incentive

_8_ Market economy

_17_ Property rights

_6_ "Invisible hand"

_2_ Market failure

_10_ Externality

_15_ Market power

_5_ Monopoly

_4_ Productivity

_11_ Inflation

_9_ Business cycle

Practice Problems

1. a. Intended: Raise the wage of low-productivity workers. Unintended: Some workers are unemployed at the higher wage.

   b. Intended: Low-income renters get a cheap apartment. Unintended: Some people find no apartment at all causing more homelessness.

   c. Intended: Reduce the deficit and use less gasoline. Unintended: Bicycle sales increase.

   d. Intended: Fewer street drugs are consumed. Unintended: More gangs and gang warfare.

   e. Intended: Increase the wolf population. Unintended: Damage to sheep and cattle herds.

   f. Intended: Improve the financial condition of U.S. sugar beet growers. Unintended: Cause South American growers to grow marijuana and coca leaves.

2. a. Susan gives up income from work (and must pay tuition).

   b. Susan gives up a college degree and the increase in income through life that it would have brought her (but doesn't have to pay tuition).

   c. Farmer Jones gives up 4,000 bushels of beans.

   d. Farmer Jones gives up 10,000 bushels of corn.

   e. Each is the opportunity cost of the other, because each decision requires giving something up.

Short-Answer Questions

1. No, you don't have to give up anything to get air. Yes, you can't have as much clean air as you want without giving up something to get it (pollution equipment on cars, etc.).

2. The items you could have enjoyed had you spent that portion of your paycheck (current consumption).

3. Taxes and welfare make us more equal but reduce incentives for hard work, lowering total output.

4. The marginal benefit of another glass of water is generally lower because we have so much water that one more glass is of little value. The opposite is true for diamonds.

5. Yes, because the marginal benefit of fixing the car is $2,500 − $2,000 = $500, and the marginal cost is $300. The original repair payment is not relevant.

6. The cost of an accident was lowered. This changed incentives, so people drive faster and have more accidents.

7. There would be more total output if the two countries specialize and trade because each is doing what it does most efficiently.

8. The butcher, brewer, and baker produce the best food possible, not out of kindness, but because it is in their best interest to do so. Self-interest can maximize social welfare.

9. We must give up consumption today.

10. Spending would double, but since the quantity of output would remain the same, prices would double.

11. Fairness would require that everyone get an equal share because they were equally talented and worked equally hard. Fairness would require that people not get an equal share because they were not equally talented and did not work equally hard.

12. They are equally self-interested. The seller will sell to the highest bidder, and the buyer will buy from the lowest offer.

True/False Questions

1. F; the economy becomes less efficient because it decreases the incentive to work hard.

2. T

3. F; the "invisible hand" refers to how markets guide self-interested people to create desirable social outcomes.

4. T

5. F; all countries gain from voluntary trade.

6. T

7. F; higher prices reduce the quantity demanded.

8. T

9. T

10. T

11. F; a reduction in inflation tends to raise unemployment.

12. F; a manufacturer should produce as long as the marginal benefit exceeds the marginal cost.

13. F; a single farmer is too small to influence the market.

14. T

15. F; workers in the United States have a high standard of living because they are productive.

Multiple-Choice Questions

1. e
2. c
3. b
4. d
5. d
6. c
7. a
8. a
9. b
10. e
11. c
12. a
13. d
14. c
15. b
16. c
17. a
18. d
19. b
20. c

Advanced Critical Thinking

1. More students would wish to park on campus.
2. It would take much longer to find a parking place.
3. No, because we would have to factor in the value of our time spent looking for a parking place.
4. No. Students that could be earning money working are giving up more while looking for a parking place. Therefore, their opportunity cost is higher.

Thinking Like an Economist

CHAPTER OVERVIEW

Context and Purpose

Chapter 2 is the second chapter in a three-chapter section that serves as the introduction of the text. Chapter 1 introduced ten principles of economics that will be revisited throughout the text. Chapter 2 develops how economists approach problems, while Chapter 3 will explain how individuals and countries gain from trade.

The purpose of Chapter 2 is to familiarize you with how economists approach economic problems. With practice, you will learn how to approach similar problems in this dispassionate systematic way. You will see how economists employ the scientific method, the role of assumptions in model building, and the application of two specific economic models. You will also learn the important distinction between two roles economists can play: as scientists when we try to explain the economic world and as policymakers when we try to improve it.

Chapter Review

Introduction Like other fields of study, economics has its own jargon and way of thinking. It is necessary to learn the special language of economics, because knowledge of the economic vocabulary will help you communicate with precision to others about economic issues. This chapter will also provide an overview of how economists look at the world.

The Economist as Scientist

While economists don't use test tubes or telescopes, they are scientists because they employ the *scientific method*—the dispassionate and objective development and testing of theories.

The scientific method: observation, theory, and more observation: Just as in other sciences, an economist observes an event, develops a theory, and collects data to test the theory. An economist observes inflation, creates a theory that excessive growth in money causes inflation, and then collects data on money growth and inflation to see if there is a relationship. Collecting data to test economic theories is difficult, however, because economists usually cannot create data from experiments.

That is, economists cannot manipulate the economy just to test a theory. Therefore, economists often use data gathered from historical economic events.

The role of assumptions: Assumptions are made to make the world easier to understand. A physicist assumes an object is falling in a vacuum when measuring acceleration due to gravity. This assumption is reasonably accurate for a marble but not for a beach ball. An economist may assume that prices are fixed (can't be changed) or may assume that prices are flexible (can move up or down in response to market pressures). Since prices often cannot be changed quickly (the menu in a restaurant is expensive to change) but can be changed easily over time, it is reasonable for economists to assume that prices are fixed in the short run but flexible in the long run. The art of scientific thinking is deciding which assumptions to make.

Economic models: Biology teachers employ plastic models of the human body. They are simpler than the actual human body but that is what makes them useful. Economists use economic models that are composed of diagrams and equations. Economic models are based on assumptions and are simplifications of economic reality.

Our first model: the circular-flow diagram: The **circular-flow diagram** shows the flow of goods and services, factors of production, and monetary payments between households and firms. Households sell the factors of production, such as land, labor, and capital to firms, in the market for factors of production. In exchange, the households receive wages, rent, and profit. Households use these dollars to buy goods and services from firms in the market for goods and services. The firms use this revenue to pay for the factors of production, and so on. This is a simplified model of the entire economy. This version of the circular-flow diagram has been simplified because it excludes international trade and the government.

Our second model: the production possibilities frontier: A **production possibilities frontier** is a graph that shows the combinations of output the economy can possibly produce given the available factors of production and the available production technology. It is drawn assuming the economy produces only two goods. This model demonstrates the following economic principles:

- If the economy is operating on the production possibilities frontier, it is operating *efficiently* because it is producing a mix of output that is the maximum possible from the resources available.

- Points inside the curve are, therefore, *inefficient*. Points outside the curve are currently unattainable.

- If the economy is operating on the production possibilities frontier, we can see the *trade-offs* society faces. To produce more of one good, it must produce less of the other. The amount of one good given up when producing more of another good is the *opportunity cost* of the additional production.

- The production possibilities frontier is bowed outward because the opportunity cost of producing more of a good increases as we near maximum production of that good. This is because we use resources better suited toward production of the other good in order to continue to expand production of the first good.

- A technological advance in production shifts the production possibilities frontier outward. This is a demonstration of *economic growth.*

Microeconomics and Macroeconomics   Economics is studied on various levels. **Microeconomics** is the study of how households and firms make decisions and how they interact in specific markets. **Macroeconomics** is the study of economy-wide phenomena such as the federal deficit, the rate of unemployment, and policies to improve our standard of living. Microeconomics and macroeconomics are related because changes in the overall economy arise from decisions of millions of individuals. Although related, the methods employed in microeconomics and macroeconomics differ enough that they are often taught in separate courses.

The Economist as Policy Advisor

When economists attempt to explain the world as it is, they act as scientists. When economists attempt to improve the world, they act as policy advisors. Correspondingly, **positive statements** describe the world *as it is*, while **normative statements** prescribe how the world *ought to be.* Positive statements can be confirmed or refuted with evidence. Normative statements involve values (ethics, religion, political philosophy) as well as facts.

For example, "Money growth causes inflation" is a positive statement (of a scientist). "The government ought to reduce inflation" is a normative statement (of a policy advisor). The two statements are related because evidence about whether money causes inflation might help us decide what tool the government should use if it chooses to reduce inflation.

Economists act as policy advisors to the government in many different areas. The president is advised by economists on the Council of Economic Advisers, the Department of the Treasury, the Department of Labor, and the Department of Justice. Congress is advised by economists from the Congressional Budget Office and the Federal Reserve.

Why Economists Disagree

There are two reasons why economists have a reputation for giving conflicting advice to policymakers.

- Economists may have different scientific judgments. That is, economists may disagree about the validity of alternative positive theories regarding how the world works. For example, economists differ in their views of the sensitivity of household saving to changes in the after-tax return to saving.

- Economists may have different values. That is, economists may have different normative views about what policy should try to accomplish. For example, economists differ in their views of whether taxes should be used to redistribute income.

In reality, although there are legitimate disagreements among economists on many issues, there is tremendous agreement on many basic principles of economics.

Let's Get Going

In the next chapter, we will begin to apply the ideas and methods of economics. As you begin to think like an economist, you will use a variety of skills—mathematics, history, politics, philosophy—with the objectivity of a scientist.

Helpful Hints

1. Opportunity costs are usually not constant along a production possibilities frontier. Notice that the production possibilities frontier shown in Exhibit 1 is bowed outward. It shows the production trade-offs for an economy that produces only paper and pencils.

    If we start at the point where the economy is using all of its resources to produce paper, producing 100 units of pencils only requires a trade-off or an opportunity cost of 25 units of paper (point A to point B). This is because when we move resources from paper to pencil production, we first move those resources best suited for pencil production and poorly suited for paper production.

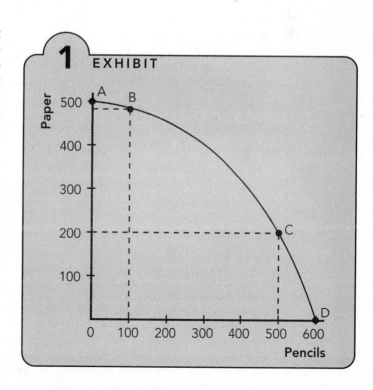

Therefore, pencil production increases with very little decrease in paper production. However, if the economy were operating at point C, the opportunity cost of an additional 100 pencils (point C to D) is 200 units of paper. This is because we now move resources toward pencil production that were extremely well suited for paper production and are poorly suited for pencil production. Therefore, as we produce more and more of any particular good, the opportunity cost per unit tends to rise because resources are specialized. That is, resources are not equally well suited for producing each output.

The argument above applies when moving either direction on the production possibilities frontier. For example, if we start at point D (maximum production of pencils), a small reduction in pencil production (100 units) releases enough resources to increase production of paper by a large amount (200 units). However, moving from point B to point A only increases paper production by 25 units.

2. A production possibilities frontier only shows the choices available—not which point of production is best. A common mistake made by students when using production possibilities frontiers is to look at a production possibilities frontier and suggest that a point somewhere near the middle "looks best." Students make this subjective judgment because the middle point appears to provide the biggest total number of units of production of the two goods. However, ask yourself the following question. Using the production possibilities frontier in Exhibit 1, what production point would be best if paper were worth $10 per sheet and pencils were worth 1 cent per dozen? We would move our resources toward paper production. What if paper were worth 1 cent per sheet and pencils were worth $50 each? We would move our resources toward pencil production. Clearly, what we actually choose to produce depends on the price of each good. Therefore, a production possibilities frontier only provides the choices available; it alone cannot determine which choice is best.

3. Economic disagreement is interesting but economic consensus is more important. Economists have a reputation for disagreeing with one another because we tend to highlight our differences. While our disagreements are interesting to us, the matters on which we agree are more important to you. There are a great number of economic principles for which there is near unanimous support within the economics profession. The aim of this text is to concentrate on the areas of agreement within the profession as opposed to the areas of disagreement.

Terms and Definitions

Choose a definition for each key term.

Key Terms

_____ Scientific method

_____ Economic models

_____ Circular-flow diagram

_____ Factors of production

_____ Production possibilities frontier

_____ Opportunity cost

_____ Efficiency

_____ Microeconomics

_____ Macroeconomics

_____ Positive statements

_____ Normative statements

Definitions

1. Inputs such as land, labor, and capital

2. The study of economy-wide phenomena

3. Objective development and testing of theories

4. Whatever is given up to get something else

5. Prescription for how the world ought to be

6. Getting maximum output from the resources available

7. Descriptions of the world as it is

8. Simplifications of reality based on assumptions

9. A graph that shows the combinations of output the economy can possibly produce given the available factors of production and the available production technology

10. The study of how households and firms make decisions and how they interact in markets

11. A diagram of the economy that shows the flow of goods and services, factors of production, and monetary payments between households and firms

PROBLEMS AND SHORT-ANSWER QUESTIONS

Practice Problems

1. Identify the parts of the circular-flow diagram immediately involved in the following transactions.
    a. Mary buys a car from General Motors for $20,000.

    _____

    _____

    _____

    _____

    _____

    _____

    b. General Motors pays Joe $5,000/month for work on the assembly line.

    _____

    _____

    _____

    _____

    _____

    _____

    c. Joe gets a $15 haircut.

    _____

    _____

    _____

    _____

    _____

    d. Mary receives $10,000 of dividends on her General Motors stock.

    _____

    _____

    _____

    _____

    _____

    _____

2. The following table provides information about the production possibilities frontier of Athletic Country.

Bats	Rackets
0	420
100	400
200	360
300	300
400	200
500	0

2 EXHIBIT

a. In Exhibit 2, plot and connect these points to create Athletic Country's production possibilities frontier.

b. If Athletic Country currently produces 100 bats and 400 rackets, what is the opportunity cost of an additional 100 bats?

_____

_____

_____

_____

_____

_____

c. If Athletic Country currently produces 300 bats and 300 rackets, what is the opportunity cost of an additional 100 bats?

_____

_____

d. Why does the additional production of 100 bats in part c cause a greater trade-off than the additional production of 100 bats in part *b*?

_____

_____

_____

e. Suppose Athletic Country is currently producing 200 bats and 200 rackets. How many additional bats could they produce without giving up any rackets? How many additional rackets could they produce without giving up any bats?

_____

_____

f. Is the production of 200 bats and 200 rackets efficient? Explain.

_____

_____

3. The production possibilities frontier in Exhibit 3 shows the available trade-offs between consumption goods and capital goods. Suppose two countries face this identical production possibilities frontier.

a. Suppose Party Country chooses to produce at point A, while Parsimonious Country chooses to produce at point B. Which country will experience more growth in the future? Why?

_____

_____

_____

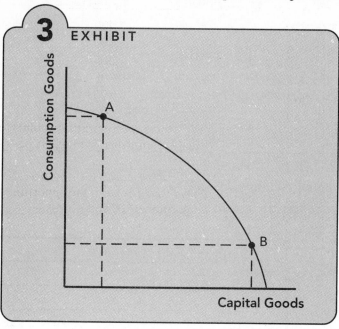

b. In this model, what is the opportunity cost of future growth?

_____

_____

_____

c. Demonstrate in Exhibit 4 the impact of growth on a production possibilities frontier such as the one shown above. Would the production possibilities frontier for Parsimonious Country shift more or less than that for Party Country? Why?

_____

_____

_____

d. On the graph in Exhibit 5, show the shift in the production possibilities curve if there was an increase in technology that only affected the production of capital goods.

e. Does the shift in part *d* above imply that all additional production must be in the form of capital goods? Why?

_____

_____

Short-Answer Questions

1. Describe the scientific method.

    _____

    _____

2. What is the role of assumptions in any science?

    _____

    _____

3. Is a more realistic model always better?

    _____

    _____

    _____

4. Why does a production possibilities frontier have a negative slope (slope down and to the right)?

    _____

    _____

    _____

5. Why is the production possibilities frontier bowed outward?

    _____

    _____

    _____

6. What are the two subfields within economics? Which is more likely to be a building block of the other? Why?

    _____

    _____

    _____

7. When an economist makes a normative statement, is she more likely to be acting as a scientist or a policy advisor? Why?

    _____

    _____

8. Which statements are testable: positive statements or normative statements? Why?

    _____

    _____

9. Name two reasons why economists disagree.

    _____

    _____

10. Name two economic propositions for which more than 90 percent of economists agree.

    _____

    _____

SELF-TEST

True/False Questions

_____ 1. Economic models must mirror reality or they are of no value.

_____ 2. Assumptions make the world easier to understand because they simplify reality and focus our attention.

_____ 3. It is reasonable to assume that the world is composed of only one person when modeling international trade.

_____ 4. When people act as scientists, they must try to be objective.

_____ 5. If an economy is operating on its production possibilities frontier, it must be using its resources efficiently.

_____ 6. If an economy is operating on its production possibilities frontier, it must produce less of one good if it produces more of another.

_____ 7. Points outside the production possibilities frontier are attainable but inefficient.

_____ 8. If an economy were experiencing substantial unemployment, the economy is producing inside the production possibilities frontier.

_____ 9. The production possibilities frontier is bowed outward because the trade-off between the production of any two goods is constant.

_____ 10. An advance in production technology would cause the production possibilities curve to shift outward.

_____ 11. Macroeconomics is concerned with the study of how households and firms make decisions and how they interact in specific markets.

_____ 12. The statement, "An increase in inflation tends to cause unemployment to fall in the short run," is normative.

_____ 13. When economists make positive statements, they are more likely to be acting as scientists.

_____ 14. Normative statements can be refuted with evidence.

_____ 15. Most economists believe that tariffs and import quotas usually reduce general economic welfare.

Multiple-Choice Questions

1. The scientific method requires that
   a. the scientist use test tubes and have a clean lab.
   b. the scientist be objective.
   c. the scientist use precision equipment.
   d. only incorrect theories are tested.
   e. only correct theories are tested.

2. Which of the following is most likely to produce scientific evidence about a theory?
   a. an economist employed by the AFL/CIO doing research on the impact of trade restrictions on workers' wages
   b. a radio talk show host collecting data on how capital markets respond to taxation
   c. a tenured economist employed at a leading university analyzing the impact of bank regulations on rural lending
   d. a lawyer employed by General Motors addressing the impact of air bags on passenger safety

3. Which of the following statements regarding the circular-flow diagram is true?
   a. The factors of production are owned by households.
   b. If Susan works for IBM and receives a paycheck, the transaction takes place in the market for goods and services.
   c. If IBM sells a computer, the transaction takes place in the market for factors of production.
   d. The factors of production are owned by firms.
   e. None of the above is true.

4. In which of the following cases is the assumption most reasonable?
   a. To estimate the speed at which a beach ball falls, a physicist assumes that it falls in a vacuum.
   b. To address the impact of money growth on inflation, an economist assumes that money is strictly coins.
   c. To address the impact of taxes on income distribution, an economist assumes that everyone earns the same income.
   d. To address the benefits of trade, an economist assumes that there are two people and two goods.

5. Economic models are
   a. created to duplicate reality.
   b. built with assumptions.
   c. usually made of wood and plastic.
   d. useless if they are simple.

6. Which of the following is not a factor of production?
   a. land
   b. labor
   c. capital
   d. money
   e. All of the above are factors of production.

7. Points on the production possibilities frontier are
   a. efficient.
   b. inefficient.
   c. unattainable.
   d. normative.
   e. none of the above.

8. Which of the following will not shift a country's production possibilities frontier outward?
    a. an increase in the capital stock
    b. an advance in technology
    c. a reduction in unemployment
    d. an increase in the labor force

9. Economic growth is depicted by
    a. a movement along a production possibilities frontier toward capital goods.
    b. a shift in the production possibilities frontier outward.
    c. a shift in the production possibilities frontier inward.
    d. a movement from inside the curve toward the curve.

Use Exhibit 6 to answer questions 10 through 13.

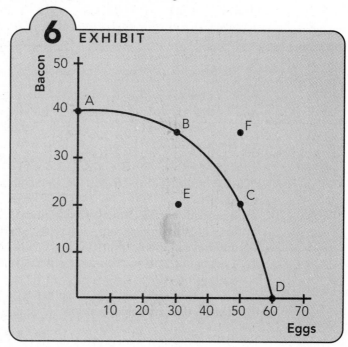

10. If the economy is operating at point C, the opportunity cost of producing an additional 15 units of bacon is
     a. 10 units of eggs.
     b. 20 units of eggs.
     c. 30 units of eggs.
     d. 40 units of eggs.
     e. 50 units of eggs.

11. If the economy were operating at point E,
     a. the opportunity cost of 20 additional units of eggs is 10 units of bacon.
     b. the opportunity cost of 20 additional units of eggs is 20 units of bacon.
     c. the opportunity cost of 20 additional units of eggs is 30 units of bacon.
     d. 20 additional units of eggs can be produced with no impact on bacon production.

12. Point F represents
     a. a combination of production that can be reached if we reduce the production of eggs by 20 units.
     b. a combination of production that is inefficient because there are unemployed resources.
     c. a combination of production that can be reached if there is a sufficient advance in technology.
     d. none of the above.

13. As we move from point A to point D,
    a. the opportunity cost of eggs in terms of bacon is constant.
    b. the opportunity cost of eggs in terms of bacon falls.
    c. the opportunity cost of eggs in terms of bacon rises.
    d. the economy becomes more efficient.
    e. the economy becomes less efficient.

14. Which of the following issues is related to microeconomics?
    a. the impact of money on inflation
    b. the impact of technology on economic growth
    c. the impact of the deficit on saving
    d. the impact of oil prices on auto production

15. Which of the following statements about microeconomics and macroeconomics is not true?
    a. The study of very large industries is a topic within macroeconomics.
    b. Macroeconomics is concerned with economy-wide phenomena.
    c. Microeconomics is a building block for macroeconomics.
    d. Microeconomics and macroeconomics cannot be entirely separated.

16. Which of the following statements is normative?
    a. Printing too much money causes inflation.
    b. People work harder if the wage is higher.
    c. The unemployment rate should be lower.
    d. Large government deficits cause an economy to grow more slowly.

17. In making which of the following statements is an economist acting more like a scientist?
    a. A reduction in unemployment benefits will reduce the unemployment rate.
    b. The unemployment rate should be reduced because unemployment robs individuals of their dignity.
    c. The rate of inflation should be reduced because it robs the elderly of their savings.
    d. The state should increase subsidies to universities because the future of our country depends on education.

18. Positive statements are
    a. microeconomic.
    b. macroeconomic.
    c. statements of prescription that involve value judgments.
    d. statements of description that can be tested.

19. Suppose two economists are arguing about policies that deal with unemployment. One economist says, "The government should fight unemployment because it is the greatest social evil." The other economist responds, "Hogwash. Inflation is the greatest social evil." These economists
    a. disagree because they have different scientific judgments.
    b. disagree because they have different values.
    c. really don't disagree at all. It just looks that way.
    d. do none of the above.

20. Suppose two economists are arguing about policies that deal with unemployment. One economist says, "The government could lower unemployment by one percentage point if it would just increase government spending by 50 billion dollars." The other economist responds, "Hogwash. If the government spent an additional 50 billion dollars, it would reduce unemployment by only one tenth of one percent, and that effect would only be temporary!" These economists
    a. disagree because they have different scientific judgments.
    b. disagree because they have different values.
    c. really don't disagree at all. It just looks that way.
    d. do none of the above.

ADVANCED CRITICAL THINKING

You are watching *NewsHour with Jim Lehrer* on public television. The first focus segment is a discussion of the pros and cons of free trade (lack of obstructions to international trade). For balance, there are two economists present—one in support of free trade and one opposed. Your roommate says, "Those economists have no idea what's going on. They can't agree on anything. One says free trade makes us rich. The other says it will drive us into poverty. If the experts don't know, how is the average person ever going to know whether free trade is best?"

1. Can you give your roommate any insight into why economists might disagree on this issue?

2. Suppose you discover that 93 percent of economists believe that free trade is generally best (which is the greatest agreement on any single issue). Could you now give a more precise answer as to why economists might disagree on this issue?

3. What if you later discovered that the economist opposed to free trade worked for a labor union. Would that help you explain why there appears to be a difference of opinion on this issue?

SOLUTIONS

Terms and Definitions

 _3_ Scientific method

 _8_ Economic models

 _11_ Circular-flow diagram

 _1_ Factors of production

 _9_ Production possibilities frontier

 _4_ Opportunity cost

 _6_ Efficiency

 _10_ Microeconomics

 _2_ Macroeconomics

 _7_ Positive statements

 _5_ Normative statements

Practice Problems

1. a. $20,000 of spending from households to market for goods and services. Car moves from market for goods and services to household. $20,000 of revenue from market for goods and services to firms while car moves from firm to market for goods and services.

   b. $5,000 of wages from firms to market for factors of production. Inputs move from market for factors of production to firms. Labor moves from households to market for factors of production while $5,000 income moves from market for factors to households.

   c. $15 of spending from households to market for goods and services. Service moves from market for goods and services to household. Service moves from firms to market for goods and services in return for $15 revenue.

   d. $10,000 of profit from firms to market for factors of production. Inputs move from market for factors of production to firms. Capital services move from households to market for factors of production in return for $10,000 income.

2. a. See Exhibit 7.

   b. 40 rackets

   c. 100 rackets

   d. Because as we produce more bats, the resources best suited for making bats are already being used. Therefore it takes even more resources to produce 100 bats and greater reductions in racket production.

   e. 200 bats; 160 rackets

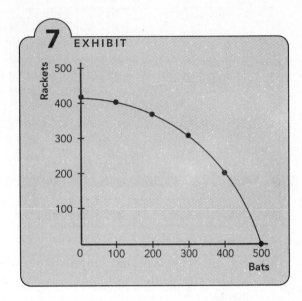

f. No. Resources were not used efficiently if production can be increased with no opportunity cost.

3. a. Parsimonious country. Capital (plant and equipment) is a factor of production and producing more of it now will increase future production.

   b. Fewer consumption goods are produced now.

   c. See Exhibit 8. The production possibilities curve will shift more for Parsimonious Country because they have experienced a greater increase in factors of production (capital).

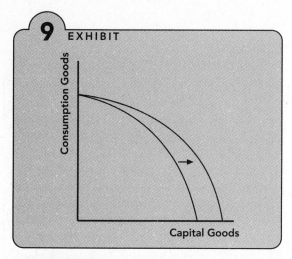

9 EXHIBIT

d. See Exhibit 9.

e. No, the outward shift improves choices available for both consumption and capital goods.

Short-Answer Questions

1. The dispassionate development and testing of theory by observing, testing, and observing again.

2. To simplify reality so that we can focus our thinking on what is actually important.

3. Not necessarily. Realistic models are more complex. They may be confusing and they may fail to focus on what is important.

4. Because if an economy is operating efficiently, production choices have opportunity costs. If we want more of one thing, we must have less of another.

5. Because resources are specialized and, thus, are not equally well-suited for producing different outputs.

6. Microeconomics and macroeconomics. Micro-economics is more of a building block of macro because when we address macro issues (say unemployment) we have to consider how individuals respond to work incentives such as wages and welfare.

7. As a policy advisor because normative statements are prescriptions about what ought to be and are somewhat based on value judgments.

8. Positive statements are statements of fact and are refutable by examining evidence.

9. Economists may have different scientific judgments. Economists may have different values.

10. A ceiling on rents reduces the quantity and quality of housing available. Tariffs and import quotas usually reduce general economic welfare.

True/False Questions

1. F; economic models are simplifications of reality.
2. T
3. F; there must be at least two individuals for trade.
4. T
5. T
6. T
7. F; points outside the production possibilities frontier cannot yet be attained.
8. T
9. F; it is bowed outward because the trade-offs are not constant.
10. T
11. F; macroeconomics is the study of economy-wide phenomena.
12. F; this statement is positive.
13. T
14. F; normative statements cannot be refuted.
15. T

Multiple-Choice Questions

1. b
2. c
3. a
4. d
5. b
6. d
7. a
8. c
9. b
10. b
11. d
12. c
13. c
14. d
15. a
16. c
17. a
18. d
19. b
20. a

ADVANCED CRITICAL THINKING

1. Economists may have different scientific judgments. Economists may have different values. There may not really be any real disagreement because the majority of economists may actually agree.

2. Those opposed to free trade are likely to have different values than the majority of economists. There is not much disagreement on this issue among the mainstream economics profession.

3. Yes. It suggests that impediments to international trade may benefit some groups (organized labor) but these impediments are unlikely to benefit the public in general. Supporters of these policies are promoting their own interests.

APPENDIX

Practice Problems

1. The following ordered pairs of price and quantity demanded describe Joe's demand for cups of gourmet coffee.

Price per cup of coffee	Quantity demanded of coffee
$5	2 cups
4	4 cups
3	6 cups
2	8 cups
1	10 cups

a. Plot and connect the ordered pairs on the graph in Exhibit 10.

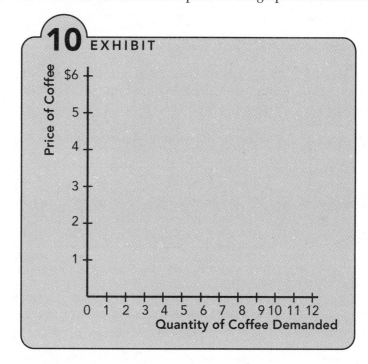

b. What is the slope of Joe's demand curve for coffee in the price range of $5 and $4?

_____

c. What is the slope of Joe's demand curve for coffee in the price range of $2 and $1?

_____

d. Are the price of coffee and Joe's quantity demanded of coffee positively correlated or negatively correlated? How can you tell?

_____

e. If the price of coffee moves from $2 per cup to $4 per cup, what happens to the quantity demanded? Is this a movement along a curve or a shift in the curve?

_____

_____

f. Suppose Joe's income doubles from $20,000 per year to $40,000 per year. Now the following ordered pairs describe Joe's demand for gourmet coffee. Plot these ordered pairs on the graph provided in part (a) above.

Price per cup of coffee	Quantity demanded of coffee
$5	4 cups
4	6 cups
3	8 cups
2	10 cups
1	12 cups

g. Did the doubling of Joe's income cause a movement along his demand curve or a shift in his demand curve? Why?

_____

_____

2. An alien lands on earth and observes the following: on mornings when people carry umbrellas, it tends to rain later in the day. The alien concludes that umbrellas cause rain.

a. What error has the alien committed?

_____

_____

b. What role did expectations play in the alien's error?

_____

_____

c. If rain is truly caused by humidity, temperature, wind currents, and so on, what additional type of error has the alien committed when it decided that umbrellas cause rain?

_____

_____

True/False Questions

_____ 1. When graphing in the coordinate system, the x-coordinate tells us the horizontal location while the y-coordinate tells us the vertical location of the point.

_____ 2. When a line slopes upward in the x, y coordinate system, the two variables measured on each axis are positively correlated.

_____ 3. Price and quantity demanded for most goods are positively related.

_____ 4. If three variables are related, one of them must be held constant when graphing the other two in the x, y coordinate system.

_____ 5. If three variables are related, a change in the variable not represented on the x, y coordinate system will cause a movement along the curve drawn in the x, y coordinate system.

_____ 6. The slope of a line is equal to the change in y divided by the change in x along the line.

_____ 7. When a line has negative slope, the two variables measured on each axis are positively correlated.

_____ 8. There is a positive correlation between lying down and death. If we conclude from this evidence that it is unsafe to lie down, we have an omitted variable problem because critically ill people tend to lie down.

_____ 9. Reverse causality means that while we think A causes B, B may actually cause A.

_____ 10. Since people carry umbrellas to work in the morning and it rains later in the afternoon, carrying umbrellas must cause rain.

SOLUTIONS FOR APPENDIX

Practice Problems

1. a. See Exhibit 11.
   b. –1/2
   c. –1/2
   d. Negatively correlated, because an increase in price is associated with a decrease in quantity demanded. That is, the demand curve slopes negatively.
   e. Decrease by four cups. Movement along curve.
   f. See Exhibit 12.
   g. Shift in curve because a variable changed (income) which is not measured on either axis.

2. a. Reverse causality.
   b. Since rain can be predicted, people's expectation of rain causes them to carry umbrellas before it rains, making it appear as if umbrellas cause rain.
   c. Omitted variables.

True/False Questions

1. T
2. T
3. F; they are negatively correlated.
4. T
5. F; a change in a variable not represented on the graph will cause a shift in the curve.
6. T
7. F; negative slope implies negative correlation.
8. T
9. T
10. F; this is an example of reverse causation.

3

Interdependence and the Gains from Trade

GOALS

In this chapter you will

- Consider how everyone can benefit when people trade with one another

- Learn the meaning of absolute advantage and comparative advantage

- See how comparative advantage explains the gains from trade

- Apply the theory of comparative advantage to everyday life and national policy

OUTCOMES

After accomplishing these goals, you should be able to

- Show how total production rises when individuals specialize in the production of goods for which they have a comparative advantage

- Explain why all people have a comparative advantage even if they have no absolute advantage

- Demonstrate the link between comparative advantage and opportunity cost

- Explain why people who are good at everything still tend to specialize

CHAPTER OVERVIEW

Context and Purpose

Chapter 3 is the third chapter in the three-chapter section that serves as the introduction of the text. The first chapter introduced ten fundamental principles of economics. The second chapter developed how economists approach problems. This chapter shows how people and countries gain from trade (which is one of the ten principles discussed in Chapter 1).

The purpose of Chapter 3 is to demonstrate how everyone can gain from trade. Trade allows people to specialize in the production of goods for which they have a comparative advantage and then trade for goods other people produce. Because of specialization, total output rises, and through trade, we are all able to share in the bounty. This is as true for countries as it is for individuals. Since everyone can gain from trade, restrictions on trade tend to reduce welfare.

Chapter Review

Introduction Each of us consumes products every day that were produced in a number of different countries. Complex products contain components that were produced in many different countries so these products have no single country of origin. Those who produce are neither generous nor ordered by government to produce. People produce because they wish to trade and get something in return. Hence, trade makes us interdependent.

A Parable for the Modern Economy

Imagine a simple economy. There are two people—a cattle rancher and a potato farmer. There are two goods—meat and potatoes.

- If each can produce only one product (the rancher can produce only meat and the farmer potatoes), they will trade just to increase the variety of products they consume. Each benefits because of increased variety.

- If each can produce both goods, but each is more efficient than the other at producing one good, then each will specialize in what he or she does best (again the rancher produces meat and the farmer produces potatoes), total output will rise, and they will trade.

Trade allows each to benefit because trade allows for specialization, and specialization increases the total production available to share.

- If one producer is better than the other at producing both meat and potatoes, there are the same advantages to trade but it is more difficult to see. Again, trade allows each to benefit because trade allows for specialization, and specialization increases the total production available to share. To understand the source of the gains from trade when one producer is better at producing both products, we must understand the concept of comparative advantage.

Comparative Advantage: The Driving Force of Specialization

To understand **comparative advantage,** we begin with the concept of **absolute advantage.** Absolute advantage compares the quantity of inputs required to produce a good. The producer that requires fewer resources (say fewer hours worked) to produce a good is said to have an absolute advantage in the production of that good. That is, the most efficient producer (the one with the highest productivity) has an absolute advantage.

While absolute advantage compares the actual cost of production for each producer, comparative advantage compares **opportunity costs** of production for each producer. The producer with the lower opportunity cost of production is said to have a comparative advantage. Regardless of absolute advantage, if producers have different opportunity costs of production for each good, each should specialize in the production of the good for which their opportunity cost of production is lower. That is, each producer should produce the item for which they have a comparative advantage. They can then trade some of their output for the other good. Trade makes both producers better off because trade allows for specialization, and specialization increases the total production available to be shared. Both producers gain when they trade at a price that lies between their domestic opportunity costs.

The decision to specialize and the resulting gains from trade are based on comparative advantage, not absolute advantage. Although a single producer can have an absolute advantage in the production of both goods, he cannot have a comparative advantage in the production of both goods because a low opportunity cost of producing one good implies a high opportunity cost of producing the other good.

In summary, trade allows producers to exploit the differences in their opportunity costs of production. Each specializes in the production of the good for which they have the lower opportunity cost of production and, thus, a comparative advantage. This increases total production and makes the economic pie larger. Everyone can benefit. The additional production generated by specialization is the gain from trade.

Adam Smith in his 1776 book, *An Inquiry into the Nature and Causes of the Wealth of Nations,* and David Ricardo in his 1817 book, *Principles of Political Economy and Taxation,* both recognized the gains from trade through specialization and the principle of comparative advantage. Current arguments for free trade are still based on their work.

Applications of Comparative Advantage

The principle of comparative advantage applies to individuals as well as countries. Recall, absolute advantage does not determine specialization in production. For example, Tiger Woods may have an absolute advantage in both golf and lawn mowing. However, because he can earn $5,000/hour playing golf, he is better off paying someone to mow his lawn (even if they do it more slowly than he) as long as he can get someone to do it for less than $5,000/hour. This is because the opportunity cost of an hour of mowing for Tiger Woods is $5,000. Tiger Woods will likely specialize in golf and trade for other services. He does this because he has a comparative advantage in golf and a comparative disadvantage in lawn mowing even though he has an absolute advantage in both.

Trade between countries is subject to the same principle of comparative advantage. Goods produced abroad and sold domestically are called **imports.** Goods produced domestically and sold abroad are called **exports.** Even if the United States has an absolute advantage in the production of both cars and food, it should specialize in the production of the item for which it has a comparative advantage. Since the opportunity cost of food is low in the United States (better land) and high in Japan, the United States should produce more food and export it to Japan in exchange for imports of autos from Japan. While the United States gains from trade, the impact of trade on U.S. autoworkers is different from the impact of trade on U.S. farmers.

A reduction in barriers to free trade improves the welfare of the importing country as a whole, but it does not improve the welfare of the domestic producers in the importing country. For this reason, domestic producers lobby their governments to maintain (or increase) barriers to free trade.

Helpful Hints

1. A step-by-step example of comparative advantage will demonstrate most of the concepts discussed in Chapter 3. It will give you a pattern to follow when answering questions at the end of the chapter in your text and for the problems that follow in this Study Guide.

Suppose we have the following information about the productivity of industry in Japan and Korea. The data are the units of output per hour of work.

	Steel	Televisions
Japan	6	3
Korea	8	2

A Japanese worker can produce 6 units of steel or 3 televisions per hour. A Korean worker can produce 8 units of steel or 2 televisions per hour.

We can plot the production possibilities frontier for each country assuming each country has only one worker and the worker works only one hour. To plot the frontier, plot the end points and connect them with a line. For example, Japan can produce 6 units of steel with its worker or 3 televisions. It can also allocate one half hour to the production of each and get 3 units of steel and 1 1/2 televisions. Any other proportion of the hour can be allocated to the two productive activities. The production possibilities frontier is linear in these cases because the labor resource can be moved from the production of one good to the other at a constant rate. We can do the same for Korea. Without trade, the production possibilities frontier is also the consumption possibilities frontier.

Comparative advantage determines specialization and trade. The opportunity cost of a television in Japan is 2 units of steel, which is shown by the slope of the production possibilities frontier in Exhibit 1. Alternatively, the opportunity cost of one unit of steel in Japan is 1/2 of a television. In Korea, the opportunity cost of a television is 4 units of steel and the cost of a unit of steel is 1/4 of a television. Since the opportunity cost of a television is lower in Japan, Japan has a comparative advantage in television production and should specialize in televisions. Since the opportunity cost of steel is lower in Korea, Korea has a comparative advantage in steel production and should specialize in steel.

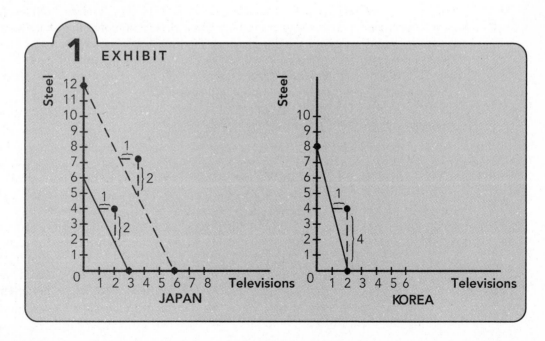

What is the range of prices at which each country would be willing to exchange? If Japan specializes in television production and produces 3 televisions, it would be willing to trade televisions for steel as long as the price of steel is below 1/2 television per unit of steel because that was the Japanese price for a unit of steel prior to trade. Korea would be willing to specialize in steel production and trade for televisions as long as the price of a television is less than 4 units of steel because that was the Korean price of a television prior to trade. In short, the final price must be between the original trade-offs each faced in the absence of trade. One television will cost between 2 and 4 units of steel. One unit of steel will cost between 1/2 and 1/4 of a television.

2. Trade allows countries to consume outside their original production possibilities frontier. Suppose that Japan and Korea settle on a trading price of 3 units of steel for 1 television (or 1/3 of a television for 1 unit of steel). (I am giving you this price. There is nothing in the problem that would let you calculate the final trading price. You can only calculate the range in which it must lie.) This price is halfway between the two prices that each faces in the absence of trade. The range for the trading price is 4 units of steel for 1 television to 2 units of steel for 1 television.

    If Japan specializes in television production, produces 3 televisions, and exports 1 television for 3 units of steel, Japan will be able to consume 2 televisions and 3 units of steel. If we plot this point (2 televisions and 3 steel) on Japan's graph, we see that it lies outside its production possibilities frontier. If Korea specializes, produces 8 units of steel, and exports 3 units for 1 television, Korea will be able to consume 5 units of steel and 1 television. If we plot this point (5 steel and 1 television) on Korea's graph, we see that it also lies outside its production possibilities frontier.

    This is the gain from trade. Trade allows countries (and people) to specialize. Specialization increases world output. After trading, countries consume outside their individual production possibilities frontiers. In this way, trade is like an improvement in technology. It allows countries to move beyond their current production possibilities frontiers.

3. Only comparative advantage matters—absolute advantage is irrelevant. In the previous example, Japan had an absolute advantage in the production of televisions because it could produce 3 per hour while Korea could only produce 2. Korea had an absolute advantage in the production of steel because it could produce 8 units per hour compared to 6 for Japan.

    To demonstrate that comparative advantage, not absolute advantage, determines specialization and trade, we alter the previous example so that Japan has an absolute advantage in the production of both goods. To this end, suppose Japan becomes twice as productive as in the previous table. That is, a worker can now produce 12 units of steel or 6 televisions per hour.

	Steel	Televisions
Japan	12	6
Korea	8	2

Now Japan has an absolute advantage in the production of both goods. Japan's new production possibilities frontier is the dashed line in Exhibit 1. Will this change the analysis? Not at all. The opportunity cost of each good within Japan is the same—2 units of steel per television or 1/2 television per unit of steel (and Korea is unaffected). For this reason, Japan still has the identical comparative advantage as before, and it will specialize in television production while Korea will specialize in steel. However, since productivity has doubled in Japan, its entire set of choices has improved, and thus, its material welfare has improved.

Terms and Definitions

Choose a definition for each key term.

Key Terms

_____Absolute advantage

_____Comparative advantage

_____Gains from trade

_____Opportunity cost

_____Imports

_____Exports

Definitions

1. Whatever is given up to obtain some item

2. The ability to produce a good at a lower opportunity cost than another producer

3. Goods produced domestically and sold abroad

4. Goods produced abroad and sold domestically

5. The ability to produce a good using fewer inputs than another producer

6. The increase in total production due to specialization allowed by trade

PROBLEMS AND SHORT-ANSWER QUESTIONS

Practice Problems

1. Angela is a college student. She takes a full load of classes and has only 5 hours per week for her hobby. Angela is artistic and can make 2 clay pots per hour or 4 coffee mugs per hour.

   a. Draw Angela's production possibilities frontier for pots and mugs.

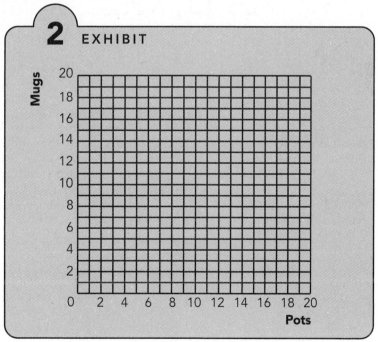

2 EXHIBIT

   b. What is Angela's opportunity cost of 1 pot? 10 pots?

   _____

   c. What is Angela's opportunity cost of 1 mug? 10 mugs?

   _____

d. Why is her production possibilities frontier a straight line instead of bowed out like those presented in Chapter 2?

_____

_____

2. Suppose a worker in Germany can produce 15 computers or 5 tons of grain per month. Suppose a worker in Poland can produce 4 computers or 4 tons of grain per month. For simplicity, assume that each country has only one worker.

a. Fill out the following table:

	Computers	**Grain**
Germany	_____	_____
Poland	_____	_____

b. Graph the production possibilities frontier for each country in Exhibit 3.

3 EXHIBIT

GERMANY   POLAND

c. What is the opportunity cost of a computer in Germany? What is the opportunity cost of a ton of grain in Germany?

_____

_____

d. What is the opportunity cost of a computer in Poland? What is the opportunity cost of a ton of grain in Poland?

_____

_____

e. Which country has the absolute advantage in producing computers? grain?

_____

_____

f. Which country has the comparative advantage in producing computers? grain?

_____

_____

_____

g. Each country should tend toward specialization in the production of which good? Why?

_____

_____

_____

h. What is the range of prices for computers and grain for which both countries would benefit?

_____

_____

_____

i. Suppose Germany and Poland settle on a price of 2 computers for 1 ton of grain or 1/2 ton of grain for a computer. Suppose each country specializes in production and they trade 4 computers for 2 tons of grain. Plot the final consumption points on the graphs you made in part b above. Are these countries consuming inside or outside of their production possibilities frontier?

_____

_____

j. Suppose the productivity of a worker in Poland doubles so that a worker can produce 8 computers or 8 tons of grain per month. Which country has the absolute advantage in producing computers? grain?

_____

_____

k. After the doubling of productivity in Poland, which country has a comparative advantage in producing computers? grain? Has the comparative advantage changed? Has the material welfare of either country changed?

_____

_____

_____

l. How would your analysis change if you assumed, more realistically, that each country had 10 million workers?

_____

_____

_____

3. Suppose a worker in the United States can produce 4 cars or 20 computers per month while a worker in Russia can produce 1 car or 5 computers per month. Again, for simplicity, assume each country has only one worker.

a. Fill out the following table:

	Cars	Computers
United States	_____	_____
Russia	_____	_____

b. Which country has the absolute advantage in the production of cars? computers?

_____

_____

c. Which country has the comparative advantage in the production of cars? computers?

_____

_____

_____

d. Are there any gains to be made from trade? Why?

_____

_____

e. Does your answer in *d* above help you pinpoint a source for gains from trade?

_____

_____

_____

f. What might make two countries have different opportunity costs of production? (Use your imagination. This was not directly discussed in Chapter 3.)

_____

_____

_____

Short-Answer Questions

1. Why do people choose to become interdependent as opposed to self-sufficient?

_____

_____

_____

2. Why is comparative advantage important in determining trade instead of absolute advantage?

_____

_____

_____

3. What are the gains from trade?

_____

_____

_____

4. Why is a restriction of trade likely to reduce material welfare?

_____

_____

5. Suppose a lawyer that earns $200 per hour can also type at 200 words per minute. Should the lawyer hire a secretary who can only type 50 words per minute? Why?

_____

_____

_____

6. Evaluate this statement: A technologically advanced country, which is better than its neighbor at producing everything, would be better off if it closed its borders to trade because the less productive country is a burden to the advanced country.

_____

_____

_____

SELF-TEST

True/False Questions

_____ 1. If Japan has an absolute advantage in the production of an item, it must also have a comparative advantage in the production of that item.

_____ 2. Comparative advantage, not absolute advantage, determines the decision to specialize in production.

_____ 3. Absolute advantage is a comparison among producers based on productivity.

_____ 4. Self-sufficiency is the best way to increase one's material welfare.

_____ 5. Comparative advantage is a comparison among producers based on opportunity cost.

_____ 6. If a producer is self-sufficient, the production possibilities frontier is also the consumption possibilities frontier.

_____ 7. If a country's workers can produce 5 hamburgers per hour or 10 bags of French fries per hour, absent trade, the price of 1 bag of fries is 2 hamburgers.

_____ 8. If producers have different opportunity costs of production, trade will allow them to consume outside their production possibilities frontiers.

_____ 9. If trade benefits one country, its trading partner must be worse off due to trade.

_____ 10. Talented people that are the best at everything have a comparative advantage in the production of everything.

_____ 11. The gains from trade can be measured by the increase in total production that comes from specialization.

_____ 12. When a country removes a specific import restriction, it always benefits every worker in that country.

_____ 13. If Germany's productivity doubles for everything it produces, this will not alter its prior pattern of specialization because it has not altered its comparative advantage.

_____ 14. If an advanced country has an absolute advantage in the production of everything, it will benefit if it eliminates trade with less developed countries and becomes completely self-sufficient.

_____ 15. If gains from trade are based solely on comparative advantage, and if all countries have the same opportunity costs of production, then there are no gains from trade.

Multiple-Choice Questions

1. If a nation has an absolute advantage in the production of a good,
   a. it can produce that good at a lower opportunity cost than its trading partner.
   b. it can produce that good using fewer resources than its trading partner.
   c. it can benefit by restricting imports of that good.
   d. it will specialize in the production of that good and export it.
   e. none of the above is true.

2. If a nation has a comparative advantage in the production of a good,
   a. it can produce that good at a lower opportunity cost than its trading partner.
   b. it can produce that good using fewer resources than its trading partner.
   c. it can benefit by restricting imports of that good.
   d. it must be the only country with the ability to produce that good.
   e. none of the above is true.

3. Which of the following statements about trade is true?
   a. Unrestricted international trade benefits every person in a country equally.
   b. People that are skilled at all activities cannot benefit from trade.
   c. Trade can benefit everyone in society because it allows people to specialize in activities in which they have an absolute advantage.
   d. Trade can benefit everyone in society because it allows people to specialize in activities in which they have a comparative advantage.

4. According to the principle of comparative advantage,
   a. countries with a comparative advantage in the production of every good need not specialize.
   b. countries should specialize in the production of goods that they enjoy consuming.
   c. countries should specialize in the production of goods for which they use fewer resources in production than their trading partners.
   d. countries should specialize in the production of goods for which they have a lower opportunity cost of production than their trading partners.

5. Which of the following statements is true?
   a. Self-sufficiency is the road to prosperity for most countries.
   b. A self-sufficient country consumes outside its production possibilities frontier.
   c. A self-sufficient country can, at best, consume on its production possibilities frontier.
   d. Only countries with an absolute advantage in the production of every good should strive to be self-sufficient.

6. Suppose a country's workers can produce 4 watches per hour or 12 rings per hour. If there is no trade,
   a. the domestic price of 1 ring is 3 watches.
   b. the domestic price of 1 ring is 1 1/3 of a watch.
   c. the domestic price of 1 ring is 4 watches.
   d. the domestic price of 1 ring is 1/4 of a watch.
   e. the domestic price of 1 ring is 12 watches.

7. Suppose a country's workers can produce 4 watches per hour or 12 rings per hour. If there is no trade,
   a. the opportunity cost of 1 watch is 3 rings.
   b. the opportunity cost of 1 watch is 1/3 of a ring.
   c. the opportunity cost of 1 watch is 4 rings.
   d. the opportunity cost of 1 watch is 1/4 of a ring.
   e. the opportunity cost of 1 watch is 12 rings.

The following table shows the units of output a worker can produce per month in Australia and Korea. Use this table to answer questions 8 through 15.

	Food	Electronics
Australia	20	5
Korea	8	4

8. Which of the following statements about absolute advantage is true?
   a. Australia has an absolute advantage in the production of food while Korea has an absolute advantage in the production of electronics.
   b. Korea has an absolute advantage in the production of food while Australia has an absolute advantage in the production of electronics.
   c. Australia has an absolute advantage in the production of both food and electronics.
   d. Korea has an absolute advantage in the production of both food and electronics.

9. The opportunity cost of 1 unit of electronics in Australia is
   a. 5 units of food.
   b. 1/5 of a unit of food.
   c. 4 units of food.
   d. 1/4 of a unit of food.

10. The opportunity cost of 1 unit of electronics in Korea is
    a. 2 units of food.
    b. 1/2 of a unit of food.
    c. 4 units of food.
    d. 1/4 of a unit of food.

11. The opportunity cost of 1 unit of food in Australia is
    a. 5 units of electronics.
    b. 1/5 of a unit of electronics.
    c. 4 units of electronics.
    d. 1/4 of a unit of electronics.

12. The opportunity cost of 1 unit of food in Korea is
    a. 2 units of electronics.
    b. 1/2 of a unit of electronics.
    c. 4 units of electronics.
    d. 1/4 of a unit of electronics.

13. Which of the following statements about comparative advantage is true?
    a. Australia has a comparative advantage in the production of food while Korea has a comparative advantage in the production of electronics.
    b. Korea has a comparative advantage in the production of food while Australia has a comparative advantage in the production of electronics.
    c. Australia has a comparative advantage in the production of both food and electronics.
    d. Korea has a comparative advantage in the production of both food and electronics.
    e. Neither country has a comparative advantage.

14. Korea should
    a. specialize in food production, export food, and import electronics.
    b. specialize in electronics production, export electronics, and import food.
    c. produce both goods because neither country has a comparative advantage.
    d. produce neither good because it has an absolute disadvantage in the production of both goods.

15. Prices of electronics can be stated in terms of units of food. What is the range of prices of electronics for which both countries could gain from trade?
    a. The price must be greater than 1/5 of a unit of food but less than 1/4 of a unit of food.
    b. The price must be greater than 4 units of food but less than 5 units of food.
    c. The price must be greater than 1/4 of a unit of food but less than 1/2 of a unit of food.
    d. The price must be greater than 2 units of food but less than 4 units of food.

16. Suppose the world consists of two countries—the United States and Mexico. Further, suppose there are only two goods—food and clothing. Which of the following statements is true?
    a. If the United States has an absolute advantage in the production of food, then Mexico must have an absolute advantage in the production of clothing.
    b. If the United States has a comparative advantage in the production of food, then Mexico must have a comparative advantage in the production of clothing.
    c. If the United States has a comparative advantage in the production of food, it must also have a comparative advantage in the production of clothing.
    d. If the United States has a comparative advantage in the production of food, Mexico might also have a comparative advantage in the production of food.
    e. None of the above is true.

Use the production possibilities frontiers in Exhibit 4 to answer questions 17 through 19. Assume each country has the same number of workers, say 20 million, and that each axis is measured in metric tons per month.

17. Argentina has a comparative advantage in the production of
    a. both fruit and beef.
    b. fruit.
    c. beef.
    d. neither fruit nor beef.

18. Peru will export
    a. both fruit and beef.
    b. fruit.
    c. beef.
    d. neither fruit nor beef.

19. The opportunity cost of producing a metric ton of beef in Peru is
    a. 1/3 ton of fruit.
    b. 1 ton of fruit.
    c. 2 tons of fruit.
    d. 3 tons of fruit.
    e. 6 tons of fruit.

20. Joe is a tax accountant. He receives $100 per hour doing tax returns. He can type 10,000 characters per hour into spreadsheets. He can hire an assistant who types 2,500 characters per hour into spreadsheets. Which of the following statements is true?
    a. Joe should not hire an assistant because the assistant cannot type as fast as he.
    b. Joe should hire the assistant as long as he pays the assistant less than $100 per hour.
    c. Joe should hire the assistant as long as he pays the assistant less than $25 per hour.
    d. None of the above is true.

ADVANCED CRITICAL THINKING

You are watching an election debate on television. A candidate says, "We need to stop the flow of foreign automobiles into our country. If we limit the importation of autos, our domestic auto production will rise and the United States will be better off."

1. Is it likely that the United States will be better off if we limit auto imports? Explain.

    _____

    _____

    _____

2. Will anyone in the United States be better off if we limit auto imports? Explain.

    _____

    _____

    _____

3. In the real world, does every person in the country gain when restrictions on imports are reduced? Explain.

    _____

    _____

    _____

SOLUTIONS

Terms and Definitions

_5_ Absolute advantage

_2_ Comparative advantage

_6_ Gains from trade

_1_ Opportunity cost

_4_ Imports

_3_ Exports

Practice Problems

1. a.

5 EXHIBIT

b. 2 mugs. 20 mugs.

c. 1/2 pot. 5 pots.

d. Because here resources can be moved from the production of one good to another at a constant rate.

2. a.

	Computers	Grain
Germany	15	5
Poland	4	4

b. See Exhibit 6.

c. 1/3 ton grain. 3 computers.

d. 1 ton grain. 1 computer.

e. Germany because one worker can produce 15 computers compared to 4. Germany because one worker can produce 5 tons of grain compared to 4.

f. Germany because a computer has the opportunity cost of only 1/3 ton of grain compared to 1 ton of grain in Poland. Poland because a ton of grain has the opportunity

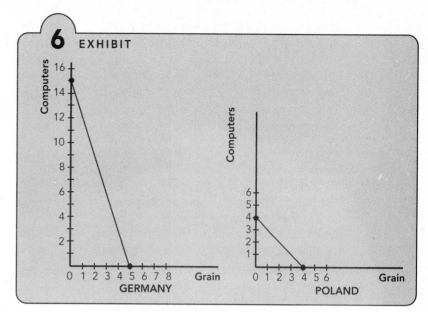

6 EXHIBIT

cost of only 1 computer compared to 3 computers in Germany.

g. Germany should produce computers while Poland should produce grain because the opportunity cost of computers is lower in Germany and the opportunity cost of grain is lower in Poland. That is, each has a comparative advantage in those goods.

h. Grain must cost less than 3 computers to Germany. Computers must cost less than 1 ton of grain to Poland.

i. See Exhibit 7. They are consuming outside their production possibilities frontier.

j. Germany because one worker can produce 15 compared to 8. Poland because one worker can produce 8 compared to 5.

k. Germany has comparative advantage in computers. Poland has comparative advantage

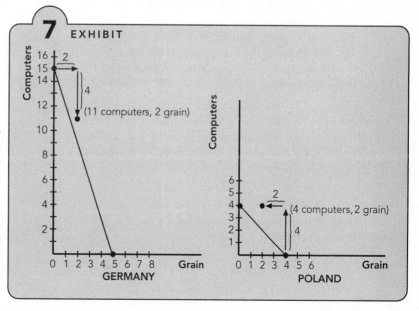

7 EXHIBIT

in grain. No change in comparative advantage. Poland is better off, however, because it now has a larger set of choices.

1. It would not change absolute advantage or comparative advantage. It would change the scale in the previous two graphs by a factor of 10 million.

3. a.

	Cars	Computers
United States	4	20
Russia	1	5

b. United States because one worker can produce 4 cars compared to 1. The United States because one worker can produce 20 computers compared to 5.

c. In both, the opportunity cost of 1 car is 5 computers. In both, the opportunity cost of 1 computer is 1/5 of a car. Therefore, neither has a comparative advantage in either good.

d. No. Each can get the same trade-off between goods domestically.

e. Yes. There needs to be differences in opportunity costs of producing goods across countries for there to be gains from trade.

f. The availability of resources or technology might be different across countries. That is, workers could have different levels of education, land could be of different quality, capital could be of different quality, or the available technology might be different.

Short-Answer Questions

1. Because a consumer gets a greater variety of goods at a much lower cost than they could produce by themselves. That is, there are gains from trade.

2. What is important in trade is how a country's costs without trade differ from each other. This is determined by the relative opportunity costs across countries.

3. The additional output that comes from countries with different opportunity costs of production specializing in the production of the item for which they have the lower domestic opportunity cost.

4. Because it forces people to produce at a higher cost than they pay when they trade.

5. Yes, as long as the secretary earns less than $50/hour, the lawyer is ahead.

6. This is not true. All countries can gain from trade if their opportunity costs of production differ. Even the least productive country will

have a comparative advantage at producing something, and it can trade this good to the advanced country for less than the advanced country's opportunity cost.

True/False Questions

1. F; absolute advantage compares the quantities of inputs used in production while comparative advantage compares the opportunity costs.
2. T
3. T
4. F; restricting trade eliminates gains from trade.
5. T
6. T
7. F; the price of 1 bag of fries is 1/2 of a hamburger.
8. T
9. F; voluntary trade benefits both traders.
10. F; a low opportunity cost of producing one good implies a high opportunity cost of producing the other good.
11. T
12. F; it may harm those involved in that industry.
13. T
14. F; voluntary trade benefits all traders.
15. T

Multiple-Choice Questions

1. b
2. a
3. d
4. d
5. c
6. b
7. a
8. c
9. c
10. a
11. d
12. b
13. a
14. b
15. d
16. b
17. c
18. b
19. d
20. c

Advanced Critical Thinking

1. No. If we import autos, it is because the opportunity cost of producing them elsewhere is lower than in the United States.

2. Yes. Those associated with the domestic auto industry—stockholders of domestic auto producers and autoworkers.

3. No. When we reduce restrictions on imports, the country gains from the increased trade but individuals in the affected domestic industry may lose.

The Market Forces of Supply and Demand

CHAPTER OVERVIEW

Context and Purpose

Chapter 4 is the first chapter in a three-chapter sequence that deals with supply and demand and how markets work. Chapter 4 shows how supply and demand for a good determine both the quantity produced and the price at which the good sells. Chapter 5 will add precision to our discussion of supply and demand by addressing the concept of elasticity—the sensitivity of the quantity supplied and quantity demanded to changes in economic variables. Chapter 6 will address the impact of government policies on prices and quantities in markets.

The purpose of Chapter 4 is to establish the model of supply and demand. The model of supply and demand is the foundation for our discussion for the remainder of this text. For this reason, time spent studying the concepts in this chapter will return benefits to you throughout your study of economics. Many instructors would argue that this chapter is the most important chapter in the text.

Chapter Review

Introduction In a market economy, supply and demand determine both the quantity of each good produced and the price at which each good is sold. In this chapter, we develop the determinants of supply and demand. We also address how changes in supply and demand alter prices and change the allocation of the economy's resources.

Markets and Competition

A **market** is a group of buyers and sellers of a particular good or service. It can be highly organized like a stock market or less organized like the market for ice cream. A **competitive market** is a market in which there are many buyers and sellers so that each has a negligible impact on the market price.

A *perfectly competitive* market has two main characteristics:

- The goods offered for sale are all exactly the same.

- The buyers and sellers are so numerous that no one buyer or seller can influence the price.

If a market is perfectly competitive, both buyers and sellers are said to be *price takers* because they cannot influence the price. The assumption of perfect competition applies well to agricultural markets because the product is similar and no individual buyer or seller can influence the price.

If a market has only one seller, the market is known as a *monopoly*. Other types of markets fall between the extremes of perfect competition and monopoly.

Demand

The behavior of buyers is captured by the concept of demand. The **quantity demanded** is the amount of a good that buyers are willing and able to purchase. While many things determine the quantity demanded of a good, the *price* of the good plays a central role. Other things equal, an increase in the price of a good reduces the quantity demanded. This negative relationship between the price of a good and the quantity demanded of a good is known as the **law of demand.**

The **demand schedule** is a table that shows the relationship between the price of a good and the quantity demanded. The **demand curve** is a graph of this relationship with the price on the vertical axis and the quantity demanded on the horizontal axis. The demand curve is downward sloping due to the law of demand.

Market demand is the sum of the quantities demanded for each individual buyer at each price. That is, the market demand curve is the horizontal sum of the individual demand curves. The market demand curve shows the total quantity demanded of a good at each price, while all other factors that affect how much buyers wish to buy are held constant.

Shifts in the Demand Curve When people change how much they wish to buy at each price, the demand curve shifts. If buyers increase the quantity demanded at each price, the demand curve shifts right, which is called an *increase in demand*. Alternatively, if buyers decrease the quantity demanded at each price, the demand curve shifts left, which is called a *decrease in demand*. The most important factors that shift demand curves are:

- *Income:* A **normal good** is a good for which an increase in income leads to an increase in demand. An **inferior good** is a good for which an increase in income leads to a decrease in demand.

- *Prices of Related Goods:* If two goods can be used in place of one another, they are known as **substitutes.** When two goods are substitutes, an increase in the price of one good leads to an increase in the demand for the other good. If two goods are used together, they are known as **complements.** When two goods are complements, an increase in the price of one good leads to a decrease in the demand for the other good.

- *Tastes:* If your preferences shift toward a good, it will lead to an increase in the demand for that good.

- *Expectations:* Expectations about future income or prices will affect the demand for a good today.

- *Number of Buyers:* An increase in the number of buyers will lead to an increase in the market demand for a good because there are more individual demand curves to horizontally sum.

A demand curve is drawn with price on the vertical axis and quantity demanded on the horizontal axis while holding other things equal. Therefore, a change in the price of a good represents a movement along the demand curve while a change in income, prices of related goods, tastes, expectations, and the number of buyers causes a shift in the demand curve.

Supply

The behavior of sellers is captured by the concept of supply. The **quantity supplied** is the amount of a good that sellers are willing and able to sell. While many things determine the quantity supplied of a good, the *price* of the good is central. Other things equal, an increase in the price makes production more profitable and increases the quantity supplied. This positive relationship between the price of a good and the quantity supplied is known as the **law of supply.**

The **supply schedule** is a table that shows the relationship between the price of a good and the quantity supplied. The **supply curve** is a graph of this relationship with the price on the vertical axis and the quantity supplied on the horizontal axis. The supply curve is upward sloping due to the law of supply.

Market supply is the sum of the quantity supplied for each individual seller at each price. That is, the market supply curve is the horizontal sum of the individual supply curves. The market supply curve shows the total quantity supplied of a good at each price, while all other factors that affect how much producers wish to sell are held constant.

Shifts in the Supply Curve When producers change how much they wish to sell at each price, the supply curve shifts. If producers increase the quantity supplied at each price, the supply curve shifts right, which is called an *increase in supply*. Alternatively, if producers decrease the quantity supplied at each price, the supply curve shifts left, which is called a *decrease in supply*. The most important factors that shift supply curves are:

- *Input Prices:* A decrease in the price of an input makes production more profitable and increases supply.

- *Technology:* An improvement in technology reduces costs, makes production more profitable, and increases supply.

- *Expectations:* Expectations about the future will affect the supply of a good today.

- *Number of Sellers:* An increase in the number of sellers will lead to an increase in the market supply for a good because there are more individual supply curves to horizontally sum.

A supply curve is drawn with price on the vertical axis and quantity supplied on the horizontal axis while holding other things equal. Therefore, a change in the price of a good represents a movement along the supply curve while a change in input prices, technology, expectations, and the number of sellers causes a shift in the supply curve.

Supply and Demand Together

When placed on the same graph, the intersection of supply and demand is called the market's **equilibrium.** Equilibrium is a situation in which the price has reached the level where quantity supplied equals quantity demanded. The **equilibrium price,** or the market-clearing price, is the price that balances the quantity demanded and the quantity supplied. When the quantity supplied equals the quantity demanded at the equilibrium price, we have determined the **equilibrium quantity.**

The market naturally moves toward its equilibrium. If the price is above the equilibrium price, the quantity supplied exceeds the quantity demanded and there is a **surplus,** or an excess supply of the good. A surplus causes the price to fall until it reaches equilibrium. If the price is below the equilibrium price, the quantity demanded exceeds the quantity supplied and there is a **shortage,** or an excess demand for the good. A shortage causes the price to rise until it reaches equilibrium. This natural adjustment of the price to bring the quantity supplied and the quantity demanded into balance is known as the **law of supply and demand.**

When an economic event shifts the supply or the demand curve, the equilibrium in the market changes, resulting in a new equilibrium price and quantity. When analyzing the impact of some event on the market equilibrium, employ the following three steps:

- Decide whether the event shifts the supply curve or demand curve or both.

- Decide which direction the curve shifts.

- Use the supply-and-demand diagram to see how the shift changes the equilibrium price and quantity.

A shift in the demand curve is called a "change in demand." It is caused by a change in a variable that affects the amount people wish to purchase of a good *other than the price of the good*. A change in the price of a good causes a movement along a given demand curve and is called a "change in the quantity demanded." Likewise, a shift in the supply curve is called a "change in supply." It is caused by a change in a variable that affects the amount producers wish to supply of a good *other than the price of the good*. A change in the price of a good causes a movement along a supply curve and is called a "change in the quantity supplied."

For example, a frost that destroys much of the orange crop causes a decrease in the supply of oranges (supply of oranges shifts to the left). This increases the price of oranges and decreases the quantity demanded of oranges. In other words, a decrease in the supply of oranges increases the price of oranges and decreases the quantity of oranges purchased.

If both supply and demand shift at the same time, there may be more than one possible outcome for the changes in the equilibrium price and quantity. For example, if demand were to increase (shift right) while supply were to decrease (shift left), the price will certainly rise but the impact on the equilibrium quantity is ambiguous. In this case, the change in the equilibrium quantity depends on the magnitudes of the shifts in supply and demand.

Conclusion: How Prices Allocate Resources

Markets generate equilibrium prices. These prices are the signals that guide the allocation of scarce resources. Prices of products rise to the level necessary to allocate the products to those who are willing to pay for them. Prices of inputs (say labor) rise to the level necessary to induce people to do the jobs that need to get done. Prices coordinate decentralized decision making so that no jobs go undone, and there is no shortage of goods and services for those willing and able to pay for them.

Helpful Hints

1. By far, the greatest difficulty students have when studying supply and demand is distinguishing between a "change in demand" and a "change in the quantity demanded" and between a "change in supply" and a "change in the quantity supplied." It helps to remember that "demand" is the entire relationship between price and quantity demanded. That is, demand is the entire demand curve, not a point on a demand curve. Therefore, a change in demand is a shift in the entire demand curve, which can only be caused by a change in a determinant of demand other than the price of the good. A change in the quantity demanded is a movement along the demand curve and is caused by a change in the price of the good. Likewise, "supply" refers to the entire supply curve, not a point on the supply curve. Therefore, a change in supply is a shift in the entire supply curve, which can only be caused by a change in a determinant of supply other than the price of the good. A change in the quantity supplied is a movement along the supply curve and is caused by a change in the price of the good.

2. If both supply and demand shift at the same time and we do not know the magnitude of each shift, then the change in either the price or the quantity must be ambiguous. For example, if there is an increase in supply (supply shifts right) and an increase in demand (demand shifts right), the equilibrium quantity must certainly rise, but the change in the equilibrium price is ambiguous. Do this for all four possible combinations of changes in supply and demand. You will find that if you know the impact on the equilibrium price with certainty, then the impact on the equilibrium quantity must be ambiguous. If you know the impact on the equilibrium quantity with certainty, then the impact on the equilibrium price must be ambiguous.

Terms and Definitions

Choose a definition for each key term.

Key Terms

_____ Market

_____ Competitive market

_____ Monopoly

_____ Quantity demanded

_____ Law of demand

_____ Demand schedule

_____ Demand curve

_____ Normal good

_____ Inferior good

_____ Substitutes

_____ Complements

_____ Quantity supplied

_____ Law of supply

_____ Supply schedule

_____ Supply curve

_____ Equilibrium

_____ Equilibrium price

_____ Equilibrium quantity

_____ Surplus

_____ Shortage

_____ Law of supply and demand

Definitions

1. The quantity supplied and the quantity demanded at the equilibrium price

2. A table that shows the relationship between the price of a good and the quantity demanded

3. A table that shows the relationship between the price of a good and the quantity supplied

4. Two goods for which an increase in the price of one leads to an increase in the demand for the other

5. A group of buyers and sellers of a particular good or service

6. Market with only one seller

7. A good for which, other things equal, an increase in income leads to a decrease in demand

8. A situation in which quantity demanded is greater than quantity supplied

9. A situation in which quantity supplied is greater than quantity demanded

10. The amount of a good that buyers are willing and able to purchase

11. A situation in which the price has reached the level where quantity supplied equals quantity demanded

12. A market in which there are many buyers and sellers so that each has a negligible impact on the market price

13. The claim that, other things equal, the quantity demanded of a good falls when the price of the good rises

14. A graph of the relationship between the price of a good and the quantity demanded

15. The price that balances quantity supplied and quantity demanded

16. The amount of a good that sellers are willing and able to sell

17. The claim that, other things equal, the quantity supplied of a good rises when the price of the good rises

18. The claim that the price of any good adjusts to bring the quantity supplied and quantity demanded for that good into balance

19. Two goods for which an increase in the price of one leads to a decrease in the demand for the other

20. A good for which, other things equal, an increase in income leads to an increase in demand

21. A graph of the relationship between the price of a good and the quantity supplied

PROBLEMS AND SHORT-ANSWER QUESTIONS

Practice Problems

1. Suppose we have the following market supply and demand schedules for bicycles:

Price	Quantity Demanded	Quantity Supplied
$100	70	30
200	60	40
300	50	50
400	40	60
500	30	70
600	20	80

a. Plot the supply curve and the demand curve for bicycles in Exhibit 1.

b. What is the equilibrium price of bicycles?

_____

c. What is the equilibrium quantity of bicycles?

_____

d. If the price of bicycles were $100, is there a surplus or a shortage? How many units of surplus or shortage are there? Will this cause the price to rise or fall?

_____

_____

_____

e. If the price of bicycles were $400, is there a surplus or a shortage? How many units of surplus or shortage are there? Will this cause the price to rise or fall?

_____

_____

_____

f. Suppose that the bicycle maker's labor union bargains for an increase in its wages. Further, suppose this event raises the cost of production, makes bicycle manufacturing less profitable, and reduces the quantity supplied of bicycles by 20 units at each price of bicycles. Plot the new supply curve and the original supply and demand curves in Exhibit 2. What is the new equilibrium price and quantity in the market for bicycles?

_____

2.   Each of the events listed below has an impact on the market for bicycles. For each event, which curve is affected (supply or demand for bicycles), what direction is it shifted, and what is the resulting impact on the equilibrium price and quantity of bicycles?
   a.   The price of automobiles increases.

   _____

   _____

   b.   Consumers' incomes decrease and bicycles are a normal good.

   _____

   _____

   c.   The price of steel used to make bicycle frames increases.

   _____

   _____

   d.   An environmental movement shifts tastes toward bicycling.

   _____

   _____

   e.   Consumers expect the price of bicycles to fall in the future.

   _____

   _____

   f.   A technological advance in the manufacture of bicycles occurs.

   _____

   _____

   g.   The prices of bicycle helmets and shoes are reduced.

   _____

   _____

   h.   Consumers' incomes decrease and bicycles are an inferior good.

   _____

   _____

3.   The following questions address a market when both supply and demand shift.
   a.   What would happen to the equilibrium price and quantity in the bicycle market if there is an increase in both the supply and the demand for bicycles?

   _____

   _____

   b.   What would happen to the equilibrium price and quantity in the bicycle market if the demand for bicycles increases more than the increase in the supply of bicycles?

   _____

   _____

Short-Answer Questions

1. What are the two main characteristics of a perfectly competitive market?

   _____

   _____

2. Explain the law of demand.

   _____

3. What are the variables that should affect the amount of a good that consumers wish to buy, other than its price?

   _____

4. What is the difference between a normal good and an inferior good?

   _____

   _____

5. Explain the law of supply.

   _____

6. What are the variables that should affect the amount of a good that producers wish to sell, other than its price?

   _____

7. Suppose *suppliers* of corn expect the price of corn to rise in the future. How would this affect the supply and demand for corn and the equilibrium price and quantity of corn?

   _____

   _____

   _____

8. If there is a surplus of a good, is the price above or below the equilibrium price for that good?

   _____

9. Suppose there is an increase in consumers' incomes. In the market for automobiles (a normal good), does this event cause an increase in demand or an increase in quantity demanded? Does this cause an increase in supply or an increase in quantity supplied? Explain.

   _____

   _____

   _____

   _____

10. Suppose there is an advance in the technology employed to produce automobiles. In the market for automobiles, does this event cause an increase in supply or an increase in the quantity supplied? Does this cause an increase in demand or an increase in the quantity demanded? Explain.

_____

_____

_____

_____

SELF-TEST

True/False Questions

_____ 1. A perfectly competitive market consists of products that are all slightly different from one another.

_____ 2. A monopolistic market has only one seller.

_____ 3. The law of demand states that an increase in the price of a good decreases the demand for that good.

_____ 4. If apples and oranges are substitutes, an increase in the price of apples will decrease the demand for oranges.

_____ 5. If golf clubs and golf balls are complements, an increase in the price of golf clubs will decrease the demand for golf balls.

_____ 6. If consumers expect the price of shoes to rise, there will be an increase in the demand for shoes today.

_____ 7. The law of supply states that an increase in the price of a good increases the quantity supplied of that good.

_____ 8. An increase in the price of steel will shift the supply of automobiles to the right.

_____ 9. When the price of a good is below the equilibrium price, it causes a surplus.

_____ 10. The market supply curve is the horizontal summation of the individual supply curves.

_____ 11. If there is a shortage of a good, then the price of that good tends to fall.

_____ 12. If pencils and paper are complements, an increase in the price of pencils causes the demand for paper to decrease or shift to the left.

_____ 13. If Coca-Cola and Pepsi are substitutes, an increase in the price of Coca-Cola will cause an increase in the equilibrium price and quantity in the market for Pepsi.

_____ 14. An advance in the technology employed to manufacture Rollerblades™ will result in a decrease in the equilibrium price and an increase in the equilibrium quantity in the market for Rollerblades™.

_____ 15. If there is an increase in supply accompanied by a decrease in demand for coffee, then there will be a decrease in both the equilibrium price and quantity in the market for coffee.

Multiple-Choice Questions

1. A perfectly competitive market has
    a. only one seller.
    b. at least a few sellers.
    c. many buyers and sellers.
    d. firms that set their own prices.
    e. none of the above.

2. If an increase in the price of blue jeans leads to an increase in the demand for tennis shoes, then blue jeans and tennis shoes are
    a. substitutes.
    b. complements.
    c. normal goods.
    d. inferior goods.
    e. none of the above.

3. The *law of demand* states that an increase in the price of a good
    a. decreases the demand for that good.
    b. decreases the quantity demanded for that good.
    c. increases the supply of that good.
    d. increases the quantity supplied of that good.
    e. does none of the above.

4. The *law of supply* states that an increase in the price of a good
    a. decreases the demand for that good.
    b. decreases the quantity demanded for that good.
    c. increases the supply of that good.
    d. increases the quantity supplied of that good.
    e. does none of the above.

5. If an increase in consumer incomes leads to a decrease in the demand for camping equipment, then camping equipment is
    a. a complementary good.
    b. a substitute good.
    c. a normal good.
    d. an inferior good.
    e. none of the above.

6. A monopolistic market has
    a. only one seller.
    b. at least a few sellers.
    c. many buyers and sellers.
    d. firms that are price takers.
    e. none of the above.

7. Which of the following shifts the demand for watches to the right?
    a. a decrease in the price of watches
    b. a decrease in consumer incomes if watches are a normal good
    c. a decrease in the price of watch batteries if watch batteries and watches are complements
    d. an increase in the price of watches
    e. none of the above

8. All of the following shift the supply of watches to the right except
    a. an increase in the price of watches.
    b. an advance in the technology used to manufacture watches.
    c. a decrease in the wage of workers employed to manufacture watches.
    d   manufacturers' expectations of lower watch prices in the future.
    e. All of the above cause an increase in the supply of watches.

9. If the price of a good is above the equilibrium price,
    a. there is a surplus and the price will rise.
    b. there is a surplus and the price will fall.
    c. there is a shortage and the price will rise.
    d. there is a shortage and the price will fall.
    e. the quantity demanded is equal to the quantity supplied and the price remains unchanged.

10. If the price of a good is below the equilibrium price,
    a. there is a surplus and the price will rise.
    b. there is a surplus and the price will fall.
    c. there is a shortage and the price will rise.
    d. there is a shortage and the price will fall.
    e. the quantity demanded is equal to the quantity supplied and the price remains unchanged.

11. If the price of a good is equal to the equilibrium price,
    a. there is a surplus and the price will rise.
    b. there is a surplus and the price will fall.
    c. there is a shortage and the price will rise.
    d. there is a shortage and the price will fall.
    e. the quantity demanded is equal to the quantity supplied and the price remains unchanged.

12. An increase (rightward shift) in the demand for a good will tend to cause
    a. an increase in the equilibrium price and quantity.
    b. a decrease in the equilibrium price and quantity.
    c. an increase in the equilibrium price and a decrease in the equilibrium quantity.
    d. a decrease in the equilibrium price and an increase in the equilibrium quantity.
    e. none of the above.

13. A decrease (leftward shift) in the supply for a good will tend to cause
    a. an increase in the equilibrium price and quantity.
    b. a decrease in the equilibrium price and quantity.
    c. an increase in the equilibrium price and a decrease in the equilibrium quantity.
    d. a decrease in the equilibrium price and an increase in the equilibrium quantity.
    e. none of the above.

14. Suppose there is an increase in both the supply and demand for personal computers. In the market for personal computers, we would expect the
    a. equilibrium quantity to rise and the equilibrium price to rise.
    b. equilibrium quantity to rise and the equilibrium price to fall.
    c. equilibrium quantity to rise and the equilibrium price to remain constant.
    d. equilibrium quantity to rise and the change in the equilibrium price to be ambiguous.
    e. change in the equilibrium quantity to be ambiguous and the equilibrium price to rise.

15. Suppose there is an increase in both the supply and demand for personal computers. Further, suppose the supply of personal computers increases more than demand for personal computers. In the market for personal computers, we would expect the
    a. equilibrium quantity to rise and the equilibrium price to rise.
    b. equilibrium quantity to rise and the equilibrium price to fall.
    c. equilibrium quantity to rise and the equilibrium price to remain constant.
    d. equilibrium quantity to rise and the change in the equilibrium price to be ambiguous.
    e. change in the equilibrium quantity to be ambiguous and the equilibrium price to fall.

16. Which of the following statements is true about the impact of an increase in the price of lettuce?
    a. The demand for lettuce will decrease.
    b. The supply of lettuce will decrease.
    c. The equilibrium price and quantity of salad dressing will rise.
    d. The equilibrium price and quantity of salad dressing will fall.
    e. Both *a* and *d* are true.

17. Suppose a frost destroys much of the Florida orange crop. At the same time, suppose consumer tastes shift toward orange juice. What would we expect to happen to the equilibrium price and quantity in the market for orange juice?
    a. Price will increase; quantity is ambiguous.
    b. Price will increase; quantity will increase.
    c. Price will increase; quantity will decrease.
    d. Price will decrease; quantity is ambiguous.
    e. The impact on both price and quantity is ambiguous.

18. Suppose consumer tastes shift toward the consumption of apples. Which of the following statements is an accurate description of the impact of this event on the market for apples?
    a. There is an increase in the demand for apples and an increase in the quantity supplied of apples.
    b. There is an increase in the demand and supply of apples.
    c. There is an increase in the quantity demanded of apples and in the supply for apples.
    d. There is an increase in the demand for apples and a decrease in the supply of apples.
    e. There is a decrease in the quantity demanded of apples and an increase in the supply for apples.

19. Suppose both buyers and sellers of wheat expect the price of wheat to rise in the near future. What would we expect to happen to the equilibrium price and quantity in the market for wheat today?
    a. The impact on both price and quantity is ambiguous.
    b. Price will increase; quantity is ambiguous.
    c. Price will increase; quantity will increase.
    d. Price will increase; quantity will decrease.
    e. Price will decrease; quantity is ambiguous.

20. An inferior good is one for which an increase in income causes a(n)
    a. increase in supply.
    b. decrease in supply.
    c. increase in demand.
    d. decrease in demand.

ADVANCED CRITICAL THINKING

You are watching a national news broadcast. It is reported that a typhoon is heading for the Washington coast and that it will likely destroy much of this year's apple crop. Your roommate says, "If there are going to be fewer apples available, I'll bet that apple prices will rise. We should buy enormous quantities of apples now and put them in storage. Later we will sell them and make a killing."

1. If this information about the storm is publicly available so that all buyers and sellers in the apple market expect the price of apples to rise in the future, what will happen immediately to the supply and demand for apples and the equilibrium price and quantity of apples?

    _____

    _____

2. Can you "beat the market" with public information? That is, can you use publicly available information to help you buy something cheap and quickly sell it at a higher price? Why or why not?

    _____

    _____

3. Suppose a friend of yours works for the U.S. Weather Bureau. She calls you and provides you with inside information about the approaching storm—information not available to the public. Can you "beat the market" with inside information? Why?

    _____

    _____

SOLUTIONS

Terms and Definitions

_5_ Market
12 Competitive market
_6_ Monopoly
10 Quantity demanded
13 Law of demand
_2_ Demand schedule
14 Demand curve
20 Normal good
_7_ Inferior good
_4_ Substitutes
19 Complements
16 Quantity supplied
17 Law of supply
_3_ Supply schedule
21 Supply curve
11 Equilibrium
15 Equilibrium price
_1_ Equilibrium quantity
_9_ Surplus
_8_ Shortage
18 Law of supply and demand

Practice Problems

1. a. See Exhibit 3.

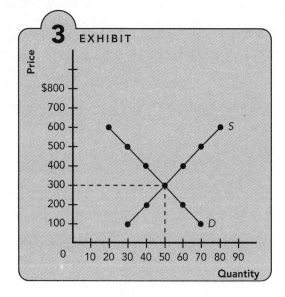

   b. $300
   c. 50 bicycles
   d. Shortage, 70 − 30 = 40 units, the price will rise
   e. Surplus, 60 − 40 = 20 units, the price will fall

   f. See Exhibit 4. equilibrium price = $400, equilibrium quantity = 40 bicycles

2. a. demand, shifts right, equilibrium price and quantity rise
   b. demand, shifts left, equilibrium price and quantity fall
   c. supply, shifts left, equilibrium price rises and equilibrium quantity falls
   d. demand, shifts right, equilibrium price and quantity rise
   e. demand, shifts left, equilibrium price and quantity fall
   f. supply, shifts right, equilibrium price falls and equilibrium quantity rises
   g. demand, shifts right, equilibrium price and quantity rise
   h. demand, shifts right, equilibrium price and quantity rise

3. a. equilibrium quantity will rise, equilibrium price is ambiguous
   b. equilibrium price and quantity will rise

Short-Answer Questions

1. The goods offered for sale are all the same, and the buyers and sellers are so numerous that no one buyer or seller can influence the price.

2. Other things equal, price and quantity demanded of a good are negatively related.

3. Income, prices of related goods, tastes, expectations, and number of buyers in the market.

4. When income rises, demand for a normal good increases or shifts right. When income rises, demand for an inferior good decreases or shifts left.

5. Other things equal, price and quantity supplied of a good are positively related.

6. The variables are input prices, technology, expectations, and number of sellers in the market.

7. The supply of corn in today's market would decrease (shift left) as sellers hold back their offerings in anticipation of greater profits if the price rises in the future. If only suppliers expect higher prices, demand would be unaffected. The equilibrium price would rise and the equilibrium quantity would fall.

8. The price must be above the equilibrium price.

9. There would be an *increase in the demand* for automobiles, which means that the entire demand curve shifts to the right. This implies a movement along the fixed supply curve as the price rises. The increase in price causes an *increase in the quantity supplied* of automobiles, but there is no increase in the supply of automobiles.

10. There would be an *increase in the supply* of automobiles, which means that the entire supply curve shifts to the right. This implies a movement along the fixed demand curve as the price falls. The decrease in price causes an *increase in the quantity demanded* of automobiles, but there is no increase in the demand for automobiles.

True/False Questions

1. F; a perfectly competitive market consists of goods offered for sale that are all exactly the same.
2. T
3. F; the law of demand states that an increase in the price of a good decreases the *quantity demanded* of that good (a movement along the demand curve).
4. F; it will increase the demand for oranges.
5. T
6. T
7. T
8. F; an increase in the price of an input shifts the supply curve for the output to the left.
9. F; it causes an excess demand.
10. T
11. F; an excess demand causes the price to rise.
12. T
13. T
14. T
15. F; there will be a decrease in the equilibrium price, but the impact on the equilibrium quantity is ambiguous.

Multiple-Choice Questions

1. c
2. a
3. b
4. d
5. d
6. a
7. c
8. a
9. b
10. c
11. e
12. a
13. c
14. d
15. b
16. d
17. a
18. a
19. b
20. d

Advanced Critical Thinking

1. Sellers reduce supply (supply shifts left) in the hope of selling apples later at a higher price, and buyers increase demand (demand shifts right) in the hope of buying apples now before the price goes up. The price will immediately rise and the quantity exchanged is ambiguous.

2. No. Usually the market immediately adjusts so that the price has already moved to its new equilibrium value before the amateur speculator can make his or her purchase.

3. Yes. In this case, you can make your purchase before the market responds to the information about the storm.

5

Elasticity and Its Application

CHAPTER OVERVIEW

Context and Purpose

Chapter 5 is the second chapter of a three-chapter sequence that deals with supply and demand and how markets work. Chapter 4 introduced supply and demand. Chapter 5 shows how much buyers and sellers respond to changes in market conditions. Chapter 6 will address the impact of government policies on competitive markets.

The purpose of Chapter 5 is to add precision to our supply and demand model. We introduce the concept of elasticity, which measures the responsiveness of buyers and sellers to changes in economic variables such as prices and income. The concept of elasticity allows us to make quantitative observations about the impact of changes in supply and demand on equilibrium prices and quantities.

Chapter Review

Introduction In Chapter 4, we learned that an increase in price reduces the quantity demanded and increases the quantity supplied in a market. In this chapter, we will develop the concept of elasticity so that we can address how much the quantity demanded and the quantity supplied responds to changes in market conditions such as price.

The Elasticity of Demand

To measure the response of demand to its determinants, we use the concept of **elasticity**. **Price elasticity of demand** measures how much the quantity demanded responds to a change in the price of that good, computed as the percentage change in quantity demanded divided by the percentage change in price.

If the quantity demanded changes substantially from a change in price, demand is *elastic*. If the quantity demanded changes little from a change in price, demand is *inelastic*. Whether a demand curve tends to be price elastic or inelastic depends on the following:

- *Availability of close substitutes:* The demand for goods with close substitutes is more sensitive to changes in prices and, thus, is more price elastic.

GOALS

In this chapter you will

■ Learn the meaning of the elasticity of demand

■ Examine what determines the elasticity of demand

■ Learn the meaning of the elasticity of supply

■ Examine what determines the elasticity of supply

■ Apply the concept of elasticity in three very different markets

OUTCOMES

After accomplishing these goals, you should be able to

■ Calculate the price and income elasticity of demand

■ Distinguish between the price elasticity of demand for necessities and luxuries

■ Calculate the price elasticity of supply

■ Distinguish between an inelastic and elastic supply curve

■ Demonstrate the impact of the price elasticity of demand on total revenue

- *Necessities versus luxuries:* The demand for necessities is inelastic while the demand for luxuries is elastic. Since one cannot do without a necessity, an increase in the price has little impact on the quantity demanded. However, an increase in price greatly reduces the quantity demanded of a luxury.

- *Definition of the market:* The more narrowly we define the market, the more likely there are to be close substitutes and the more price elastic the demand curve.

- *Time horizon:* The longer the time period considered, the greater the availability of close substitutes and the more price elastic the demand curve.

The formula for computing the price elasticity of demand is:

$$\text{Price elasticity of demand} = \frac{\text{Percentage change in quantity demanded}}{\text{Percentage change in price}}.$$

Since price elasticity of demand is always negative, it is customary to drop the negative sign.

When we compute price elasticity between any two points on a demand curve, we get a different answer depending on our chosen starting point and our chosen finishing point if we take the change in price and quantity as a percent of the starting value for each. To avoid this problem, economists often employ the *midpoint method* to calculate elasticities. With this method, the percentage changes in quantity and price are calculated by dividing the change in the variable by the *average* or midpoint value of the two points on the curve, not the starting point on the curve. Thus, the formula for the price elasticity of demand using the midpoint method is:

$$\text{Price elasticity of demand} = \frac{(Q_2 - Q_1) / [(Q_2 + Q_1) / 2]}{(P_2 - P_1) / [(P_2 + P_1) / 2]}.$$

If price elasticity of demand is greater than one, demand is elastic. If elasticity is less than one, demand is inelastic. If elasticity is equal to one, demand is said to have unit elasticity. If elasticity is zero, demand is perfectly inelastic (vertical). If elasticity is infinite, demand is perfectly elastic (horizontal). In general, the flatter the demand curve, the more elastic. The steeper the demand curve, the more inelastic.

Total revenue is the amount paid by buyers and received by sellers, computed simply as price times quantity. The elasticity of demand determines the impact of a change in price on total revenue:

- If demand is price inelastic (less than 1), an increase in price increases total revenue because the price increase is proportionately larger than the reduction in quantity demanded.

- If demand is price elastic (greater than 1), an increase in price decreases total revenue because the decrease in the quantity demanded is proportionately larger than the increase in price.

- If demand is unit price elastic (exactly equal to 1), a change in price has no impact on total revenue because the increase in price is proportionately equal to the decrease in quantity.

Along a linear demand curve, price elasticity is not constant. When price is high and quantity low, price elasticity is large because a change in price causes a larger *percentage* change in quantity. When price is low and quantity high, price elasticity is small because a change in price causes a smaller *percentage* change in quantity.

There are additional demand elasticities. The **income elasticity of demand** is a measure of how much the quantity demanded responds to a change in consumers' income, computed as the percentage change in quantity demanded divided by the percentage change in income or:

$$\text{Income elasticity of demand} = \frac{\text{Percentage change in quantity demanded}}{\text{Percentage change in income}}.$$

For *normal goods*, income elasticity is positive. For *inferior goods*, income elasticity is negative. Within the group of normal goods, necessities like food have small income elasticities because the quantity demanded changes little when income changes. Luxuries have larger income elasticities.

The **cross-price elasticity of demand** is a measure of the response of the quantity demanded of one good to a change in the price of another good, computed as the percentage change in the quantity demanded of one good divided by the percentage change in the price of another good or:

$$\text{Cross-price elasticity of demand} = \frac{\text{Percentage change in quantity demanded of good 1}}{\text{Percentage change in the price of good 2}}.$$

The cross-price elasticity of demand is positive for *substitutes* and negative for *complements*.

The Elasticity of Supply

Price elasticity of supply measures how much the quantity supplied responds to a change in the price of that good, computed as the percentage change in quantity supplied divided by the percentage change in price.

If the quantity supplied changes substantially from a change in price, supply is *elastic*. If the quantity supplied changes little from a change in price, supply is *inelastic*. Supply is more elastic when the sellers have greater flexibility to change the amount of a good they produce in response to a change in price. Generally, the shorter the time period considered, the less flexibility the seller has in choosing how much to produce and the more inelastic the supply curve.

The formula for computing the price elasticity of supply is:

$$\text{Price elasticity of supply} = \frac{\text{Percentage change in quantity supplied}}{\text{Percentage change in price}}.$$

If price elasticity of supply is greater than one, supply is elastic. If elasticity is less than one, supply is inelastic. If elasticity is equal to one, supply is said to have unit elasticity. If elasticity is zero, supply is perfectly inelastic (vertical). If elasticity is infinite, supply is perfectly elastic (horizontal). In general, the flatter the supply curve, the more elastic. The steeper the supply curve, the more inelastic.

Price elasticity of supply may not be constant along a given supply curve. At low quantities, a small increase in price may stimulate a large increase in quantity supplied because there is excess capacity in the production facility. Therefore, price elasticity is large. At high quantities, a large increase in price may cause only a small increase in quantity supplied because the production facility is at full capacity. Therefore, price elasticity is small.

Three Applications of Supply, Demand, and Elasticity

- *The market for agricultural products:* Advances in technology have shifted the supply curve for agricultural products to the right. The demand for food, however, is generally inelastic (steep) because food is inexpensive and a necessity. As a result, the rightward shift in supply has caused a great reduction in the equilibrium price and a small increase in the equilibrium quantity. Thus, ironically, technological advances in agriculture reduce total revenue paid to farmers as a group.

- *The market for oil:* In the 1970s and early 1980s, the Organization of Petroleum Exporting Countries (OPEC) reduced the supply of oil in order to raise its price. In the short run, the demand for oil tends to be inelastic (steep) because consumers cannot easily find substitutes. Thus, the decrease in supply raised the price substantially and increased total revenue to the producers. In the long run, however, consumers found substitutes and drove more fuel-efficient cars causing the demand for oil to become more elastic, and producers searched for more oil causing supply to become more elastic. As a result, while the price of oil rose a great deal in the short run, it did not rise much in the long run.

- *The market for illegal drugs:* In the short run, the demand for illegal addictive drugs is relatively inelastic. As a result, drug interdiction policies that reduce the supply of drugs tend to greatly increase the price of drugs while reducing the quantity consumed very little, and thus, total revenue paid by drug users increases. This need for additional funds by drug users may cause drug-related crime to rise. This increase in total revenue and in crime is likely to be smaller in the long run because the demand for illegal drugs becomes more elastic as time passes. Alternatively, policies aimed at reducing the demand for drugs reduce total revenue in the drug market and reduce drug-related crime.

Conclusion

The tools of supply and demand allow you to analyze the most important events and policies that shape the economy.

Helpful Hints

1. An easy way to remember the difference between the terms elastic and inelastic is to substitute the word *sensitivity* for elasticity. For example, price elasticity of demand becomes price *sensitivity* of demand. If the quantity demanded is sensitive to a change in price (demand is relatively flat), demand is elastic. If the quantity demanded is insensitive to a change in price (demand is relatively steep), demand is inelastic. The same is true for the price elasticity of supply. If the quantity supplied is sensitive to a change in price, supply is elastic. If the quantity supplied is insensitive to a change in price, supply is inelastic.

2. While elasticity and slope are similar, they are not the same. Along a straight line, slope is constant. Slope (rise over run) is the same anywhere on the line and is measured as the change in the dependent variable divided by the change in the independent variable. Elasticity, however, is measured as the *percent* change in the dependent variable divided by the *percent* change in the independent variable. This value changes as we move along a line, because a one-unit change in a variable is a larger percentage change when the initial values are small as opposed to when they are large. In practice, however, it is still reasonable to suggest that flatter curves tend to be more elastic and steeper curves tend to be more inelastic.

3. The term "elasticity" is used to describe how much the quantity stretches (or changes) in response to some economic event such as a change in price or income. If the quantity stretches a great deal in response to a change in price or income, it is considered elastic. This mental picture should also help you to remember how to calculate an elasticity—in the numerator, you will always find the percent change in quantity, and in the denominator, you will always find the percent change in the variable that is the source of the change in quantity.

Terms and Definitions

Choose a definition for each key term.

Key Terms

_____ Elasticity

_____ Price elasticity of demand

_____ Elastic

_____ Inelastic

_____ Total revenue

_____ Income elasticity of demand

_____ Cross-price elasticity of demand

_____ Price elasticity of supply

_____ Normal good

_____ Inferior good

Definitions

1. A measure of how much the quantity demanded of a good responds to a change in consumers' income.

2. When the quantity demanded or supplied responds substantially to a change in one of its determinants.

3. A good characterized by a negative income elasticity.

4. A measure of the responsiveness of the quantity demanded or quantity supplied to one of its determinants.

5. A good characterized by a positive income elasticity.

6. A measure of how much the quantity supplied of a good responds to a change in the price of that good.

7. When the quantity demanded or supplied responds only slightly to a change in one of its determinants.

8. The amount paid by buyers and received by sellers of a good computed as $P \times Q$.

9. A measure of how much the quantity demanded of a good responds to a change in the price of that good.

10. A measure of how much the quantity demanded of one good responds to a change in the price of another good.

PROBLEMS AND SHORT-ANSWER QUESTIONS

Practice Problems

1. For each pair of goods listed below, which good would you expect to have the more elastic demand? Why?
   a. cigarettes; a trip to Florida over spring break

   _____

   _____

   b. an AIDS vaccine over the next month; an AIDS vaccine over the next five years

   _____

   _____

   c. beer; Budweiser

   _____

   _____

   d. insulin; aspirin

   _____

   _____

2. Suppose the *Daily Newspaper* estimates that if it raises the price of its newspaper from $1.00 to $1.50 then the number of subscribers will fall from 50,000 to 40,000.
   a. What is the price elasticity of demand for the *Daily Newspaper* when elasticity is calculated using the midpoint method?

   _____

   _____

   b. What is the advantage of using the midpoint method?

   _____

   _____

   c. If the *Daily Newspaper*'s only concern is to maximize total revenue, should it raise the price of a newspaper from $1.00 to $1.50? Why or why not?

   _____

   _____

3. The table below provides the demand schedule for motel rooms at Small Town Motel. Use the information provided to complete the table. Answer the following questions based on your responses in the table. Use the midpoint method to calculate the percentage changes used to generate the elasticities.

Price	Quantity Demanded	Total Revenue	% Change In Price	% Change In Quantity	Elasticity
$ 20	24	_____			
40	20	_____	_____	_____	_____
60	16	_____	_____	_____	_____
80	12	_____	_____	_____	_____
100	8	_____	_____	_____	_____
120	4	_____	_____	_____	_____

a. Over what range of prices is the demand for motel rooms elastic? To maximize total revenue, should Small Town Motel raise or lower the price within this range?

_____

_____

b. Over what range of prices is the demand for motel rooms inelastic? To maximize total revenue, should Small Town Motel raise or lower the price within this range?

_____

_____

c. Over what range of prices is the demand for motel rooms unit elastic? To maximize total revenue, should Small Town Motel raise or lower the price within this range?

_____

_____

4. The demand schedule from question 3 above is reproduced below along with another demand schedule when consumer incomes have risen to $60,000 from $50,000. Use this information to answer the following questions. Use the midpoint method to calculate the percentage changes used to generate the elasticities.

Price	Quantity Demanded When Income is $50,000	Quantity Demanded When Income is $60,000
$ 20	24	34
40	20	30
60	16	26
80	12	22
100	8	18
120	4	14

    a. What is the income elasticity of demand when motel rooms rent for $40?

_____

_____

    b. What is the income elasticity of demand when motel rooms rent for $100?

_____

_____

    c. Are motel rooms normal or inferior goods? Why?

_____

_____

    d. Are motel rooms likely to be necessities or luxuries? Why?

_____

_____

5. For each pair of goods listed below, which good would you expect to have the more elastic supply? Why?
    a. televisions; beachfront property

_____

_____

    b. crude oil over the next week; crude oil over the next year

_____

_____

    c. a painting by van Gogh; a print of the same painting by van Gogh

_____

_____

Short-Answer Questions

1. What are the four major determinants of the price elasticity of demand?

_____

_____

_____

2. If demand is inelastic, will an increase in price raise or lower total revenue? Why?

_____

_____

3. If the price of soda doubles from $1.00 per can to $2.00 per can and you buy the same amount, what is your price elasticity of demand for soda, and is it considered elastic or inelastic?

_____

_____

4. If the price of Pepsi increases by one cent and this induces you to stop buying Pepsi altogether and switch to Coca-Cola, what is your price elasticity of demand for Pepsi, and is it considered elastic or inelastic?

_____

_____

5. Suppose your income rises by 20 percent and your quantity demanded of eggs falls by 10 percent. What is the value of your income elasticity of demand for eggs? Are eggs normal or inferior goods to you?

_____

_____

6. Suppose a firm is operating at half capacity. Is its supply curve for output likely to be relatively elastic or inelastic? Why?

_____

_____

7. Is the price elasticity of supply for fresh fish likely to be elastic or inelastic when measured over the time period of one day? Why?

_____

_____

8. If a demand curve is linear, is the elasticity constant along the demand curve? Which part tends to be elastic and which part tends to be inelastic? Why?

_____

_____

_____

9. Suppose that at a price of $2.00 per bushel, the quantity supplied of corn is 25 million metric tons. At a price of $3.00 per bushel, the quantity supplied is 30 million metric tons. What is the elasticity of supply for corn? Is supply elastic or inelastic?

_____

_____

10. Suppose that when the price of apples rises by 20 percent, the quantity demanded of oranges rises by 6 percent. What is the cross-price elasticity of demand between apples and oranges? Are these two goods substitutes or complements?

_____

_____

SELF-TEST

True/False Questions

_____ 1. If the quantity demanded of a good is sensitive to a change in the price of that good, demand is said to be price inelastic.

_____ 2. Using the midpoint method to calculate elasticity, if an increase in the price of pencils from 10 cents to 20 cents reduces the quantity demanded from 1,000 pencils to 500 pencils, then the demand for pencils is unit price elastic.

_____ 3. The demand for tires should be more inelastic than the demand for Goodyear brand tires.

_____ 4. The demand for aspirin this month should be more elastic than the demand for aspirin this year.

_____ 5. The price elasticity of demand is defined as the percentage change in the price of that good divided by the percentage change in quantity demanded of that good.

_____ 6. If the cross-price elasticity of demand between two goods is positive, the goods are likely to be complements.

_____ 7. If the demand for a good is price inelastic, an increase in its price will increase total revenue in that market.

_____ 8. The demand for a necessity such as insulin tends to be elastic.

_____ 9. If a demand curve is linear, the price elasticity of demand is constant along it.

_____ 10. If the income elasticity of demand for a bus ride is negative, then a bus ride is an inferior good.

_____ 11. The supply of automobiles for this week is likely to be more price inelastic than the supply of automobiles for this year.

_____ 12. If the price elasticity of supply for blue jeans is 1.3, an increase of 10 percent in the price of blue jeans would increase the quantity supplied of blue jeans by 13 percent.

_____ 13. The price elasticity of supply tends to be more inelastic as the firm's production facility reaches maximum capacity.

_____ 14. An advance in technology that shifts the market supply curve to the right always increases total revenue received by producers.

_____ 15. The income elasticity of demand for luxury items, such as diamonds, tends to be large (greater than 1).

Multiple-Choice Questions

1. If a small percentage increase in the price of a good greatly reduces the quantity demanded for that good, the demand for that good is
   a. price inelastic.
   b. price elastic.
   c. unit price elastic.
   d. income inelastic.
   e. income elastic.

2. The price elasticity of demand is defined as
   a. the percentage change in price of a good divided by the percentage change in the quantity demanded of that good.
   b. the percentage change in income divided by the percentage change in the quantity demanded.
   c. the percentage change in the quantity demanded of a good divided by the percentage change in the price of that good.
   d. the percentage change in the quantity demanded divided by the percentage change in income.
   e. none of the above.

3. In general, a flatter demand curve is more likely to be
   a. price elastic.
   b. price inelastic.
   c. unit price elastic.
   d. none of the above.

4. In general, a steeper supply curve is more likely to be
   a. price elastic.
   b. price inelastic.
   c. unit price elastic.
   d. none of the above.

5. Which of the following would cause a demand curve for a good to be price inelastic?
   a. There are a great number of substitutes for the good.
   b. The good is inferior.
   c. The good is a luxury.
   d. The good is a necessity.

6. The demand for which of the following is likely to be the most price inelastic?
   a. airline tickets
   b. bus tickets
   c. taxi rides
   d. transportation

7. If the cross-price elasticity between two goods is negative, the two goods are likely to be
   a. luxuries.
   b. necessities.
   c. complements.
   d. substitutes.

8. If a supply curve for a good is price elastic, then
   a. the quantity supplied is sensitive to changes in the price of that good.
   b. the quantity supplied is insensitive to changes in the price of that good.
   c. the quantity demanded is sensitive to changes in the price of that good.
   d. the quantity demanded is insensitive to changes in the price of that good.
   e. none of the above.

9. If a fisherman must sell all of his daily catch before it spoils for whatever price he is offered, once the fish are caught, the fisherman's price elasticity of supply for fresh fish is
   a. zero.
   b. one.
   c. infinite.
   d. unable to be determined from this information.

10. A decrease in supply (shift to the left) will increase total revenue in that market if
    a. supply is price elastic.
    b. supply is price inelastic.
    c. demand is price elastic.
    d. demand is price inelastic.

11. If an increase in the price of a good has no impact on the total revenue in that market, demand must be
    a. price inelastic.
    b. price elastic.
    c. unit price elastic.
    d. all of the above.

12. If consumers always spend 15 percent of their income on food, then the income elasticity of demand for food is
    a. 0.15.
    b. 1.00.
    c. 1.15.
    d. 1.50.
    e. none of the above.

13. Technological improvements in agriculture that shift the supply of agricultural commodities to the right tend to
    a. reduce total revenue to farmers as a whole because the demand for food is inelastic.
    b. reduce total revenue to farmers as a whole because the demand for food is elastic.
    c. increase total revenue to farmers as a whole because the demand for food is inelastic.
    d. increase total revenue to farmers as a whole because the demand for food is elastic.

14. If supply is price inelastic, the value of the price elasticity of supply must be
    a. zero.
    b. less than 1.
    c. greater than 1.
    d. infinite.
    e. none of the above.

15. If there is excess capacity in a production facility, it is likely that the firm's supply curve is
    a. price inelastic.
    b. price elastic.
    c. unit price elastic.
    d. none of the above.

Use the following information to answer questions 16 and 17. Suppose that at a price of $30 per month, there are 30,000 subscribers to cable television in Small Town. If Small Town Cablevision raises its price to $40 per month, the number of subscribers will fall to 20,000.

16. Using the midpoint method for calculating the elasticity, what is the price elasticity of demand for cable television in Small Town?
    a. 0.66
    b. 0.75
    c. 1.0
    d. 1.4
    e. 2.0

17. At which of the following prices does Small Town Cablevision earn the greatest total revenue?
    a. either $30 or $40 per month because the price elasticity of demand is 1.0
    b. $30 per month
    c. $40 per month
    d. $0 per month

18. If demand is linear (a straight line), then price elasticity of demand is
    a. constant along the demand curve.
    b. inelastic in the upper portion and elastic in the lower portion.
    c. elastic in the upper portion and inelastic in the lower portion.
    d. elastic throughout.
    e. inelastic throughout.

19. If the income elasticity of demand for a good is negative, it must be
    a. a luxury good.
    b. a normal good.
    c. an inferior good.
    d. an elastic good.

20. If consumers think that there are very few substitutes for a good, then
    a. supply would tend to be price elastic.
    b. supply would tend to be price inelastic.
    c. demand would tend to be price elastic.
    d. demand would tend to be price inelastic.
    e. none of the above is true.

ADVANCED CRITICAL THINKING

In order to reduce teen smoking, the government places a $2 per pack tax on cigarettes. After one month, while the price to the consumer has increased a great deal, the quantity demanded of cigarettes has been reduced only slightly.

1. Is the demand for cigarettes over the period of one month elastic or inelastic?

    _____

    _____

2. Suppose you are in charge of pricing for a tobacco firm. The president of your firm suggests that the evidence received over the last month demonstrates that the cigarette industry should get together and raise the price of cigarettes further because total revenue to the tobacco industry will certainly rise. Is the president of your firm correct? Why?

    _____

    _____

    _____

3. As an alternative, suppose the president of your tobacco firm suggests that your firm raise the price of your cigarettes independent of the other tobacco firms because the evidence clearly shows that smokers are insensitive to changes in the price of cigarettes. Is the president of your firm correct if it is his desire to maximize total revenue? Why?

    _____

    _____

    _____

SOLUTIONS

Terms and Definitions

 4 Elasticity
 9 Price elasticity of demand
 2 Elastic
 7 Inelastic
 8 Total revenue
 1 Income elasticity of demand
10 Cross-price elasticity of demand
 6 Price elasticity of supply
 5 Normal good
 3 Inferior good

Practice Problems

1. a. a trip to Florida because it is a luxury while cigarettes are a necessity (to smokers)

   b. an AIDS vaccine over the next five years because there are likely to be more substitutes (alternative medications) developed over this time period and consumers' behavior may be modified over longer time periods

   c. Budweiser because it is a more narrowly defined market than beer so there are more substitutes for Budweiser than for beer

   d. aspirin because there are many substitutes for aspirin but few substitutes for insulin

2. a. $(10,000/45,000)/(\$0.50/\$1.25) = 0.56$

   b. With the midpoint method, the value of the elasticity is the same whether you begin at a price of $1.00 and raise it to $1.50 or begin at a price of $1.50 and reduce it to $1.00.

   c. Yes. Since the price elasticity of demand is less than one (inelastic), an increase in price will increase total revenue.

3.

Price	Quantity Demanded	Total Revenue	% Change In Price	% Change In Quantity	Elasticity
$ 20	24	480			
			0.67	0.18	0.27
40	20	800			
			0.40	0.22	0.55
60	16	960			
			0.29	0.29	1.00
80	12	960			
			0.22	0.40	1.82
100	8	800			
			0.18	0.67	3.72
120	4	480			

a. $80 to $120; lower its prices

b. $20 to $60; raise its prices

c. $60 to $80; it doesn't matter. For these prices, a change in price proportionately changes the quantity demanded, so total revenue is unchanged.

4. a. $(10/25)/(\$10,000/\$55,000) = 2.2$

   b. $(10/13)/(\$10,000/\$55,000) = 4.2$

   c. Normal goods, because the income elasticity of demand is positive.

   d. Luxuries, because the income elasticity of demand is large (greater than 1). In each case, an 18 percent increase in income caused a much larger increase in quantity demanded.

5. a. Televisions, because the production of televisions can be increased in response to an increase in the price of televisions while the quantity of beachfront property is fixed.

   b. Crude oil over the next year, because production of oil over the next year can more easily be increased than the production of oil over the next week.

   c. A van Gogh print, because more of them can be created in response to an increase in price while the quantity of an original work is fixed.

Short-Answer Questions

1. Whether the good is a necessity or a luxury, the availability of close substitutes, the definition of the market, and the time horizon over which demand is measured.

2. It will increase total revenue, because a large increase in price will be accompanied by only a small reduction in the quantity demanded if demand is inelastic.

3. Zero, therefore it is considered perfectly inelastic.

4. Infinite, therefore it is considered perfectly elastic.

5. $-0.10/0.20 = -1/2$. Eggs are inferior goods.

6. Elastic, because a small increase in price will induce the firm to increase production by a large amount.

7. Inelastic (nearly vertical), because once the fish are caught, the quantity offered for sale is fixed and must be sold before it spoils, regardless of the price.

8. No. The upper part tends to be elastic while the lower part tends to be inelastic. This is because on the upper part, for example, a one unit change in the price is a small percentage change while a one unit change in quantity is a large percentage change. This effect is reversed on the lower part of the demand curve.

9. $\dfrac{(30-25)/[(25+30)/2]}{(3-2)/[(2+3)/2]} = 0.45,$

   therefore supply is inelastic.

10. $0.06/0.20 = 0.30$, apples and oranges are substitutes, because the cross-price elasticity is positive (an increase in the price of apples increases the quantity demanded of oranges).

True/False Questions

1. F; demand would be price elastic.
2. T
3. T
4. F; the longer the time period considered, the more price elastic the demand curve because consumers have an opportunity to substitute or change their behavior.
5. F; the price elasticity of demand is defined as the percentage change in the quantity demanded of a good divided by the percentage change in the price of that good.
6. F; the two goods are likely to be substitutes.
7. T
8. F; the demand for necessities tends to be inelastic.
9. F; demand will be price elastic in its upper portion and price inelastic in its lower portion.
10. T
11. T
12. T
13. T
14. F; it will increase total revenue only if demand is price elastic.

15. T

Multiple-Choice Questions

1. b
2. c
3. a
4. b
5. d
6. d
7. c
8. a
9. a
10. d
11. c
12. b
13. a
14. b
15. b
16. d
17. b
18. c
19. c
20. d

Advanced Critical Thinking

1. Inelastic.
2. Not necessarily. Demand tends to be more elastic over longer periods. In the case of cigarettes, some consumers will substitute toward cigars and pipes. Others may quit or never start to smoke.
3. No. While the demand for cigarettes (the market broadly defined) may be inelastic, the demand for any one brand (market narrowly defined) is likely to be much more elastic because consumers can substitute toward other lower priced brands.

Supply, Demand, and Government Policies

6

CHAPTER OVERVIEW

Context and Purpose

Chapter 6 is the third chapter in a three-chapter sequence that deals with supply and demand and how markets work. Chapter 4 developed the model of supply and demand. Chapter 5 added precision to the model of supply and demand by developing the concept of elasticity—the sensitivity of the quantity supplied and quantity demanded to changes in economic conditions. Chapter 6 addresses the impact of government policies on competitive markets using the tools of supply and demand that you learned in Chapters 4 and 5.

The purpose of Chapter 6 is to consider two types of government policies: price controls and taxes. Price controls set the maximum or minimum price at which a good can be sold while a tax creates a wedge between what the buyer pays and the seller receives. These policies can be analyzed within the model of supply and demand. We will find that government policies sometimes produce unintended consequences.

Chapter Review

Introduction   In Chapters 4 and 5, we acted as scientists because we built the model of supply and demand to describe the world as it is. In Chapter 6, we act as policy advisors because we address how government policies are used to try to improve the world. We address two policies: price controls and taxes. Sometimes these policies produce unintended consequences.

Controls on Prices

There are two types of controls on prices: price ceilings and price floors. A **price ceiling** sets a legal maximum on the price at which a good can be sold. A **price floor** sets a legal minimum on the price at which a good can be sold.

Price Ceilings   Suppose the government is persuaded by buyers to set a price ceiling. If the price ceiling is set above the equilibrium price, it is *not binding*. That is, it has no impact on the market because the price can move to equilibrium without restriction. If the price ceiling is set below the equilibrium price, it is a *binding constraint* because it does not allow the market to reach equilibrium. A binding price

GOALS

In this chapter you will

- Examine the effects of government policies that place a ceiling on prices

- Examine the effects of government policies that put a floor under prices

- Consider how a tax on a good affects the price of the good and the quantity sold

- Learn that taxes levied on buyers and taxes levied on sellers are equivalent

- See how the burden of a tax is split between buyers and sellers

OUTCOMES

After accomplishing these goals, you should be able to

- Describe the conditions necessary for a price ceiling to be a binding constraint

- Explain why a binding price floor creates a surplus

- Demonstrate why a tax placed on a good generally reduces the quantity of the good sold

- Demonstrate why the results are the same when a tax is placed on the buyers or sellers of a good

- Show whether the buyers or sellers of a good bear the burden of the tax when demand is inelastic and supply is elastic ceiling causes the quantity demanded to exceed the quantity supplied, or a shortage. Since there is a shortage, methods develop to ration the small quantity supplied across a large number of buyers. Buyers willing to wait in long lines might get the good, or sellers could sell only to their friends, family, or members of the same race. Lines are inefficient, and discrimination is both inefficient and unfair. Free markets are impersonal and ration goods with prices.

Price ceilings are commonly found in the markets for gasoline and apartments. When OPEC restricted the quantity of petroleum in 1973, the supply of gasoline was reduced and the equilibrium price rose above the price ceiling and the price ceiling became binding. This caused a shortage of gas and long lines at the pump. In response, the price ceilings were later repealed. Price ceilings on apartments are known as rent controls. Binding rent controls create a shortage of housing. Both the demand and supply of housing are inelastic in the short run, so the initial shortage is small. In the long run, however, the supply and demand for housing become more elastic, and the shortage is more apparent. This causes waiting lists for apartments, bribes to landlords, unclean and unsafe buildings, and lower quality housing. Once established, however, rent controls are politically difficult to remove.

Price Floors   Suppose the government is persuaded by sellers to set a price floor. If the price floor is set below the equilibrium price, it is *not binding*. That is, it has no impact on the market because the price can move to equilibrium without restriction. If the price floor is set above the equilibrium price, it is a *binding constraint* because it does not allow the market to reach equilibrium. A binding price floor causes the quantity supplied to exceed the quantity demanded, or a surplus. In order to eliminate the surplus, sellers may appeal to the biases of the buyers and sell to buyers that are family, friends, or members of the same race. Free markets are impersonal and ration goods with prices.

An important example of a price floor is the minimum wage. The minimum wage is a binding constraint in the market for young and unskilled workers. When the wage is set above the market equilibrium wage, the quantity supplied of labor exceeds the quantity demanded. The result is unemployment. Studies show that a 10 percent increase in the minimum wage depresses teenage employment by 1 to 3 percent. The minimum wage also causes teenagers to look for work and drop out of school.

Price controls often hurt those they are trying to help—usually the poor. The minimum wage may help those who find work at the minimum wage but harm those who become unemployed as a result of the minimum wage. Rent controls reduce the quality and availability of housing.

Taxes

Governments use taxes to raise revenue. A tax on a good will affect the quantity sold and both the price paid by buyers and the price received by sellers. If the tax is collected from the buyers, demand shifts downward by the size of the tax per unit. As a result of the decrease in demand, the quantity sold decreases, the price paid by the buyer increases, and the price received by the seller decreases. If the tax is collected from the sellers, supply shifts upward by the size of the tax per unit. As a result of the decrease in supply, the quantity sold decreases, the price paid by the buyer increases, and the price received by the seller decreases. Therefore, a tax collected from buyers has the same effect as a tax collected from sellers. After a tax has been placed on a good, the difference between what the buyer pays and the seller receives is the tax per unit and is known as the *tax wedge*. In summary:

- A tax discourages market activity. That is, the quantity sold is reduced.

- Buyers and sellers share the burden of a tax because the price paid by the buyers increases while the price received by the sellers decreases.

- The effect of a tax collected from buyers is equivalent to a tax collected from sellers.

- The government cannot legislate the relative burden of the tax between buyers and sellers. The relative burden of a tax is determined by the elasticity of supply and demand in that market.

Tax incidence is the manner in which the burden of a tax is shared among participants in a market. When a tax wedge is placed between buyers and sellers, the tax burden falls more heavily on the side of the market that is less elastic. That is, the tax burden falls more heavily on the side of the market that is less willing to leave the market when price movements are unfavorable to them. For example, in the market for cigarettes, since cigarettes are addictive, demand is likely to be less elastic than supply. Therefore, a tax on cigarettes tends to raise the price paid by buyers more than it reduces the price received by sellers, and as a result, the burden of a cigarette tax falls more heavily on the buyers of cigarettes. With regard to the payroll tax (Social Security and Medicare tax), since labor supply is less elastic than labor demand, most of the tax burden is borne by the workers as opposed to the 50–50 split intended by lawmakers.

Conclusion

Supply and demand can be utilized to analyze the impact of government policies such as price controls and taxes.

Helpful Hints

1. Price ceilings and price floors only matter if they are binding constraints. Price ceilings do not automatically cause a shortage. A price ceiling only causes a shortage if the price ceiling is set below the equilibrium price. In a similar manner, a price floor only causes a surplus if the price floor is set above the equilibrium price.

2. It is useful to think of taxes as causing vertical shifts in demand and supply. Since demand is the maximum buyers are willing to pay for each quantity, a tax imposed on the buyers in a market reduces or shifts downward the demand faced by sellers by precisely the size of the tax per unit. That is, the buyers now offer the sellers an amount that has been reduced by precisely the size of the tax per unit. Alternatively, since supply is the minimum sellers are willing to accept for each quantity, a tax imposed on the sellers in a market reduces or shifts upward the supply faced by buyers by precisely the size of the tax per unit. This is because the sellers now require an additional amount from the buyers that is precisely the size of the tax per unit.

Terms and Definitions

Choose a definition for each key term.

Key Terms

_____ Price ceiling

_____ Price floor

_____ Tax incidence

_____ Tax wedge

Definitions

1. The manner in which the burden of a tax is shared among participants in a market

2. A legal maximum on the price at which a good can be sold

3. The difference between what the buyer pays and the seller receives after a tax has been imposed

4. A legal minimum on the price at which a good can be sold

PROBLEMS AND SHORT-ANSWER QUESTIONS

Practice Problems

1. Use the following supply and demand schedules for bicycles to answer the questions below.

Price	Quantity Demanded	Quantity Supplied
$300	60	30
400	55	40
500	50	50
600	45	60
700	40	70
800	35	80

a. In response to lobbying by the Bicycle Riders Association, Congress places a price ceiling of $700 on bicycles. What effect will this have on the market for bicycles? Why?

_____

_____

_____

b. In response to lobbying by the Bicycle Riders Association, Congress places a price ceiling of $400 on bicycles. Use the information provided above to plot the supply and demand curves for bicycles in Exhibit 1. Impose the price ceiling. What is the result of a price ceiling of $400 on bicycles?

_____

_____

_____

c. Does a price ceiling of $400 on bicycles make all bicycle buyers better off? Why or why not?

_____

_____

_____

d. Suppose instead, in response to lobbying by the Bicycle Manufacturers Association, Congress imposes a price floor on bicycles of $700. Use the information provided above to plot the supply and demand curves for bicycles in Exhibit 2. Impose the $700 price floor. What is the result of the $700 price floor?

_____

_____

2 EXHIBIT

2. Use the following supply and demand schedules for bicycles to answer the questions below.

Price	Quantity Demanded	Quantity Supplied
$300	60	30
400	55	40
500	50	50
600	45	60
700	40	70
800	35	80

a. Plot the supply and demand curves for bicycles in Exhibit 3. On the graph, impose a tax of $300 per bicycle to be collected from the sellers. After the tax, what has happened to the price paid by the buyers, the price received by the sellers, and the quantity sold when compared to the free market equilibrium?

_____

_____

_____

b. Again, plot the supply and demand curves for bicycles in Exhibit 4. On the graph, impose a tax of $300 per bicycle to be collected from the buyers. After the tax, what has happened to the price paid by the buyers, the price received by the sellers, and the quantity sold when compared to the free market equilibrium?

_____

_____

_____

4 EXHIBIT

c. Compare your answers to questions *a* and *b* above. What conclusion do you draw from this comparison?

_____

_____

d. Who bears the greater burden of this tax, the buyers or the sellers? Why?

_____

_____

_____

Short-Answer Questions

1. What is the impact on the price and quantity in a market if a price ceiling is set above the equilibrium price? Why?

_____

_____

2. What is the impact on the price and quantity in a market if a price ceiling is set below the equilibrium price?

_____

3. What are some of the problems created by a binding price ceiling?

    _____

    _____

    _____

4. Is the impact of a binding price ceiling greater in the short run or the long run? Why?

    _____

    _____

    _____

5. What is the impact on the price and quantity in a market if a price floor is set below the equilibrium price? Why?

    _____

    _____

6. What is the impact on the price and quantity in a market if a price floor is set above the equilibrium price?

    _____

7. When we use the model of supply and demand to analyze a tax that is collected from the buyers, which way do we shift the demand curve? Why?

    _____

    _____

    _____

8. When we use the model of supply and demand to analyze a tax that is collected from the sellers, which way do we shift the supply curve? Why?

    _____

    _____

    _____

9. Why is a tax collected from the buyers equivalent to a tax collected from the sellers?

    _____

    _____

    _____

10. Suppose a gas-guzzler tax is placed on luxury automobiles. Who will likely bear the greater burden of the tax, the buyers of luxury autos or the sellers? Why?

_____

_____

_____

SELF-TEST

True/False Questions

_____ 1. If the equilibrium price of gasoline is $1.00 per gallon and the government places a price ceiling on gasoline of $1.50 per gallon, the result will be a shortage of gasoline.

_____ 2. A price ceiling set below the equilibrium price causes a surplus.

_____ 3. A price floor set above the equilibrium price is a binding constraint.

_____ 4. The shortage of housing caused by a binding rent control is likely to be more severe in the long run when compared to the short run.

_____ 5. The minimum wage helps all teenagers because they receive higher wages than they would otherwise.

_____ 6. A 10 percent increase in the minimum wage causes a 10 percent reduction in teenage employment.

_____ 7. A price ceiling that is not a binding constraint today could cause a shortage in the future if demand were to increase and raise the equilibrium price above the fixed price ceiling.

_____ 8. A price floor in a market always creates a surplus in that market.

_____ 9. A $10 tax on baseball gloves will always raise the price that the buyers pay for baseball gloves by $10.

_____ 10. The ultimate burden of a tax lands most heavily on the side of the market that is less elastic.

_____ 11. If medicine is a necessity, the burden of a tax on medicine will likely land more heavily on the buyers of medicine.

_____ 12. When we use the model of supply and demand to analyze a tax collected from the buyers, we shift the demand curve upward by the size of the tax.

_____ 13. A tax collected from buyers has an equivalent impact to a same size tax collected from sellers.

_____ 14. A tax creates a tax wedge between a buyer and a seller. This causes the price paid by the buyer to rise, the price received by the seller to fall, and the quantity sold to fall.

_____ 15. The government can choose to place the burden of a tax on the buyers in a market by collecting the tax from the buyers rather than the sellers.

Multiple-Choice Questions

1. For a price ceiling to be a binding constraint on the market, the government must set it
   a. above the equilibrium price.
   b. below the equilibrium price.
   c. precisely at the equilibrium price.
   d. at any price because all price ceilings are binding constraints.

2. A binding price ceiling creates
   a. a shortage.
   b. a surplus.
   c. an equilibrium.
   d. a shortage or a surplus depending on whether the price ceiling is set above or below the equilibrium price.

3. Suppose the equilibrium price for apartments is $500 per month and the government imposes rent controls of $250. Which of the following is *unlikely* to occur as a result of the rent controls?
   a. There will be a shortage of housing.
   b. Landlords may discriminate among apartment renters.
   c. Landlords may be offered bribes to rent apartments.
   d. The quality of apartments will improve.
   e. There may be long lines of buyers waiting for apartments.

4. A price floor
   a. sets a legal maximum on the price at which a good can be sold.
   b. sets a legal minimum on the price at which a good can be sold.
   c. always determines the price at which a good must be sold.
   d. is not a binding constraint if it is set above the equilibrium price.

5. Which of the following statements about a binding price ceiling is true?
   a. The surplus created by the price ceiling is greater in the short run than in the long run.
   b. The surplus created by the price ceiling is greater in the long run than in the short run.
   c. The shortage created by the price ceiling is greater in the short run than in the long run.
   d. The shortage created by the price ceiling is greater in the long run than in the short run.

6. Which side of the market is more likely to lobby government for a price floor?
   a. Neither buyers or sellers desire a price floor.
   b. Both buyers and sellers desire a price floor.
   c. the sellers
   d. the buyers

7. The surplus caused by a binding price floor will be greatest if
   a. both supply and demand are elastic.
   b. both supply and demand are inelastic.
   c. supply is inelastic and demand is elastic.
   d. demand is inelastic and supply is elastic.

8. Which of the following is an example of a price floor?
   a. rent controls
   b. restricting gasoline prices to $1.00 per gallon when the equilibrium price is $1.50 per gallon
   c. the minimum wage
   d. All of the above are price floors.

9. Which of the following statements is true if the government places a price ceiling on gasoline at $1.50 per gallon and the equilibrium price is $1.00 per gallon?
   a. There will be a shortage of gasoline.
   b. There will be a surplus of gasoline.
   c. A significant increase in the supply of gasoline could cause the price ceiling to become a binding constraint.
   d. A significant increase in the demand for gasoline could cause the price ceiling to become a binding constraint.

10. Studies show that a 10 percent increase in the minimum wage
    a. decreases teenage employment by about 10 to 15 percent.
    b. increases teenage employment by about 10 to 15 percent.
    c. decreases teenage employment by about 1 to 3 percent.
    d. increases teenage employment by about 1 to 3 percent.

11. Within the supply-and-demand model, a tax collected from the buyers of a good shifts the
    a. demand curve upward by the size of the tax per unit.
    b. demand curve downward by the size of the tax per unit.
    c. supply curve upward by the size of the tax per unit.
    d. supply curve downward by the size of the tax per unit.

12. Within the supply-and-demand model, a tax collected from the sellers of a good shifts the
    a. demand curve upward by the size of the tax per unit.
    b. demand curve downward by the size of the tax per unit.
    c. supply curve upward by the size of the tax per unit.
    d. supply curve downward by the size of the tax per unit.

13. Which of the following takes place when a tax is placed on a good?
    a. an increase in the price buyers pay, a decrease in the price sellers receive, and a decrease in the quantity sold
    b. an increase in the price buyers pay, a decrease in the price sellers receive, and an increase in the quantity sold
    c. a decrease in the price buyers pay, an increase in the price sellers receive, and a decrease in the quantity sold
    d. a decrease in the price buyers pay, an increase in the price sellers receive, and an increase in the quantity sold

14. When a tax is collected from the buyers in a market,
    a. the buyers bear the burden of the tax.
    b. the sellers bear the burden of the tax.
    c. the tax burden on the buyers and sellers is the same as an equivalent tax collected from the sellers.
    d. the tax burden falls most heavily on the buyers.

15. A tax of $1.00 per gallon on gasoline
    a. increases the price the buyers pay by $1.00 per gallon.
    b. decreases the price the sellers receive by $1.00 per gallon.
    c. increases the price the buyers pay by precisely $0.50 and reduces the price received by sellers by precisely $0.50.
    d. places a tax wedge of $1.00 between the price the buyers pay and the price the sellers receive.

16. The burden of a tax falls more heavily on the sellers in a market when
    a. demand is inelastic and supply is elastic.
    b. demand is elastic and supply is inelastic.
    c. both supply and demand are elastic.
    d. both supply and demand are inelastic.

17. A tax placed on a good that is a necessity for consumers will likely generate a tax burden that
    a. falls more heavily on buyers.
    b. falls more heavily on sellers.
    c. is evenly distributed between buyers and sellers.
    d. falls entirely on sellers.

18. The burden of a tax falls more heavily on the buyers in a market when
    a. demand is inelastic and supply is elastic.
    b. demand is elastic and supply is inelastic.
    c. both supply and demand are elastic.
    d. both supply and demand are inelastic.

19. Which of the following statements about the burden of a tax is correct?
    a. The tax burden generated from a tax placed on a good consumers perceive to be a necessity will fall most heavily on the sellers of the good.
    b. The tax burden falls most heavily on the side of the market (buyers or sellers) that is most willing to leave the market when price movements are unfavorable to them.
    c. The burden of a tax lands on the side of the market (buyers or sellers) from which it is collected.
    d. The distribution of the burden of a tax is determined by the relative elasticities of supply and demand and is not determined by legislation.

20. For which of the following products would the burden of a tax likely fall more heavily on the sellers?
    a. food
    b. entertainment
    c. clothing
    d. housing

ADVANCED CRITICAL THINKING

Suppose that the government needs to raise tax revenue. A politician suggests that the government place a tax on food because everyone must eat and, thus, a food tax would surely raise a great deal of tax revenue. However, since the poor spend a large proportion of their income on food, the tax should be collected only from the sellers of food (grocery stores) and not from the buyers of food. The politician argues that this type of tax would place the burden of the tax on corporate grocery store chains and not on poor consumers.

1. Can the government legislate that the burden of a food tax will fall only on the sellers of food? Why or why not?

_____

_____

_____

2. Do you think the burden of a food tax will tend to fall on the sellers of food or the buyers of food? Why?

_____

_____

_____

SOLUTIONS

Terms and Definitions

_2_ Price ceiling
_4_ Price floor
_1_ Tax incidence
_3_ Tax wedge

Practice Problems

1. a. It will have no effect. The price ceiling is not binding because the equilibrium price is $500 and the price ceiling is set at $700.

   b. See Exhibit 5. The quantity demanded rises to 55 units, the quantity supplied falls to 40 units, and there is a shortage of 15 units.

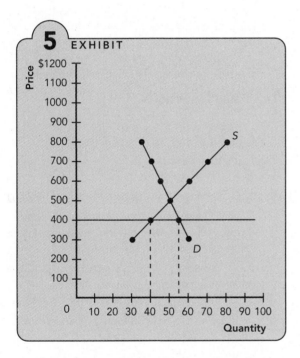

   c. No. It may make those bicycle buyers better off that actually get a bicycle. However, some buyers are unable to get a bike, must wait in line, pay a bribe, or accept a lower quality bicycle.

   d. See Exhibit 6. The quantity supplied rises to 70 units, the quantity demanded falls to 40 units, and there is a surplus of 30 units.

2. a. See Exhibit 7. The price paid by the buyers rises to $700, the price received by the sellers falls to $400, and the quantity sold falls to 40 units.

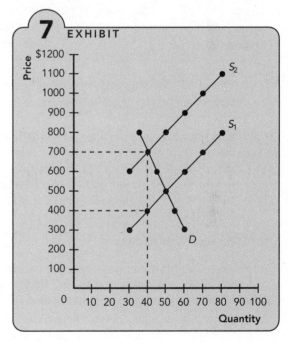

b. See Exhibit 8. The price paid by the buyers rises to $700, the price received by the sellers falls to $400, and the quantity sold falls to 40 units.

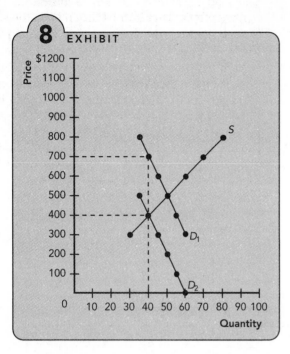

8   EXHIBIT

c. The impact of a tax collected from sellers is equivalent to the impact of a tax collected from buyers.

d. The greater burden of the tax has fallen on the buyers. The free market equilibrium price was $500. After the tax, the price the buyers pay has risen $200 while the price the sellers receive has fallen $100. This is because demand is less elastic than supply.

Short-Answer Questions

1. There is no impact because the price can move to equilibrium without restriction. That is, the price ceiling is not a binding constraint.

2. The quantity supplied decreases and the quantity demanded increases, causing a shortage.

3. There will be a shortage, buyers may wait in lines, sellers may be able to discriminate among buyers, the quality of the product may be reduced, and bribes may be paid to sellers.

4. The impact is greater in the long run because both supply and demand tend to be more elastic in the long run. As a result, the shortage becomes more severe in the long run.

5. There is no impact because the price can move to equilibrium without restriction. That is, the price floor is not a binding constraint.

6. The quantity supplied increases and the quantity demanded decreases, causing a surplus.

7. The demand curve is shifted downward by the size of the tax because the amount the buyer is willing to offer the seller has been reduced precisely by the size of the tax.

8. The supply curve is shifted upward by the size of the tax because the amount the seller requires from the buyer has been increased by precisely the size of the tax.

9. A tax places a wedge between what the buyer pays and the seller receives. Whether the buyer or the seller actually hands the tax to the government makes no difference whatsoever.

10. The sellers will bear the greater burden because the demand for luxuries tends to be highly elastic. That is, when the price buyers pay rises due to the tax, wealthy buyers can easily shift their purchases toward alternative items while producers cannot quickly reduce production when the price they receive falls. The burden falls on the side of the market that is less elastic.

True/False Questions

1. F; a price ceiling set above the equilibrium price is not binding.

2. F; it causes a shortage.

3. T

4. T

5. F; some may be helped but others become unemployed and still others quit school to earn what appears to a teenager to be a good wage.

6. F; it causes a 1 to 3 percent reduction in employment.

7. T

8. F; it creates a surplus only if the floor is set above the equilibrium price.

9. F; the difference between what the sellers receive and the buyers pay will be $10, but the price received by the sellers usually will fall some so the price paid by the buyers will rise by less than $10.

10. T

11. T

12. F; we shift the demand curve downward by the size of the tax.

13. T

14. T

15. F; the burden of a tax is determined by the relative elasticities of supply and demand.

Multiple-Choice Questions

1. b
2. a
3. d
4. b
5. d
6. c
7. a
8. c
9. d
10. c
11. b
12. c
13. a
14. c
15. d
16. b
17. a
18. a
19. d
20. b

Advanced Critical Thinking

1. No. The tax burden is determined by the elasticity of supply and demand. The burden of a tax falls most heavily on the side of the market that is less elastic. That is, the burden is on the side of the market least willing to leave the market when the price moves unfavorably.

2. The burden will fall most heavily on the buyers of food regardless of whether the tax is collected from the buyers or the sellers. Food is a necessity, and therefore, the demand for food is relatively inelastic. When the price rises due to the tax, people still must eat. Grocery chains can sell another product line when the price they receive for food falls due to the tax.

Consumers, Producers, and the Efficiency of Markets

GOALS

In this chapter you will

- Examine the link between buyers' willingness to pay for a good and the demand curve

- Learn how to define and measure consumer surplus

- Examine the link between sellers' costs of producing a good and the supply curve

- Learn how to define and measure producer surplus

- See that the equilibrium of supply and demand maximizes total surplus in a market

CHAPTER OVERVIEW

Context and Purpose

Chapter 7 is the first chapter in a three-chapter sequence on welfare economics and market efficiency. Chapter 7 employs the supply-and-demand model to develop consumer surplus and producer surplus as a measure of welfare and market efficiency. These concepts are then utilized in Chapters 8 and 9 to determine the winners and losers from taxation and restrictions on international trade.

The purpose of Chapter 7 is to develop *welfare economics*—the study of how the allocation of resources affects economic well-being. Chapters 4 through 6 employed supply and demand in a positive framework when we asked the question, "What is the equilibrium price and quantity in a market?" We now address the normative question, "Is the equilibrium price and quantity in a market the best possible solution to the resource allocation problem or is it simply the price and quantity that balances supply and demand?" We will discover that under most circumstances the equilibrium price and quantity is also the one that maximizes welfare.

Chapter Review

Introduction In this chapter, we address **welfare economics**—the study of how the allocation of resources affects economic well-being. We measure the benefits that buyers and sellers receive from taking part in a market, and we discover that the equilibrium price and quantity in a market maximizes the total benefits received by buyers and sellers.

Consumer Surplus

Consumer surplus measures the benefits received by buyers from participating in a market. Each potential buyer in a market has some **willingness to pay** for a good. This willingness to pay is the maximum amount that a buyer will pay for the good. If we plot the value of the greatest willingness to pay for the first unit followed by the next greatest willingness to pay for the second unit and so on (on a price and quantity graph), we have plotted the market demand curve for the good. That is, the height of the demand curve is the marginal

OUTCOMES

After accomplishing these goals, you should be able to

- Derive a demand curve from a group of individual buyers' willingness to pay schedules

- Locate consumer surplus on a supply and demand graph

- Derive a supply curve from a group of individual sellers' cost of production schedules

- Locate producer surplus on a supply-and-demand graph

- Demonstrate why all quantities other than the equilibrium quantity fail to maximize total surplus in a market buyers' willingness to pay. Since some buyers value a good more than other buyers, the demand curve is downward sloping.

Consumer surplus is the amount a buyer is willing to pay for a good minus the amount the buyer actually pays for it. For example, if you are willing to pay $20 for a new CD by your favorite music artist and you are able to purchase it for $15, you receive consumer surplus on that CD of $5. In general, since the height of the demand curve measures the value buyers place on a good measured by the buyers' willingness to pay, *consumer surplus in a market is the area below the demand curve and above the price.*

When the price of a good falls, consumer surplus increases for two reasons. First, existing buyers receive greater surplus because they are allowed to pay less for the quantities they were already going to purchase, and second, new buyers are brought into the market because the price is now lower than their willingness to pay.

Note that since the height of the demand curve is the value buyers place on a good measured by their willingness to pay, consumer surplus measures the benefits received by buyers *as the buyers themselves perceive it*. Therefore, consumer surplus is an appropriate measure of buyers' benefits if policymakers respect the preferences of buyers. Economists generally believe that buyers are rational and that buyer preferences should be respected except possibly in cases of drug addiction and so on.

Producer Surplus

Producer surplus measures the benefits received by sellers from participating in a market. Each potential seller in a market has some *cost* of production. This **cost** is the value of everything a seller must give up to produce a good, and it should be interpreted as the producers' opportunity cost of production—actual out-of-pocket expenses plus the value of the producers' time. The cost of production is the minimum amount a seller is willing to accept in order to produce the good. If we plot the cost of the least cost producer of the first unit, then the next least cost producer of the second unit, and so on (on a price and quantity graph), we have plotted the market supply curve for the good. That is, the height of the supply curve is the marginal sellers' cost of production. Since some sellers have a lower cost than other sellers, the supply curve is upward sloping.

Producer surplus is the amount a seller is paid for a good minus the seller's cost of providing it. For example, if a musician can produce a CD for a cost of $10 and sell it for $15, the musician receives a producer surplus of $5 on that CD. In general, since the height of the supply curve measures the sellers' costs, *producer surplus in a market is the area below the price and above the supply curve.*

When the price of a good rises, producer surplus increases for two reasons. First, existing sellers receive greater surplus because they receive more for the quantities they were already going to sell, and second, new sellers are brought into the market because the price is now higher than their cost.

Market Efficiency

We measure economic well-being with *total surplus*—the sum of consumer and producer surplus.

$$\frac{\text{Total}}{\text{surplus}} = (\text{value to buyers} - \text{amount paid by buyers}) + (\text{amount received by sellers} - \text{cost to sellers}).$$

$$\frac{\text{Total}}{\text{surplus}} = \text{value to buyers} - \text{cost to sellers}.$$

Graphically, total surplus is the area below the demand curve and above the supply curve. Resource allocation is said to exhibit **efficiency** if it maximizes the total surplus received by all members of society. Free market equilibrium is efficient because it maximizes total surplus. This efficiency is demonstrated by the following observations:

- Free markets allocate output to the buyers who value it the most—those with a willingness to pay greater than or equal to the equilibrium price. Therefore, consumer surplus cannot be increased by moving consumption from a current buyer to any other nonbuyer.

- Free markets allocate buyers for goods to the sellers who can produce at least cost—those with a cost of production less than or equal to the equilibrium price. Therefore, producer surplus cannot be increased by moving production from a current seller to any other nonseller.

- Free markets produce the quantity of goods that maximizes the sum of consumer and producer surplus or total surplus. If we produce less than the equilibrium quantity, we fail to produce units where the value to the marginal buyer exceeds the cost to the marginal seller. If we produce more than the equilibrium quantity, we produce units where the cost to the marginal seller exceeds the value to the marginal buyer.

Economists generally advocate free markets because they are efficient. Since markets are efficient, many believe that government policy should be *laissez-faire*, which means "allow them to do." Adam Smith's "invisible hand" of the marketplace guides buyers and sellers to an allocation of resources that maximizes total surplus. The efficient outcome cannot be improved upon by a benevolent social planner. Many economists argue that free markets for scalped tickets (and possibly even markets for organs for transplant) maximize total surplus. In addition to efficiency, policymakers may also be concerned with **equity**—the fairness of the distribution of well-being among the members of society. The issue of equity involves normative judgments that go beyond the realm of economics.

Conclusion: Market Efficiency and Market Failure

There are two main reasons a free market may not be efficient:

- A market may not be perfectly competitive. If individual buyers or sellers (or small groups of them) can influence the price, they have *market power* and they may be able to keep the price and quantity away from equilibrium.

- A market may generate side effects, or *externalities*, which affect people who are not participants in the market at all. These side effects, such as pollution, are not taken into account by buyers and sellers in a market, so the market equilibrium may not be efficient for society as a whole.

Market power and externalities are the two main types of *market failure*—the inability of some unregulated markets to allocate resources efficiently.

Helpful Hints

1. To better understand "willingness to pay" for the buyer and "cost" to seller, read both demand and supply "backward." That is, read both demand and supply from the quantity axis to the price or dollar axis. When we read demand from quantity to price, we find that the potential buyer for the first unit has a very high willingness to pay because that buyer places a great value on the good. As we move farther out along the quantity axis, the buyers for those quantities have a somewhat lower willingness to pay, and thus, the demand curve slopes negatively. When we read supply from quantity to price, we find that the potential seller for the first unit is extremely efficient and, accordingly, has a very low cost of production. As we move farther out along the quantity axis, the sellers for those quantities have somewhat higher costs, and thus, the supply curve slopes upward. At equilibrium between supply and demand, only those units are produced that generate a value to buyers which exceeds the cost to the sellers.

2. Consumer surplus exists, in part, because in a competitive market, there is one price and all participants are price takers. With a single market price determined by the interactions of many buyers and sellers, individual buyers may have a willingness to pay that exceeds the price, and as a result, some buyers receive consumer surplus. If, however, sellers are aware of the buyers' willingness to pay and the sellers engage in price discrimination, that is, charge each buyer their willingness to pay, there would be no consumer surplus. Each buyer would be forced to pay their individual willingness to pay. This issue will be addressed in later chapters.

Terms and Definitions

Choose a definition for each key term.

Key Terms

_____ Welfare economics

_____ Willingness to pay

_____ Consumer surplus

_____ Cost

_____ Producer surplus

_____ Efficiency

_____ Equity

_____ Market failure

Definitions

1. The amount a buyer is willing to pay for a good minus the amount the buyer actually pays for it

2. The property of a resource allocation of maximizing the total surplus received by all members of society

3. The study of how the allocation of resources affects economic well-being

4. The inability of some unregulated markets to allocate resources efficiently

5. The fairness of the distribution of well-being among the members of society

6. The amount a seller is paid for a good minus the seller's cost of providing it

7. The maximum amount that a buyer will pay for a good

8. The value of everything a seller must give up to produce a good

PROBLEMS AND SHORT-ANSWER QUESTIONS

Practice Problems

1. The following information describes the value Lori Landlord places on having her five apartment houses repainted. She values the repainting of each apartment house at a different amount depending on how badly it needs repainting.

Value of new paint on first apartment house	$5,000
Value of new paint on second apartment house	4,000
Value of new paint on third apartment house	3,000
Value of new paint on fourth apartment house	2,000
Value of new paint on fifth apartment house	1,000

a. Plot Lori Landlord's willingness to pay in Exhibit 1.

b. If the price to repaint her apartments is $5,000 each, how many will she repaint? What is the value of her consumer surplus?

_____

_____

_____

c. Suppose the price to repaint her apartments falls to $2,000 each. How many apartments will Lori choose to have repainted? What is the value of her consumer surplus?

_____

_____

d. What happened to Ms. Landlord's consumer surplus when the price of having her apartments repainted fell? Why?

_____

_____

_____

2. The following information shows the costs incurred by Peter Painter when he paints apartments. Because painting is backbreaking work, the more he paints, the higher the costs he incurs in both pain and chiropractic bills.

Cost of painting first apartment house	$1,000
Cost of painting second apartment house	2,000
Cost of painting third apartment house	3,000
Cost of painting fourth apartment house	4,000
Cost of painting fifth apartment house	5,000

a. Plot Peter Painter's cost in Exhibit 2.
b. If the price of painting apartment houses is $2,000 each, how many will he paint? What is the value of his producer surplus?

_____

_____

_____

c. Suppose the price to paint apartments rises to $4,000 each. How many apartments will Peter choose to repaint? What is the value of his producer surplus?

_____

_____

_____

d. What happened to Mr. Painter's producer surplus when the price to paint apartments rose? Why?

_____

_____

_____

3. Use the information about willingness to pay and cost from questions *1* and *2* above to answer the following questions.

a. If a benevolent social planner sets the price for painting apartment houses at $5,000, what is the value of consumer surplus? producer surplus? total surplus?

_____

_____

b. If a benevolent social planner sets the price for painting apartment houses at $1,000, what is the value of consumer surplus? producer surplus? total surplus?

_____

_____

c. If the price for painting apartment houses is allowed to move to its free market equilibrium price of $3,000, what is the value of consumer surplus, producer surplus, and total surplus in the market? How does total surplus in the free market compare to the total surplus generated by the social planner?

_____

_____

_____

4. In Exhibit 3, plot the linear supply and demand curves for painting apartments implied by the information in questions *1* and *2* above (draw them so that they contact the vertical axis). Show consumer and producer surplus for the free market equilibrium price and quantity. Is this allocation of resources efficient? Why?

_____

_____

_____

_____

_____

_____

_____

_____

_____

3 EXHIBIT

5. Suppose Lori Landlord has difficulty renting her dilapidated apartments so she increases her willingness to pay for painting by $2,000 per apartment. Plot Lori's new willingness to pay along with Peter's cost in Exhibit 4. If the equilibrium price rises to $4,000, what is the value of consumer surplus, producer surplus, and total surplus? Show consumer and producer surplus on the graph. Compare your answer to the answer you found in *3c* above.

_____

_____

_____

Short-Answer Questions

1. What is the relationship between the buyers' willingness to pay for a good and the demand curve for that good?

    _____

    _____

2. What is consumer surplus and how is it measured?

    _____

    _____

3. What is the value of consumer surplus for the marginal buyer? Why?

    _____

    _____

4. If the cost for Moe to mow a lawn is $5, for Larry to mow a lawn is $7, and for Curly to mow a lawn is $9, what is the value of their producer surplus if each mows a lawn and the price for lawn mowing is $10?

_____

_____

5. What is the relationship between the sellers' cost to produce a good and the supply curve for that good?

_____

_____

6. What is producer surplus and how is it measured?

_____

_____

7. When the price of a good rises, what happens to producer surplus? Why?

_____

_____

_____

8. Can a benevolent social planner choose a quantity that provides greater economic welfare than the equilibrium quantity generated in a competitive market? Why?

_____

_____

_____

9. What does an economist mean by "efficiency"?

_____

_____

10. Is a competitive market efficient? Why?

_____

_____

11. How does a competitive market choose which producers will produce and sell a product?

_____

_____

_____

SELF-TEST

True/False Questions

_____ 1. Consumer surplus is the amount a buyer is willing to pay for a good minus the seller's cost.

_____ 2. If the demand curve in a market is stationary, consumer surplus decreases when the price in that market increases.

_____ 3. If your willingness to pay for a hamburger is $3.00 and the price is $2.00, your consumer surplus is $5.00.

_____ 4. Producer surplus is a measure of the unsold inventories of suppliers in a market.

_____ 5. Consumer surplus is a good measure of buyers' benefits if buyers are rational.

_____ 6. Cost to the seller includes the opportunity cost of the seller's time.

_____ 7. The height of the supply curve is the marginal seller's cost.

_____ 8. Total surplus is the cost to sellers minus the value to buyers.

_____ 9. Free markets are efficient because they allocate output to buyers who have a willingness to pay that is below the price.

_____ 10. Producer surplus is the area above the supply curve and below the price.

_____ 11. The major advantage of allowing free markets to allocate resources is that the outcome of the allocation is efficient.

_____ 12. Equilibrium in a competitive market maximizes total surplus.

_____ 13. The two main types of market failure are market power and externalities.

_____ 14. Externalities are side effects, such as pollution, that are not taken into account by the buyers and sellers in a market.

_____ 15. Producing more of a product always adds to total surplus.

Multiple-Choice Questions

1. Consumer surplus is the area
   a. above the supply curve and below the price.
   b. below the supply curve and above the price.
   c. above the demand curve and below the price.
   d. below the demand curve and above the price.
   e. below the demand curve and above the supply curve.

2. A buyer's willingness to pay is
   a. that buyer's consumer surplus.
   b. that buyer's producer surplus.
   c. that buyer's maximum amount they are willing to pay for a good.
   d. that buyer's minimum amount they are willing to pay for a good.
   e. none of the above.

3. If a buyer's willingness to pay for a new Honda is $20,000 and she is able to actually buy it for $18,000, her consumer surplus is
   a. $0.
   b. $2,000.
   c. $18,000.
   d. $20,000.
   e. $38,000.

4. An increase in the price of a good along a stationary demand curve
   a. increases consumer surplus.
   b. decreases consumer surplus.
   c. improves the material welfare of the buyers.
   d. improves market efficiency.

5. Suppose there are three identical vases available to be purchased. Buyer 1 is willing to pay $30 for one, buyer 2 is willing to pay $25 for one, and buyer 3 is willing to pay $20 for one. If the price is $25, how many vases will be sold and what is the value of consumer surplus in this market?
   a. One vase will be sold, and consumer surplus is $30.
   b. One vase will be sold, and consumer surplus is $5.
   c. Two vases will be sold, and consumer surplus is $5.
   d. Three vases will be sold, and consumer surplus is $0.
   e. Three vases will be sold, and consumer surplus is $80.

6. Producer surplus is the area
   a. above the supply curve and below the price.
   b. below the supply curve and above the price.
   c. above the demand curve and below the price.
   d. below the demand curve and above the price.
   e. below the demand curve and above the supply curve.

7. If a benevolent social planner chooses to produce less than the equilibrium quantity of a good, then
   a. producer surplus is maximized.
   b. consumer surplus is maximized.
   c. total surplus is maximized.
   d. the value placed on the last unit of production by buyers exceeds the cost of production.
   e. the cost of production on the last unit produced exceeds the value placed on it by buyers.

8. If a benevolent social planner chooses to produce more than the equilibrium quantity of a good, then
   a. producer surplus is maximized.
   b. consumer surplus is maximized.
   c. total surplus is maximized.
   d. the value placed on the last unit of production by buyers exceeds the cost of production.
   e. the cost of production on the last unit produced exceeds the value placed on it by buyers.

9. The seller's cost of production is
   a. the seller's consumer surplus.
   b. the seller's producer surplus.
   c. the maximum amount the seller is willing to accept for a good.
   d. the minimum amount the seller is willing to accept for a good.
   e. none of the above.

10. Total surplus is the area
    a. above the supply curve and below the price.
    b. below the supply curve and above the price.
    c. above the demand curve and below the price.
    d. below the demand curve and above the price.
    e. below the demand curve and above the supply curve.

11. An increase in the price of a good along a stationary supply curve
    a. increases producer surplus.
    b. decreases producer surplus.
    c. improves market equity.
    d. does all of the above.

12. Adam Smith's "invisible hand" concept suggests that a competitive market outcome
    a. minimizes total surplus.
    b. maximizes total surplus.
    c. generates equality among the members of society.
    d. does both *b* and *c*.

13. In general, if a benevolent social planner wanted to maximize the total benefits received by buyers and sellers in a market, the planner should
    a. choose a price above the market equilibrium price.
    b. choose a price below the market equilibrium price.
    c. allow the market to seek equilibrium on its own.
    d. choose any price the planner wants because the losses to the sellers (buyers) from any change in price are exactly offset by the gains to the buyers (sellers).

14. If buyers are rational and there is no market failure,
    a. free market solutions are efficient.
    b. free market solutions are equitable.
    c. free market solutions maximize total surplus.
    d. all of the above are true.
    e. *a* and *c* are correct.

15. If a producer has market power (can influence the price of the product in the market) then free market solutions
    a. are equitable.
    b. are efficient.
    c. are inefficient.
    d. maximize consumer surplus.

16. If a market is efficient, then
    a. the market allocates output to the buyers that value it the most.
    b. the market allocates buyers to the sellers who can produce the good at least cost.
    c. the quantity produced in the market maximizes the sum of consumer and producer surplus.
    d. all of the above are true.
    e. none of the above is true.

17. If a market generates a side effect or externality, then free market solutions
    a. are equitable.
    b. are efficient.
    c. are inefficient.
    d. maximize producer surplus.

18. Medical care clearly enhances people's lives. Therefore, we should consume medical care until
   a. everyone has as much as they would like.
   b. the benefit buyers place on medical care is equal to the cost of producing it.
   c. buyers receive no benefit from another unit of medical care.
   d. we must cut back on the consumption of other goods.

19. Joe has 10 baseball gloves and Sue has none. A baseball glove costs $50 to produce. If Joe values an additional baseball glove at $100 and Sue values a baseball glove at $40, then to maximize
   a. efficiency, Joe should receive the glove.
   b. efficiency, Sue should receive the glove.
   c. consumer surplus, both should receive a glove.
   d. equity, Joe should receive the glove.

20. Suppose that the price of a new bicycle is $300. Sue values a new bicycle at $400. It costs $200 for the seller to produce the new bicycle. What is the value of total surplus if Sue buys a new bike?
   a. $100
   b. $200
   c. $300
   d. $400
   e. $500

ADVANCED CRITICAL THINKING

Suppose you are having an argument with your roommate about whether the federal government should subsidize the production of food. Your roommate argues that since food is something that is unambiguously good (unlike liquor, guns, and drugs which may be considered inherently evil by some members of society), we simply cannot have too much of it. That is, since food is clearly good, having more of it must always improve our economic well-being.

5 EXHIBIT

Price

0

Quantity

1. Is it true that you cannot have too much of a good thing? Conversely, is it possible to overproduce unambiguously good things such as food, clothing, and shelter? Why?

   _____

   _____

   _____

   _____

2. In Exhibit 5, demonstrate your answer to question *1* above with a supply-and-demand graph for food by showing the impact on economic well-being of producing quantities in excess of the equilibrium quantity.

SOLUTIONS

Terms and Definitions

_3_ Welfare economics

_7_ Willingness to pay

_1_ Consumer surplus

_8_ Cost

_6_ Producer surplus

_2_ Efficiency

_5_ Equity

_4_ Market failure

Practice Problems

1. a. See Exhibit 6.

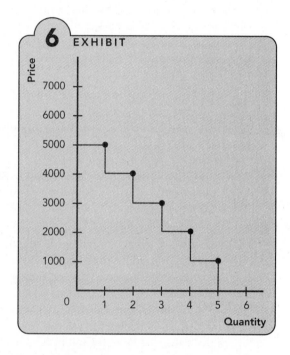

   6 EXHIBIT

   b. One apartment painted. $5,000 – $5,000 = $0, therefore she has no consumer surplus.
   c. Four apartments painted. ($5,000 – $2,000) + ($4,000 – $2,000) + ($3,000 – $2,000) + ($2,000 – $2,000) = $6,000 of consumer surplus.
   d. Her consumer surplus rose because she gains surplus on the unit she would have already purchased at the old price plus she gains surplus on the new units she now purchases due to the lower price.

2. a. See Exhibit 7.
   b. Two. ($2,000 – $1,000) + ($2,000 – $2,000) = $1,000 of producer surplus.

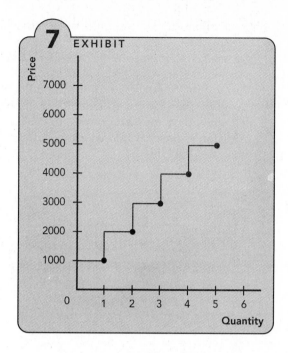

7 EXHIBIT

   c. Four apartments. ($4,000 – $1,000) + ($4,000 – $2,000) + ($4,000 – $3,000) + ($4,000 – $4,000) = $6,000 of producer surplus.
   d. He received greater producer surplus on the unit he would have produced anyway plus additional surplus on the units he now chooses to produce due to the increase in price.

3. a. Only one unit will be purchased, so consumer surplus = ($5,000 – $5,000) = $0, producer surplus = ($5,000 – $1,000) = $4,000, and total surplus = $0 + $4,000 = $4,000.
   b. Only one unit will be produced, so consumer surplus = ($5,000 – $1,000) = $4,000, producer surplus = ($1,000 – $1,000) = $0, and total surplus = $4,000 + $0 = $4,000.
   c. Consumer surplus = ($5,000 – $3,000) + ($4,000 – $3,000) + ($3,000 – $3,000) = $3,000. Producer surplus = ($3,000 – $1,000) + ($3,000 – $2,000) + ($3,000 – $3,000) = $3,000. Total surplus = $3,000 + $3,000 = $6,000. Free market total surplus is greater than social planner total surplus.

4. See Exhibit 8. Yes, it is efficient because at a quantity that is less than the equilibrium quantity, we fail to produce units that buyers value more than their cost. At a quantity above the equilibrium quantity, we produce units that cost more than the buyers value them. At equilibrium, we produce all possible units that are valued in excess of what they cost, which maximizes total surplus.

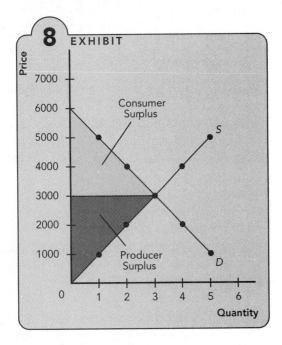

5. See Exhibit 9. Consumer surplus = $3,000 + $2,000 + $1,000 + $0 = $6,000.

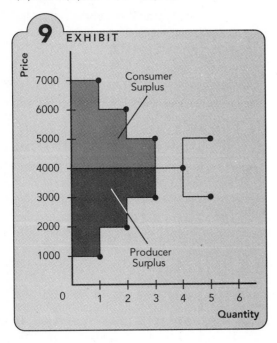

Producer surplus = $3,000 + $2,000 + $1,000 + $0 = $6,000.

Total surplus = $6,000 + $6,000 = $12,000.

Consumer surplus, producer surplus, and total surplus have all increased.

Short-Answer Questions

1. The height of the demand curve at any quantity is the marginal buyer's willingness to pay. Therefore, a plot of buyers' willingness to pay for each quantity is a plot of the demand curve.

2. Consumer surplus is the amount a buyer is willing to pay for a good minus the amount the buyer actually pays. It is measured as the area below the demand curve and above the price.

3. Zero, because the marginal buyer is the buyer who would leave the market if the price were any higher. Therefore, they are paying their willingness to pay and are receiving no surplus.

4. ($10 − $5) + ($10 − $7) + ($10 − $9) = $9

5. The height of the supply curve at any quantity is the marginal seller's cost. Therefore, a plot of the sellers' cost for each quantity is a plot of the supply curve.

6. Producer surplus is the amount a seller is paid for a good minus the seller's cost of providing it. It is measured as the area below the price and above the supply curve.

7. Producer surplus increases because existing sellers receive a greater surplus on the units they were already going to sell and new sellers enter the market because the price is now above their cost.

8. Generally, no. At any quantity below the equilibrium quantity, the market fails to produce units where the value to the marginal buyer exceeds the cost. At any quantity above the equilibrium quantity, the market produces units where the cost to the marginal producer exceeds the value to the buyers.

9. It is a resource allocation that maximizes the total surplus received by all members of society.

10. Yes, because it maximizes the area below the demand curve and above the supply curve, or total surplus.

11. Only those producers who have costs at or below the market price will be able to produce and sell that good.

True/False Questions

1. F; consumer surplus is the amount a buyer is willing to pay for a good minus the amount the buyer actually pays.
2. T
3. F; $3.00 − $2.00 = $1.00.
4. F; it is a measure of the benefits of market participation to the sellers in a market.
5. T
6. T
7. T
8. F; total surplus is the value to buyers minus the cost to sellers.
9. F; free markets allocate output to buyers who have a willingness to pay that is above the price.
10. T
11. T
12. T
13. T
14. T
15. F; producing above the equilibrium quantity reduces total surplus because units are produced for which cost exceeds the value to buyers.

Multiple-Choice Questions

1. d
2. c
3. b
4. b
5. c
6. a
7. d
8. e
9. d
10. e
11. a
12. b
13. c
14. e
15. c
16. d
17. c
18. b
19. a
20. b

Advanced Critical Thinking

1. You can have too much of a good thing. Yes, any good with a positive cost and a declining willingness to pay from the consumer can be overproduced. This is because at some point of production, the cost per unit will exceed the value to the buyer and there will be a loss to total surplus associated with additional production.
2. See Exhibit 10.

10 EXHIBIT

Application: The Costs of Taxation

8

GOALS

In this chapter you will

- Examine how taxes reduce consumer and producer surplus

- Learn the meaning and causes of the deadweight loss of a tax

- Consider why some taxes have larger deadweight losses than others

- Examine how tax revenue and deadweight loss vary with the size of a tax

OUTCOMES

After accomplishing these goals, you should be able to

- Place a tax wedge in a supply-and-demand graph and determine the tax revenue and the levels of consumer and producer surplus

- Place a tax wedge in a supply-and-demand graph and determine the value of the deadweight loss

- Show why a given tax will generate a greater deadweight loss if supply and demand are elastic than if they are inelastic

- Demonstrate why some very large taxes generate little tax revenue but a great deal of deadweight loss

CHAPTER OVERVIEW

Context and Purpose

Chapter 8 is the second chapter in a three-chapter sequence dealing with welfare economics. In the previous section on supply and demand, Chapter 6 introduced taxes and demonstrated how a tax affects the price and quantity sold in a market. Chapter 6 also described the factors that determine how the burden of the tax is divided between the buyers and sellers in a market. Chapter 7 developed welfare economics—the study of how the allocation of resources affects economic well-being. Chapter 8 combines the lessons learned in Chapters 6 and 7 and addresses the effects of taxation on welfare. Chapter 9 will address the effects of trade restrictions on welfare.

The purpose of Chapter 8 is to apply the lessons learned about welfare economics in Chapter 7 to the issue of taxation, which we addressed in Chapter 6. We will learn that the cost of a tax to buyers and sellers in a market exceeds the revenue collected by the government. We will also learn about the factors that determine the degree by which the cost of a tax exceeds the revenue collected by the government.

Chapter Review

Introduction Taxes raise the price buyers pay, reduce the price sellers receive, and reduce the quantity exchanged. Clearly, the welfare of the buyers and sellers is reduced, and the welfare of the government is increased. However, overall welfare is reduced because the cost of a tax to buyers and sellers exceeds the revenue raised by the government.

The Deadweight Loss of Taxation

Recall from Chapter 6 that a tax places a wedge between what a buyer pays and a seller receives and reduces the quantity sold regardless of whether the tax is collected from the buyer or the seller. With regard to welfare, recall from Chapter 7 that consumer surplus is the amount buyers are willing to pay minus the price they actually pay, while producer surplus is the price sellers actually receive minus their costs. The welfare or benefit to the government from a tax is the revenue it collects from the tax, which is the quantity of the good sold *after the tax is placed on the good* multiplied by the tax per unit. This benefit actually accrues to those on whom the tax revenue is spent.

Referring to Exhibit 1, without a tax the price is P_0 and the quantity is Q_0. Thus, consumer surplus is the area $A + B + C$ and producer surplus is $D + E + F$. Tax revenue is zero. Total surplus is $A + B + C + D + E + F$.

With a tax, the price to buyers rises to P_B, the price to sellers falls to P_S, and the quantity falls to Q_1. Consumer surplus is now A, producer surplus is now F, and tax revenue is $B + D$. Total surplus is now $A + B + D + F$. Consumer surplus and producer surplus have both been reduced and tax revenue has been increased. However, consumer surplus and producer surplus have been reduced by $B + C + D + E$, and government

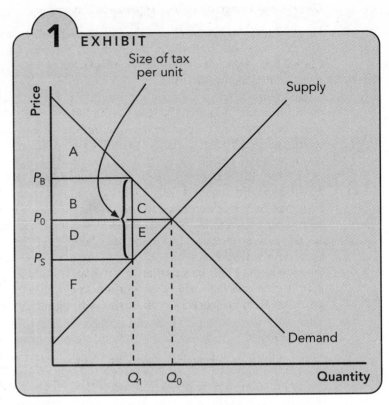

EXHIBIT 1

Size of tax per unit

revenue has been increased by only $B + D$. Therefore, losses to buyers and sellers from a tax exceed the revenue raised by the government. The reduction in total surplus that results from a tax is known as **deadweight loss** and is equal to $C + E$.

Taxes cause deadweight losses because taxes prevent buyers and sellers from realizing some of the gains from trade. That is, taxes distort incentives because taxes raise the price paid by buyers, which reduces the quantity demanded and lowers the price received by sellers, which reduces the quantity supplied. The size of the market is reduced below its optimum, and sellers fail to produce and sell goods for which the benefits to buyers exceed the costs of the producers. Deadweight loss is a loss of potential gains from trade.

The Determinants of the Deadweight Loss

The size of the deadweight loss from a tax depends on the elasticities of supply and demand. Deadweight loss from a tax is caused by the distortion in the price faced by buyers and sellers. The more buyers are sensitive to an increase in the price of the good (more elastic demand), the more they reduce their quantity demanded when a tax is placed on a good. The more sellers are sensitive to a decrease in the price of a good (more elastic supply), the more they reduce their quantity supplied when a tax is placed on a good. A greater reduction in the quantity exchanged in the market causes a greater deadweight loss. As a result, *the greater the elasticities of supply and demand, the greater the deadweight loss of a tax.*

The most important tax in the U.S. economy is the tax on labor—federal and state income taxes and Social Security taxes. Taxes on labor encourage workers to work fewer hours, second earners to stay home, the elderly to retire early, and the unscrupulous to enter the underground economy. The more elastic the supply of labor, the greater the deadweight loss of taxation and, thus, the greater the cost of any government program that relies on income tax revenue for funding. Economists and politicians argue about how elastic the supply of labor is and, thus, how large these effects are.

Henry George, a 19th-century economist, suggested that there should be a single tax on land because the supply of land is inelastic. Therefore, the burden of the tax would be entirely on the owners of land, and the tax would have no deadweight loss. Few modern economists support a single tax on land because it would not raise enough revenue and because it would need to be a tax on unimproved land (which would be difficult to implement). A tax on improved land would cause landowners to devote fewer resources toward improving their land and would create a deadweight loss.

Deadweight Loss and Tax Revenue as Taxes Vary

Deadweight loss increases as a tax increases. Indeed, deadweight loss increases at an increasing rate as a tax increases. It increases as the square of the factor of increase in the tax. For example, if a tax is doubled, the deadweight loss rises by a factor of four. If a tax is tripled, the deadweight loss rises by a factor of nine, and so on.

Tax revenue first increases and then decreases as a tax increases. This is because, at first, an increase in a tax increases the taxes collected per unit more than it reduces the units sold. At some point, however, an ever-increasing tax reduces the size of the market (the quantity sold and taxed) to such a degree that the government begins to collect a large tax on such a small quantity that tax revenue begins to fall.

The idea that a high tax rate could so shrink the market that it reduces tax revenue was expressed by Arthur Laffer in 1974. The *Laffer curve* is a diagram that shows as the size of a tax on a good is increased, revenue first rises and then falls. The implication is that if tax rates are already extremely high, a reduction in tax rates could increase tax revenue. This is a part of what has come to be called supply-side economics. Evidence has shown that this may be true for individuals who are taxed at extremely high rates, but it is less likely to be true for an entire economy. A possible exception is Sweden in the 1980s because its tax rates were about 80 percent for the typical worker. In support of supply-side concepts, note that workers in countries with low tax rates choose to work more hours per week than do workers in countries with high tax rates.

Conclusion

Taxes place a cost on market participants in two ways:

- Resources are diverted from buyers and sellers to the government.

- Taxes distort incentives so fewer goods are produced and sold than otherwise. That is, taxes cause society to lose some of the benefits of efficient markets.

Helpful Hints

1. As a tax increases, it reduces the size of the market more and more. At some point, the tax is so high that it is greater than or equal to the potential surplus even from the first unit. At that point, the tax has become a *prohibitive tax* because it eliminates the market altogether. Note that when a tax is prohibitive, the government collects no revenue at all from the tax because no units are sold. The market has reached the far side of the Laffer curve.

2. As a tax increases, the deadweight loss increases *at an increasing rate* because there are two sources to the deadweight loss and both sources are generating an increase in deadweight loss as a tax increases. First, an increase in a tax reduces the quantity exchanged and that increases deadweight loss. Second, as quantity exchanged decreases due to the tax, each successive unit that is not produced and sold *has a higher total surplus associated with it*. This further increases the deadweight loss from a tax.

Terms and Definitions

Choose a definition for each key term.

Key Terms

_____ Tax wedge

_____ Deadweight loss

_____ Laffer curve

Definitions

1. The reduction in total surplus that results from a tax

2. A graph showing the relationship between the size of a tax and the tax revenue collected

3. The difference between what the buyer pays and the seller receives when a tax is placed in a market

PROBLEMS AND SHORT-ANSWER QUESTIONS

Practice Problems

1. Exhibit 2 shows the market for tires. Suppose that a $12 road-use tax is placed on each tire sold.
   a. In Exhibit 2, locate consumer surplus, producer surplus, tax revenue, and the deadweight loss.

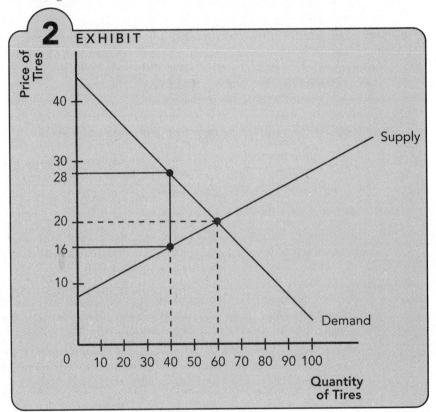

   b. Why is there a deadweight loss in the market for tires after the tax is imposed?

   _____

   c. What is the value of the tax revenue collected by the government? Why wasn't the government able to collect $12 per tire on 60 tires sold (the original equilibrium quantity)?

   _____

   _____

   _____

   d. What is the value of the tax revenue collected from the buyers? What is the value of the tax revenue collected from the sellers? Did the burden of the tax fall more heavily on the buyers or the sellers? Why?

   _____

   _____

   _____

e. Suppose over time, buyers of tires are able to substitute away from auto tires (they walk and ride bicycles). Because of this, their demand for tires becomes more elastic. What will happen to the size of the deadweight loss in the market for tires? Why?

_____

_____

_____

2. Use Exhibit 3, which shows the market for music CDs, to answer the following questions.

3 EXHIBIT

a. Complete the table. (Note: To calculate deadweight loss, the area of a triangle is 1/2 base × height).

Tax per unit	Tax revenue collected	Deadweight loss
$ 0	_____	_____
3	_____	_____
6	_____	_____
9	_____	_____
12	_____	_____
15	_____	_____
18	_____	_____

b. As the tax is increased, what happens to the amount of tax revenue collected? Why?

_____

_____

_____

c. At a tax of $18 per CD, how much tax revenue is collected? Why?

_____

_____

_____

d. If the government wanted to maximize tax revenue, what tax per unit should it impose?

_____

e. If the government wanted to maximize efficiency (total surplus), what tax per unit should it impose?

_____

f. What happens to the deadweight loss due to the tax as the tax is increased? Why?

_____

_____

_____

Short-Answer Questions

1. Why does a tax reduce consumer surplus?

_____

_____

2. Why does a tax reduce producer surplus?

_____

_____

3. Why does a tax generally produce a deadweight loss?

_____

_____

_____

4. Under what conditions would a tax fail to produce a deadweight loss?

_____

_____

5. When a tax is placed on a good, does the government collect revenue equal to the loss in total surplus due to the tax? Why?

_____

_____

_____

_____

_____

6. Suppose Rachel values having her house painted at $1,000. The cost for Paul to paint her house is $700. What is the value of the total surplus or the gains from trade on this transaction? What is the size of the tax that would eliminate this trade? What is the deadweight loss from this tax? What generalization can you make from this exercise?

_____

_____

_____

7. Would you expect a tax on gasoline to have a greater deadweight loss in the short run or the long run? Why?

_____

_____

_____

_____

8. Would a tax on unimproved land generate a large deadweight loss? Why? Who would bear the burden of the tax, the renter or the landlord? Why?

_____

_____

_____

9. As a tax on a good increases, what happens to tax revenue? Why?

_____

_____

_____

_____

10. As a tax on a good increases, what happens to the deadweight loss from the tax? Why?

_____

_____

_____

_____

SELF-TEST

True/False Questions

_____ 1. In general, a tax raises the price the buyers pay, lowers the price the sellers receive, and reduces the quantity sold.

_____ 2. If a tax is placed on a good and it reduces the quantity sold, there must be a deadweight loss from the tax.

_____ 3. Deadweight loss is the reduction in consumer surplus that results from a tax.

_____ 4. When a tax is placed on a good, the revenue the government collects is exactly equal to the loss of consumer and producer surplus from the tax.

_____ 5. If John values having his hair cut at $20 and Mary's cost of providing the haircut is $10, any tax on haircuts larger than $10 will eliminate the gains from trade and cause a $20 loss of total surplus.

_____ 6. If a tax is placed on a good in a market where supply is perfectly inelastic, there is no deadweight loss and the sellers bear the entire burden of the tax.

_____ 7. A tax on cigarettes would likely generate a larger deadweight loss than a tax on luxury boats.

_____ 8. A tax will generate a greater deadweight loss if supply and demand are inelastic.

_____ 9. A tax causes a deadweight loss because it eliminates some of the potential gains from trade.

_____ 10. A larger tax always generates more tax revenue.

_____ 11. A larger tax always generates a larger deadweight loss.

_____ 12. If an income tax rate is high enough, a reduction in the tax rate could increase tax revenue.

_____ 13. A tax collected from buyers generates a smaller deadweight loss than a tax collected from sellers.

_____ 14. If a tax is doubled, the deadweight loss from the tax more than doubles.

_____ 15. A deadweight loss results when a tax causes market participants to fail to produce and consume units on which the benefits to the buyers exceed the costs to the sellers.

Multiple-Choice Questions

Use Exhibit 4 to answer questions 1 through 10.

1. If there is no tax placed on the product in this market, consumer surplus is the area
   a. A + B + C.
   b. D + C + B.
   c. A + B + E.
   d. C + D + F.
   e. A.

4 EXHIBIT

Size of tax per unit

Price

Supply

P_B
P_0
P_S

A
B
C
D
E
F

Demand

Q_1 Q_0 Quantity

2. If there is no tax placed on the product in this market, producer surplus is the area
   a. A + B + C + D.
   b. C + D + F.
   c. D.
   d. C + F.
   e. A + B + E.

3. If a tax is placed on the product in this market, consumer surplus is the area
   a. A.
   b. A + B.
   c. A + B + E.
   d. A + B + C + D.
   e. D.

4. If a tax is placed on the product in this market, producer surplus is the area
   a. A.
   b. A + B + E.
   c. C + D + F.
   d. D.
   e. A + B + C + D.

5. If a tax is placed on the product in this market, tax revenue paid by the buyers is the area
   a. A.
   b. B.
   c. C.
   d. B + C.
   e. B + C + E + F.

6. If a tax is placed on the product in this market, tax revenue paid by the sellers is the area
   a. A.
   b. B.
   c. C.
   d. C + F.
   e. B + C + E + F.

7. If there is no tax placed on the product in this market, total surplus is the area
   a. A + B + C + D.
   b. A + B + C + D + E + F.
   c. B + C + E + F.
   d. E + F.
   e. A + D + E + F.

8. If a tax is placed on the product in this market, total surplus is the area
   a. A + B + C + D.
   b. A + B + C + D + E + F.
   c. B + C + E + F.
   d. E + F.
   e. A + D.

9. If a tax is placed on the product in this market, deadweight loss is the area
   a. B + C.
   b. B + C + E + F.
   c. A + B + C + D.
   d. E + F.
   e. A + D.

10. Which of the following is true with regard to the burden of the tax in Exhibit 4?
    a. The buyers pay a larger portion of the tax because demand is more inelastic than supply.
    b. The buyers pay a larger portion of the tax because demand is more elastic than supply.
    c. The sellers pay a larger portion of the tax because supply is more elastic than demand.
    d. The sellers pay a larger portion of the tax because supply is more inelastic than demand.

11. Which of the following would likely cause the greatest deadweight loss?
    a. a tax on cigarettes
    b. a tax on salt
    c. a tax on cruise line tickets
    d. a tax on gasoline

12. A tax on gasoline is likely to
    a. cause a greater deadweight loss in the long run when compared to the short run.
    b. cause a greater deadweight loss in the short run when compared to the long run.
    c. generate a deadweight loss that is unaffected by the time period over which it is measured.
    d. None of the above is correct.

13. Deadweight loss is greatest when
    a. both supply and demand are relatively inelastic.
    b. both supply and demand are relatively elastic.
    c. supply is elastic and demand is perfectly inelastic.
    d. demand is elastic and supply is perfectly inelastic.

14. Since the supply of unimproved land is relatively inelastic, a tax on unimproved land would generate a
    a. large deadweight loss and the burden of the tax would fall on the renter.
    b. small deadweight loss and the burden of the tax would fall on the renter.
    c. large deadweight loss and the burden of the tax would fall on the landlord.
    d. small deadweight loss and the burden of the tax would fall on the landlord.

15. Taxes on labor income tend to encourage
    a. workers to work fewer hours.
    b. second earners to stay home.
    c. the elderly to retire early.
    d. the unscrupulous to enter the underground economy.
    e. all of the above.

16. When a tax on a good starts small and is gradually increased, tax revenue will
    a. rise.
    b. fall.
    c. first rise and then fall.
    d. first fall and then rise.
    e. do none of the above.

17. The graph that shows the relationship between the size of a tax and the tax revenue collected by the government is known as a
    a. Keynesian curve.
    b. Henry George curve.
    c. Laffer curve.
    d. Reagan curve.
    e. None of the above is correct.

18. If a tax on a good is doubled, the deadweight loss from the tax
    a. stays the same.
    b. doubles.
    c. increases by a factor of four.
    d. could rise or fall.

19. The reduction of a tax
    a. could increase tax revenue if the tax had been extremely high.
    b. will always reduce tax revenue regardless of the prior size of the tax.
    c. will have no impact on tax revenue.
    d. causes a market to become less efficient.

20. When a tax distorts incentives to buyers and sellers so that fewer goods are produced and sold, the tax has
    a. increased efficiency.
    b. decreased equity.
    c. generated no tax revenue.
    d. caused a deadweight loss.

ADVANCED CRITICAL THINKING

You are watching the local news report on television with your roommate. The news anchor reports that the state budget has a deficit of $100 million. Since the state currently collects exactly $100 million from its 5 percent sales tax, your roommate says, "I can tell them how to fix their deficit. They should simply double the sales tax to 10 percent. That will double their tax revenue from $100 million to $200 million and provide the needed $100 million."

1. Is it true that doubling a tax will always double tax revenue? Why?

    _____

    _____

    _____

    _____

2. Will doubling the sales tax affect the tax revenue and the deadweight loss in all markets to the same degree? Explain?

    _____

    _____

    _____

    _____

    _____

    _____

SOLUTIONS

Terms and Definitions

_3_ Tax wedge
_1_ Deadweight loss
_2_ Laffer curve

Practice Problems

1. a. See Exhibit 5.

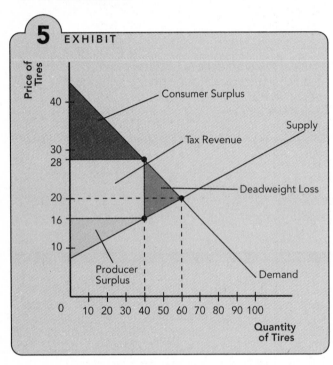

5 EXHIBIT

b. The tax raises the price paid by buyers and lowers the price received by sellers causing them to reduce their quantities demanded and supplied. Therefore, they fail to produce and exchange units where the value to buyers exceeds the cost to sellers.

c. $12 × 40 = $480. The tax distorted prices to the buyers and sellers so that the quantity supplied and demanded with the tax is reduced to 40 units from 60 units.

d. $8 × 40 = $320 from buyers. $4 × 40 = $160 from sellers. The burden fell more heavily on the buyers because the demand for tires was less elastic than the supply of tires.

e. Deadweight loss will increase because when buyers are more sensitive to an increase in price (due to the tax), they will reduce their quantity demanded even more and shrink the market more. Thus, even fewer units that are valued by buyers in excess of their cost will be sold.

2. a.

Tax per unit	Tax revenue collected	Deadweight loss
$ 0	$ 0	$0
3	30	($3 × 2)/2 = $3
6	48	($6 × 4)/2 = $12
9	54	($9 × 6)/2 = $27
12	48	($12 × 8)/2 = $48
15	30	($15 × 10)/2 = $75
18	0	($18 × 12)/2 = $108

b. It first rises, then falls. At first, as the tax is increased tax revenue rises. At some point, the tax reduces the size of the market to such a degree that the government is collecting a large tax on such a small quantity that tax revenue begins to fall.

c. No tax revenue is collected because the tax is as large as the total surplus on the first unit. Therefore, there is no incentive to produce and consume even one unit and the entire market is eliminated.

d. $9 per unit.

e. $0 per unit which causes the market to return to its free market equilibrium.

f. It increases. Indeed, it increases at an increasing rate. This is because as the tax increases, it causes the quantity exchanged to be reduced on units that have an ever larger potential surplus attached to them.

Short-Answer Questions

1. Consumer surplus is what the buyer is willing to pay for a good minus what the buyer actually pays and a tax raises the price the buyer actually pays.

2. Producer surplus is the amount the seller receives for a good minus the seller's cost and a tax reduces what the seller receives for a good.

3. A tax raises the price buyers pay and lowers the price sellers receive. This price distortion reduces the quantity demanded and supplied so we fail to produce and consume units where the benefits to the buyers exceed the costs to the sellers.

4. If either supply or demand were perfectly inelastic (insensitive to a change in price), then a tax would fail to reduce the quantity exchanged and the market would not shrink.

5. No. The tax distorts prices to buyers and sellers and causes them to reduce their quantities demanded and supplied. Taxes are collected only on the units sold after the tax is imposed. Those units that are no longer produced and sold

generate no tax revenue but those units would have added to total surplus because they were valued by buyers in excess of their cost to sellers. The reduction in total surplus is the deadweight loss.

6. Total surplus = $300. Any tax larger than $300. Deadweight loss would be $300. A tax that is greater than the potential gains from trade will eliminate trade and create a deadweight loss equal to the lost gains from trade.

7. There would be a greater deadweight loss in the long run. This is because both demand and supply tend to be more elastic in the long run as consumers and producers are able to substitute away from this market when prices move in an adverse direction. The more a market shrinks from a tax, the greater the deadweight loss.

8. No, because the supply of unimproved land is highly inelastic, so the quantity supplied is not responsive to a decrease in the price received by the seller. The landlord would bear the burden of the tax for the same reason—supply of unimproved land is highly inelastic.

9. First tax revenue increases. At some point tax revenue decreases as the distortion in prices to buyers and sellers causes the market to shrink and large taxes are collected on a small number of units exchanged.

10. Deadweight loss increases continuously because as a tax increases, the distortion in prices caused by the tax causes the market to shrink continuously. Thus, we fail to produce more and more units where the benefits to buyers exceed the costs to sellers.

True/False Questions

1. T
2. T
3. F; deadweight loss is the reduction in *total surplus* that results from a tax.
4. F; the loss of producer and consumer surplus exceeds the revenue from the tax. The difference is deadweight loss.
5. F; the loss in total surplus is the buyer's value minus the seller's cost or $20 – $10 = $10.
6. T
7. F; the more elastic the demand curve, the greater the deadweight loss, and the demand for cigarettes (a necessity) should be more inelastic than the demand for luxury boats (a luxury).
8. F; a tax generates a greater deadweight loss when supply and demand are more elastic.
9. T

10. F; as a tax increases, revenue first rises and then falls as the tax shrinks the market to a point where all trades are eliminated and tax revenue is zero.
11. T
12. T
13. F; taxes collected from either the buyers or the sellers are equivalent. That is why economists simply use a tax wedge when analyzing a tax and avoid the issue altogether.
14. T
15. T

Multiple-Choice Questions

1. c
2. b
3. a
4. d
5. b
6. c
7. b
8. a
9. d
10. d
11. c
12. a
13. b
14. d
15. e
16. c
17. c
18. c
19. a
20. d

Advanced Critical Thinking

1. No. Usually an increase in a tax will reduce the size of the market, because the tax will increase the price to buyers causing them to reduce their quantity demanded and will decrease the price to sellers causing them to reduce their quantity supplied. Therefore, when taxes double, the government collects twice as much per unit on many fewer units, so tax revenue will increase by less than double and could, in some extreme cases, even go down.

2. No. Some markets may have extremely elastic supply-and-demand curves. In these markets, an increase in a tax causes market participants to leave the market, and little revenue is generated from the tax increase but deadweight loss

increases a great deal. Other markets may have inelastic supply-and-demand curves. In these markets, an increase in a tax fails to cause market participants to leave the market and a great deal of additional tax revenue is generated with little increase in deadweight loss.

Application: International Trade

GOALS

In this chapter you will

- Consider what determines whether a country imports or exports a good

- Examine who wins and who loses from international trade

- Learn that the gains to winners from international trade exceed the losses to losers

- Analyze the welfare effects of tariffs

- Examine the arguments people use to advocate trade restrictions

OUTCOMES

After accomplishing these goals, you should be able to

- Determine whether a country imports or exports a good if the world price is greater than the before-trade domestic price

- Show that the consumer wins and the producer loses when a country imports a good

- Use consumer and producer surplus to show that the gains of the consumer exceed the losses of the producer when a country imports a good

- Show the deadweight loss associated with a tariff

- Defeat the arguments made in support of trade restrictions

CHAPTER OVERVIEW

Context and Purpose

Chapter 9 is the third chapter in a three-chapter sequence dealing with welfare economics. Chapter 7 introduced welfare economics—the study of how the allocation of resources affects economic well-being. Chapter 8 applied the lessons of welfare economics to taxation. Chapter 9 applies the tools of welfare economics from Chapter 7 to the study of international trade, a topic that was first introduced in Chapter 3.

The purpose of Chapter 9 is to use our knowledge of welfare economics to address the gains from trade more precisely than we did in Chapter 3 when we studied comparative advantage and the gains from trade. We will develop the conditions that determine whether a country imports or exports a good and discover who wins and who loses when a country imports or exports a good. We will find that when free trade is allowed, the gains of the winners exceed the losses of the losers. Since there are gains from trade, we will see that restrictions on free trade reduce the gains from trade and cause deadweight losses similar to those generated by a tax.

Chapter Review

Introduction This chapter employs welfare economics to address the following questions:

- How does international trade affect economic well-being?

- Who gains and who loses from free international trade?

- How do the gains from trade compare to the losses from trade?

The Determinants of Trade

In the absence of international trade, a market generates a domestic price that equates the domestic quantity supplied and domestic quantity demanded in that market. The **world price** is the price of the good that prevails in the world market for that good. Prices represent opportunity costs. Therefore, comparing the world price and the domestic price of a good before trade indicates whether a country has the lower opportunity cost of production and, thus, a comparative advantage in the production of a good or if other countries have a comparative advantage in the production of the good.

- If the world price is above the domestic price for a good, the country has a comparative advantage in the production of that good and that good should be exported if trade is allowed.

- If the world price is below the domestic price for a good, foreign countries have a comparative advantage in the production of that good and that good should be imported if trade is allowed.

The Winners and Losers from Trade

Assume that the country being analyzed is a small country and is, therefore, a *price taker* on world markets. This means that the country takes the world price as given and cannot influence the world price.

Exhibit 1 depicts a situation where the world price is higher than the before-trade domestic price. This country has a comparative advantage in the production of this good. If free trade is allowed, the domestic price will rise to the world price and it will export the difference between the domestic quantity supplied and the domestic quantity demanded.

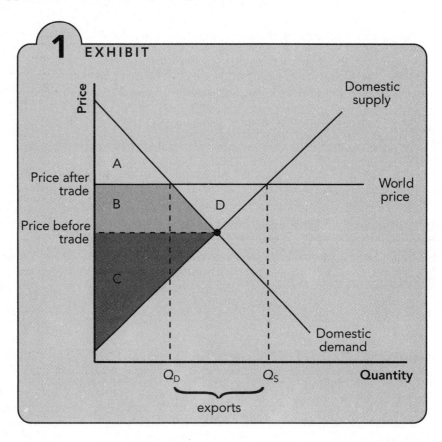

1 EXHIBIT

With regard to gains and losses to an exporting country from trade, before-trade consumer surplus was A + B and producer surplus was C, so total surplus was A + B + C. After trade, consumer surplus is A and producer surplus is B + C + D (the area below the price and above the supply curve). Total surplus is now A + B + C + D for a gain of area D. This analysis generates two conclusions:

- When a country allows trade and becomes an exporter of a good, domestic producers are better off and domestic consumers are worse off.

- Trade increases the economic well-being of a nation because the gains of the winners exceed the losses of the losers.

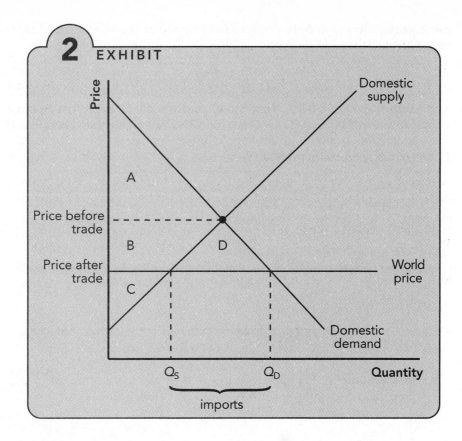

2 EXHIBIT

Exhibit 2 depicts a situation where the world price is lower than the before-trade domestic price. Other countries have a comparative advantage in the production of this good. If free trade is allowed, the domestic price will fall to the world price, and it will import the difference between the domestic quantity supplied and the domestic quantity demanded.

With regard to gains and losses to an importing country from trade, before-trade consumer surplus was A and producer surplus was B + C, so total surplus was A + B + C. After trade, consumer surplus is A + B + D (the area below the demand curve and above the price) and producer surplus is C. Total surplus is now A + B + C + D for a gain of area D. This analysis generates two conclusions:

- When a country allows trade and becomes an importer of a good, domestic consumers are better off and domestic producers are worse off.

- Trade increases the economic well-being of a nation because the gains of the winners exceed the losses of the losers.

Trade can make everyone better off if the winners compensate the losers. Compensation is rarely paid, so the losers lobby for trade restrictions, such as tariffs. When import restrictions were lifted on Chinese textiles, clothing prices fell in the United States, domestic consumers gained, and U.S. producers lost.

Tariffs restrict international trade. A **tariff** is a tax on goods produced abroad and sold domestically. Therefore, a tariff is placed on a good only if the country is an importer of that good. A tariff raises the price of the good, reduces the domestic quantity demanded, increases the domestic quantity supplied, and, thus, reduces the quantity of imports. A tariff moves the market closer to the no-trade equilibrium.

A tariff increases producer surplus and government revenue but reduces consumer surplus by a greater amount than the increase in producer surplus and government revenue. Therefore, a tariff creates a deadweight loss because total surplus is reduced. The deadweight loss comes from two sources. The increase in the price due to the tariff causes the production of units that cost more to produce than the world price (overproduction) and causes consumers to fail to consume units where the value to the consumer is greater than world price (underconsumption).

An import quota sets a limit on the quantity of a good that can be produced abroad and sold domestically. To accomplish this, a government can distribute a limited number of import licenses. As with a tariff, an import quota reduces the quantity of imports, raises the domestic price of the good, decreases the welfare of domestic consumers, increases the welfare of domestic producers, and causes deadweight losses. It moves the market closer to the no-trade equilibrium.

Note that the results of a tariff and an import quota are nearly the same except that the government collects revenue from a tariff. If the import licenses are given away, the license holders earn the surplus generated from the world price being below the domestic price. If the government sells the import licenses for the maximum possible amount, it will collect revenue equal to the tariff revenue and a tariff and a quota become identical. If quotas are "voluntary" in the sense that they are imposed by the exporting country, the revenue from the quota accrues to the foreign firms or governments.

Tariffs cause deadweight losses. Therefore, if economic efficiency is a policy goal, countries should allow free trade and avoid using tariffs.

Free trade offers benefits beyond efficiency. Free trade increases variety for consumers, allows firms to take advantage of economies of scale, makes markets more competitive, and facilitates the spread of technology.

The Arguments for Restricting Trade Opponents of free trade (often producers hurt by free trade) offer the following arguments in support of trade restrictions:

The Jobs Argument Opponents of free trade argue that trade destroys domestic jobs. However, while free trade does destroy inefficient jobs in the importing sector, it creates more efficient jobs in the export sector, industries where the country has a comparative advantage. This is always true because each country has a comparative advantage in the production of something.

The National-Security Argument Some industries argue that their product is vital for national security so it should be protected from international competition. The danger of this argument is that it runs the risk of being overused, particularly when the argument is made by representatives of industry rather than the defense establishment.

The Infant-Industry Argument New industries argue that they need temporary protection from international competition until they become mature enough to compete. However, there is a problem choosing which new industries to protect, and once protected, temporary protection often becomes permanent. In addition, industries government truly expects to be competitive in the future don't need protection because the owners will accept short-term losses.

The Unfair-Competition Argument Opponents of free trade argue that other countries provide their industries with unfair advantages such as subsidies, tax breaks, and lower environmental restrictions. However, the gains of consumers in the importing country will exceed the losses of the producers in that country, and the country will gain when importing subsidized production.

The Protection-as-a-Bargaining-Chip Argument Opponents of free trade argue that the threat of trade restrictions may result in other countries lowering their trade restrictions. However, if this does not work, the threatening country must back down or reduce trade—neither of which is desirable.

When countries choose to reduce trade restrictions, they can take a *unilateral* approach and remove trade restrictions on their own. Alternatively, they can take a *multilateral* approach and reduce trade restrictions along with other countries. Examples of the multilateral approach are NAFTA and GATT. The rules of GATT are enforced by the WTO. The multilateral approach has advantages in that it provides freer overall trade because many countries do it together, and thus, it is sometimes more easily accomplished politically. However, it may fail if negotiations between countries break down. Many economists suggest a unilateral approach because there will be gains to the domestic economy and this will cause other countries to emulate it.

Globalization is blamed by the uninformed for low wages and poor working conditions in less-developed countries. Economists argue, however, that low wages in poor countries are due to such things as low productivity. Attempts to increase wages in poor countries by restricting trade cause workers in poor countries to lose their jobs, which makes the poor even poorer.

Conclusion

Economists overwhelmingly support free trade. Free trade between states in the United States improves welfare by allowing each area of the country to specialize in the production of goods for which they have a comparative advantage. In the same manner, free trade between countries allows each country to enjoy the benefits of comparative advantage and the gains from trade.

Helpful Hints

1. Countries that restrict trade usually restrict imports rather than exports. This is because producers lose from imports and gain from exports, and producers are better organized to lobby the government to protect their interests. For example, when a country imports a product, consumers win and producers lose. Consumers are less likely to organize and lobby the government than the affected producers so imports may be restricted. When a country exports a product, producers win and consumers lose. But again, consumers are less likely to organize and lobby the government to restrict exports so exports are rarely restricted.

2. The overwhelming majority of economists find no sound *economic* argument in opposition to free trade. The only argument against free trade that may not be defeated on economic grounds is the "national-security argument." This is because it is the only argument against free trade that is not based on economics but rather is based on other strategic objectives.

3. A *prohibitive* tariff or import quota is one that is so restrictive that it returns the domestic market to its original no-trade equilibrium. This occurs if the tariff is greater than or equal to the difference between the world price and the no-trade domestic price or if the import quota is set at zero.

Terms and Definitions

Choose a definition for each key term.

Key Terms

_____ World price

_____ Price takers

_____ Tariff

Definitions

1. Market participants that cannot influence the price so they view the price as given

2. The price of a good that prevails in the world market for that good

3. A tax on goods produced abroad and sold domestically

PROBLEMS AND SHORT-ANSWER QUESTIONS

Practice Problems

1. Use Exhibit 3 to answer the following questions.

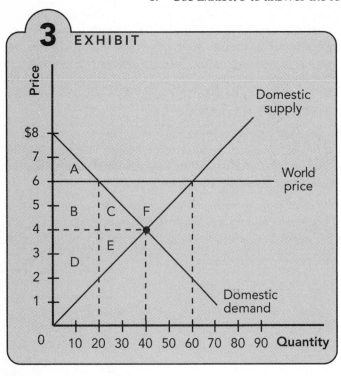

a. If trade is not allowed, what is the equilibrium price and quantity in this market?

_____

_____

b. If trade is allowed, will this country import or export this commodity? Why?

_____

_____

c. If trade is allowed, what is the price at which the good is sold, the domestic quantity supplied and demanded, and the quantity imported or exported?

_____

_____

d. What area corresponds to consumer surplus if no trade is allowed?

_____

e. What area corresponds to consumer surplus if trade is allowed?

_____

f. What area corresponds to producer surplus if no trade is allowed?

_____

g. What area corresponds to producer surplus if trade is allowed?

_____

h. If free trade is allowed, who gains and who loses, the consumers or the producers, and what area corresponds to their gain or loss?

_____

_____

i. What area corresponds to the gains from trade?

_____

2. Use Exhibit 4 to answer the following questions.

a. If trade is not allowed, what is the equilibrium price and quantity in this market?

_____

_____

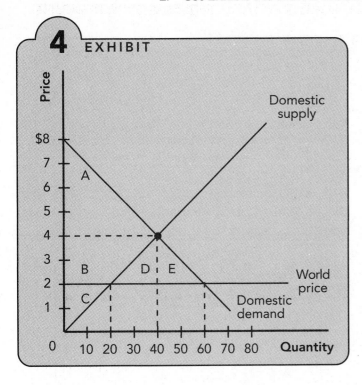

b. If trade is allowed, will this country import or export this commodity? Why?

_____

_____

c. If trade is allowed, what is the price at which the good is sold, the domestic quantity supplied and demanded, and the quantity imported or exported?

_____

_____

d. What area corresponds to consumer surplus if no trade is allowed?

_____

e. What area corresponds to consumer surplus if trade is allowed?

_____

f. What area corresponds to producer surplus if no trade is allowed?

_____

g. What area corresponds to producer surplus if trade is allowed?

_____

h. If free trade is allowed, who gains and who loses, the consumers or the producers, and what area corresponds to their gain or loss?

_____

_____

i. What area corresponds to the gains from trade?

_____

3. Use Exhibit 5 to answer the following questions.

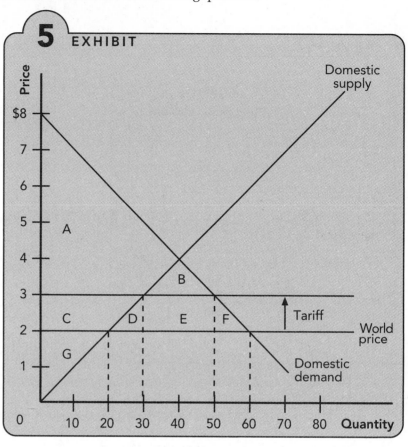

a. If free trade is allowed, what is the domestic quantity supplied, domestic quantity demanded, and the quantity imported?

_____

_____

b. If a $1 tariff is placed on this good, what is the domestic quantity supplied, domestic quantity demanded, and the quantity imported?

_____

_____

c. What area corresponds to consumer and producer surplus before the tariff is applied?

_____

_____

d. What area corresponds to consumer surplus, producer surplus, and government revenue after the tariff is applied?

_____

_____

e. What area corresponds to the deadweight loss associated with the tariff?

_____

f. Describe in words the sources of the deadweight loss from a tariff.

_____

_____

_____

g. What is the size of the tariff that would eliminate trade altogether (i.e., that would return the market to its no-trade domestic solution)?

_____

Short-Answer Questions

The following table shows the amount of output a worker can produce per hour in Partyland and Laborland.

	Beer	Pizza
Partyland	2	4
Laborland	4	12

1. If free trade is allowed, which good will each country export to the other? Why? (Explain in terms of each country's opportunity cost of production.)

_____

_____

_____

2. If the world price for a good is above a country's before-trade domestic price, will this country import or export this good? Why?

_____

_____

3. If residents of a country are allowed to import a good, who gains and who loses when compared to the before-trade equilibrium, the producers or the consumers? Why?

_____

_____

4. Describe in words the source of the gains from trade (the additional total surplus) received by an exporting country.

_____

_____

5. Describe in words the source of the gains from trade (the additional total surplus) received by an importing country.

_____

_____

6. Describe in words the source of the deadweight loss from restricting trade.

_____

_____

_____

7. For every tariff there is an import quota that will generate a similar result. What are the shortcomings of using an import quota to restrict trade versus using a tariff?

_____

_____

_____

8. What arguments are made to support trade restrictions?

_____

_____

_____

9. Present the free-trade response to the argument that imports should be restricted on goods that a country needs for national security.

_____

_____

10. If tariffs reduce total surplus and, therefore, total economic well-being, why do governments employ them?

_____

_____

_____

11. List other benefits of free trade beyond those suggested by our standard analysis.

_____

_____

_____

SELF-TEST

True/False Questions

_____ 1. If the world price for a good exceeds a country's before-trade domestic price for that good, the country should import that good.

_____ 2. Countries should import products for which they have a comparative advantage in production.

_____ 3. If a worker in Brazil can produce 6 oranges or 2 apples in an hour while a worker in Mexico can produce 2 oranges or 1 apple in an hour, then Brazil should export oranges and Mexico should export apples.

_____ 4. If free trade is allowed and a country imports wheat, domestic buyers of bread are better off and domestic farmers are worse off when compared to the before-trade domestic equilibrium.

_____ 5. If free trade is allowed and a country exports a good, domestic producers of the good are worse off and domestic consumers of the good are better off when compared to the before-trade domestic equilibrium.

_____ 6. If free trade is allowed and a country exports a good, the gains of domestic producers exceed the losses of domestic consumers and total surplus rises.

_____ 7. Trade makes everyone better off.

_____ 8. Trade can make everyone better off if the winners from trade compensate the losers from trade.

_____ 9. Trade increases the economic well-being of a nation because the gains of the winners exceed the losses of the losers.

_____ 10. Tariffs tend to benefit consumers.

_____ 11. A tariff raises the price of a good, reduces the domestic quantity demanded, increases the domestic quantity supplied, and increases the quantity imported.

_____ 12. An import quota that restricts imports to the same degree as an equivalent tariff raises the same amount of government revenue as the equivalent tariff, even if the government gives away the import licenses.

_____ 13. Opponents of free trade often argue that free trade destroys domestic jobs.

_____ 14. If a foreign country subsidizes its export industries, its taxpayers are paying to improve the welfare of consumers in the importing countries.

_____ 15. Tariffs cause deadweight losses because they raise the price of the imported good and cause overproduction and underconsumption of the good in the importing country.

Multiple-Choice Questions

1. If free trade is allowed, a country will export a good if the world price is
   a. below the before-trade domestic price of the good.
   b. above the before-trade domestic price of the good.
   c. equal to the before-trade domestic price of the good.
   d. none of the above.

2. Suppose the world price is below the before-trade domestic price for a good. If a country allows free trade in this good,
   a. consumers will gain and producers will lose.
   b. producers will gain and consumers will lose.
   c. both producers and consumers will gain.
   d. both producers and consumers will lose.

The following table shows the amount of output a worker can produce per hour in the United States and Canada.

	Pens	**Pencils**
United States	8	4
Canada	8	2

3. Which of the following statements about free trade between the United States and Canada is true?
   a. The United States will export pencils but there will be no trade in pens because neither country has a comparative advantage in the production of pens.
   b. The United States will export pens and Canada will export pencils.
   c. The United States will export pencils and Canada will export pens.
   d. The United States will export both pens and pencils.

4. If the world price for a good exceeds the before-trade domestic price for a good, then that country must have
   a. an absolute advantage in the production of the good.
   b. an absolute disadvantage in the production of the good.
   c. a comparative advantage in the production of the good.
   d. a comparative disadvantage in the production of the good.

Use Exhibit 6 to answer questions 5 through 9.

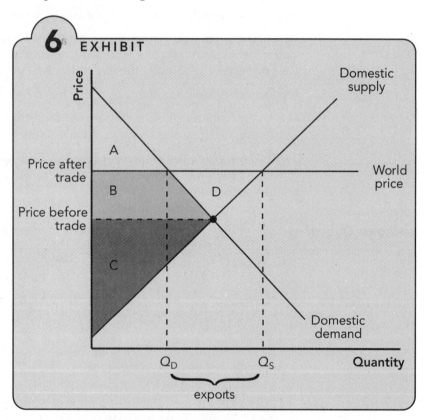

5. If trade is not allowed, consumer surplus is the area
    a. A.
    b. A + B.
    c. A + B + C.
    d. A + B + D.
    e. A + B + C + D.

6. If free trade is allowed, consumer surplus is the area
    a. A.
    b. A + B.
    c. A + B + C.
    d. A + B + D.
    e. A + B + C + D.

7. If trade is not allowed, producer surplus is the area
    a. C.
    b. B + C.
    c. B + C + D.
    d. A + B + C.
    e. A + B + C + D.

8. If free trade is allowed, producer surplus is the area
    a. C.
    b. B + C.
    c. B + C + D.
    d. A + B + C.
    e. A + B + C + D.

9. The gains from trade correspond to the area
    a. A.
    b. B.
    c. C.
    d. D.
    e. B + D.

10. When a country allows trade and exports a good,
    a. domestic consumers are better off, domestic producers are worse off, and the nation is worse off because the losses of the losers exceed the gains of the winners.
    b. domestic consumers are better off, domestic producers are worse off, and the nation is better off because the gains of the winners exceed the losses of the losers.
    c. domestic producers are better off, domestic consumers are worse off, and the nation is worse off because the losses of the losers exceed the gains of the winners.
    d. domestic producers are better off, domestic consumers are worse off, and the nation is better off because the gains of the winners exceed the losses of the losers.

Use Exhibit 7 to answer questions 11 through 16.

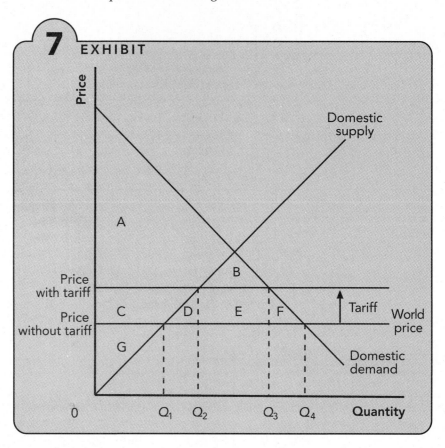

11. If free trade is allowed, consumer surplus is the area
    a. A.
    b. A + B.
    c. A + B + C.
    d. A + B + C + D + E + F.
    e. A + B + C + D + E + F + G.

12. If a tariff is placed on this good, consumer surplus is the area
    a. A.
    b. A + B.
    c. A + B + C.
    d. A + B + C + D + E + F.
    e. A + B + C + D + E + F + G.

13. Government revenue from the tariff is the area
    a. C + D + E + F.
    b. D + E + F.
    c. D + F.
    d. G.
    e. E.

14. If a tariff is placed on this good, producer surplus is the area
    a. G.
    b. G + C.
    c. G + C + D + E + F.
    d. G + C + D + E + F + B.
    e. G + C + E.

15. The deadweight loss from the tariff is the area
    a. B + D + E + F.
    b. B.
    c. D + E + F.
    d. D + F.
    e. E.

16. When politicians argue that outsourcing or offshoring of technical support to India by Dell Computer Corporation is harmful to the U.S. economy, they are employing which of the following arguments for restricting trade?
    a. the infant-industry argument
    b. the jobs argument
    c. the national-security argument
    d. the deadweight loss argument

17. Which of the following statements about a tariff is true?
    a. A tariff increases producer surplus, decreases consumer surplus, increases revenue to the government, and reduces total surplus.
    b. A tariff increases consumer surplus, decreases producer surplus, increases revenue to the government, and reduces total surplus.
    c. A tariff increases producer surplus, decreases consumer surplus, increases revenue to the government, and increases total surplus.
    d. A tariff increases consumer surplus, decreases producer surplus, increases revenue to the government, and increases total surplus.

18. Which of the following statements about import quotas is true?
    a. Import quotas are preferred to tariffs because they raise more revenue for the imposing government.
    b. Voluntary quotas established by the exporting country generate no deadweight loss for the importing country.
    c. For every tariff, there is an import quota that could have generated a similar result.
    d. An import quota reduces the price to the domestic consumers.

19. Which of the following is not employed as an argument in support of trade restrictions?
    a. Free trade destroys domestic jobs.
    b. Free trade harms the national security if vital products are imported.
    c. Free trade is harmful to importing countries if foreign countries subsidize their exporting industries.
    d. Free trade harms both domestic producers and domestic consumers and therefore reduces total surplus.
    e. Free trade harms infant industries in an importing country.

20. Because producers are better able to organize than consumers, we would expect there to be political pressure to create
    a. free trade.
    b. import restrictions.
    c. export restrictions.
    d. none of the above.

ADVANCED CRITICAL THINKING

You are watching the nightly news. A political candidate being interviewed says, "I'm for free trade, but it must be fair trade. If our foreign competitors will not raise their environmental regulations, reduce subsidies to their export industries, and lower tariffs on their imports of our goods, we should retaliate with tariffs and import quotas on their goods to show them that we won't be played for fools!"

1. If a foreign country artificially lowers the cost of production for its producers with lax environmental regulations and direct subsidies and then exports the products to us, who gains and who loses in our country, producers or consumers?

   _____

   _____

2. Continuing from question 1 above, does our country gain or lose? Why?

   _____

   _____

3. If a foreign country subsidizes the production of a good exported to the United States, who bears the burden of their mistaken policy?

   _____

4. What happens to our overall economic well-being if we restrict trade with a country that subsidizes its export industries? Explain.

   _____

   _____

   _____

5. Is there any difference in the analysis of our importation of a good sold at the cost of production or sold at a subsidized price? Why?

   _____

   _____

   _____

6. Is it a good policy to threaten trade restrictions in the hope that foreign governments will reduce their trade restrictions? Explain.

   _____

   _____

   _____

SOLUTIONS

Terms and Definitions

_2_ World price

_1_ Price takers

_3_ Tariff

Practice Problems

1. a. Price = $4, quantity = 40 units.

   b. Export because the world price is above the domestic price, which implies that this country has a comparative advantage in the production of this good.

   c. Price = $6, quantity supplied = 60 units, quantity demanded = 20 units, quantity exported = 40 units.

   d. A + B + C

   e. A

   f. D + E

   g. B + C + D + E + F

   h. Consumers lose B + C, producers gain B + C + F

   i. F

2. a. Price = $4, quantity = 40 units.

   b. Import because the world price is below the domestic price, which implies that other countries have a comparative advantage in the production of this good.

   c. Price = $2, quantity supplied = 20 units, quantity demanded = 60 units, quantity imported = 40 units.

   d. A

   e. A + B + D + E

   f. B + C

   g. C

   h. Consumers gain B + D + E, producers lose B

   i. D + E

3. a. Quantity supplied = 20 units, quantity demanded = 60 units, quantity imported = 40 units.

   b. Quantity supplied = 30 units, quantity demanded = 50 units, quantity imported = 20 units.

   c. Consumer surplus = A + B + C + D + E + F, producer surplus = G

   d. Consumer surplus = A + B, producer surplus = C + G, government revenue = E

   e. D + F

f. First, the rise in the price due to the tariff causes _overproduction_ because units are produced that cost more than the world price. Second, the rise in price causes _underconsumption_ because consumers fail to consume units where the value to consumers is greater than the world price.

g. A $2 tariff would raise the price to $4 (the no-trade domestic price) and eliminate trade.

Short-Answer Questions

1. In Partyland, the opportunity cost of 1 beer is 2 pizzas. In Laborland, the opportunity cost of 1 beer is 3 pizzas. Partyland has the lower opportunity cost of beer and, thus, a comparative advantage in beer production, and it will export beer. In Laborland, the opportunity cost of 1 pizza is 1/3 of a beer. In Partyland, the opportunity cost of 1 pizza is 1/2 of a beer. Laborland has the lower opportunity cost of pizza and, thus, a comparative advantage in pizza production, and it will export pizza. The fact that Laborland is more efficient at both is irrelevant.

2. Export, because the domestic opportunity cost of production is lower than the opportunity cost of production in other countries.

3. Consumers gain and producers lose because, if trade is allowed, the domestic price falls to the world price.

4. The gains are the additional value placed on the exported units by buyers in the rest of the world in excess of the domestic cost of production.

5. The gains are the additional value placed by domestic buyers on the imported units in excess of their cost of production in the rest of the world.

6. The rise in price from restricting trade causes overproduction of the good (production of units that cost more than the world price) and underconsumption of the good (failure to consume units valued more than the world price).

7. The revenue from an import quota will accrue to the license holders or foreign firms and governments unless the domestic government sells the import licenses for the maximum possible amount.

8. Free trade will destroy domestic jobs, reduce national security, harm infant industries, force domestic producers to compete with foreign companies that have unfair advantages, and allow other countries to have trade restrictions while our country does not.

9. The danger is that nearly any good (far beyond standard military items) can be argued by representatives of industry to be necessary for national security.
10. Tariffs harm domestic consumers while helping domestic producers. Producers are better able to organize than are consumers, and thus, they are better able to lobby the government on their behalf.
11. Free trade increases the variety of goods for consumers, allows firms to take advantage of economies of scale, makes markets more competitive, and facilitates the spread of technology.

True/False Questions

1. F; the country should *export* that good.
2. F; countries should export goods for which they have a comparative advantage in production.
3. T
4. T
5. F; producers gain, consumers lose.
6. T
7. F; some gain and some lose but the gains of the winners outweigh the losses of the losers.
8. T
9. T
10. F; tariffs benefit producers.
11. F; tariffs decrease imports.
12. F; at most, a quota can raise the same revenue if the government sells the import licenses for the maximum amount possible (the difference between the world price and the domestic price).
13. T
14. T
15. T

Multiple-Choice Questions

1. b
2. a
3. c
4. c
5. b
6. a
7. a
8. c
9. d
10. d
11. d
12. b
13. e
14. b
15. d
16. b
17. a
18. c
19. d
20. b

Advanced Critical Thinking

1. Consumers gain, producers lose.
2. Our country gains because the gains of the consumers exceed the losses of the producers.
3. The taxpayers of the foreign country.
4. Producers gain, consumers lose, but consumers lose more than producers gain so total surplus is reduced and there is a deadweight loss. The result is no different than restricting trade when the foreign producer has no unfair advantage.
5. No. In either case, the world price is lower than the before-trade domestic price, causing consumers to gain and producers to lose from trade. Also, restrictions on trade cause consumers to lose more than producers gain whether the production of the good was subsidized or not.
6. Usually not. If the other country fails to give in to the threat, the threatening country has to choose between backing down and reducing trade—neither of which is desirable.

Externalities

GOALS

In this chapter you will

- Learn what an externality is

- See why externalities can make market outcomes inefficient

- Examine how people can sometimes solve the problem of externalities on their own

- Consider why private solutions to externalities sometimes do not work

- Examine the various government policies aimed at solving the problem of externalities

OUTCOMES

After accomplishing these goals, you should be able to

- Distinguish between a positive and a negative externality

- Demonstrate why the optimal quantity and the market quantity differ in the presence of an externality

- Define the Coase theorem

- Explain how transaction costs may impede a private solution to an externality

- Demonstrate the potential equality of a corrective tax and pollution permits

CHAPTER OVERVIEW

Context and Purpose

Chapter 10 is the first chapter in the microeconomic section of the text. It is the first chapter in a three-chapter sequence on the economics of the public sector. Chapter 10 addresses externalities—the uncompensated impact of one person's actions on the well-being of a bystander. Chapter 11 will address public goods and common resources (goods that will be defined in Chapter 11), and Chapter 12 will address the tax system.

In Chapter 10, we address different sources of externalities and a variety of potential cures for externalities. Markets maximize total surplus to buyers and sellers in a market. However, if a market generates an externality (a cost or benefit to someone external to the market), the market equilibrium may not maximize the total benefit to society. Thus, in Chapter 10 we will see that while markets are usually a good way to organize economic activity, governments can sometimes improve market outcomes.

Chapter Review

Introduction   An **externality** is the uncompensated impact of one person's actions on the well-being of a bystander. If the effect is beneficial, it is called a _positive externality_. If the effect is adverse, it is called a _negative externality_. Markets maximize total surplus to buyers and sellers in a market and this is usually efficient. However, if a market generates an externality, the market equilibrium may not maximize the total benefit to society as a whole, and thus, the market is inefficient. Government policy may be needed to improve efficiency.

Examples of negative externalities are pollution from exhaust and noise. Examples of positive externalities are historic building restorations and research into new technologies.

Externalities and Market Inefficiency

The height of the demand curve measures the value of the good to the marginal consumer. The height of the supply curve measures the cost to the marginal producer. If there is no government intervention, the price adjusts to balance supply and demand. The quantity produced maximizes consumer and producer surplus. If there is no externality, the market solution is efficient because it maximizes the well-being of buyers and sellers in the market and their well-being is all that matters. However, if there is an externality and bystanders are affected by this market, the market does not maximize the total benefit to society as a whole because others beyond just the buyers and sellers in the market are affected.

There are two types of externalities:

- Negative externality: When the production of a good generates pollution, costs accrue to society beyond those that accrue to the producing firm. Thus, the **social cost** exceeds the private cost of production, and graphically, the social cost curve is above the supply curve (private cost curve). Total surplus is the value to the consumers minus the true social cost of production. Therefore, the optimal quantity that maximizes total surplus is less than the equilibrium quantity generated by the market.

- Positive externality: A good such as education generates benefits to people beyond just the buyers of education. As a result, the social value of education exceeds the private value. Graphically, the social value curve is above the demand curve (private value curve). Total surplus is the true social value minus the cost to producers. Therefore, the optimal quantity that maximizes total surplus is greater than the equilibrium quantity generated by the market.

Internalizing an externality is the altering of incentives so that people take into account the external effects of their actions. To internalize externalities, the government can create taxes and subsidies to shift the supply and demand curves until they are the same as the true social cost and social value curves. This will make the equilibrium quantity and the optimal quantity the same, and the market becomes efficient. Negative externalities can be internalized with taxes while positive externalities can be internalized with subsidies.

High technology production (robotics, etc.) generates a positive externality for other producers known as a technology spillover. Some economists consider this spillover effect to be so pervasive that they believe the government should have an industrial policy—government intervention to promote technology-enhancing industries. Other economists are skeptical. At present, the U.S. government provides a property right for new ideas in the form of patent protection, and offers special tax breaks for expenditures on research and development.

Private Solutions to Externalities

Government action is not always needed to solve the externality problem. Some private solutions to the externality problem are as follows:

- Moral codes and social sanctions: People "do the right thing" and do not litter.

- Charities: People give tax-deductible gifts to environmental groups and private colleges and universities.

- Private markets that harness self-interest and cause efficient mergers: The bee keeper merges with the apple orchard, and the resulting firm produces more apples and more honey.

- Private markets that harness self-interest and create contracts among affected parties: The apple orchard and the bee keeper can agree to produce the optimal combined quantity of apples and honey.

The **Coase theorem** is the proposition that if private parties can bargain without cost over the allocation of resources, they can solve the problem of externalities on their own. In other words, regardless of the initial distribution of rights, the interested parties can always reach a bargain in which everyone is better off and the outcome is efficient. For example, if the value of peace and quiet exceeds the value of owning a barking dog, the party desiring quiet will buy the right to quiet from the dog owner and remove the dog, or the dog owner will fail to buy the right to own a barking dog from the owner of quiet space. Regardless of whether one has the property right to peace and quiet or the other has the right to make noise, there is no barking dog, which, in this case, is efficient. The result is the opposite and is also efficient if the value of owning a dog exceeds the value of peace and quiet.

Private parties often fail to reach efficient agreements, however, due to **transaction costs.** Transaction costs are the costs that parties incur in the process of agreeing and following through on a bargain. If transaction costs exceed the potential gains from the agreement, no private solution will occur. Some sources of high transaction costs are

- lawyers' fees to write the agreement.

- costs of enforcing the agreement.

- a breakdown in bargaining when there is a range of prices that would create efficiency.

- a large number of interested parties.

Public Policies toward Externalities

When private bargaining does not work, the government can sometimes improve the outcome by responding in one of two ways: command-and-control policies or market-based policies.

- Command-and-control policies are regulations that require or prohibit (or limit) certain behaviors. The problem here is that the regulator must know all of the details of an industry and alternative technologies in order to create the efficient rules. Prohibiting a behavior altogether can be best if the cost of a particular type of pollution is enormous.

- Market-based policies align private incentives with social efficiency. There are two types of market-based policies: **corrective taxes** and subsidies, and tradable pollution permits.

A tax enacted to correct the effects of a negative externality is known as a corrective tax or Pigovian tax. An ideal corrective tax or subsidy would equal the external cost or benefit from the activity generating the externality. Corrective taxes can reduce negative externalities at a lower cost than regulations because the tax essentially places a price on a negative externality, say pollution. Those firms that can reduce their pollution with the least cost reduce their pollution a great deal while other firms that have higher costs of reducing their pollution reduce their pollution very little. The same amount of total reduction in pollution can be achieved with the tax as with regulation but at lower cost. In addition, with the tax firms have incentive to develop cleaner technologies and reduce pollution even further than the regulation would have required. Unlike other taxes, corrective taxes enhance efficiency rather than reduce efficiency. For example, the tax on gasoline is a corrective tax because, rather than causing a deadweight loss, it causes there to be less traffic congestion, safer roads, and a cleaner environment. Gasoline taxes are politically unpopular.

Tradable pollution permits allow the holder of the permit to pollute a certain amount. Those firms that have a high cost of reducing their pollution will be willing to pay a high price for the permits, and those firms that can reduce pollution at a low cost will sell their permits and will instead reduce their pollution. The initial allocation of the permits among industries does not affect the efficient outcome. This method is similar to a corrective tax. While a corrective tax sets the price of pollution (the tax), tradable pollution permits set the quantity of pollution permitted. In the market for pollution, either method can reach the efficient solution. Tradable pollution permits may be superior because the regulator does not need to know the demand to pollute in order to restrict pollution to a particular quantity. The EPA is increasingly and successfully using pollution permits to reduce pollution.

Some people object to an economic analysis of pollution. They feel that any pollution is too much and that putting a price on pollution is immoral. Since all economic activity creates pollution to some degree and all activities involve trade-offs, economists have little sympathy for this argument. Rich productive countries demand a cleaner environment, and market-based policies reduce pollution at a lower cost than alternatives, further increasing the demand for a clean environment.

Conclusion

Markets maximize total surplus to buyers and sellers in a market and this is usually efficient. However, if a market generates an externality, the market equilibrium may not maximize the total benefit to society as a whole, and thus, the market is inefficient. The Coase theorem says that people can bargain among themselves and reach an efficient solution. If transaction costs are high, however, government policy may be needed to improve efficiency. Corrective taxes and pollution permits are preferred to command-and-control policies because they reduce pollution at a lower cost and, therefore, increase the quantity demanded of a clean environment.

Helpful Hints

1. Why do we use the word "externality" to refer to the uncompensated impact of one person's actions on the well-being of a bystander? An easy way to remember is to know that the word externality refers to the "external effects" of a market transaction or to costs and benefits that land on a bystander who is "external to the market."

2. Negative externalities cause the socially optimal quantity of a good to be less than the quantity produced by the market. Positive externalities cause the socially optimal quantity of a good to be greater than the quantity produced by the market. To remedy the problem, the government can tax goods that produce negative externalities by the size of the external cost, and subsidize goods that produce positive externalities by the size of the external benefit.

Terms and Definitions

Choose a definition for each key term.

Key Terms

_____ Externality

_____ Positive externality

_____ Negative externality

_____ Social cost

_____ Internalizing an externality

_____ Coase theorem

_____ Transaction costs

_____ Corrective tax

Definitions

1. The proposition that if private parties can bargain without cost over the allocation of resources, they can solve the problem of externalities on their own

2. The costs that parties incur in the process of agreeing and following through on a bargain

3. A situation when a person's actions have an adverse impact on a bystander

4. A tax designed to induce private decision makers to take into account the social costs that arise from a negative externality

5. The uncompensated impact of one person's actions on the well-being of a bystander

6. Altering incentives so that people take into account the external effects of their actions

7. The sum of private costs and external costs

8. A situation when a person's actions have a beneficial impact on a bystander

PROBLEMS AND SHORT-ANSWER QUESTIONS

Practice Problems

1. The information below provides the prices and quantities in a hypothetical market for automobile antifreeze.

Price per gallon	Quantity demanded	Quantity supplied
$1	700	300
2	600	400
3	500	500
4	400	600
5	300	700
6	200	800
7	100	900
8	0	1,000

1 EXHIBIT

a. Plot the supply and demand curves for antifreeze in Exhibit 1.
b. What is the equilibrium price and quantity generated by buyers and sellers in the market?

_____

_____

c. Suppose that the production of antifreeze generates pollution in the form of chemical runoff and that the pollution imposes a $2 cost on society for each gallon of antifreeze produced. Plot the social cost curve in Exhibit 1.
d. What is the optimal quantity of antifreeze production? Does the market overproduce or underproduce antifreeze?

_____

_____

e. If the government were to intervene to make this market efficient, should it impose a corrective tax or a subsidy? What is the value of the appropriate tax or subsidy?

_____

_____

2. Suppose citizens living around Metropolitan Airport value peace and quiet at a value of $3 billion.
a. If it costs the airlines $4 billion to make their planes quieter (the airlines value noise at $4 billion), is it efficient for the government to require that the planes be muffled? Why?

_____

_____

_____

b. If it costs the airlines $2 billion to make their planes quieter, is it efficient for the government to require that the planes be muffled? Why?

_____

_____

c. Suppose there are no transaction costs and suppose that people have the right to peace and quiet. If it costs the airlines $2 billion to make their planes quieter, what is the private solution to the problem?

_____

_____

d. Suppose there are no transaction costs and suppose that airlines have the right to make as much noise as they please. If it costs the airlines $2 billion to make their planes quieter, what is the private solution to the problem?

_____

_____

e. Compare your answers to c and d above. What are the similarities, and what are the differences? What general rule can you make from the comparison?

_____

_____

_____

f. Suppose it costs the airlines $2 billion to make their planes quieter. If a private solution to the noise problem requires an additional $2 billion of transaction costs (due to legal fees, the large number of affected parties, and enforcement costs), can there be a private solution to the problem? Why?

_____

_____

3. Suppose there are four firms that each wish to dump one barrel of waste chemicals into the river. Firm 1 produces a product that is so valued by society and sells for such a high price that it is willing to pay $8 million to dump a barrel. Firm 2 produces a somewhat less valuable product and is only willing to pay $6 million to dump a barrel. In similar fashion, suppose firm 3 is willing to pay $4 million to dump a barrel and firm 4 will pay $2 million.

a. Draw the demand for the right to pollute in Exhibit 2.

b. Suppose the EPA estimates that the safe level of pollutants in the river is 3 barrels. At what value should they set a corrective tax?

_____

c. Suppose the EPA estimates that the safe level of pollutants in the river is 3 barrels. How many tradable pollution permits should they allocate? At what price will the permits trade?

_____

2 EXHIBIT

d. Compare parts *b* and *c* above. How many barrels are dumped in each case? What is the price paid to pollute in each case? Is there an advantage to one method of internalizing the externality compared to the other?

_____

_____

_____

Short-Answer Questions

Use the following information for questions 1 through 3:

Suppose that a commercial apple orchard uses pesticides in the production of apples. In the process, dangerous fumes drift across a nearby neighborhood.

1. Is this an example of a positive or a negative externality? Explain.

_____

_____

_____

2. If this externality is not internalized, does the market overproduce or underproduce apples? What does it mean to overproduce or underproduce a product?

_____

_____

_____

3. To internalize this externality, should the government tax or subsidize apples? Why?

_____

_____

_____

4. Suppose an individual enjoys lawn care and gardening a great deal. He uses pesticides to control insects and the harmful residue drifts across the neighborhood. He values the use of the pesticides at $10,000 and the neighborhood values clean air at $15,000. What does the Coase theorem suggest will take place?

_____

_____

_____

5. In question 4 above, how large would the transaction costs need to be in order to ensure that no private solution to the problem can be found?

_____

6. What are the sources of transaction costs when affected parties try to eliminate an externality?

_____

_____

_____

7. What are some types of private solutions to externalities?

_____

_____

_____

8. What are the two types of public policies toward externalities? Describe them. Which one do economists prefer? Why?

_____

_____

_____

9. Does a corrective tax reduce or increase efficiency? Why?

_____

_____

_____

10. Why are tradable pollution permits considered superior to corrective taxes at reducing pollution?

_____

_____

_____

SELF-TEST

True/False Questions

_____ 1. A positive externality is an external benefit that accrues to the buyers in a market while a negative externality is an external cost that accrues to the sellers in a market.

_____ 2. If a market generates a negative externality, the social cost curve is above the supply curve (private cost curve).

_____ 3. If a market generates a positive externality, the social value curve is above the demand curve (private value curve).

_____ 4. A market that generates a negative externality that has not been internalized generates an equilibrium quantity that is less than the optimal quantity.

_____ 5. If a market generates a negative externality, a corrective tax will move the market toward a more efficient outcome.

_____ 6. According to the Coase theorem, an externality always requires government intervention in order to internalize the externality.

_____ 7. To reduce pollution by some targeted amount, it is most efficient if each firm that pollutes reduces its pollution by an equal amount.

_____ 8. When Smokey the Bear says, "Only you can prevent forest fires," society is attempting to use moral codes and social sanctions to internalize the externality associated with using fire while camping.

_____ 9. A tax always makes a market less efficient.

_____10. If Bob values smoking in a restaurant at $10 and Sue values clean air while she eats at $15, according to the Coase theorem, Bob will not smoke in the restaurant only if Sue owns the right to clean air.

_____11. If transaction costs exceed the potential gains from an agreement between affected parties to an externality, there will be no private solution to the externality.

_____12. A corrective tax sets the price of pollution while tradable pollution permits set the quantity of pollution.

_____13. An advantage of using tradable pollution permits to reduce pollution is that the regulator need not know anything about the demand for pollution rights.

_____14. The majority of economists do not like the idea of putting a price on polluting the environment.

_____15. For any given demand curve for pollution, a regulator can achieve the same level of pollution with either a corrective tax or by allocating tradable pollution permits.

Multiple-Choice Questions

1. An externality is
   a. the benefit that accrues to the buyer in a market.
   b. the cost that accrues to the seller in a market.
   c. the uncompensated impact of one person's actions on the well-being of a bystander.
   d. the compensation paid to a firm's external consultants.
   e. none of the above.

2. A negative externality generates
   a. a social cost curve that is above the supply curve (private cost curve) for a good.
   b. a social cost curve that is below the supply curve (private cost curve) for a good.
   c. a social value curve that is above the demand curve (private value curve) for a good.
   d. none of the above.

3. A positive externality generates
   a. a social cost curve that is above the supply curve (private cost curve) for a good.
   b. a social value curve that is above the demand curve (private value curve) for a good.
   c. a social value curve that is below the demand curve (private value curve) for a good.
   d. none of the above.

4. A negative externality (that has not been internalized) causes the
   a. optimal quantity to exceed the equilibrium quantity.
   b. equilibrium quantity to exceed the optimal quantity.
   c. equilibrium quantity to equal the optimal quantity.
   d. equilibrium quantity to be either above or below the optimal quantity.

5. A positive externality (that has not been internalized) causes the
   a. optimal quantity to exceed the equilibrium quantity.
   b. equilibrium quantity to exceed the optimal quantity.
   c. equilibrium quantity to equal the optimal quantity.
   d. equilibrium quantity to be either above or below the optimal quantity.

6. To internalize a negative externality, an appropriate public policy response would be to
   a. ban the production of all goods creating negative externalities.
   b. have the government take over the production of the good causing the externality.
   c. subsidize the good.
   d. tax the good.

7. The government engages in an industrial policy
   a. to internalize the negative externality associated with industrial pollution.
   b. to internalize the positive externality associated with technology-enhancing industries.
   c. to help stimulate private solutions to the technology externality.
   d. by allocating tradable technology permits to high technology industry.

8. When an individual buys a car in a congested urban area, it generates
   a. an efficient market outcome.
   b. a technology spillover.
   c. a positive externality.
   d. a negative externality.

9. The most efficient pollution control system would ensure that
   a. each polluter reduce its pollution an equal amount.
   b. the polluters with the lowest cost of reducing pollution reduce their pollution the greatest amount.
   c. no pollution of the environment is tolerated.
   d. the regulators decide how much each polluter should reduce its pollution.

10. According to the Coase theorem, private parties can solve the problem of externalities if
    a. each affected party has equal power in the negotiations.
    b. the party affected by the externality has the initial property right to be left alone.
    c. there are no transaction costs.
    d. the government requires them to negotiate with each other.
    e. there are a large number of affected parties.

11. To internalize a positive externality, an appropriate public policy response would be to
    a. ban the good creating the externality.
    b. have the government produce the good until the value of an additional unit is zero.
    c. subsidize the good.
    d. tax the good.

12. Which of the following is not considered a transaction cost incurred by parties in the process of contracting to eliminate a pollution externality?
    a. costs incurred to reduce the pollution
    b. costs incurred due to lawyers' fees
    c. costs incurred to enforce the agreement
    d. costs incurred due to a large number of parties affected by the externality
    e. All of the above are considered transaction costs.

13. Bob and Tom live in a university dorm. Bob values playing loud music at a value of $100. Tom values peace and quiet at a value of $150. Which of the following statements is true?
    a. It is efficient for Bob to continue to play loud music.
    b. It is efficient for Bob to stop playing loud music only if Tom has the property right to peace and quiet.
    c. It is efficient for Bob to stop playing loud music only if Bob has the property right to play loud music.
    d. It is efficient for Bob to stop playing loud music regardless of who has the property right to the level of sound.

14. Bob and Tom live in a university dorm. Bob values playing loud music at a value of $100. Tom values peace and quiet at a value of $150. Which of the following statements is true about an efficient solution to this externality problem if Bob has the right to play loud music and if there are no transaction costs?
    a. Bob will pay Tom $100 and Bob will stop playing loud music.
    b. Tom will pay Bob between $100 and $150 and Bob will stop playing loud music.
    c. Bob will pay Tom $150 and Bob will continue to play loud music.
    d. Tom will pay Bob between $100 and $150 and Bob will continue to play loud music.

15. Which of the following is true regarding tradable pollution permits and corrective taxes?
    a. Corrective taxes are more likely to reduce pollution to a targeted amount than tradable pollution permits.
    b. Tradable pollution permits efficiently reduce pollution only if they are initially distributed to the firms that can reduce pollution at the lowest cost.
    c. To set the quantity of pollution with tradable pollution permits, the regulator must know everything about the demand for pollution rights.
    d. Corrective taxes and tradable pollution permits create an efficient market for pollution.
    e. All of the above are true.

16. The gas-guzzler tax that is placed on new vehicles that get very poor mileage is an example of
    a. a tradable pollution permit.
    b. an application of the Coase theorem.
    c. an attempt to internalize a positive externality.
    d. an attempt to internalize a negative externality.

17. A corrective tax on pollution
    a. sets the price of pollution.
    b. sets the quantity of pollution.
    c. determines the demand for pollution rights.
    d. reduces the incentive for technological innovations to further reduce pollution.

18. Tradable pollution permits
    a. set the price of pollution.
    b. set the quantity of pollution.
    c. determine the demand for pollution rights.
    d. reduce the incentive for technological innovations to further reduce pollution.

19. When wealthy alumni provide charitable contributions to their alma mater to reduce the tuition payments of current students, it is an example of
    a. an attempt to internalize a positive externality.
    b. an attempt to internalize a negative externality.
    c. a corrective tax.
    d. a command-and-control policy.

20. Suppose an industry emits a negative externality such as pollution, and the possible methods to internalize the externality are command-and-control policies, corrective taxes, and tradable pollution permits. If economists were to rank these methods for internalizing a negative externality based on efficiency, ease of implementation, and the incentive for the industry to further reduce pollution in the future, they would likely rank them in the following order (from most favored to least favored):
    a. corrective taxes, command-and-control policies, tradable pollution permits.
    b. command-and-control policies, tradable pollution permits, corrective taxes.
    c. tradable pollution permits, corrective taxes, command-and-control policies.
    d. tradable pollution permits, command-and-control policies, corrective taxes.
    e. They would all rank equally high because the same result can be obtained from any one of the policies.

ADVANCED CRITICAL THINKING

You are home for semester break. Your father opens the mail. One of the letters is your parents' property tax bill. On the property tax bill, there is a deduction if the property owner has done anything to beautify his/her property. The property owner can deduct 50 percent of any expenditure on things such as landscaping from his/her property taxes. For example, if your parents spent $2,000 on landscaping, they can reduce their tax bill by $0.50 \times \$2,000 = \$1,000$ so that the true cost of the landscaping was only $1,000. Your father announces, "This is an outrage. If someone wants to improve their house, it is no one's business but their own. I remember some of my college economics and I know that taxes and subsidies are always inefficient."

1. What is the city government trying to subsidize with this tax break?

_____

_____

_____

2. What is the externality that this subsidy is trying to internalize?

    _____

    _____

    _____

3. While taxes and subsidies usually create inefficiencies, are taxes and subsidies always inefficient? Why?

    _____

    _____

    _____

SOLUTIONS

Terms and Definitions

_5_ Externality

_8_ Positive externality

_3_ Negative externality

_7_ Social cost

_6_ Internalizing an externality

_1_ Coase theorem

_2_ Transaction costs

_4_ Corrective tax

Practice Problems

1. a. See Exhibit 3.

3 EXHIBIT

b. Price = $3, quantity = 500 units.

c. See Exhibit 4.

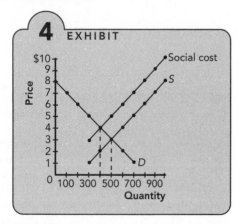

4 EXHIBIT

d. 400 units. The market overproduces because the market quantity is 500 while the optimal quantity is 400 units.

e. The government should impose a corrective tax of $2 per unit.

2. a. No, because the cost of correcting the externality exceeds the value placed on it by the affected parties.

b. Yes, because the value placed on peace and quiet exceeds the cost of muffling the planes.

c. The airlines could spend $2 billion and make their planes quieter or buy the right to make noise for $3 billion, so they will choose to make the planes quieter for $2 billion.

d. The affected citizens must pay at least $2 billion and are willing to pay up to $3 billion to the airlines to have the planes made quieter.

e. Similarities: The planes will be made quieter regardless of the original property rights because it is efficient. Differences: If the citizens have the right to quiet, citizens gain and airlines lose. If the airlines have the right to make noise, airlines gain and citizens lose.

f. No, because the transaction costs exceed the potential gains from trade. (The potential gains are the $3 billion value of quiet minus the $2 billion cost to quiet the planes, or $1 billion.)

3. a. See Exhibit 5.

5 EXHIBIT

b. $4 million per barrel

c. Three permits should be sold. They will trade at a price of $4 million per permit.

d. three barrels. $4 million per barrel. Yes, with the tradable pollution permits, the regulator does not need to know anything about the demand for pollution in this market in order to target pollution at 3 barrels and the initial allocation of pollution permits will not have an impact on the efficient solution.

Short-Answer Questions

1. Negative externality, because the social cost of producing apples exceeds the private cost of producing apples.

2. Overproduce. To overproduce is to produce units where the true cost exceeds the true val-

ue. To underproduce is to fail to produce units where the true value exceeds the true cost.

3. Tax apples because to internalize this externality, it requires that the supply curve for apples be shifted upward until it equals the true social cost curve.

4. No pesticides will be used and the air will be clean, regardless of whether the individual owns the right to use pesticides or the neighborhood residents own the right to clean air. Either the individual will fail to buy the right to pollute or the neighborhood residents will pay the individual not to pollute.

5. There are $15,000 – $10,000 = $5,000 of potential benefits. If transaction costs exceed this amount, there will be no private solution.

6. Lawyers' fees, costs of enforcement, a breakdown in bargaining when there is a range of prices that would create efficiency, and a large number of interested parties.

7. Moral codes and social sanctions, charities, mergers between affected firms, contracts between affected firms.

8. Command-and-control policies are regulations that prohibit certain behaviors. Market-based policies align private incentives with social efficiency. Economists prefer market-based policies because they are more efficient and they provide incentives for even further reduction in, say, pollution through advances in technology.

9. It increases efficiency by shifting the supply or demand curve toward the true social cost or value curve, thereby making the market solution equal to the optimal or efficient solution.

10. The regulator doesn't need to know anything about the demand to pollute in order to arrive at the targeted amount of pollution.

True/False Questions

1. F; a positive externality is a benefit that accrues to a bystander, and a negative externality is a cost that accrues to a bystander.
2. T
3. T
4. F; the equilibrium quantity is greater than the optimal quantity.
5. T
6. F; the Coase theorem suggests that private parties can solve the problem of an externality on their own if there are no transaction costs.
7. F; firms that can reduce pollution at a lower cost should reduce their pollution more than firms that can reduce pollution at a greater cost.

8. T
9. F; corrective taxes can make a market more efficient.
10. F; the original distribution of property rights to the air will not affect the efficient solution.
11. T
12. T
13. T
14. F; economists generally think that a market for pollution will reduce pollution most efficiently.
15. T

Multiple-Choice Questions

1. c
2. a
3. b
4. b
5. a
6. d
7. b
8. d
9. b
10. c
11. c
12. a
13. d
14. b
15. d
16. d
17. a
18. b
19. a
20. c

Advanced Critical Thinking

1. Expenditures on home improvement.
2. When a house is well maintained, it raises the value (or fails to reduce the value) of the nearby property. Individual buyers and sellers in the market for home repair do not take this into account when choosing the quantity of home repair, and thus, the optimal quantity exceeds the equilibrium quantity.
3. No. Appropriate corrective taxes and subsidies move a market closer to efficiency because the market equilibrium is inefficient to begin with.

Public Goods and Common Resources

CHAPTER OVERVIEW

Context and Purpose

Chapter 11 is the second chapter in a three-chapter sequence on the economics of the public sector. Chapter 10 addressed externalities. Chapter 11 addresses public goods and common resources—goods for which it is difficult to charge prices to users. Chapter 12 will address the tax system.

The purpose of Chapter 11 is to address a group of goods that are free to the consumer. When goods are free, market forces that normally allocate resources are absent. Therefore, free goods, such as playgrounds and public parks, may not be produced and consumed in the proper amounts. Government can potentially remedy this market failure and improve economic well-being.

Chapter Review

Introduction Some goods are free to the consumer—beaches, lakes, playgrounds. When goods are free, market forces that normally allocate resources are absent. Therefore, free goods, such as playgrounds and public parks, may not be produced and consumed in the proper amounts. Government can potentially remedy this market failure and improve economic well-being.

The Different Kinds of Goods

There are two characteristics of goods that are useful when defining types of goods:

- **Excludability:** the property of a good whereby a person can be prevented from using it. A good is excludable if a seller can exclude nonpayers from using it (food in the grocery store) and not excludable if a seller cannot exclude nonpayers from using it (broadcast television or radio signal).

- **Rivalry in consumption:** the property of a good whereby one person's use of a good diminishes other people's use. A good is rival in consumption if only one person can consume the good (food) and not rival if the good can be consumed by more than one at the same time (streetlight).

GOALS

In this chapter you will

- Learn the defining characteristics of public goods and common resources
- Examine why private markets fail to provide public goods
- Consider some of the important public goods in our economy
- See why the cost–benefit analysis of public goods is both necessary and difficult
- Examine why people tend to use common resources too much
- Consider some of the important common resources in our economy

OUTCOMES

After accomplishing these goals, you should be able to

- Classify goods into the categories of public goods, private goods, common resources, or goods produced by a natural monopoly
- Explain why production of public goods is unprofitable to private industry
- Explain the public good nature of national defense
- Explain why surveys to determine the benefits of public goods are a less precise valuation of benefits than prices of private goods
- Tell the story of the Tragedy of the Commons
- Explain why fish and wildlife are common resources

With these characteristics, goods can be divided into four categories:

1. **Private goods:** Goods that are both excludable and rival in consumption. Most goods like bread and blue jeans are private goods and are allocated efficiently by supply and demand in markets.

2. **Public goods:** Goods that are neither excludable nor rival in consumption, such as national defense and streetlights.

3. **Common resources:** Goods that are rival in consumption but not excludable, such as fish in the ocean.

4. Goods produced by a *natural monopoly:* Goods that are excludable but not rival in consumption, such as fire protection and cable television. Natural monopolies will be addressed in Chapter 15.

This chapter examines the two types of goods that are not excludable and, thus, are free: public goods and common resources.

Public Goods

Public goods are difficult for a private market to provide because of the *free-rider problem*. A **free rider** is a person who receives the benefit of a good but avoids paying for it. Since public goods are not excludable, firms cannot prevent nonpayers from consuming the good, and thus, there is no incentive for a firm to produce a public good. The outcome of a public good is similar to that of a positive externality because consumers of a good fail to consume the efficient quantity of the good because they do not take into account the benefit to others.

For example, a streetlight may be valued by each of ten homeowners in a neighborhood at $1,000. If the cost is $5,000, no individual will buy a streetlight because no one can sell the right to use the light to their neighbors for $1,000 each. This is because after the streetlight is in place, their neighbors can consume the light whether they pay or not. Even though the neighborhood values the streetlight at a total value of $10,000 and the cost of a streetlight is only $5,000, the private market will not be able to provide it. Public goods are related to positive externalities in that each neighbor ignores the external benefit provided to others when deciding whether to buy a streetlight. Often government steps in and provides goods, such as streetlights, where benefits exceed the costs and pays for them with tax revenue. In this case, the government could provide the streetlight and tax each resident $500 and everyone would be better off.

Some important public goods are national defense, basic research that produces general knowledge, and programs to fight poverty.

Some goods can switch between being public goods and private goods depending on the circumstances. A lighthouse is a public good if the owner cannot charge each ship as it passes the light. A lighthouse becomes a private good if the owner can charge the port to which the ships are traveling.

When a private market cannot produce a public good, governments must decide whether to produce the good. Their decision tool is often **cost–benefit analysis:** a study that compares the costs and benefits to society of providing a public good. There are two problems with cost–benefit analysis:

*   Quantifying benefits is difficult using the results of a questionnaire.

*   Respondents have little incentive to tell the truth.

When governments decide whether to spend money on additional safety measures such as stoplights and stop signs, they must consider the value of a human life because the benefit of such an expenditure is the probability of saving a life times the value of a life. Studies suggest that the value of a human life is about $10 million.

Common Resources

Common resources are not excludable but are rival (fish in the ocean). Therefore, common resources are free, but when one person uses it, it diminishes other people's enjoyment of it. The outcome of a common resource is similar to that of a negative externality because consumers of a good do not take into account the negative impact on others from their consumption. The result is that common resources are used excessively.

The **Tragedy of the Commons** is a parable that illustrates why common resources get used more than is desirable from the standpoint of society as a whole. The town common (open land to be grazed) will be overgrazed to the point where it becomes barren because, since it is free, private incentives suggest that each individual should graze as many sheep as possible, yet this is overgrazing from a social perspective. Possible solutions are to regulate the number of sheep grazed, tax sheep, auction off sheep-grazing permits, or divide the land and sell it to individual sheep herders making grazing land a private good.

Some important common resources are clean air and water, congested nontoll roads, fish, whales, and other wildlife. Private decision makers use a common resource too much, so governments regulate behavior or impose fees to reduce the problem of overuse.

Conclusion: The Importance of Property Rights

In the case of public goods and common resources, markets fail to allocate resources efficiently because property rights are not clearly established. With private markets, no one owns the clean air so no one can charge people when they pollute. The result is that people pollute too much or use too much clean air (common resource example). Further, no one can charge those who are protected by national defense for the benefit they receive so people produce too little national defense (public good example).

The government can potentially solve these problems by selling pollution permits, regulating private behavior, or providing the public good.

Helpful Hints

1. In general, public goods are underproduced and common resources are overconsumed. This is because they are both free. Since public goods are free, it is not profitable to produce them (streetlights and national defense). Since common resources are free, people overconsume them (clean air and fish in the ocean).

2. Public goods are defined by their characteristics, not by who provides them. A streetlight is a public good because it is not excludable and not rival in consumption. This is true even if, as an individual, I choose to buy one and put it in my front yard. Once in my front yard, I cannot charge you for standing near it, and when you do, it does not reduce my benefits from using it. Therefore, a streetlight is a public good whether I buy it or the city government buys it. Further, if the city government sets up a food stand and sells hot dogs, the hot dogs are private goods even though they are provided by the government because the hot dogs are both excludable and rival in consumption.

3. When governments use cost–benefit analysis as a tool to help them decide whether to produce a public good, we noted that it is difficult to collect data on the true benefits that people would receive from a public good. This is because they have an incentive to exaggerate their benefit if they would use the public good and underreport their benefit if they don't plan to use the public good very much. This is sometimes called the *liars problem*.

Terms and Definitions

Choose a definition for each key term.

Key Terms

_____ Excludability

_____ Rivalry in consumption

_____ Private goods

_____ Public goods

_____ Common resources

_____ Natural monopoly

_____ Free rider

_____ Cost–benefit analysis

_____ Tragedy of the Commons

Definitions

1. Goods that are both excludable and rival in consumption

2. The property of a good whereby one person's use diminishes other people's use

3. A person who receives the benefit of a good but avoids paying for it

4. A study that compares the costs and benefits to society of providing a public good

5. Goods that are rival in consumption but not excludable

6. The property of a good whereby a person can be prevented from using it

7. A parable that illustrates why common resources get used more than is desirable from the standpoint of society as a whole

8. Goods that are neither excludable nor rival in consumption

9. Firm that produces goods that are excludable but not rival in consumption

PROBLEMS AND SHORT-ANSWER QUESTIONS

Practice Problems

1. Consider the rivalry in consumption and excludability of each of the following goods. Use this information to determine whether the goods are public goods, private goods, common resources, or produced by a natural monopoly. Explain.

   a. Fish in a private pond

   _____

   _____

   b. Fish in the ocean

   _____

   _____

   c. Broadcast television signals

   _____

   _____

   _____

    d. Cable television signals

_____

_____

    e. Basic research on lifestyle and cholesterol levels

_____

_____

    f. Specific research on a cholesterol-lowering drug for which a patent can be obtained

_____

_____

    g. An uncongested highway (no tolls)

_____

_____

    h. A congested highway (no tolls)

_____

_____

    i. An uncongested toll road

_____

_____

    j. A hot dog served at a private party

_____

_____

    k. A hot dog sold at a stand owned by the city government

_____

_____

2. Suppose the city of Roadville is debating whether to build a new highway from its airport to the downtown area. The city surveys its citizens and finds that, on average, each of the one million residents values the new highway at a value of $50 and the highway costs $40 million to construct.

    a. Assuming the survey was accurate, is building a new highway efficient? Why?

_____

_____

    b. Under what conditions would private industry build the road?

_____

_____

c. Is it likely that private industry will build the road? Why?

_____

_____

d. Should the city build the road? On average, how much should it increase each resident's tax bill to pay for the road?

_____

_____

e. Is it certain that building the highway is efficient? That is, what are the problems associated with using cost–benefit analysis as a tool for deciding whether to provide a public good?

_____

_____

Short-Answer Questions

1. What does it mean to say that a good is excludable?

_____

_____

2. Why is it difficult for private industry to provide public goods?

_____

_____

3. How is a streetlight (a public good) related to a positive externality?

_____

_____

4. Suppose the value of a human life is $10 million. Suppose the use of airbags in cars reduces the probability of dying in a car accident over one's lifetime from 0.2 percent to 0.1 percent. Further, suppose that a lifetime supply of airbags will cost the average consumer $12,000. If these numbers were accurate, would it be efficient for the government to require airbags in cars? Why?

_____

_____

5. What type of problem are hunting and fishing licenses intended to relieve? Explain.

_____

_____

_____

6. How are fish in the ocean (a common resource) related to a negative externality?

_____

_____

_____

7. How can the establishment of individual property rights eliminate the problems associated with a common resource?

_____

_____

8. Food is more important than roads to the public, yet the government provides roads for the public and rarely provides food. Why?

_____

_____

_____

9. Why did buffalo almost become extinct while cows (a similar animal) are unlikely to ever become extinct?

_____

_____

10. Were the buffalo hunters that almost made the buffalo extinct behaving irrationally? Explain.

_____

_____

_____

SELF-TEST

True/False Questions

_____ 1. A public good is both rival in consumption and excludable.

_____ 2. A common resource is neither rival in consumption nor excludable.

_____ 3. An apple sold in a grocery store is a private good.

_____ 4. Goods produced by a natural monopoly are free to the consumer of the good.

_____ 5. Private markets have difficulty providing public goods due to the free-rider problem.

_____ 6. If the city government sells apples at a roadside stand, the apples are public goods because they are provided by the government.

_____ 7. Public goods are related to positive externalities because the potential buyers of public goods ignore the external benefits those goods provide to other consumers when they make their decision about whether to purchase public goods.

_____ 8. Common resources are overused because common resources are free to the consumer.

_____ 9. The socially optimal price for a fishing license is zero.

_____ 10. The government should continue to spend to improve the safety of our highways until there are no deaths from auto accidents.

_____ 11. Common resources are related to negative externalities because consumers of common resources ignore the negative impact of their consumption on other consumers of the common resource.

_____ 12. If someone owned the property rights to clean air, that person could charge for the use of the clean air in a market for clean air, and thus, air pollution could be reduced to the optimal level.

_____ 13. A fireworks display at a private amusement park is a good provided by a natural monopoly.

_____ 14. When the government uses cost–benefit analysis to decide whether to provide a public good, the potential benefit of the public good can easily be established by surveying the potential consumers of the public good.

_____ 15. National defense is a classic example of a common resource.

Multiple-Choice Questions

1. If one person's consumption of a good diminishes other people's use of the good, the good is said to be
   a. a common resource.
   b. a good produced by a natural monopoly.
   c. rival in consumption.
   d. excludable.

2. A public good is
   a. both rival in consumption and excludable.
   b. neither rival in consumption nor excludable.
   c. rival in consumption but not excludable.
   d. not rival in consumption but excludable.

3. A private good is
   a. both rival in consumption and excludable.
   b. neither rival in consumption nor excludable.
   c. rival in consumption but not excludable.
   d. not rival in consumption but excludable.

4. A good produced by a natural monopoly is
   a. both rival in consumption and excludable.
   b. neither rival in consumption nor excludable.
   c. rival in consumption but not excludable.
   d. not rival in consumption but excludable.

5. A common resource is
   a. both rival in consumption and excludable.
   b. neither rival in consumption nor excludable.
   c. rival in consumption but not excludable.
   d. not rival in consumption but excludable.

6. Public goods are difficult for a private market to provide due to
    a. the public goods problem.
    b. the rivalness problem.
    c. the Tragedy of the Commons.
    d. the free-rider problem.

7. Suppose each of 20 neighbors on a street values street repairs at $3,000. The cost of the street repair is $40,000. Which of the following statements is true?
    a. It is not efficient to have the street repaired.
    b. It is efficient for each neighbor to pay $3,000 to repair the section of street in front of his/her home.
    c. It is efficient for the government to tax the residents $2,000 each and repair the road.
    d. None of the above is true.

8. A free rider is a person who
    a. receives the benefit of a good but avoids paying for it.
    b. produces a good but fails to receive payment for the good.
    c. pays for a good but fails to receive any benefit from the good.
    d. fails to produce goods but is allowed to consume goods.

9. Which of the following is an example of a public good?
    a. whales in the ocean
    b. apples on a tree in a public park
    c. hot dogs at a picnic
    d. national defense

10. A positive externality affects market efficiency in a manner similar to a
    a. private good.
    b. public good.
    c. common resource.
    d. rival good.

11. Suppose that requiring motorcycle riders to wear helmets reduces the probability of a motorcycle fatality from 0.3 percent to 0.2 percent over the lifetime of a motorcycle rider and that the cost of a lifetime supply of helmets is $500. It is efficient for the government to require riders to wear helmets if human life is valued at
    a. $100 or more.
    b. $150 or more.
    c. $500 or more.
    d. $50,000 or more.
    e. $500,000 or more.

12. A negative externality affects market efficiency in a manner similar to
    a. a private good.
    b. a public good.
    c. a common resource.
    d. an excludable good.

13. When governments employ cost–benefit analysis to help them decide whether to provide a public good, measuring benefits is difficult because
    a. one can never place a value on human life or the environment.
    b. respondents to questionnaires have little incentive to tell the truth.
    c. there are no benefits to the public since a public good is not excludable.
    d. the benefits are infinite because a public good is not rival in consumption and an infinite amount of people can consume it at the same time.

14. Which of the following is an example of a common resource?
    a. a national park
    b. a fireworks display
    c. national defense
    d. iron ore

15. The Tragedy of the Commons is a parable that illustrates why
    a. public goods are underproduced.
    b. private goods are underconsumed.
    c. common resources are overconsumed.
    d. natural monopolies overproduce goods.

16. Which of the following are potential solutions to the problem of air pollution?
    a. auction off pollution permits
    b. grant rights of the clean air to citizens so that firms must purchase the right to pollute
    c. regulate the amount of pollutants that firms can put in the air
    d. all of the above

17. When markets fail to allocate resources efficiently, the ultimate source of the problem is usually
    a. that prices are not high enough so people overconsume.
    b. that prices are not low enough so firms overproduce.
    c. that property rights have not been well established.
    d. government regulation.

18. If a person can be prevented from using a good, the good is said to be
    a. a common resource.
    b. a public good.
    c. rival in consumption.
    d. excludable.

19. A congested toll road is
    a. a private good.
    b. a public good.
    c. a common resource.
    d. a good produced by a natural monopoly.

20. A person who regularly watches public television but fails to contribute to public television's fund-raising drives is known as
    a. a common resource.
    b. a costly rider.
    c. a free rider.
    d. an unwelcome rider.
    e. excess baggage.

ADVANCED CRITICAL THINKING

Broadcast television and broadcast radio send out signals that can be received by an infinite number of receivers without reducing the quality of the reception of other consumers of the signal and it is not possible to charge any of the consumers of the signal.

1. What type of good (private, public, common resource, produced by a natural monopoly) is a broadcast television or broadcast radio signal? Explain.

    _____

    _____

    _____

2. Is this type of good normally provided by private industry? Why?

    _____

    _____

    _____

3. Private companies have been providing broadcast television and radio since the invention of the medium. How do they make it profitable if they cannot charge the recipient of the signal?

    _____

    _____

    _____

4. What are the "recent" alternatives to traditional commercial television and commercial radio?

    _____

    _____

    _____

5. What type of good (private, public, common resource, produced by a natural monopoly) is this newer type of television and music provision?

    _____

    _____

    _____

SOLUTIONS

Terms and Definitions

_6_ Excludability

_2_ Rivalry in consumption

_1_ Private goods

_8_ Public goods

_5_ Common resources

_9_ Natural monopoly

_3_ Free rider

_4_ Cost–benefit analysis

_7_ Tragedy of the Commons

Practice Problems

1. a. Rival in consumption and excludable, private good. Only one can eat a fish. Since it is private, nonpayers can be excluded from fishing.

   b. Rival in consumption but not excludable, common resource. Only one can eat a fish but the ocean is not privately owned so nonpayers cannot be excluded.

   c. Not rival in consumption and not excludable, public good. Additional viewers can turn on their television without reducing the benefits to other consumers and nonpayers cannot be excluded.

   d. Not rival in consumption but excludable, produced by a natural monopoly. More houses can be wired without reducing the benefit to other consumers and the cable company can exclude nonpayers.

   e. Not rival in consumption and not excludable, public good. Once discovered, additional people can benefit from the knowledge without reducing the benefit to other consumers of the knowledge, and once in the public domain, nonpayers cannot be excluded.

   f. Not rival in consumption but excludable, produced by a natural monopoly. Additional users of the knowledge could use it without reducing the benefit to other consumers; therefore, it is not rival. If a patent can be obtained, no one else can produce the anticholesterol pill so it is excludable.

   g. Not rival in consumption and not excludable, public good. Additional cars can travel the road without reducing the benefit to other consumers, and the additional cars cannot be forced to pay for the road.

   h. Rival in consumption but not excludable, common resource. Additional cars reduce the benefits of current users but they cannot be forced to pay for the use of the highway.

   i. Not rival in consumption but excludable, produced by a natural monopoly. Additional cars do not reduce the benefits to current users but they can be excluded if they don't pay the toll.

   j. Rival in consumption but not excludable, common resource. If one eats the hot dog, another cannot. However, once provided, partygoers cannot be charged for eating the hot dogs.

   k. Rival in consumption and excludable, private good. If one eats the hot dog, another cannot. Even though it is supplied by the government, it is being sold so nonpayers can be excluded.

2. a. Yes, because the total benefit is $50 × 1,000,000 = $50 million while the cost is $40 million.

   b. If the road could be built as a toll road, then private industry could make the road excludable and the project could be profitable.

   c. No. Toll roads are usually in rural areas where they can be made as limited-access roads and, therefore, excludable. It would be very difficult to make a downtown urban road limited-access or excludable.

   d. Yes. $40.

   e. No. Quantifying benefits is difficult using the results from a questionnaire and respondents have little incentive to tell the truth. Therefore, those who would use the road exaggerate their benefit, and those that would rarely use it understate their benefit.

Short-Answer Questions

1. It means that those who do not pay for the good can be excluded from consuming it.

2. Because public goods are not excludable, the free-rider problem makes it unprofitable for private industry to produce public goods.

3. When people consider buying a streetlight, they fail to consider the external benefit it would provide to others and only consider their personal benefit. Thus, there is an underproduction and consumption of both public goods and goods that generate positive externalities.

4. No, because the expected benefit from airbags is $(0.2 − 0.1) × $10,000,000 = $10,000$ while the cost is $12,000.

5. The overconsumption of common resources. Since common resources are free, people use them excessively. Selling a limited number of

hunting or fishing licenses restricts the number of users.

6. A common resource is free so it is over-consumed. Each consumer of fish fails to take into account the negative impact on others of their consumption causing overuse of the resource from a social perspective.

7. People overuse common resources because their benefit is positive and their cost is zero. If ownership over the resource exists, the cost of using the resource is realized and a socially optimal price is generated.

8. Food is both rival in consumption and excludable so it can be efficiently provided by the private market. Roads are often neither rival in consumption nor excludable so they will not be provided by private markets and may be most efficiently provided by government.

9. Buffalo were a common resource and over-consumed. Cows are private goods and are produced and sold at the socially efficient price and quantity.

10. No. Because the buffalo were a common property resource, the buffalo were free. Each hunter pursued his own best interest but failed to take into account the impact of his actions on other people.

True/False Questions

1. F; it is neither rival in consumption nor excludable.
2. F; it is rival in consumption but not excludable.
3. T
4. F; they are excludable so a price must be paid to receive them but they are not rival in consumption so they can be enjoyed by many at the same time.
5. T
6. F; goods are categorized as public or private based on their characteristics, not who provided them, so an apple sold to a consumer is private regardless who provided the apple.
7. T
8. T
9. F; a positive price is optimal so that the price reduces the quantity demanded of fish to the socially optimal level.
10. F; at some point, the cost of increasing safety (reducing highway deaths) exceeds the value of a life.
11. T
12. T
13. T
14. F; quantifying benefits is difficult and respondents have little incentive to tell the truth.
15. F; national defense is an example of a public good.

Multiple-Choice Questions

1. c
2. b
3. a
4. d
5. c
6. d
7. c
8. a
9. d
10. b
11. e
12. c
13. b
14. a
15. c
16. d
17. c
18. d
19. a
20. c

Advanced Critical Thinking

1. Public good. A broadcast signal is not rival in consumption and not excludable.
2. No, because it is not profitable to produce a good for which nonpayers cannot be excluded from consuming it.
3. Broadcasters charge advertisers for the commercials they show during the broadcasters' programming. That is why it is called commercial television or commercial radio.
4. Cable television, pay-per-view television, and cable music included with cable television.
5. Produced by a natural monopoly because it is not rival in consumption but is excludable.

The Design of the Tax System

12

CHAPTER OVERVIEW

Context and Purpose

Chapter 12 is the third chapter in a three-chapter sequence on the economics of the public sector. Chapter 10 addressed externalities. Chapter 11 addressed public goods and common resources. Chapter 12 addresses the tax system. Taxes are inevitable because when the government remedies an externality, provides a public good, or regulates the use of a common resource, it needs tax revenue to perform these functions.

The purpose of Chapter 12 is to build on the lessons learned about taxes in previous chapters. We have seen that a tax reduces the quantity sold in a market, that the distribution of the burden of a tax depends on the relative elasticities of supply and demand, and that taxes cause deadweight losses. We expand our study of taxes in Chapter 12 by addressing how the U.S. government raises and spends money. We then address the difficulty of making a tax system both efficient and equitable.

Chapter Review

Introduction Taxes are inevitable because when the government remedies an externality, provides a public good, or regulates the use of a common resource, it needs tax revenue to perform these functions. In previous chapters that dealt with taxation, we learned that a tax reduces the quantity sold in a market, that the distribution of the burden of a tax depends on the relative elasticities of supply and demand, and that taxes cause deadweight losses. We now address how the U.S. government raises and spends money and how difficult it is to make a tax system both efficient and equitable.

A Financial Overview of the U.S. Government

The government is composed of federal, state, and local governments. Over time, the government has taken a larger share of total income in taxes—from 7 percent in 1902 to around 30 percent in recent years. The tax burden in the United States as measured by the central government's tax revenue as a percent of GDP is 19 percent. The U.S. tax burden is about average when compared to other countries. Euro-

GOALS

In this chapter you will

- Get an overview of how the U.S. government raises and spends money

- Examine the efficiency costs of taxes

- Learn alternative ways to judge the equity of a tax system

- See why studying tax incidence is crucial for evaluating tax equity

- Consider the trade-off between efficiency and equity in the design of a tax system

OUTCOMES

After accomplishing these goals, you should be able to

- List the four largest sources of tax revenue to the U.S. government from the largest to the smallest source

- Describe the administrative burdens of a tax

- Compare the benefits principle to the ability-to-pay principle of allocating a tax burden

- Explain why the burden of a tax often lands on someone other than the person from whom the tax is collected

- Discuss the efficiency and equity of a flat tax

pean countries have a higher tax burden, and less-developed countries have a lower tax burden than the United States. As countries become wealthier, the tax burden tends to increase.

The U.S. federal government collects about two-thirds of the taxes in our economy. In 2004, the average American paid $6,397 in taxes to the federal government. The largest source of tax revenue for the federal government is individual income taxes (43 percent), followed by social insurance taxes or payroll taxes (39 percent), corporate income taxes (10 percent), and all other taxes (8 percent). A family's tax liability is a percentage of income after deductions (mortgage interest payments, state and local tax payments, and charitable giving) and is based on the number of dependents. Corporate profits are taxed twice—once as corporate income and once as individual income when profits are paid out as dividends. The category of "other taxes" includes excise taxes (taxes on specific goods), estate taxes, and customs duties.

In 2004, the federal government's greatest spending was on Social Security (22 percent) followed by national defense (20 percent), income security or welfare (15 percent), Medicare (12 percent), health (mostly Medicaid, 10 percent), net interest (7 percent), and all others that included the federal court system, space program, farm-support programs, and congressional salaries (15 percent). Social Security and income security are *transfer payments*—payments for which the government does not receive a good or service in return.

A **budget deficit** is an excess of government spending over government receipts. A **budget surplus** is an excess of government receipts over government spending. Under current law, the budget deficit will continue to grow because of rising social security and Medicare payments to the elderly and a reduction in the number of taxpayers.

State and local governments collect about 40 percent of all taxes paid. Their greatest source of revenue is sales taxes (19 percent), followed by property taxes (17 percent), individual income taxes (12 percent), corporate income taxes (2 percent), from the federal government (21 percent), and all others that include license fees, tolls, and fares for public transportation (29 percent).

State and local governments spend the greatest share of their funds on education (34 percent), public welfare (16 percent), highways (7 percent), and all others that include libraries, police, trash and snow removal, fire protection, and park maintenance (43 percent).

Taxes and Efficiency

A tax system should be both *efficient* and *equitable*. Here we address efficiency. A tax is more efficient than another if it raises the same amount of revenue at a smaller cost to taxpayers. The cost of a tax includes the actual tax payment itself plus the following:

- the deadweight loss that results when taxes distort private decisions

- the administrative burden taxpayers bear when they comply with the tax laws

Recall from Chapter 8 that the deadweight loss from a tax is the reduction in economic well-being of taxpayers in excess of the amount of revenue raised by the government. The loss is generated when buyers and sellers allocate resources according to the prices they face after the tax rather than the true costs and benefits of the goods. As a result of a tax, we fail to produce and consume goods on which the benefits exceed the cost of production. Many European countries employ a value-added tax (VAT), which is a consumption tax collected at various stages of production.

Income taxes place a tax on interest income and, therefore, discourage saving. A consumption tax would not distort people's saving decisions.

The administrative burden of a tax includes the time spent filling out tax forms, the time spent throughout the year keeping records for tax purposes, and the resources the government uses to enforce the tax laws. Simplifying the tax laws would reduce the administrative burden but would require the elimination of many favorite loopholes of taxpayers.

The **average tax rate** is total taxes paid divided by total income. The **marginal tax rate** is the extra taxes paid on an additional dollar of income. The average tax rate is most appropriate for gauging the sacrifice made by a taxpayer. The marginal tax rate, however, is most appropriate for gauging how much the tax system distorts incentives and, thus, how inefficient the tax is. Since people think at the margin, a high marginal tax rate discourages hard work and causes a large deadweight loss.

Rational people think at the margin and respond to incentives. In Iceland, when the government moved from collecting taxes based on the previous year's income to collecting taxes on the current year's income, a year of income had a zero marginal tax rate. As expected, hours worked and production rose during the year with the zero marginal tax rate. As an additional example, when marginal tax rates were reduced in the United States, there was an increase in the percentage of married women who chose to work and the number of hours worked increased for those women who already had jobs.

A **lump-sum tax** is a tax that is the same amount for every person, regardless of income. A lump-sum tax is the most efficient tax because a lump-sum tax does the following:

- generates a marginal tax rate of zero so it does not distort decision making and thus creates no deadweight loss;

- imposes the minimum administrative burden.

We rarely see lump-sum taxes, however, because many perceive them as unfair or not equitable since rich and poor pay the same amount.

Taxes and Equity

There are different principles on which taxes can be based to generate fairness or equity. The **benefits principle** states that people should pay taxes based on the benefits they receive from government services. This principle can be used to justify gasoline taxes to pay for roads and to justify that the rich should pay more taxes than the poor because the rich benefit more from fire and police protection, national defense, and the court system. This principle can also be used to justify antipoverty programs paid for by the rich because the rich may benefit more than the middle class from not living in a society with poverty.

The **ability-to-pay principle** states that taxes should be levied on a person according to how well that person can shoulder the burden. This principle suggests that all taxpayers should make an "equal sacrifice" to support the government. The concept of "equal sacrifice" leads to two notions of equity: vertical equity and horizontal equity. **Vertical equity** states that taxpayers with a greater ability to pay taxes should pay larger amounts, and **horizontal equity** states that taxpayers with similar abilities to pay taxes should pay the same amount.

A **proportional tax** is a tax for which high-income and low-income taxpayers pay the same fraction of income. A **regressive tax** is a tax for which high-income taxpayers pay a smaller fraction of their income than do low-income taxpayers. A **progressive tax** is a tax for which high-income taxpayers pay a larger fraction of their income than do low-income taxpayers. If taxes are based on the ability-to-pay principle, then vertical equity requires that the rich pay more taxes than the poor, and thus, taxes should be progressive. The U.S. tax system is progressive because the highest income quintile of American families pays 26.3 percent of their income in taxes while the lowest income quintile pays 5.5 percent. After taking account of government transfers, the poorest quintile pays a negative 30 percent in taxes (they receive more than they pay).

A **flat tax** is an income tax that has the same marginal rate for all taxpayers. It is simple and can be progressive if a threshold amount of income is exempt from taxation.

Horizontal equity is difficult to accomplish because it is difficult to determine when two families truly have similar abilities to pay. For example, married couples are taxed as if they were a single taxpayer. Since they get only one exclusion (income that is not taxed), a greater amount of a married couple's combined income is taxed than when each member of the couple was single. This is the so-called "marriage tax."

It is necessary to address tax incidence in order to evaluate tax equity. This is because the person from whom the tax is collected often is not the person that bears the burden of the tax. The *flypaper theory* of tax incidence ignores the true burden of the tax and mistakenly assumes that the person from whom the tax is collected is also the one that bears the burden of the tax. For example, the corporate income tax is collected from corporations but it is actually paid by the owners, customers, and workers of the corporation.

Conclusion: The Trade-Off between Equity and Efficiency

The goals of equity and efficiency for the tax system often conflict, and people attach different weights to these two goals. President Reagan was concerned with the efficiency of the tax system so he proposed lowering marginal tax rates. President Clinton was more concerned with equity of the tax system so he proposed raising marginal tax rates. George W. Bush plans to reduce the highest rate to 35 percent.

Helpful Hints

1. The benefits principle of taxation suggests that people should pay taxes based on the benefits they receive from government services. This is similar to having the government utilize a *user fee* (a price charged by the government for using a public good) when it supplies a public good. For example, the government can charge people a direct user fee when they use a government-owned toll road. Alternatively, the government can utilize a gasoline tax as an indirect user fee to pay for the entire road system. Either way, the people who benefit from the road pay for the road.

2. Remember, only people pay taxes. When we tax a business such as a corporation, the corporation is a tax collector, not a taxpayer. The burden of the tax will be shifted to the owners, customers, and workers of the corporation based on the elasticities of supply and demand in the relevant markets for the corporation's labor, capital, and products.

Terms and Definitions

Choose a definition for each key term.

Key Terms

_____ Budget deficit

_____ Budget surplus

_____ Average tax rate

_____ Marginal tax rate

_____ Lump-sum tax

_____ Benefits principle

_____ Ability-to-pay principle

_____ Vertical equity

_____ Horizontal equity

_____ Proportional tax

_____ Regressive tax

_____ Progressive tax

Definitions

1. A tax for which high-income and low-income taxpayers pay the same fraction of income

2. The idea that taxes should be levied on a person according to how well that person can shoulder the burden

3. The extra taxes paid on an additional dollar of income

4. A tax that is the same amount for every person

5. An excess of government receipts over government spending

6. The idea that taxpayers with a greater ability to pay taxes should pay larger amounts

7. A tax for which high-income taxpayers pay a larger fraction of their income than do low-income taxpayers

8. An excess of government spending over government receipts

9. The idea that taxpayers with similar abilities to pay taxes should pay the same amount

10. The idea that people should pay taxes based on the benefits they receive from government services

11. Total taxes paid divided by total income

12. A tax for which high-income taxpayers pay a smaller fraction of their income than do low-income taxpayers

PROBLEMS AND SHORT-ANSWER QUESTIONS

Practice Problems

1. a. Fill out the table below assuming that the government taxes 20 percent of the first $30,000 of income and 50 percent of all income above $30,000.

Income	Taxes Paid	Average Tax Rate	Marginal Tax Rate
$10,000	_____	_____	_____
20,000	_____	_____	_____
30,000	_____	_____	_____
40,000	_____	_____	_____
50,000	_____	_____	_____

   b. Compare the taxes for someone making $10,000 to those of someone making $50,000 in part *a* above. Is this tax system progressive, regressive, or proportional? Explain.

   _____

   _____

   _____

   _____

2. a. Fill out the table below assuming that the government imposes a lump-sum tax of $6,000 on all individuals.

Income	Taxes Paid	Average Tax Rate	Marginal Tax Rate
$10,000	_____	_____	_____
20,000	_____	_____	_____
30,000	_____	_____	_____
40,000	_____	_____	_____
50,000	_____	_____	_____

   b. Compare the taxes for someone making $10,000 to those of someone making $50,000 in part *a* above. Is this tax system progressive, regressive, or proportional? Explain.

   _____

   _____

   _____

   _____

3. a. Fill out the table below assuming that the government taxes 20 percent of all income.

Income	Taxes Paid	Average Tax Rate	Marginal Tax Rate
$10,000	_____	_____	_____
20,000	_____	_____	_____
30,000	_____	_____	_____
40,000	_____	_____	_____
50,000	_____	_____	_____

b. Compare the taxes for someone making $10,000 to those of someone making $50,000 in part *a* above. Is this tax system progressive, regressive, or proportional? Explain.

_____

_____

_____

4. a. Fill out the table below assuming that the government taxes 40 percent of the first $10,000 of income and 10 percent of all income above $10,000.

Income	Taxes Paid	Average Tax Rate	Marginal Tax Rate
$10,000	_____	_____	_____
20,000	_____	_____	_____
30,000	_____	_____	_____
40,000	_____	_____	_____
50,000	_____	_____	_____

b. Compare the taxes for someone making $10,000 to those of someone making $50,000 in part *a* above. Is this tax system progressive, regressive, or proportional? Explain.

_____

_____

5. a. Suppose the only objective of the tax system is to collect $6,000 from people who make $30,000. Which of the tax systems described in questions 1 through 4 is best? Why?

_____

_____

_____

b. Suppose the only objective of the tax system is to be efficient. Which of the tax systems described in questions 1 through 4 is best? Why?

_____

_____

_____

_____

c. Suppose the only objective of the tax system is to be vertically equitable based on the ability-to-pay principle. Which of the tax systems described in questions 1 through 4 is best? Why?

_____

_____

_____

_____

Short-Answer Questions

1. List the sources of revenue for the federal government from the largest source to the smallest.

    _____

    _____

2. List the categories of spending by the federal government from the largest to the smallest.

    _____

    _____

    _____

3. List the sources of revenue for state and local governments from the largest source to the smallest.

    _____

    _____

    _____

4. List the categories of spending by state and local governments from the largest to the smallest.

    _____

    _____

5. What does it mean to say that a tax is *efficient*? What makes a tax efficient?

    _____

    _____

    _____

6. Is a consumption tax efficient? Explain.

    _____

    _____

    _____

7. Is a lump-sum tax efficient? Explain. Why do we rarely see lump-sum taxes in the real world?

_____

_____

_____

_____

8. Explain the difference between the benefits principle and the ability-to-pay principle of taxation. Which principle of taxation stresses vertical equity? Explain.

_____

_____

_____

_____

9. Are corporate income taxes truly paid by the corporation? That is, is the burden of the tax on the corporation? Explain.

_____

_____

_____

10. What is a flat tax? Can it be made to be progressive? If yes, how?

_____

_____

SELF-TEST

True/False Questions

_____ 1. The largest source of revenue for the federal government is the individual income tax.

_____ 2. An excise tax is a tax on income.

_____ 3. Expenditures on national defense are an example of a government transfer payment.

_____ 4. To judge the vertical equity of a tax system, one should look at the average tax rate of taxpayers of differing income levels.

_____ 5. The marginal tax rate is the appropriate tax rate to judge how much a particular tax system distorts economic decision making.

_____ 6. A lump-sum tax is a progressive tax.

_____ 7. Lump-sum taxes are equitable but not efficient.

_____ 8. More taxes are collected by state and local governments than by the federal government.

_____ 9. An efficient tax is one that generates minimal deadweight losses and minimal administrative burdens.

_____ 10. The federal income tax system in the United States is regressive.

_____ 11. The horizontal inequity of the federal income tax system is demonstrated by the fact that when two individuals marry, their combined income tax bill will increase.

_____ 12. Corporations bear the burden of the corporate income tax.

_____ 13. A tax system with a low marginal tax rate generates less deadweight loss and is more efficient than a similar tax system with a higher marginal tax rate.

_____ 14. If the government runs a budget deficit, it means that there is an excess of government spending over government receipts.

_____ 15. The marginal tax rate is total taxes paid divided by total income.

Multiple-Choice Questions

1. Which of the following lists the sources of tax revenue to the federal government from the largest source to the smallest source?
   a. individual income taxes, corporate income taxes, social insurance taxes
   b. corporate income taxes, individual income taxes, social insurance taxes
   c. individual income taxes, social insurance taxes, corporate income taxes
   d. social insurance taxes, individual income taxes, corporate income taxes
   e. None of the above is correct.

2. In the United States, the tax system is
   a. progressive.
   b. regressive.
   c. proportional.
   d. lump sum.

3. In 2004, the average American paid federal taxes of a little more than
   a. $4,000.
   b. $5,000.
   c. $6,000.
   d. $7,000.
   e. $8,000.

4. Which of the following lists the spending by the federal government from the largest category to the smallest category?
   a. Social Security, national defense, income security, Medicare, health, net interest
   b. national defense, net interest, Social Security, income security, health, Medicare
   c. health, national defense, net interest, Social Security, income security, Medicare
   d. net interest, Social Security, national defense, health, Medicare, income security
   e. None of the above is correct.

5. Which one of the following statements regarding the taxes and spending of state and local governments is true?
   a. State and local governments collect more tax revenue than the federal government.
   b. The greatest expenditure of state and local governments is on education.
   c. Corporate income taxes are a greater source of tax revenue to state and local governments than individual income taxes.
   d. The greatest source of tax revenue to state and local governments is property taxes.

6. If the federal government runs a budget surplus, there is a(n)
   a. excess of government spending over government receipts.
   b. excess of government receipts over government spending.
   c. equality of government spending and receipts.
   d. surplus of government workers.

7. Susan values a pair of blue jeans at $40. If the price is $35, Susan buys the jeans and generates consumer surplus of $5. Suppose a tax is placed on blue jeans that causes the price of blue jeans to rise to $45. Now Susan fails to buy a pair of jeans. This example has demonstrated
   a. the administrative burden of a tax.
   b. horizontal equity.
   c. the ability-to-pay principle.
   d. the benefits principle.
   e. the deadweight loss from a tax.

8. A tax for which high-income taxpayers pay a smaller fraction of their income than do low-income taxpayers is known as a(n)
   a. proportional tax.
   b. progressive tax.
   c. regressive tax.
   d. equitable tax.

9. An efficient tax
   a. raises revenue at the smallest possible cost to taxpayers.
   b. minimizes the deadweight loss from the tax.
   c. minimizes the administrative burden from the tax.
   d. does all of the above.

10. The marginal tax rate is
    a. total taxes paid divided by total income.
    b. the taxes paid by the marginal worker.
    c. the extra taxes paid on an additional dollar of income.
    d. total income divided by total taxes paid.

11. The appropriate tax rate to employ to judge the vertical equity of a tax system is the
    a. marginal tax rate.
    b. average tax rate.
    c. proportional tax rate.
    d. horizontal tax rate.

12. The average tax rate is
    a. total taxes paid divided by total income.
    b. the taxes paid by the marginal worker.
    c. the extra taxes paid on an additional dollar of income.
    d. total income divided by total taxes paid.

13. Which of the following taxes is the most efficient tax?
    a. a proportional income tax
    b. a progressive income tax
    c. a consumption tax
    d. a lump-sum tax

14. A progressive tax system is one where
    a. marginal tax rates are low.
    b. marginal tax rates are high.
    c. higher income taxpayers pay more taxes than do lower income taxpayers.
    d. higher income taxpayers pay a greater percentage of their income in taxes than do lower income taxpayers.

Use the following information about a tax system to answer questions 15 through 17.

Income	Amount of Tax
$10,000	$1,000
20,000	2,000
30,000	5,000
40,000	15,000

15. The average tax rate for a taxpayer earning $20,000 is
    a. 0 percent.
    b. 5 percent.
    c. 10 percent.
    d. 20 percent.
    e. none of the above.

16. This tax system is
    a. progressive.
    b. lump-sum.
    c. regressive.
    d. proportional.

17. The marginal tax rate for a taxpayer whose earnings rise from $30,000 to $40,000 is
    a. 0 percent.
    b. 16.7 percent.
    c. 37.5 percent.
    d. 100 percent.
    e. none of the above.

18. The ability-to-pay principle of taxation suggests that if a tax system is to be vertically equitable, it should be
    a. regressive.
    b. proportional.
    c. progressive.
    d. efficient.
    e. lump-sum.

19. Which of the following taxes can be supported by the benefits principle of taxation?
    a. gasoline taxes used to pay for roads
    b. progressive income taxes used to pay for national defense
    c. property taxes used to pay for police and the court system
    d. progressive income taxes used to pay for antipoverty programs
    e. All of the above can be supported by the benefits principle of taxation.

20. The appropriate tax rate to employ to gauge how much the tax system distorts incentives and decision making is the
    a. marginal tax rate.
    b. average tax rate.
    c. proportional tax rate.
    d. horizontal tax rate.
    e. vertical tax rate.

ADVANCED CRITICAL THINKING

You are having a political debate with a friend. The discussion centers on taxation. You show your friend some data from your economics textbook that suggests that the average American paid about $6,000 in federal income tax in 2004. Your friend says, "If $6,000 per person is what it takes to run this country, then I think that it would be much simpler if we just billed each American $6,000 and eliminated the complex tax code."

1. What type of tax is your friend suggesting? What is its appeal?

   _____

   _____

2. Is this type of tax supported by the "benefits principle" of tax equity? Explain.

   _____

   _____

3. Is this type of tax supported by the "ability-to-pay" principle of tax equity? Is it vertically equitable? Is it horizontally equitable?

   _____

   _____

   _____

   _____

4. Since your friend agrees that the tax she suggested is not equitable, she now suggests that we simply tax rich corporations since they can clearly afford it and then people wouldn't have to pay any taxes. Is she correct? Who would actually pay the taxes? Explain how she mistakenly employed the *flypaper theory* of taxation.

   _____

   _____

   _____

   _____

SOLUTIONS

Terms and Definitions

_8_ Budget deficit

_5_ Budget surplus

_11_ Average tax rate

_3_ Marginal tax rate

_4_ Lump-sum tax

_10_ Benefits principle

_2_ Ability-to-pay principle

_6_ Vertical equity

_9_ Horizontal equity

_1_ Proportional tax

_12_ Regressive tax

_7_ Progressive tax

Practice Problems

1. a.

Income	Taxes Paid	Average Tax Rate	Marginal Tax Rate
$10,000	$2,000	20%	20%
20,000	4,000	20	20
30,000	6,000	20	20
40,000	11,000	27.5	50
50,000	16,000	32	50

b. Progressive, because the average tax rate for a person making $50,000 exceeds the average tax rate for a person making $10,000. That is, the rich pay a larger fraction of their income than do poor people.

2. a.

Income	Taxes Paid	Average Tax Rate	Marginal Tax Rate
$10,000	$6,000	60%	0%
20,000	6,000	30	0
30,000	6,000	20	0
40,000	6,000	15	0
50,000	6,000	12	0

b. Regressive, because the average tax rate for a person making $10,000 exceeds the average tax rate for a person making $50,000. That is, the poor pay a larger fraction of their income than do rich people.

3. a.

Income	Taxes Paid	Average Tax Rate	Marginal Tax Rate
$10,000	$2,000	20%	20%
20,000	4,000	20	20
30,000	6,000	20	20
40,000	8,000	20	20
50,000	10,000	20	20

b. Proportional, because the average tax rate for a person making $10,000 is equal to that of a person making $50,000.

4. a.

Income	Taxes Paid	Average Tax Rate	Marginal Tax Rate
$10,000	$4,000	40%	10%
20,000	5,000	25	10
30,000	6,000	20	10
40,000	7,000	17.5	10
50,000	8,000	16	10

b. Regressive, because the average tax rate for a person making $10,000 is greater than that of a person making $50,000.

5. a. They are all equally suitable because each system generates $6,000 tax revenue from people making $30,000.

b. Taxes are more efficient if they generate smaller deadweight losses and smaller administrative burdens. The lump-sum tax in question 2 has a zero marginal rate, so it does not distort economic decision making (no deadweight loss) and is simple (small administrative burden), therefore, it is most efficient. However, it is regressive.

c. The tax system in question 1, because it is the only one that is progressive.

Short-Answer Questions

1. individual income taxes, social insurance taxes, corporate income taxes, and other taxes

2. Social Security, national defense, income security, Medicare, health, net interest, and other spending

3. sales taxes, property taxes, individual income taxes, and corporate income taxes; they also receive money from the federal government and other fees (license fees, tolls, fares, etc.).

4. education, public welfare, highways, and other spending (libraries, police, trash and snow removal, fire protection, park maintenance)

5. A tax is efficient if it raises the same amount of revenue at a smaller cost to taxpayers. It should

generate a small deadweight loss and a small administrative burden.

6. Yes. It is more efficient than an income tax because a consumption tax does not tax saving and, thus, does not distort the saving decision. An income tax does tax saving, so it does distort the saving decision and causes a deadweight loss.

7. Yes. The marginal tax rate associated with a lump-sum tax is zero, so a lump-sum tax does not distort decision making at the margin and, thus, generates no deadweight loss. It is rarely used because it is regressive.

8. The benefits principle argues that people should pay taxes based on the benefits they receive while the ability-to-pay principle argues that taxes should be based on how well a person can shoulder the burden. The ability-to-pay principle stresses vertical equity because vertical equity requires that taxpayers with a greater ability-to-pay should pay larger taxes.

9. No. Corporate income taxes are collected from the corporation but only people pay taxes. The tax burden is actually divided between the shareholders, the workers, and customers of the corporation.

10. It is an income tax with the same marginal rate for all taxpayers. Yes. Make a threshold amount of income exempt from taxation.

True/False Questions

1. T
2. F; an excise tax is a tax on a specific good such as gasoline or liquor.
3. F; a transfer payment is an expenditure for which no good or service is received in return.
4. T
5. T
6. F; a lump-sum tax is regressive.
7. F; lump-sum taxes are efficient but not equitable.
8. F; state and local governments collect about 40 percent of the taxes.
9. T
10. F; it is progressive because higher income people pay a larger percentage of their income in taxes.
11. T
12. F; the corporation's shareholders, workers, and purchasers of the corporation's products bear the burden of the corporate income tax.
13. T
14. T

15. F; the marginal tax rate is the extra taxes paid on an additional dollar of income.

Multiple-Choice Questions

1. c
2. a
3. c
4. a
5. b
6. b
7. e
8. c
9. d
10. c
11. b
12. a
13. d
14. d
15. c
16. a
17. d
18. c
19. e
20. a

Advanced Critical Thinking

1. Lump-sum tax. It is the most efficient tax—its marginal rate is zero so it does not distort incentives, and it imposes the minimum administrative burden.

2. No, if wealthy people benefit more from public services such as police and national defense, they should pay more in taxes.

3. No, wealthy people have a greater ability to pay. Therefore, it is not vertically equitable. However, it is horizontally equitable in that people with the same ability to pay are paying the same amount because all pay the same amount.

4. No, only people pay taxes—corporations collect taxes. The taxes are paid by the owners, workers, and customers of the corporations. The flypaper theory of taxation mistakenly says that the burden of a tax is on the person or company from whom the taxes are collected.

13

The Costs of Production

CHAPTER OVERVIEW

Context and Purpose

Chapter 13 is the first chapter in a five-chapter sequence dealing with firm behavior and the organization of industry. It is important that you become comfortable with the material in Chapter 13 because Chapters 14 through 17 are based on the concepts developed in Chapter 13. To be more specific, Chapter 13 develops the cost curves on which firm behavior is based. The remaining chapters in this section (Chapters 14 through 17) utilize these cost curves to develop the behavior of firms in a variety of different market structures—competitive, monopolistic, oligopolistic, and monopolistically competitive.

The purpose of Chapter 13 is to address the costs of production and develop the firm's cost curves. These cost curves underlie the firm's supply curve. In previous chapters, we summarized the firm's production decisions by starting with the supply curve. While this is suitable for answering many questions, it is now necessary to address the costs that underlie the supply curve in order to address the part of economics known as *industrial organization*—the study of how firms' decisions about prices and quantities depend on the market conditions they face.

Chapter Review

Introduction In previous chapters, we summarized the firm's production decisions by starting with the supply curve. While this is suitable for answering many questions, it is now necessary to address the costs that underlie the supply curve in order to address the part of economics known as *industrial organization*—the study of how firms' decisions about prices and quantities depend on the market conditions they face.

What Are Costs?

Economists generally assume that the goal of a firm is to maximize **profits**.

Profit = total revenue – total cost.

Total revenue is the quantity of output the firm produces times the price at which it sells the output. **Total cost** is more complex. An

GOALS

In this chapter you will

■ Examine what items are included in a firm's costs of production

■ Analyze the link between a firm's production process and its total costs

■ Learn the meaning of average total cost and marginal cost and how they are related

■ Consider the shape of a typical firm's cost curves

■ Examine the relationship between short-run and long-run costs

OUTCOMES

After accomplishing these goals, you should be able to

■ Explain the difference between economic profit and accounting profit

■ Utilize a production function to derive a total-cost curve

■ Explain why the marginal-cost curve must intersect the average total-cost curve at the minimum point of the average total-cost curve

■ Explain why a production function might exhibit increasing marginal product at low levels of output and decreasing marginal product at high levels of output

■ Explain why, as a firm expands its scale of operation, it tends to first exhibit economies of scale, then constant returns to scale, then diseconomies of scale economist considers the firm's cost of production to include all of the *opportunity costs* of producing its output. The total opportunity cost of production is the sum of the *explicit* and *implicit* costs of production. **Explicit costs** are input costs that require an outlay of money by the firm, such as when money flows out of a firm to pay for raw materials, workers' wages, rent, and so on. **Implicit costs** are input costs that do not require an outlay of money by the firm. Implicit costs include the value of the income forgone by the owner of the firm had the owner worked for someone else plus the forgone interest on the financial capital that the owner invested in the firm.

Accountants are only concerned with the firm's flow of money so they record only explicit costs. Economists are concerned with the firm's decision making, so they are concerned with total opportunity costs, which are the sum of explicit costs and implicit costs. Since accountants and economists view costs differently, they view profits differently:

- **Economic profit** = total revenue – (explicit costs + implicit costs)

- **Accounting profit** = total revenue – explicit costs

Because an accountant ignores implicit costs, accounting profit is greater than economic profit. A firm's decision about supplying goods and services is motivated by *economic* profits.

Production and Costs

For the following discussion, we assume that the size of the production facility (factory) is fixed in the short run. Therefore, this analysis describes production decisions in the short run.

A firm's costs reflect its production process. A **production function** shows the relationship between the quantity of inputs used to make a good (horizontal axis) and the quantity of output of that good (vertical axis). The **marginal product** of any input is the increase in output that arises from an additional unit of that input. The marginal product of an input can be measured as the slope of the production function or "rise over run." Production functions exhibit **diminishing marginal product**—the property whereby the marginal product of an input declines as the quantity of the input increases. Hence, the slope of a production function gets flatter as more and more inputs are added to the production process.

The *total-cost curve* shows the relationship between the quantity of output produced and the total cost of production. Since the production process exhibits diminishing marginal product, the quantity of inputs necessary to produce equal increments of output rises as we produce more output, and thus, the total-cost curve rises at an increasing rate or gets steeper as the amount produced increases.

The Various Measures of Cost

Several measures of cost can be derived from data on the firm's total cost. Costs can be divided into fixed costs and variable costs. **Fixed costs** are costs that do not vary with the quantity of output produced—for example, rent. **Variable costs** are costs that do vary with the quantity of output produced—for example, expenditures on raw materials and temporary workers. The sum of fixed and variable costs equals total costs.

In order to choose the optimal amount of output to produce, the producer needs to know the cost of the typical unit of output and the cost of producing one additional unit. The cost of the typical unit of output is measured by **average total cost**, which is total cost divided by the quantity of output. Average total cost is the sum of **average fixed cost** (fixed costs divided by the quantity of output) and **average variable cost** (variable costs divided by the quantity of output). **Marginal cost** is the cost of producing one additional unit. It is measured as the increase in total costs that arises from an extra unit of production. In symbols, if Q = quantity, TC = total cost, ATC = average total cost, FC = fixed costs, AFC = average fixed costs, VC = variable costs, AVC = average variable costs, and MC = marginal cost, then:

$ATC = TC/Q$,

$AVC = VC/Q$,

$AFC = FC/Q$,

$MC = \Delta TC/\Delta Q$.

When these cost curves are plotted on a graph with cost on the vertical axis and quantity produced on the horizontal axis, these cost curves will have predictable shapes. At low levels of production, the marginal product of an extra worker is large so the marginal cost of another unit of output is small. At high levels of production, the marginal product of a worker is small so the marginal cost of another unit is large. Therefore, because of diminishing marginal product, the marginal-cost curve is increasing or upward sloping. The average-total-cost curve is U-shaped because at low levels of output, average costs are high due to high fixed costs. As output increases, average costs fall because fixed costs are spread across additional units of output. However, at some point, diminishing returns begin to increase average costs again. The **efficient scale** of the firm is the quantity of output that minimizes average total cost. Whenever marginal cost is less than average total cost, average total cost is falling. Whenever marginal cost is greater than average total cost, average total cost is rising. Therefore, the marginal-cost curve crosses the average-total-cost curve at the efficient scale.

To this point, we have assumed that the production function exhibits diminishing marginal product at all levels of output, and therefore, there are rising marginal costs at all levels of output. Often, however, production first exhibits increasing marginal product and decreasing marginal costs at very low levels of output as the addition of workers allows for specialization of skills. At higher levels of output, diminishing returns eventually set in and marginal costs begin to rise, causing all cost-curve relationships previously described to continue to hold. In particular:

- Marginal cost eventually rises with the quantity of output.

- The average-total-cost curve is U-shaped.

- The marginal-cost curve crosses the average-total-cost curve at the minimum of average total cost.

Costs in the Short Run and in the Long Run

The division of costs between fixed and variable depends on the time horizon. In the short run, the size of the factory is fixed, and for many firms, the only way to vary output is hiring or firing workers. In the long run, the firm can change the size of the factory and all costs are variable. The long-run average-total-cost curve, although flatter than the short-run average-total-cost curves, is still U-shaped. For each particular factory size, there is a short-run average-total-cost curve that lies on or above the long-run average-total-cost curve. In the long run, the firm gets to choose on which short-run curve it wants to operate. In the short run, it must operate on the short-run curve it chose in the past. Some firms reach the long run faster than do others because some firms can change the size of their factory relatively easily.

At low levels of output, firms tend to have **economies of scale**—the property whereby long-run average total cost falls as the quantity of output increases. At high levels of output, firms tend to have **diseconomies of scale**—the property whereby long-run average total cost rises as the quantity of output increases. At intermediate levels of output, firms tend to have **constant returns to scale**—the property whereby long-run average total cost stays the same as the quantity of output changes. Economies of scale may be caused by increased *specialization* among workers as the factory gets larger while diseconomies of scale may be caused by *coordination problems* inherent in extremely large organizations. Adam Smith, 200 years ago, recognized the efficiencies captured by large factories that allowed workers to specialize in particular jobs.

Conclusion

This chapter developed a typical firm's cost curves. These cost curves will be used in the following chapters to see how firms make production and pricing decisions.

Helpful Hints

1. Since accountants and economists view costs and, thus, profits differently, it is possible for a firm that appears profitable according to an accountant to be unprofitable according to an economist. For example, suppose a firm incurs $20,000 in explicit costs to produce output that is sold for total revenue of $30,000. According to the accountant, the firm's profit is $10,000. However, suppose that the owner/manager of the firm could have worked for another firm and earned $15,000 during this period. While the accountant would still record the firm's profits at $30,000 – $20,000 = $10,000, the economist would argue that the firm is not profitable because the total explicit and implicit costs are $20,000 + $15,000 = $35,000, which exceeds the $30,000 of total revenue.

2. In the case of discrete numerical examples, marginal values are determined over a range of a variable rather than at a point. Therefore, when we plot a marginal value, we plot it halfway between the two end points of the range of the variable of concern. For example, if we are plotting the marginal cost of production as we move from the fifth unit to the sixth unit of production, we calculate the change in cost as we move from producing five units to producing six units, and then we plot this marginal cost as if it is for the fifth and a half unit. Notice the marginal-cost curves in your text. Each marginal-cost curve is plotted in this manner. Similarly, if we were plotting the marginal cost of production as we move from producing 50 units to producing 60 units, we would plot the marginal cost of that change in production as if it were for the 55th unit.

3. The long run is usually defined as the period of time necessary for all inputs to become variable. That is, the long run is the period of time necessary for the firm to be able to change the size of the production facility or factory. Note that this period of time differs across industries. For example, it may take many years for all of the inputs of a railroad to become variable because the railroad tracks are quite permanent and the right-of-way for new track is difficult to obtain. However, an ice cream shop could add on to its production facility in just a matter of months. Thus, it takes longer for a railroad to reach the long run than it does for an ice cream shop.

Terms and Definitions

Choose a definition for each key term.

Key Terms

_____ Total revenue

_____ Total cost

_____ Profit

_____ Explicit costs

_____ Implicit costs

_____ Economic profit

_____ Accounting profit

_____ Production function

_____ Marginal product

_____ Diminishing marginal product

_____ Fixed costs

_____ Variable costs

_____ Average total cost

_____ Average fixed cost

_____ Average variable cost

_____ Marginal cost

_____ Efficient scale

_____ Economies of scale

_____ Diseconomies of scale

_____ Constant returns to scale

Definitions

1. Costs that do not vary with the quantity of output produced

2. Total revenue minus total cost

3. The increase in total cost that arises from an extra unit of production

4. The property whereby long-run average total cost falls as the quantity of output increases

5. The property whereby long-run average total cost stays the same as the quantity of output changes

6. Input costs that do not require an outlay of money by the firm

7. The increase in output that arises from an additional unit of input

8. The market value of the inputs a firm uses in production

9. The property whereby long-run average total cost rises as the quantity of output increases

10. Fixed costs divided by the quantity of output

11. Costs that vary with the quantity of output produced

12. The quantity of output that minimizes average total cost

13. The amount a firm receives for the sale of its output

14. The relationship between quantity of inputs used to make a good and the quantity of output of that good

15. Variable costs divided by the quantity of output

16. Total cost divided by the quantity of output

17. The property whereby the marginal product of an input declines as the quantity of the input increases

18. Total revenue minus total cost, including both explicit and implicit costs

19. Total revenue minus total explicit cost

20. Input costs that require an outlay of money by the firm

PROBLEMS AND SHORT-ANSWER QUESTIONS

Practice Problems

1. Joe runs a small boat factory. He can make ten boats per year and sell them for $25,000 each. It costs Joe $150,000 for the raw materials (fiberglass, wood, paint, and so on) to build the ten boats. Joe has invested $400,000 in the factory and equipment needed to produce the boats: $200,000 from his own savings and $200,000 borrowed at 10 percent interest (assume that Joe could have loaned his money out at 10 percent, too). Joe can work at a competing boat factory for $70,000 per year.

   a. What is the total revenue Joe can earn in a year?

   _____

   _____

   b. What are the explicit costs Joe incurs while producing ten boats?

   _____

   _____

   c. What are the total opportunity costs of producing ten boats (explicit and implicit)?

   _____

   _____

   d. What is the value of Joe's accounting profit?

   _____

   _____

   e. What is the value of Joe's economic profit?

   _____

   _____

   f. Is it truly profitable for Joe to operate his boat factory? Explain.

   _____

   _____

   _____

   _____

2. a. Complete the following table. It describes the production and cost of hamburgers at a roadside stand. All figures are measured per hour.

Number of Workers	Output	Marginal Product of Labor	Cost of Factory	Cost of Workers	Total Cost
0	0		$25	$0	_____
1	6	_____	25	5	_____
2	11	_____	25	10	_____
3	15	_____	25	15	_____
4	18	_____	25	20	_____
5	20	_____	25	25	_____

b. Plot the production function in Exhibit 1.
c. What happens to the marginal product of labor as more workers are added to the production facility? Why? Use this information about the marginal product of labor to explain the slope of the production function you plotted above.

_____

_____

_____

_____

_____

_____

_____

_____

1 EXHIBIT

d. Plot the total-cost curve in Exhibit 2.
e. Explain the shape of the total-cost curve.

_____

_____

_____

_____

_____

_____

2 EXHIBIT

3. a. The information below is for Bob's blue jeans manufacturing plant. All data are per hour. Complete the table. Note the following abbreviations: *FC* (fixed cost), *VC* (variable cost), *TC* (total cost), *AFC* (average fixed cost), *AVC* (average variable cost), *ATC* (average total cost), *MC* (marginal cost).

Quantity	FC	VC	TC	AFC	AVC	ATC	MC
0	$16	$0	___	___	___	___	
1	16	18	___	___	___	___	___
2	16	31	___	___	___	___	___
3	16	41	___	___	___	___	___
4	16	49	___	___	___	___	___
5	16	59	___	___	___	___	___
6	16	72	___	___	___	___	___
7	16	90	___	___	___	___	___
8	16	114	___	___	___	___	___
9	16	145	___	___	___	___	___
10	16	184	___	___	___	___	___

b. Plot *AFC, AVC, ATC,* and *MC* in Exhibit 3. (Note: Read Helpful Hint 2 above before plotting *MC*).

c. Explain the shape of each of the curves you plotted in part *b* above.

_____

_____

_____

_____

_____

_____

3 EXHIBIT

d. Explain the relationship between *ATC* and *MC*.

_____

_____

_____

e. Explain the relationship between *ATC, AFC,* and *AVC*.

_____

_____

_____

    f. What is Bob's efficient scale? How do you find the efficient scale? Explain.

_____

_____

_____

Short-Answer Questions

1. What is profit?

_____

2. How does economic profit differ from accounting profit?

_____

_____

_____

3. Suppose you own and operate your own business. Further, suppose that interest rates rise and another firm offers you a job paying twice what you thought you were worth in the labor market. What has happened to your accounting profit? What has happened to your economic profit? Are you more or less likely to continue to operate your own firm?

_____

_____

_____

_____

4. Explain the relationship between the production function and the total-cost curve.

_____

_____

_____

_____

5. Is the salary of management in a firm a fixed cost or a variable cost? Why?

_____

_____

6. What is the efficient scale of a firm?

_____

_____

7. Explain the relationship between marginal cost and average total cost.

_____

_____

_____

_____

8. What is the shape of the marginal-cost curve in the typical firm? Why is it shaped this way?

_____

_____

_____

_____

_____

_____

9. If a firm is operating in the area of constant returns to scale, what will happen to average total costs in the short run if the firm expands production? Why? What will happen to average total costs in the long run? Why?

_____

_____

_____

_____

10. When a small firm expands the scale of its operation, why does it usually first experience increasing returns to scale? When the same firm grows to be extremely large, why might a further expansion of the scale of operation generate decreasing returns to scale?

_____

_____

_____

_____

SELF-TEST

True/False Questions

_____ 1. Total revenue equals the quantity of output the firm produces times the price at which it sells its output.

_____ 2. Wages and salaries paid to workers are an example of implicit costs of production.

_____ 3. If total revenue is $100, explicit costs are $50, and implicit costs are $30, then accounting profit equals $50.

_____ 4. If there are implicit costs of production, accounting profits will exceed economic profits.

_____ 5. When a production function gets flatter, the marginal product is increasing.

_____ 6. If a firm continues to employ more workers within the same size factory, it will eventually experience diminishing marginal product.

_____ 7. If the production function for a firm exhibits diminishing marginal product, the corresponding total-cost curve for the firm will become flatter as the quantity of output expands.

_____ 8. Fixed costs plus variable costs equal total costs.

_____ 9. Average total costs are total costs divided by marginal costs.

_____10. When marginal costs are below average total costs, average total costs must be falling.

_____11. If, as the quantity produced increases, a production function first exhibits increasing marginal product and later diminishing marginal product, the corresponding marginal-cost curve will be U-shaped.

_____12. The average-total-cost curve crosses the marginal-cost curve at the minimum of the marginal-cost curve.

_____13. The average-total-cost curve in the long run is flatter than the average-total-cost curve in the short run.

_____14. The efficient scale for a firm is the quantity of output that minimizes marginal cost.

_____15. In the long run, as a firm expands its production facilities, it generally first experiences diseconomies of scale, then constant returns to scale, and finally economies of scale.

Multiple-Choice Questions

1. Accounting profit is equal to total revenue minus
    a. implicit costs.
    b. explicit costs.
    c. the sum of implicit and explicit costs.
    d. marginal costs.
    e. variable costs.

2. Economic profit is equal to total revenue minus
    a. implicit costs.
    b. explicit costs.
    c. the sum of implicit and explicit costs.
    d. marginal costs.
    e. variable costs.

Use the following information to answer questions 3 and 4. Madelyn owns a small pottery factory. She can make 1,000 pieces of pottery per year and sell them for $100 each. It costs Madelyn $20,000 for the raw materials to produce the 1,000 pieces of pottery. She has invested $100,000 in her factory and equipment: $50,000 from her savings and $50,000 borrowed at 10 percent (assume that she could have loaned her money out at 10 percent, too). Madelyn can work at a competing pottery factory for $40,000 per year.

3. The accounting profit at Madelyn's pottery factory is
    a. $30,000.
    b. $35,000.
    c. $70,000.
    d. $75,000.
    e. $80,000.

4. The economic profit at Madelyn's pottery factory is
    a. $30,000.
    b. $35,000.
    c. $70,000.
    d. $75,000.
    e. $80,000.

5. If there are implicit costs of production,
    a. economic profit will exceed accounting profit.
    b. accounting profit will exceed economic profit.
    c. economic profit and accounting profit will be equal.
    d. economic profit will always be zero.
    e. accounting profit will always be zero.

6. If a production function exhibits diminishing marginal product, its slope
    a. becomes flatter as the quantity of the input increases.
    b. becomes steeper as the quantity of the input increases.
    c. is linear (a straight line).
    d. could be any of the above.

7. If a production function exhibits diminishing marginal product, the slope of the corresponding total-cost curve
    a. becomes flatter as the quantity of output increases.
    b. becomes steeper as the quantity of output increases.
    c. is linear (a straight line).
    d. could be any of the above.

Use the following information to answer questions 8 and 9.

Number of Workers	Output
0	0
1	23
2	40
3	50

8. The marginal product of labor as production moves from employing one worker to employing two workers is
    a. 0.
    b. 10.
    c. 17.
    d. 23.
    e. 40.

9. The production process described above exhibits
    a. constant marginal product of labor.
    b. increasing marginal product of labor.
    c. diminishing marginal product of labor.
    d. increasing returns to scale.
    e. decreasing returns to scale.

10. Which of the following is a variable cost in the short run?
    a. wages paid to factory labor
    b. payment on the lease for factory equipment
    c. rent on the factory
    d. interest payments on borrowed financial capital
    e. salaries paid to upper management

Use the following information to answer questions 11 through 14.

Quantity of Output	Fixed Costs	Variable Costs	Total Costs	Marginal Costs
0	$10	$0	_____	
				_____
1	10	5	_____	
				_____
2	10	11	_____	
				_____
3	10	18	_____	
				_____
4	10	26	_____	
				_____
5	10	36	_____	

11. The average fixed cost of producing four units is
    a. $26.
    b. $10.
    c. $5.
    d. $2.50.
    e. none of the above.

12. The average total cost of producing three units is
    a. $3.33.
    b. $6.
    c. $9.33.
    d. $18.
    e. $28.

13. The marginal cost of changing production from three units to four units is
    a. $5.
    b. $6.
    c. $7.
    d. $8.
    e. $9.

14. The efficient scale of production is
    a. one unit.
    b. two units.
    c. three units.
    d. four units.
    e. five units.

15. When marginal costs are below average total costs,
    a. average fixed costs are rising.
    b. average total costs are falling.
    c. average total costs are rising.
    d. average total costs are minimized.

16. If marginal costs equal average total costs,
    a. average total costs are rising.
    b. average total costs are falling.
    c. average total costs are minimized.
    d. average total costs are maximized.

17. If, as the quantity produced increases, a production function first exhibits increasing marginal product and later diminishing marginal product, the corresponding marginal-cost curve will
    a. slope upward.
    b. be U-shaped.
    c. slope downward.
    d. be flat (horizontal).

18. In the long run, if a very small factory were to expand its scale of operations, it is likely that it would initially experience
    a. economies of scale.
    b. constant returns to scale.
    c. diseconomies of scale.
    d. an increase in average total costs.

19. The efficient scale of production is the quantity of output that minimizes
    a. average total cost.
    b. marginal cost.
    c. average fixed cost.
    d. average variable cost.

20. Which of the following statements is true?
    a. All costs are fixed in the long run.
    b. All costs are variable in the long run.
    c. All costs are fixed in the short run.
    d. All costs are variable in the short run.

ADVANCED CRITICAL THINKING

Your friend has a large garden and grows fresh fruit and vegetables to be sold at a local "farmer's market." Your friend comments, "I hired a college student who was on summer vacation to help me this summer and my production more than doubled. Next summer, I think I'll hire two or maybe three helpers and my output should go up more than three- or fourfold."

1. If all production processes eventually exhibit diminishing marginal product of the variable inputs, could it be true that your friend hired a helper (doubled the labor) and more than doubled his production? Why?

_____

_____

_____

_____

2. Is it likely that he could hire more workers and continue to reap greater than proportional increases in production? Why?

_____

_____

_____

3. In the long run, what must your friend do to the scale of his operation if he wants to continue to hire workers and have those workers generate proportional increases in production? Explain. Even in the long run, could your friend expand his scale of operation forever and continue to keep average total costs at a minimum? Explain.

_____

_____

_____

_____

_____

_____

SOLUTIONS

Terms and Definitions

13 Total revenue

_8_ Total cost

_2_ Profit

20 Explicit costs

_6_ Implicit costs

18 Economic profit

19 Accounting profit

14 Production function

_7_ Marginal product

17 Diminishing marginal product

_1_ Fixed costs

11 Variable costs

16 Average total cost

10 Average fixed cost

15 Average variable cost

_3_ Marginal cost

12 Efficient scale

_4_ Economies of scale

_9_ Diseconomies of scale

_5_ Constant returns to scale

Practice Problems

1. a. $10 \times \$25,000 = \$250,000$

   b. $\$150,000 + (\$200,000 \times 0.10) = \$170,000$

   c. $\$150,000 + (\$400,000 \times 0.10) + \$70,000 = \$260,000$

   d. $\$250,000 - \$170,000 = \$80,000$

   e. $\$250,000 - \$260,000 = -\$10,000$

   f. No. Joe could make $70,000 plus 10 percent interest on his $200,000 financial capital for a total of $90,000 if he worked for the competition instead of running his own factory. His factory makes an accounting profit of only $80,000 per year, so it costs him $10,000 to run his own factory (the size of the economic loss).

2. a.

b. See Exhibit 4.

4 EXHIBIT

c. It diminishes because additional workers have to share the production equipment and the work area becomes more crowded. The slope of the production function is the change in output from a change in a unit of input, which is the marginal product of labor. Since it is diminishing, the slope of the production function gets flatter as a greater number of inputs are used.

d. See Exhibit 5.

5 EXHIBIT

e. The total-cost curve gets steeper as the quantity produced rises due to the diminishing marginal product of labor. That is, in order

Number of Workers	Output	Marginal Product of Labor	Cost of Factory	Cost of Workers	Total Cost
0	0		$25	$0	$25
		6			
1	6		25	5	30
		5			
2	11		25	10	35
		4			
3	15		25	15	40
		3			
4	18		25	20	45
		2			
5	20		25	25	50

to produce additional equal increments of output, the firm must employ ever greater amounts of inputs and costs rise at an increasing rate.

3. a.

Quantity	FC	VC	TC	AFC	AVC	ATC	MC
0	$16	$0	$16	—	—	—	
							$18
1	16	18	34	$16.00	$18.00	$34.00	
							13
2	16	31	47	8.00	15.50	23.50	
							10
3	16	41	57	5.33	13.67	19.00	
							8
4	16	49	65	4.00	12.25	16.25	
							10
5	16	59	75	3.20	11.80	15.00	
							13
6	16	72	88	2.67	12.00	14.67	
							18
7	16	90	106	2.29	12.86	15.14	
							24
8	16	114	130	2.00	14.25	16.25	
							31
9	16	145	161	1.78	16.11	17.88	
							39
10	16	184	200	1.60	18.40	20.00	

b. See Exhibit 6.

6 EXHIBIT

c. *AFC* declines as the quantity goes up because a fixed cost is spread across a greater number of units. *MC* declines for the first four units due to an increasing marginal product of the variable input. *MC* rises thereafter due to decreasing marginal product. *AVC* is U-shaped for the same reason as *MC*. *ATC* declines due to falling *AFC* and increasing

marginal product. *ATC* rises at higher levels of production due to decreasing marginal product.

d. When *MC* is below *ATC*, *ATC* must be declining. When *MC* is above *ATC*, *ATC* must be rising. Therefore, *MC* crosses *ATC* at the minimum of *ATC*.

e. *AFC* plus *AVC* equals *ATC*.

f. Six pairs of blue jeans. Efficient scale is the output that minimizes *ATC*. It is also the place where *MC* crosses the average-total-cost curve.

Short-Answer Questions

1. Profit = total revenue – total cost.

2. Economic profit is total revenue minus explicit costs and *implicit costs*. Accounting profit is total revenue minus explicit costs.

3. Accounting profit is unchanged. Economic profit is reduced because implicit costs have risen—the opportunity cost of your invested money and of your time both went up. You are less likely to continue to operate your own firm because it is less profitable.

4. The total-cost curve reflects the production function. When an input exhibits diminishing marginal product, the production function gets flatter because additional increments of inputs increase output by ever smaller amounts. Correspondingly, the total-cost curve gets steeper as the amount produced rises.

5. It is a fixed cost because the salary paid to management doesn't vary with the quantity produced.

6. It is the quantity of production that minimizes average total cost.

7. When marginal cost is below average total cost, the average-total-cost curve must be falling. When marginal cost is above average total cost, the average-total-cost curve must be rising. Thus, the marginal-cost curve crosses the average-total-cost curve at the minimum of average total cost.

8. Typically, the marginal-cost curve is U-shaped. The firm often experiences increasing marginal product at very small levels of output as workers are allowed to specialize in their activities. Thus, marginal cost falls. At some point, the firm will experience diminishing marginal product and the marginal-cost curve will begin to rise.

9. In the short run, the size of the production facility is fixed so the firm will experience diminishing returns and increasing average total costs when adding additional workers. In the long run, the firm will expand the size of the factory and the number of workers together, and if the firm experiences constant returns to scale, average total costs will remain fixed at the minimum.

10. As a small firm expands the scale of operation, the higher production level allows for greater specialization of the workers and long-run average total costs fall. As an enormous firm continues to expand, it will likely develop coordination problems and long-run average total costs begin to increase.

True/False Questions

1. T
2. F; wages and salaries are explicit costs of production because dollars flow out of the firm.
3. T
4. T
5. F; marginal product is the slope of the production function, so marginal product is decreasing when the production function gets flatter.
6. T

7. F; diminishing marginal product means that it requires ever greater amounts of an input to produce equal increments of output so total costs rise at an increasing rate.
8. T
9. F; average total costs are total costs divided by the quantity of output.
10. T
11. T
12. F; the marginal-cost curve crosses the average-total-cost curve at the minimum of the average-total-cost curve.
13. T
14. F; efficient scale minimizes average total costs.
15. F; a firm generally experiences economies of scale, constant returns to scale, and diseconomies of scale as the scale of production expands.

Multiple-Choice Questions

1. b
2. c
3. d
4. a
5. b
6. a
7. b
8. c
9. c
10. a
11. d
12. c
13. d
14. d
15. b
16. c
17. b
18. a
19. a
20. b

Advanced Critical Thinking

1. Yes. Many production processes first exhibit increasing marginal product of the variable inputs (in this case, workers). This result may occur due to specialization of labor. After the second worker is hired, one worker specializes in weeding while the other specializes in watering.

2. No. At some point, if any input is fixed (say, the size of the garden), the firm will experience

diminishing marginal product of the variable inputs. That is, at some point, the garden will become crowded and additional workers will add smaller and smaller amounts to output.

3. It is likely that the garden is small enough that the firm would experience economies of scale if it increased its scale of operation by expanding the size of the garden and hiring more workers. No, your friend cannot expand his scale of operation forever because, at some point, the firm becomes so large that it develops coordination problems and the firm experiences diseconomies of scale.

$$14$$

Firms in Competitive Markets

GOALS

In this chapter you will

■ Learn what characteristics make a market competitive

■ Examine how competitive firms decide how much output to produce

■ Examine how competitive firms decide when to shut down production temporarily

■ Examine how competitive firms decide whether to exit or enter a market

■ See how firm behavior determines a market's short-run and long-run supply curves

OUTCOMES

After accomplishing these goals, you should be able to

■ List up to three conditions that characterize a competitive market

■ Locate the supply curve for a competitive firm on a graph of its cost curves

■ Demonstrate why firms temporarily shut down if the price they receive for their output is less than average variable cost

■ Demonstrate why firms exit a market permanently if the price they receive for their output is less than average total cost

■ Show why the long-run supply curve in a competitive market is more elastic than the short-run supply curve

CHAPTER OVERVIEW

Context and Purpose

Chapter 14 is the second chapter in a five-chapter sequence dealing with firm behavior and the organization of industry. Chapter 13 developed the cost curves on which firm behavior is based. These cost curves are employed in Chapter 14 to show how a competitive firm responds to changes in market conditions. Chapters 15 through 17 will employ these cost curves to see how firms with market power (monopolistic, oligopolistic, and monopolistically competitive firms) respond to changes in market conditions.

The purpose of Chapter 14 is to examine the behavior of competitive firms—firms that do not have market power. The cost curves developed in the previous chapter shed light on the decisions that lie behind the supply curve in a competitive market.

Chapter Review

Introduction   In this chapter, we examine the behavior of competitive firms—firms that do not have *market power*. Firms that have market power can influence the market price of the goods they sell. The cost curves developed in the previous chapter shed light on the decisions that lie behind the supply curve in a competitive market.

What Is a Competitive Market?

A **competitive market** has two main characteristics:

• There are many buyers and sellers in the market.

• The goods offered for sale are largely the same.

The result of these two conditions is that each buyer and seller is a *price taker*. A third condition sometimes thought to characterize perfectly competitive markets is:

• Firms can freely enter or exit the market.

Firms in competitive markets try to maximize profits, which equals total revenue minus total cost. Total revenue (TR) is $P \times Q$. Since a competitive firm is small compared to the market, it takes the price as given. Thus, total revenue is proportional to the amount of output sold—doubling output sold doubles total revenue.

Average revenue (AR) equals total revenue (TR) divided by the quantity of output (Q) or $AR = TR/Q$. Since $TR = P \times Q$, then $AR = (P \times Q)/Q = P$. That is, for all firms, *average revenue equals the price of the good*.

Marginal revenue (MR) equals the change in total revenue from the sale of an additional unit of output or $MR = \Delta TR/\Delta Q$. When Q rises by one unit, total revenue rises by P dollars. Therefore, for competitive firms, *marginal revenue equals the price of the good*.

Profit Maximization and the Competitive Firm's Supply Curve

Firms maximize profit by comparing marginal revenue and marginal cost. For the competitive firm, marginal revenue is fixed at the price of the good and marginal cost is increasing as output rises. There are three general rules for profit maximization:

- If marginal revenue exceeds marginal cost, the firm should increase output to increase profit.

- If marginal cost exceeds marginal revenue, the firm should decrease output to increase profit.

- At the profit-maximizing level of output, marginal revenue and marginal cost are exactly equal.

Assume that we have a firm with typical cost curves. Graphically, marginal cost (MC) is upward sloping, average total cost (ATC) is U-shaped, and MC crosses ATC at the minimum of ATC. If we draw $P = AR = MR$ on this graph, we can see that the firm will choose to produce a quantity that will maximize profit based on the intersection of MR and MC. That is, the firm will choose to produce the quantity where $MR = MC$. At any quantity lower than the optimal quantity, $MR > MC$ and profit is increased if output is increased. At any quantity above the optimal quantity, $MC > MR$ and profit is increased if output is reduced.

If the price were to increase, the firm would respond by increasing production to the point where the new higher $P = AR = MR$ is equal to MC. That is, the firm moves up its MC curve until $MR = MC$ again. Therefore, *because the firm's marginal-cost curve determines how much the firm is willing to supply at any price, it is the competitive firm's supply curve*.

A firm will temporarily *shut down* (produce nothing) *if the revenue that it would get from producing is less than the variable costs (VC) of production*. Examples of temporary shutdowns are farmers leaving land idle for a season and restaurants closing for lunch. For the temporary shutdown decision, the firm ignores fixed costs because these are considered to be **sunk costs**, or costs that are not recoverable because the firm must pay them whether they produce output or not. Mathematically, the firm should temporarily shut down if $TR < VC$. Divide by Q and get $TR/Q < VC/Q$, which is $AR = MR = P < AVC$. That is, the firm should shut down if $P < AVC$. Therefore, *the competitive firm's short-run supply curve is the portion of its marginal-cost curve that lies above the average-variable-cost curve*.

In general, beyond the example of a competitive firm, all rational decision makers think at the margin and ignore sunk costs when making economic decisions. Rational decision makers undertake activities where the marginal benefit exceeds the marginal cost.

In the long run, a firm will *exit the market* (permanently cease operations) *if the revenue it would get from producing is less than its total costs*. If the firm exits the industry, it avoids both its fixed and variable costs, or total costs. Mathematically, the firm should exit if $TR < TC$. Divide by Q and get $TR/Q = TC/Q$, which is $AR = MR = P < ATC$. That is, the firm should exit if $P < ATC$. Therefore, *the competitive firm's long-run supply curve is the portion of its marginal-cost curve that lies above the average-total-cost curve*.

A competitive firm's profit = $TR - TC$. Divide and multiply by Q and get profit = $(TR/Q - TC/Q) \times Q$ or profit = $(P - ATC) \times Q$. If price is above ATC, the firm is profitable. If price is below ATC, the firm generates losses and would eventually choose to exit the market.

The Supply Curve in a Competitive Market

In the short run, the number of firms in the market is fixed because firms cannot quickly enter or exit the market. Therefore, in the short run, the market supply curve is the horizontal sum of the portion of the individual firm's marginal-cost curves that lie above their average-variable-cost curves. That is, the market supply curve is simply the sum of the quantities supplied by each firm in the market at each price. Since the individual marginal-cost curves are upward sloping, *the short-run market supply curve is also upward sloping*.

In the long run, firms are able to enter and exit the market. Suppose all firms have the same cost curves. If firms in the market are making profits, new firms will enter the market, increasing the quantity supplied and causing the price to fall until economic profits are zero. If firms in the market are making losses, some existing firms will exit the market, decreasing the quantity supplied and causing the price to rise until economic profits are zero. In the long run, *firms that remain in the market must be making zero economic profit*. Since profit = $(P - ATC) \times Q$, *profit equals zero only when P = ATC*. Since for the competitive firm $P = MC$ and MC intersects ATC at the minimum of ATC, *the long-run equilibrium of a competitive market with free entry and exit must have firms operating at their efficient scale*. Also, since firms enter or exit the market if the price is above or below minimum ATC, the price always returns to the minimum of ATC for each firm but the total quantity supplied in the market rises and falls with the number of firms. Thus, there is only one price consistent with zero profits, and *the long-run market supply curve must be horizontal* (perfectly elastic) at that price.

Competitive firms stay in business even though they are making zero economic profits in the long run. Recall that economists define total costs to include all the opportunity costs of the firm, so the zero-profit equilibrium is compensating the owners of the firm for their time and their money invested.

In the short run, an increase in demand increases the price of a good and existing firms make economic profits. In the long run, this attracts new firms to enter the market causing a corresponding increase in the market supply. This increase in supply reduces the price to its original level consistent with zero profits but the quantity sold in the market is now higher. Thus, if at present firms are earning high profits in a competitive industry, they can expect new firms to enter the market and prices and profits to fall in the future.

While the standard case is one where the long-run market supply curve is perfectly elastic, the long-run market supply curve might be upward sloping for two reasons:

- If an input necessary for production is in limited supply, an expansion of firms in that industry will raise the costs for all existing firms and increase the price as output supplied increases.

- If firms have different costs (some are more efficient than others) in order to induce new less efficient firms to enter the market, the price must increase to cover the less efficient firm's costs. In this case, only the *marginal firm* earns zero economic profits while more efficient firms earn profits in the long run.

Regardless, because firms can enter and exit more easily in the long run than in the short run, *the long-run market supply curve is more elastic than the short-run market supply curve*.

Conclusion: Behind the Supply Curve

The supply decision is based on marginal analysis. Profit maximizing firms that supply goods in competitive markets produce where marginal cost equals price equals minimum average total cost.

Helpful Hints

1. We have determined that, in the short run, the firm will produce the quantity of output where $P = MC$ as long as the price equals or exceeds average variable cost. An additional way to see the logic of this behavior is to recognize that since fixed costs must be paid regardless of the level of production, any time the firm can at least cover its variable costs, any additional revenue beyond its variable costs can be applied to its fixed costs. Therefore, in the short run, the firm loses less money than it would if it shut down if the price exceeds its average variable costs. As a result, the short-run supply curve for the firm is the portion of the marginal-cost curve that is above the average-variable-cost curve.

2. Recall that rational decision makers think at the margin. The decision rule for any action is that we should do things for which the marginal benefit exceeds the marginal cost and continue to do that thing until the marginal benefit equals the marginal cost. This decision rule translates directly to the firm's production decision in that the firm should continue to produce additional output until marginal revenue (the marginal benefit to the firm) equals marginal cost.

3. In this chapter, we derived the equation for profit as profit = $(P - ATC) \times Q$. It helps to remember that, in words, this formula says that profit simply equals the average profit per unit times the number of units sold. This holds true even in the case of losses. If the price is less than average total cost, then we have the average loss per unit times the number of units sold.

Terms and Definitions

Choose a definition for each key term.

Key Terms

_____ Price takers

_____ Competitive market

_____ Average revenue

_____ Marginal revenue

_____ Shut down

_____ Exit

_____ Sunk cost

Definitions

1. A short-run decision to temporarily cease production during a specific period of time due to current market conditions

2. A market with many buyers and sellers trading identical products so that each buyer and seller is a price taker

3. Total revenue divided by the quantity sold

4. A cost to which one is already committed and is not recoverable

5. The change in total revenue from an additional unit sold

6. Buyers and sellers in a competitive market that must accept the price that the market determines

7. A long-run decision to permanently cease production and leave the market

PROBLEMS AND SHORT-ANSWER QUESTIONS

Practice Problems

1. Are the following markets likely to be perfectly competitive? Explain.
    a. The market for gasoline

    _____

    _____

    _____

    b. The market for blue jeans

    _____

    _____

    _____

c. The market for agricultural products such as corn and beans

_____

_____

_____

d. The market for the common stock of IBM

_____

_____

_____

e. The market for electricity

_____

_____

_____

f. The market for cable television

_____

_____

2. a. The following table contains information about the revenues and costs for Barry's Baseball Manufacturing. All data are per hour. Complete the first group of columns which correspond to Barry's production if $P = \$3$. ($TR =$ total revenue, $TC =$ total cost, $MR =$ marginal revenue, $MC =$ marginal cost)

Q	TR, P = $3	TC	Profit	MR	MC	TR, P = $2	Profit	MR
0	_____	$1	_____			_____	_____	
1	_____	$2	_____	_____	_____	_____	_____	_____
2	_____	$4	_____	_____	_____	_____	_____	_____
3	_____	$7	_____	_____	_____	_____	_____	_____
4	_____	$11	_____	_____	_____	_____	_____	_____
5	_____	$16	_____	_____	_____	_____	_____	_____

b. If the price is $3 per baseball, what is Barry's optimal level of production? What criteria did you use to determine the optimal level of production?

_____

_____

c. Is $3 per baseball a long-run equilibrium price in the market for baseballs? Explain. What adjustment will take place in the market for baseballs, and what will happen to the price in the long run?

_____

_____

d. Suppose the price of baseballs falls to $2. Fill out the remaining three columns of the table above. What is the profit-maximizing level of output when the price is $2 per baseball? How much profit does Barry's Baseball Manufacturing earn when the price of baseballs is $2?

_____

_____

_____

e. Is $2 per baseball a long-run equilibrium price in the market for baseballs? Explain. Why would Barry continue to produce at this level of profit?

_____

_____

_____

f. Describe the slope of the short-run supply curve for the market for baseballs. Describe the slope of the long-run supply curve in the market for baseballs.

_____

_____

_____

3. a. In Exhibit 1, show the cost curves of a representative firm in long-run equilibrium alongside the corresponding market equilibrium.
    b. Suppose there is a *decrease* in the demand for this product. In Exhibit 2, show the shift in demand in the market for this product and the corresponding profit or loss on the cost curves of the representative firm.
    c. In Exhibit 3, show the adjustment that takes place in order to return the market and firm to long-run equilibrium.
    d. After the market has returned to long-run equilibrium, is the price higher, lower, or the same as the initial price? Are there more, fewer, or the same number of firms producing in the market?

_____

_____

2 EXHIBIT

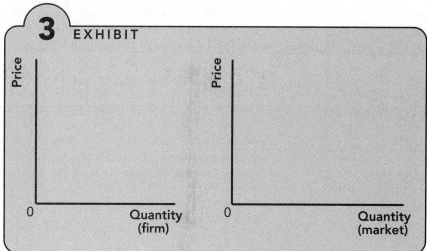

3 EXHIBIT

Short-Answer Questions

1. What are the three conditions that characterize a competitive market?

   _____

   _____

2. If a firm is in a competitive market, what happens to its total revenue if it doubles its output? Why?

   _____

   _____

3. If a firm is producing a level of output where marginal revenue exceeds marginal cost, would it improve profits by increasing output, decreasing output, or keeping output unchanged? Why?

   _____

   _____

4. What constitutes a competitive firm's short-run supply curve? Explain.

_____

_____

_____

5. What constitutes a competitive firm's long-run supply curve? Explain.

_____

_____

_____

6. You go to your campus bookstore and see a coffee mug emblazoned with your university's shield. It costs $5 and you value it at $8, so you buy it. On the way to your car, you drop it and it breaks into pieces. Should you buy another one or should you go home because the total expenditure of $10 now exceeds the $8 value that you place on it? Why?

_____

_____

_____

7. Suppose the price for a firm's output is above the average variable cost of production but below the average total cost of production. Will the firm shut down in the short run? Explain. Will the firm exit the market in the long run? Explain.

_____

_____

_____

8. Why must the long-run equilibrium in a competitive market (with free entry and exit) have all firms operating at their efficient scale?

_____

_____

_____

9. Why is the short-run market supply curve upward sloping while the standard long-run market supply curve is perfectly elastic?

_____

_____

_____

10. Under what conditions would the long-run market supply curve be upward sloping?

_____

_____

SELF-TEST

True/False Questions

_____ 1.   The only requirement for a market to be perfectly competitive is for the market to have many buyers and sellers.

_____ 2.   For a competitive firm, marginal revenue equals the price of the good it sells.

_____ 3.   If a competitive firm sells three times the amount of output, its total revenue also increases by a factor of three.

_____ 4.   A firm maximizes profit when it produces output up to the point where marginal cost equals marginal revenue.

_____ 5.   If marginal cost exceeds marginal revenue at a firm's current level of output, the firm can increase profit if it increases its level of output.

_____ 6.   A competitive firm's short-run supply curve is the portion of its marginal-cost curve that lies above its average-total-cost curve.

_____ 7.   A competitive firm's long-run supply curve is the portion of its marginal-cost curve that lies above its average-variable-cost curve.

_____ 8.   In the short run, if the price a firm receives for a good is above its average variable costs but below its average total costs of production, the firm will temporarily shut down.

_____ 9.   In a competitive market, both buyers and sellers are price takers.

_____10.   In the long run, if the price firms receive for their output is below their average total costs of production, some firms will exit the market.

_____11.   In the short run, the market supply curve for a good is the sum of the quantities supplied by each firm at each price.

_____12.   The short-run market supply curve is more elastic than the long-run market supply curve.

_____13.   In the long run, perfectly competitive firms earn small but positive economic profits.

_____14.   In the long run, if firms are identical and there is free entry and exit in the market, all firms in the market operate at their efficient scale.

_____15.   If the price of a good rises above the minimum average total cost of production, positive economic profits will cause new firms to enter the market, which drives the price back down to the minimum average total cost of production.

Multiple-Choice Questions

1.   Which of the following is _not_ a characteristic of a competitive market?
   a.   There are many buyers and sellers in the market.
   b.   The goods offered for sale are largely the same.
   c.   Firms can freely enter or exit the market.
   d.   Firms generate small but positive economic profits in the long run.
   e.   All of the above are characteristics of a competitive market.

2. Which of the following markets would most closely satisfy the requirements for a competitive market?
    a. gold bullion
    b. electricity
    c. cable television
    d. soda
    e. All of the above represent competitive markets.

3. If a competitive firm doubles its output, its total revenue
    a. more than doubles.
    b. doubles.
    c. less than doubles.
    d. cannot be determined because the price of the good may rise or fall.

4. For a competitive firm, marginal revenue is
    a. equal to the price of the good sold.
    b. average revenue divided by the quantity sold.
    c. total revenue divided by the quantity sold.
    d. equal to the quantity of the good sold.

5. The competitive firm maximizes profit when it produces output up to the point where
    a. marginal cost equals total revenue.
    b. marginal revenue equals average revenue.
    c. marginal cost equals marginal revenue.
    d. price equals average variable cost.

6. If a competitive firm is producing a level of output where marginal revenue exceeds marginal cost, the firm could increase profits if it
    a. increased production.
    b. decreased production.
    c. maintained production at the current level.
    d. temporarily shut down.

Use Exhibit 4 to answer questions 7 through 11.

7. If the price is P_4, a competitive firm will maximize profits if it produces
    a. Q_1.
    b. Q_2.
    c. Q_3.
    d. Q_4.
    e. Q_5.

8. If the price is P_4, the firm will earn profits equal to the area
    a. $(P_2 - P_1) \times Q_2$.
    b. $(P_3 - P_2) \times Q_3$.
    c. $(P_4 - P_2) \times Q_4$.
    d. $(P_4 - P_3) \times Q_3$.
    e. None of the above is correct.

9. In the short run, competitive firms will temporarily shut down production if the price falls below
    a. P_1.
    b. P_2.
    c. P_3.
    d. P_4.

10. In the long run, some competitive firms will exit the market if the price is below
    a. P_1.
    b. P_2.
    c. P_3.
    d. P_4.

11. In the long run, the competitive equilibrium is
    a. P_1, Q_1.
    b. P_2, Q_2.
    c. P_4, Q_3.
    d. P_4, Q_4.
    e. P_4, Q_5.

12. In the short run, the competitive firm's supply curve is the
    a. entire marginal-cost curve.
    b. portion of the marginal-cost curve that lies above the average-total-cost curve.
    c. portion of the marginal-cost curve that lies above the average-variable-cost curve.
    d. upward-sloping portion of the average-total-cost curve.
    e. upward-sloping portion of the average-variable-cost curve.

13. In the long run, the competitive firm's supply curve is the
    a. entire marginal-cost curve.
    b. portion of the marginal-cost curve that lies above the average-total-cost curve.
    c. portion of the marginal-cost curve that lies above the average-variable-cost curve.
    d. upward-sloping portion of the average-total-cost curve.
    e. upward-sloping portion of the average-variable-cost curve.

14. A grocery store should close at night if the
    a. total costs of staying open are greater than the total revenue due to staying open.
    b. total costs of staying open are less than the total revenue due to staying open.
    c. variable costs of staying open are greater than the total revenue due to staying open.
    d. variable costs of staying open are less than the total revenue due to staying open.

15. The long-run market supply curve
    a. is always more elastic than the short-run market supply curve.
    b. is always less elastic than the short-run market supply curve.
    c. has the same elasticity as the short-run market supply curve.
    d. is always perfectly elastic.

16. In the long run, some firms will exit the market if the price of the good offered for sale is less than
    a. marginal revenue.
    b. marginal cost.
    c. average revenue.
    d. average total cost.

17. If all firms in a market have identical cost structures and if inputs used in the production of the good in that market are readily available, then the long-run market supply curve for that good should be
    a. perfectly elastic.
    b. downward sloping.
    c. upward sloping.
    d. perfectly inelastic.

18. If an input necessary for production is in limited supply so that an expansion of the industry raises costs for all existing firms in the market, then the long-run market supply curve for a good could be
    a. perfectly elastic.
    b. downward sloping.
    c. upward sloping.
    d. perfectly inelastic.

19. If the long-run market supply curve for a good is perfectly elastic, an increase in the demand for that good will, in the long run, cause
    a. an increase in the price of the good and an increase in the number of firms in the market.
    b. an increase in the price of the good but no increase in the number of firms in the market.
    c. an increase in the number of firms in the market but no increase in the price of the good.
    d. no impact on either the price of the good or the number of firms in the market.

20. In long-run equilibrium in a competitive market, firms are operating at
    a. the minimum of their average-total-cost curves.
    b. the intersection of marginal cost and marginal revenue.
    c. their efficient scale.
    d. zero economic profit.
    e. all of the above.

ADVANCED CRITICAL THINKING

In some regions of the country, it is common for Wal-Mart stores and large supermarkets to stay open 24 hours a day, 365 days a year.

1. You walk into a Wal-Mart store at 2:00 A.M. with a friend to buy some VCR tapes. Your friend says, "I can't believe that these stores stay open all night. Only one out of fifteen checkout lines is open. There can't be more than ten shoppers in this store. It just doesn't make any sense for this store to be open all night." Explain to your friend what conditions must be true for it to be to the advantage of Wal-Mart to stay open all night.

_____

_____

_____

2. Are the costs of rent, equipment, fixtures, salaries of management, and so on relevant when Wal-Mart makes the decision whether to stay open all night? Why?

   _____

   _____

3. If Wal-Mart had the same number of customers during its daytime hours as you observed during its nighttime hours, do you think it would continue to operate? Explain.

   _____

   _____

   _____

   _____

SOLUTIONS

Terms and Definitions

__6__ Price takers

__2__ Competitive market

__3__ Average revenue

__5__ Marginal revenue

__1__ Shut down

__7__ Exit

__4__ Sunk cost

Practice Problems

1. a. Yes, many buyers and sellers and the product of different sellers is nearly identical.

   b. Probably not, many buyers and sellers but the product is not identical (Levi's vs. Lee), so each seller is not a price taker.

   c. Yes, many buyers and sellers and the product of different sellers is identical.

   d. Yes, many buyers and sellers and the product of different sellers is identical.

   e. No, few sellers (often only one). If there were multiple sellers, the product would be identical.

   f. No, few sellers (often only one). If there were multiple sellers, the product would be nearly identical.

b. Optimal production is either two or three baseballs per hour. This level of production maximizes profit (at $2) and it is the level of output where $MC = MR$ (at $3).

c. No, because Barry is earning positive economic profits of $2. These profits will attract new firms to enter the market for baseballs, the market supply will increase, and the price will fall until economic profits are zero.

d. See answers for the table in part *a* above. Optimal production is either one or two baseballs per hour. Zero economic profit is earned by Barry.

e. Yes. Economic profits are zero and firms neither enter nor exit the industry. Zero economic profits means that Barry doesn't earn anything beyond his opportunity costs of production but his revenues do cover the cost of his inputs and the value of his time and money.

f. The slope of the short-run supply curve is positive because when $P = 2, quantity supplied is one or two units per firm and when $P = 3, quantity supplied is two or three units per firm. In the long run, supply is horizontal (perfectly elastic) at $P = 2 because any price above $2 causes firms to enter and drives the price back to $2.

2. a.

Q	TR, P = $3	TC	Profit	MR	MC	TR, P = $2	Profit	MR
0	$0	$1	−$1				$0	−$1	
				$3	$1				$2
1	3	2	1				2	0	
				3	2				2
2	6	4	2				4	0	
				3	3				2
3	9	7	2				6	−1	
				3	4				2
4	12	11	1				8	−3	
				3	5				2
5	15	16	−1				10	−6	

3. a. See Exhibit 5.

b. See Exhibit 6.

c. See Exhibit 7.

d. The price has returned to its initial level. There are fewer firms producing in this market.

Short-Answer Questions

1. There are many buyers and sellers, the goods offered for sale are largely the same, and firms can freely enter or exit the market.

2. Total revenue doubles. This is because, in a competitive market, the price is unaffected by the amount sold by any individual firm.

3. If $MR > MC$, increasing output will increase profits because an additional unit of production increases revenue more than it increases costs.

4. It is the portion of the firm's marginal-cost curve that lies above its average-variable-cost curve because the firm maximizes profit where $P = MC$, and in the short run, fixed or sunk costs are irrelevant and the firm must only cover its variable costs.

5. It is the portion of the firm's marginal-cost curve that lies above its average-total-cost curve because the firm maximizes profit where $P = MC$,

and in the long run, the firm must cover its total costs or it should exit the market.

6. You should buy another mug because the marginal benefit ($8) still exceeds the marginal cost ($5). The broken mug is a sunk cost and is not recoverable. Therefore, it is irrelevant.

7. No. In the short run, the firm's fixed costs are sunk costs so the firm will not shut down because it only needs to cover its variable costs. Yes. In the long run, the firm must cover total costs, and if $P < ATC$, the firm generates losses in the long run and it will exit the market.

8. In the long-run equilibrium, firms must be making zero economic profits so that firms are not entering or exiting the industry. Zero profits occur when $P = ATC$ and for the competitive firm $P = MC$ determines the production level. $P = ATC = MC$ only at the minimum of ATC.

9. In the short run, firms cannot exit or enter the market so the market supply curve is the horizontal sum of the upward-sloping MC curves of the existing firms. However, in the long run, if the price is above or below minimum ATC, firms will enter or exit the market causing the price to always return to minimum ATC for each firm, but the total quantity supplied in the market rises and falls with the number of firms. Thus, the market supply curve is horizontal.

10. If an input necessary for production is in limited supply or if firms have different costs.

True/False Questions

1. F; the goods offered for sale are largely the same and (possibly) firms can freely enter or exit the market.
2. T
3. T
4. T
5. F; the firm increases profits if it reduces output.
6. F; it is the portion of the MC curve that lies above its average-variable-cost curve.
7. F; it is the portion of the MC curve that lies above its average-total-cost curve.
8. F; the firm will continue to operate in the short run as long as price exceeds average variable costs.
9. T
10. T
11. T
12. F; the long-run market supply curve is more elastic than the short-run market supply curve.

13. F; they earn zero economic profits in the long run.
14. T
15. T

Multiple-Choice Questions

1. d
2. a
3. b
4. a
5. c
6. a
7. c
8. d
9. a
10. b
11. b
12. c
13. b
14. c
15. a
16. d
17. a
18. c
19. c
20. e

Advanced Critical Thinking

1. For Wal-Mart to stay open all night (and not undertake a temporary shutdown), it must be true that its total revenue at night must equal or exceed its *variable costs* incurred from staying open the additional hours (electricity, wages of night shift workers, . . .).

2. No. These costs are fixed costs or sunk costs—costs that cannot be recovered even if Wal-Mart chooses not to operate at night.

3. It is unlikely. This is because the temporary shutdown decision (staying open additional hours at night) depends on whether total revenue equals or exceeds *variable costs*, but the decision to remain in the market in the long-run depends on whether total revenue equals or exceeds *total costs*. It is unlikely that the revenue earned at night covers total costs (both fixed and variable costs).

Monopoly

GOALS

In this chapter you will

- Learn why some markets have only one seller

- Analyze how a monopoly determines the quantity to produce and the price to charge

- See how the monopoly's decisions affect economic well-being

- Consider the various public policies aimed at solving the problem of monopoly

- See why monopolies try to charge different prices to different customers

OUTCOMES

After accomplishing these goals, you should be able to

- List three reasons why a monopoly can remain the sole seller of a product in a market

- Use a monopolist's cost curves and the demand curve it faces to show the profit earned by a monopolist

- Show the deadweight loss from a monopolist's production decision

- Show why forcing a natural monopoly to charge its marginal cost of production creates losses for the monopolist

- Demonstrate the surprising result that price discrimination by a monopolist can raise economic welfare above that generated by standard monopoly pricing

CHAPTER OVERVIEW

Context and Purpose

Chapter 15 is the third chapter in a five-chapter sequence dealing with firm behavior and the organization of industry. Chapter 13 developed the cost curves on which firm behavior is based. These cost curves were employed in Chapter 14 to show how a competitive firm responds to changes in market conditions. In Chapter 15, these cost curves are again employed, this time to show how a monopolistic firm chooses the quantity to produce and the price to charge. Chapters 16 and 17 will address the decisions made by oligopolistic and monopolistically competitive firms.

A monopolist is the sole seller of a product without close substitutes. As such, it has market power because it can influence the price of its output. That is, a monopolist is a price maker as opposed to a price taker. The purpose of Chapter 15 is to examine the production and pricing decisions of monopolists, the social implications of their market power, and the ways in which governments might respond to the problems caused by monopolists.

Chapter Review

Introduction   Monopolists have market power because they can influence the price of their output. That is, monopolists are *price makers* as opposed to *price takers*. While competitive firms choose to produce a quantity of output such that the given market price equals the marginal cost of production, monopolists charge prices that exceed marginal cost. In this chapter, we examine the production and pricing decisions of monopolists, the social implications of their market power, and the ways in which governments might respond to the problems caused by monopolists.

Why Monopolies Arise

A **monopoly** is a firm that is the sole seller of a product without close substitutes. A monopoly is able to remain the only seller in a market only if there are *barriers to entry*. That is, other firms are unable to enter the market and compete with it. There are three sources of barriers to entry:

- *A key resource is owned by a single firm.* For example, if a firm owns the only well in town, it has a monopoly for the sale of water. DeBeers essentially has a monopoly in the market for diamonds because it controls 80 percent of the world's production of diamonds. This source of monopoly is somewhat rare.

- *The government gives a single firm the exclusive right to produce some good.* When the government grants patents (which last for 20 years) to inventors and copyrights to authors, it is giving someone the right to be the sole producer of that good. The benefit is that it increases incentives for creative activity. The costs will be discussed later in this chapter.

- *The costs of production make a single producer more efficient than a large number of producers.* A **natural monopoly** arises when a single firm can supply a good to an entire market at a smaller cost than could two or more firms. This happens when there are economies of scale over the relevant range of output. That is, the average-total-cost curve for an individual firm continually declines at least to the quantity that could supply the entire market. This cost advantage is a natural barrier to entry because firms with higher costs find it undesirable to enter the market. Common examples are utilities such as water and electricity distribution.

How Monopolies Make Production and Pricing Decisions

A competitive firm is small relative to the market, so it takes the price of the good it produces as given. Since it can sell as much as it chooses at the given market price, the competitive firm faces a demand curve that is perfectly elastic at the market price. A monopoly is the sole producer in its market, so it faces the entire downward-sloping market demand curve. The monopolist can choose any price/quantity combination on the demand curve by choosing the quantity and seeing what price buyers will pay. As with competitive firms, monopolies choose a quantity of output that maximizes profit (total revenue minus total cost).

Since the monopolist faces a downward-sloping demand curve, it must lower the price of the good if it wishes to sell a greater quantity. Therefore, when it sells an additional unit, the sale of the additional unit has two effects on total revenue ($P \times Q$):

- *The output effect*: Q is higher.

- *The price effect*: P is lower (on the marginal unit *and on the units it was already selling*).

Since the monopolist must reduce the price on every unit it sells when it expands output by one unit, marginal revenue ($\Delta TR/\Delta Q$) for the monopolist declines as Q increases and marginal revenue is always less than the price of the good.

As with a competitive firm, the monopolist maximizes profit at the level of output where marginal revenue (MR) equals marginal cost (MC). As Q increases, MR decreases and MC increases. Therefore, at low levels of output, $MR > MC$ and an increase in Q increases profit. At high levels of output, $MC > MR$ and a decrease in output increases profit. The monopolist, therefore, should produce up to the point where $MR = MC$. That is, the profit-maximizing level of output is determined by the intersection of the marginal-revenue and marginal-cost curves. Since the MR curve lies below the demand curve, the price the monopolist charges is found by reading up to the demand curve from the $MR = MC$ intersection.

Recall that for the competitive firm, since the demand curve facing the firm is perfectly elastic so that $P = MR$, the profit-maximizing equilibrium requires that $P = MR = MC$. However, for the monopoly firm, $MR < P$, so the profit-maximizing equilibrium requires that $P > MR = MC$. As a result, *in competitive markets, price equals marginal cost while in monopolized markets, price exceeds marginal cost.*

Evidence from the pharmaceutical drug market is consistent with our theory. While the patent is enforced, the price of a drug is high. When the patent expires and generic drugs become available, the price falls substantially.

As with the competitive firm, profit = $(P - ATC) \times Q$, or profit equals the average profit per unit times the number of units sold.

The Welfare Cost of Monopoly

Does a monopoly market maximize economic well-being as measured by total surplus? Recall that total surplus is the sum of consumer surplus and producer surplus. Equilibrium of supply and demand in a competitive market naturally maximizes total surplus because all units are produced where the value to buyers is greater than or equal to the cost of production to the sellers.

For a monopolist to produce the socially efficient quantity (maximize total surplus by producing all units where the value to buyers exceeds or equals the cost of production), it would have to produce the level of output where the marginal-cost curve intersects the demand curve. However, the monopolist chooses to produce the level of output where the marginal-revenue curve intersects the marginal-cost curve. Since for the monopolist the marginal-revenue curve is always below the demand curve, *the monopolist produces less than the socially efficient quantity of output*.

The small quantity produced by the monopolist allows the monopolist to charge a price that exceeds the marginal cost of production. Therefore, the monopolist generates a *deadweight loss* because, at the high monopoly price, consumers fail to buy units of output where the value to them exceeds the cost to the monopolist.

The deadweight loss from a monopoly is similar to the deadweight loss from a tax, and the monopolist's profit is similar to tax revenue except that the revenue is received by a private firm. Since the profit earned by a monopolist is simply a transfer of consumer surplus to producer surplus, a monopoly's profit is not a social cost. The social cost of a monopoly is the deadweight loss generated when the monopolist produces a quantity of output below that which is efficient.

Public Policy toward Monopolies

Monopolies fail to allocate resources efficiently because they produce less than the socially optimal quantity of output and charge prices that exceed marginal cost. Policymakers can respond to the problem of monopoly in one of four ways:

- *By trying to make monopolized industries more competitive.* The Justice Department can employ antitrust laws (statutes aimed at reducing monopoly power) to prevent mergers that reduce competition, break up extremely large companies to increase competition, and prevent companies from colluding. However, some mergers result in synergies that reduce costs and raise efficiency. Therefore, it is difficult for government to know which mergers to block and which ones to allow.

- *By regulating the behavior of the monopolies.* The prices charged by natural monopolies such as utilities are often regulated by government. If a natural monopoly is required to set its price equal to its marginal cost, the efficient quantity will be consumed but the monopoly will lose money because marginal cost must be below average variable cost if average variable cost is declining. Thus, the monopolist will exit the industry. In response, regulators can subsidize a natural monopoly with tax revenue (which creates its own deadweight loss) or allow average-total-cost pricing which is an improvement over monopoly pricing but it is not as efficient as marginal-cost pricing. Another problem with regulating prices is that monopolists have no incentive to reduce costs because their prices are reduced when their costs are reduced.

- *By turning some private monopolies into public enterprises.* Instead of regulating the prices charged by a natural monopoly, the government can run the monopoly itself. The Postal Service is an example. Economists generally prefer private ownership to government ownership because private owners have a greater incentive to minimize costs.

- *By doing nothing at all.* Since each of the solutions above has its own shortcomings, some economists urge that monopolies be left alone. They believe that the "political failure" in the real world is more costly than the "market failure" caused by monopoly pricing.

Price Discrimination

Price discrimination is the business practice of selling the same good at different prices to different customers. Price discrimination can only be practiced by a firm with market power such as a monopolist. There are three lessons to note about price discrimination:

- Price discrimination is a rational strategy for a profit-maximizing monopolist because a monopolist's profits are increased when it charges each customer a price closer to his or her individual willingness to pay.

- Price discrimination is only possible if the monopolist is able to separate customers according to their willingness to pay—by age, income, location, etc. If there is *arbitrage*—the process of buying a good in one market at a low price and selling it in another market at a higher price—price discrimination is not possible.

- Price discrimination can raise economic welfare because output increases beyond that which would result under monopoly pricing. However, the additional surplus (reduced deadweight loss) is received by the producer, not the consumer.

Perfect price discrimination occurs when a monopolist charges each customer his or her exact willingness to pay. In this case, the efficient quantity is produced and consumed and there is no deadweight loss. However, total surplus goes to the monopolist in the form of profit. In reality, perfect price discrimination cannot be accomplished. Imperfect price discrimination may raise, lower, or leave unchanged total surplus in a market.

Examples of price discrimination include movie tickets, airline tickets, discount coupons, financial aid for college tuition, quantity discounts, and tickets for Broadway shows.

Conclusion: The Prevalence of Monopoly

In one sense, monopolies are common because most firms have some control over the prices they charge. On the other hand, firms with substantial monopoly power are rare. Monopoly power is a matter of degree.

Helpful Hints

1. A monopolist can choose the quantity and see what price buyers will pay or can choose the price and see what quantity buyers will purchase. That is, a monopolist is still subject to the demand curve for its product. The monopolist cannot choose both a high price and a large quantity if that combination does not lie on the demand curve facing the monopolist.

2. A monopolist is not guaranteed to earn profits. Any one of us can be the monopolist in the production of gold-plated textbook covers (since there is currently no producer of such a product), but the demand for such a product is likely to be too low to cover the costs of production. In like manner, gaining a patent on a product does not guarantee the holder of the patent future profits.

Terms and Definitions

Choose a definition for each key term.

Key Terms

_____ Monopoly

_____ Natural monopoly

_____ Price discrimination

_____ Arbitrage

_____ Perfect price discrimination

Definitions

1. A monopoly that arises because a single firm can supply a good or service to an entire market at a smaller cost than could two or more firms

2. A firm that is the sole seller of a product without close substitutes

3. A situation in which the monopolist is able to charge each customer precisely his or her willingness to pay

4. The business practice of selling the same good at different prices to different customers

5. The process of buying a good in one market at a low price and selling it in another market at a higher price

PROBLEMS AND SHORT-ANSWER QUESTIONS

Practice Problems

1. a. What are the three sources of the barriers to entry that allow a monopoly to remain the sole seller of a product?

    _____

    _____

    b. What is the entry barrier that is the source of the monopoly power for the following products or producers? List some competitors that keep these products or producers from having absolute monopoly power.

    (1) United States Postal Service

    _____

    _____

    (2) Perrier Spring Water

    _____

    _____

    (3) Prozac (a brand-name drug)

    _____

    _____

    (4) DeBeers Diamonds

    _____

    _____

    (5) *Principles of Economics,* by N. Gregory Mankiw (your textbook)

    _____

    _____

    (6) Edison Power Company

    _____

    _____

2. Suppose a firm has a patent on a special process to make a unique smoked salmon. The following table provides information about the demand facing this firm for this unique product.

Pounds of Salmon	Price	(P × Q) Total Revenue	(ΔTR/ΔQ) Marginal Revenue
0	$20	_____	
			_____
1	18	_____	
			_____
2	16	_____	
			_____
3	14	_____	
			_____
4	12	_____	
			_____
5	10	_____	
			_____
6	8	_____	
			_____
7	6	_____	

a. Complete the table above.
b. Plot the demand curve and the marginal-revenue curve in Exhibit 1. (Read Helpful Hint 2 in Chapter 13 of this study guide for a reminder on how to plot marginal values.)

1 EXHIBIT

c. Suppose that there are no fixed costs and that the marginal cost of production of smoked salmon is constant at $6 per pound. (Thus, the average total cost is also constant at $6 per pound.) What is the quantity and price chosen by the monopolist? What is the profit earned by the monopolist? Show your solution on the graph you created in part *b* above.

d. What is the price and quantity that maximizes total surplus?

_____

e. Compare the monopoly solution and the efficient solution. That is, is the monopolist's price too high or too low? Is the monopolist's quantity too high or too low? Why?

_____

_____

_____

f. Is there a deadweight loss in this market if the monopolist charges the monopoly price? Explain.

_____

_____

_____

g. If the monopolist is able to costlessly and perfectly price discriminate, is the outcome efficient? Explain. What is the value of consumer surplus, producer surplus, and total surplus? Explain.

_____

_____

_____

3. a. What type of market is represented in Exhibit 2: perfect competition, monopoly, or natural monopoly? Explain.

_____

_____

b. Show the profit or loss generated by this firm in Exhibit 2 assuming that the firm maximizes profit.

c. Suppose government regulators force this firm to set the price equal to its marginal cost in order to improve efficiency in this market. In Exhibit 3, show the profit or loss generated by this firm.

d. In the long run, will forcing this firm to charge a price equal to its marginal cost improve efficiency? Explain.

_____

_____

_____

Short-Answer Questions

1. What is a *barrier to entry*? What are the three sources of barriers to entry that allow a monopoly to remain the sole seller in a market?

   _____

   _____

   _____

2. If a natural monopoly is forced through regulation to charge a price equal to its marginal cost, will the outcome be efficient? Why?

   _____

   _____

   _____

3. Does a monopolist charge the highest possible price for its output? Why? How does a monopolist choose the price it will charge for its product?

   _____

   _____

   _____

4. Why does a monopolist produce less than the socially efficient quantity of output?

_____

_____

_____

5. Are the monopolist's profits part of the social cost of monopoly? Explain.

_____

_____

_____

6. What are the four ways that policymakers can respond to the problem of monopoly?

_____

_____

_____

_____

7. Should antitrust laws be utilized to stop all mergers? Why?

_____

_____

_____

8. What are some of the problems associated with regulating the price charged by a natural monopoly?

_____

_____

_____

9. Is perfect price discrimination efficient? Explain. Who receives the surplus?

_____

_____

_____

10. What is the necessary condition for a monopolist to be able to price discriminate?

_____

_____

_____

SELF-TEST

True/False Questions

_____ 1. Monopolists are price takers.

_____ 2. The most common source of a barrier to entry into a monopolist's market is that the monopolist owns a key resource necessary for production of that good.

_____ 3. A monopoly is the sole seller of a product with no close substitutes.

_____ 4. A natural monopoly is a monopoly that uses its ownership of natural resources as a barrier to entry into its market.

_____ 5. The demand curve facing a monopolist is the market demand curve for its product.

_____ 6. For the monopolist, marginal revenue is always less than the price of the good.

_____ 7. The monopolist chooses the quantity of output at which marginal revenue equals marginal cost and then uses the demand curve to find the price that will induce consumers to buy that quantity.

_____ 8. The supply curve for a monopolist is always positively sloped.

_____ 9. A monopolist produces an efficient quantity of output but it is still inefficient because it charges a price that exceeds marginal cost and the resulting profit is a social cost.

_____ 10. Using regulations to force a natural monopoly to charge a price equal to its marginal cost of production will cause the monopoly to lose money and exit the industry.

_____ 11. Most economists argue that the most efficient solution to the problem of monopoly is that the monopoly should be publicly owned.

_____ 12. Price discrimination is only possible if there is no arbitrage.

_____ 13. Price discrimination can raise economic welfare because output increases beyond that which would result under monopoly pricing.

_____ 14. Perfect price discrimination is efficient but all of the surplus is received by the consumer.

_____ 15. Universities are engaging in price discrimination when they charge different levels of tuition to poor and wealthy students.

Multiple-Choice Questions

1. Which of the following is *not* a barrier to entry in a monopolized market?
   a. The government gives a single firm the exclusive right to produce some good.
   b. The costs of production make a single producer more efficient than a large number of producers.
   c. A key resource is owned by a single firm.
   d. A single firm is very large.

2. A firm whose average total cost continually declines at least to the quantity that could supply the entire market is known as a
   a. perfect competitor.
   b. natural monopoly.
   c. government monopoly.
   d. regulated monopoly.

3. When a monopolist produces an additional unit, the marginal revenue generated by that unit must be
   a. above the price because the output effect outweighs the price effect.
   b. above the price because the price effect outweighs the output effect.
   c. below the price because the output effect outweighs the price effect.
   d. below the price because the price effect outweighs the output effect.

4. A monopolist maximizes profit by producing the quantity at which
   a. marginal revenue equals marginal cost.
   b. marginal revenue equals price.
   c. marginal cost equals price.
   d. marginal cost equals demand.
   e. none of the above occurs.

5. Which of the following statements about price and marginal cost in competitive and monopolized markets is true?
   a. In competitive markets, price equals marginal cost; in monopolized markets, price equals marginal cost.
   b. In competitive markets, price exceeds marginal cost; in monopolized markets, price exceeds marginal cost.
   c. In competitive markets, price equals marginal cost; in monopolized markets, price exceeds marginal cost.
   d. In competitive markets, price exceeds marginal cost; in monopolized markets, price equals marginal cost.

6. South-Western is a monopolist in the production of your textbook because
   a. South-Western owns a key resource in the production of textbooks.
   b. South-Western is a natural monopoly.
   c. the government has granted South-Western exclusive rights to produce this textbook.
   d. South-Western is a very large company.

Use Exhibit 4 to answer questions 7 through 10.

7. The profit-maximizing monopolist will choose the price and quantity represented by point
   a. A.
   b. B.
   c. C.
   d. D.
   e. None of the above is correct.

8. The profit earned by the profit-maximizing monopolist is represented by the area
   a. P_4ABP_2.
   b. P_4ACP_1.
   c. P_4AQ_10.
   d. P_3DQ_20.
   e. None of the above is correct.

9. The deadweight loss associated with monopoly pricing is represented by the area
   a. P_4ABP_2.
   b. P_4ACP_1.
   c. ABD.
   d. P_2BCP_1.
   e. None of the above is correct.

10. The efficient price and quantity are represented by point
    a. A.
    b. B.
    c. C.
    d. D.
    e. None of the above is correct.

11. The inefficiency associated with monopoly is due to
    a. the monopoly's profits.
    b. the monopoly's losses.
    c. overproduction of the good.
    d. underproduction of the good.

12. Compared to a perfectly competitive market, a monopoly market will usually generate
    a. higher prices and higher output.
    b. higher prices and lower output.
    c. lower prices and lower output.
    d. lower prices and higher output.

13. The monopolist's supply curve
    a. is the marginal-cost curve above average variable cost.
    b. is the marginal-cost curve above average total cost.
    c. is the upward-sloping portion of the average-total-cost curve.
    d. is the upward-sloping portion of the average variable cost.
    e. does not exist.

14. Using government regulations to force a natural monopoly to charge a price equal to its marginal cost will
    a. improve efficiency.
    b. raise the price of the good.
    c. attract additional firms to enter the market.
    d. cause the monopolist to exit the market.

15. The purpose of antitrust laws is to
    a. regulate the prices charged by a monopoly.
    b. increase competition in an industry by preventing mergers and breaking up large firms.
    c. increase merger activity to help generate synergies that reduce costs and raise efficiency.
    d. create public ownership of natural monopolies.
    e. do all of the above.

16. Public ownership of natural monopolies
    a. tends to be inefficient.
    b. usually lowers the cost of production dramatically.
    c. creates synergies between the newly acquired firm and other government-owned companies.
    d. does none of the above.

17. Which of the following statements about price discrimination is *not* true?
    a. Price discrimination can raise economic welfare.
    b. Price discrimination requires that the seller be able to separate buyers according to their willingness to pay.
    c. Perfect price discrimination generates a deadweight loss.
    d. Price discrimination increases a monopolist's profits.
    e. For a monopolist to engage in price discrimination, buyers must be unable to engage in arbitrage.

18. If regulators break up a natural monopoly into many smaller firms, the cost of production
    a. will fall.
    b. will rise.
    c. will remain the same.
    d. could either rise or fall depending on the elasticity of the monopolist's supply curve.

19. A monopoly is able to continue to generate economic profits in the long run because
   a. potential competitors sometimes don't notice the profits.
   b. there is some barrier to entry to that market.
   c. the monopolist is financially powerful.
   d. antitrust laws eliminate competitors for a specified number of years.
   e. of all of the above.

20. If marginal revenue exceeds marginal cost, a monopolist should
   a. increase output.
   b. decrease output.
   c. keep output the same because profits are maximized when marginal revenue exceeds marginal cost.
   d. raise the price.

ADVANCED CRITICAL THINKING

You are watching a television news show. A consumer advocate is discussing the airline industry. He says, "There are so many rates offered by airlines that it is technically possible for a 747 to be carrying a full load of passengers where no two of them paid the same price for their tickets. This is clearly unfair and inefficient." He continues, "In addition, the profits of the airlines have doubled in the last few years since they began this practice, and these additional profits are clearly a social burden. We need legislation that requires airlines to charge all passengers on an airplane the same price for their travel."

1. List some of the ways airlines divide their customers according to their willingness to pay.

   _____

   _____

   _____

2. Is it necessarily inefficient for airlines to charge different prices to different customers? Why?

   _____

   _____

   _____

3. Is the increase in profits generated by this type of price discrimination a social cost? Explain.

   _____

   _____

   _____

SOLUTIONS

Terms and Definitions

<u>2</u> Monopoly

<u>1</u> Natural monopoly

<u>4</u> Price discrimination

<u>5</u> Arbitrage

<u>3</u> Perfect price discrimination

Practice Problems

1. a. A key resource is owned by a single firm (monopoly resource), the government gives a single firm the exclusive right to produce a good (government-created monopoly), the costs of production make a single producer more efficient (natural monopoly).

    b. (1) Natural monopoly. E-mail, Fax machines, telephone, private delivery such as FedEx.

    (2) Monopoly resource. Other bottled water, soft drinks.

    (3) Government-created monopoly due to a patent. Other drugs for depression, generic drugs when the patent expires.

    (4) Monopoly resource. Other gems such as emeralds, rubies, sapphires.

    (5) Government-created monopoly due to copyright. Other principles of economics texts.

    (6) Natural monopoly. Wood-burning stoves, gas lanterns, home generators.

2. a.

Pounds of Salmon	Price	(P × Q) Total Revenue	(ΔTR/ΔQ) Marginal Revenue
0	$20	0	
			18
1	18	18	
			14
2	16	32	
			10
3	14	42	
			6
4	12	48	
			2
5	10	50	
			−2
6	8	48	
			−6
7	6	42	

b. See Exhibit 5.

c. Q = between 3 and 4 units (say 3.5), P = between $12 and $14 (say $13). Profit = $TR - TC$ or profit = $(3.5 \times \$13) - (3.5 \times \$6)$ = $45.50 − $21.00 = $24.50. (Or profit = $(P - ATC) \times Q = (\$13 - \$6) \times 3.5 = \$24.50$.) See Exhibit 6.

d. Seven units at $6 each. (The efficient solution is where the market produces all units where benefits exceed or equal costs of production, which is where demand intersects MC.)

e. The monopolist's price is too high and quantity produced too low because the monopolist faces a downward-sloping demand curve that makes $MR < P$. Therefore, when the profit-maximizing monopolist sets $MR = MC$ and the MR curve is below the demand curve, the quantity is less than optimal and the price charged exceeds the MC of production.

f. Yes. Units from 3.5 to 7, or an additional 3.5 pounds of salmon are valued by the consumer at values in excess of the $6 per pound MC of production and these units are not produced and consumed when the price is $13. (Deadweight loss = the deadweight loss triangle = 1/2 (7 − 3.5) × ($13 − $6) = $12.25.)

   g. Yes, all units are produced where the value to buyers is greater than or is equal to the cost of production (7 units). Total surplus is now producer surplus, and there is no consumer surplus. Total surplus and producer surplus is the area under the demand curve and above the price or 1/2($20 − $6) × 7 = $49. Consumer surplus = $0.

3. a. Natural monopoly because *ATC* is still declining at the quantity that could satisfy the entire market.

   b. See Exhibit 7.

c. See Exhibit 8.

d. No. Since marginal cost must be below average total cost if average total cost is declining, this firm will generate losses if forced to charge a price equal to marginal cost. It will simply exit the market, which eliminates all surplus associated with this market.

Short-Answer Questions

1. Anything that restricts new firms from entering a market. A key resource is owned by a single firm, the government gives a single firm the exclusive right to produce a good, or the costs of production make a single producer more efficient than a large number of producers.

2. No. The monopolist will generate losses and will exit the market.

3. No. Even a monopolist is subject to the demand for its product, so a high price would cause buyers to buy very little of the good. The monopolist chooses its price by first choosing the optimal quantity based on the intersection of *MR* and *MC* and then charging the price consistent with that quantity.

4. For a monopolist, *P* > *MR* because for a monopolist to sell another unit, it must reduce the price on the marginal unit *and all of its previous units*. Therefore, while a monopolist equates *MR* and *MC*, it charges a price that is greater than *MC*, which causes consumers to buy less than the efficient amount of the good.

5. No. The monopolist's profits are a redistribution of consumer surplus to producer surplus. The social cost of monopoly is the deadweight loss associated with the reduced production of output.

6. Try to make monopolized industries more competitive, regulate the behavior of the monopolies, turn private monopolies into public enterprises, or do nothing at all.

7. No, many mergers capture synergies between the merging firms that reduce costs and increase efficiency.

8. The monopolist may lose money and exit the market. Subsidies to prevent this require taxes that also generate deadweight losses. Regulated monopolists have little incentive to reduce costs.

9. Yes, because every unit is produced where the value to buyers is greater than or equal to the cost to the producer. However, the entire total surplus is received by the producer (the monopolist).

10. The monopolist must be able to separate buyers according to their willingness to pay.

True/False Questions

1. F; monopolists are price makers.
2. F; owning a key resource is the rarest source of barriers to entry.

3. T

4. F; a natural monopoly is a firm with an average total cost curve that continually declines at least to the quantity that satisfies the entire market.

5. T

6. T

7. T

8. F; monopolists have no supply curve.

9. F; the inefficiency generated by a monopoly results from the failure of the monopolist to produce units of output where the value to consumers equals or exceeds the cost of production. The monopolist's profits are not a cost to society but are just a redistribution from consumer surplus to producer surplus.

10. T

11. F; economists usually prefer private ownership to public ownership because private owners have a greater incentive to reduce costs.

12. T

13. T

14. F; all of the surplus is received by the producer.

15. T

Multiple-Choice Questions

1. d
2. b
3. d
4. a
5. c
6. c
7. a
8. b
9. c
10. d
11. d
12. b
13. e
14. d
15. b
16. a
17. c
18. b
19. b
20. a

Advanced Critical Thinking

1. Airlines segment people by age (young and old fly cheaper), by location (more competitive routes are cheaper), by length of time between leaving and returning (tourists fly cheaper than business travelers), by length of time of advance booking (later bookings can be more expensive until the very last minute when it may become cheaper again), and so on.

2. No. Price discrimination can improve efficiency. By charging buyers their willingness to pay, the monopolist increases production to the point where all units are produced where the value to buyers is greater than or equal to the cost of production.

3. No. Some of the additional profits are from the creation of additional surplus that accrues entirely to the producer, and some of the profits are a redistribution of surplus from consumer surplus to producer surplus.

16

Oligopoly

CHAPTER OVERVIEW

Context and Purpose

Chapter 16 is the fourth chapter in a five-chapter sequence dealing with firm behavior and the organization of industry. The previous two chapters discussed the two extreme forms of market structure—competition and monopoly. The market structure that lies between competition and monopoly is known as *imperfect competition*. There are two types of imperfect competition—oligopoly and monopolistic competition. Chapter 16 addresses oligopoly while the final chapter in this sequence, Chapter 17, addresses monopolistic competition.

The purpose of Chapter 16 is to discuss *oligopoly*—a market structure in which only a few sellers offer similar or identical products. Since there are only a few sellers in an oligopolistic market, oligopolistic firms are interdependent while competitive firms are not. That is, in a competitive market, the decisions of one firm have no impact on the other firms in the market while in an oligopolistic market, the decisions of any one firm may affect the pricing and production decisions of the other firms in the market.

Chapter Review

Introduction   The market structure that lies between competition and monopoly is known as *imperfect competition*. One type of imperfectly competitive market is **oligopoly**—a market structure in which only a few sellers offer similar or identical products. Oligopoly differs from competition because in a competitive market, the decisions of one firm have no impact on the other firms in the market while in an oligopolistic market, the decisions of any one firm may affect the pricing and production decisions of other firms in the market. Oligopolistic firms are interdependent.

Between Monopoly and Perfect Competition

Competitive firms charge a price equal to marginal cost, and in the long run, this is equal to average total cost, causing each firm to earn no economic profits. A monopolist charges a price that exceeds marginal cost. This reduces output and causes a deadweight loss. The market structure that lies between the extremes of competition and monopoly and contains elements of both is known as imperfect competition. There are two types of imperfect competition—oligopoly

GOALS

In this chapter you will

- See what market structures lie between monopoly and competition

- Examine what outcomes are possible when a market is an oligopoly

- Learn about the prisoners' dilemma and how it applies to oligopoly and other issues

- Consider how the antitrust laws try to foster competition in oligopolistic markets

OUTCOMES

After accomplishing these goals, you should be able to

- Describe the characteristics of oligopoly and monopolistic competition

- Describe the conditions under which an oligopolistic market generates the same outcome as a monopolistic market

- Show why the outcome of the prisoners' dilemma may change if the game is repeated

- Show why some business practices that appear to reduce competition may have a legitimate business purpose and monopolistic competition. *Oligopoly* is a market structure in which only a few sellers offer similar or identical products. Firms in markets with four-firm *concentration ratios* in excess of 50 percent are often oligopolies because four firms supply more than 50 percent of the output of the entire industry. **Monopolistic competition** is a market structure in which many firms sell products that are similar but not identical. To summarize the distinguishing characteristics of the various market structures:

- Monopoly has only one firm.

- Oligopoly has a few firms selling similar or identical products.

- Perfect competition has many firms selling identical products.

- Monopolistic competition has many firms selling differentiated products.

It is often difficult to decide which structure best describes a particular market. Oligopolies may become a larger portion of the economy because high-tech industries have high fixed costs and small marginal costs, so mergers are particularly attractive. We observe this effect in cable television, publishing, and Web site providers.

Markets with Only a Few Sellers

A *duopoly* is an oligopoly with only two firms. If a market were perfectly competitive, the price of output would equal marginal cost. If a market were monopolistic, the profit-maximizing price would exceed marginal cost and the result would be inefficient.

Collusion is an agreement among firms in a market about quantities to produce or prices to charge. A **cartel** is a group of firms acting in unison. If duopolists collude and form a cartel, the market solution is the same as if it were served by a monopolist and the two firms divide the monopoly profits. Cartels are illegal in most nations, and authorities in different countries often work together to fight cartels.

Oligopolists may fail to cooperate because antitrust laws prohibit collusion or because self-interest makes it difficult to agree on how to divide the profits. Without a binding agreement, each oligopolist will maximize its profit given the production levels of the other firms. A **Nash equilibrium** is a situation in which economic actors interacting with one another each choose their best strategy given the strategies that all the other actors have chosen. A Nash equilibrium is a type of oligopolistic equilibrium. When oligopolists individually choose production levels to maximize individual profits, they produce a quantity that is greater than the level produced by monopoly but less than that produced by competition and they will charge a price that is less than the monopoly price but greater than the competitive price.

The larger the oligopoly (more firms), the more difficult it is for them to form a cartel and behave as a monopolist. If they each choose their own level of production to maximize individual profits, they will make the marginal decision of whether to produce an additional unit based on the following:

- *The output effect*: Because price is above marginal cost, selling one more unit at the going price will raise profit.

- *The price effect*: Raising production one unit will increase the total sold, but it will lower the price and the profit on all of the other units sold.

If the output effect exceeds the price effect, the oligopolist will produce another unit and it will continue to expand output until these two effects balance. The greater the number of sellers in an oligopoly, the smaller the price effect because each individual firm's impact on the price is small. Thus, the level of output increases. As the number of sellers in an oligopoly grows larger, the price approaches marginal cost and the quantity approaches the socially efficient level. When there are a large number of firms, the price effect disappears altogether and the market becomes competitive.

Unrestricted international trade increases the number of firms in domestic oligopolies and moves the outcome of the market closer to the competitive solution where prices are equal to marginal cost.

An example of a cartel is OPEC (Organization of Petroleum Exporting Countries), which limits the production of oil.

Game Theory and the Economics of Cooperation

Game theory is the study of how people behave in strategic situations. Strategic situations are when decision makers must consider how others might respond to their actions. The **prisoners' dilemma**

is a particular "game" between two captured prisoners that illustrates why cooperation is difficult to maintain even when it is mutually beneficial. The game applies to oligopoly because oligopolistic firms would always be better off to cooperate yet they often do not.

An example of a prisoners' dilemma is the following: Two criminals are captured. If one confesses and the other does not, the confessor goes free while the other receives a long sentence. If both confess, they each receive an intermediate term. If neither confesses, they each receive a very short term. If the two could cooperate, the best strategy is for each to keep quiet. However, since they cannot guarantee cooperation after they are caught, the best strategy for each is to confess. That is, confessing is a **dominant strategy**—a strategy that is best for a player in a game regardless of the strategies chosen by the other players.

The prisoners' dilemma applies to oligopoly in the following manner: Two oligopolists are better off if they cooperate by keeping production low and sharing the monopoly profits. However, after the agreement is made, the dominant strategy for each is to cheat and produce more than they agreed to produce to enhance their individual profits. The result is that profits fall for both. Self-interest makes it difficult to maintain cooperation.

The prisoners' dilemma applies to the following:

- *Arms races:* Each country prefers to live in a safe world, but the dominant strategy is to increase armaments and the world is less safe.

- *Common resources:* Users of a common resource would find it more profitable to jointly limit their use of the resource, but the dominant strategy is to overuse the resource and joint profits fall.

Lack of cooperation in the cases above is harmful to society. However, lack of cooperation between oligopolists regarding the level of production may be bad for the oligopolists but it is good from the standpoint of society as a whole.

While cooperation is difficult to maintain, it is not impossible. If the game is repeated, the prisoners' dilemma can be solved and agreements can be maintained. For example, oligopolies may include a penalty for violation of the agreement. If the penalty is that they all maintain high production forever if someone cheats, then all should maintain low production levels and share monopoly profits. If the game is played on a periodic basis (each week, month, or year new production levels are chosen), then a simple strategy of tit-for-tat generates the greatest likelihood of cooperation. *Tit-for-tat* is when a player in a game starts by cooperating and then does whatever the other player did last period. If the first player cooperated last period, then the second player should cooperate the next period. If the first player defected (cheated) last period, then the second player should cheat the next period, and so on.

Public Policy toward Oligopolies

Since cooperating oligopolists reduce output and raise prices, policymakers try to induce firms in an oligopoly market to compete rather than cooperate. The Sherman Antitrust Act of 1890 makes agreements to not compete (to reduce quantities or raise prices) a criminal conspiracy. The Clayton Act of 1914 allows individuals harmed by such agreements the right to sue for triple damages. Price fixing clearly reduces economic welfare and is illegal.

There is some disagreement over the use of antitrust laws against some business practices that appear like price fixing. For example:

- *Resale price maintenance* or *fair trade* is when a manufacturer requires retailers to charge a certain price. This appears to prevent retailers from competing on price. However, some economists defend the practice as legitimate because (1) if the manufacturer has market power, it is at wholesale not retail, and the manufacturer would not gain from eliminating competition at the retail level, and (2) resale price maintenance stops discount retailers from free riding on the services provided by full-service retailers.

- *Predatory pricing* occurs when a firm cuts prices with the intention of driving competitors out of the market so that the firm can become a monopolist and later raise prices. Some economists think that this behavior is unlikely because it hurts the firm that is engaged in predatory pricing the most.

- *Tying* occurs when a manufacturer bundles two products together and sells them for one price. Courts argue that tying gives the firm more market power by connecting a weak product with a strong product. Some economists disagree. They suggest that it allows the firm to price discriminate, which may actually increase efficiency. Tying remains controversial.

An antitrust case has been brought against Microsoft for tying its browser to its operating system. Some economists argue that future antitrust suits should take into account that the new high-tech industries may be natural monopolies—firms whose costs continue to decline at least to the quantity that satisfies the entire market.

Conclusion

Oligopolies will look more like a competitive market if there are a large number of firms and more like a monopoly if there are a small number of firms. The prisoners' dilemma shows why cooperation is difficult to maintain even when it is in the best interest of the oligopolists. The use of antitrust laws against price fixing improves economic efficiency but their use in other areas is more controversial.

Helpful Hints

1. Oligopoly lies between monopoly and perfect competition. If oligopolists are able to collude and form a cartel, the market solution is the same as that for a monopoly. If oligopolists are unable to collude and form a cartel, the production and pricing in the market depend on the number of firms. The fewer the number of firms, the more the result appears like monopoly where the price exceeds marginal cost and the quantity is below the efficient level. The greater the number of firms, the more the result appears like competition where the price equals marginal cost and the quantity is efficient.

Terms and Definitions

Choose a definition for each key term.

Key Terms

_____ Imperfect competition

_____ Oligopoly

_____ Monopolistic competition

_____ Duopoly

_____ Collusion

_____ Cartel

_____ Nash equilibrium

_____ Game theory

_____ Prisoners' dilemma

_____ Dominant strategy

Definitions

1. The study of how people behave in strategic situations

2. A market structure in which many firms sell products that are similar but not identical

3. An agreement among firms in a market about quantities to produce or prices to charge

4. A strategy that is best for a player in a game regardless of the strategies chosen by the other players

5. The market structure that lies between competition and monopoly

6. An oligopoly with only two firms

7. A market structure in which only a few sellers offer similar or identical products

8. A particular "game" between two captured prisoners that illustrates why cooperation is difficult to maintain even when it is mutually beneficial

9. A situation in which economic actors interacting with one another each choose their best strategy given the strategies that all the other actors have chosen

10. A group of firms acting in unison

PROBLEMS AND SHORT-ANSWER QUESTIONS

Practice Problems

1. In which market structure—monopoly, oligopoly, monopolistic competition, or perfect competition—would you place each of the following products? Why?
    a. Retail market for electricity

    _____

    b. Principles of economics textbooks

    _____

    c. *Principles of Economics*, by N. Gregory Mankiw

    _____

    d. Photographic film

    _____

    e. Retail market for gasoline

    _____

    f. Restaurants in a large city

    _____

    g. Auto tires

    _____

    h. Trash collection

    _____

    i. Legal services in a metropolitan area

    _____

    j. Breakfast cereal

    _____

    k. Gold bullion

    _____

    l. Air travel from any one airport

    _____

2. The following information describes the demand schedule for a unique type of apple. This type of apple can only be produced by two firms because they own the land on which these unique trees spontaneously grow. As a result, the

marginal cost of production is zero for these duopolists, causing total revenue to equal profit.

a. Complete the following table.

Price per Bushel	Quantity (in bushels)	Total Revenue (profit)
$12	0	_____
11	5	_____
10	10	_____
9	15	_____
8	20	_____
7	25	_____
6	30	_____
5	35	_____
4	40	_____
3	45	_____
2	50	_____
1	55	_____
0	60	_____

b. If the market were perfectly competitive, what price and quantity would be generated by this market? Explain.

_____

c. If these two firms colluded and formed a cartel, what price and quantity would be generated by this market, what is the level of profit generated by the market, and what is the level of profit generated by each firm?

_____

_____

d. If one firm cheats and produces one additional increment (five units) of production, what is the level of profit generated by each firm?

_____

e. If both firms cheat and each produces one additional increment (five units) of production (compared to the cooperative solution), what is the level of profit generated by each firm?

_____

f. If both firms are cheating and producing one additional increment of output (five additional units compared to the cooperative solution), will either firm choose to produce an additional increment (five more units)? Why? What is the value of the Nash equilibrium in this duopoly market?

_____

_____

g. Compare the competitive equilibrium to the Nash equilibrium. In which situation is society better off? Explain.

_____

_____

_____

h. What would happen to the price and quantity in this market (qualitatively) if an additional firm were able to grow these unique apples?

_____

i. Use the data from the duopoly example above to fill in the boxes of the prisoners' dilemma. Place the value of the profits earned by each duopolist in the appropriate box in Exhibit 1.

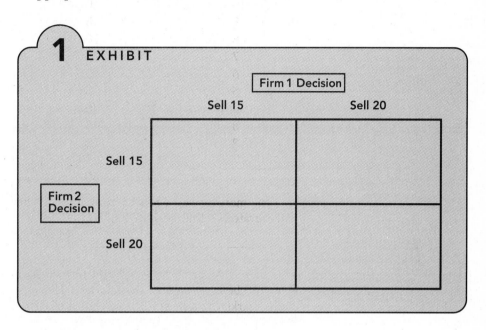

j. What is the solution to this prisoners' dilemma? Explain.

_____

k. What might the solution be if the participants were able to repeat the "game"? Why? What simple strategy might they use to maintain their cartel?

_____

_____

Short-Answer Questions

1. What are the two types of imperfect competition? Describe them.

_____

_____

2. The market for vitamins and dietary supplements is dominated by five firms. What type of market structure does it represent? Explain.

_____

3. What is the outcome in an oligopolistic market if the oligopolists collude and form a cartel? Explain.

_____

_____

4. Suppose a group of oligopolists does not collude but instead reaches a Nash equilibrium. What price and quantity will result in this oligopolist market when compared to the monopolistic or competitive result?

_____

_____

5. Referring to question 4 above, what would happen to the price and quantity in the Nash equilibrium if an additional firm were to join the oligopoly? Why?

_____

_____

6. If oligopolists would be better off if they collude, why do they so often fail to cooperate?

_____

_____

7. Is it better for society as a whole if oligopolists cooperate? Explain. What measures do we take to try to prevent cooperation between oligopolists?

_____

_____

8. Suppose High-Tech Software sells two products—a word processing package and a spreadsheet package. Suppose that the business community values the word processing package at $100 per unit and the spreadsheet package at $250 per unit while the university community values the word processing package at $125 and the spreadsheet at $200. (Assume that the marginal cost of each unit is zero.) What are the profit-maximizing prices that High-Tech should charge if they sell each product separately and what is the total price of the two goods? If High-Tech is able to engage in tying, what is the profit-maximizing price for the two products as a bundle? Should this be legal?

_____

_____

SELF-TEST

True/False Questions

_____ 1. An oligopoly is a market structure in which many firms sell products that are similar but not identical.

_____ 2. The market for crude oil is an example of an oligopolistic market.

_____ 3. The unique feature of an oligopoly market is that the actions of one seller have a significant impact on the profits of all of the other sellers in the market.

_____ 4. When firms cooperate with one another, it is generally good for society as a whole.

_____ 5. When firms cooperate with one another, it is generally good for the cooperating firms.

_____ 6. When oligopolists collude and form a cartel, the outcome in the market is similar to that generated by a perfectly competitive market.

_____ 7. The price and quantity generated by a Nash equilibrium is closer to the competitive solution than the price and quantity generated by a cartel.

_____ 8. The greater the number of firms in the oligopoly, the more the outcome of the market looks like that generated by a monopoly.

_____ 9. Cooperation is easily maintained in an oligopoly because cooperation maximizes each individual firm's profits.

_____10. The prisoners' dilemma demonstrates why it is difficult to maintain cooperation even when cooperation is mutually beneficial.

_____11. There is a constant tension in an oligopoly between cooperation and self-interest because after an agreement to reduce production is reached, it is profitable for each individual firm to cheat and produce more.

_____12. The dominant strategy for an oligopolist is to cooperate with the group and maintain low production regardless of what the other oligopolists do.

_____13. Antitrust laws require manufacturers to engage in resale price maintenance or fair trade.

_____14. Predatory pricing occurs when a firm cuts prices with the intention of driving competitors out of the market so that the firm can become a monopolist and later raise prices.

_____15. If a prisoners' dilemma game is repeated, the participants are more likely to independently maximize their profits and reach a Nash equilibrium.

Multiple-Choice Questions

1. The market for hand tools (such as hammers and screwdrivers) is dominanted by Black & Decker, Stanley, and Craftsman. This market is best described as
   a. competitive.
   b. a monopoly.
   c. an oligopoly.
   d. monopolistically competitive.

2. A market structure in which many firms sell products that are similar but not identical is known as
   a. perfect competition.
   b. monopoly.
   c. oligopoly.
   d. monopolistic competition.

3. If oligopolists engage in collusion and successfully form a cartel, the market outcome is
   a. the same as if it were served by a monopoly.
   b. the same as if it were served by competitive firms.
   c. efficient because cooperation improves efficiency.
   d. known as a Nash equilibrium.

4. Suppose an oligopolist individually maximizes its profits. When calculating profits, if the output effect exceeds the price effect on the marginal unit of production, then the oligopolist
    a. has maximized profits.
    b. should produce more units.
    c. should produce fewer units.
    d. should exit the industry.
    e. is in a Nash equilibrium.

5. As the number of sellers in an oligopoly grow larger, an oligopolistic market looks more like
    a. a monopoly.
    b. monopolistic competition.
    c. a competitive market.
    d. a collusion solution.

6. When an oligopolist individually chooses its level of production to maximize its profits, it produces an output that is
    a. more than the level produced by a monopoly and less than the level produced by a competitive market.
    b. less than the level produced by a monopoly and more than the level produced by a competitive market.
    c. more than the level produced by either a monopoly or a competitive market.
    d. less than the level produced by either a monopoly or a competitive market.

7. When an oligopolist individually chooses its level of production to maximize its profits, it charges a price that is
    a. more than the price charged by a monopoly and less than the price charged by a competitive market.
    b. less than the price charged by a monopoly and more than the price charged by a competitive market.
    c. more than the price charged by either a monopoly or a competitive market.
    d. less than the price charged by either a monopoly or a competitive market.

8. As the number of sellers in an oligopoly increases,
    a. collusion is more likely to occur because a larger number of firms can place pressure on any firm that defects.
    b. output in the market tends to fall because each firm must cut back on production.
    c. the price in the market moves further from marginal cost.
    d. the price in the market moves closer to marginal cost.

9. A situation in which oligopolists interacting with one another each choose their best strategy given the strategies that all the other oligopolists have chosen is known as a
    a. collusion solution.
    b. cartel.
    c. Nash equilibrium.
    d. dominant strategy.

Use the table below to answer questions 10 through 13. The table shows the demand schedule for tickets to watch amateur baseball games in a medium-sized town. The city provides the ballparks, and the players play for free, so the marginal cost of providing the games is zero. The city has authorized two companies to provide baseball games in two stadiums, and the public considers the games in each stadium to be equivalent.

Price	Quantity
$6	0
5	1,000
4	2,000
3	3,000
2	4,000
1	5,000
0	6,000

10. Under competition, the price and quantity in this market would be
    a. $4; 2,000.
    b. $3; 3,000.
    c. $2; 4,000.
    d. $1; 5,000.
    e. $0; 6,000.

11. If the duopolists in this baseball market collude and successfully form a cartel, what is the price that each should charge in order to maximize profits?
    a. $5
    b. $4
    c. $3
    d. $2
    e. $1

12. If the duopolists in this baseball market collude and successfully form a cartel, how much profit will *each* earn?
    a. $1,500
    b. $3,000
    c. $4,000
    d. $4,500
    e. $9,000

13. Suppose that the duopolists are unable to collude, and both companies cheat on the production agreement. If both alter production *together* by 500-unit increments so that total production changes by 1,000-unit increments, how much profit will *each* earn when the market reaches a Nash equilibrium?
    a. $2,500
    b. $4,000
    c. $4,500
    d. $8,000
    e. $9,000

Use the prisoners' dilemma game in Exhibit 2 to answer questions 14 and 15. It shows the possible profits for duopolists that are the only two restaurants in town. Each firm can choose how many hours to be open for business.

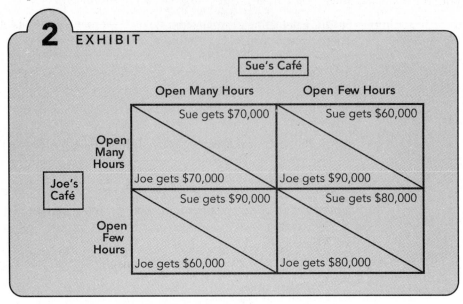

14. The dominant strategy for Sue and Joe is for
    a. both to be open for many hours.
    b. both to be open for a few hours.
    c. Sue to be open for many hours while Joe is open for few hours.
    d. Sue to be open for few hours while Joe is open for many hours.
    e. There is no dominant strategy in this prisoners' dilemma game.

15. Suppose Sue and Joe agreed to collude and jointly maximize their profits. If Sue and Joe were to be able to repeatedly play the game shown above and they agreed on a penalty for defecting from their agreement, what is the likely outcome of the game?
    a. Both are open for many hours.
    b. Both are open for a few hours.
    c. Sue is open for many hours while Joe is open for few hours.
    d. Sue is open for few hours while Joe is open for many hours.

16. Many economists argue that resale price maintenance
    a. is price fixing and, therefore, is prohibited by law.
    b. enhances the market power of the producer.
    c. has a legitimate purpose of stopping discount retailers from free riding on the services provided by full-service retailers.
    d. is both *a* and *b*.

17. Collusion is difficult for an oligopoly to maintain
    a. because antitrust laws make collusion illegal.
    b. because, in the case of oligopoly, self-interest is in conflict with cooperation.
    c. if additional firms enter of the oligopoly.
    d. for all of the above reasons.

Use the following information to answer questions 18 and 19: Suppose that ABC Publishing sells an economics textbook and an accompanying study guide. Bob is willing to pay $75 for the text and $15 for the study guide. Mary is willing to spend $60 for the text and $25 for the study guide. Suppose both the book and study guide have a zero marginal cost of production.

18. If ABC Publishing charges separate prices for both products, its best strategy is to charge prices that, when combined, total
   a. $60.
   b. $75.
   c. $80.
   d. $85.
   e. $90.

19. If ABC Publishing engages in tying, its best strategy is to charge a combined price of
   a. $60.
   b. $75.
   c. $80.
   d. $85.
   e. $90.

20. Laws that make it illegal for firms to conspire to raise prices or reduce production are known as
   a. pro-competition laws.
   b. antitrust laws.
   c. antimonopoly laws.
   d. anticollusion laws.
   e. all of the above.

ADVANCED CRITICAL THINKING

You are watching television. An advertisement begins, "Come on down to Warehouse Electronics. We've got deals so great you won't believe it! National brand 13-inch color television sets for $99. The price is so low that we can't tell you the name of the manufacturer!"

1. Why would Warehouse Electronics be unable to reveal the name of the manufacturer when it advertises its television sets for an unusually low price?

   _____

   _____

2. Although this activity appears like price fixing, is the objective of this practice to reduce competition? Why?

   _____

   _____

3. Why would the manufacturer place this type of restriction on the retailers that sell its products?

   _____

   _____

SOLUTIONS

Terms and Definitions

5 Imperfect competition

7 Oligopoly

2 Monopolistic competition

6 Duopoly

3 Collusion

10 Cartel

9 Nash equilibrium

1 Game theory

8 Prisoners' dilemma

4 Dominant strategy

Practice Problems

1. a. Monopoly, only one firm from which to purchase.

   b. Monopolistic competition, many firms each selling differentiated products.

   c. Monopoly, only one firm can produce it due to copyright laws.

   d. Oligopoly, few firms (Fuji, Kodak) selling similar products.

   e. Perfect competition, many firms selling identical products.

   f. Monopolistic competition, many firms each selling differentiated products.

   g. Oligopoly, few firms (Goodyear, Firestone, Michelin) selling very similar products.

   h. Monopoly, only one firm from which to purchase.

   i. Monopolistic competition, many firms each selling differentiated products.

   j. Oligopoly, few firms (Kellogg Company, Post, General Mills, Quaker Oats) selling similar products.

   k. Perfect competition, many firms selling identical products.

   l. Oligopoly, few airlines from which to choose at any one airport, similar product.

   Note: While monopoly and competition are more easily distinguished, the line between oligopoly and monopolistic competition is not as sharp. For example, (b) might be considered to be an oligopoly since there are relatively few publishers and economic textbooks may be considered to be very similar, and (j) might be considered to be monopolistic competition if the products are considered to be differentiated, and so on.

2. a.

Price per Bushel	Quantity (in bushels)	Total Revenue (profit)
$12	0	$0
11	5	55
10	10	100
9	15	135
8	20	160
7	25	175
6	30	180
5	35	175
4	40	160
3	45	135
2	50	100
1	55	55
0	60	0

   b. In a competitive market, competition reduces the price until it equals marginal cost (which is zero in this case), therefore $P = \$0$ and $Q = 60$.

   c. These duopolists would behave as a monopolist, produce at the level that maximizes profit, and agree to divide the production levels and profit. Therefore, $P = \$6$, $Q = 30$ for the market. Profit $= \$6 \times 30 = \$180$. Each firm produces 15 units at $6 and receives profit of $90 (half of the $180).

   d. Cheating firm: $20 \times \$5 = \$100$, other firm: $15 \times \$5 = \$75$.

   e. Each firm: $20 \times \$4 = \$80$.

   f. No, because the profit would fall for the cheater to $25 \times \$3 = \$75$, which is below $80 profit from part e above. Therefore, the Nash equilibrium is each firm producing 20 units (40 for the market) at a price of $4, creating $160 of profit for the market, and each duopolist receives $80 profit.

   g. The Nash equilibrium has a higher price ($4 compared to $0) and a smaller quantity (40 units compared to 60 units). Society is better off with competitive equilibrium.

   h. The new Nash equilibrium would have a lower price and a larger quantity. It would move toward the competitive solution.

   i. See Exhibit 3.

   j. The dominant strategy for each is to cheat and sell 20 units because each firm's profit is greater when it sells 20 units regardless of whether the other firm sells 15 or 20 units.

   k. They might be able to maintain the cooperative (monopoly) production level of 30 units and each produce 15 units because if

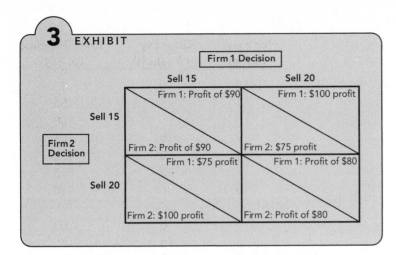

3 EXHIBIT

Firm 1 Decision

Sell 15 | Sell 20

Firm 2 Decision

Sell 15
- Firm 1: Profit of $90
- Firm 2: Profit of $90
- Firm 1: $100 profit
- Firm 2: $75 profit

Sell 20
- Firm 1: $75 profit
- Firm 2: $100 profit
- Firm 1: Profit of $80
- Firm 2: Profit of $80

the game is repeated, the participants can devise a penalty for cheating. The simplest penalty is "tit-for-tat."

Short-Answer Questions

1. Oligopoly and monopolistic competition. Oligopoly is a market structure in which only a few sellers offer similar or identical products. Monopolistic competition is when many firms sell products that are similar but not identical.

2. Oligopoly, because there are few firms and the products are similar or identical.

3. The outcome is the same as if the market were served by a monopolist. Monopoly profits are divided among the firms, and production levels are limited by agreement to the level that a monopoly would produce.

4. The price will be lower than monopoly but higher than competition. The quantity sold will be greater than monopoly but less than competition.

5. The price would fall and the quantity sold would rise. This is because with the addition of another firm, the individual firm's impact on the price is reduced, which causes the output effect to exceed the price effect and the profit-maximizing output level of the group is increased. As members are added, the outcome approaches a competitive solution.

6. Once an agreement to reduce production is made, it is always profitable for the individual firm to cheat and produce in excess of the agreement regardless of whether the others cheat or maintain the agreement. Cheating is a dominant strategy. This is the prisoners' dilemma.

7. It is better if they do not cooperate because the Nash equilibrium is closer to the efficient competitive solution than the monopoly solution would have been. Antitrust laws make it illegal for firms to make agreements not to compete.

8. Word processing price = $100, spreadsheet price = $200, total = $300. If tying the two together, price = $325. Maybe, because it may be just a method of price discrimination which, recall, increases total surplus (is more efficient) but it moves surplus from the consumer to the producer.

True/False Questions

1. F; an oligopoly is where a few sellers offer similar or identical products.

2. T

3. T

4. F; it raises prices above marginal cost and reduces output below the socially optimal level.

5. T

6. F; it is the same as that generated by a monopoly.

7. T

8. F; the greater the number of firms, the more the market approaches the competitive solution.

9. F; cooperation maximizes the profits of the group and the individual firms if none of the oligopolists violates the agreement. However, once the agreement is made, an individual firm will increase its profits if it cheats and produces more.

10. T

11. T

12. F; the dominant strategy is to increase production regardless of the choices of the other firms.

13. F; sometimes courts view retail price maintenance as price fixing and declare it illegal.

14. T

15. F; repeated games are more likely to generate cooperation because a penalty for cheating can be enforced.

Multiple-Choice Questions

1. c
2. d
3. a
4. b
5. c
6. a
7. b
8. d
9. c
10. e
11. c
12. d
13. b
14. a
15. b
16. c
17. d
18. b
19. d
20. b

Advanced Critical Thinking

1. The manufacturer may be engaging in "resale price maintenance" or "fair trade" practices with its retailers (including Warehouse Electronics). This may restrict the retailer's right to advertise a price below the suggested retail price for the product.

2. No, because any reduction in competition at the retail level generates market power for the retailer and fewer units will be sold. This is not in the interest of the manufacturer.

3. The purpose is to stop discount retailers from free riding on the services provided by full-service retailers—retailers with a knowledgeable sales force, a repair shop, and so on.

17

Monopolistic Competition

GOALS

In this chapter you will

- Analyze competition among firms that sell differentiated products

- Compare the outcome under monopolistic competition and under perfect competition

- Consider the desirability of outcomes in monopolistically competitive markets

- Examine the debate over the effects of advertising

- Examine the debate over the role of brand names

OUTCOMES

After accomplishing these goals, you should be able to

- Show the long-run adjustment that takes place in a monopolistically competitive market when a firm generates economic profits

- Show why monopolistically competitive firms produce at less than efficient scale in the long run

- Discuss the inefficiencies of monopolistically competitive markets

- Provide an argument in support of and in opposition to the use of advertising

- Provide an argument in support of and in opposition to the use of brand names

CHAPTER OVERVIEW

Context and Purpose

Chapter 17 is the final chapter in a five-chapter sequence dealing with firm behavior and the organization of industry. Chapters 14 and 15 developed the two extreme forms of market structure—competition and monopoly. The market structure that lies between competition and monopoly is known as imperfect competition. There are two types of imperfect competition—oligopoly, which we addressed in the previous chapter, and monopolistic competition, which is the topic of the current chapter. The analysis in this chapter is again based on the cost curves developed in Chapter 13.

The purpose of Chapter 17 is to address *monopolistic competition*—a market structure in which many firms sell products that are similar but not identical. Recall, oligopoly differs from perfect competition because there are only a few sellers in the market. Monopolistic competition differs from perfect competition because each of the many sellers offers a somewhat different product. As a result, monopolistically competitive firms face a downward-sloping demand curve while competitive firms face a horizontal demand curve at the market price. Monopolistic competition is extremely common.

Chapter Review

Introduction **Monopolistic competition** shares some features of competition and monopoly:

- *Many sellers:* This is in common with competition.

- *Product differentiation:* This is in common with monopoly—each firm's product is slightly different, so each firm is a price maker and faces a downward-sloping demand for its product.

- *Free entry:* This is in common with competition—firms can enter or exit without restriction so economic profits are driven to zero.

Examples of monopolistically competitive markets are the market for books, CDs, movies, restaurants, and so on. Monopolistically competitive markets are common.

Oligopoly differs from perfect competition because there are only a few sellers in the market. Monopolistic competition differs from perfect competition because each of the many sellers offers a somewhat different product. As a result, monopolistically competitive firms face a downward-sloping demand curve while competitive firms face a horizontal demand curve at the market price.

Competition with Differentiated Products

Similar to a monopolist, a monopolistically competitive firm faces a downward-sloping demand curve for its product. Therefore, it follows the same rule for profit maximization as a monopolist—it produces the quantity at which marginal cost equals marginal revenue and then uses the demand curve to determine the price consistent with this quantity. In the short run, if the price exceeds average total cost, the firm makes economic profits. If the price is below average total cost, the firm generates losses.

As in a competitive market, if the firm is making profits, new firms have incentive to enter the market. Entry reduces the demand faced by each firm already in the market (shifts their demand curves to the left) and reduces their profits in the long run. If the firm is generating losses, incumbent firms have incentive to exit the market. Exit increases the demand faced by each firm that remains in the market (shifts their demand curves to the right) and reduces their losses. Entry and exit continue until the firms in the market are making zero economic profits. In long-run equilibrium, the demand curve facing the firm must be tangent to the average-total-cost curve so that $P = ATC$ and profits are zero.

The long-run equilibrium for a monopolistically competitive firm exhibits the following:

- As in monopoly, price exceeds marginal cost because profit maximization requires that $MR = MC$, and MR is always less than demand if demand is downward sloping.

- As in competition, price equals average total cost so economic profits equal zero because, unlike in monopoly, free entry drives profits to zero.

The long-run equilibrium under monopolistic competition differs from the long-run equilibrium under perfect competition in two ways:

- *Excess capacity:* Monopolistically competitive firms produce in the downward-sloping portion of their average-total-cost curve. Therefore, they produce a quantity that is less than that which would be produced at the *efficient scale* (minimum ATC) of the firm. As a result, they are said to have *excess capacity*. Competitive firms produce at the efficient scale.

- *Markup over marginal cost:* A monopolistically competitive firm charges a price that exceeds its marginal cost. A competitive firm charges a price that equals its marginal cost. As a result, if a monopolistically competitive firm could attract another customer, it would increase its profits.

Monopolistic competition may be inefficient for two reasons:

- Since price exceeds marginal cost, some units that buyers valued in excess of the cost of production are not produced and consumed. This is the standard deadweight loss associated with monopoly. Regulating a monopolistically competitive firm in order to reduce the deadweight loss is not easily accomplished—the task is similar to regulating a natural monopoly.

- The number of firms in the market may not be "ideal" because the entering firm only considers its own profits but its entry generates two external effects:

  (1) *The product-variety externality*: Entry creates consumer surplus in the new market, which is a positive externality.

  (2) *The business-stealing externality*: Entry causes other firms to lose customers and profits and reduces existing surplus, which is a negative externality.

Therefore, the entry of new firms into a monopolistically competitive market can raise or lower social surplus.

Monopolistically competitive markets do not ensure the maximization of total surplus. However, there is no easy way for public policy to improve the market outcome.

Advertising

Since monopolistically competitive firms sell differentiated products at prices above marginal cost, each firm has incentive to advertise to attract more buyers. Firms that sell highly differentiated consumer products spend 10 to 20 percent of revenue on advertising; firms that sell industrial products spend little; and firms that sell undifferentiated products spend nothing at all. About 2 percent of firm revenue, or about $240 billion per year, is spent on advertising. That spending is largely on commercials on television and radio, space in newspapers and magazines, direct mail, the yellow pages, billboards, and the Internet.

Economists debate the social value of advertising. Critics argue that advertising manipulates people's tastes to create a desire that otherwise would not exist and that advertising impedes competition by increasing the perception of product differentiation, which increases brand loyalty, causes demand to be more inelastic, and allows the firm to charge a greater markup over marginal cost. Defenders of advertising argue that advertising provides information to customers about prices, the existence of new products, and the location of retail outlets. This information increases competition because consumers are aware of price differentials and it provides new firms with the means to attract customers from existing firms. Evidence suggests that advertising increases competition and reduces prices for consumers.

Advertising that appears to contain little information may be useful because it provides a *signal* of product quality. Firms are likely to spend a great deal on advertising only if they think their product is of high quality. Therefore, consumers may be rational to try new products that are expensively advertised because it signals that the product is of high quality. The content of the ad is irrelevant. What is important is that the ad is expensive.

Advertising is related to *brand names*. Critics of brand names argue that brand names cause consumers to perceive differences between goods that do not exist. Defenders of brand names argue that brand names ensure that the product is of high quality because (1) brand names provide *information* about the quality of a product and (2) brand names give firms the *incentive* to maintain high quality.

Conclusion

Monopolistic competition contains characteristics of both monopoly and competition. Like monopoly, firms face downward-sloping demand curves and charge prices above marginal cost. Like competition, entry and exit drive profits to zero in the long run. Many markets are monopolistically competitive. The allocation of resources under monopolistic competition is not perfect, but policymakers may not be able to improve on it.

Helpful Hints

1. A source of inefficiency in monopolistic competition is underproduction. That is, some units are not produced that buyers value in excess of the cost of production. The monopolistically competitive firm charges a price that exceeds marginal cost while the competitive firm charges a price equal to marginal cost. However, the higher price charged by the monopolistically competitive firm is not the source of inefficiency. As with monopoly, it is the lower quantity demanded that results from the higher price that is the source of inefficiency. By itself, the higher price simply redistributes surplus from the buyer to the seller but it does not reduce total surplus.

Terms and Definitions

Choose a definition for each key term.

Key Terms

_____ Monopolistic competition

_____ Free entry

_____ Efficient scale

Definitions

1. A situation where firms can enter the market without restriction

2. The quantity that minimizes average total cost

3. A market structure in which many firms sell products that are similar but not identical

PROBLEMS AND SHORT-ANSWER QUESTIONS

Practice Problems

1. Categorize each of the following markets as either competitive, monopolistic, or monopolistically competitive. Explain.
   a. toothpaste

   _____

   b. cable television

   _____

   c. gasoline at retail

   _____

   d. local newspapers

   _____

   e. magazines

   _____

   f. wheat

   _____

   g. video games

   _____

   h. beer

   _____

2. Suppose that there are many restaurants in the city and that each has a somewhat different menu.

 a. In Exhibit 1, draw the diagram of the cost curves (average total cost and marginal cost), demand curve, and marginal-revenue curve for Mario's Pizza when it is in long-run equilibrium.

 b. Is Mario's Pizza profitable in the long run? Explain.

 _____

 _____

 _____

 c. Is Mario's Pizza producing at the efficient scale? Explain. Why doesn't Mario's expand its output if it has excess capacity?

 _____

 _____

 _____

 d. In Exhibit 1, show the deadweight loss associated with Mario's level of output. Does this deadweight loss occur because the price is higher than a competitive firm would charge or because the quantity is smaller than a competitive firm would produce? Explain.

 _____

 _____

 _____

e. Suppose that Mario's engages in an advertising campaign that is a huge success. In Exhibit 2, draw the diagram of Mario's cost curves, demand curve, and marginal-revenue curve and show Mario's profit in the short run. Can this situation be maintained in the long run? Explain.

_____

_____

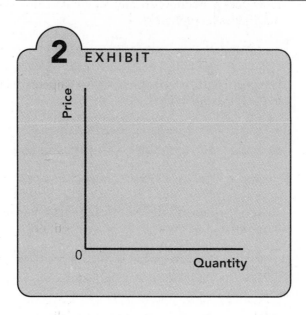

3. For each of the following pairs of firms, which firm would likely spend a higher proportion of its revenue on advertising? Explain.
   a. the maker of Bayer Aspirin or the maker of generic aspirin

   _____

   b. a firm introducing a low-quality ice cream or a firm introducing a high-quality ice cream that each cost about the same to make

   _____

   c. John Deere farm tractor division or John Deere lawn mower division

   _____

   d. the bakery that bakes Old Home Wheat Bread or a wheat farmer

   _____

Short-Answer Questions

1. What characteristics does monopolistic competition have in common with a monopoly?

   _____

   _____

2. What characteristics does monopolistic competition have in common with perfect competition?

_____

_____

3. How does a monopolistically competitive firm choose the quantity and price that maximizes its profits?

_____

4. Is it possible for a monopolistically competitive firm to generate economic profits in the long run? Why?

_____

_____

_____

5. How does the long-run equilibrium in monopolistic competition differ from the long-run equilibrium in perfect competition?

_____

_____

6. Is the long-run equilibrium in monopolistic competition efficient? Explain.

_____

_____

_____

_____

7. Summarize the arguments in support of advertising and brand names.

_____

_____

_____

8. Summarize the arguments in opposition to advertising and brand names.

_____

_____

_____

SELF-TEST

True/False Questions

_____ 1. Monopolistic competition is a market structure in which few firms sell similar products.

_____ 2. Similar to firms in perfectly competitive markets, firms in monopolistically competitive markets can enter and exit the market without restriction so profits are driven to zero in the long run.

_____ 3. In the long run, firms in monopolistically competitive markets produce at the minimum of their average-total-cost curves.

_____ 4. Similar to a monopolist, a monopolistically competitive firm faces a downward-sloping demand curve for its product.

_____ 5. Both monopolists and monopolistically competitive firms produce the quantity at which marginal revenue equals marginal cost and then use the demand curve facing the firm to determine the price consistent with that quantity.

_____ 6. Since a monopolistically competitive firm charges a price that exceeds marginal cost, the firm fails to produce some units that the buyers value in excess of the cost of production, and thus, monopolistic competition is inefficient.

_____ 7. In the long run, a monopolistically competitive firm charges a price that exceeds average total cost.

_____ 8. Economists generally agree that monopolistically competitive firms should be regulated in order to increase economic efficiency.

_____ 9. Firms that sell highly differentiated consumer products are more likely to spend a large percentage of their revenue on advertising.

_____ 10. Advertising must be socially wasteful because advertising simply adds to the cost of producing a product.

_____ 11. Critics of advertising argue that advertising decreases competition while defenders of advertising argue that advertising increases competition and reduces prices to consumers.

_____ 12. Even advertising that appears to contain little information about the product may be useful because it provides a signal about the quality of the product.

_____ 13. Brand names allow firms to make economic profits in the long run because they are able to sell inferior products based on the apparent connection of those products to the firm's unrelated high-quality products.

_____ 14. Policymakers are starting to view restrictions on advertising by professionals such as doctors, lawyers, and pharmacists as anticompetitive.

_____ 15. In the long run, a monopolistically competitive firm produces at the efficient scale while a competitive firm has excess capacity.

Multiple-Choice Questions

1. Which of the following is not a characteristic of a monopolistically competitive market?
    a. many sellers
    b. differentiated products
    c. long-run economic profits
    d. free entry and exit

2. Which of the following products is least likely to be sold in a monopolistically competitive market?
    a. video games
    b. breakfast cereal
    c. beer
    d. cotton

3. Which of the following is true regarding the similarities and differences in monopolistic competition and monopoly?
    a. The monopolist faces a downward-sloping demand curve while the monopolistic competitor faces an elastic demand curve.
    b. The monopolist makes economic profits in the long run while the monopolistic competitor makes zero economic profits in the long run.
    c. Both the monopolist and the monopolistic competitor operate at the efficient scale.
    d. The monopolist charges a price above marginal cost while the monopolistic competitor charges a price equal to marginal cost.

4. In the short run, if the price is above average total cost in a monopolistically competitive market, the firm makes
    a. losses and firms enter the market.
    b. losses and firms exit the market.
    c. profits and firms enter the market.
    d. profits and firms exit the market.

5. If the monopolistic competitor described by Exhibit 3 is producing at the profit-maximizing (loss-minimizing) level of output, it
    a. is generating losses.
    b. is generating profits.
    c. is generating zero profits.
    d. could be generating either profits or losses depending on what quantity it chooses to produce.

6. The monopolistically competitive market shown in Exhibit 3 will, in the long run,
    a. attract new producers into the market, which will shift the demand faced by incumbent firms to the right.
    b. attract new producers into the market, which will shift the demand faced by incumbent firms to the left.
    c. cause producers to exit the market, which will shift the demand faced by incumbent firms to the right.
    d. cause producers to exit the market, which will shift the demand faced by incumbent firms to the left.

7. Which of the following is true regarding the production and pricing decisions of monopolistically competitive firms? Monopolistically competitive firms choose the quantity at which marginal cost equals
    a. average total cost and then use the demand curve to determine the price consistent with this quantity.
    b. marginal revenue and then use the demand curve to determine the price consistent with this quantity.
    c. average total cost and then use the supply curve to determine the price consistent with this quantity.
    d. marginal revenue and then use the supply curve to determine the price consistent with this quantity.

8. Exhibit 4 depicts a monopolistically competitive firm
    a. generating profits in the short run.
    b. generating losses in the short run.
    c. generating zero profits in the long run.
    d. It is impossible to determine from this graph whether the firm is generating profits or losses.

9. Which of the following is true with regard to monopolistically competitive firms' scale of production and pricing decisions? Monopolistically competitive firms produce
    a. at the efficient scale and charge a price equal to marginal cost.
    b. at the efficient scale and charge a price above marginal cost.
    c. with excess capacity and charge a price equal to marginal cost.
    d. with excess capacity and charge a price above marginal cost.

10. One source of inefficiency in monopolistic competition is that
    a. since price is above marginal cost, surplus is redistributed from buyers to sellers.
    b. since price is above marginal cost, some units are not produced that buyers value in excess of the cost of production and this causes a deadweight loss.
    c. monopolistically competitive firms produce beyond their efficient scale.
    d. monopolistically competitive firms earn economic profits in the long run.

11. When firms enter a monopolistically competitive market and the business-stealing externality is larger than the product-variety externality, then
    a. there are too many firms in the market and market efficiency could be increased if firms exited the market.
    b. there are too few firms in the market and market efficiency could be increased with additional entry.
    c. the number of firms in the market is optimal and the market is efficient.
    d. the only way to improve efficiency in this market is for the government to regulate it like a natural monopoly.

12. The use of the word "competition" in the name of the market structure called "monopolistic competition" refers to the fact that
    a. monopolistically competitive firms charge prices equal to the minimum of their average total cost just like competitive firms.
    b. monopolistically competitive firms face a downward-sloping demand curve just like competitive firms.
    c. the products are differentiated in a monopolistically competitive market just like in a competitive market.
    d. there are many sellers in a monopolistically competitive market and there is free entry and exit in the market just like a competitive market.

13. The use of the word "monopoly" in the name of the market structure called "monopolistic competition" refers to the fact that
    a. a monopolistically competitive firm faces a downward-sloping demand curve for its differentiated product and so does a monopolist.
    b. monopolistically competitive markets have free entry and exit just like a monopolistic market.
    c. monopolistically competitive firms charge prices equal to their marginal costs just like monopolists.
    d. monopolistically competitive firms produce beyond their efficient scale and so do monopolists.

14. Which of the following firms is most likely to spend a large percentage of their revenue on advertising?
    a. the manufacturer of an undifferentiated commodity
    b. a perfect competitor
    c. the manufacturer of an industrial product
    d. the producer of a highly differentiated consumer product
    e. the producer of a low-quality product that costs the same to produce as a similar high-quality product.

15. For the economy as a whole, what percentage of firm revenue is spent on advertising?
    a. 1 percent
    b. 2 percent
    c. 4 percent
    d. 6 percent
    e. 10 percent

16. Which of the following is *not* put forth as a criticism of advertising and brand names?
    a. Advertising manipulates people's tastes to create a desire that otherwise would not exist.
    b. Advertising increases competition, which causes unnecessary bankruptcies and layoffs.
    c. Advertising increases brand loyalty, causes demand to be more inelastic, and thus, increases markup over marginal cost.
    d. Brand names cause consumers to perceive differences between goods that do not exist.
    e. All of the above are criticisms of advertising and brand names.

17. Expensive television commercials that appear to provide no specific information about the product being advertised
    a. are most likely used by firms that are perfect competitors.
    b. should be banned by regulators because they add to the cost of the product without providing the consumer with any useful information about the product.
    c. may be useful because they provide a signal to the consumer about the quality of the product.
    d. only affect the buying habits of irrational consumers.

18. Which of the following is *not* an argument put forth by economists in support of the use of advertising?
    a. Advertising provides information to customers about prices, new products, and location of retail outlets.
    b. Advertising provides a creative outlet for artists and writers.
    c. Advertising increases competition.
    d. Advertising provides new firms with the means to attract customers from existing firms.

19. Defenders of the use of brand names argue that brand names
    a. provide information about the quality of the product.
    b. give firms incentive to maintain high quality.
    c. are useful even in socialist economies such as the former Soviet Union.
    d. do all of the above.

20. Which of the following firms has the least incentive to advertise?
    a. a manufacturer of home heating and air conditioning
    b. a manufacturer of breakfast cereal
    c. a wholesaler of crude oil
    d. a restaurant

ADVANCED CRITICAL THINKING

You are watching a sporting event on television. An advertisement featuring Tiger Woods (a famous golfer) is broadcast during a commercial break. In the ad, Tiger Woods does nothing but hit golf balls. He never speaks. There is no written copy. At the end of the advertisement, the Nike "swoosh" appears on the screen along with the words "Nike Golf." A short time earlier, you read in a newspaper that Tiger Woods received $40 million to be the spokesperson for Nike golf equipment.

1. A friend watches the Nike advertisement with you and says, "What a waste of society's resources. I didn't learn anything about Nike golf equipment from that ad. I think there should be government regulations requiring ads to be informative in some way." Explain to your friend what you did learn from Tiger Woods' presence in this ad.

_____

_____

_____

_____

_____

2. Did the use of the Nike name and the Nike "swoosh" provide any information? Explain.

_____

_____

_____

_____

3. In general, does advertising tend to decrease competition and raise prices to consumers or increase competition and reduce prices to consumers? Why?

_____

_____

_____

_____

SOLUTIONS

Terms and Definitions

_3_ Monopolistic competition

_1_ Free entry

_2_ Efficient scale

Practice Problems

1. a. monopolistically competitive—many firms, differentiated products, free entry

   b. monopoly—one firm

   c. competitive—many firms, identical products

   d. monopoly—one firm (Could be a natural monopoly because one firm can satisfy the entire market on the downward-sloping portion of its _ATC_ curve.)

   e. monopolistically competitive—many firms, differentiated products, free entry

   f. competitive—many firms, identical products

   g. monopolistically competitive—many firms, differentiated products, free entry

   h. monopolistically competitive—many firms, differentiated products, free entry

2. a. See Exhibit 5.

   b. No. Since there is free entry, profit causes firms to enter the industry, which reduces the existing demand faced by profitable firms until $P = ATC$ and profit is zero.

   c. No. Profits attract new firms, which reduces the demand for an incumbent firm's product to the point where its demand is tangent to its _ATC_ curve causing $P = ATC$ and profits equal zero. Since the tangency of demand and _ATC_ is in the negatively sloping portion of _ATC_, the firm is operating at less than the efficient scale. If Mario's expanded output,

MC would exceed MR and $P < ATC$ so profits would be negative.

   d. See Exhibit 6. The deadweight loss occurs because firms fail to produce units that the buyer values in excess of the cost of production. That is, the loss is due to the reduced quantity in monopolistic competition.

   e. See Exhibit 7. No. Profits attract entry, which reduces the demand faced by each firm to the point where it is again tangent to its _ATC_ curve.

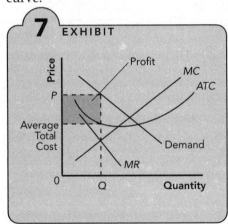

3. a. Bayer Aspirin, because it is a branded or differentiated consumer good.

   b. The firm generating high-quality ice cream because advertising is more profitable if there are repeat buyers.

   c. John Deere lawn mower division because lawn mowers are sold to consumers as opposed to industry.

   d. The bakery of Old Home Wheat Bread because it is differentiated. Wheat is not differentiated.

Short-Answer Questions

1. Both market structures involve a differentiated product so firms face downward-sloping de-

mand curves, equate *MC* and *MR*, and charge a price above *MC*.

2. Both market structures have many sellers and free entry and exit. Thus, profits are driven to zero in the long run.

3. It chooses the quantity by equating *MC* and *MR* and then uses the demand curve to find the price that is consistent with this quantity (just like a monopolist).

4. No. Profits attract new firms to the market, which reduces the demand faced by each of the incumbent firms until the demand faced by each firm is tangent to its *ATC* curve and profits are zero.

5. Monopolistic competition has excess capacity because monopolistically competitive firms produce at less than efficient scale and they charge prices in excess of marginal cost. Competitive firms produce at the efficient scale and charge prices equal to marginal cost.

6. No. Since price exceeds marginal cost, there is underproduction—some units that buyers value in excess of marginal cost are not produced. Also, the number of firms in the market may not be ideal because entry into the industry creates the positive product-variety externality and the negative business-stealing externality.

7. Advertising provides information about prices, new products, and the location of retail outlets; provides new firms with the means to attract customers from existing firms; and can be a signal of high quality. Brand names provide information about the quality of the product and provide incentive for the producer to maintain high quality.

8. The use of advertising and brand names manipulates people's tastes, impedes competition, and creates brand loyalty when there is no difference among goods. This allows for a higher markup over marginal cost and increases inefficiency.

True/False Questions

1. F; monopolistic competition is a market structure in which many firms sell differentiated products.
2. T
3. F; monopolistic competitors produce in the downward-sloping portion of their *ATC* curve where the *ATC* curve is tangent to the demand curve faced by the firm.
4. T
5. T
6. T

7. F; monopolistically competitive firms charge a price equal to *ATC*.
8. F; it is not clear how one would regulate a monopolistically competitive firm in order to increase efficiency.
9. T
10. F; advertising may increase competition, which could increase social welfare.
11. T
12. T
13. F; brand names give the firm incentive to maintain high quality.
14. T
15. F; monopolistically competitive firms have excess capacity while competitive firms produce at the efficient scale.

Multiple-Choice Questions

1. c
2. d
3. b
4. c
5. a
6. c
7. b
8. c
9. d
10. b
11. a
12. d
13. a
14. d
15. b
16. b
17. c
18. b
19. d
20. c

Advanced Critical Thinking

1. Viewers learned that Nike was willing to spend an enormous amount of money to promote their new line of golf equipment. This signals that their market research suggests that they have a high-quality product that will generate repeat sales.

2. Yes. The use of the brand name provides information that the product is of high quality and that the firm has incentive to maintain high quality. Nike is a multibillion-dollar company that would not want to risk losing existing sales

of shoes and athletic ware by marketing poor-quality golf equipment marked with the Nike brand name.

3. Advertising tends to increase competition and decrease prices to consumers because it often provides information about prices, the existence of new products, and the location of retail outlets and it provides new firms with the means to attract customers from existing firms.

The Markets for the Factors of Production

CHAPTER OVERVIEW

Context and Purpose

Chapter 18 is the first chapter in a three-chapter sequence that addresses the economics of labor markets. Chapter 18 develops and analyzes the markets for the factors of production—labor, land, and capital. Chapter 19 builds on Chapter 18 and explains in more detail why some workers earn more than do others. Chapter 20 addresses the distribution of income and the role the government can play in altering the distribution of income.

The purpose of Chapter 18 is to provide the basic theory for the analysis of factor markets—the markets for labor, land, and capital. As you might expect, we find that the wages earned by the factors of production depend on the supply and demand for the factor. What is new in our analysis is that the demand for a factor is a *derived demand*. That is, a firm's demand for a factor is determined by its decision to supply a good in another market.

Chapter Review

Introduction   The **factors of production** are the inputs used to produce goods and services. The most important inputs are labor, land, and capital. This chapter provides the basic theory for the analysis of factor markets. We will find that the supply and demand for a factor determine the wage earned by that factor. What is new in our analysis is that the demand for a factor is a *derived demand*. That is, a firm's demand for a factor is determined by its decision to supply a good in another market. In this chapter, we analyze the factor demand of competitive profit-maximizing firms.

The Demand for Labor

The wage of labor is determined by the supply and demand for labor. The demand for labor is a derived demand in that it depends on the firm's decision to supply output in another market. Suppose that a firm is *competitive* in both its output market and in the market for labor. Also, suppose that the firm is *profit-maximizing*. In order to derive the demand for labor, we first have to determine how the use of labor affects the amount of output the firm produces. A **production function** shows the relationship between the quantity of inputs used to make a good and the quantity of output of that good. Since rational decision makers think at the margin, we derive the **marginal product of labor**—the increase in the amount of output from an additional unit of labor holding all other inputs fixed—from the production function. Production functions exhibit **diminishing marginal product**, which is the property whereby the marginal product of an input declines as the quantity of the input increases.

The firm is concerned with the *value* of the output generated by each worker rather than the output itself. Thus, we calculate the **value of the marginal product**, which is the marginal product of an input times the price of the output. Another name for the value of the marginal product is *marginal revenue product*. Since the output is sold in a competitive market, the price is constant regardless of the amount produced and sold, and therefore, the *value* of the marginal product declines in concert with the decline in the marginal product as the quantity of the input increases.

Since the firm is also a competitor in the market for labor, it takes the wage as given. It is profitable for the firm to hire a worker if the value of the marginal product of that worker is greater than the wage. This analysis implies that:

- a competitive, profit-maximizing firm hires workers up to the point where the value of the marginal product of labor equals the wage, and

- the value-of-marginal-product curve *is* the labor-demand curve for a competitive, profit-maximizing firm.

Since the demand for labor is the value-of-marginal-product curve, the demand for labor shifts when the value of the marginal product of labor changes due to changes in the following:

- *The output price*: An increase in the price of output increases the value of the marginal product and shifts labor demand right.

- *Technological change*: An advance in technology typically raises the marginal product of labor and shifts labor demand right. *Labor-saving* technological change could shift labor demand left, but the evidence shows that most technological change is *labor-augmenting*, which shifts labor demand right. "Luddites" oppose technological progress because they mistakenly think it destroys jobs.

- *The supply of other factors*: An increase in the supply of a factor used with labor in production increases the marginal product of labor and shifts labor demand to the right.

For a competitive, profit-maximizing firm, the demand for a factor is closely related to its supply of output because the production function links inputs and output. If W is the wage, MC is marginal cost, and MPL is the marginal product of labor, then $MC = W/MPL$. Thus, diminishing marginal product is associated with increasing marginal cost. In terms of inputs, a profit-maximizing firm hires until the value of the marginal product of labor equals the wage or $P \times MPL = W$. Rearranging, we get $P = W/MPL$. Substituting MC for W/MPL from above, we get $P = MC$. Thus, when a competitive firm hires labor up to the point at which the value of the marginal product equals the wage, it also produces up to the point at which the price equals marginal cost.

The Supply of Labor

The supply of labor arises from individuals' trade-off between work and leisure. An upward-sloping labor-supply curve means that people respond to an increase in the wage by enjoying less leisure and working more hours. While labor supply need not be upward sloping in all cases, for now we will assume that it is upward sloping.

The following events will cause the labor-supply curve to shift:

- *Changes in tastes*: Changes in attitudes toward working such that women are more likely to work outside the home will shift the supply of labor to the right.

- *Changes in alternative opportunities*: If better opportunities arise in alternative labor markets, labor supply will decrease in the market under consideration.

- *Immigration*: When immigrants come to the United States, the U.S. supply of labor shifts to the right.

Equilibrium in the Labor Market

In competitive labor markets:

- The wage adjusts to balance the supply and demand for labor, and

- The wage equals the value of the marginal product of labor.

As a result, any event that changes the supply or demand for labor must change the equilibrium wage and the value of the marginal product by the same amount because these must always be equal.

For example, suppose that immigration causes an increase in the supply of labor (supply of labor shifts right). This reduces the equilibrium wage, increases the quantity demanded of labor because it is profitable for firms to hire additional workers, and reduces the marginal product of labor (and the value of the marginal product of labor) as the number of workers employed rises. In the new equilibrium, both the wage and the value of the marginal product of labor have fallen.

Alternatively, suppose there is an increase in the demand for the output produced by firms in an industry. This causes an increase in the price of the good and increases the *value* of the marginal product of labor. This event increases the demand for labor (rightward shift in the labor-demand curve), increases the equilibrium wage, and increases employment. Again, the value of the marginal product of labor and the wage move together (both increase in this case). When there is a change in the demand for a firm's output, the prosperity of firms and their workers moves together.

Our analysis of labor demand shows that the wage equals the value of the marginal product of labor. Therefore, highly productive workers should earn more than less productive workers. In addition, real wages should increase in relation to the increase in productivity. Statistics support this conclusion. When productivity grows quickly, real wages grow quickly. Since 1959, productivity has grown at 2.1 percent per year and real wages at 2 percent per year. Since 1995, productivity and real wages have grown at 3 percent per year. The surge in productivity in the United States since 1995 may be due to the spread of computers and information technology.

A market with only a single buyer is called a *monopsony*. When a firm is a monopsonist in a labor market, the firm uses its market power to reduce the number of workers hired, reduce the wage it pays, and increase its profits. As in monopoly, the market is smaller than is socially optimal, which causes deadweight losses.

The Other Factors of Production: Land and Capital

A firm's factors of production fall into three categories—labor, land, and capital. **Capital** is the stock of equipment and structures used to produce goods and services. The *rental price* of a factor is the price one pays to use the factor for a limited period of time while the *purchase price* of a factor is the price one pays to own that factor indefinitely.

Since the wage is the rental price of labor, we can apply the theory of factor demand we used for the labor market to the markets for land and capital. For both land and capital, the firm increases the quantity hired until the value of the factor's marginal product equals the factor's price, and thus, the demand curve for each factor is the factor's value-of-marginal-product curve. As a result, labor, land, and capital each earn the value of their marginal contribution to the production process because each factor's rental price is equal to the value of its marginal product.

Capital is often owned by firms as opposed to being owned directly by households. Therefore, capital income is often paid first to a firm. Capital income is later paid to those households that have lent money to the firm in the form of *interest* and to those households that own stock in the firm in the form of *dividends*. Alternatively, the firm retains some of its capital income to buy more capital. This portion of capital income is known as *retained earnings*. Regardless of how capital income is allocated, its total value equals the value of the marginal product of capital.

The purchase price of land and capital is based on the stream of rental income it generates. Thus, the purchase price of land or capital depends on both the current and expected future value of the marginal product of that factor.

Because of diminishing returns, a factor in abundant supply has a low marginal product and a low price while a factor in scarce supply has a high marginal product and a high price. When the supply of a factor changes, however, it has an effect on other factor markets because factors are used together in production. For example, the destruction of capital in an industry increases the rental price of the remaining capital. In the labor market, the workers are now working with less capital, which reduces their marginal product. This reduces the demand for labor and reduces the wage of workers. In a real world example, the bubonic plague reduced the labor force by one-third and increased the wage of the remaining scarce workers. This event decreased the rental price of land because the marginal product of land fell due to the reduction in workers available to farm the land.

Conclusion

The theory developed in this chapter of how labor, land, and capital are compensated is known as the *neoclassical theory of distribution*. It suggests that the amount earned by a factor depends on supply and demand and that the demand for a factor depends on its marginal productivity. In equilibrium, each factor earns the value of its marginal product. This theory is widely accepted.

Helpful Hints

1. Your text provides examples of the impact of an increase in the supply of labor and an increase in the demand for labor on the marginal product of labor and the wage. The same logic used in those examples can be applied to the cases of a decrease in the supply of labor or a decrease in the demand for labor. For example, a decrease in the supply of labor (leftward shift in the labor-supply curve) increases the equilibrium wage, decreases the quantity demanded of labor because it is profitable for firms to hire fewer workers, and increases the marginal product of labor (and the value of the marginal product of labor) as the number of workers employed decreases. In the new equilibrium, both the wage and the value of the marginal product of labor have risen. Alternatively, suppose there is a decrease in the demand for the output produced by firms in an industry. This causes a decrease in the price of the good and decreases the *value* of the marginal product of labor. This event decreases the demand for labor (leftward shift in the labor-demand curve), decreases the equilibrium wage, and decreases employment.

2. The categories of the factors of production are labor, land, and capital. In this context, land is more than just the land on which one might grow crops. Land is generally considered to be "nature's bounty" and is all forms of natural resources that have not yet been altered by people. This would include rivers, oil reserves, minerals, and land itself.

3. To see the impact of a change in the quantity employed of one factor on the earnings of a second factor, always look at the impact on the marginal product of the second factor. For example, an increase in the available capital will reduce the marginal product of capital and its rental rate. The increase in capital, however, will increase the marginal product of labor because workers have additional capital with which to work and their wages will rise accordingly.

Terms and Definitions

Choose a definition for each key term.

Key Terms

_____ Factors of production

_____ Derived demand

_____ Production function

_____ Marginal product of labor

_____ Diminishing marginal product

_____ Value of the marginal product

_____ Capital

_____ Rental price (of a factor)

Definitions

1. The property whereby the marginal product of an input declines as the quantity of the input increases

2. The equipment and structures used to produce goods and services

3. The inputs used to produce goods and services

4. The increase in the amount of output from an additional unit of labor

5. The relationship between the quantity of inputs used to make a good and the quantity of output of that good

6. The price a person pays to use a factor for a limited period of time

7. The marginal product of an input times the price of the output

8. The demand for a factor of production, which is derived from the firm's decision to supply another good

PROBLEMS AND SHORT-ANSWER QUESTIONS

Practice Problems

1. Suppose that labor is the only variable input in the production process for a competitive profit-maximizing firm that produces coffee mugs. The firm's production function is shown below.

Labor (number of workers)	Output per Hour	Marginal Product of Labor	Value of MPL when P = $3	Value of MPL when P = $5
0	0			
1	9	_____	_____	_____
2	17	_____	_____	_____
3	24	_____	_____	_____
4	30	_____	_____	_____
5	35	_____	_____	_____
6	39	_____	_____	_____
7	42	_____	_____	_____
8	44	_____	_____	_____

a. Fill out columns three and four of the table above (the marginal product of labor and the value of the marginal product of labor when the price of output equals $3 per mug).

b. Suppose that the competitive wage for workers who can make coffee mugs is $19 per hour. How many workers should this firm hire? Why?

_____

_____

c. Suppose that schools that teach pottery skills increase the supply of workers that can make coffee mugs and that this event lowers the competitive wage for coffee mug workers to $13 per hour. How many workers should this firm hire? Why? Does this represent a shift in the firm's demand for labor or a movement along the firm's demand for labor? Explain.

_____

_____

_____

_____

d. Suppose there is an increase in the demand for coffee mugs and that the price of coffee mugs rises to $5 per mug. Fill out the last column of the table above to show the value of the marginal product of labor when the price of mugs is $5 per mug.

e. Suppose that the competitive wage for coffee mug workers remains at $13 per hour and the price of mugs is $5 per mug. How many workers should this firm now hire? Why? Does this represent a shift in the firm's demand for labor or a movement along the firm's demand for labor? Explain.

_____

_____

_____

_____

2. Suppose there is an increase in the demand for lumber, which raises the price of lumber.

a. Show the impact of the increase in the price of lumber on the market for lumberjacks in Exhibit 1.

b. What did the increase in the price of lumber do to the value of the marginal product of lumberjacks and the wage of lumberjacks? Explain.

_____

_____

c. What will happen to the value of the marginal product and the rental rate for timberland and for capital that is used for cutting and shipping timber? Explain.

_____

_____

d. How has this event affected the prosperity of the firm and the owners of the factors of production employed by the firm? Explain.

_____

_____

3. Suppose that an enormous amount of forest land is cleared for agricultural use in Brazil.

   a. Show the impact of this event on the market for agricultural land in Brazil in Exhibit 2. What has happened to the marginal product of land and the rental price of land in Brazil?

   _____

   _____

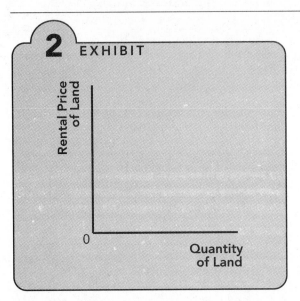

b. Show the impact of this event on the market for Brazilian farmworkers in Exhibit 3. What has happened to the marginal product of farm labor and the wage of farm labor?

   _____

   _____

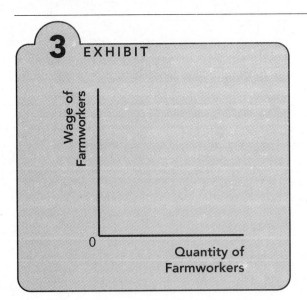

4. Describe the impact of the following events on the market for autoworkers in Tennessee. (Note that Honda operates a factory in Tennessee.)

a. Honda adds on to its factory in Tennessee.

_____

b. *Consumer Reports* declares Honda to be the best-made automobile in its class.

_____

_____

c. Refugees with manufacturing skills from war-torn Bosnia and Kosovo are relocated to Tennessee.

_____

Short-Answer Questions

1. Why is the firm's demand curve for labor the value of the marginal product of labor?

_____

_____

_____

2. Why does the firm's demand curve for labor slope downward (that is, why does it slope negatively)?

_____

_____

_____

3. Prove that when a competitive firm hires up to the point at which the value of the marginal product equals the wage, it also produces up to the point at which price equals marginal cost.

_____

_____

_____

4. Why must the equilibrium wage in the market for labor equal the value of the marginal product of labor for each firm?

_____

_____

5. Suppose there is an increase in college enrollments, which causes an increase in the demand for textbooks. What should happen in the markets for labor and capital employed in the manufacturing of textbooks? Explain.

_____

_____

6. Why does an increase in the amount of capital reduce the rental rate of capital? Why does this same event increase the wage of labor?

_____

_____

_____

7. Explain the difference between the rental price of a factor and the purchase price of a factor. How are they related?

_____

_____

_____

_____

8. When households own capital directly, capital income is in the form of rental payments to households. In what form is capital income paid when businesses own capital?

_____

_____

_____

9. What events will shift the demand for labor to the right?

_____

_____

_____

10. What events will shift the supply of labor to the right?

_____

_____

_____

SELF-TEST

True/False Questions

_____ 1. The factors of production are labor, land, and money.

_____ 2. The demand for a factor is considered to be a derived demand because it is derived from the firm's decision to supply output in another market.

_____ 3. For a competitive profit-maximizing firm, the demand curve for a factor is the value-of-the-marginal-product curve for that factor.

_____ 4. A factor exhibits diminishing marginal productivity if employing additional units of the factor reduces output.

_____ 5. If there is an increase in the equilibrium wage, there must have been an increase in the value of the marginal product of labor.

_____ 6. An increase in the demand for textbooks will increase the value of the marginal product of textbook writers.

_____ 7. A decrease in the supply of labor reduces the value of the marginal product of labor, decreases the wage, and decreases employment.

_____ 8. The only way for the value of the marginal product of a factor to rise is for the price of the output produced by the factor to rise.

_____ 9. An increase in the demand for pencils will likely improve the fortunes of both the pencil factory and the workers in the pencil factory.

_____ 10. The demand for labor is downward sloping because the production function exhibits diminishing marginal productivity of labor.

_____ 11. In equilibrium, when a competitive firm hires labor up to the point at which the value of the marginal product of labor equals the wage, it also produces up to the point at which the price equals marginal cost.

_____ 12. An increase in the supply of capital will increase the marginal product of capital and the rental rate of capital.

_____ 13. If capital is owned by firms as opposed to being owned directly by households, then capital income will be in the form of stocks, bonds, and retained interest.

_____ 14. The value of the marginal product of land is the marginal product of land multiplied by the price of the output produced on the land.

_____ 15. An increase in the supply of capital decreases the value of the marginal product of capital, reduces the rental rate of capital, and decreases the value of the marginal product of labor, which reduces the wage of labor.

Multiple-Choice Questions

1. The most important factors of production are
   a. money, stocks, and bonds.
   b. water, earth, and knowledge.
   c. management, finance, and marketing.
   d. labor, land, and capital.

2. If a factor exhibits diminishing marginal product, hiring additional units of the factor will
   a. generate ever smaller amounts of output.
   b. cause a reduction in output.
   c. have no effect on output.
   d. increase the marginal product of the factor.

Use the following table to answer questions 3 through 5.

Labor (number of workers)	Output per Hour	Marginal Product of Labor	Value of the MPL
0	0		
1	5		
2	9		
3	12		
4	14		
5	15		

3. What is the marginal product of labor as the firm moves from using three workers to using four workers?
   a. 0
   b. 2
   c. 12
   d. 14
   e. None of the above is correct.

4. If the price of output is $4 per unit, what is the value of the marginal product of labor as the firm moves from using four workers to using five workers?
   a. $4
   b. $8
   c. $12
   d. $56
   e. $60

5. If this profit-maximizing firm sells its output in a competitive market for $3 per unit and hires labor in a competitive market for $8 per hour, then this firm should hire
   a. one worker.
   b. two workers.
   c. three workers.
   d. four workers.
   e. five workers.

6. The value of the marginal product of labor is
   a. the price of the output times the wage of labor.
   b. the wage of labor times the quantity of labor.
   c. the price of the output times the marginal product of labor.
   d. the wage of labor times the marginal product of labor.
   e. none of the above.

7. For a competitive, profit-maximizing firm, the value-of-the-marginal-product curve for capital is the firm's
   a. production function.
   b. marginal-cost curve.
   c. supply curve of capital.
   d. demand curve for capital.

8. An increase in the supply of labor
   a. increases the value of the marginal product of labor and increases the wage.
   b. decreases the value of the marginal product of labor and decreases the wage.
   c. increases the value of the marginal product of labor and decreases the wage.
   d. decreases the value of the marginal product of labor and increases the wage.

9. A decrease in the demand for fish
   a. decreases the value of the marginal product of fishermen, reduces their wage, and reduces employment in the fishing industry.
   b. increases the value of the marginal product of fishermen, increases their wage, and increases employment in the fishing industry.
   c. decreases the value of the marginal product of fishermen, reduces their wage, and increases employment in the fishing industry.
   d. increases the value of the marginal product of fishermen, increases their wage, and decreases employment in the fishing industry.

10. What will a decrease in the supply of fishermen do to the market for capital employed in the fishing industry?
   a. increase the demand for fishing boats and increase rental rates on fishing boats
   b. decrease the demand for fishing boats and decrease rental rates on fishing boats
   c. increase the demand for fishing boats and decrease rental rates on fishing boats
   d. decrease the demand for fishing boats and increase rental rates on fishing boats

11. An increase in the demand for apples will cause all but which of the following?
   a. an increase in the price of apples
   b. an increase in the value of the marginal product of apple pickers
   c. an increase in the wage of apple pickers
   d. a decrease in the number of apple pickers employed

12. A decrease in the supply of farm tractors will cause all but which of the following?
   a. an increase in the rental rate for tractors
   b. an increase in the value of the marginal product of tractors
   c. an increase in the wage of farmworkers
   d. a decrease in the rental rate of farmland

13. If both input and output markets are competitive and firms are profit maximizing, then in equilibrium, each factor of production earns
   a. an equal share of output.
   b. the value of its marginal product.
   c. the amount allocated by the political process.
   d. an amount equal to the price of output times total output.

14. An individual firm's demand for a factor of production
    a. slopes downward due to the factor's diminishing marginal product.
    b. slopes downward because an increase in the production of output reduces the price at which the output can be sold in a competitive market, thereby reducing the value of the marginal product as more of the factor is used.
    c. slopes upward due to the factor's increasing marginal product.
    d. is perfectly elastic (horizontal) if the factor market is perfectly competitive.

15. An increase in the demand for a firm's output
    a. increases the prosperity of the firm but decreases the prosperity of the factors hired by the firm.
    b. decreases the prosperity of the firm but increases the prosperity of the factors hired by the firm.
    c. increases the prosperity of both the firm and the factors hired by the firm.
    d. decreases the prosperity of both the firm and the factors hired by the firm.

16. A competitive, profit-maximizing firm should hire workers up to the point where
    a. the wage, the rental price of capital, and the rental price of land are all equal.
    b. the marginal product of labor equals zero and the production function is maximized.
    c. the marginal product of labor equals the wage.
    d. the value of the marginal product of labor equals the wage.

17. Which of the following is not true with regard to workers who have a high value of marginal product? These workers
    a. are usually highly paid.
    b. usually have little capital with which to work.
    c. have skills that are in relatively scarce supply.
    d. produce output for which there is great demand.

18. An increase in the price of automobiles shifts the demand for autoworkers to the
    a. right and increases the wage.
    b. left and decreases the wage.
    c. right and decreases the wage.
    d. left and increases the wage.

19. When capital is owned by the firm as opposed to being directly owned by households, capital income may take any of the following forms except
    a. retained earnings.
    b. interest.
    c. dividends.
    d. stock.

20. Suppose that a war is fought with biological weapons. The weapons destroy people but not capital. What is likely to happen to equilibrium wages and rental rates after the war when compared to their values before the war?
    a. Wages rise and rental rates rise.
    b. Wages fall and rental rates fall.
    c. Wages rise and rental rates fall.
    d. Wages fall and rental rates rise.

ADVANCED CRITICAL THINKING

You are watching a debate about immigration on public television with a friend. The participants represent two camps—organized labor and corporate industry. Organized labor argues against open immigration while U.S. industry argues in favor of more open immigration. Your friend says, "I can't believe that these two groups can't get together on this issue. Both firms and workers join forces to produce our industrial output. I would think that their interests would be similar. Maybe a better arbitrator could help these groups find a position on immigration that would satisfy both groups."

1. If there were open immigration, what would happen to the value of the marginal product of labor and the wage?

_____

2. If there were open immigration, what would happen to the value of the marginal product of capital and land and their rental rates?

_____

3. Are the positions that each group takes on immigration consistent with their interests? Explain. Is there likely to be a solution that satisfies both?

_____

_____

_____

_____

SOLUTIONS

Terms and Definitions

_3_ Factors of production

_8_ Derived demand

_5_ Production function

_4_ Marginal product of labor

_1_ Diminishing marginal product

_7_ Value of the marginal product

_2_ Capital

_6_ Rental price (of a factor)

Practice Problems

1. a.

Labor (number of workers)	Output per Hour	Marginal Product of Labor	Value of MPL when P = $3	Value of MPL when P = $5
0	0			
		9	$27	$45
1	9			
		8	24	40
2	17			
		7	21	35
3	24			
		6	18	30
4	30			
		5	15	25
5	35			
		4	12	20
6	39			
		3	9	15
7	42			
		2	6	10
8	44			

b. Three workers because the value of the marginal product of each of the first three workers exceeds the $19 wage, so each worker adds to profits but the fourth worker only has a value of marginal product of $18 so hiring the fourth worker would reduce profits.

c. Five workers because the value of the marginal product of each of the first five workers now exceeds the $13 wage, but the sixth worker only has a value of marginal product of $12 so hiring the sixth worker would reduce profits. This is a movement along the firm's demand curve for labor because the value of the marginal product of labor for each worker is remaining the same but the wage facing the firm has changed.

d. See the fifth column in the table in part *a* above.

e. Seven workers because the value of the marginal product of each of the first seven workers exceeds the $13 wage, but the eighth worker only has a value of marginal product of $10 so it would be unprofitable to hire that worker. This is a shift in the demand curve for labor because the value of the marginal product of labor has increased for each worker because the price of output rose. Thus, the firm demands more workers at the same $13 wage.

2. a. See Exhibit 4.

b. Increase the value of the marginal product of labor and the wage.

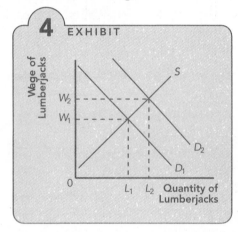

4 EXHIBIT

c. When the price of output rises, the value of the marginal product of all of the inputs increases accordingly. Thus, the value of the marginal product of both land and capital will rise and so will their rental rates.

d. When the price of output changes, the prosperity of the firm and the inputs move together. In this case, the prosperity of the firm and the inputs are increased.

3. a. See Exhibit 5. This event increases the supply of agricultural land and decreases the

5 EXHIBIT

marginal product of land and the rental price of land.

b. See Exhibit 6. The increase in the supply of agricultural land increases the marginal product of labor and shifts the demand for farm labor to the right which increases the wage.

6   EXHIBIT

4. a. The increase in capital available for workers increases the marginal product of labor, shifts the demand for labor to the right, and increases the wage.

b. This event increases the demand for Hondas and increases the price of Hondas. The increase in the price of Hondas increases the value of the marginal product of labor, shifts the demand for labor to the right, and increases the wage.

c. This event increases the supply of labor, decreases the marginal product of labor, and decreases the wage.

Short-Answer Questions

1. The profit-maximizing firm will hire workers up to the point where the value of the marginal product of labor is equal to the wage. Beyond that point, additional workers cost more than the value of their marginal product and their employment would reduce profit. Since the value-of-the-marginal-product curve determines how many workers the firm will hire at each wage, it *is* the demand curve for labor.

2. The marginal product of labor is diminishing as more labor is added to the production process. Since the price of output is given in a competitive market, it follows that the *value* of the marginal product also declines as the quantity of labor is increased.

3. Given: $MC = W/MPL$. If the firm hires up to the point where the wage equals the value of

the marginal product, then $P \times MPL = W$, or $P = W/MPL$. Substituting MC for W/MPL, we get $P = MC$.

4. The equilibrium wage is determined by supply and demand for labor in the market for labor. Each firm then hires workers up to the point where that wage equals the value of the marginal product of labor in each firm.

5. The value of the marginal product of both labor and capital employed in the production of textbooks should rise because the price of the output produced by them has risen. Therefore, the wage and rental rate paid to each should also rise.

6. Since there is a declining marginal product of capital as more capital is used, an increase in capital reduces the marginal product of capital and its rental rate. The increase in capital, however, increases the marginal product of labor and increases its wage.

7. The rental price is the price one pays to use the factor for a limited period of time while the purchase price of a factor is the price one pays to own that factor indefinitely. The purchase price of a factor depends on the current and expected future value of the marginal product of the factor.

8. Interest, dividends, and retained earnings.

9. An increase in the price of output produced by labor, an advance in labor-augmenting technology used in production, and an increase in the supply of factors used with labor in production.

10. A shift in tastes toward working outside the home, a reduction in alternative opportunities for employment, and immigration.

True/False Questions

1. F; the factors are labor, land, and capital.

2. T

3. T

4. F; a factor exhibits diminishing marginal productivity if the increase in output generated from an additional unit of input diminishes as the quantity of the input increases.

5. T

6. T

7. F; a decrease in the supply of labor increases the value of the marginal product of labor, increases the wage, and decreases employment.

8. F; the marginal product of the factor could rise from a reduction in the supply of the factor

(more scarce) or from an increase in the productivity of that factor.

9. T
10. T
11. T
12. F; an increase in the supply of capital will decrease the value of the marginal product of capital and decrease the rental rate.
13. F; capital income will be in the form of interest, dividends, and retained earnings.
14. T
15. F; it increases the value of the marginal product of labor and the wage.

Multiple-Choice Questions

1. d
2. a
3. b
4. a
5. c
6. c
7. d
8. b
9. a
10. b
11. d
12. c
13. b
14. a
15. c
16. d
17. b
18. a
19. d
20. c

Advanced Critical Thinking

1. Labor would be less scarce so the value of the marginal product of labor would decrease and so would the wage.
2. Additional labor could be applied to capital and land, which would increase the value of the marginal product of capital and land and increase their rental rates.
3. Yes. Organized labor wishes to keep the wage of labor high so they hope to restrict immigration. Corporate interests wish to raise the return to capital and land so it hopes to allow open immigration. No.

19

Earnings and Discrimination

GOALS

In this chapter you will

- Examine how wages compensate for differences in job characteristics
- Learn and compare the human-capital and signaling theories of education
- Examine why in some occupations a few superstars earn tremendous incomes
- Learn why wages rise above the level that balances supply and demand
- Consider why it is difficult to measure the impact of discrimination on wages
- See when market forces can and cannot provide a natural remedy for discrimination

OUTCOMES

After accomplishing these goals, you should be able to

- Explain why an economics professor earns less than a corporate economist of similar age, background, and training
- Explain the differing impact of policies aimed at increasing the educational attainment of all workers under the signaling and the human-capital view of education
- List the characteristics of a market where superstars can arise
- List three reasons why a wage can rise above the equilibrium wage
- Explain why differences in wages among groups does not by itself say anything about how much discrimination there is in the labor market
- Explain why competitive employers are unlikely to discriminate against groups of employees unless the customers or the government demands it

CHAPTER OVERVIEW

Context and Purpose

Chapter 19 is the second chapter in a three-chapter sequence that addresses the economics of labor markets. Chapter 18 developed the markets for the factors of production. Chapter 19 goes beyond the supply-and-demand models developed in Chapter 18 to help explain the wide variation in wages we find in the economy. Chapter 20 addresses the distribution of income and the role the government can play in altering the distribution of income.

The purpose of Chapter 19 is to extend the basic neoclassical theory of the labor market that we developed in Chapter 18. Neoclassical theory argues that wages depend on the supply and demand for labor and that labor demand depends on the value of the marginal productivity of labor. To address the wide variation in the wages that we observe, we must examine more precisely what determines the supply and demand for various types of labor.

Chapter Review

Introduction   Chapter 19 extends the basic neoclassical theory of the labor market that we developed in Chapter 18. Neoclassical theory argues that wages depend on the supply and demand for labor and that labor demand depends on the value of the marginal productivity of labor. To address the wide variation in the wages that we observe, Chapter 19 examines more precisely what determines the supply and demand for various types of labor.

Some Determinants of Equilibrium Wages

Workers differ from one another. Jobs also differ in terms of the wages they pay and their nonmonetary characteristics. These differences affect labor supply, labor demand, and equilibrium wages.

Some jobs are easy, fun, and safe while others are hard, dull, and dangerous. If the wages were the same, most people would prefer to do easy, fun, and safe jobs. Therefore, workers require a higher wage in order to be induced to do a hard, dull, and dangerous job. A **compensating differential** is the difference in wages that arises to offset the nonmonetary characteristics of different jobs. For example, people who work in coal mines or on the night shift receive a compensating differential to compensate for the disagreeable nature of their work.

Capital is a factor of production that itself has been produced. Capital includes the economy's accumulation of equipment and structures and also includes a less tangible form of capital known as human capital. **Human capital** is the accumulation of investments in people, such as education and on-the-job training. Workers with more human capital earn more than those with less for the following reasons: With regard to labor demand, educated workers have a higher marginal product, so firms are willing to pay more for them. With regard to labor supply, workers are only willing to educate themselves if they are rewarded for doing so. In effect, there is a compensating differential between educated and uneducated workers to compensate for the cost of becoming educated. In 1980, male college graduates earned 44 percent more than workers with a high school diploma. By 2003, the difference was 82 percent. For women, the differential rose from 35 percent to 72 percent. There are two hypotheses that may explain the increased differential. First, the growth in international trade has allowed the United States to import goods made by unskilled workers in foreign countries where unskilled workers are plentiful and export goods produced by skilled labor. In the domestic economy, this increases the demand for skilled workers and decreases the demand for unskilled workers. Second, increases in technology have increased the demand for skilled workers and decreased the demand for unskilled workers. Both hypotheses may be true. People gain more than just human capital when they go to college. The greater an individual's educational attainment, the greater the individual's overall satisfaction with life, including satisfaction with one's love life.

Natural ability, effort, and chance help explain wages. Some people are smarter and stronger than others and they are paid for their natural ability. Some people work harder than others and are compensated for their effort. Chance plays a role in that someone's education and experience can be made valueless if there is a change in technology that eliminates that person's job. Beauty may be a natural ability because attractiveness may make an actor or waiter more productive. It may also be a sign of an intelligent person who expends effort to successfully appear attractive and this may suggest that the individual may be successful at other things, too. Alternatively, a wage premium for beauty may simply be a type of discrimination. Attractive people do earn a premium over less attractive people.

The human-capital view of education argues that workers with more education are paid more because the education made them more productive. As an alternative, the *signaling* view of education argues that firms use education as a method of sorting high-ability workers from low-ability workers. Educational attainment signals high ability because it is easier for high-ability people to earn a college degree than it is for low-ability people, and firms are willing to pay more for high-ability people. Just as with the signaling theory of advertising where the advertisement itself contains no real information, the signaling theory of education suggests that schooling has no real productivity benefit. According to the human-capital view of education, a policy of increasing educational attainment for all workers should raise all workers' wages. According to the signaling view of education, additional education would not affect productivity or wages. The benefits of education are probably a combination of both human-capital and signaling effects.

A few superstars earn astronomical salaries. These superstars are often performers such as athletes, actors, writers, and so on. Superstars arise in markets that have two characteristics:

- Every customer in the market wants to enjoy the good supplied by the best producer.

- The good is produced with a technology that makes it possible for the best producer to supply every customer at low cost.

So far, we have addressed why workers might earn different equilibrium wages. Some workers, however, may earn higher wages because their wages are held above equilibrium due to the following:

- *Minimum-wage laws.* This mostly affects less-experienced and less-skilled workers.

- *The market power of labor unions.* A **union** is a worker association that bargains with employers over wages and working conditions. The union can hold wages 10 to 20 percent above equilibrium because they can threaten to **strike** or withhold labor from the firm.

- *Efficiency wages.* **Efficiency wages** occur when firms choose to hold wages above equilibrium to increase productivity because high wages reduce worker turnover, increase worker effort, and raise the quality of workers that apply for jobs at the firm.

Whenever the wage is held above equilibrium, the result is unemployment.

The Economics of Discrimination

Wages can differ due to discrimination. **Discrimination** is the offering of different opportunities to similar individuals who differ only by race, ethnic group, sex, age, or other personal characteristics. Discrimination is an emotional issue.

Wages differ across races and sexes for a number of reasons. Whites have more human capital on average than blacks due to more years of schooling and better schools. Men generally have more years of education and more job experience than women. In school, women may have been directed away from science and math courses. Men may also receive a compensating differential for doing more unpleasant jobs than women choose to do. While some of the wage differentials are likely to be due to discrimination, there is no agreement with regard to how much. Economists would agree that *because the differences in average wages among groups in part reflect differences in human capital and job characteristics, they do not by themselves say anything about how much discrimination there is in the labor market*.

A recent study suggests that job candidates with names common in the African-American community receive less interest from employers than candidates with names common in the white community.

While it is difficult to measure discrimination, suppose we have evidence that there is discrimination in the labor market. If some employers discriminate against certain groups of employees, then the demand for the services of those that are discriminated against will be low and their wages will be low while the demand for those workers not discriminated against will be high and their wages will be high. In a competitive market, employers that discriminate against certain groups of employees will be at a competitive disadvantage because their labor costs will be higher. Firms that care only about profits and do not discriminate will tend to replace those that do discriminate because they will be more profitable. The firms that do not discriminate will increase the demand for the labor services of the group that was discriminated against, decrease the demand for the group not discriminated against, and the wages will be equalized across groups. Thus, competitive markets can be a cure for employer discrimination.

If customers or governments demand discrimination, however, then competition and the profit motive of firms may not correct the wage differential. If bigoted customers are willing to pay extra to be served by a certain group in a restaurant and are not willing to be served by another group, then the wage differential can persist even in a competitive market. If the government mandates discriminatory practices, then competition will again fail to equalize a discriminatory wage differential. There is evidence that, in some professional sports, white athletes are paid more than black athletes of comparable ability and that attendance is greater for teams with a greater proportion of white players. This suggests that sports fans are willing to pay a premium to watch white players. Since black players are less profitable, this wage differential can persist even if owners care only about profits. If a wage differential persists in a competitive market, it is because bigoted customers are willing to pay for it or because the government requires it. The wage differential cannot be maintained by a bigoted employer alone.

Conclusion

In competitive markets, workers earn a wage equal to the value of their marginal product. The workers' value of marginal product is higher if they are more talented, diligent, experienced, and educated. Firms pay less to those workers against whom customers discriminate because they are less profitable to the firm.

Helpful Hints

1. The wage is explained by supply and demand. Characteristics of both people and jobs affect supply, demand, and the wage for labor in each labor market. For example, education, experience, and hard work increase the value of the marginal productivity of workers, increase the demand for their services, and increase their wage. An increase in the disagreeable nature of the work, the expense of training, and the required ability to do the job reduce the pool of workers willing and able to do a particular job, reduce the supply of labor in that market, and increase the wage. Even the market for superstars can be explained with supply and demand. Since superstars can satisfy every customer at the same time through television, movies, music CDs, and so on, the value of their marginal product is enormous and so is the demand for their services.

2. Different pay for different groups of people is not, by itself, evidence of labor market discrimination because differences in pay among groups in part reflects differences in human capital and job characteristics. What seems to be discrimination may simply be a compensating differential that is paid for the disagreeable nature of a job. In addition, a wage differential could be due to a difference in the average productivity across groups of workers.

Terms and Definitions

Choose a definition for each key term.

Key Terms

_____ Compensating differential

_____ Human capital

_____ Union

_____ Strike

_____ Efficiency wages

_____ Discrimination

Definitions

1. The offering of different opportunities to similar individuals who differ only by race, ethnic group, sex, age, or other personal characteristics

2. A difference in wages that arises to offset the nonmonetary characteristics of different jobs

3. The organized withdrawal of labor from a firm by a union

4. The accumulation of investments in people, such as education and on-the-job training

5. Above-equilibrium wages paid by firms in order to increase worker productivity

6. A worker association that bargains with employers over wages and working conditions

PROBLEMS AND SHORT-ANSWER QUESTIONS

Practice Problems

1. Within each of the following pairs of workers, which worker is likely to earn more and why? (It may be obvious which one is paid more. The real issue is to explain why one is paid more than the other.)
    a. a carpenter working at the top of a 600-foot cooling tower of a nuclear power plant or a carpenter who frames houses

    _____

    _____

b. a clerk in a grocery store or a lawyer

_____

_____

c. a lawyer with one year of experience or a lawyer with six years of experience

_____

_____

d. an attractive salesperson or a homely salesperson

_____

_____

e. an autoworker in a factory who works the day shift or an autoworker in a factory who works the night shift

_____

_____

f. an economics professor or a corporate economist

_____

_____

g. a history professor or an economics professor

_____

_____

h. someone trained as a keypunch operator (typist who types input commands on cards to be read by a mainframe computer prior to the existence of computer terminals) or someone trained as a personal computer specialist

_____

_____

i. your favorite local blues band that plays regularly at a nearby campus bar or David Bowie

_____

_____

j. a lazy, stupid plumber or a hardworking, bright plumber

_____

_____

k. the best carpenter on the planet or the best writer on the planet

_____

_____

2. a. Explain the human-capital view of education and the signaling view of education.

    _____

    _____

    b. What are the implications for education policy under each view?

    _____

    _____

    c. Which of the above is true? Explain.

    _____

    _____

3. a. How can a competitive market eliminate discrimination in the labor market?

    _____

    _____

    _____

    b. What limits a competitive market's ability to reduce discrimination? Explain.

    _____

    _____

    _____

Short-Answer Questions

1. Why does someone who has a great amount of human capital that was acquired through education earn more than someone with a small amount of human capital?

    _____

    _____

2. Name some characteristics of a job that might require a positive compensating differential.

    _____

    _____

3. What has happened to the relative wages of skilled and unskilled workers in the United States over the last 20 years? Why?

    _____

    _____

    _____

4. What are the necessary conditions for a superstar to arise in a market? Explain.

    _____

    _____

    _____

5. Does a difference in average wages among groups, by itself, suggest that there is discrimination in the labor market? Explain.

    _____

    _____

    _____

6. If a discriminatory wage differential persists in a competitive market, is it due to discrimination on the part of the employer or must it be from some other source? Explain.

    _____

    _____

    _____

7. Is there discrimination in professional sports? Is the employer the source of the discrimination? Explain.

    _____

    _____

    _____

    _____

8. List the professions of most superstars. What do these professions have in common?

    _____

    _____

    _____

9. Why is a plumber's apprentice paid less than a master plumber?

    _____

    _____

10. Provide three reasons why wages might be set above the equilibrium wage. Explain.

    _____

    _____

    _____

    _____

SELF-TEST

True/False Questions

_____ 1. A compensating differential is the difference in wages paid to workers who are discriminated against and those who are not discriminated against.

_____ 2. Workers on the night shift receive a compensating differential to offset the disagreeable nature of working at night.

_____ 3. In the last 20 years in the United States, the gap between the wages of unskilled workers and skilled workers has been closing.

_____ 4. Firms are willing to pay more for workers with greater human capital because workers with greater human capital have a greater value of marginal product.

_____ 5. Human capital is increased by education and on-the-job training.

_____ 6. An apprentice will work for a relatively low wage because some of the apprentice's pay is in terms of on-the-job training.

_____ 7. Some superstars can earn astronomical salaries because, in some markets, everyone wants the good supplied by the best producer and technology has made it possible for the best producer to satisfy every customer at low cost.

_____ 8. If the signaling view of education is true, a policy of increasing the education of workers will increase the wages of all workers.

_____ 9. The evidence that attractive people are paid more than unattractive people clearly demonstrates that the labor market discriminates against unattractive people.

_____ 10. Ability, effort, and chance must play an important role in wage determination since less than half of the variation in wages can be explained by workers' education, experience, age, and job characteristics.

_____ 11. If a company in a competitive market persistently pays a discriminatory wage to a certain group, it must be because the employer is a bigot.

_____ 12. If there is a difference in wages among groups, it is evidence that there is discrimination in the labor market.

_____ 13. If it were not for minimum-wage laws, workers would always be paid the equilibrium wage.

_____ 14. Competition will tend to eliminate discrimination in the labor market if customers are not bigoted and if government does not require discrimination.

_____ 15. At least some of the differences in pay between men and women can be explained by the fact that, on average, men have attained more and better schooling, have more job experience, and may do more unpleasant jobs.

Multiple-Choice Questions

1. If a person who works in a coal mine gets paid more than a person with a similar background and skills who works in a safer job, then
   a. we have evidence of discrimination against workers outside the coal mine.
   b. we have observed a compensating differential.
   c. coal miners must have greater human capital than others.
   d. coal miners must be more attractive than other workers.

2. According to the human-capital view of education, education
    a. increases human capital and the wages of workers.
    b. only helps firms sort workers into high-ability and low-ability workers.
    c. has no impact on the human capital of workers.
    d. can make any worker into a superstar.

3. Which of the following is not part of a worker's human capital?
    a. education
    b. on-the-job training
    c. experience
    d. effort
    e. All of the above are parts of a worker's human capital.

4. According to the signaling view of education, education
    a. increases human capital and the wages of workers.
    b. only helps firms sort workers into high-ability and low-ability workers.
    c. reduces the wage gap between high-skilled and low-skilled workers.
    d. can make any worker into a superstar.

5. All of the following would tend to increase a worker's wage except
    a. more education.
    b. working the night shift.
    c. doing a job that is fun.
    d. having a greater amount of natural ability.
    e. working harder.

6. In a competitive market, which of the following is least likely to be the source of a persistent discriminatory wage differential?
    a. the customer
    b. the government
    c. the employer
    d. All of the above could be the source of a persistent discriminatory wage differential.

7. If two jobs require the same amount of skills and experience, the job that pays the most is most likely to be the one that is
    a. unpleasant.
    b. safe.
    c. easy.
    d. fun.
    e. all of the above.

8. In the last 20 years, the gap between the wages of skilled and unskilled workers in the United States has
    a. decreased.
    b. increased.
    c. stayed the same.
    d. first increased and is now decreasing.

9. Which of the following is true regarding the earnings of attractive versus unattractive workers?
    a. Attractive people tend to earn less because attractive people are viewed as shallow and more self-absorbed and, therefore, as less productive.
    b. Attractive people tend to earn less because attractive people usually have less human capital.
    c. Attractive people tend to earn more because they may actually have a larger value of marginal product.
    d. Attractive people tend to earn more because attractive people usually have greater human capital.

10. The relative wage of unskilled workers has fallen in the United States likely as a result of a relative
    a. increase in the number of unskilled workers available because workers are more poorly educated.
    b. increase in the number of unskilled workers available due to immigration into the United States.
    c. decrease in the demand for unskilled workers because workers are more poorly educated.
    d. decrease in the demand for unskilled workers because of increases in technology and increases in international trade.

11. Which of the following professionals is most likely to be able to generate the income of a superstar?
    a. the best medical doctor
    b. the best professor
    c. the best accountant
    d. the best writer
    e. All of the above participate in markets that could generate a superstar.

12. It is *not* considered discrimination when an employer offers different opportunities to individuals that differ only by their
    a. race.
    b. sex.
    c. productivity.
    d. age.

13. In order for a market to support superstars, it must have which of the following characteristics?
    a. It must be involved in professional athletics.
    b. Every customer must want the good supplied by the best producer, and the technology must exist for the best producer to supply every customer at low cost.
    c. Every customer must be willing to pay an enormous amount for the product, and the product must be a necessity.
    d. Every customer must be indifferent to the price they pay, and the seller must be a competitor in the market for the product.

14. Which of the following statements regarding discrimination is true?
    a. Discrimination cannot exist in a competitive labor market.
    b. Discrimination can only persist in a competitive labor market if customers are willing to pay to maintain the discriminatory practice or the government requires discrimination.
    c. Bigoted employers are the main source of a persistent discriminatory wage differential in a competitive market.
    d. The existence of a wage differential among groups is strong evidence of discrimination in the labor market.

15. Competitive markets tend to
    a. reduce labor market discrimination because nondiscriminating firms will employ cheaper labor, earn more profits, and drive discriminating firms out of the market.
    b. have no impact on labor market discrimination.
    c. increase labor market discrimination because bigoted employers can charge any price they want in a competitive market to cover the cost of their discrimination.
    d. increase labor market discrimination because some workers can charge more for their services than other workers in a competitive market.

16. A wage differential among groups may not by itself be evidence of discrimination in the labor market because different groups have
     a. different levels of education.
     b. different preferences for the type of work they are willing to do.
     c. different levels of job experience.
     d. all of the above.

17. Which of the following is *not* a reason why some workers are paid above the equilibrium wage?
     a. minimum-wage laws
     b. beauty
     c. unions
     d. efficiency wages

18. Which of the following is likely to generate a compensating differential?
     a. One employee is more attractive than another.
     b. One employee works harder than another.
     c. One employee is willing to work the night shift while another is not.
     d. One employee is more educated than another.
     e. All of the above generate compensating differentials.

19. Which of the following explanations of wage differentials is *not* likely to be true?
     a. Men have more human capital than women.
     b. Whites have more human capital than blacks.
     c. Employers in competitive markets are bigots.
     d. Men have more job experience than women.

20. Which of the following could result in women being paid less than men?
     a. customers preferring to deal with men
     b. women preferring to work in pleasant, clean, safe, workplaces
     c. women entering and leaving the labor force to care for children
     d. women obtaining less human capital because they don't plan to work continuously to the age of retirement
     e. all of the above

ADVANCED CRITICAL THINKING

You are at a political rally with some friends. A candidate for state office states that working women earn about 60 cents for each dollar that working men earn. The candidate says, "This is clearly evidence that employers discriminate against women. This gap between the earnings of men and women will never close because professions women tend to choose are traditionally low-paying and the professions men choose are traditionally high-paying. I will propose that the government create a panel to decide what jobs should pay so that people of similar skills and education earn the same amount."

1. Suppose a secretary and a truck driver are judged to require the same level of education and skills, yet a secretary earns $30,000 while a truck driver earns $40,000. What would happen to the quantities supplied and demanded in the market for secretaries and truck drivers if the wage for these professions were set by law at $35,000?

_____

_____

_____

_____

2. What would happen to the level of effort and natural ability of the workers available in each market in question 1? What would happen to the quality of work generated in each market?

_____

_____

_____

_____

3. Suppose it is true that the skills and education required to do each job in question 1 are, in fact, nearly identical. What explanation would an economist likely propose to explain why the equilibrium wage differs by $10,000 across these markets?

_____

_____

_____

_____

SOLUTIONS

Terms and Definitions

_2_ Compensating differential

_4_ Human capital

_6_ Union

_3_ Strike

_5_ Efficiency wages

_1_ Discrimination

Practice Problems

1. a. The carpenter working at the 600-foot height because he/she will likely require a compensating differential for the danger of the job.

   b. A lawyer because the lawyer has greater human capital from years of education and the lawyer requires a compensating differential to compensate for the cost and effort of becoming educated.

   c. A lawyer with six years of experience because work experience is part of human capital.

   d. An attractive salesperson because they may have a higher value of marginal product due to being attractive or because they have signaled that they may be successful at a variety of things when they succeeded at the task of making themselves look attractive. Alternatively, it may be due to discrimination against homely people.

   e. The night-shift worker because the night shift is disagreeable and the worker requires a compensating differential.

   f. The corporate economist because the corporate economist requires a compensating differential to compensate for the disagreeable nature of the work. Also, the corporate economist may have a greater value of marginal product.

   g. An economics professor because the market wage for economists is higher due to the economist's higher value of marginal product in the corporate labor market.

   h. A personal computer specialist because, through chance, technology has changed such that keypunch operators are no longer needed while PC specialists are needed.

   i. Superstar David Bowie because through technology he is able to satisfy the entire market at the same time. (He is the first rock star to have a net worth in excess of one billion dollars.)

   j. The hardworking, bright plumber because the value of the marginal product is higher for people with ability and who work hard.

   k. The best writer because the writer is in a market that can support a superstar while the carpenter is not.

2. a. Education increases human capital and raises the value of the marginal product of labor and, thus, the wage. Alternatively, education is only a signal of high ability.

   b. According to the human-capital view, policies that increase educational attainment for all will increase all wages. According to the signaling view, an increase in educational attainment will not affect wages because education does not increase productivity.

   c. Probably both are true. It is unclear regarding the relative sizes of these two effects.

3. a. Firms only interested in profit will hire the group of workers that is discriminated against. Since their wages are relatively low, the firms that do not discriminate will have a competitive advantage over the discriminatory firms. As the nondiscriminating firms replace the discriminatory firms, the relative demand for workers previously discriminated against will increase, which will remove the discriminatory wage differential.

   b. If bigoted customers are willing to pay higher prices to firms that discriminate, or if the government requires discrimination, the competitive market cannot eliminate discrimination.

Short-Answer Questions

1. Because workers with greater human capital are more productive and firms are willing to pay more for workers with a greater value of marginal product. In addition, workers must be compensated for the cost of educating themselves.

2. A compensating differential is paid for the disagreeable, unpleasant nature of a job. Other things being equal, jobs will pay more if they are dirty, noisy, smelly, solitary, unsafe, hard, require travel, require working odd hours such as the night shift or swing shift, require working with unpleasant people, etc.

3. The gap between skilled and unskilled wages has risen, possibly because the growth in international trade has allowed the United States to import goods made by unskilled workers in countries where unskilled labor is plentiful and export goods made by skilled workers. This

would increase the relative demand for skilled workers. Or it could be that increases in technology have increased the relative demand for skilled workers.

4. Every customer in the market wants to enjoy the good supplied by the best producer and the good is produced with a technology that makes it possible for the best producer to supply every customer at low cost.

5. No. Since average wages among groups are in part based on differences in human capital and job characteristics, a wage differential among groups alone tells us nothing about discrimination.

6. If customers are not bigoted and government does not require discrimination, competition will ensure that employers cannot continuously discriminate. If a wage differential persists, it must be because the customers are willing to pay for it (they are bigoted) or the government requires it. It cannot simply be due to a bigoted employer.

7. Evidence suggests that in some professional sports, white players are paid more than equivalent black players. The source is likely to be the sports fan (the customer).

8. Writers, athletes, television and movie actors, movie directors, musicians, artists, software creators, motivational speakers, etc. Customers want only the best, and technology allows the seller to satisfy all customers at low cost.

9. Because the apprentice's value of marginal product is less and because the apprentice is being paid, in part, with on-the-job training that increases the apprentice's human capital and future earnings.

10. Minimum-wage laws (government-imposed wage floor), the market power of labor unions (threat of strike raises wage), and efficiency wages (firms pay above equilibrium wage to increase productivity because high wages reduce turnover, increase effort, and raise the quality of job applicants).

True/False Questions

1. F; it is the difference in wages that arises to off-set the nonmonetary characteristics of different jobs.
2. T
3. F; the gap has been widening.
4. T
5. T
6. T
7. T
8. F; education would not increase productivity and would have no effect on wages.
9. F; attractive people may have a larger value of marginal product or attractive people may have signaled that since they are good at making themselves attractive they may also be good at other tasks.
10. T
11. F; it must be because the customer is willing to pay for the discrimination or because the government requires it.
12. F; the difference in wages may be due to differences in human capital or job characteristics.
13. F; unions may pressure firms to raise wages above equilibrium, and firms may choose to pay efficiency wages, which are above equilibrium.
14. T
15. T

Multiple-Choice Questions

1. b
2. a
3. d
4. b
5. c
6. c
7. a
8. b
9. c
10. d
11. d
12. c
13. b
14. b
15. a
16. d
17. b
18. c
19. c
20. e

Advanced Critical Thinking

1. There will be a surplus of secretaries and a shortage of truck drivers. That is, it will increase the quantity supplied of secretaries and decrease the quantity demanded while it will decrease the quantity supplied of truck drivers and increase the quantity demanded.

2. Hardworking, high-ability workers would avoid the truck-driving market and the quality

of truck driving would be reduced. Hardworking, high-ability workers would be attracted to the secretary market and the quality of secretarial services would be increased.

3. An economist would argue that $10,000 is the compensating differential necessary to get someone to undertake the disagreeable nature of truck driving—working alone, overnight travel away from children, less clean and less safe work environment, etc.

Income Inequality and Poverty

GOALS

In this chapter you will

- Examine the degree of economic inequality in our society

- Consider some problems that arise when measuring economic inequality

- See how political philosophers view the government's role in redistributing income

- Consider the various policies aimed at helping poor families escape poverty

OUTCOMES

After accomplishing these goals, you should be able to

- Explain why the gap in earnings between skilled and unskilled workers is growing in the United States

- Name some factors that cause the measurement of income distribution to exaggerate the degree of income inequality

- Compare and contrast utilitarianism, liberalism, and libertarianism

- Explain the concept of a negative income tax

CHAPTER OVERVIEW

Context and Purpose

Chapter 20 is the third chapter in a three-chapter sequence that addresses the economics of labor markets. Chapter 18 developed the markets for the factors of production. Chapter 19 extended the basic supply-and-demand model to help explain the wide variation in wages we find in the economy. Chapter 20 addresses the measurement of the distribution of income and looks at the role the government plays in altering the distribution of income.

The purpose of Chapter 20 is to address income distribution. The discussion proceeds by answering three questions. First, how much inequality is there? Second, what do different political philosophies have to say about the proper role of government in altering the distribution of income? And third, what are the various government policies that are used to help the poor?

Chapter Review

Introduction This chapter addresses the distribution of income by answering three questions. First, how much inequality is there? Second, what do different political philosophies have to say about the proper role of government in altering the distribution of income? And third, what are the various government policies that are used to help the poor? We will find that governments may be able to improve on the distribution of income generated by the market but at the expense of a distortion in incentives and a reduction in efficiency.

The Measurement of Inequality

There are a variety of ways to describe the distribution of income. One way is to show what percent of total before-tax income is earned by families in each fifth and the top 5 percent of the income distribution. The top fifth earns about 47.6 percent of total income while the bottom fifth earns about 4.1 percent. That is, the top fifth earns more than ten times what the bottom fifth earns. The top 5 percent earns more than the bottom 40 percent.

The distribution of income is remarkably stable over time. Over the past 65 years, the bottom fifth has generally earned between 4 and 5 percent while the top fifth has earned between 40 and 50 percent. However, from 1935 to 1970, the income distribution narrowed slightly, and from 1970 to 2003, it has grown slightly wider. The increase in income inequality may be because of increases in international trade. Increases in technology have reduced the demand for unskilled workers while raising the demand for skilled workers, which has caused a change in relative wages.

When countries are ranked by inequality, the United States ranks about average. Japan, Germany, and Canada have greater income equality than the United States while South Africa, Brazil, and Mexico have greater income inequality. As a result of globalization, global income inequality is decreasing. That is, developing nations are growing more rapidly than developed countries.

Another measure of the distribution of income is the **poverty rate**—the percentage of the population whose family income falls below an absolute level called the **poverty line.** The poverty line is an absolute level of income set by the federal government for each family size below which a family is deemed to be in poverty. It is set at approximately three times the cost of providing an adequate diet. In 2003, the median family had an income of $52,680 while 12.5 percent of the population was in families with incomes below the poverty line of $18,810. The poverty rate fell from 1959 to 1973, but it has not declined since then. Poverty rates demonstrate three facts:

- *Poverty is correlated with race.* Blacks and Hispanics are three times more likely than whites to live in poverty.

- *Poverty is correlated with age.* Children are more likely than average and the elderly are less likely than average to live in poverty.

- *Poverty is correlated with family composition.* Families headed by females with no husband present are five times as likely to live in poverty as a family headed by a married couple.

There are problems associated with measuring inequality. Although data on the income distribution and the poverty rate are useful in measuring inequality, these measures are not perfect measures of someone's ability to maintain a standard of living for the following reasons:

- **In-kind transfers** are transfers to the poor given in the form of goods and services rather than cash. They are not accounted for in the standard measures of income inequality.

- The economic **life cycle** is the regular pattern of income variation over a person's life. Young and old may earn little income, but the young can borrow and the old can live off past saving. Standard measures of income inequality exaggerate the variation in living standards because annual income has greater variation than living standards.

- *Transitory versus permanent income.* Incomes vary due to random and transitory forces. That is, events can cause income to be unusually high or low for any given year. Again, people can borrow and lend so that they can maintain stable living standards even when there is variation in income. A family's living standard depends largely on its permanent income. **Permanent income** is a person's normal, or average, income.

For each of the reasons listed above, standard measures of income distribution exaggerate the inequality of living standards.

Economic mobility in the United States is high. During any ten-year period, 25 percent of families fall below the poverty line in at least one year but only 3 percent of families are poor for eight or more years. At the other extreme, if a father earns income 20 percent above average, his son will earn income only 8 percent above average and his grandson will earn an average income. Further, four out of five millionaires made their money on their own rather than inheriting it. These data suggest that deviations from average income tend to be somewhat temporary, and again, measures of income inequality tend to exaggerate the inequality in living standards.

The Political Philosophy of Redistributing Income

Economics alone cannot tell us whether governments *should* do anything about economic inequality. For this, we must address various schools of political philosophy:

- **Utilitarianism:** The political philosophy according to which the government should choose policies to maximize the total utility of everyone in society. **Utility** is a measure of happiness or satisfaction and is assumed to be the ultimate objective of all actions. If there is diminishing marginal utility for each additional dollar of income, then taking away a dollar from a rich person and giving it to a poor person lowers the rich person's utility less than the gain in utility received by the poor person. Utilitarians reject complete equalization of income because they realize that people respond to incentives, and thus, taxes create deadweight losses and there is less total income to be redistributed. The founders of this philosophy are the English philosophers Jeremy Bentham and John Stuart Mill.

- **Liberalism:** The political philosophy according to which the government should choose policies deemed to be just, as evaluated by an impartial observer behind a "veil of ignorance." This means that the only objective measure of economic justice is to set the rules for society as if every person were ignorant about the station in life each will end up filling—top, bottom, or middle. John Rawls, the originator of this theory of justice, argues that we would be concerned about being at the bottom of the income distribution so we would create a social rule known as the **maximin criterion**—the claim that the government should aim to maximize the well-being of the worst-off person in society. As a result, redistribution of income is a type of **social insurance**. Although not equalizing income completely, it would require greater redistribution than utilitarianism. Critics argue that rational people behind a veil of ignorance would not necessarily be so risk averse as to follow the maximin criterion.

- **Libertarianism:** The political philosophy according to which the government should punish crimes and enforce voluntary agreements but not redistribute income. Libertarians, such as Robert Nozick, argue that society earns no income—only individuals earn income. Therefore, income is not a shared resource to be distributed by a social planner. To a libertarian, if the *process* is fair, the *outcome* is fair, no matter how unequal. Thus, the government should punish stealing and cheating to make a fair playing field but should not be concerned with the final score if the rules were fair. Equality of opportunity is more important than equality of incomes.

Policies to Reduce Poverty

Regardless of political philosophy, most people think that the government should help the most needy because the poor are more likely to experience homelessness, drug dependency, domestic violence, health problems, teenage pregnancy, illiteracy, unemployment, and low educational attainment and are more likely to commit crimes and be victims of crime. Here are some policy options:

- *Minimum-wage laws:* Advocates argue that it helps the poor without any cost to government. Critics argue that it raises the wage above equilibrium for the lowest skilled workers and causes unemployment among those workers. Those that keep their jobs gain while those that become unemployed lose. The more elastic the demand for labor, the greater the job loss from a minimum wage. In addition, many minimum-wage workers are teenagers from middle-class families so the program is poorly targeted to the poor.

- *Welfare:* **Welfare** is a broad term that encompasses various government programs that supplement the incomes of the needy. These programs are cash assistance for people who have low incomes and have demonstrated a "need" such as having small children at home (Temporary Assistance for Needy Families, formerly known as Aid to Families with Dependent Children) or have a disability (Supplemental Security Income or SSI). Critics argue that these programs encourage the problems they hope to cure. Eligibility for assistance requires that the father not be in the household. This encourages fathers to abandon their families, causing broken homes, and may encourage unwed women to have illegitimate children. Evidence does not support the claim that welfare caused the decline in the two-parent family.

- *Negative income tax:* A **negative income tax** is a tax system that collects revenue from high-income households and gives transfers to low-income households. Under this tax system, a progressive income tax on the rich would be used to subsidize or provide a "negative tax" to low-income families. Poor families would not have to demonstrate need beyond simply being poor. This would not subsidize the breakup of families or subsidize illegitimate births, but it would subsidize those that are just lazy. The Earned Income Tax Credit is similar to a negative income tax but it only applies to the working poor, not the unemployed or sick.

- *In-kind transfers:* In-kind transfers occur when the poor are directly provided goods and services as opposed to being provided cash payments. Food stamps and Medicaid are examples. Supporters argue that this method ensures that the poor actually receive what they need as opposed to giving them money that they could spend on alcohol, drugs, and so on. Advocates of cash payments argue that in-kind transfers are inefficient because the government doesn't know what the poor need most. In addition, they argue that it is insulting to the poor to be forced to accept in-kind transfers.

Some antipoverty programs have the unintended effect of reducing the incentive for the poor to work. For example, suppose the government were to guarantee a fixed minimum level of income. If anyone below that income level were to work and earn a dollar, then the government would simply reduce that person's benefits one dollar. As a result, the effective tax rate is 100 percent on any new income, and there is no incentive to work. Welfare, Medicaid, food stamps, and the Earned Income Tax Credit are all reduced when a recipient earns more income. This discourages work and may create a "culture of poverty." That is, welfare recipients lose their job skills, their children fail to see the benefits of work, and multiple generations of families become dependent on government. If benefits are reduced gradually as income rises, the incentive to work is not reduced as much. However, this increases the cost of fighting poverty because families above the poverty line will receive some benefits.

Work disincentives created by antipoverty programs can be reduced by *workfare*—programs requiring any person collecting benefits to accept a government-provided job. Another possibility is to limit the number of years a person can collect welfare. This method was used by the 1996 welfare reform bill that limits lifetime welfare to five years. Welfare rolls have decreased.

In developing countries, poverty, not culture, seems to be the cause of child labor.

Conclusion

It is difficult to measure inequality, and there is little agreement about what to do about it. If we choose to do something about inequality, we should remember there is a trade-off between equity and efficiency. That is, the more equally the pie is divided, the smaller the pie becomes.

Helpful Hints

1. People in poverty are more likely to experience homelessness, drug dependency, domestic violence, health problems, teenage pregnancy, illiteracy, unemployment, and low educational attainment and are more likely to commit crimes and be victims of crime. Note, however, that while it is clear that poverty is associated with these social ills, it is unclear whether poverty causes these social ills or whether these social ills cause poverty. That is, it may be that drug dependency, health problems, having children while young and out of wedlock, illiteracy, and so on are as much a cause of poverty as they are an effect of poverty.

2. There are a variety of reasons why an individual's current annual income can differ from his or her average lifetime income. The individual's income will depend on whether they are young, middle age, or old, and whether they have had an unusually productive or unproductive year. Since people can borrow and lend, standards of living are more stable than incomes, and thus, standard measures of income distribution will exaggerate the degree of economic inequality.

3. An additional reason why some people prefer the government to provide for the poor using in-kind transfers instead of cash payments is that in-kind transfers are thought to generate less fraud. This is because there is little incentive for an individual to file a fraudulent claim to receive medical benefits that the individual doesn't need but there may be a great incentive to file a fraudulent welfare claim to receive cash.

Terms and Definitions

Choose a definition for each key term.

Key Terms	Definitions

Key Terms

_____ Poverty rate

_____ Poverty line

_____ In-kind transfers

_____ Life cycle

_____ Permanent income

_____ Utilitarianism

_____ Utility

_____ Liberalism

_____ Maximin criterion

_____ Social insurance

_____ Libertarianism

_____ Welfare

_____ Negative income tax

Definitions

1. A measure of happiness or satisfaction

2. A person's normal income

3. Government programs that supplement the incomes of the needy

4. Transfers to the poor given in the form of goods and services rather than cash

5. The political philosophy according to which the government should choose policies to maximize the total utility of everyone in society

6. The percentage of the population whose family income falls below an absolute level called the poverty line

7. A tax system that collects revenue from high-income households and gives transfers to low-income households

8. The political philosophy according to which the government should choose policies deemed to be just, as evaluated by an impartial observer behind a "veil of ignorance"

9. The political philosophy according to which the government should punish crimes and enforce voluntary agreements but not redistribute income

10. An absolute level of income set by the federal government for each family size below which a family is deemed to be in poverty

11. The claim that the government should aim to maximize the well-being of the worst-off person in society

12. The regular pattern of income variation over a person's life

13. Government policy aimed at protecting people against the risk of adverse events

PROBLEMS AND SHORT-ANSWER QUESTIONS

Practice Problems

1. Use Table 2 from Chapter 20 in your text to answer this question.
   a. In the most recent year available, what percent of income did the bottom fifth of the income distribution earn? What percent of income did the top fifth of the distribution earn? Roughly, what is the relationship between what the bottom fifth earns and what the top fifth earns?

   _____

   _____

   b. What is the range of the percent of income earned by the bottom fifth of the income distribution over the last 68 years? What is the range for the top fifth? Describe the trend for each group over the last 68 years. Provide some explanations for the trends you described.

   _____

   _____

   _____

   _____

   _____

   _____

   c. Describe three reasons why the measure of income distribution expressed in Table 2 in Chapter 20 may not truly measure someone's ability to maintain a certain standard of living. As a result, are the standard measures of income distribution likely to exaggerate or understate the true distribution of the standard of living? Explain.

   _____

   _____

   _____

   _____

   d. What is permanent income? Why might we wish to use permanent income when measuring the distribution of income? If we used permanent income instead of current annual income when measuring the distribution of income, would this tend to exaggerate or understate the true distribution of the standard of living? Explain. (Hint: If you are a full-time student, can you borrow as much as you want in order to perfectly smooth out your lifetime consumption?)

   _____

   _____

   _____

2. Susan earns five times as much as Joe.
   a. What would the political philosophy of utilitarianism, liberalism, and libertarianism likely suggest should be done in this situation? Explain.

   _____

   _____

   _____

   _____

   _____

   b. Compare the degree of redistribution each suggests.

   _____

   _____

   _____

   _____

   _____

3. Suppose the government has to choose between two antipoverty programs. Each program guarantees that every family has at least $15,000 of income. One scheme establishes a negative income tax where: Taxes = (0.50 of income) – $15,000. The other scheme is for the government to guarantee every family at least $15,000 to spend, and if a family falls short, the government will simply make up the difference.
   a. Using the negative income tax scheme described above, fill out the following table.

Earned Income	Taxes Paid	After-Tax Income
$ 0	_____	_____
5,000	_____	_____
10,000	_____	_____
20,000	_____	_____
30,000	_____	_____
40,000	_____	_____

   b. What is the value of income for which this family neither receives a subsidy nor pays any tax? (That is, how high does income have to be for the family to stop receiving a subsidy?)

   _____

   _____

   _____

   _____

   c. Under the second scheme where the government simply guarantees at least $15,000 to every family, what is the level of income at which a family stops receiving a subsidy? Explain.

   _____

   _____

d. Which plan is likely to be more expensive to the government? Explain.

_____

_____

e. Suppose a poor family that only earns $5,000 per year decides to plant a garden and sell the produce in a "farmer's market" in the city. Suppose the family earns an additional $5,000 selling the produce. What is the family's final income under each scheme? What is the effective tax rate on the $5,000 earned by the family under each scheme? Which scheme promotes a work ethic among the poor and which one discourages work? Explain.

_____

_____

_____

_____

Short-Answer Questions

1. How does the income distribution in the United States compare with the income distribution in other countries? Explain.

_____

_____

2. Does poverty affect all groups within the population the same? Explain.

_____

_____

_____

3. If the poverty rate is 12 percent, does it mean that about 12 percent of the population live their entire lives in poverty? Explain.

_____

_____

_____

4. Of the three political philosophies discussed in your text, which one differs the most from the other two and why? What does each school of thought suggest about income redistribution?

_____

_____

_____

_____

_____

5. Why don't the political philosophies of utilitarianism and liberalism suggest that income be completely equalized across the population?

_____

_____

6. Suppose there is a minimum wage. Under which of the following conditions is employment of unskilled workers reduced by the greatest amount: when labor demand is relatively inelastic or when labor demand is relatively elastic? Why? Is labor demand likely to be more elastic or inelastic in the long run? Why?

_____

_____

_____

_____

_____

_____

7. How could welfare programs exacerbate the problems they are supposed to cure?

_____

_____

_____

_____

8. What are some examples of in-kind transfers? Why do some people prefer that the government provide cash payments to the needy instead of in-kind transfers?

_____

_____

_____

_____

SELF-TEST

True/False Questions

_____ 1. In the United States, the earnings of families in the top fifth of the income distribution are more than ten times the earnings of the bottom fifth of the income distribution.

_____ 2. The income distribution in the United States grew much wider from 1935 to 1970 but has narrowed since 1970.

_____ 3. The poverty line is set at approximately three times the cost of providing an adequate diet.

_____ 4. Most child labor in developing countries is employed in manufacturing in the factories of multinational corporations.

_____ 5. Children are more likely than average and the elderly are less likely than average to live in poverty.

_____ 6. Because of in-kind transfers to the poor and because people's incomes vary from year to year and across their lifetimes, standard measures of income distribution exaggerate the degree of inequality in standards of living.

_____ 7. Since about 12 percent of families are below the poverty line, then it follows that about 12 percent of families live their entire lives in poverty.

_____ 8. The political philosophies of utilitarianism and liberalism both suggest that income should be equalized across the population.

_____ 9. Libertarians are more concerned with equal opportunity than with equal outcome.

_____10. Robert Nozick argues that economic justice would result if society chose a set of rules for the redistribution of income from behind a "veil of ignorance," and he argues that the set of rules would be the maximin criterion.

_____11. If the demand for labor is relatively inelastic, an increase in the minimum wage will increase unemployment among unskilled workers by a relatively small amount.

_____12. When compared to other welfare programs such as Temporary Assistance for Needy Families and SSI, a negative income tax would be more costly to the government but it would provide a greater incentive for the poor to work.

_____13. Critics of Temporary Assistance for Needy Families argue that since eligibility for this program requires that the father not be in the household, the program encourages families to break up.

_____14. It is more efficient for the government to provide in-kind transfers instead of cash payments.

_____15. If permanent income were utilized to measure the income distribution instead of current annual income, the income distribution would appear to be wider.

Multiple-Choice Questions

1. In the United States, the top 5 percent of the income distribution earns
   a. more than the bottom 40 percent of the income distribution.
   b. about ten times what the bottom fifth of the income distribution earns.
   c. about the same as the bottom fifth of the income distribution.
   d. about half of all income.

2. The poverty line is set at
   a. two times the price of a new car.
   b. five times the value of average rent.
   c. three times the cost of providing an adequate diet.
   d. one-third of average family income.

3. Compared to other countries, the income distribution in the United States is
   a. about average.
   b. a little narrower than most.
   c. the most equal.
   d. the most unequal.

4. Which of the following is *not* an explanation for the slight widening of the income distribution in the United States since 1970?
   a. The increase in technology has decreased the demand for unskilled workers and increased the demand for skilled workers, causing the gap between their wages to widen.
   b. An increase in international trade has decreased the demand for unskilled workers and increased the demand for skilled workers, causing the gap between their wages to widen.
   c. An increase in discrimination against unskilled immigrant labor has reduced the demand for unskilled workers and caused an increase in the gap between the wages of unskilled and skilled workers.

5. In the United States, the top fifth of the income distribution earns a little more than
   a. what the bottom fifth earns.
   b. two times what the bottom fifth earns.
   c. five times what the bottom fifth earns.
   d. ten times what the bottom fifth earns.
   e. twenty times what the bottom fifth earns.

6. Which of the following statements about poverty rates is *not* true?
   a. Blacks and Hispanics are three times more likely to live in poverty than whites.
   b. Children are more likely than average to live in poverty.
   c. The elderly are more likely than average to live in poverty.
   d. Families headed by females with no husband present are five times as likely to live in poverty as a family headed by a married couple.

7. Since 1935, the income distribution in the United States has
   a. been unchanged.
   b. narrowed slightly from 1935 to 1970 and then widened slightly from 1970 to today.
   c. widened slightly from 1935 to 1970 and then narrowed slightly from 1970 to today.
   d. slowly widened.
   e. slowly narrowed.

8. Because in-kind transfers are not accounted for in standard measures of income distribution, the standard measures of income distribution
   a. exaggerate the inequality of living standards.
   b. understate the inequality of living standards.
   c. accurately represent the true inequality of living standards.
   d. could exaggerate or understate the inequality of living standards depending on whether the transfers are goods or services.

9. Permanent income is
   a. Social Security income of the elderly and disabled.
   b. equal to the minimum wage.
   c. a person's normal, or average, income.
   d. wages fixed by a union or other labor contract.
   e. none of the above.

10. Because people's incomes vary over the life cycle and because there are transitory shocks to people's incomes, the standard measures of income distribution
    a. exaggerate the inequality of living standards.
    b. understate the inequality of living standards.
    c. accurately represent the true inequality of living standards.
    d. could exaggerate or understate the inequality of living standards depending on whether the transitory shocks are positive or negative.

11. If people can borrow and lend to perfectly smooth out their lifetime living standards, then
    a. current annual income is a good measure of the distribution of living standards.
    b. permanent income is a good measure of the distribution of living standards.
    c. transitory income is a good measure of the distribution of living standards.
    d. life-cycle income is a good measure of the distribution of living standards.
    e. none of the above is true.

12. Jill earns more than Bob and she came by her income fairly and honestly. Which of the following political philosophies would argue against the redistribution of income from Jill to Bob?
    a. utilitarianism
    b. liberalism
    c. libertarianism
    d. all of the above
    e. none of the above

13. The maximin criterion suggested by Rawls' theory of justice argues that the government should aim to
    a. minimize the difference between the rich and poor.
    b. maximize the total utility of society.
    c. minimize the well-being of the best-off person in society.
    d. maximize the well-being of the worst-off person in society.
    e. maximize the economic freedom of individuals by minimizing government interference in private decision making.

14. Rank utilitarianism, liberalism, and libertarianism in sequence from the political philosophy that would redistribute income the greatest to the one that would redistribute income the least.
    a. utilitarianism, liberalism, libertarianism
    b. libertarianism, liberalism, utilitarianism
    c. liberalism, libertarianism, utilitarianism
    d. liberalism, utilitarianism, libertarianism
    e. All three political philosophies argue for similar degrees of income redistribution.

15. Utilitarianism suggests that the government should choose policies that maximize the total utility of everyone in society by
    a. allowing each individual to maximize their own utility without interference from the government.
    b. redistributing income from rich to poor because, due to the diminishing marginal utility of income, taking a dollar from the rich reduces their utility by less than the gain in utility generated by giving a dollar to the poor.
    c. redistributing income from rich to poor because this would maximize the well-being of the worst-off person in society.
    d. redistributing income from rich to poor because this is what the members of society would choose to do if they were behind a "veil of ignorance."

16. To which of the following policies is the Earned Income Tax Credit most closely related?
    a. minimum-wage laws
    b. welfare
    c. negative income tax
    d. in-kind transfers

17. An increase in the minimum wage will cause a relatively large increase in unemployment among
    a. unskilled workers if the demand for labor is relatively elastic.
    b. unskilled workers if the demand for labor is relatively inelastic.
    c. skilled workers if the demand for labor is relatively elastic.
    d. skilled workers if the demand for labor is relatively inelastic.

18. Current antipoverty programs discourage work because
    a. they make recipients more comfortable than most middle-class Americans.
    b. benefits are reduced at such a high rate when recipients earn more income that there is little or no incentive to work once one is receiving benefits.
    c. antipoverty programs attract naturally lazy people to begin with.
    d. in order to be eligible for benefits, a recipient cannot have a job.

19. The greatest advantage of a negative income tax is that it
    a. reduces the cost to the government of fighting poverty.
    b. generates a smaller disincentive to work than most alternative antipoverty programs.
    c. would not provide benefits to lazy people.
    d. ensures that the poor actually receive what the government thinks they need.
    e. does all of the above.

20. Temporary Assistance for Needy Families
    a. has eliminated poverty in the United States.
    b. provides almost no disincentive to work because the benefits are very gradually reduced as a recipient's income from work increases.
    c. may lead to the break up of families because fathers may not be in the home if single mothers are receiving benefits.
    d. provides in-kind transfers, such as food stamps and Medicaid, to single mothers and their children.
    e. does all of the above.

ADVANCED CRITICAL THINKING

Suppose a friend comments to you, "I think welfare recipients are simply lazy spendthrifts. I have a friend who receives Temporary Assistance for Needy Families and when she was offered a part-time job, she turned it down."

1. What happens to a welfare recipient's benefits if they increase their earnings?

   _____

   _____

2. What is the effective tax rate on their additional income if they were to lose $1 in benefits for each dollar of additional income?

    _____

    _____

    _____

    _____

    _____

3. How does this system affect a welfare recipient's incentive to work? Is a welfare recipient necessarily lazy if they turn down a part-time job?

    _____

    _____

    _____

    _____

SOLUTIONS

Terms and Definitions

_6_ Poverty rate

_10_ Poverty line

_4_ In-kind transfers

_12_ Life cycle

_2_ Permanent income

_5_ Utilitarianism

_1_ Utility

_8_ Liberalism

_11_ Maximin criterion

_13_ Social insurance

_9_ Libertarianism

_3_ Welfare

_7_ Negative income tax

Practice Problems

1. a. Bottom fifth = 4.1 percent. Top fifth = 47.6 percent. The top fifth earns more than ten times what the bottom fifth earns.

   b. Bottom fifth range is from 4.1 percent to 5.5 percent. Top fifth range is from 40.9 percent to 51.7 percent. For the bottom fifth, their share grew until 1970 and fell thereafter. For the top fifth, their share fell until 1970 and grew thereafter. Since 1970, the increase in international trade and the increase in technology has decreased the demand for unskilled labor and increased the demand for skilled labor, increasing the relative wages of the already higher income workers.

   c. In-kind transfers are not included, the economic life-cycle is not recognized, and transitory versus permanent income is not recognized. All three problems suggest that standard measures exaggerate economic inequality because the poor receive transfers in the form of goods and services and because the variation in income can be smoothed by borrowing and lending.

   d. Permanent income is a person's normal, or average, income. Using it removes the life-cycle effects and the transitory effects that cause any given year's income to be nonrepresentative of the person's true standard of living. This would probably tend to understate the true distribution of the standard of living because, in reality, we cannot fully smooth our living standards by borrowing when young or when we have a bad year.

2. a. Utilitarianism: Since there is diminishing marginal utility of income as income grows large, it would harm Susan less than it would help Joe if we redistributed income from Susan to Joe. Thus, to maximize total utility, redistribute from Susan to Joe. Liberalism: Both Susan and Joe would agree that if they didn't know their station in life, they would choose to socially insure each other with a maximin system in case they were to be the one on the bottom end of the income distribution. So, redistribute from Susan to Joe. Libertarian: Since equal opportunity is more important than equal outcome, if each came by their income fairly and honestly, then no redistribution need take place.

   b. From least redistribution to most, libertarianism, utilitarianism, liberalism.

3. a.

Earned Income	Taxes Paid	After-Tax Income
$ 0	–$15,000	$15,000
5,000	–12,500	17,500
10,000	–10,000	20,000
20,000	–5,000	25,000
30,000	0	30,000
40,000	5,000	35,000

   b. $30,000

   c. $15,000. The government simply guarantees each family has $15,000, so once a family reaches that level, it fails to receive a subsidy.

   d. The negative income tax because, under this tax scheme, the government will continue to subsidize families in the $15,000 to $30,000 range.

   e. If negative income tax, final income = $10,000 earned income + $10,000 subsidy = $20,000. If $15,000 guarantee, final income = $10,000 + $5,000 subsidy = $15,000. If negative income tax, tax rate equals .50 because when income went up $5,000, take-home pay went up $2,500 or $2,500/$5,000 = .50. If $15,000 guarantee, tax rate equals 100 percent, because when income went up $5,000, final take-home pay stayed the same at $15,000 because benefits were reduced by $5,000 or $5,000/$5,000 = 100 percent. The $15,000 guarantee discourages work because there is no gain whatsoever from working when income is in the $0 to $15,000 range.

Short-Answer Questions

1. The United States ranks about average. Japan, Germany, India, Canada, and the United Kingdom have greater income equality than the United States while Russia, China, Nigeria, Mexico, Brazil, and South Africa have greater income inequality.

2. No. With regard to race, blacks and Hispanics are more likely to live in poverty. With regard to age, young are more likely than average and old are less likely than average to live in poverty. With regard to family composition, families headed by females are more likely to live in poverty.

3. No. There is a great deal of variation in a person's income from year to year and a great deal of variation in a person's income over their life cycle. There is also variation from generation to generation within a family. As a result, a much larger portion of the population than 12 percent lives some small portion of their lives in poverty, and very few live a large portion of their lives in poverty.

4. Libertarianism differs from both utilitarianism and liberalism because libertarianism argues that income is earned only by individuals and not by society, so no social planner has the right to alter the distribution of income if it was generated by a fair playing field. Utilitarianism redistributes income because of the diminishing marginal utility of income, and liberalism redistributes income because of a maximin criterion for social insurance.

5. Because they recognize that taxes cause disincentives to work so that too much redistribution causes the pie to become so small that both rich and poor lose.

6. When labor demand is relatively elastic because an increase in the wage causes a large reduction in labor demand. More elastic in the long run because firms have time to adjust production in response to the rise in wages.

7. Welfare programs could cause families to break up and unwed mothers to have children. They can cause disincentives to work. Children fail to see the advantages of work, and multiple generations become dependent on government.

8. Food stamps and Medicaid. Some argue that in-kind transfers are inefficient because the government doesn't know what the poor need most and they argue that in-kind transfers are insulting to the poor.

True/False Questions

1. T
2. F; it grew narrower from 1935 to 1970 and has grown wider since.
3. T
4. F; most child labor is in agriculture and is employed by their parents.
5. T
6. T
7. F; because of the variation in incomes from year to year and across the life cycle, only 3 percent of families are below the poverty line for eight out of ten years.
8. F; both schools of thought recognize the disincentive to work and the reduction in total output caused by a tax system that would perfectly equalize income. Complete equality would cause both rich and poor to be worse off.
9. T
10. F; John Rawls has made this argument.
11. T
12. T
13. T
14. F; it is more efficient to provide cash payments but recipients may spend it on things taxpayers don't appreciate.
15. F; income distribution would appear to be narrower.

Multiple-Choice Questions

1. a
2. c
3. a
4. c
5. d
6. c
7. b
8. a
9. c
10. a
11. b
12. c
13. d
14. d
15. b
16. c
17. a
18. b
19. b
20. c

Advanced Critical Thinking

1. They tend to lose benefits at a very high rate.

2. The tax rate would be 100 percent on the additional income.

3. Once one is on welfare, there is little or no incentive to work. Once on welfare, one need not be lazy to remain on it. It may be rational to remain on welfare if every time a person makes a dollar, the person loses a dollar in benefits.

The Theory of Consumer Choice

CHAPTER OVERVIEW

Context and Purpose

Chapter 21 is the first of two unrelated chapters that introduce you to some advanced topics in microeconomics. These two chapters are intended to whet your appetite for further study in economics. Chapter 21 is devoted to an advanced topic known as the theory of consumer choice.

The purpose of Chapter 21 is to develop the theory that describes how consumers make decisions about what to buy. So far, we have summarized these decisions with the demand curve. We now look at the theory of consumer choice, which underlies the demand curve. After developing the theory, we apply the theory to a number of questions about how the economy works.

Chapter Review

Introduction Chapter 21 develops the theory that describes how consumers make decisions about what to buy. So far, we have summarized these decisions with the demand curve. We now look at the theory of consumer choice, which underlies the demand curve. After developing the theory, we apply the theory to the following questions:

- Do all demand curves slope downward?

- How do wages affect labor supply?

- How do interest rates affect household saving?

The Budget Constraint: What the Consumer Can Afford

A **budget constraint** is the limit on the consumption bundles that a consumer can afford (given the consumer's income and the prices of the goods the consumer wishes to buy). On a graph that measures the quantity of a consumption good on each axis, a budget constraint is a straight line connecting the maximum amounts that could be purchased of each commodity given the prices of each commodity and the consumer's income. For example, if a consumer has income of $1,000 and the price of Pepsi is $2 per pint, the maximum amount of

GOALS

In this chapter you will

- See how a budget constraint represents the choices a consumer can afford
- Learn how indifference curves can be used to represent a consumer's preferences
- Analyze how a consumer's optimal choices are determined
- See how a consumer responds to changes in income and changes in prices
- Decompose the impact of a price change into an income effect and a substitution effect
- Apply the theory of consumer choice to three questions about household behavior

OUTCOMES

After accomplishing these goals, you should be able to

- Draw a budget constraint on a graph if you are given the value of income and the prices of the goods
- Explain why indifference curves must slope downward if the two products considered are "goods"
- Explain the relationship between the relative prices and the marginal rate of substitution between two goods at the consumer's optimum
- Shift the budget constraint when the price of a good increases
- Demonstrate the income and substitution effect on a graph using indifference curves and budget constraints
- Show why someone's labor-supply curve might be backward sloping

Pepsi that could be purchased is $1,000/$2 = 500 pints. If the price of pizza is $10, the maximum amount of pizza that could be purchased is $1,000/$10 = 100 pizzas.

The slope of the budget constraint is the *relative price* of the two goods. In this case since a pizza costs five times what a pint of Pepsi costs, the consumer can trade one pizza for five pints of Pepsi. If the quantity of Pepsi is plotted on the vertical axis and the quantity of pizza on the horizontal axis, the slope of the budget constraint (rise/run) is 5/1, which equals the price of pizza divided by the price of Pepsi or $10/$2 = 5. Since the budget constraint always slopes downward or negatively, we often ignore the negative sign.

Preferences: What the Consumer Wants

A consumer's preferences can be represented with indifference curves. If two bundles of commodities suit a consumer's tastes equally well, the consumer is indifferent between them. Graphically, an **indifference curve** is a curve that shows consumption bundles that give the consumer the same level of satisfaction. When drawn on a graph that measures the quantity consumed of each good on each axis, an indifference curve must be downward sloping because if consumption of one good is reduced, the consumption of the other good must be increased for the consumer to be equally happy. The slope at any point on an indifference curve is known as the **marginal rate of substitution** or *MRS*. The *MRS* is the rate at which a consumer is willing to trade one good for another while maintaining a constant level of satisfaction.

There are four properties of indifference curves:

- Higher indifference curves (further from the origin) are preferred to lower ones because people prefer more goods rather than fewer.

- Indifference curves are downward sloping because if consumption of one good is reduced, the consumption of the other good must be increased for the consumer to be equally happy.

- Indifference curves do not cross because it would suggest that a consumer's preferences are contradictory.

- Indifference curves are bowed inward because a consumer is willing to trade a greater amount of a good for another good if they have an abundance of the good they are trading away and they are willing to trade a lesser amount of a good for another good if they have very little of the good they are trading away.

When it is easy to substitute two goods for each other, indifference curves are bowed inward very little. When it is difficult to substitute two goods for each other, indifference curves are bowed inward a great deal. This is demonstrated by two extreme cases:

- **Perfect substitutes:** two goods with straight-line indifference curves. An example of perfect substitutes is nickels and dimes—two nickels for each dime.

- **Perfect complements:** two goods with right-angle indifference curves. An example of perfect complements is right shoes and left shoes—additional shoes that don't come in pairs do not increase satisfaction.

Optimization: What the Consumer Chooses

When we combine the budget constraint and the consumer's indifference curves, we are able to determine the amount of each commodity that the consumer will buy. The consumer will try to reach the highest indifference curve subject to remaining on the budget constraint. The point where an indifference curve just touches the budget constraint determines the *optimum* amount of purchases of each good. At the optimum, the indifference curve is *tangent* to the budget constraint and the slope of the indifference curve and the budget constraint are the same. Thus, the consumer chooses consumption of the two goods so that the marginal rate of substitution (slope of the indifference curve) equals the relative price of the two goods (slope of the budget constraint). At the optimum, the trade-off between the goods that the consumer is willing to make (slope of the indifference curve) is equal to the trade-off between the goods that the market is willing to make (slope of the budget constraint).

An alternative way to describe preferences and optimization is with the concept of utility. Utility is an abstract measure of the happiness or satisfaction a consumer receives from consuming a bundle of goods. Therefore, an indifference curve is actually an "equal-utility" curve. The *marginal utility* of a good is the increase in utility one gets from consuming an additional unit of that good. Goods exhibit *diminishing marginal utility* as more of any good is consumed. Since the marginal rate of substitution (the slope of the indifference curve) is the trade-off between two goods that the consumer is willing to make, it must also equal the marginal utility of one good divided by the marginal utility of the other good. Therefore, for two goods X and Y, at the optimum:

$$MRS = P_x/P_y = MU_x/MU_y$$

or,

$$MU_x/P_x = MU_y/P_y.$$

At the optimum, the marginal utility of a dollar spent on X must be equal to the marginal utility of a dollar spent on Y. Similarly, one can say that, at the optimum, the indifference curve is tangent to the budget constraint.

Suppose the income of the consumer were to increase. Because the consumer can now consume more of both goods and because the relative price of the two goods remains unchanged, an increase in income shifts the budget constraint outward in a parallel fashion. The consumer can now reach a new optimum on a higher indifference curve. It is most common that the consumer will choose to consume more of both goods. Thus, a **normal good** is a good for which an increase in income raises the quantity demanded. Alternatively, an **inferior good** is a good for which an increase in income reduces the quantity demanded. Bus rides are an inferior good.

Suppose the price of one of the goods were to fall. If the consumer allocates all of his income to the good whose price has fallen, the consumer can buy more of that good. If the consumer allocates all of his income to the good whose price is unchanged, the maximum amount he can purchase remains unchanged. This causes the budget constraint to rotate outward. That is, the budget constraint only shifts outward on the axis of the good whose price has fallen. The consumer can now reach a new optimum on a higher indifference curve.

The impact of a change in the price of a good can be decomposed into two effects: an income effect and a substitution effect. The **income effect** is the change in consumption that results when a price change moves the consumer to a higher or lower indifference curve. The *substitution effect* is the change in consumption that results when a price change moves the consumer along a given indifference curve to a point with a new marginal rate of substitution. Graphically, the substitution effect is the change in consumption that results from the change in relative prices, which rotates the budget line along a given indifference curve. The income effect is the change in consumption that results from the parallel shift in the budget constraint to the new optimum on the new indifference curve.

A demand curve can be derived from the consumer's optimizing decisions that result from the consumer's budget constraint and indifference curves. The combined income and substitution effect shows the total change in quantity demanded from a change in the price of a good. When these values are plotted on a price/quantity graph, the points form the consumer's demand curve.

Three Applications

- *Do all demand curves slope downward?* Theoretically, demand can sometimes slope upward. If an increase in the price of an inferior good has a larger income effect than substitution effect (the good is very strongly inferior), then an increase in the price of the good would cause the quantity demanded to rise. A **Giffen good** is a good for which an increase in the price raises the quantity demanded. Giffen goods are so rare that economists are not certain that one has ever existed.

- *How do wages affect labor supply?* The theory of consumer choice can be applied to the allocation decision between work and leisure. In this case, the two goods are consumption and leisure. The maximum amount of leisure is the number of hours available. The maximum amount of consumption is the number of hours available times the wage. The individual's indifference curves determine an optimum amount of leisure and consumption. Suppose the wage were to rise. The substitution effect induces more consumption and less leisure (more work). However, if both leisure and consumption are normal goods, the income effect suggests that the individual will wish to have both more consumption and more leisure (less work). If the substitution effect outweighs the income effect, an increase in wages will increase the quantity of labor supplied and labor supply is upward sloping. If the income effect outweighs the substitution effect, an increase in wages will decrease the quantity of labor supplied and labor supply slopes backward. Evidence that the workweek is getting shorter suggests that the income effect is very strong and the labor supply curve bends backward when measured over long periods of time. Evidence on the behavior of lottery winners and people who receive large bequests suggests that, at high income levels, the labor-supply curve is backward sloping.

- *How do interest rates affect household saving?* The theory of consumer choice can be applied to the decision of how much income to consume today and how much to save for tomorrow. In this case, we measure consumption when young on the horizontal axis and consumption when old on the vertical axis. A person can consume all of his earnings when young and have nothing when old, or consume nothing when young, save all of his income, earn interest on the saving, and consume a greater amount when old. A person's preferences determine the optimal amounts of consumption in each period. If the interest rate rises, the budget constraint becomes steeper because the maximum possible consumption when old increases. When the interest rate rises, the substitution effect suggests that the consumer should increase consumption when old and decrease consumption when young (save more) because consumption when old has become relatively cheaper. However, if consumption in both periods is a normal good, the income effect suggests that the individual should consume more in both periods (save less). If the substitution effect outweighs the income effect, an increase in the interest rate will cause the individual to save more. If the income effect outweighs the substitution effect, an increase in the interest rate will cause the individual to save less. Evidence on this issue is mixed, so there is no clear recommendation for public policy toward the taxation of interest.

Conclusion: Do People Really Think This Way?

While consumers may not literally make decisions in the manner suggested by the theory of consumer choice, the model of consumer choice describes a process that permits economic analysis. The theory is useful in many applications.

Helpful Hints

1. We have noted that the slope of the budget constraint is equal to the relative prices of the two goods represented on the graph. But which price should we put in the numerator and which price should we put in the denominator of the slope? Place the price of the good represented on the horizontal axis in the numerator and the price of the good represented on the vertical axis in the denominator of the slope. For example, if the quantity of popcorn is measured on the horizontal axis and the quantity of candy bars is measured on the vertical axis, and if the price of a bag of popcorn is $2 while the price of a candy bar is $1, then two candy bars can be exchanged for one bag of popcorn. The slope of the budget constraint is $2/$1 or 2. (Again, the slope of the budget constraint is always negative so we often ignore the sign.)

2. A mapping of an individual's preferences generates an infinite set of indifference curves. Each indifference curve divides the commodity space into three areas—points preferred to those on the indifference curve (points outside the indifference curve or away from the origin), points inferior to the indifference curve (points inside the indifference curve or toward the origin), or points of equal satisfaction as those on the indifference curve (points on the indifference curve). While there are an infinite set of indifference curves, it is customary to represent on a graph only those indifference curves that are tangent to a budget constraint, and thus, only those indifference curves that determine an optimum.

3. The slope of the indifference curve is the marginal rate of substitution, which is the marginal utility of one good compared to the marginal utility of the other good. The slope of the budget constraint is equal to the relative prices of the two goods. Since at the optimum, the indifference curve is tangent to the budget constraint, it follows that at the optimum the relative prices of the two goods equal the relative marginal utilities of the two goods. Thus, at the optimum, the additional utility gained by the consumer from an additional dollar's worth of one good is the same as the additional utility gained by the consumer from an additional dollar's worth of the other good. That is, at the optimum, the consumer cannot increase his total satisfaction by moving expenditures from one good to the other good.

Terms and Definitions

Choose a definition for each key term.

Key Terms

_____ Budget constraint

_____ Indifference curve

_____ Marginal rate of substitution

_____ Perfect substitutes

_____ Perfect complements

_____ Normal good

_____ Inferior good

_____ Income effect

_____ Substitution effect

_____ Giffen good

Definitions

1. The change in consumption that results when a price change moves the consumer to a higher or lower indifference curve

2. The rate at which a consumer is willing to trade one good for another

3. The limit on the consumption bundles that a consumer can afford

4. A good for which an increase in income raises the quantity demanded

5. A good for which an increase in the price raises the quantity demanded

6. Two goods with right-angle indifference curves

7. A curve that shows consumption bundles that give the consumer the same level of satisfaction

8. A good for which an increase in income reduces the quantity demanded

9. Two goods with straight-line indifference curves

10. The change in consumption that results when a price change moves the consumer along a given indifference curve to a point with a new marginal rate of substitution

PROBLEMS AND SHORT-ANSWER QUESTIONS

Practice Problems

1. Suppose a consumer only buys two goods—hot dogs and hamburgers. Suppose the price of hot dogs is $1, the price of hamburgers is $2, and the consumer's income is $20.

   a. Plot the consumer's budget constraint in Exhibit 1. Measure the quantity of hot dogs on the vertical axis and the quantity of hamburgers on the horizontal axis. Explicitly plot the points on the budget constraint associated with the even-numbered quantities of hamburgers (0, 2, 4, 6 . . .).

   b. Suppose the individual chooses to consume six hamburgers. What is the maximum amount of hot dogs that he can afford? Draw an indifference curve on the figure above that establishes this bundle of goods as the optimum.

   _____

   c. What is the slope of the budget constraint? What is the slope of the consumer's indifference curve at the optimum? What is the relationship between the slope of the budget constraint and the slope of the indifference curve at the optimum? What is the economic interpretation of this relationship?

   _____

   _____

   _____

   _____

   d. Explain why any other point on the budget constraint must be inferior to the optimum.

   _____

   _____

   _____

   _____

2. Use Exhibit 2 to answer the following questions.

a. Suppose the price of a magazine is $2, the price of a book is $10, and the consumer's income is $100. Which point on the graph represents the consumer's optimum—x, y, or z? What are the optimal quantities of books and magazines this individual chooses to consume?

_____

_____

b. Suppose the price of books falls to $5. What are the two optimum points on the graph that represent the substitution effect (in sequence)? What is the change in the consumption of books due to the substitution effect?

_____

_____

_____

c. Again, suppose the price of books falls to $5. What are the two optimum points on the graph that represent the income effect (in sequence)? What is the change in the consumption of books due to the income effect? Is a book a normal good or an inferior good for this consumer? Explain.

_____

_____

_____

d. For this consumer, what is the total change in the quantity of books purchased when the price of books fell from $10 to $5?

_____

e. Use the information in this problem to plot the consumer's demand curve for books in Exhibit 3.

Short-Answer Questions

1. Suppose that there are two goods available to the consumer—pens and pencils. Suppose that the price of a pen is $2.00 while the price of a pencil is $0.50. If we measure the quantity of pens on the horizontal axis and the quantity of pencils on the vertical axis, what is the slope of the budget constraint? Do you need to know the income of the consumer to answer this question? Why?

_____

_____

_____

2. If we measure "goods" on each axis, is an indifference curve positively (upward) sloped or negatively (downward) sloped? Why? If we measure a "good" on one axis but a "bad" (such as pollution) on the other axis, what type of slope do you think an indifference curve would have? Why?

_____

_____

_____

_____

3. Why are most indifference curves bowed inward?

_____

_____

_____

_____

4. Consider the following two pairs of goods:

    • Graduation caps and graduation gowns

    • Gasoline at an Exxon station and gasoline at a Shell station

    Which of the pairs of goods above is likely to be nearly perfect substitutes, and which is likely to be nearly perfect complements? Explain.

    _____

    _____

    _____

    _____

5. Referring to question 4 above, what is the shape of the indifference curves that you would expect each pair of goods to generate, straight-line or right-angle? For which pair of goods would you observe the greatest substitution effect if the relative prices of the two goods were to change? Why?

    _____

    _____

    _____

    _____

6. Suppose there are two goods available to the consumer—coffee and tea. Suppose that the price of coffee decreases. What impact will the substitution effect and income effect have on the quantity demanded of coffee if coffee is a normal good? Explain. What impact will the substitution effect and income effect have on the quantity demanded of coffee if coffee is an inferior good? Explain.

    _____

    _____

    _____

    _____

    _____

7. Suppose there are only two goods available to you, apples and oranges. Suppose that the prices of apples and oranges double and that your income also doubles. What will happen to the amount of apples and oranges that you choose to consume? Explain. (Hint: What has happened to the slope of the budget constraint? What has happened to the maximum amount of apples or oranges that you could consume if you allocated all of your income to one good or the other?)

    _____

    _____

    _____

    _____

8. Some people argue that the tax rate should be reduced on interest earned from saving because it will increase the after-tax return to saving, increase the quantity of saving supplied, and increase economic growth. Are we certain that a decrease in the tax rate on interest earned from saving will increase the quantity of saving? Explain.

_____

_____

_____

_____

SELF-TEST

True/False Questions

_____ 1. If we measure the quantity of French fries on the horizontal axis and the quantity of hamburgers on the vertical axis, and if the price of French fries is $0.60 and the price of a hamburger is $2.40, then the slope of the budget constraint is 1/4 (and it is negative).

_____ 2. A budget constraint is a set of commodity bundles that provide the consumer with the same level of satisfaction.

_____ 3. Indifference curves measure the consumer's willingness to trade one good for another good while maintaining a constant level of satisfaction.

_____ 4. When drawn on a graph that measures the quantity of a good on each axis, indifference curves are usually straight lines that slope downward (negatively).

_____ 5. If two goods are perfect complements, indifference curves associated with these two goods would cross each other at the optimum.

_____ 6. Indifference curves tend to be bowed inward because a consumer is willing to trade a greater amount of a good for another if they have an abundance of the good they are trading away.

_____ 7. At the consumer's optimum point, the marginal rate of substitution of apples for oranges is equal to the ratio of the price of oranges to the price of apples.

_____ 8. The more difficult it is to substitute one good for another, the more bowed inward indifference curves become.

_____ 9. If the price of a good falls, the substitution effect always causes an increase in the quantity demanded of that good.

_____10. If the price of a good falls and the good is a normal good, the income effect causes a decrease in the quantity demanded of that good.

_____11. If the price of a good falls and the good is an inferior good, the income effect causes a decrease in the quantity demanded of that good.

_____12. The income effect is measured as the change in consumption that results when a price change moves the consumer along a given indifference curve to a point with a new marginal rate of substitution.

_____13. An increase in the interest rate will always lead to a greater amount of saving.

_____14. A Giffen good is an extremely inferior good.

_____15. The theory of consumer choice can be used to demonstrate that labor supply curves must be upward sloping.

Multiple-Choice Questions

1. The limit on the consumption bundles that a consumer can afford is known as
   a. an indifference curve.
   b. the marginal rate of substitution.
   c. the budget constraint.
   d. the consumption limit.

2. A change in the relative prices of which of the following pairs of goods would likely cause the smallest substitution effect?
   a. gasoline from 7-Eleven and gasoline from Quick Stop
   b. right shoes and left shoes
   c. Coca-Cola and Pepsi
   d. Bud Light and Coors Light

3. Indifference curves for perfect substitutes are
   a. straight lines.
   b. bowed inward.
   c. bowed outward.
   d. right angles.
   e. nonexistent.

4. Suppose a consumer must choose between the consumption of sandwiches and pizza. If we measure the quantity of pizza on the horizontal axis and the quantity of sandwiches on the vertical axis, and if the price of a pizza is $10 and the price of a sandwich is $5, then the slope of the budget constraint is
   a. 5.
   b. 10.
   c. 2.
   d. 1/2.

5. The slope at any point on an indifference curve is known as
   a. the trade-off rate.
   b. the marginal rate of substitution.
   c. the marginal rate of trade-off.
   d. the marginal rate of indifference.

6. Which of the following statements is _not_ true with regard to the standard properties of indifference curves?
   a. Indifference curves are downward sloping.
   b. Indifference curves do not cross each other.
   c. Higher indifference curves are preferred to lower ones.
   d. Indifference curves are bowed outward.

7. The consumer's optimal purchase of any two goods is the point where
   a. the consumer reaches the highest indifference curve subject to remaining on the budget constraint.
   b. the consumer has reached the highest indifference curve.
   c. the two highest indifference curves cross.
   d. the budget constraint crosses the indifference curve.

8. Which of the following is true about the consumer's optimum consumption bundle? At the optimum,
   a. the indifference curve is tangent to the budget constraint.
   b. the slope of the indifference curve equals the slope of the budget constraint.
   c. the relative prices of the two goods equals the marginal rate of substitution.
   d. all of the above are true.
   e. none of the above is true.

9. Suppose we measure the quantity of good X on the horizontal axis and the quantity of good Y on the vertical axis. If indifference curves are bowed inward, as we move from having an abundance of good X to having an abundance of good Y, the marginal rate of substitution of good Y for good X (the slope of the indifference curve)
   a. rises.
   b. falls.
   c. stays the same.
   d. could rise or fall depending on the relative prices of the two goods.

10. If an increase in a consumer's income causes the consumer to increase his quantity demanded of a good, then the good is
    a. an inferior good.
    b. a normal good.
    c. a substitute good.
    d. a complementary good.

11. If an increase in a consumer's income causes the consumer to decrease her quantity demanded of a good, then the good is
    a. an inferior good.
    b. a normal good.
    c. a substitute good.
    d. a complementary good.

Suppose that the consumer must choose between buying socks and belts. Also, suppose that the consumer's income is $100. Use Exhibit 4 to answer questions 12 through 15.

12. If the price of a belt is $10 and the price of a pair of socks is $5, the consumer will choose to buy the commodity bundle represented by point
    a. x.
    b. y.
    c. z.
    d. The optimal point cannot be determined from this graph.

13. Suppose that the price of a pair of socks falls from $5 to $2. The substitution effect is represented by the movement from point
    a. y to point x.
    b. x to point y.
    c. z to point x.
    d. x to point z.

14. Suppose that the price of a pair of socks has falls from $5 to $2. The income effect is represented by the movement from point
    a. y to point x.
    b. x to point y.
    c. z to point x.
    d. x to point z.

15. A pair of socks is
    a. an inferior good.
    b. a normal good.
    c. a Giffen good.
    d. none of the above.

16. The change in consumption that results when a price change moves the consumer along a given indifference curve is known as the
    a. complementary effect.
    b. normal effect.
    c. income effect.
    d. substitution effect.
    e. inferior effect.

17. If income and prices were both to double, the budget line would
    a. shift outward in a parallel fashion.
    b. shift inward in a parallel fashion.
    c. stay the same.
    d. rotate inward.
    e. rotate outward.

18. If leisure is a normal good, an increase in the wage
    a. will always increase the quantity of labor supplied.
    b. will always decrease the amount of labor supplied.
    c. will increase the amount of labor supplied if the income effect outweighs the substitution effect.
    d. will increase the amount of labor supplied if the substitution effect outweighs the income effect.

19. If consumption when young and when old are both normal goods, an increase in the interest rate
    a. will always increase the quantity of saving.
    b. will always decrease the quantity of saving.
    c. will increase the quantity of saving if the substitution effect outweighs the income effect.
    d. will increase the quantity of saving if the income effect outweighs the substitution effect.

20. Which of the following is *not* true regarding the outcome of a consumer's optimization process?
    a. The consumer has reached his highest indifference curve subject to his budget constraint.
    b. The marginal utility per dollar spent on each good is the same.
    c. The consumer is indifferent between any two points on his budget constraint.
    d. The marginal rate of substitution between goods is equal to the ratio of the prices between goods.
    e. The consumer's indifference curve is tangent to his budget constraint.

ADVANCED CRITICAL THINKING

Suppose you have a wealthy aunt. Your aunt dies and leaves you a great deal of money (potentially). When you attend the reading of the will, you discover that she has bequeathed her millions to a "family incentive trust." As the lawyer reads the will, you discover that you only get the money if you get married, have children, stay with your spouse and raise your children, don't become dependent on drugs or alcohol, and if you *continuously have a full-time job.* (Note: Family incentive trusts are real and becoming very common.)

1. Why might your aunt include the requirement that you continuously have a full-time job?

    _____

    _____

2. Does the evidence about how people behave after they receive an inheritance suggest that your aunt's concerns are well-founded, or is she just a control freak who wants to control the lives of her relatives even after she is gone? Explain.

    _____

    _____

    _____

3. What does this evidence suggest about the slope of the labor-supply curve? Explain.

    _____

    _____

    _____

    _____

    _____

SOLUTIONS

Terms and Definitions

_3_ Budget constraint

_7_ Indifference curve

_2_ Marginal rate of substitution

_9_ Perfect substitutes

_6_ Perfect complements

_4_ Normal good

_8_ Inferior good

_1_ Income effect

_10_ Substitution effect

_5_ Giffen good

Practice Problems

1. a. See Exhibit 5.

5 EXHIBIT

b. Eight. For the indifference curve, see Exhibit 5.

c. Rise over run = 2/1. This is also the price ratio of price of hamburgers to price of hot dogs = $2/$1. The slope of the indifference curve is also 2/1. (Note: All of these slopes are negative.) At the optimum, the indifference curve is tangent to the budget constraint so their slopes are equal. Thus, the trade-off between the goods that the individual is willing to undertake (_MRS_) is the same as the trade-off that the market requires (slope of budget constraint).

d. Since the highest indifference curve reachable is tangent to the budget constraint, any other point on the budget constraint must have an indifference curve running through it that is below the optimal indifference curve, so that point must be inferior to the optimum.

2. a. Point z. 25 books and 5 magazines.

b. From point z to point x. From five books to 8 books.

c. From point x to point y. From eight books to 6 books. Books are inferior because an increase in income decreases the quantity demanded of books.

d. The quantity demanded increased from 5 books to 6 books.

e. See Exhibit 6.

6 EXHIBIT

Short-Answer Questions

1. Slope = rise/run = 4/1 or 4. It is also the ratio of the price of pens to the price of pencils or $2.00/$0.50 = 4. (All slopes are negative.) No. Income simply must be any positive amount. A change in income shifts the budget constraint in or out but does not change its slope.

2. Negatively sloped because, for a consumer to be equally happy, if consumption of one good is reduced, the consumption of the other good must be increased. Positively sloped because, for a consumer to be equally happy, if consumption of the bad item is increased, the consumption of the good item must also be increased.

3. Because the marginal rate of substitution (_MRS_) is not constant along most indifference curves. A consumer is willing to trade a greater amount of a good for another if they have an abundance of the good they are trading away. They are willing to trade a lesser amount away if they have very little of the good they are trading away.

4. Exxon gas and Shell gas are nearly perfect substitutes because the marginal rate of substitution is fixed at about one—one gallon of Exxon gas for one gallon of Shell gas. Graduation caps and gowns are nearly perfect complements because additional units of caps without gowns or additional units of gowns without caps provide little or no additional satisfaction.

5. Exxon gas and Shell gas would have nearly straight-line indifference curves while graduation caps and gowns would have nearly right-angle indifference curves. A change in the relative prices of gas would cause a great substitution between gas at each station while a change in the relative prices of caps and gowns would cause little or no substitution of caps for gowns or gowns for caps.

6. The substitution effect will cause an increase in the quantity demanded of coffee regardless of whether coffee is normal or inferior. If coffee is normal, the income effect will cause an increase in the quantity demanded of coffee. If coffee is inferior, the income effect will cause a decrease in the quantity demanded of coffee.

7. There will be no impact because the slope of the budget constraint is unaltered (relative prices are the same so the market trade-off is the same) and the position of the budget constraint is unaltered (the maximum amount of each good that can be purchased is unaltered so the end points of the budget constraint are the same).

8. No. An increase in the return to saving should increase consumption when old (substitution effect increases saving), but an increase in the return to saving increases income and should increase consumption when young and old (income effect decreases saving). If the income effect outweighs the substitution effect, a greater after-tax return on saving would decrease saving.

True/False Questions

1. T
2. F; a budget constraint is the limit on the consumption bundles that a consumer can afford.
3. T
4. F; indifference curves are negatively sloped but they are usually bowed inward.
5. F; indifference curves for perfect complements are right angles but still never cross another indifference curve.
6. T
7. T
8. T
9. T
10. F; the income effect would cause an increase in the quantity demanded.
11. T
12. F; the income effect is measured as the change in consumption that results when a change in

price moves the consumer to a higher or lower indifference curve.
13. F; if the income effect from a change in interest rates outweighs the substitution effect, the individual will save less.
14. T
15. F; labor supply curves can be backward sloping if the income effect from a change in the wage outweighs the substitution effect.

Multiple-Choice Questions

1. c
2. b
3. a
4. c
5. b
6. d
7. a
8. d
9. a
10. b
11. a
12. c
13. c
14. b
15. b
16. d
17. c
18. d
19. c
20. c

Advanced Critical Thinking

1. She is probably afraid that her gift of millions would tempt you to be lazy and cause you to lead a less useful life than you would otherwise.

2. Her concerns may be well-founded. People who win lotteries or receive large inheritances often quit work or reduce the hours they work.

3. This evidence suggests that the labor supply curve may be backward sloping. We generally assume that a higher wage increases the quantity supplied of labor (upward sloping labor supply), but in fact, a higher wage may decrease the quantity of labor supplied (backward sloping labor supply) if leisure is a normal good and the income effect of an increase in the wage outweighs the substitution effect.

Frontiers of Microeconomics

GOALS

In this chapter you will

- Examine the problems caused by asymmetric information

- Learn about market solutions to asymmetric information

- Consider why democratic voting systems may not represent the preferences of society

- Consider why people may not always behave as rational maximizers

OUTCOMES

After accomplishing these goals, you should be able to

- Describe the information asymmetry in the labor market

- Explain why insurance companies screen potential customers

- Generate an example of the Condorcet voting paradox

- Explain why people are willing to sign contracts that require them to contribute a portion of their paychecks to a retirement savings program

CHAPTER OVERVIEW

Context and Purpose

Chapter 22 is the last chapter in the microeconomics portion of the text. It is the second of two unrelated chapters that introduce you to some advanced topics in microeconomics. These two chapters are intended to whet your appetite for further study in economics.

The purpose of Chapter 22 is to give you a taste of three topics on the frontier of microeconomic research. The first topic we address is *asymmetric information*, a situation when one person in an economic relationship has more relevant knowledge than the other person. The second topic is *political economy*, the application of economic tools to the understanding of the functioning of government. The third topic we address is *behavioral economics*, the introduction of psychology into the study of economic issues.

Chapter Review

Introduction The study of economics is always seeking to expand the understanding of human behavior and society. This chapter addresses three areas on the frontier of economic study. The first topic we address is *asymmetric information*, a situation when one person in an economic relationship has more relevant knowledge than the other person. The second topic is *political economy*, the application of economic tools to the understanding of the functioning of government. The third topic we address is *behavioral economics*, the introduction of psychology into the study of economic issues.

Asymmetric Information

A difference in access to relevant knowledge is called an *information asymmetry*. We address two types of information asymmetries: *hidden actions* and *hidden characteristics*.

Hidden Actions and Moral Hazard
Hidden actions may occur when a person (called the **agent**) performs some task on behalf of another person (called the **principal**); generally, the agent knows more about his effort and performance than the principal. The problem of **moral hazard** arises if the principal cannot perfectly monitor the agent, so the agent tends to engage in dishonest or undesirable behavior (he shirks his responsibilities). In the employment relationship, the employer is the principal and the worker is the agent. Employers respond to the moral hazard problem with the following:

- *Better monitoring*: Employers use video cameras to catch irresponsible behavior or workers.

- *High wages*: Firms pay efficiency wages (above equilibrium wages) to raise the cost to the worker of being fired and make the worker less likely to shirk.

- *Delayed payment*: Year-end bonuses and higher pay later in life reduce shirking today.

Insurance can generate moral hazard because the insured may have little incentive to reduce the risk of an accident.

There is a principal-agent problem in the corporate structure because there is a separation of ownership (the principal) and management (the agent). Shareholders hire a board of directors to oversee management and create incentives for management to maximize profits rather than pursue their own objectives. Sometimes corporate managers are sent to prison for taking advantage of shareholders.

Hidden Characteristics and Adverse Selection   Hidden characteristics are when a seller knows more than the buyer about the good being sold. Hidden characteristics may generate a problem known as **adverse selection**—the buyer risks selecting goods of low quality. Adverse selection may occur in the market for the following:

- *Used cars*. Buyers may choose not to buy even slightly used cars because they surmise that sellers know something bad about the cars. This is known as the "lemons" problem.

- *Labor*. If a firm reduces the wage it pays, high-productivity workers tend to quit and the firm is left with low-productivity workers.

- *Insurance*. People with hidden health problems are more likely to want to buy health insurance than people with average or good health.

When markets suffer from adverse selection, people may continue to drive used cars they would rather sell, firms may pay wages above equilibrium and cause unemployment, and relatively healthy people may fail to purchase health insurance because it is too expensive. That is, markets may become inefficient.

Markets respond to asymmetric information in several ways:

Signaling   **Signaling** is when an informed party takes actions to reveal information to an uninformed party. Recall from previous chapters that firms spend money on expensive advertising to signal that they sell high-quality products. Students attend high-quality schools to signal that they are high-ability people. For a signal to be effective, it must be costly but less costly to the person with the higher-quality product. Signaling is rational for both the buyer and seller. A personal gift qualifies as a signal of love because it is costly (it takes time to purchase), and if someone loves another the most, they know what to buy (takes less time to buy than it would for a simple acquaintance).

Screening   **Screening** is when an uninformed party acts to induce an informed party to reveal information. Buyers of used cars may have their mechanic check out a used car. Auto insurers may check a driver's driving history or offer different policies that have different degrees of appeal to risky and safe drivers so the two kinds of drivers will reveal their driving characteristics.

Although markets may fail to allocate resources efficiently when there is asymmetric information, it is not clear that public policy actions can improve market outcomes because of the following:

- Private markets can sometimes deal with the problem by using signaling and screening.

- The government rarely has more information than private parties, so it cannot improve upon the current imperfect allocation of resources. Thus, the market is not first-best, but is second-best.

- The government itself is an imperfect institution.

Political Economy

Political economy, also known as *public choice*, applies the methods of economics to study how the government works. Before we choose to have the government attempt to improve market outcomes, we must recognize that government is also imperfect.

The Condorcet Voting Paradox   The Condorcet voting paradox is the failure of majority rule to produce transitive preferences for society. Transitivity is the property that if A is preferred to B, and B preferred to C, then A must be preferred to C. When society has to choose between more than two outcomes, majority rule democracy may not tell us which alternative society really wants because pair-wise voting across three or more alternatives does not guarantee transitivity, a phenomenon known as the **Condorcet paradox.** That is, it is possible under pair-wise voting that A is preferred to B, and B preferred to C, yet C preferred to A. Because the property of transitivity is required for majority-rule democracy to accurately aggregate preferences, two conclusions can be drawn: (1) Majority-rule voting does not necessarily tell us what society wants, and (2) setting the order in which items are voted on can affect the outcome.

Arrow's Impossibility Theorem   **Arrow's impossibility theorem** is a mathematical result showing that, under certain assumed conditions, there is no scheme for aggregating individual preferences into a valid set of social preferences. Due to the Condorcet paradox, alternative voting systems have been proposed. A Borda count allows voters to rank and give points to possible outcomes when there are more than two outcomes—like sports team rankings. However, Arrow has shown that no voting system can satisfy the following properties required of a perfect voting scheme:

- *Unanimity*: If everyone prefers A to B, then A should beat B.

- *Transitivity*: If A beats B, and B beats C, then A should beat C.

- *Independence of irrelevant alternatives*: The rankings between any two outcomes should not depend on whether some third outcome is available.

- *No dictators*: There is no person that always gets his way.

For example, majority rule does not always satisfy transitivity, and the Borda count does not always satisfy the independence of irrelevant alternatives. While democracy should not be abandoned, all voting schemes are flawed mechanisms for social choice.

The median voter is king.   The **median voter theorem** is a mathematical result showing that if voters are choosing a point along a line and each voter wants the point closest to his most preferred point, then majority rule will pick the most preferred point of the median voter. The median voter is the voter exactly in the middle of the distribution. Majority rule voting will always generate an outcome that is preferred by the median voter if each voter votes for the outcome that is closest to his most preferred outcome. This outcome will not necessarily be the average preferred outcome or the modal outcome. In addition, minority views are not given much weight.

Politicians may be self-interested. Self-interest may cause politicians to maximize their own well-being as opposed to maximizing the well-being of society. Some politicians may act out of greed, and others may sacrifice the national interest to improve their local popularity. Therefore, actual economic policy often fails to resemble the ideal policy derived in economic textbooks.

Behavioral Economics

In *behavioral economics*, economists make use of basic psychological insights. People aren't always rational. Economists generally assume that people and firms behave rationally. But people may not act as rational maximizers but instead as *satisficers*. Or people may exhibit "near rationality" or "bounded rationality." People make the following systematic errors:

- People are overconfident.

- People give too much weight to a small number of vivid observations.

- People are reluctant to change their minds.

   Regardless of these issues, economic models based on rationality may be good approximations of reality.

People care about fairness.   The *ultimatum game* is a game where one player decides what portion of $100 to give to another player. The second player must either accept the split or both get nothing. Rational wealth maximizers would choose $99 and offer $1. The second player would accept this offer because $1 is better than nothing. In experiments, however, the first player tends to give much more than $1 (but less than $50) to the second player, and the second player usually rejects small offerings. People may be driven by a sense of fairness as opposed to their normal self-interest. As a result, firms may pay above equilibrium wages during profitable years to be fair or to avoid retaliation on the part of workers.

People are inconsistent over time. People tend to desire instant gratification as opposed to delayed gratification. Therefore, they fail to follow through on plans to do things that are dreary, take effort, or cause discomfort. For example, people often save less than they plan. To help follow through on a plan, people may restrict their future behavior: Smokers throw away their cigarettes, dieters put a lock on the refrigerator, and workers sign up for a retirement plan.

Conclusion

This chapter introduced areas of continuing economic research. Asymmetric information should make us more wary of market outcomes. Political economy should make us more wary of government solutions. Behavioral economics should make us more wary of human decision making.

Helpful Hints

1. The market for insurance demonstrates many of the problems and market solutions generated by asymmetric information. For auto insurance, firms first screen prospective customers to reduce *adverse selection*—the problem of selling insurance to worse than average drivers. After the sale of the insurance, auto insurance companies require a deductible or co-payment on collision insurance. This reduces *moral hazard*—the problem of insured drivers driving more recklessly once they are insured.

2. No method of economic decision making is always perfect. Markets may not maximize total surplus due to externalities, public goods, imperfect competition, and asymmetric information. In addition, people and firms may not always rationally maximize their own well-being. But government may not be able to improve upon the situation because governments may not have any better information than markets, all voting schemes are imperfect, and politicians may choose to maximize their own well-being instead of the well-being of society.

Terms and Definitions

Choose a definition for each key term.

Key Terms	Definitions
_____ Moral hazard	1. An action taken by an informed party to reveal private information to an uninformed party
_____ Agent	2. The failure of majority rule to produce transitive preferences for society
_____ Principal	3. A person for whom another person, called the agent, is performing some act
_____ Adverse selection	4. The tendency of a person who is imperfectly monitored to engage in dishonest or otherwise undesirable behavior
_____ Signaling	5. A mathematical result showing that if voters are choosing a point along a line and each voter wants the point closest to his most preferred point, then majority rule will pick the most preferred point of the median voter
_____ Screening	
_____ Condorcet paradox	6. A mathematical result showing that, under certain assumed conditions, there is no scheme for aggregating individual preferences into a valid set of social preferences
_____ Arrow's impossibility theorem	7. The tendency for the mix of unobserved attributes to become undesirable from the standpoint of an uninformed party
_____ Median voter theorem	8. A person who is performing an act for another person, called the principal
	9. An action taken by an uninformed party to induce an informed party to reveal information

PROBLEMS AND SHORT-ANSWER QUESTIONS

Practice Problems

1. For each of the following situations, identify the principal and the agent, describe the information asymmetry involved, and explain how moral hazard has been reduced.
   a. Dental insurance companies offer free annual checkups

   _____

   _____

   b. Firms compensate traveling salespersons with commissions (a percentage of the value of the sales)

   _____

   _____

   c. Agricultural seed companies pay migrant workers bonuses if they work the entire summer season

   _____

   _____

   d. McDonald's pays twice the minimum wage to high school students

   _____

   _____

2. For each of the following situations, describe the information asymmetry involved, name the type of action that has been taken to reduce adverse selection (signaling or screening), and explain how adverse selection has been reduced.
   a. McDonald's only hires high school students with good grades

   _____

   _____

   b. Hyundai (a Korean auto manufacturer) provides a 100,000-mile warranty on its new cars

   _____

   _____

   c. A health insurance company requires a prospective customer to take a physical examination

   _____

   _____

   d. Budweiser sponsors the Super Bowl half-time show

   _____

   _____

3. Answer the questions regarding the Condorcet paradox for the three sets of voting preferences below.

Case 1

	Voter Type		
	Type 1	**Type 2**	**Type 3**
Percent of Electorate	15	40	45
First Choice	C	A	B
Second Choice	A	B	C
Third Choice	B	C	A

a. If voters must choose between A and B, what are the percentages of votes that each outcome receives and which outcome wins?

_____

b. If voters must choose between B and C, what are the percentages of votes that each outcome receives and which outcome wins?

_____

c. If voters must choose between C and A, what are the percentages of votes that each outcome receives and which outcome wins?

_____

d. Do these preferences exhibit transitivity? Explain.

_____

e. If the voters choose between A and B and then compare to C, which outcome wins?

_____

If the voters choose between B and C and then compare to A, which outcome wins?

_____

_____

If the voters choose between A and C, and then compare to B, which outcome wins?

_____

_____

Does the order in which items are voted on matter in this case? Why?

_____

_____

Case 2

	Voter Type		
	Type 1	**Type 2**	**Type 3**
Percent of Electorate	30	15	55
First Choice	A	B	C
Second Choice	B	C	A
Third Choice	C	A	B

a. If voters must choose between A and B, what are the percentages of votes that each outcome receives and which outcome wins?

_____

b. If voters must choose between B and C, what are the percentages of votes that each outcome receives and which outcome wins?

_____

c. If voters must choose between C and A, what are the percentages of votes that each outcome receives and which outcome wins?

_____

d. Do these preferences exhibit transitivity? Explain.

_____

_____

_____

e. If the voters choose between A and B and then compare to C, which outcome wins?

_____

_____

If the voters choose between B and C and then compare to A, which outcome wins?

_____

_____

If the voters choose between A and C and then compare to B, which outcome wins?

_____

_____

Does the order in which items are voted on matter in this case? Why?

_____

_____

_____

_____

Case 3

	Voter type		
	Type 1	**Type 2**	**Type 3**
Percent of Electorate	25	35	40
First Choice	A	B	C
Second Choice	B	A	A
Third Choice	C	C	B

a. If voters must choose between A and B, what are the percentages of votes that each outcome receives and which outcome wins?

_____

b. If voters must choose between B and C, what are the percentages of votes that each outcome receives and which outcome wins?

_____

c. If voters must choose between C and A, what are the percentages of votes that each outcome receives and which outcome wins?

_____

d. Do these preferences exhibit transitivity? Explain.

_____

_____

e. If the voters choose between A and B and then compare to C, which outcome wins?

_____

_____

If the voters choose between B and C and then compare to A, which outcome wins?

_____

If the voters choose between A and C and then compare to B, which outcome wins?

_____

_____

Does the order in which items are voted on matter in this case? Why?

_____

_____

Is the winning outcome the first choice of a large portion of the population? How can this be?

_____

_____

4. a. For Case 1 in problem 3 above, which outcome wins if you use a Borda count to determine the winner among outcomes A, B, and C, and what are the scores for each outcome?

_____

_____

b. For Case 1 in problem 3 above, eliminate outcome C and use a Borda count to find the winner from the remaining choices of A and B. What property required of a perfect voting system has been violated? Explain.

_____

_____

c. Compare the results of Case 1 in problem 3 under simple majority rule, a Borda count with three choices, and a Borda count with two choices. What conclusions can you draw from these results?

_____

_____

5. In each of the following situations, describe the behavior that suggests that people may not always behave as self-interested rational maximizers.
   a. Workers agree to a labor contract that gives them a 5 percent raise for each of the next three years. After one year passes, they discover that the firm's profits have increased by 100 percent. The workers go on strike and receive no income during the strike.

_____

_____

b. A worker plans to start saving 20 percent of his income starting three months from now because he has to first pay off some overdue bills. After three months pass, the worker saves nothing and instead spends all of his monthly income.

_____

_____

c. After a famous rock star dies in a plane crash, many people decide to ride the train rather than fly.

_____

_____

d. Joe wants to go on a Canadian fishing trip, and his wife, Sue, wishes to take a different type of trip. The newspaper reports that the size and number of fish being caught in the area where they plan to fish is greater than normal because the temperature has become unseasonably cool. Joe is more sure about his choice of the fishing trip, and Sue is more sure about her desire to go on a different type of trip.

_____

_____

Short-Answer Questions

1. What is *moral hazard*? What steps might a firm take to avoid moral hazard in the employment relationship?

   _____

   _____

   _____

2. What is *adverse selection*? Would you pay as much for a home that is only a year old (but has been lived in by people that have since built another home in the local area) as you would for a brand new home that has yet to be lived in? Why? What steps might you take to avoid adverse selection?

   _____

   _____

   _____

3. Would you expect the buyers of auto insurance to have a higher or lower than average probability of having an auto accident? Why? How does the insurance company address the adverse selection in this market? How does it address the moral hazard in this market?

   _____

   _____

   _____

4. To reduce adverse selection, firms signal high quality with expensive advertising. What are the necessary characteristics of an effective signal? Why don't firms producing low-quality goods use expensive advertising to falsely signal high quality?

   _____

   _____

   _____

5. Why does choosing a good gift qualify as a signal of love and concern to the recipient?

   _____

   _____

   _____

6. Suppose that 30 percent of the voters want to spend $10,000 on a new park, 30 percent want to spend $11,000, and 40 percent wish to spend $25,000. How much does the average voter want to spend? How much does the median voter want to spend? If each voter chooses the point closest to his most preferred choice, what will be the final choice among these three choices of a majority rule? Does the Condorcet paradox arise?

_____

_____

_____

7. Use the median voter theorem to explain why the Republican presidential nominee is more conservative during the primaries than during the general election and the Democratic nominee is more liberal during the primaries than during the general election.

_____

_____

_____

_____

8. Do politicians always choose policies that maximize the well-being of society? Why?

_____

_____

_____

9. If people were rational wealth maximizers, what result would we expect from the "ultimatum game"? What results do we actually find in experiments? What does this imply about wage determination?

_____

_____

_____

_____

10. The most popular major on campus is economics. Your best friend takes an introductory economics class and tells you that it was the worst class she has ever taken. You avoid taking any economics. Is this rational? Explain.

_____

_____

_____

_____

SELF-TEST

True/False Questions

_____ 1. Asymmetric information is a problem that occurs when one person in a transaction knows more about what is going on than the other.

_____ 2. In the principal-agent relationship, the principal performs a task on behalf of the agent.

_____ 3. Employers may pay higher than equilibrium wages to avoid moral hazard in the employment relationship by raising the cost of shirking.

_____ 4. To avoid the problem of adverse selection, insurance companies screen their prospective customers to discover hidden health problems.

_____ 5. Signals to convey high quality are most effective when they are costless to all firms in the industry.

_____ 6. If A is preferred to B, B preferred to C, and A is preferred to C, then these preferences exhibit the property of unanimity.

_____ 7. The Condorcet paradox shows that majority-rule voting always tells us the outcome that society really wants.

_____ 8. Arrow's impossibility theorem shows that no voting system can satisfy the properties required of a perfect voting system.

_____ 9. According to the median voter theorem, majority rule will produce the average preferred outcome.

_____ 10. Politicians do not always choose the ideal economic policy because some politicians are corrupt and greedy, and others are willing to sacrifice the national interest for local popularity.

_____ 11. In the real world, people always behave rationally when making economic decisions.

_____ 12. The ultimatum game demonstrates that people will always make choices according to their self-interest.

_____ 13. Since people tend to care about fairness, firms may give bonuses during particularly profitable years to be fair and to avoid retaliation from the workers.

_____ 14. People seem to naturally engage in delayed gratification and they tend to follow through on plans made today to do something unpleasant in the future.

_____ 15. Since people are reluctant to change their minds in the face of new information, we can conclude that people do not always behave as rational maximizers.

Multiple-Choice Questions

1. John's car is in need of repair, so John decides to sell it to avoid the repair bill. Unaware of the problem, Susan buys the car. This is an example of
   a. adverse selection.
   b. moral hazard.
   c. efficiency wages.
   d. hidden actions.

2. Judy wants to avoid buying a car that is a lemon. She takes a car she would like to buy to her mechanic before she purchases it. This is known as
    a. moral hazard.
    b. adverse selection.
    c. signaling.
    d. screening.

3. Chris is a traveling salesman for an apparel company. In this employment relationship, Chris is the
    a. principal.
    b. agent.
    c. signaler.
    d. screener.

4. Which of the following must be true about a signal that is used to reveal private information in order for the signal to be effective?
    a. It must be free to the informed party.
    b. It must be costly to the informed party but less costly to the party with the higher-quality product.
    c. It must be "as seen on TV."
    d. It must be applied to an inexpensive product.

5. Which of the following is an example of a signal that is used to reveal private information?
    a. Bob carefully chooses a special gift for Carolyn.
    b. Lexus advertises its cars during the Super Bowl.
    c. Madelyn earns her MBA from the Harvard Business School.
    d. All of the above are correct.

6. Which of the following is *not* a method firms use to avoid the moral hazard problem in the employment relationship?
    a. paying above equilibrium wages
    b. putting hidden video cameras in the workplace
    c. buying life insurance on their workers
    d. paying employees with delayed compensation such as a year-end bonus

7. Which of the following best demonstrates the problem of moral hazard?
    a. Karen doesn't buy health insurance because it is too expensive and she is healthy.
    b. Rachel chooses to attend a well-respected college.
    c. Dick drives more recklessly after he buys auto insurance.
    d. A life insurance company forces Fred to have a physical prior to selling him insurance.

8. Under pair-wise majority voting, if A is preferred to B and B is preferred to C, then A should be preferred to C. This is known as the property of
    a. unanimity.
    b. transitivity.
    c. independence.
    d. impossibility.

Use the following set of voter preferences to answer questions 9 through 12.

	Voter type		
	Type 1	Type 2	Type 3
Percent of Electorate	35	25	40
First Choice	C	A	B
Second Choice	A	B	C
Third Choice	B	C	A

9. What percent of the population votes for A when the choice is between A and B?
    a. 25 percent
    b. 35 percent
    c. 40 percent
    d. 60 percent
    e. 75 percent

10. Under pair-wise majority voting, which outcome wins?
    a. A
    b. B
    c. C
    d. These preferences suffer from the Condorcet paradox, so there is no clear winner.

11. If we first compare A to C, and then compare the winner to B, which outcome is the winner?
    a. A
    b. B
    c. C
    d. These preferences suffer from the Condorcet paradox, so there is no clear winner.

12. Using a Borda count, which outcome is preferred?
    a. A
    b. B
    c. C
    d. These preferences do not exhibit transitivity, so there is no clear winner.

13. Which of the following is *not* a property required of a perfect voting system?
    a. The median voter always wins.
    b. transitivity
    c. no dictators
    d. independence of irrelevant alternatives

14. Suppose that 40 percent of the voting population wish to spend $1,000 for artwork in City Hall, 25 percent wish to spend $20,000, and 35 percent wish to spend $22,000. What is the median preferred outcome, the average preferred outcome, and the modal preferred outcome?
    a. $1,000; $14,333; $1,000
    b. $20,000; $20,000; $22,000
    c. $20,000; $13,100; $1,000
    d. $1,000; $20,000; $22,000

15. Which of the following is true under pair-wise majority rule if people vote for the outcome closest to their most preferred outcome?
    a. The average preferred outcome wins.
    b. The outcome preferred by the median voter wins.
    c. The outcome preferred by the greatest number of voters wins.
    d. There is no clear winner due to Arrow's impossibility theorem.

16. Which of the following is *not* true about how people make decisions?
    a. People are sometimes too sure of their own abilities.
    b. People are reluctant to change their minds in the face of new information.
    c. People give too much weight to a small number of vivid observations.
    d. People are always rational maximizers.
    e. All of the above are actually true statements about how people make decisions.

17. In the *ultimatum game*, what split would be rational for both the person proposing the split and the person who must accept or reject the split?
    a. 99/1
    b. 75/25
    c. 50/50
    d. 1/99
    e. There is no rational solution.

18. Which of the following helps explain why firms pay bonuses to workers during particularly profitable years to prevent workers from becoming disgruntled?
    a. People are rational maximizers.
    b. People are inconsistent over time.
    c. People care about fairness.
    d. People are reluctant to change their minds.

19. John's friend dies of a sudden heart attack. John rushes to his doctor for an expensive physical examination. This response demonstrates that
    a. people give too much weight to a small number of vivid observations.
    b. people easily change their minds when confronted with new information.
    c. people tend to plan ahead and follow through on their plans.
    d. people enjoy going to the doctor.

20. Which of the following is a response to people's inconsistent behavior over time?
    a. efficiency wages
    b. year-end bonuses
    c. forced contributions to a retirement plan
    d. all of the above

ADVANCED CRITICAL THINKING

You are watching a television news story about the AIDS crisis with a friend. Your friend says, "I think it is terrible that people infected with AIDS often can't buy health insurance. People that are ill are the ones that really need health insurance. Even worse, once someone gets health insurance, they often have to pay a deductible equal to 20 percent of the first $3,000 of their medical bills each year. Only then does the insurance company cover the remainder of the medical bills."

1. What problem caused by asymmetric information are insurance companies trying to avoid when they deny coverage to someone who may already be ill? What would happen if the insurance companies did not deny coverage to people who are already ill?

_____

_____

_____

_____

2. What problem does charging a deductible help solve? What might happen if insurance companies didn't require a deductible?

_____

_____

_____

_____

3. How might public policy address the problems in the market for health insurance? What are some of the shortcomings of a public policy solution?

_____

_____

_____

_____

SOLUTIONS

Terms and Definitions

_4_ Moral hazard

_8_ Agent

_3_ Principal

_7_ Adverse selection

_1_ Signaling

_9_ Screening

_2_ Condorcet paradox

_6_ Arrow's impossibility theorem

_5_ Median voter theorem

Practice Problems

1. a. The insurance company is the principal; the insured is the agent. Only the agent knows how well he takes care of his teeth. By checking the insured's teeth each year, the insurance company can better monitor the behavior of the insured and reduce major future claims.

    b. The firm is the principal; the salesperson is the agent. The firm does not know how hard the salesperson works. By only paying the salesperson a commission, the firm is able to better monitor the salesperson's work habits, and the worker is less likely to shirk.

    c. The firm is the principal; the worker is the agent. The firm does not know how hard the migrant worker works. By paying a large bonus for completing the season, the firm raises the cost of shirking and the cost of being fired. The worker is less likely to shirk.

    d. McDonald's is the principal; the student is the agent. McDonald's does not know how hard the student works. By paying above market wages, McDonald's increases the cost of shirking and the cost of being fired. The worker is less likely to shirk.

2. a. McDonald's doesn't know the abilities of the potential workers as well as do the workers. McDonald's _screens_ potential workers using past educational performance, and it is able to select high-ability workers.

    b. Buyers don't know the quality of Hyundai cars because they are relatively new to this market. Hyundai _signals_ high quality with a long warranty, and buyers are able to select high-quality cars.

    c. The insurance company does not know as much about the health of the insurance buyer as does the buyer. The insurance company

screens prospective customers with physical exams to find hidden health problems so its insurance pool is not sicker than average.

    d. Beer buyers don't know the quality of Budweiser as well as Budweiser. Budweiser _signals_ high quality with expensive advertising because they could only afford to do it if they could generate repeat buyers. Customers are able to choose a high-quality beer.

3. Case 1:

    a. A = 15 + 40 = 55, B = 45. A beats B.

    b. B = 40 + 45 = 85, C = 15. B beats C.

    c. C = 15 + 45 = 60, A = 40. C beats A.

    d. No. A beats B and B beats C, so transitivity requires that A beats C but, in fact, C beats A.

    e. A beats B, so compare A to C and C wins.
        B beats C, so compare B to A and A wins.
        C beats A, so compare C to B and B wins.
        Yes, because these preferences do not exhibit transitivity.

    Case 2:

    a. A = 30 + 55 = 85, B = 15. A beats B.

    b. B = 30 + 15 = 45, C = 55. C beats B.

    c. A = 30, C = 15 + 55 = 70. C beats A.

    d. Yes. C beats A and A beats B. Transitivity requires that C beats B and it does.

    e. A beats B, so compare B to C and C wins.
        C beats B, so compare C to A and C wins.
        C beats A, so compare C to B and C wins.
        No, because these preferences exhibit transitivity.

    Case 3:

    a. A = 25 + 40 = 65, B = 35. A beats B.

    b. B = 25 + 35 = 60, C = 40. B beats C.

    c. A = 25 + 35 = 60, C = 40. A beats C.

    d. Yes. A beats B and B beats C. Transitivity requires that A beats C and it does.

    e. A beats B, so compare A to C and A wins.
        B beats C, so compare B to A and A wins.
        A beats C, so compare A to B and A wins.
        No, because these preferences exhibit transitivity. No, only 25 percent of the population chooses A as their first choice, but most of the population greatly dislikes C and none of the population greatly dislikes A.

4. a. If choosing between A, B, and C, A = 30 + 120 + 45 = 195, B = 15 + 80 + 135 = 230, C = 45 + 40 + 90 = 175 and B wins.

    b. If choosing between only A and B, A = 30 + 80 + 45 = 155, B = 15 + 40 + 90 = 145 and

A wins. Independence of irrelevant alternatives: The rankings of A and B shouldn't change when C is removed, but the ranking did change.

c. A wins, then B wins, then A wins again. Thus, majority voting does not necessarily tell us what society wants, and deciding the order on which items are voted may affect the outcome.

5. a. People care about fairness and may be willing to accept nothing so that their adversary gets nothing if they think the split was unfair.

b. People are inconsistent over time. From three months away, saving seems like a good idea, but as that date approaches, the desire for immediate gratification takes over.

c. People give too much weight to a small number of vivid observations. The probability of a plane crash has probably not changed yet people are more afraid to fly due to one highly publicized case.

d. People are reluctant to change their minds. Both Joe and Sue use the same information to defend their original opinion.

Short-Answer Questions

1. The tendency of a person who is imperfectly monitored to engage in immoral behavior. Better monitoring and paying higher wages or delaying some payment to raise the cost of shirking.

2. When unobserved attributes become undesirable from the standpoint of the uninformed party. No. Because you might assume that the sellers know something bad about the house—flooding, poor construction, bad neighbors or schools, etc. Have the house inspected and check out the neighborhood and schools.

3. Higher, because buyers of insurance know more about their probability of an accident, and those with a high probability of having accidents will need insurance. Insurance companies check a driver's driving history and offer policies that appeal differently to risky and safe drivers, and then they charge higher premiums to risky drivers. They require a deductible to avoid moral hazard.

4. It must be costly but less costly to the individual with the higher-quality product. Since low-quality firms will not generate repeat purchases from their advertising, it is not cost-effective for them to engage in expensive advertising.

5. Because it takes time (is costly), but it takes less time for someone that is knowledgeable about the recipient.

6. $0.3(\$10,000) + 0.3(\$11,000) + 0.4(\$25,000) = \$16,300$. Median voter wants to spend \$11,000. \$11,000 wins. No. Take any pair, find the winner, and then compare it to the remaining choice and \$11,000 always wins.

7. Each candidate first must win the nomination through the primaries. To do that, they must capture the median voter within their party—conservative for the Republicans and liberal for the Democrats. After being nominated, they must capture the overall median voter, which requires each to move to the center—Republicans become more liberal and Democrats become more conservative.

8. No. Some politicians may act out of greed and others may sacrifice the national interest to improve their local popularity.

9. The first person would take \$99 and give \$1 to the other, and the other would accept. The first person usually offers more than \$1 and the second person rejects small offers. Firms that are having particularly profitable years may pay above equilibrium wages to be fair or to avoid retaliation.

10. No. People give too much weight to a small number of vivid observations. In this case, the friend is just one additional observation out of thousands.

True/False Questions

1. T
2. F; the agent performs a task on behalf of the principal.
3. T
4. T
5. F; signals must be costly yet less costly to the person with the higher-quality product.
6. F; these preferences exhibit transitivity.
7. F; it shows that the order in which items are voted on can determine the outcome; therefore, majority-rule voting does not always tell us what society wants.
8. T
9. F; it will produce the outcome preferred by the median voter.
10. T
11. F; there is evidence that people are only "near rational."
12. F; it shows that people care about fairness.

13. T
14. F; people tend to seek instant gratification and fail to follow through on unpleasant tasks.
15. T

Multiple-Choice Questions

1. a
2. d
3. b
4. b
5. d
6. c
7. c
8. b
9. d
10. d
11. b
12. c
13. a
14. c
15. b
16. d
17. a
18. c
19. a
20. c

Advanced Critical Thinking

1. Adverse selection. People who are already ill would seek to buy insurance. Their medical bills would be far higher than average, causing premiums to rise. At the artificially high price for insurance, fewer healthy people would buy insurance because the cost would exceed their expected bills. When healthy people drop out of the market, the price rises even further for the remaining participants, further reducing the size of the insurance market.

2. Moral hazard. Without a deductible, people might go to the doctor even if they don't really need medical attention. They also have little incentive to take care of themselves to avoid illness because they bear no cost of the illness. As above, this raises the cost of insurance above the expected bills of healthy people and many will fail to buy insurance.

3. Some people advocate government-provided health insurance where everyone (sick and healthy) would be forced to participate. Majority-rule democratic institutions may not generate the amount of health care that people want. Self-interested politicians may choose to provide an amount of health care that is different than what people actually want.

Measuring a Nation's Income

GOALS

In this chapter you will

- Consider why an economy's total income equals its total expenditure

- Learn how gross domestic product (GDP) is defined and calculated

- See the breakdown of GDP into its four major components

- Learn the distinction between real GDP and nominal GDP

- Consider whether GDP is a good measure of economic well-being

OUTCOMES

After accomplishing these goals, you should be able to

- Demonstrate why income equals expenditure equals output

- Explain the key words and phrases in the definition of GDP

- Define consumption, investment, government purchases, and net exports

- Calculate real and nominal GDP using base year and current year prices

- List a number of welfare-enhancing activities that are not captured by GDP

CHAPTER OVERVIEW

Context and Purpose

Chapter 23 is the first chapter in the macroeconomic section of the text. It is the first of a two-chapter sequence that introduces you to two vital statistics that economists use to monitor the macroeconomy—GDP and the consumer price index. Chapter 23 develops how economists measure production and income in the macroeconomy. Chapter 24 develops how economists measure the level of prices in the macroeconomy. Taken together, Chapter 23 concentrates on the _quantity_ of output in the macroeconomy while Chapter 24 concentrates on the _price_ of output in the macroeconomy.

The purpose of this chapter is to provide you with an understanding of the measurement and the use of gross domestic product (GDP). GDP is the single most important measure of the health of the macroeconomy. Indeed, it is the most widely reported statistic in every developed economy.

Chapter Review

Introduction **Microeconomics** is the study of individual markets and the decision making of individual firms and households that meet in those markets. **Macroeconomics** is the study of the entire economy as a whole. This chapter, and the remainder of this text, deals with macroeconomics.

The Economy's Income and Expenditure

In a nation's macroeconomy, income must equal expenditure. This is true because, in every transaction, the income of the seller must be equal to the expenditure of the buyer. Gross domestic product (GDP) is a measure of the _total income_ or total output in the economy. Since income equals expenditure, GDP can be measured by adding up the income earned in the economy (wages, rent, and profit) or the expenditure on goods and services produced in the economy. That is, income equals expenditure equals GDP.

The Measurement of Gross Domestic Product

GDP is defined as the market value of all final goods and services produced within a country in a given period of time.

- "Market value" means that production is valued at the price paid for the output. Hence, items sold at higher prices are more heavily weighted in GDP.

- "Of all" means that GDP attempts to measure all production in the economy that is legally sold in markets. For example, GDP excludes the production and sale of illegal drugs and household production such as when homeowners clean their own houses. However, in an attempt to be comprehensive, GDP does include the estimated rental value of owner-occupied housing as an expenditure on housing services.

- "Final" means that GDP includes only goods and services that are sold to the end user. Thus, GDP counts the sale of a Ford Taurus when it is sold at retail, but it excludes Ford's purchases of intermediate goods such as glass, steel, and tires used up during the production of the car. *Intermediate goods* are goods that are produced by one firm to be further processed by another firm. Counting only final goods and services avoids double counting *intermediate production.*

- "Goods and services" means that while GDP clearly includes tangible manufactured items such as cars and trucks, it also includes intangible items such as lawyers' and doctors' services.

- "Produced" means that we exclude the sale of used items that were produced (and counted) in a previous period. Again, this avoids double counting.

- "Within a country" means that GDP measures the value of production within the geographic borders of a country.

- "In a given period of time" means that we measure GDP per year or per quarter.

GDP data are statistically "seasonally adjusted" to eliminate the systematic variations in the data that are caused by seasonal events such as Christmas and crop harvest. Our definition of GDP focuses on expenditures. The government also adds up income to measure GDP. The difference between the two calculations is statistical discrepancy.

Other measures of income besides GDP are listed below, from largest to smallest.

- *Gross national product (GNP):* GNP measures the income or production of a nation's permanent residents or "nationals" (both people and their factories) no matter where they are located.

- *Net national product (NNP):* NNP is the total income of a nation's residents (GNP) minus depreciation. *Depreciation* is the value of the wear and tear on the economy's capital stock.

- *National income:* National income is the total income earned by a nation's residents. It is NNP less indirect business taxes plus business subsidies.

- *Personal income:* Personal income is the income of households and noncorporate businesses. It excludes retained earnings (corporate income not paid out as dividends) but includes interest income households receive from government debt and government *transfer payments* (welfare and social security).

- *Disposable personal income:* This is income of households and nonincorporated businesses after they pay their obligations to the government (taxes, traffic tickets).

The Components of GDP

GDP can be measured by adding up the value of the expenditures on final goods and services. Economists divide expenditures into four components: consumption (*C*), investment (*I*), government purchases (*G*), and net exports (*NX*).

- **Consumption** is spending by households on goods and services, with the exception of new housing.

- **Investment** is spending on capital equipment, inventories, and structures such as new housing. Investment does not include spending on stocks, bonds, and mutual funds.

- **Government purchases** is spending on goods and services by all levels of government (federal, state, and local). Government purchases do not include *transfer payments* such as government payments for Social Security, welfare, and *unemployment* benefits because the government does not receive any product or service in return.

- **Net exports** is the value of foreign purchases of U.S. domestic production (exports) minus U.S. domestic purchases of foreign production (imports). Imports must be subtracted because consumption, investment, and government purchases include expenditures on all goods, foreign and domestic, and the foreign component must be removed so that only spending on domestic production remains.

Denoting GDP as Y, we can say that $Y = C + I + G + NX$. The variables are defined in such a way that this equation is an identity.

Real versus Nominal GDP

Nominal GDP is the value of output measured in the prices that existed during the year in which the output was produced (current prices). **Real GDP** is the value of output measured in the prices that prevailed in some arbitrary (but fixed) *base year* (constant prices). If we observe that nominal GDP has risen from one year to the next, we are unable to determine whether the quantity of goods and services has risen or whether the prices of goods and services have risen. However, if we observe that real GDP has risen, we are certain that the quantity of goods and services has risen because the output from each year is valued in terms of the same base year prices. Thus, real GDP is the better measure of production in the economy.

The GDP deflator = (nominal GDP/real GDP) × 100. The **GDP deflator** is a price index that measures the level of prices in the current year relative to the level of prices in the base year. The percentage increase in the price level as measured by the GDP deflator is the rate of **inflation.**

In the United States, real GDP has grown on average at a rate of 3.2 percent per year since 1965. Occasional periods of decline in real GDP are known as *recessions.*

Is GDP a Good Measure of Economic Well-Being?

Real GDP is a strong indicator of the economic well-being of a society because countries with a large real GDP per person tend to have better educational systems, better health care systems, more literate citizens, better housing, a better diet, a longer life expectancy, and so on. A country with a larger GDP even wins more Olympic medals. That is, a larger real GDP per person generally indicates a larger consumption per person. However, GDP is not a perfect measure of material well-being because it excludes leisure, the quality of the environment, and goods and services produced at home and not sold in markets such as child rearing, housework, and volunteer work. In addition, GDP says nothing about the *distribution* of income. GDP also fails to capture the underground or shadow economy—the portion of the economy that does not report its economic activity. For example, GDP does not measure illegal drug sales or income that is unreported to avoid taxation. The underground economy is relatively small in the United States.

Helpful Hints

1. GDP measures production. When we set out to measure GDP, we must first remember that we are measuring *production* (and the income earned from producing it) over a period of time. If we can remember that, we will generally account for unusual types of production correctly. Examples:

    - How should we handle the measurement of the production of a cruise ship that takes three years to build and is sold at the end of the third year? Logically, we should count the portion of the ship that was completed during each year and apply it to that year's GDP. In fact, that is what economists do. If we had accounted for the entire ship in the year in which it was sold, we would have overestimated GDP in the third year and underestimated GDP in the previous two years.

- Similarly, if a new house were built during one year but sold for the first time during the next year, we should account for it during the first year because that is when it was produced. That is, the builder "purchased" the finished home during the first year and added it to his or her inventory of homes.

While in general we only wish to count final goods and services, we do count the production of intermediate goods that were not used during the period but were added to a firm's inventory because this production will not be captured by counting all of the final goods.

2. GDP does not include all expenditures. We have learned that we can measure GDP by adding the expenditures on final goods and services ($Y = C + I + G + NX$). Once we have learned the expenditure approach, however, we must not forget the words "on final goods and services" and mistakenly count all expenditures. When we include expenditures on used items, intermediate goods, stocks and bonds, or government transfer payments, we get a very large dollar value, but it has nothing to do with GDP. The dollar value of total transactions in the economy is enormous and many times that of GDP.

3. Intermediate goods and final goods are distinct. It should be helpful to clarify the distinction between intermediate goods and final goods with an example. Recall:

- Intermediate goods are goods that are produced by one firm to be further processed by another firm.

- Final goods are sold to the end user.

GDP only includes the value of the final goods and services because the value of the intermediate goods used in the production of a final good or service is fully captured in the price of the final good or service. If we include the value of intermediate production in GDP, we would double count the intermediate goods.

If we understand this distinction, can we list the items in the economy that are intermediate or final? For example, is a tire an intermediate good or a final good? The answer is: It depends on who bought it. When General Motors buys a tire from Goodyear, the tire is an intermediate good because General Motors will attach it to a car and sell it. When you buy a tire from your Goodyear dealer, it is a final good and should be counted in GDP. Thus, it is difficult to list items in the economy that are intermediate or final without knowledge of the buyer.

4. Comparisons of GDP across countries and time can be biased. We should be cautious when we compare GDP across nations of different levels of market development and when we compare GDP across long periods of time within a single nation. This is because GDP excludes most non-market activities. Clearly, a greater proportion of the output of lesser-developed nations is likely to be household production such as when someone does their own farming, cleaning, sewing, and maybe even home construction. Since these activities are not captured by a market transaction, they are not recorded in lesser-developed nations or in earlier periods of industrialized nations when market development was less extensive. The result is an even lower estimate of their GDP.

Terms and Definitions

Choose a definition for each key term.

Key Terms

_____Inflation

_____Unemployment

_____Macroeconomics

_____Microeconomics

_____Total income

_____Total expenditure

_____Gross domestic product

_____Intermediate production

_____Final production

_____Gross national product

_____Depreciation

_____Consumption

_____Investment

_____Government purchases

_____Net exports

_____Transfer payment

_____Real GDP

_____Nominal GDP

_____Base year

_____GDP deflator

_____Recession

Definitions

1. The production of goods and services valued at current year prices

2. Spending by households on goods and services, excluding new housing

3. Spending on domestically produced goods by foreigners (exports) minus spending on foreign goods by domestic residents (imports)

4. Period of decline in GDP

5. Market value of all final goods and services produced within a country in a given period of time

6. Wages, rent, and profit

7. The rate at which prices are rising

8. Market value of all final goods and services produced by a nation's residents in a given period of time

9. Spending on capital equipment, inventories, and structures, including household purchases of new housing

10. Spending on goods and services by all levels of government

11. A measure of the price level calculated as the ratio of nominal GDP to real GDP then multiplied by 100

12. Expenditures by government for which they receive no goods or services

13. Percent of the labor force that is out of work

14. The study of how households and firms make decisions and how they interact in markets

15. Goods that are produced by one firm to be further processed by another firm

16. The study of economy-wide phenomena

17. The production of goods and services valued at base year prices

18. Finished products sold to the end user

19. Consumption, investment, government purchases, and net exports

20. The year from which prices are used to measure real GDP

21. Value of worn-out equipment and structures

PROBLEMS AND SHORT-ANSWER QUESTIONS

Practice Problems

1. a. Complete the following table.

	Year 1	Year 2	Year 3
Gross Domestic Product	4,532	4,804	
Consumption		3,320	3,544
Investment	589	629	673
Government Purchases	861		977
Net Exports	–45	–58	–54

   b. What is the largest expenditure component of GDP?

   _____

   _____

   c. Does investment include the purchase of stocks and bonds? Why?

   _____

   _____

   _____

   d. Do government purchases include government spending on unemployment checks? Why?

   _____

   _____

   _____

   e. What does it mean to say that net exports are negative?

   _____

   _____

2. Suppose the base year in the following table is 2003.

Year	Production of X	Price per Unit of X
2003	20 units	$ 5
2004	20 units	10
2005	20 units	20

   a. What is nominal GDP for 2003, 2004, and 2005?

   _____

   b. What is real GDP for 2003, 2004, and 2005?

   _____

3. Suppose the following table records the total output and prices for an entire economy. Further, suppose the base year in the following table is 2003.

Year	Price of Soda	Quantity of Soda	Price of Jeans	Quantity of Jeans
2003	$1.00	200	$10.00	50
2004	1.00	220	11.00	50

a. What is the value of nominal GDP in 2003?

b. What is the value of real GDP in 2003?

c. What is the value of nominal GDP in 2004?

d. What is the value of real GDP in 2004?

e. What is the value of the GDP deflator in 2003?

f. What is the value of the GDP deflator in 2004?

g. From 2003 to 2004, prices rose approximately what percentage?

h. Was the increase in nominal GDP from 2003 to 2004 mostly due to an increase in real output or due to an increase in prices?

4. Complete the following table.

Year	Nominal GDP	Real GDP	GDP Deflator
1		$100	100
2	$120		120
3	150	125	

a. What year is the base year? How can you tell?

b. From year 1 to year 2, did real output rise or did prices rise? Explain?

c. From year 2 to year 3, did real output rise or did prices rise? Explain?

Short-Answer Questions

1. Why does income = expenditure = GDP?

    _____

    _____

    _____

    _____

2. Define GDP and explain the important terms in the definition.

    _____

    _____

    _____

    _____

    _____

3. What are the components of expenditure? Provide an example of each.

    _____

    _____

    _____

    _____

    _____

4. Provide an example of a transfer payment. Do we include it in GDP? Why?

    _____

    _____

    _____

5. If nominal GDP in 2005 exceeds nominal GDP in 2004, did real output rise? Did prices rise?

    _____

    _____

    _____

6. If real GDP in 2005 exceeds real GDP in 2004, did real output rise? Did prices rise?

    _____

    _____

    _____

7. If you buy a $20,000 Toyota that was produced entirely in Japan, does this affect U.S. GDP? Show how this transaction would affect the appropriate expenditure categories that make up GDP.

    _____

    _____

    _____

8. Explain the difference between GDP and GNP. If the residents of the United States generate as much production in the rest of the world as the rest of the world produces in the United States, what should be true about U.S. GDP and GNP?

    _____

    _____

    _____

9. Which contributes more when measuring GDP, a new diamond necklace purchased by a wealthy person or a soda purchased by a thirsty person? Why?

    _____

    _____

    _____

10. If your neighbor hires you to mow her lawn instead of doing it herself, what will happen to GDP? Why? Did output change?

    _____

    _____

    _____

SELF-TEST

True/False Questions

_____ 1. For an economy as a whole, income equals expenditure because the income of the seller must be equal to the expenditure of the buyer.

_____ 2. The production of an apple contributes more to GDP than the production of a gold ring because food is necessary for life itself.

_____ 3. If the lumberyard sells $1,000 of lumber to a carpenter and the carpenter uses the lumber to build a garage that he sells for $5,000, the contribution to GDP is $6,000.

_____ 4. A country with a larger GDP per person generally has a greater standard of living or quality of life than a country with a smaller GDP per person.

_____ 5. If nominal GDP in 2006 exceeds nominal GDP in 2005, real output must have risen.

_____ 6. If U.S. GDP exceeds U.S. GNP, then foreigners produce more in the United States than U.S. citizens produce in the rest of the world.

_____ 7. Wages are an example of a transfer payment because there is a transfer of payment from the firm to the worker.

_____ 8. In the United States, investment is the largest component of GDP.

_____ 9. Nominal GDP employs current prices to value output while real GDP employs constant base-year prices to value output.

_____ 10. A new car produced in 2005, but first sold in 2006, should be counted in 2006 GDP because that is when it was first sold as a final good.

_____ 11. When the city of Chicago purchases a new school building, the investment component of GDP increases.

_____ 12. A recession occurs when real GDP declines.

_____ 13. Depreciation is the value of the wear and tear on the economy's equipment and structures.

_____ 14. Cigarettes should be valued in GDP at $3.50 per pack even though $1.00 of that price is tax because the buyers paid $3.50 per pack.

_____ 15. Net national product always exceeds a nation's total income because of depreciation and taxes.

Multiple-Choice Questions

1. An example of a transfer payment is
   a. wages.
   b. profit.
   c. rent.
   d. government purchases.
   e. unemployment benefits.

2. The value of plant and equipment worn out in the process of manufacturing goods and services is measured by
   a. consumption.
   b. depreciation.
   c. Net national product.
   d. investment.
   e. intermediate production.

3. Which of the following would be excluded from 1989 GDP? The sale of
   a. a 1989 Honda made in Tennessee.
   b. a haircut.
   c. a realtor's services.
   d. a home built in 1988 and first sold in 1989.
   e. All of the above should be counted in 1989 GDP.

4. Gross domestic product can be measured as the sum of
    a. consumption, investment, government purchases, and net exports.
    b. consumption, transfer payments, wages, and profits.
    c. investment, wages, profits, and intermediate production.
    d. final goods and services, intermediate goods, transfer payments, and rent.
    e. net national product, gross national product, and disposable personal income.

5. U.S. gross domestic product (in contrast to gross national product) measures the production and income of
    a. Americans and their factories no matter where they are located in the world.
    b. people and factories located within the borders of the United States.
    c. the domestic service sector only.
    d. the domestic manufacturing sector only.
    e. none of the above.

6. Gross domestic product is the sum of the market value of the
    a. intermediate goods.
    b. manufactured goods.
    c. normal goods and services.
    d. inferior goods and services.
    e. final goods and services.

7. If nominal GDP in 2005 exceeds nominal GDP in 2004, then the production of output must have
    a. risen.
    b. fallen.
    c. stayed the same.
    d. risen or fallen because there is not enough information to determine what happened to real output.

8. If a cobbler buys leather for $100 and thread for $50 and uses them to produce and sell $500 worth of shoes to consumers, the contribution to GDP is
    a. $50.
    b. $100.
    c. $500.
    d. $600.
    e. $650.

9. GDP would include which of the following?
    a. housework
    b. illegal drug sales
    c. intermediate sales
    d. consulting services
    e. the value of taking a day off from work

10. Real GDP is measured in _____ prices while nominal GDP is measured in _____ prices.
    a. current year; base year
    b. base year; current year
    c. intermediate; final
    d. domestic; foreign
    e. foreign; domestic

The following table contains information about an economy that produces only pens and books. The base year is 2002. Use this information to answer questions 11 through 16.

Year	Price of Pens	Quantity of Pens	Price of Books	Quantity of Books
2002	$3	100	$10	50
2003	3	120	12	70
2004	4	120	14	70

11. What is the value of nominal GDP for 2003?
    a. $800
    b. $1,060
    c. $1,200
    d. $1,460
    e. none of the above

12. What is the value of real GDP for 2003?
    a. $800
    b. $1,060
    c. $1,200
    d. $1,460
    e. none of the above

13. What is the value of the GDP deflator in 2003?
    a. 100
    b. 113
    c. 116
    d. 119
    e. 138

14. What is the percentage increase in prices from 2002 to 2003?
    a. 0 percent
    b. 13 percent
    c. 16 percent
    d. 22 percent
    e. 38 percent

15. What is the approximate percentage increase in prices from 2003 to 2004?
    a. 0 percent
    b. 13 percent
    c. 16 percent
    d. 22 percent
    e. 38 percent

16. What is the percentage increase in real GDP from 2003 to 2004?
    a. 0 percent
    b. 7 percent
    c. 22 percent
    d. 27 percent
    e. 32 percent

17. If U.S. GDP exceeds U.S. GNP, then
    a. foreigners are producing more in the United States than Americans are producing in foreign countries.
    b. Americans are producing more in foreign countries than foreigners are producing in the United States.
    c. real GDP exceeds nominal GDP.
    d. real GNP exceeds nominal GNP.
    e. intermediate production exceeds final production.

18. U.S. GDP would exclude which of the following?
    a. lawyer services purchased by a home buyer
    b. lawn care services purchased by a home owner
    c. a new bridge purchased by the state of Texas
    d. cotton purchased by Lee Jeans
    e. the purchase of a new Mazda produced in Illinois

19. How is your purchase of a $40,000 BMW automobile that was produced entirely in Germany recorded in the U.S. GDP accounts?
    a. Investment increases by $40,000 and net exports increase by $40,000.
    b. Consumption increases by $40,000 and net exports decrease by $40,000.
    c. Net exports decrease by $40,000.
    d. Net exports increase by $40,000.
    e. There is no impact because this transaction does not involve domestic production.

20. If your grandparents buy a new retirement home, this transaction would affect
    a. consumption.
    b. investment.
    c. government purchases.
    d. net exports.
    e. none of the above.

ADVANCED CRITICAL THINKING

You are watching a news report with your father. The news anchor points out that a certain troubled Caribbean nation generates a GDP per capita of only $350 per year. Since your father knows that U.S. GDP per capita is approximately $35,000, he suggests that we are materially 100 times better off in the United States than in the Caribbean nation.

1. Is your father's statement accurate?

   _____

   _____

2. What general category of production is not captured by GDP in both the United States and the Caribbean nation?

   _____

   _____

   _____

   _____

3. Provide some examples of this type of activity.

   _____

   _____

   _____

   _____

4. Why would the exclusion of this type of production affect the measurement of Caribbean output more than U.S. output?

_____

_____

_____

_____

5. Does this mean that residents of the Caribbean nation are actually as well off materially as residents in the United States?

_____

_____

_____

_____

SOLUTIONS

Terms and Definitions

_7_ Inflation

_13_ Unemployment

_16_ Macroeconomics

_14_ Microeconomics

_6_ Total income

_19_ Total expenditure

_5_ Gross domestic product

_15_ Intermediate production

_18_ Final production

_8_ Gross national product

_21_ Depreciation

_2_ Consumption

_9_ Investment

_10_ Government purchases

_3_ Net exports

_12_ Transfer payment

_17_ Real GDP

_1_ Nominal GDP

_20_ Base year

_11_ GDP deflator

_4_ Recession

Practice Problems

1. a.

	Year 1	Year 2	Year 3
Gross Domestic Product	4,532	4,804	5,140
Consumption	3,127	3,320	3,544
Investment	589	629	673
Government Purchases	861	913	977
Net Exports	−45	−58	−54

   b. consumption

   c. No, because that transaction is a purchase of an asset, not a purchase of currently produced capital goods.

   d. No, because unemployment benefits are expenditures for which the government receives no production in return.

   e. It means that imports exceed exports.

2. a. $100, $200, $400
    b. $100, $100, $100

3. a. $700
    b. $700

   c. $770

   d. $720

   e. 100

   f. 107

   g. $(107 - 100)/100 = 0.07 = 7\%$

   h. Percent increase in nominal = ($770 − $700)/700 = 0.10 = 10%. Percent increase in prices = 7%; therefore, most of the increase was due to prices.

4.

Year	Nominal GDP	Real GDP	GDP Deflator
1	$100	$100	100
2	120	100	120
3	150	125	120

   a. Year 1, because the deflator = 100.

   b. Prices rose 20 percent and real output stayed the same.

   c. Prices stayed the same and real output rose 25 percent.

Short-Answer Questions

1. Because the income of the seller equals the expenditure of the buyer and GDP can be measured with either one.

2. Market value of all final goods and services produced within a country in a given period of time. "Market value" = price paid, "of all" = all legal production, "final" = to end users, "goods and services" = includes services, "produced" = no used items, "within a country" = inside borders, "in a given period" = per quarter or year.

3. Consumption (food), investment (factory), government purchases (military equipment), net exports (sale of a Ford to France minus purchase of a Toyota from Japan).

4. Social Security payments. No, because the government received no good or service in return.

5. We can't be certain which rose, prices or real output, because an increase in either prices or real output will cause nominal output to rise.

6. Real output rose because the value of output in each year is measured in constant base year prices. We have no information on prices.

7. No. Consumption would increase by $20,000 and net exports would decrease by $20,000. As a result, U.S. GDP is unaffected.

8. GDP is the production within the borders of the United States. GNP is the production of

Americans no matter where the production takes place. They should be equal.

9. A diamond necklace because GDP measures market value.

10. GDP will rise because the mowing of the lawn was a market transaction. However, output didn't really rise.

True/False Questions

1. T
2. F; contribution is based on market value.
3. F; the garage is the final good, valued at $5,000.
4. T
5. F; prices or real output could have risen.
6. T
7. F; transfer payments are expenditures for which no good or service is received in return.
8. F; consumption is the largest component of GDP.
9. T
10. F; goods are counted in the year produced.
11. F; the purchase is included in government purchases.
12. T
13. T
14. T
15. F; total income – depreciation = NNP.

Multiple-Choice Questions

1. e
2. b
3. d
4. a
5. b
6. e
7. d
8. c
9. d
10. b
11. c
12. b
13. b
14. b
15. d
16. a
17. a
18. d
19. b
20. b

Advanced Critical Thinking

1. No.
2. Nonmarket activities such as household production.
3. Household production done by an individual without pay such as gardening, cleaning, sewing, home improvement or construction, child supervision, etc.
4. A greater proportion of the output produced by less-developed nations is nonmarket output. That is, it is not sold and recorded as a market transaction.
5. No. It just means that quantitative comparisons between nations of greatly different levels of development are very difficult to do and are often inaccurate.

Measuring the Cost of Living

GOALS

In this chapter you will

- Learn how the consumer price index (CPI) is constructed

- Consider why the CPI is an imperfect measure of the cost of living

- Compare the CPI and the GDP deflator as a measure of the overall price level

- See how to use a price index to compare dollar amounts from different times

- Learn the distinction between real and nominal interest rates

OUTCOMES

After accomplishing these goals, you should be able to

- List the five steps necessary to calculate the inflation rate

- Discuss three reasons why the CPI may be biased

- Describe two differences between the CPI and GDP deflator

- Convert a value measured in 1965 dollars to its value measured in 1990 dollars

- Explain the relationship between the real interest rate, the nominal interest rate, and the inflation rate

CHAPTER OVERVIEW

Context and Purpose

Chapter 24 is the second chapter of a two-chapter sequence that deals with how economists measure output and prices in the macroeconomy. Chapter 23 addressed how economists measure output. Chapter 24 develops how economists measure the overall price level in the macroeconomy.

The purpose of Chapter 24 is twofold: first, to show you how to generate a price index and, second, to teach you how to employ a price index to compare dollar figures from different points in time and to adjust interest rates for inflation. In addition, you will learn some of the shortcomings of using the consumer price index as a measure of the cost of living.

Chapter Review

Introduction To compare the income of a worker in, say, 1930 to the income of a worker today, we must first convert the dollar amount of each of their incomes into a comparable measure of purchasing power because there has been inflation over this time period. This chapter explains how economists correct economic variables for the effects of inflation. Inflation is generally measured by the consumer price index (CPI).

The Consumer Price Index

The **consumer price index** is a measure of the overall cost of the goods and services bought by a typical consumer. It is calculated by the _Bureau of Labor Statistics._

There are five steps to calculating a CPI:

- _Fix the basket._ Estimate the _quantities_ of the products purchased by the typical consumer (i.e., the _basket of goods and services_).

- _Find the prices._ Locate the prices of each item in the basket for each point in time (each year for an annual CPI).

- _Compute the basket's cost._ Use the prices and quantities to calculate the cost of the basket for each year.

- *Choose a base year and compute the index.* Choose a year as the benchmark against which the other years can be compared (i.e., the *base year*). The choice of the base year is arbitrary. Make a ratio of the cost of the basket for each year to the cost in the base year. Multiply each ratio times 100. Each resulting number is the value of the index for that year.

- *Compute inflation.* Inflation is the percentage change in the price index from the preceding year. For example:

Inflation rate in 2004 = [(CPI in year 2004 − CPI in year 2003)/CPI in year 2003] × 100

The actual CPI is calculated both monthly and annually. In addition, the Bureau of Labor Statistics calculates a **producer price index** (PPI), which measures the cost of a basket of goods and services purchased by firms. Changes in the PPI usually precede changes in the CPI because firms often pass on higher costs in the form of higher consumer prices.

The major categories in the CPI basket are housing (42 percent), transportation (17 percent), food and beverages (15 percent), medical care (6 percent), recreation (6 percent), education and communication (6 percent), apparel (4 percent), and other goods and services (4 percent).

The *cost of living* is the amount by which incomes must rise in order to maintain a constant *standard of living*. There are three problems with using the CPI to measure changes in the cost of living:

- *Substitution bias:* Over time, some prices rise more than others. Consumers will substitute toward goods that have become relatively less expensive. The CPI, however, is based on a fixed basket of purchases. Because the CPI fails to acknowledge the consumer's substitution of less expensive products for more expensive products, the CPI overstates the increase in the cost of living.

- *Introduction of new goods:* When new goods are introduced, a dollar has increased in value because it can buy a greater variety of products. Because the CPI is based on a fixed consumer basket, it does not reflect this increase in the purchasing power of the dollar (equivalent to a reduction in prices). Thus, again, the CPI overstates the increase in the cost of living.

- *Unmeasured quality change:* If the quality of a good rises from year to year, as with tires and computers, then the value of a dollar is rising even if actual prices are constant. This is equivalent to a reduction in prices. To the degree that an increase in quality is not accounted for by the Bureau of Labor Statistics, the CPI overstates the increase in the cost of living. The opposite is true for a deterioration of quality.

Economists believe that these three factors have caused the CPI to overestimate inflation by about 1 percent each year. This small overestimation of inflation may cause overpayment of Social Security benefits because Social Security benefits are tied to the CPI. Recent technical changes to the CPI may have reduced the upward bias in the CPI by about half.

Recall that the *GDP deflator* is the ratio of *nominal GDP* (current output valued at current prices) to *real GDP* (current output valued at base-year prices). Thus, the GDP deflator is a price index, too. It differs from the CPI in two ways:

- First, the basket of goods is different. The GDP deflator utilizes the prices of all goods and services produced domestically. The CPI utilizes the prices of goods and services *bought by consumers* only, regardless of where the goods were produced. Therefore, a change in the price of foreign oil, which raises the price of gasoline, is captured by the CPI but not by the GDP deflator, while a change in the price of a domestically produced nuclear missile is captured by the GDP deflator but not by the CPI.

- Second, the GDP deflator utilizes the quantities of goods and services in *current* output, so the "basket" changes each year. The CPI utilizes the quantities in a *fixed* basket, so the basket changes only when the Bureau of Labor Statistics chooses. Although the CPI and GDP deflator should track each other very closely, the CPI may tend to rise slightly faster due to its inherent substitution bias and the bias associated with the introduction of new goods.

Correcting Economic Variables for the Effects of Inflation

Economists use the CPI to correct *dollar figures*, such as income, and *interest rates* for the effects of inflation.

We correct income for inflation so that we can compare income from different years. The general formula for comparing dollar values from different years is as follows:

Value in year X dollars = Value in year Y dollars × (CPI in year X/CPI in year Y)

In words, to make the above conversion, multiply the dollar value you wish to adjust by the ratio of the ending price level to the starting price level. Your value will now be measured in dollars consistent with the ending price level.

For example, suppose your aunt earned $17,000 in 1969 and earned $55,000 in 1994. Over those 25 years, has her standard of living increased?

CPI in 1969 = 36.7

CPI in 1994 = 148.2

$17,000 × (148.2/36.7) = $68,649 > $55,000

A $17,000 salary in 1969 would buy as much as a $68,649 salary in 1994. Since your aunt only earned $55,000 in 1994, her real income fell and her standard of living actually decreased.

When a dollar amount, for example a Social Security payment, is automatically adjusted for inflation, we say that it has been *indexed* for inflation. A contract with this provision is said to contain a *COLA* or *cost-of-living allowance.*

We also correct interest rates for inflation. A correction is necessary because, if prices have risen during the term of a loan, the dollars used for repayment will not buy as much as the dollars originally borrowed.

The **nominal interest rate** is the interest rate uncorrected for the effects of inflation. The **real interest rate** is the interest rate corrected for the effects of inflation. The formula for correcting the nominal interest rate for inflation is:

real interest rate = nominal interest rate − inflation rate

For example, if the bank paid you a nominal interest rate of 4 percent on your account, and the inflation rate were 3 percent, the real interest rate on your account would be only 1 percent: 4% − 3% = 1%.

Helpful Hints

1. Your particular consumption basket may not be typical. Since the GDP deflator and the CPI are based on different baskets of goods and services, each will provide a slightly different measurement of the cost of living. Continuing in this same line of thinking, your particular consumption basket may differ from the typical consumption basket used by the Bureau of Labor Statistics when they calculate the CPI. For example, when you are a young adult, your basket may be more heavily weighted toward electronics and clothing. If clothing prices are rising faster than average, young people may have a greater increase in the cost of living than is suggested by the CPI. In like manner, when you become old, your consumption basket may be more heavily weighted toward medicine and travel. Exceptional increases in these prices may cause the cost of living for the elderly to rise more quickly than suggested by the CPI.

2. Dollar values can be adjusted backward in time as well as adjusted forward. In the earlier section, there is a numerical example that converts $17,000 of income in 1969 into the amount of income that would be necessary in 1994 to generate the same purchasing power. We discovered that it would take $68,649 for your aunt to have the same standard of living in 1994 as she had in 1969. Because she only made $55,000 in 1994, we argued that her standard of living actually fell over the 25-year period.

    Alternatively, we can convert her 1994 salary of $55,000 into its equivalent purchasing power measured in 1969 dollars and compare the resulting figure with her $17,000 income in 1969. We arrive at the same conclusion—she was better off in 1969.

    $55,000 × (36.7/148.2) = $13,620 < $17,000

Her $55,000 income in 1994 is equivalent to (or generates the same standard of living as) a $13,620 income in 1969. Since she actually made $17,000 in 1969, she had a higher standard of living in 1969.

3. When correcting interest rates for inflation, think like a lender. If you loan someone $100 for one year, and you charge them 7 percent interest, you will receive $107 at the end of the year. Did you receive 7 additional dollars of purchasing power? Suppose inflation was 4 percent. You would need to receive $104 at the end of the year just to break even. That is, you would need $104 just to be able to buy the same set of goods and services that you could have purchased for $100 at the time you granted the loan. In this sense, you received only 3 additional dollars of purchasing power for having made the $100 loan, or a 3 percent real return. Thus, the *real interest rate* on the loan is 3 percent. Using your formula:

$$7\% - 4\% = 3\%$$

Terms and Definitions

Choose a definition for each key term.

Key Terms

_____ Consumer price index

_____ Inflation rate

_____ GDP deflator

_____ Basket (of goods and services)

_____ Base year

_____ Bureau of Labor Statistics

_____ Producer price index

_____ Cost of living

_____ Standard of living

_____ Substitution bias

_____ Nominal GDP

_____ Real GDP

_____ Indexed contract

_____ Cost-of-living allowance (COLA)

_____ Nominal interest rate

_____ Real interest rate

Definitions

1. The income necessary to maintain a constant standard of living

2. A contract that requires that a dollar amount be automatically corrected for inflation

3. The ratio of the value of the fixed basket purchased by the typical consumer to the basket's value in the base year multiplied by 100

4. The quantities of each item purchased by the typical consumer

5. The ratio of the value of a fixed basket of goods and services purchased by firms to the basket's value in the base year multiplied by 100

6. The percent change in a price index

7. The interest rate corrected for the effects of inflation

8. An automatic increase in income in order to maintain a constant standard of living

9. The inability of the CPI to account for consumers' substitution toward relatively cheaper goods and services

10. Material well-being

11. Output valued at base-year prices

12. Output valued at current prices

13. The ratio of nominal GDP to real GDP multiplied by 100

14. The interest rate uncorrected for the effects of inflation

15. The benchmark year against which other years are compared

16. The government agency responsible for tracking prices

PROBLEMS AND SHORT-ANSWER QUESTIONS

Practice Problems

1. The following table shows the prices and the quantities consumed in the country known as the University States. Suppose the base year is 2002. *Also, suppose that 2002 is the year the typical consumption basket was determined, so the quantities consumed during 2002 are the only quantities needed to calculate the CPI in every year.*

Year	Price of Books	Quantity of Books	Price of Pencils	Quantity of Pencils	Price of Pens	Quantity of Pens
2002	$50	10	$1.00	100	$5	100
2003	50	12	1.00	200	10	50
2004	60	12	1.50	250	20	20

a. What is the value of the CPI in 2002?

_____

b. What is the value of the CPI in 2003?

_____

c. What is the value of the CPI in 2004?

_____

d. What is the inflation rate in 2003?

_____

e. What is the inflation rate in 2004?

_____

f. What type of bias do you observe in the CPI and corresponding inflation rates you generated above? Explain.

_____

_____

_____

g. If you had a COLA clause in your wage contract based on the CPI calculated above, would your standard of living likely increase, decrease, or stay the same during the years 2002 through 2004? Why?

_____

_____

_____

h. Again, suppose you had a COLA clause in your wage contract based on the CPI calculated above. If you personally only consume pens (no paper or pencils), would your standard of living likely increase, decrease, or stay the same during the years 2002 through 2004? Why?

_____

_____

_____

2. The following table contains the CPI and the Federal Minimum Hourly Wage Rates for the period 1965 through 2000.

Year	CPI	Minimum Wage
1965	31.5	$1.25
1966	32.4	1.25
1967	33.4	1.40
1968	34.8	1.60
1969	36.7	1.60
1970	38.8	1.60
1971	40.5	1.60
1972	41.8	1.60
1973	44.4	1.60
1974	49.3	2.00
1975	53.8	2.10
1976	56.9	2.30
1977	60.6	2.30
1978	65.2	2.65
1979	72.6	2.90
1980	82.4	3.10
1981	90.9	3.35
1982	96.5	3.35
1983	99.6	3.35
1984	103.9	3.35
1985	107.6	3.35
1986	109.6	3.35
1987	113.6	3.35
1988	118.3	3.35
1989	124.0	3.35
1990	130.7	3.80
1991	136.2	4.25
1992	140.3	4.25
1993	144.5	4.25
1994	148.2	4.25
1995	152.4	4.25
1996	156.9	4.75
1997	160.5	5.15
1998	163.0	5.15
1999	166.6	5.15
2000	172.2	5.15

a. Inflate the 1965 minimum wage to its equivalent value measured in 1990 prices.

_____

_____

b. What happened to the standard of living of minimum-wage workers over this 25-year period?

_____

_____

c. Deflate the 1990 minimum wage to its equivalent value measured in 1965 prices.

_____

_____

d. Do these two methods give you consistent results with regard to the standard of living of minimum-wage workers over time?

_____

_____

e. The minimum wage did not change over the eight-year period from 1981 to 1989. By what percentage did the purchasing power of the minimum wage decline over this period? (Hint: Inflate the value of the minimum wage in 1981 to its equivalent in 1989. Then generate the percent change.)

_____

_____

f. What happened to the standard of living of minimum-wage workers over the period from 1990 to 2000? (Inflate the 1990 minimum wage and compare it to the 2000 minimum wage.)

_____

_____

3. Suppose that you lend your roommate $100 for one year at 9 percent nominal interest.
   a. How many dollars of interest will your roommate pay you at the end of the year?

   _____

   _____

   b. Suppose at the time you both agreed to the terms of the loan, you both expected the inflation rate to be 5 percent during the year of the loan. What do you both expect the real interest rate to be on the loan?

   _____

   _____

c. Suppose at the end of the year, you are surprised to discover that the actual inflation rate over the year was 8 percent. What was the actual real interest rate generated by this loan?

_____

d. In the case described above, actual inflation turned out to be higher than expected. Which of the two of you had the unexpected gain or loss—your roommate (the borrower) or you (the lender)? Why?

_____

_____

_____

e. What would the real interest rate on the loan have been if the actual inflation rate had turned out to be a whopping 11 percent?

_____

_____

f. Explain what it means to have a negative real interest rate.

_____

_____

_____

_____

Short-Answer Questions

1. What does the consumer price index attempt to measure?

_____

2. What are the steps that one must go through in order to construct a consumer price index?

_____

_____

_____

3. Which would have a greater impact on the CPI: a 20 percent increase in the price of Rolex watches or a 20 percent increase in the price of new cars? Why?

_____

_____

_____

4. Suppose there is an increase in the price of imported BMW automobiles (which are produced in Germany). Would this have a larger impact on the CPI or the GDP deflator? Why?

_____

_____

_____

5. If the Bureau of Labor Statistics failed to recognize the increase in memory, power, and speed of newer model computers, in which direction would the CPI be biased? What do we call this type of bias?

_____

_____

6. From 1978 to 1979, the minimum wage increased 25 cents. Did minimum-wage workers see an increase in their standard of living? (Use the data from question 2 in the Practice Problems above.)

_____

7. What does the real interest rate measure?

_____

8. Suppose you lend money to your sister at a nominal interest rate of 10 percent because you both expect the inflation rate to be 6 percent. Further, suppose that after the loan has been repaid, you discover that the actual inflation rate over the life of the loan was only 2 percent. Who gained at the other's expense—you or your sister? Why?

_____

_____

_____

9. Paying close attention to question 8, make a general statement with regard to who gains or loses (the borrower or the lender) on a loan contract when inflation turns out to be either higher or lower than expected.

_____

_____

_____

10. If workers and firms negotiate a wage increase based on their expectation of inflation, who gains or loses (the workers or the firms) if actual inflation turns out to be higher than expected? Why?

_____

_____

_____

SELF-TEST

True/False Questions

_____ 1. An increase in the price of imported cameras is captured by the CPI but not by the GDP deflator.

_____ 2. An increase in the price of helicopters purchased by the U.S. military is captured by the CPI.

_____ 3. Because an increase in gasoline prices causes consumers to ride their bikes more and drive their cars less, the CPI tends to underestimate the cost of living.

_____ 4. An increase in the price of diamonds will have a greater impact on the CPI than an equal percentage increase in the price of food because diamonds are so much more expensive.

_____ 5. The "base year" in a price index is the benchmark year against which other years are compared.

_____ 6. If the CPI rises at 5 percent per year, then every individual in the country needs exactly a 5 percent increase in their income for their standard of living to remain constant.

_____ 7. The producer price index (PPI) is constructed to measure the change in price of total production.

_____ 8. If the Bureau of Labor Statistics fails to recognize that recently produced automobiles can be driven for many more miles than older models, then the CPI tends to overestimate the cost of living.

_____ 9. If your wage rises from $5.00 to $6.25 while the CPI rises from 112 to 121, you should feel an increase in your standard of living.

_____ 10. The largest category of goods and services in the CPI is medical care.

_____ 11. It is impossible for real interest rates to be negative.

_____ 12. If the nominal interest rate is 12 percent and the rate of inflation is 7 percent, then the real rate of interest is 5 percent.

_____ 13. If lenders demand a real rate of return of 4 percent and they expect inflation to be 5 percent, then they should charge 9 percent interest when they extend loans.

_____ 14. If borrowers and lenders agree on a nominal interest rate and inflation turns out to be greater than they had anticipated, lenders will gain at the expense of borrowers.

_____ 15. If workers and firms agree on an increase in wages based on their expectations of inflation and inflation turns out to be less than they expected, workers will gain at the expense of firms.

Multiple-Choice Questions

1. Inflation can be measured by all of the following except the
   a. GDP deflator.
   b. consumer price index.
   c. producer price index.
   d. finished goods price index.
   e. All of the above are used to measure inflation.

2. The CPI will be most influenced by a 10 percent increase in the price of which of the following consumption categories?
   a. housing
   b. transportation
   c. medical care
   d. food and beverages
   e. All of the above would produce the same impact.

3. In 1989, the CPI was 124.0. In 1990, it was 130.7. What was the rate of inflation over this period?
   a. 5.1 percent
   b. 5.4 percent
   c. 6.7 percent
   d. 30.7 percent
   e. You can't tell without knowing the base year.

4. Which of the following would likely cause the CPI to rise more than the GDP deflator?
   a. an increase in the price of Fords
   b. an increase in the price of tanks purchased by the military
   c. an increase in the price of domestically produced fighter planes sold exclusively to Israel
   d. an increase in the price of Hondas produced in Japan and sold in the United States
   e. an increase in the price of John Deere tractors

5. The "basket" on which the CPI is based is composed of
   a. raw materials purchased by firms.
   b. total current production.
   c. products purchased by the typical consumer.
   d. consumer production.
   e. none of the above.

6. If there is an increase in the price of apples that causes consumers to purchase fewer pounds of apples and more pounds of oranges, the CPI will suffer from
   a. substitution bias.
   b. bias due to the introduction of new goods.
   c. bias due to unmeasured quality change.
   d. base-year bias.
   e. none of the above.

Use the following table to answer questions 7 through 12. The table shows the prices and the quantities consumed in Carnivore Country. Suppose the base year is 2003. *Also, suppose that 2003 is the year the typical consumption basket was determined, so the quantities consumed in 2003 are the only quantities needed to calculate the CPI in each year.*

Year	Price of Beef	Quantity of Beef	Price of Pork	Quantity of Pork
2003	$2.00	100	$1.00	100
2004	2.50	90	0.90	120
2005	2.75	105	1.00	130

7. What is the value of the basket in the base year?
   a. $300
   b. $333
   c. $418.75
   d. $459.25
   e. none of the above

8. What are the values of the CPI in 2003, 2004, and 2005, respectively?
   a. 100, 111, 139.6
   b. 100, 109.2, 116
   c. 100, 113.3, 125
   d. 83.5, 94.2, 100
   e. none of the above

9. What is the inflation rate for 2004?
   a. 0 percent
   b. 9.2 percent
   c. 11 percent
   d. 13.3 percent
   e. none of the above

10. What is the inflation rate for 2005?
    a. 0 percent
    b. 10.3 percent
    c. 11 percent
    d. 13.3 percent
    e. none of the above

11. The table shows that the 2004 inflation rate is biased upward because of
    a. bias due to the introduction of new goods.
    b. bias due to unmeasured quality change.
    c. substitution bias.
    d. base-year bias.
    e. none of the above.

12. Suppose the base year is changed in the table from 2003 to 2005. Also, suppose that the typical consumption basket was now determined in 2005 (now use the 2005 consumption basket). What is the new value of the CPI in 2004?
    a. 90.6
    b. 100.0
    c. 114.7
    d. 134.3
    e. none of the above

13. Suppose your income rises from $19,000 to $31,000 while the CPI rises from 122 to 169. Your standard of living has likely
    a. fallen.
    b. risen.
    c. stayed the same.
    d. You can't tell without knowing the base year.

14. If the nominal interest rate is 7 percent and the inflation rate is 3 percent, then the real interest rate is
    a. –4 percent.
    b. 3 percent.
    c. 4 percent.
    d. 10 percent.
    e. 21 percent.

15. Which of the following statements is correct?
    a. The real interest rate is the sum of the nominal interest rate and the inflation rate.
    b. The real interest rate is the nominal interest rate minus the inflation rate.
    c. The nominal interest rate is the inflation rate minus the real interest rate.
    d. The nominal interest rate is the real interest rate minus the inflation rate.
    e. None of the above is true.

16. If inflation is 8 percent and the real interest rate is 3 percent, then the nominal interest rate should be
    a. 3/8 percent.
    b. 5 percent.
    c. 11 percent.
    d. 24 percent.
    e. –5 percent.

17. Under which of the following conditions would you prefer to be the lender?
    a. The nominal rate of interest is 20 percent and the inflation rate is 25 percent.
    b. The nominal rate of interest is 15 percent and the inflation rate is 14 percent.
    c. The nominal rate of interest is 12 percent and the inflation rate is 9 percent.
    d. The nominal rate of interest is 5 percent and the inflation rate is 1 percent.

18. Under which of the following conditions would you prefer to be the borrower?
    a. The nominal rate of interest is 20 percent and the inflation rate is 25 percent.
    b. The nominal rate of interest is 15 percent and the inflation rate is 14 percent.
    c. The nominal rate of interest is 12 percent and the inflation rate is 9 percent.
    d. The nominal rate of interest is 5 percent and the inflation rate is 1 percent.

19. If borrowers and lenders agree on a nominal interest rate and inflation turns out to be less than they had expected,
    a. borrowers will gain at the expense of lenders.
    b. lenders will gain at the expense of borrowers.
    c. neither borrowers nor lenders will gain because the nominal interest rate has been fixed by contract.
    d. none of the above is true.

20. If workers and firms agree on an increase in wages based on their expectations of inflation and inflation turns out to be more than they expected,
    a. firms will gain at the expense of workers.
    b. workers will gain at the expense of firms.
    c. neither workers nor firms will gain because the increase in wages is fixed in the labor agreement.
    d. none of the above is true.

ADVANCED CRITICAL THINKING

Your father quit smoking cigarettes in 1995. When you ask him why he quit, you get a surprising answer. Instead of reciting the health benefits of quitting smoking, he says, "I quit because it was just getting too expensive. I started smoking in 1965 in Vietnam and cigarettes were only 45 cents a pack. The last pack I bought was $2.00 and I just couldn't justify spending more than four times as much on cigarettes as I used to."

1. In 1965, the CPI was 31.5. In 1995 the CPI was 152.4. While it is commendable that your father quit smoking, what is wrong with his explanation?

   _____

   _____

2. What is the equivalent cost of a 1965 pack of cigarettes measured in 1995 prices?

   _____

   _____

3. What is the equivalent cost of a 1995 pack of cigarettes measured in 1965 prices?

   _____

   _____

4. Do both methods give you the same conclusion?

   _____

   _____

5. The preceding example demonstrates what economists refer to as "money illusion." Why do you think economists might choose the phrase "money illusion" to describe this behavior?

   _____

   _____

   _____

SOLUTIONS

Terms and Definitions

_3_ Consumer price index

_6_ Inflation rate

13 GDP deflator

_4_ Basket (of goods and services)

15 Base year

16 Bureau of Labor Statistics

_5_ Producer price index

_1_ Cost of living

10 Standard of living

_9_ Substitution bias

12 Nominal GDP

11 Real GDP

_2_ Indexed contract

_8_ Cost-of-living allowance (COLA)

14 Nominal interest rate

_7_ Real interest rate

Practice Problems

1. a. ($1,100/$1,100) × 100 = 100
    b. ($1,600/$1,100) × 100 = 145.5
    c. ($2,750/$1,100) × 100 = 250
    d. [(145.5 − 100)/100] × 100 = 45.5 percent
    e. [(250 − 145.5)/145.5] × 100 = 71.8 percent
    f. Substitution bias, because as the price of pens increased, the quantity consumed declined significantly.
    g. Increase, because this CPI overstates the increase in the cost of living.
    h. Decrease, because the price of pens has increased a greater percentage than the CPI.

2. a. $1.25 × (130.7/31.5) = $5.19
    b. It went down because $5.19 > $3.80
    c. $3.80 × (31.5/130.7) = $0.92
    d. Yes, because $0.92 < $1.25. Minimum-wage workers were better off in 1965.
    e. $3.35 × (124.0/90.9) = $4.57
        Further, ($3.35 − $4.57)/$4.57 = −27%
        Alternatively, you can deflate the minimum wage from 1989 to 1981 and get the same result.
    f. $3.80 × (172.2/130.7) = $5.01 < $5.15, so the standard of living of a worker earning the minimum wage improved slightly during the 1990s.

3. a. $9
    b. 9 percent − 5 percent = 4 percent
    c. 9 percent − 8 percent = 1 percent
    d. Your roommate (the borrower) gained; you lost because the borrower repaid the loan with dollars of surprisingly little value.
    e. 9% − 11% = −2%
    f. Because of inflation, the interest payment is not large enough to allow the lender to break even (maintain constant purchasing power compared to the day the loan was made).

Short-Answer Questions

1. The overall cost of the goods and services purchased by the typical consumer.
2. Fix the basket, find the prices, compute the basket's cost, choose a base year, and compute the index.
3. New cars, because there are a greater number of new cars in the typical consumption basket.
4. The CPI, because BMWs are in the typical consumption basket, but BMWs are not included in U.S. GDP.
5. Upward, unmeasured quality change.
6. No, $2.65 × (72.6/65.2) = $2.95, which is greater than $2.90.
7. The interest rate adjusted for the effects of inflation.
8. Expected real interest rate = 4 percent. Actual real interest rate = 8 percent. You gained and your sister lost.
9. When inflation is higher than expected, borrowers gain. When inflation is lower than expected, lenders gain.
10. Firms gain, workers lose, because wages didn't rise as much as the cost of living.

True/False Questions

1. T
2. F; military helicopters are not consumer goods.
3. F; the CPI tends to overstate the cost of living because people substitute toward cheaper goods.
4. F; prices in the CPI are weighted according to how much consumers buy of each and food is a larger portion of the consumption basket.
5. T
6. F; the CPI tends to overstate the effects of inflation.
7. F; the PPI measures the price of raw materials.
8. T
9. T
10. F; the largest category is housing.

11. F; if inflation exceeds the nominal interest rate, the real interest rate is negative.
12. T
13. T
14. F; borrowers will gain at the expense of lenders.
15. T

Multiple-Choice Questions

1. d
2. a
3. b
4. d
5. c
6. a
7. a
8. c
9. d
10. b
11. c
12. a
13. b
14. c
15. b
16. c
17. d
18. a
19. b
20. a

Advanced Critical Thinking

1. He is only looking at the cost of cigarettes uncorrected for inflation. It is likely that the real cost has not risen as much as first appears or maybe even gone down.
2. $\$0.45 \times (152.4/31.5) = \$2.18 > \$2.00$
3. $\$2.00 \times (31.5/152.4) = \$0.41 < \$0.45$
4. Yes, each method suggests that, after correcting for inflation, cigarettes were actually more expensive in 1965.
5. When people base decisions on values uncorrected for inflation, there may be an illusion that the cost of living has risen.

Production and Growth

CHAPTER OVERVIEW

Context and Purpose

Chapter 25 is the first chapter in a four-chapter sequence on the production of output in the long run. Chapter 25 addresses the determinants of the level and growth rate of output. We find that capital and labor are among the primary determinants of output. In Chapter 26, we address how saving and investment in capital goods affect the production of output, and in Chapter 27, we learn about some of the tools people and firms use when choosing capital projects in which to invest. In Chapter 28, we address the market for labor.

The purpose of Chapter 25 is to examine the long-run determinants of both the level and the growth rate of real GDP per person. Along the way, we will discover the factors that determine the productivity of workers and address what governments might do to improve the productivity of their citizens.

Chapter Review

Introduction   There is great variation in the standard of living across countries at a point in time and within a country across time—for example, between the United States and India today, and between the United States of today and the United States of 100 years ago. Growth rates also vary from country to country with East Asia growing quickly and Africa growing slowly. This chapter examines the long-run determinants of both the *level* and the *growth rate* of *real GDP per person.*

Economic Growth around the World

There is great variation across countries in both the *level* of real GDP per person and the *growth rate* of real GDP per person.

- At present, the *level* of real GDP per person in the United States is about 13 times that of India and 7 ½ times that of China.

- However, since the *growth rate* of real GDP per person also varies across countries, the ranking of countries by real GDP per person changes over time. For example, over the past 100 years, the ranking of Japan has risen relative to others because it has had an above average growth rate while the ranking of the United Kingdom has fallen due to its below average growth rate.

GOALS

In this chapter you will

- See how much economic growth differs around the world

- Consider why productivity is the key determinant of a country's standard of living

- Analyze the factors that determine a country's productivity

- Examine how a country's policies influence its productivity growth

OUTCOMES

After accomplishing these goals, you should be able to

- List the countries with the highest GDP per person and the countries whose GDP per person is growing the fastest

- Explain why production limits consumption in the long run

- List and explain the factors of production

- Explain seven areas of policy action that may influence a country's productivity and growth

Due to economic growth, the average American today enjoys conveniences, such as television, air conditioning, cars, telephones, and medicines, that the richest American didn't have 150 years ago. Since measures of inflation and output fail to fully capture the introduction of new goods, we overestimate inflation and underestimate economic growth.

Productivity: Its Role and Determinants

A country's standard of living depends directly on the productivity of its citizens because an economy's income is equal to an economy's output. **Productivity** refers to the quantity of goods and services produced from each unit of labor input. The productivity of a worker is determined by the available physical capital, human capital, natural resources, and technological knowledge. These inputs or *factors of production* are explained below:

- **Physical capital per worker** (or just capital): Physical capital is the stock of equipment and structures that are used to produce goods and services. Note that these tools and machines are themselves the output from prior human production.

- **Human capital per worker:** Human capital is the knowledge and skills that workers acquire through education, training, and experience. Note that human capital, like physical capital, is a human-made or produced factor of production.

- **Natural resources per worker:** Natural resources are inputs provided by nature's bounty, such as land, rivers, and mineral deposits. Natural resources come in two forms: *renewable* and *nonrenewable*.

- **Technological knowledge:** Technological knowledge is the understanding about the best ways to produce goods and services. Examples of advances in technology are the discovery and application of herbicides and pesticides in agriculture and of the assembly line in manufacturing.

Technological knowledge differs from human capital. Technological knowledge is society's understanding of the best production methods while human capital is the amount of understanding of these methods that has been transmitted to the labor force.

A *production function* establishes the relationship between the quantity of inputs used in production and the quantity of output from production. If a production function has *constant returns to scale*, then doubling all of the inputs doubles output.

In summary, output per worker (labor productivity) depends on physical capital per worker, human capital per worker, natural resources per worker, and the state of technology.

The only factor of production that is not a produced factor is natural resources. Since there is a fixed supply of nonrenewable natural resources, many people have argued that there is a limit to how much the world's economies can grow. So far, however, technological advances have found ways around these limits. Evidence of stable or falling prices of natural resources suggests that we are continuing to succeed at stretching our limited resources.

Economic Growth and Public Policy

Physical capital per worker, human capital per worker, natural resources per worker, and technological knowledge determine productivity. Productivity determines living standards. If a government wishes to raise the productivity and standard of living of its citizens, it should pursue policies that:

- *Encourage saving and investment.* If society consumes less and saves more, it has more resources available to invest in the production of capital. Additional capital increases productivity and living standards. This additional growth has an opportunity cost—society must give up current consumption in order to attain more growth. Investment in capital may be subject to **diminishing returns:** As the stock of capital rises, the extra output produced by an additional unit of capital declines. Thus, an additional increment of capital in a poor country increases growth more than the same increment in an already rich country. This is known as the **catch-up effect** because it is easier for a relatively poor country to grow quickly. However, because of diminishing returns to capital, higher saving and investment in a poor country will lead to higher growth only for a period of time, with growth slowing down again as the economy accumulates a higher level of capital stock.

- *Encourage investment from abroad,* by removing restrictions on the ownership of domestic capital and by providing a stable political environment. In addition to using domestic saving to invest in capital, countries can attract investment by foreigners. There are two categories of foreign investment. *Foreign direct investment* is capital investment that is owned and operated by a foreign entity. *Foreign portfolio investment* is capital investment that is financed with foreign money but is operated by domestic residents. Investment from abroad increases a country's GDP more than its GNP because the investing country earns the profits from the investment. The World Bank and the International Monetary Fund help channel foreign investment toward poor countries.

- *Encourage education.* Education is investment in human capital. Education not only increases the productivity of the recipient, it may provide a positive *externality*. An externality occurs when the actions of one person affect the well-being of a bystander. An educated individual may generate ideas that become useful to others. This is an argument for public education. Poor countries may suffer from *brain drain* when their educated workers emigrate to rich countries. Children in very poor countries may work instead of going to school because the opportunity cost of going to school is too great. Paying parents for sending their children to school may both reduce child labor and increase the education of very poor children. In very poor countries, improved health and nutrition of workers can significantly increase labor productivity.

- *Protect property rights and establish political stability. Property rights* refer to the ability of people to exercise control over their resources. For individuals to be willing to work, save and invest, and trade with others by contract, they must be confident that their production and capital will not be stolen and that their agreements will be enforced. Even a remote possibility of political instability creates uncertainty with regard to property rights because a revolutionary government might confiscate property—particularly capital.

- *Encourage free trade.* Free trade is like a technological advance. It allows a country to transform the output from its production into products that another country produces more efficiently. The *infant-industry argument* suggests that developing countries should pursue *inward-oriented policies* by restricting international trade to protect fledgling domestic industry from foreign competition. Most economists disagree with the infant-industry argument and promote *outward-oriented policies* that reduce or eliminate trade barriers.

- *Encourage research and development.* Most of the increase in the standard of living is due to an increase in technological knowledge that comes from research and development. After a time, knowledge is a *public good* in that we all can use it at the same time without diminishing another's benefits. Research and development might be encouraged with grants, tax breaks, and patents to establish temporary property rights to an invention. Alternatively, it might be encouraged by simply maintaining property rights and political stability.

- *Address population growth.* Population growth may affect productivity in both positive and negative ways. Rapid population growth may *stretch natural resources* across more people. Thomas Malthus (1766–1834) argued that population growth will always rise to the limit imposed by the food supply, causing mankind to live forever in poverty. Any attempt to alleviate poverty will simply cause the poor to have more children, returning them to subsistence living. Malthus' predictions have not come true because he underestimated the ability of technological progress to expand the food supply. Rapid population growth *dilutes the capital stock* (both physical and human capital) by spreading it across more workers. Educated women tend to have fewer children because the opportunity cost of having children increases as opportunities grow. However, a larger population may *promote technological progress*. Throughout history, most technological progress has come from larger population centers where there are more people who are able to discover things and exchange ideas.

Helpful Hints

1. A simple example more clearly defines the factors of production. The simpler the production process, the easier it is to separate and analyze the factors of production. For example, suppose output is "holes dug in the ground." Then the production function is:

$$Y = A\,F(L, K, H, N)$$

where Y is the number of holes dug, A is technological knowledge, L is labor, K is physical capital, H is human capital, and N is natural resources. If we have more workers, there is an increase in L and Y would increase. If we have more shovels, there is an increase in K and Y would increase. If workers are educated so that more of them dig with the spaded end of the shovel as opposed to digging with the handle, there is an increase in H and Y would increase. (Note: The number of workers and the number of shovels is unchanged.) If our country has softer soil so that digging is easier here, N is larger and, therefore, Y is larger. Finally, if we discover that it is more productive to dig after it rains rather than during a drought, there is an increase in A and Y should increase.

Terms and Definitions

Choose a definition for each key term.

Key Terms

_____ Real GDP per person

_____ Growth rate

_____ Productivity

_____ Physical capital

_____ Factors of production

_____ Human capital

_____ Natural resources

_____ Renewable resource

_____ Nonrenewable resource

_____ Technological knowledge

_____ Production function

_____ Constant returns to scale

_____ Diminishing returns

_____ Catch-up effect

_____ Foreign direct investment

_____ Foreign portfolio investment

_____ Externality

_____ Property rights

_____ Infant-industry argument

_____ Inward-oriented policies

_____ Outward-oriented policies

_____ Public good

Definitions

1. The knowledge and skills that workers acquire through education, training, and experience
2. Capital investment owned and operated by foreigners
3. The relationship between inputs and outputs from production
4. A good that we may all use at the same time without diminishing another's benefits
5. The ability of people to exercise control over their resources
6. The quantity of goods and services available for the average individual in the economy
7. The stock of equipment and structures used to produce output
8. When the incremental increase in output declines as equal increments of an input are added to production
9. A production process where doubling all of the inputs doubles the output
10. Natural resource that can be reproduced
11. Restricting international trade to protect fledgling domestic industry from foreign competition
12. Policies that decrease international trade restrictions
13. The property that poorer countries tend to grow more rapidly than richer countries
14. The annual percentage change in output
15. Inputs used in production, such as labor, capital, and natural resources
16. Natural resource that is limited in supply
17. When the actions of one person affect the well-being of a bystander
18. Policies that increase international trade restrictions
19. A society's understanding about the best ways to produce goods and services
20. The quantity of goods and services produced from each unit of labor input
21. Inputs into production provided by nature
22. Capital investment financed with foreign money but operated by domestic residents

PROBLEMS AND SHORT-ANSWER QUESTIONS

Practice Problems

1.

Country	Current Real GDP/Person	Current Growth Rate
Northcountry	$15,468	1.98%
Southcountry	13,690	2.03
Eastcountry	6,343	3.12
Westcountry	1,098	0.61

a. Which country is richest? How do you know?

_____

_____

b. Which country is advancing most quickly? How do you know?

_____

_____

c. Which country would likely see the greatest benefit from an increase in capital investment? Why?

_____

_____

_____

d. Referring to question *c* above: Would this country continue to see the same degree of benefits from an increase in capital investment forever? Why?

_____

_____

e. Referring to question *d* above: Why might investment in human capital and research and development fail to exhibit the same degree of diminishing returns as investment in physical capital?

_____

_____

f. Which country has the potential to grow most quickly? List some reasons why it may not be living up to potential.

_____

_____

_____

_____

g. If real GDP per person in Northcountry next year is $15,918, what is its annual growth rate?

_____

_____

2. Imagine a kitchen. It contains a cook, the cook's diploma, a recipe book, a stove and utensils, and some venison harvested from the open range.
   a. Link each object in the kitchen to a general category within the factors of production.

   _____

   _____

   _____

   b. While the different factors of production exhibit different levels of durability, which one is special in that it does not wear out?

   _____

   _____

   _____

3. a. List the policies governments might pursue to increase the productivity of their citizens.

   _____

   _____

   _____

   _____

   b. Which one is, at the very least, fundamentally necessary as a background in which the other policies may operate? Why?

   _____

   _____

   c. Does a growing population enhance or inhibit growth in productivity? Explain.

   _____

   _____

   _____

Short-Answer Questions

1. Economists measure both the level of real GDP per person and the growth rate of real GDP per person. What different concept does each statistic capture?

   _____

   _____

   _____

2. Must poor countries stay relatively poor forever and must rich countries stay relatively rich forever? Why?

_____

_____

_____

3. What factors determine productivity? Which ones are human produced?

_____

_____

4. How does human capital differ from physical capital?

_____

_____

_____

5. Explain the opportunity cost of investing in capital. Is there any difference in the opportunity cost of investing in human capital versus physical capital?

_____

_____

_____

6. Why does an increase in the rate of saving and investment only increase the rate of growth temporarily?

_____

_____

7. If foreigners buy newly issued stock in General Motors, and General Motors uses the proceeds to expand capacity by building new plants and equipment, which will rise more in the future: GDP or GNP? Why? What do we call this type of investment?

_____

_____

_____

_____

8. Some economists argue for lengthening patent protection while some economists argue for shortening it. Why might patents increase productivity? Why might they decrease productivity?

_____

_____

_____

SELF-TEST

True/False Questions

_____ 1. The United States should grow faster than Japan because the United States has a larger economy.

_____ 2. Evidence of rising prices for natural resources demonstrates that nonrenewable resources will become so scarce that economic growth will be limited.

_____ 3. The rate of economic growth is probably underestimated.

_____ 4. Human capital refers to human-made capital such as tools and machinery, as opposed to natural capital such as rivers and timber.

_____ 5. If a production function exhibits constant returns to scale, then doubling all of the inputs doubles output.

_____ 6. In very poor countries, paying parents to send their children to school may increase the education of poor children and decrease the use of child labor.

_____ 7. An increase in capital should cause the growth rate of a relatively poor country to increase more than that of a rich country.

_____ 8. An increase in the rate of saving and investment permanently increases a country's rate of growth.

_____ 9. A country can only increase its level of investment by increasing its saving.

_____10. The only factor of production that is not "produced" is natural resources.

_____11. Investment in human capital and technology may be particularly productive because of positive spillover effects.

_____12. If Germans invest in the U.S. economy by building a new Mercedes factory, in the future, U.S. GDP will rise by more than U.S. GNP.

_____13. Most economists believe that inward-oriented policies that protect infant industries improve the growth rates of developing nations.

_____14. Economic evidence supports the predictions of Thomas Malthus regarding the effects of population growth and the food supply on the standard of living.

_____15. The opportunity cost of additional growth is that someone must forgo current consumption.

Multiple-Choice Questions

1. A reasonable measure of the standard of living in a country is
   a. real GDP per person.
   b. real GDP.
   c. nominal GDP per person.
   d. nominal GDP.
   e. the growth rate of nominal GDP per person.

2. Many East Asian countries are growing very quickly because
   a. they have enormous natural resources.
   b. they are imperialists and have collected wealth from previous victories in war.
   c. they save and invest an unusually high percentage of their GDP.
   d. they have always been wealthy and will continue to be wealthy, which is known as the "snowball effect."

3. When a nation has very little GDP per person,
   a. it is doomed to being relatively poor forever.
   b. it must be a small nation.
   c. it has the potential to grow relatively quickly due to the "catch-up effect."
   d. an increase in capital will likely have little impact on output.
   e. none of the above is true.

4. Once a country is wealthy,
   a. it is nearly impossible for it to become relatively poorer.
   b. it may be harder for it to grow quickly because of the diminishing returns to capital.
   c. capital becomes more productive due to the "catch-up effect."
   d. it no longer needs any human capital.
   e. none of the above is true.

5. The opportunity cost of growth is
   a. a reduction in current investment.
   b. a reduction in current saving.
   c. a reduction in current consumption.
   d. a reduction in taxes.

6. *For a given level of technology*, we should expect an increase in labor productivity within a nation when there is an increase in each of the following *except*
   a. human capital per worker.
   b. physical capital per worker.
   c. natural resources per worker.
   d. labor.

7. Which of the following statements is true?
   a. Countries may have a different level of GDP per person, but they all grow at the same rate.
   b. Countries may have a different growth rate, but they all have the same level of GDP per person.
   c. Countries all have the same growth rate and level of output because any country can obtain the same factors of production.
   d. Countries have great variance in both the level and growth rate of GDP per person; thus, poor countries can become relatively rich over time.

8. If a production function exhibits constant returns to scale,
   a. doubling all of the inputs has absolutely no impact on output because output is constant.
   b. doubling all of the inputs doubles output.
   c. doubling all of the inputs more than doubles output due to the catch-up effect.
   d. doubling all of the inputs less than doubles output due to diminishing returns.

9. Copper is an example of
   a. human capital.
   b. physical capital.
   c. a renewable natural resource.
   d. a nonrenewable natural resource.
   e. technology.

10. Which of the following statements regarding the impact of population growth on productivity is true?
    a. There is no evidence, yet, that rapid population growth stretches natural resources to the point that it limits growth in productivity.
    b. Rapid population growth may dilute the capital stock, lowering productivity.
    c. Rapid population growth may promote technological progress, increasing productivity.
    d. All of the above are true.

11. Thomas Malthus argued that
    a. technological progress will continuously generate improvements in productivity and living standards.
    b. labor is the only true factor of production.
    c. an ever-increasing population is constrained only by the food supply, resulting in chronic famines.
    d. private charities and government aid will improve the welfare of the poor.
    e. none of the above is true.

12. Madelyn goes to college and reads many books while at school. Her education increases which of the following factors of production?
    a. human capital
    b. physical capital
    c. natural resources
    d. technology
    e. All of the above would be increased.

13. Which of the following describes an increase in technological knowledge?
    a. A farmer discovers that it is better to plant in the spring rather than in the fall.
    b. A farmer buys another tractor.
    c. A farmer hires another day laborer.
    d. A farmer sends his child to agricultural college and the child returns to work on the farm.

14. Our standard of living is most closely related to
    a. how hard we work.
    b. our supply of capital because everything of value is produced by machinery.
    c. our supply of natural resources because they limit production.
    d. our productivity because our income is equal to what we produce.

15. Which of the following is an example of foreign portfolio investment?
    a. A naturalized U.S. citizen, who was originally born in Germany, buys stock in Ford, and Ford uses the proceeds to buy a new plant.
    b. Toyota builds a new plant in Tennessee.
    c. Toyota buys stock in Ford, and Ford uses the proceeds to build a new plant in Michigan.
    d. Ford builds a new plant in Michigan.
    e. None of the above is an example of foreign portfolio investment.

16. Which of the following government policies is *least* likely to increase growth in Africa?
    a. increase expenditures on public education
    b. increase restrictions on the importing of Japanese automobiles and electronics
    c. eliminate civil war
    d. reduce restrictions on foreign capital investment
    e. All of the above would increase growth.

17. If Mazda builds a new plant in Illinois,
    a. in the future, U.S. GDP will rise more than U.S. GNP.
    b. in the future, U.S. GDP will rise less than U.S. GNP.
    c. in the future, U.S. GDP and GNP will both fall because some income from this investment will accrue to foreigners.
    d. there has been an increase in foreign portfolio investment in the United States.
    e. none of the above is true.

18. If real GDP per person in 2003 is $18,073 and real GDP per person in 2004 is $18,635, what is the growth rate of real output over this period?
    a. 3.0 percent
    b. 3.1 percent
    c. 5.62 percent
    d. 18.0 percent
    e. 18.6 percent

19. Which of the following expenditures to enhance productivity is most likely to emit a positive externality?
    a. Megabank buys a new computer.
    b. Susan pays her college tuition.
    c. Exxon leases a new oil field.
    d. General Motors buys a new drill press.

20. To increase growth, governments should do all of the following except
    a. promote free trade.
    b. encourage saving and investment.
    c. encourage foreigners to invest in your country.
    d. encourage research and development.
    e. nationalize major industries.

ADVANCED CRITICAL THINKING

You are having a discussion with other Generation Xers. The conversation turns to a supposed lack of growth and opportunity in the United States when compared to some Asian countries such as Japan, South Korea, Taiwan, and Singapore. Your roommate says, "These Asian countries must have cheated somehow. That's the only way they could have possibly grown so quickly."

1. Have you learned anything in this chapter that would make you question your roommate's assertion?

_____

_____

_____

2.   The phenomenal growth rate of Japan since World War II has often been referred to as the "Japanese miracle." Is it a miracle or is it explainable?

_____

_____

_____

3.   Are the high growth rates found in these Asian countries without cost?

_____

_____

SOLUTIONS

Terms and Definitions

_6_ Real GDP per person

_14_ Growth rate

_20_ Productivity

_7_ Physical capital

_15_ Factors of production

_1_ Human capital

_21_ Natural resources

_10_ Renewable resource

_16_ Nonrenewable resource

_19_ Technological knowledge

_3_ Production function

_9_ Constant returns to scale

_8_ Diminishing returns

_13_ Catch-up effect

_2_ Foreign direct investment

_22_ Foreign portfolio investment

_17_ Externality

_5_ Property rights

_11_ Infant-industry argument

_18_ Inward-oriented policies

_12_ Outward-oriented policies

_4_ Public good

Practice Problems

1. a. Northcountry, because it has the largest real GDP per person.

    b. Eastcountry, because it has the largest growth rate.

    c. Westcountry is the poorest and likely has the least capital. Since capital exhibits diminishing returns, it is most productive when it is relatively scarce.

    d. No. Because of diminishing returns to capital, the additional growth from increasing capital declines as a country has more capital.

    e. Human capital emits a positive externality. Research and development is a public good after dissemination.

    f. Westcountry, because it is currently the poorest and could easily benefit from additional capital. It may have trade restrictions (inward-oriented policies), a corrupt or unstable government, few courts, and a lack of established property rights, etc.

    g. ($15,918 − $15,468)/$15,468 = 0.029 = 2.9%

2. a. cook = labor, diploma = human capital, recipes = technological knowledge, stove and utensils = capital, venison = natural resource.

    b. Recipes (technological knowledge) never wear out. Labor and human capital die, the stove and utensils wear out slowly, and the venison is used up (although it is probably renewable).

3. a. Encourage saving and investment, investment from abroad, education, free trade, research and development, protect property rights, and establish political stability.

    b. Property rights and political stability are necessary for there to be any incentive to save, invest, trade, or educate.

    c. The answer is uncertain. A rapidly growing population may reduce productivity by stretching natural resources across more people and by diluting the capital stock across more workers. However, there is evidence that more technological progress takes place in areas with large populations.

Short-Answer Questions

1. Level of real GDP/person measures standard of living. Growth rate measures rate of advance of the standard of living.

2. No. Since growth rates vary widely across countries, rich can become relatively poorer and poor can become relatively richer.

3. Physical capital per worker, human capital per worker, natural resources per worker, and technological knowledge. All except natural resources.

4. Human capital is the knowledge and skills of the worker. Physical capital is the stock of equipment and structures.

5. Someone must forgo current consumption. No, someone must save instead of consume regardless of whether education or machines are purchased with the saving.

6. Because there are diminishing returns to physical capital.

7. GDP. GNP measures only the income of Americans while GDP measures income generated inside the United States. Therefore, GDP will rise more than GNP because some of the profits from the capital investment will accrue to foreigners in the form of dividends. Foreign portfolio investment.

8. Patents provide a property right to an idea; therefore, people are willing to invest in

research and development because it is more profitable. Research and development is a public good once the information is disseminated, and a patent restricts this public use.

True/False Questions

1. F; growth depends on the rate of increase in productivity.
2. F; the prices of natural resources, adjusted for inflation, are stable or falling, so our ability to conserve these resources is growing more rapidly than their supplies are dwindling.
3. T
4. F; human capital is the knowledge and skills of workers.
5. T
6. T
7. T
8. F; due to diminishing returns to capital, growth rises temporarily.
9. F; it can attract foreign investment.
10. T
11. T
12. T
13. F; most economists believe that outward-oriented policies improve growth.
14. F; Malthus underestimated technological improvements in food production. Thus, people are not doomed to live at subsistence.
15. T

Multiple-Choice Questions

1. a
2. c
3. c
4. b
5. c
6. d
7. d
8. b
9. d
10. d
11. c
12. a
13. a
14. d
15. c
16. b
17. a
18. b
19. b
20. e

Advanced Critical Thinking

1. Yes. There are many sources of growth and a country can influence all of them except natural resources.
2. Japan's growth is explainable. Indeed, all of the high-growth Asian countries have extremely high investment as a percent of GDP.
3. No. The opportunity cost of investment is that someone must forgo current consumption in order to save and invest.

Saving, Investment, and the Financial System

GOALS

In this chapter you will

- Learn about some of the important financial institutions in the U.S. economy

- Consider how the financial system is related to key macroeconomic variables

- Develop a model of the supply and demand for loanable funds in financial markets

- Use the loanable-funds model to analyze various government policies

- Consider how government budget deficits affect the U.S. economy

OUTCOMES

After accomplishing these goals, you should be able to

- List and describe four important types of financial institutions

- Describe the relationship between national saving, government deficits, and investment

- Explain the slope of the supply and demand for loanable funds

- Shift supply and demand in the loanable-funds market in response to a change in taxes on interest or investment

- Shift supply and demand in the loanable-funds market in response to a change in the government's budget deficit

CHAPTER OVERVIEW

Context and Purpose

Chapter 26 is the second chapter in a four-chapter sequence on the production of output in the long run. In Chapter 25, we found that capital and labor are among the primary determinants of output. For this reason, Chapter 26 addresses the market for saving and investment in capital, and Chapter 27 addresses the tools people and firms use when choosing capital projects in which to invest. Chapter 28 will address the market for labor.

The purpose of Chapter 26 is to show how saving and investment are coordinated by the loanable-funds market. Within the framework of the loanable-funds market, we are able to see the effects of taxes and government deficits on saving, investment, the accumulation of capital, and ultimately, the growth rate of output.

Chapter Review

Introduction Some people save some of their income and have funds that are available to loan. Some people wish to invest in capital equipment and thus need to borrow. The **financial system** consists of those institutions that help match, or balance, the lending of savers to the borrowing of investors. This is important because investment in capital contributes to economic growth.

Financial Institutions in the U.S. Economy

The financial system is made up of financial institutions that match borrowers and lenders. Financial institutions can be grouped into two categories: financial markets and financial intermediaries.

Financial markets allow firms to borrow _directly_ from those that wish to lend. The two most important financial markets are the bond market and the stock market.

- The _bond market_ allows large borrowers to borrow directly from the public. The borrower sells a **bond** (a certificate of indebtedness or IOU), which specifies the _date of maturity_ (the date the loan will be repaid), the amount of interest that will be paid periodically, and the _principal_ (the amount borrowed and to be repaid at maturity). The buyer of the bond is the lender.

Bond issues differ in three main ways:

(1) Bonds are of different *terms* (time to maturity). Longer term bonds are riskier and, thus, usually pay higher interest because the owner of the bond may need to sell it before maturity at a depressed price.

(2) Bonds have different *credit risk* (probability of default). Higher risk bonds pay higher interest. *Junk bonds* are exceptionally risky bonds.

(3) Bonds have different types of *tax treatment*. The interest received from owning a *municipal bond* (bond issued by state or local government) is tax exempt. Thus, municipal bonds pay lower interest.

- The *stock market* allows large firms to raise funds for expansion by taking on additional "partners" or owners of the firm. The sale of **stock** is called *equity finance* while the sale of bonds is called *debt finance.* Owners of stock share in the profits or losses of the firm while owners of bonds receive fixed interest payments as creditors. The stockholder accepts more risk than the bondholder but has a higher potential return. Stocks don't mature or expire and are traded on stock exchanges such as the New York Stock Exchange and NASDAQ. Stock prices are determined by supply and demand and reflect expectations of the firm's future profitability. A *stock index,* such as the Dow Jones Industrial Average, is an average of an important group of stock prices.

Financial intermediaries are financial institutions through which savers (lenders) can indirectly loan funds to borrowers. That is, financial intermediaries are middlepersons between borrowers and lenders. The two most important financial intermediaries are banks and mutual funds.

- *Banks* collect deposits from people and businesses (savers) and lend them to other people and businesses (borrowers). Banks pay interest on deposits and charge a slightly higher rate on their loans. Small businesses usually borrow from banks because they are too small to sell stock or bonds. Banks create a *medium of exchange* when they accept a deposit because individuals can write checks against the deposit to engage in transactions. Other intermediaries only offer savers a *store of value* because their saving is not as accessible.

- **Mutual funds** are institutions that sell shares to the public and use the proceeds to buy a group of stocks and/or bonds. This allows small savers to *diversify* their asset *portfolios* (own a variety of assets). It also allows small savers access to professional money managers. However, few money managers can beat *index funds,* which buy all of the stocks in a stock index without the aid of active management. There are two reasons why index funds outperform actively managed funds. First, it is hard to pick stocks whose prices will rise because the market price of a stock is already a good reflection of a company's true value. Second, index funds keep costs low by rarely buying and selling and by not having to pay the salaries of professional money managers.

Although there are many differences among these financial institutions, the overriding similarity is that they all direct resources from lenders to borrowers.

Saving and Investment in the National Income Accounts

In order to truly appreciate the role of the financial system in directing saving into investment, we must begin to understand saving and investment from a macroeconomic perspective. The national income accounts record the relationship between income, output, saving, investment, expenditures, taxes, and so on. There are a number of national income *identities* (equations that are true by definition) that expose relationships between these variables.

Recall, GDP is the value of output, the value of income earned from producing it, and *the value of expenditures* on it. Therefore,

$$Y = C + I + G + NX$$

where Y = GDP, C = consumption expenditures, I = investment expenditures, G = government purchases, and NX = net exports. To simplify, we assume there is no international sector, which means that we have a *closed economy.* (An *open economy* includes a foreign sector.) Therefore, for our example

$$Y = C + I + G.$$

National saving, or just **saving,** is the income left over after paying for consumption and government purchases. To find saving, subtract C and G from both sides.

$$Y - C - G = I$$

$$\text{or } S = I$$

which says, saving = investment.

To appreciate the impact of the government's purchases and taxes on saving, we need to define saving as above:

$$S = Y - C - G$$

which says again that saving is income left over after consumption and government purchases. Now add and subtract T (taxes) from the right side:

$$S = (Y - T - C) + (T - G).$$

This says that saving is equal to **private saving** $(Y - T - C)$, which is income left over after paying taxes and consumption, and **public saving** $(T - G)$, which is the government's **budget surplus.** Often G is greater than T, and the government runs a negative surplus or a **budget deficit.**

In summary, $S = I$ for the economy as a whole and the amount of saving available for investment is the sum of private saving and public saving. Although $S = I$ for the entire economy, it is not true for each individual. That is, some people invest less than they save and have funds to lend while others invest more than they save and need to borrow funds. These groups meet in the **market for loanable funds.** Note that saving is the income that remains after paying for consumption and government purchases while investment is the purchase of new capital.

The Market for Loanable Funds

For simplicity, imagine that there is one loanable funds market where all savers take their funds to be loaned and where all investors go to borrow funds.

- The *supply of loanable funds* comes from national saving. A higher real interest rate increases the incentive to save and increases the quantity supplied of loanable funds.

- The *demand for loanable funds* comes from households and firms that wish to borrow to invest. A higher real interest rate increases the cost of borrowing and reduces the quantity demanded of loanable funds.

The supply and demand for loanable funds combine to generate a market for loanable funds. This market determines the equilibrium real interest rate and the equilibrium quantity of funds loaned and borrowed. Since the funds that are loaned are national saving and the funds that are borrowed are used for investment, the loanable-funds market also determines the equilibrium level of saving and investment.

The following three policies increase saving, investment, and capital accumulation, and hence, these policies increase economic growth.

Reduced taxation on interest and dividends increases the return to saving for any real interest rate and, thus, increases the desire to save and loan at each real interest rate. Graphically, this policy will shift the supply of loanable funds to the right, lower the real interest rate, and raise the quantity demanded of funds for investment. Real interest rates fall while saving and investment rise.

Reduced taxation if one invests, for example an investment tax credit, will increase the return to investment in capital for any real interest rate and, thus, increase the desire to borrow and invest at each real interest rate. Graphically, this policy will shift the demand for loanable funds to the right, raise the real interest rate, and increase the quantity supplied of funds. Real interest rates, saving, and investment rise.

A reduction in government debt and deficits (or an increase in a budget surplus) increases public saving $(T - G)$ so more national saving is available at each real interest rate. Graphically, this policy will shift the supply of loanable funds to the right, decrease the real interest rate, and increase the quantity demanded of funds for investment. Real interest rates fall, and saving and investment rise.

Note that a *budget deficit* is an excess of government spending over tax revenue. The accumulation of past government borrowing is called the *government debt.* A *budget surplus* is an excess of tax revenue over government spending. When government spending equals tax revenue, there is a *balanced budget*. An increase in the deficit reduces national saving, shifts the supply of loanable funds to the left, raises the real interest rate, and reduces the quantity demanded of funds for investment. When private borrowing and investment are reduced due to government borrowing, we say that government is **crowding out** investment. Government surpluses do just the opposite of budget deficits.

The debt–GDP ratio usually rises during wars and this is considered appropriate. However, it rose during the 1980s. Policymakers from both parties viewed this with alarm and deficits were reduced during the 1990s and a surplus arose. During the George W. Bush presidency, the budget returned to deficit for a number of reasons: tax cuts, a recession, and the war on terrorism.

Helpful Hints

1. A financial intermediary is a middleperson. An intermediary is someone who gets between two groups and negotiates a solution. For example, we have intermediaries in labor negotiations that sit between a firm and a union. In like manner, a bank is a financial intermediary in that it sits between the ultimate lender (the depositor) and the ultimate borrower (the firm or home builder) and "negotiates" the terms of the loan contracts. Banks don't lend their own money. They lend the depositor's money.

2. Investment is not the purchase of stocks and bonds. In casual conversation, people use the word "investment" to mean the purchase of stocks and bonds. For example, "I just invested in ten shares of IBM." (Even an economist might say this.) However, when speaking in economic terms, *investment* is the actual purchase of capital equipment and structures. In this technical framework, when I buy ten shares of newly issued IBM stock, there has been only an exchange of assets—IBM has my money and I have their stock certificates. If IBM takes my money and buys new equipment with it, their purchase of the equipment is economic *investment*.

3. Don't include consumption loans in the supply of loanable funds. In casual conversation, people use the word "saving" to refer to their new deposit in a bank. For example, "I just saved $100 this week." (An economist might say this, too.) However, if that deposit were loaned out to a consumer who used the funds to purchase airline tickets for a vacation, there has been no increase in *national saving* (or just *saving*) in a macroeconomic sense. This is because saving, in a macroeconomic sense, is income (GDP) that remains after *national* consumption expenditures and government purchases ($S = Y - C - G$). No national saving took place if your personal saving was loaned and used for consumption expenditures by another person. Since national saving is the source of the supply of loanable funds, consumption loans do not affect the supply of loanable funds.

4. Demand for loanable funds is private demand for investment funds. The demand for loanable funds only includes private (households and firms) demand for funds to invest in capital structures and equipment. When the government runs a deficit, it does absorb national saving but it does not buy capital equipment with the funds. Therefore, when the government runs a deficit, we consider it a reduction in the supply of loanable funds, not an increase in the demand for loanable funds.

Terms and Definitions

Choose a definition for each key term.

Key Terms	Definitions

Key Terms

____ Financial system

____ Financial markets

____ Financial intermediaries

____ Bank

____ Medium of exchange

____ Bond

____ Stock

____ Mutual fund

____ Closed economy

____ National saving (saving)

____ Private saving

____ Public saving

____ Budget surplus

____ Budget deficit

____ Government debt

____ Investment

____ Market for loanable funds

____ Demand for loanable funds

____ Supply of loanable funds

____ Crowding out

Definitions

1. Spendable asset such as a checking deposit

2. A shortfall of tax revenue relative to government spending causing public saving to be negative

3. An economy with no international transactions

4. Financial institutions through which savers can indirectly lend to borrowers

5. The group of institutions in the economy that help match borrowers and lenders

6. The amount of borrowing for investment desired at each real interest rate

7. The income that remains after consumption expenditures and taxes

8. The accumulation of past budget deficits

9. The amount of saving made available for lending at each real interest rate

10. Institution that collects deposits and makes loans

11. Institution that sells shares and uses the proceeds to buy a diversified portfolio

12. Financial institutions through which savers can directly lend to borrowers

13. Certificate of ownership of a small portion of a large firm

14. An excess of tax revenue over government spending causing public saving to be positive

15. The income that remains after consumption expenditures and government purchases

16. A decrease in investment as a result of government borrowing

17. Expenditures on capital equipment and structures

18. Certificate of indebtedness or IOU

19. The market in which those who want to save supply funds and those who want to borrow to invest demand funds

20. The tax revenue that the government has left after paying for its spending

PROBLEMS AND SHORT-ANSWER QUESTIONS

Practice Problems

1. Fly-by-night Corporation is in need of capital funds to expand its production capacity. It is selling short- and long-term bonds and is issuing stock. You are considering the prospect of helping finance their expansion.

    a. If you are to buy both short- and long-term bonds from Fly-by-night, from which bond would you demand a higher rate of return: short- or long-term? Why?

    _____

    _____

    _____

    _____

    b. If Standard and Poor's lowered the credit worthiness of Fly-by-night, would this affect the rate of return you would demand when buying their bonds? Why?

    _____

    _____

    _____

    _____

    c. If Fly-by-night has exactly the same creditworthiness as Deadbeat City and each is issuing the same term to maturity bonds, which issuer must pay the higher interest rate on its bonds? Why?

    _____

    _____

    _____

    _____

    d. If Fly-by-night is issuing both stocks and bonds, from which would you expect to earn the higher rate of return over the long run? Why?

    _____

    _____

    _____

    _____

e. Which would be safer: putting all of your personal saving into Fly-by-night stock or putting all of your personal saving into a mutual fund that has some Fly-by-night stock in its portfolio? Why?

_____

_____

_____

_____

2. Use the saving and investment identities from the national income accounts to answer the following questions. Suppose the following values are from the national income accounts of a country with a closed economy (all values are in billions).

   $Y = \$6,000$

   $T = \$1,000$

   $C = \$4,000$

   $G = \$1,200$

   a. What is the value of saving and investment in this country?

   _____

   _____

   b. What is the value of private saving?

   _____

   _____

   c. What is the value of public saving?

   _____

   _____

   d. Is the government's budget policy contributing to growth in this country or harming it? Why?

   _____

   _____

   _____

   _____

3. The following information describes a loanable-funds market. Values are in billions.

Real Interest Rate	Quantity of Loanable Funds Supplied	Quantity of Loanable Funds Demanded
6%	$1,300	$700
5	1,200	800
4	1,000	1,000
3	800	1,200
2	600	1,500

a. Plot the supply and demand for loanable funds in Exhibit 1. What is the equilibrium real interest rate and the equilibrium level of saving and investment?

_____

_____

b. What "market forces" will not allow 2 percent to be the real interest rate?

_____

c. Suppose the government suddenly increases its budget deficit by $400 billion. What is the new equilibrium real interest rate and equilibrium level of saving and investment? (Show graphically in Exhibit 2.)

_____

d. Starting at the original equilibrium, suppose the government enacts an investment tax credit that stimulates the demand for loanable funds for capital investment by $400 billion at any real interest rate. What is the new equilibrium real interest rate and equilibrium level of saving and investment? (Show graphically in Exhibit 3.)

_____

e. With regard to questions *c* and *d*, which policy is most likely to increase growth? Why?

_____

_____

_____

Short-Answer Questions

1. Explain why a mutual fund is likely to be less risky than an individual stock.

_____

_____

_____

2. Which is likely to give you a greater rate of return: a checking deposit at a bank or the purchase of a corporate bond? Why?

_____

_____

_____

3. What is the difference between debt finance and equity finance? Provide an example of each.

_____

_____

_____

4. What is meant by the words "saving" and "investment" in the national income accounts and how does that use of the words differ from the casual use of the words?

    _____

    _____

    _____

    _____

5. In a closed economy, why can't investment ever exceed saving?

    _____

    _____

    _____

6. What is private saving? What is public saving?

    _____

    _____

7. Utilizing the national income identities, if government purchases were to rise, and if output, taxes, and consumption were to remain unchanged, what would happen to national saving, investment, and growth?

    _____

    _____

    _____

8. Suppose Americans become more frugal. That is, they consume a smaller percent of their income and save a larger percent. Describe the changes in the loanable-funds market. What would likely happen to growth?

    _____

    _____

    _____

    _____

9. Suppose the government runs a smaller deficit. Describe the changes in the loanable-funds market. What would likely happen to growth?

    _____

    _____

    _____

    _____

10. An increase in the government's budget deficit forces the government to borrow more. Why doesn't an increase in the deficit increase the demand for loanable funds in the loanable-funds market?

_____

_____

_____

11. What is the fundamental difference between financial markets and financial intermediaries?

_____

_____

SELF-TEST

True/False Questions

_____ 1. When a business firm sells a bond, it has engaged in equity finance.

_____ 2. People who buy stock in a firm have loaned money to the firm.

_____ 3. Mutual funds reduce a shareholder's risk by purchasing a diversified portfolio.

_____ 4. Municipal bonds pay less interest than comparable risk corporate bonds because the interest payments are tax exempt to the bondholder.

_____ 5. In a closed economy, saving is what remains after consumption expenditures and government purchases.

_____ 6. Public saving is always positive.

_____ 7. In a closed economy, investment is always equal to saving regardless of where the saving came from—public or private sources.

_____ 8. Investment is the purchase of capital equipment and structures.

_____ 9. If you save money this week and lend it to your roommate to buy food for consumption, your act of personal saving has increased national saving.

_____ 10. The quantity supplied of loanable funds is greater if real interest rates are higher.

_____ 11. If the real interest rate in the loanable-funds market is temporarily held above the equilibrium rate, desired borrowing will exceed desired lending and the real interest rate will fall.

_____ 12. A reduction in the budget deficit should shift the supply of loanable funds to the right, lower the real interest rate, and increase the quantity demanded of loanable funds.

_____ 13. Public saving and the government's budget surplus are the same thing.

_____ 14. If the government wanted to increase the rate of growth, it should raise taxes on interest and dividends to shift the supply of loanable funds to the right.

_____ 15. An increase in the budget deficit that causes the government to increase its borrowing shifts the demand for loanable funds to the right.

Multiple-Choice Questions

1. Which of the following is an example of equity finance?
   a. corporate bonds
   b. municipal bonds
   c. stock
   d. bank loan
   e. All of the above are equity finance.

2. Credit risk refers to a bond's
   a. term to maturity.
   b. probability of default.
   c. tax treatment.
   d. dividend.
   e. price-earnings ratio.

3. A financial intermediary is a middleperson between
   a. labor unions and firms.
   b. husbands and wives.
   c. buyers and sellers.
   d. borrowers and lenders.

4. National saving (or just saving) is equal to
   a. private saving + public saving.
   b. investment + consumption expenditures.
   c. GDP – government purchases.
   d. GDP + consumption expenditures + government purchases.
   e. none of the above.

5. Which of the following statements is true?
   a. A stock index is a directory used to locate information about selected stocks.
   b. Longer term bonds tend to pay less interest than shorter term bonds.
   c. Municipal bonds pay less interest than comparable corporate bonds.
   d. Mutual funds are riskier than single stock purchases because the performance of so many different firms can affect the return of a mutual fund.

6. If government spending exceeds tax collections,
   a. there is a budget surplus.
   b. there is a budget deficit.
   c. private saving is positive.
   d. public saving is positive.
   e. none of the above is true.

7. If GDP = $1,000, consumption = $600, taxes = $100, and government purchases = $200, how much is saving and investment?
   a. saving = $200, investment = $200
   b. saving = $300, investment = $300
   c. saving = $100, investment = $200
   d. saving = $200, investment = $100
   e. saving = $0, investment = $0

8. If the public consumes $100 billion less and the government purchases $100 billion more (other things unchanging), which of the following statements is true?
   a. There is an increase in saving, and the economy should grow more quickly.
   b. There is a decrease in saving, and the economy should grow more slowly.
   c. Saving is unchanged.
   d. There is not enough information to determine what will happen to saving.

9. Which of the following financial market securities would likely pay the highest interest rate?
    a. a municipal bond issued by the state of Texas
    b. a mutual fund with a portfolio of blue chip bonds
    c. a bond issued by a blue chip company
    d. a bond issued by a start-up company

10. Investment is
    a. the purchase of stocks and bonds.
    b. the purchase of capital equipment and structures.
    c. when we place our saving in the bank.
    d. the purchase of goods and services.

11. If Americans become more thrifty, we would expect
    a. the supply of loanable funds to shift to the right and the real interest rate to rise.
    b. the supply of loanable funds to shift to the right and the real interest rate to fall.
    c. the demand for loanable funds to shift to the right and the real interest rate to rise.
    d. the demand for loanable funds to shift to the right and the real interest rate to fall.

12. Which of the following sets of government policies is the most growth oriented?
    a. lower taxes on the returns to saving, provide investment tax credits, and lower the deficit
    b. lower taxes on the returns to saving, provide investment tax credits, and increase the deficit
    c. increase taxes on the returns to saving, provide investment tax credits, and lower the deficit
    d. increase taxes on the returns to saving, provide investment tax credits, and increase the deficit

13. An increase in the budget deficit that causes the government to increase its borrowing
    a. shifts the demand for loanable funds to the right.
    b. shifts the demand for loanable funds to the left.
    c. shifts the supply of loanable funds to the left.
    d. shifts the supply of loanable funds to the right.

14. An increase in the budget deficit will
    a. raise the real interest rate and decrease the quantity of loanable funds demanded for investment.
    b. raise the real interest rate and increase the quantity of loanable funds demanded for investment.
    c. lower the real interest rate and increase the quantity of loanable funds demanded for investment.
    d. lower the real interest rate and decrease the quantity of loanable funds demanded for investment.

15. If the supply of loanable funds is very inelastic (steep), which policy would likely increase saving and investment the most?
    a. an investment tax credit
    b. a reduction in the budget deficit
    c. an increase in the budget deficit
    d. none of the above

16. An increase in the budget deficit is
     a. a decrease in public saving.
     b. an increase in public saving.
     c. a decrease in private saving.
     d. an increase in private saving.
     e. none of the above.

17. If an increase in the budget deficit reduces national saving and investment, we
     have witnessed a demonstration of
     a. equity finance.
     b. the mutual fund effect.
     c. intermediation.
     d. crowding out.

18. If Americans become less concerned with the future and save less at each real
     interest rate,
     a. real interest rates fall and investment falls.
     b. real interest rates fall and investment rises.
     c. real interest rates rise and investment falls.
     d. real interest rates rise and investment rises.

19. If the government increases investment tax credits and reduces taxes on the re-
     turn to saving at the same time,
     a. the real interest rate should rise.
     b. the real interest rate should fall.
     c. the real interest rate should not change.
     d. the impact on the real interest rate is indeterminate.

20. An increase in the budget surplus
     a. shifts the demand for loanable funds to the right and increases the real inter-
         est rate.
     b. shifts the demand for loanable funds to the left and reduces the real interest
         rate.
     c. shifts the supply of loanable funds to the left and increases the real interest
         rate.
     d. shifts the supply of loanable funds to the right and reduces the real interest
         rate.

ADVANCED CRITICAL THINKING

You are watching a presidential debate. When a candidate is questioned about his position on economic growth, the presidential candidate steps forward and says, "We need to get this country growing again. We need to use tax incentives to stimulate saving and investment, and we need to get that
budget deficit down so that the government stops absorbing our nation's saving."

1. If government spending remains unchanged, what inconsistency is implied by
    the presidential candidate's statement?

    _____

    _____

    _____

    _____

2. If the presidential candidate truly wishes to decrease taxes and decrease the budget deficit, what has the candidate implied about his plans for government spending?

    _____

    _____

3. If policymakers want to increase growth, and if policymakers have to choose between tax incentives to stimulate saving and tax incentives to stimulate investment, what might they want to know about supply and demand in the loanable-funds market before making their decision? Explain.

    _____

    _____

    _____

    _____

    _____

    _____

    _____

SOLUTIONS

Terms and Definitions

_5_ Financial system

12 Financial markets

_4_ Financial intermediaries

10 Bank

_1_ Medium of exchange

18 Bond

13 Stock

11 Mutual fund

_3_ Closed economy

15 National saving (saving)

_7_ Private saving

20 Public saving

14 Budget surplus

_2_ Budget deficit

_8_ Government debt

17 Investment

19 Market for loanable funds

_6_ Demand for loanable funds

_9_ Supply of loanable funds

16 Crowding out

Practice Problems

1. a. Long term, because it is more likely that you may need to sell the long-term bond at a depressed price prior to maturity.

   b. Yes, the credit risk has increased and lenders would demand a higher rate of return.

   c. Fly-by-night. Unlike municipal bonds, interest receipts are taxable to the owners of corporate bonds.

   d. Owners of stock demand a higher rate of return because it is riskier.

   e. It is safer to put money in a mutual fund because it is diversified (not all of your eggs in one basket).

2. a. ($6,000 − $1,000 − $4,000) + ($1,000 − $1,200) = $800 billion

   b. $6,000 − $1,000 − $4,000 = $1,000 billion

   c. $1,000 − $1,200 = −$200 billion

   d. It is harming growth because public saving is negative so less is available for investment.

3. a. Equilibrium real interest rate = 4%, equilibrium S and I = $1,000 billion. (See Exhibit 4.)

   b. At 2 percent interest, the quantity demanded of loanable funds exceeds the quantity supplied by $900 billion. This excess demand for loans (borrowing) will drive interest rates up to 4 percent.

4 EXHIBIT

c. Equilibrium real interest rate = 5%, equilibrium S and I = $800 billion. (See Exhibit 5.)

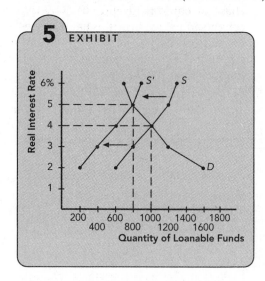

5 EXHIBIT

d. Equilibrium real interest rate = 5%, equilibrium S and I = $1,200 billion. (See Exhibit 6.)

6 EXHIBIT

e. An investment tax credit, because it shifts the demand for loanable funds to invest in capital to the right, raising the level of investment in capital and stimulating growth.

Short-Answer Questions

1. Because a mutual fund is diversified. When one stock in the fund is performing poorly, it is likely that another stock is performing well.

2. A corporate bond, because the bond is riskier and because "direct" lending through a financial market has fewer overhead costs than "indirect" lending through an intermediary.

3. Debt finance is borrowing such as when a firm sells a bond. Equity finance is taking on additional partners such as when a firm sells stock.

4. Saving is what remains after consumption and government purchases. Investment is the purchase of equipment and structures. In casual conversation, saving is what remains out of our income (even if someone else borrows it for consumption) and investment is the purchase of stocks and bonds.

5. Because saving is the GDP left over after consumption expenditures and government purchases, and this is the limit of the output available to be used to purchase equipment and structures.

6. Private saving = $Y - T - C$; public saving = $T - G$.

7. Public saving would decrease and cause national saving and investment to decrease by the same amount, slowing growth.

8. The supply of loanable funds would shift right, the real interest rate would fall, and the quantity demanded of loanable funds to purchase capital would increase. Growth would increase.

9. The supply of loanable funds would shift right, the real interest rate would fall, and the quantity demanded of loanable funds to purchase capital would increase. Growth would increase.

10. The demand for loanable funds is defined as private demand for borrowing to purchase capital equipment and structures. An increase in the deficit absorbs saving and reduces the supply of loanable funds.

11. In a financial market, savers lend directly to borrowers. Through financial intermediaries, savers lend to an intermediary who then lends to the ultimate borrower.

True/False Questions

1. F; to sell a bond is to engage in debt finance.
2. F; stockholders are owners.

3. T
4. T
5. T
6. F; public saving is negative when there is a government budget deficit.
7. T
8. T
9. F; consumption loans do not increase national saving.
10. T
11. F; desired lending exceeds desired borrowing.
12. T
13. T
14. F; it should lower taxes on interest and dividends.
15. F; it decreases the supply of loanable funds.

Multiple-Choice Questions

1. c
2. b
3. d
4. a
5. c
6. b
7. a
8. c
9. d
10. b
11. b
12. a
13. c
14. a
15. b
16. a
17. d
18. c
19. d
20. d

Advanced Critical Thinking

1. Tax incentives to stimulate saving and investment require a reduction in taxes. This would increase the deficit, which would reduce national saving and investment.

2. The candidate plans to reduce government spending.

3. Policymakers would want to know the elasticity (similar to the steepness) of the supply and demand curves. If loanable funds demand is inelastic, changes in loanable funds supply have

little effect on saving and investment, so tax incentives to increase saving at each interest rate do little for growth. If loanable funds supply is inelastic, changes in loanable funds demand have little effect on saving and investment, so tax incentives to increase investment at each interest rate do little for growth.

The Basic Tools of Finance

GOALS

In this chapter you will

- Learn the relationship between present value and future value

- Consider the effects of compound growth

- Learn how risk-averse people reduce the risk they face

- Analyze how asset prices are determined

OUTCOMES

After accomplishing these goals, you should be able to

- Choose between receiving $100 now or $120 two years from now, given an interest rate of 8 percent

- Explain why two people whose incomes grow at slightly different rates may end up with significantly different incomes after a number of years

- Explain the benefits of diversification

- Show why randomly choosing stocks may be as good as more sophisticated stock-picking methods

CHAPTER OVERVIEW

Context and Purpose

Chapter 27 is the third chapter in a four-chapter sequence on the level and growth of output in the long run. In Chapter 25, we learned that capital and labor are among the primary determinants of output and growth. In Chapter 26, we addressed how saving and investment in capital goods affect the production of output. In Chapter 27, we will learn about some of the tools people and firms use when choosing capital projects in which to invest. Since both capital and labor are among the primary determinants of output, Chapter 28 will address the market for labor.

The purpose of Chapter 27 is to introduce you to some tools that people use when they participate in financial markets. We will learn how people compare different sums of money at different points in time, how they manage risk, and how these concepts combine to help determine the value of a financial asset, such as a share of stock.

Chapter Review

Introduction Financial markets coordinate saving and investment. Financial decisions involve two elements—time and risk. For example, people and firms must make decisions today about saving and investment based on expectations of future earnings, but future returns are uncertain. The field of **finance** studies how people make decisions regarding the allocation of resources over time and the handling of risk. We will learn how people compare different sums of money at different points in time, how they manage risk, and how these concepts combine to help determine the value of a financial asset, such as a share of stock.

Present Value: Measuring the Time Value of Money

The **present value** of any future value is the amount today that would be needed, at current interest rates, to produce that future sum. The **future value** is the amount of money in the future that an amount of money today will yield, given prevailing interest rates. Suppose r = the interest rate expressed in decimal form, n = years to maturity, PV = present value, and FV = future value. Further, suppose that interest is paid annually and that the interest is put in the account to earn more interest—a process called **compounding**. Then:

(1) $PV(1 + r)n = FV$, and

(2) $FV/(1 + r)n = PV$.

For example, suppose a person deposited $100 into a bank account for three years earning 7 percent interest. Using equation (1) where $r = 0.07$, $PV = \$100$, and $n = 3$, we find that in three years the account will hold about $122.50. That is, the future value is $122.50.

Alternatively, suppose you were offered a bank deposit that would provide you with $122.50 three years from now. At an interest rate of 7 percent, what would you pay for that account today? Using equation (2) where $r = 0.07$, $FV = \$122.50$, and $n = 3$, we find that the present value of $122.50 three years from today is $100. Finding the present value of a future sum is called *discounting*.

The relationship between present value and future value demonstrates the following:

- Receiving a given sum in the present is preferred to receiving the same sum in the future. The larger the interest rate, the more pronounced is this result.

- In order to choose between two sums—a value today or a larger value at some later date—find the present value of the larger future sum and compare it to the value today.

- Firms undertake investment projects if the present value of the future returns exceeds the cost. The larger the interest rate, the less likely the project will be undertaken because the present value of the project becomes smaller. Thus, investment declines as interest rates rise.

Small differences in growth rates can make enormous differences in a country's level of income after many years. This result is also true for an individual's income or for money deposited in a bank. The concept of *compound growth* shows why. Each year's growth is based on the previous year's accumulated growth, or in the case of interest, interest is earned on previously earned interest. The effects of compound growth are demonstrated by the *rule of 70*, which states that if some variable grows at a rate of x percent per year, its value will double in approximately $70/x$ years. If your income grows at 1 percent per year, it will about double in 70 years. However, if your income grows at 4 percent, it will double in approximately 17.5 years.

Managing Risk

Most people are **risk averse,** which means that they dislike bad things more than they like comparable good things. This is because people's utility functions exhibit diminishing marginal utility of wealth. Thus, the utility lost from losing a $1,000 bet is greater than that gained from winning a $1,000 bet. People can reduce risk by buying insurance, diversifying their risk, and accepting a lower return on their assets.

- *People can reduce the risk they face by buying insurance.* Insurance allows the economy to spread the risk more efficiently because it is easier for 100 people to bear 1/100 of the group's risk of a house fire than for each to bear the entire risk of one house fire alone. There are two problems with insurance markets. *Adverse selection* occurs because a high-risk person is more likely to buy insurance than a low-risk person. *Moral hazard* occurs because after people buy insurance, they have less incentive to be careful. Some low-risk people don't buy insurance because these problems may cause the price of insurance to be too high for low-risk people. Health insurance is poorly designed because it covers routine expenses, small random expenses, and is connected with employment. These three features result from the tax exempt status of employer-provided health insurance, which leads to excessive spending on health care.

- *People can reduce the risk they face through diversification.* **Diversification** is the reduction of risk achieved by replacing a single risk with a large number of smaller unrelated risks. This is summarized by the phrase, "Don't put all of your eggs in one basket." Risk is diversified through insurance because it is easier for 100 people to bear 1/100 of the group's risk of a house fire than for each to bear the entire risk of one house fire alone. The risk on a portfolio of stocks, as measured by the *standard deviation* (volatility) of the returns, is reduced by diversifying the portfolio—

buying a small amount of a large number of stocks instead of a large amount of one stock. Diversification can eliminate **firm-specific risk**—the uncertainty associated with specific companies. It cannot eliminate **market risk**—the uncertainty associated with the entire economy, which affects all companies traded on the stock market.

- *People can reduce the risk they face by accepting a lower rate of return on their investments.* People face a trade-off between risk and return in their portfolio. In order to earn greater returns, people must accept more risk. In order to have less risk, people must accept lower returns. The optimal combination of risk and return for a person depends on the person's degree of risk aversion, which depends on the person's preferences.

Asset Valuation

The price of a share of stock is determined by supply and demand. People often try to buy stock that is *undervalued*—shares of a business whose value exceeds its price. If the price exceeds the value, the stock is considered *overvalued* and if the price and value are equal, the stock is *fairly valued*. The price of the stock is known. The value of a stock is uncertain because it is the present value of the future stream of dividends and the final sales price. The dividends and final sales price depend on the firm's future profitability. **Fundamental analysis** is a detailed analysis of a company's accounting statements and future prospects to determine its value. You can perform fundamental analysis yourself, rely on Wall Street analysts, or buy a mutual fund whose manager does fundamental analysis.

According to the **efficient markets hypothesis,** asset prices reflect all publicly available information about the value of an asset. This theory argues that professional money managers monitor news to determine a stock's value. The stock's price is set by supply and demand, so at any point in time, shares sold equal shares bought, implying that an equal number believe that the stock is overvalued as think it is undervalued. Thus, the average analyst thinks it is fairly valued all the time. According to this theory, the stock market is **informationally efficient**, which means that prices in the stock market reflect all available information in a rational way. If this is true, stock prices should follow a **random walk,** the path of which is impossible to predict from available information because all available information has already been incorporated into the price. As a result, no stock is a better buy than any other, and the best you can do is to buy a diversified portfolio.

Index funds provide evidence in support of the efficient markets hypothesis. Index funds are mutual funds that buy all of the stocks in a particular stock index. Actively managed funds use research to try to buy only the best stocks. Actively managed funds fail to outperform index funds because they trade more frequently, incurring trading costs, plus they charge fees for their alleged expertise.

Some people suggest that markets are irrational. That is, stock prices often move in ways that are hard to explain on the basis of rational analysis of news and so appear to be driven by psychological trends. However, if this were true, traders should be able to take advantage of this fact and buy better than average stocks, but beating the market is nearly impossible.

Conclusion

The concept of present value shows us that a dollar today is worth more than a dollar at a later date, and it allows us to compare sums at different points in time. Risk management shows us ways that risk-averse people can reduce their risk exposure. Asset valuation reflects a firm's future profitability. There is controversy regarding whether stock prices are a rational estimate of a company's true value.

Helpful Hints

1. Compound growth is the same as compound interest. Compound interest is when you earn interest on your previously earned interest. Assuming annual compounding, when you deposit $100 in a bank at 10 percent, you receive $110 at the end of the year. If you leave it in for two years, you receive compound interest in that you receive $121 at the end of two years—the $100 principal, $10 interest from the first year, $10 interest from the second year, *plus $1 interest on the*

first year's $10 interest payment. Next year, interest would be earned not on $100, or $110, but on $121, and so on.

In like manner, after a number of years, a faster growing economy is applying its percentage growth rate to a much larger base (size of economy), and total output accelerates away from economies that are growing more slowly. For example, applying the rule of 70, an economy that is growing at 1 percent should double in size after about 70 years (70/1). An economy growing at 4 percent should double in size every 17 1/2 years (70/4). After 70 years, the 4 percent growth economy is 16 times its original size (2^4) while the 1 percent growth economy is only twice its original size. If both economies started at the same size, the 4 percent growth economy is now eight times the size of the 1 percent growth economy thanks to compound growth.

2. Risk-averse people benefit from insurance because, due to their diminishing marginal utility of wealth, the reduction in utility from a single big expense exceeds the reduction in utility from a number of small payments into the insurance fund. For example, suppose there are 50 people in town. One house burns down each year so each person has a 1 in 50 chance of losing his entire home in any given year. People can pay 1/50 of the value of their home into the insurance fund each year, and thus, they will have paid premiums equal to the value of their home after 50 years. Alternatively, they can fail to buy insurance but they will replace their home once every 50 years due to fire. Although the expected values of these two expenses are the same, risk-averse people choose to buy insurance because the reduction in utility from paying once for one entire home exceeds the reduction in utility from paying 50 times for 1/50 of a home.

3. The volatility of the return of a stock portfolio decreases as the number of stocks in the portfolio increases. When a portfolio is comprised of just one stock, the volatility of the portfolio is the same as the volatility of the single stock. When a portfolio is comprised of two stocks, it could be that when one stock is paying a return that is less than its average, the other may be paying more than its average, and the two tend to cancel out. As a result, the portfolio has less volatility than each of the stocks in the portfolio. This effect continues as the number of stocks in the portfolio increases. However, the majority of the risk reduction occurs by the time there are 20 or 30 stocks in the portfolio. Note that in order to achieve the projected risk reduction from diversification, the risks on the stocks must be unrelated. Therefore, randomly choosing stocks should generate more risk reduction than choosing stocks of firms that are, for example, all in the same industry or all located in the same geographic area.

4. The price of a stock depends on supply and demand. The demand for a stock depends on the present value of the stream of dividend payments and the final sales price. Therefore, an increase in either the expected dividends or the final sales price, or a decrease in the prevailing interest rate, will increase the demand for a stock and increase its price. The demand for a stock also depends on risk factors associated with the stock. Because people are risk averse, an increase in aggregate risk will reduce the demand for all stocks and all stock prices should decrease. Oddly, an increase in firm-specific risk (the portion of the standard deviation in the returns on a particular stock that are associated with the specific company) should not affect the demand for the stock because this type of risk can be eliminated through diversification.

Terms and Definitions

Choose a definition for each key term.

Key Terms	Definitions

Key Terms

_____ Finance

_____ Present value

_____ Future value

_____ Compounding

_____ Risk averse

_____ Diversification

_____ Firm-specific risk

_____ Market risk

_____ Fundamental analysis

_____ Efficient markets hypothesis

_____ Informationally efficient

_____ Random walk

Definitions

1. Reflecting all available information in a rational way

2. The amount of money today that would be needed to produce, using prevailing interest rates, a given future amount of money

3. The study of a company's accounting statements and future prospects to determine its value

4. The field that studies how people make decisions regarding the allocation of resources over time and the handling of risk

5. The path of a variable whose changes are impossible to predict

6. Risk that affects only a single company

7. The accumulation of a sum of money in an account where interest is earned on previously paid interest

8. The theory according to which asset prices reflect all publicly available information about the value of an asset

9. The amount of money in the future that an amount of money today will yield, given prevailing interest rates

10. The reduction of risk achieved by replacing a single risk with a large number of smaller unrelated risks

11. Risk that affects all companies in the stock market

12. Exhibiting a dislike of uncertainty

PROBLEMS AND SHORT-ANSWER QUESTIONS

Practice Problems

1. Whitewater Raft Tour Company can purchase rafts today for $100,000. They will earn a $40,000 return on the rafts at the end of each of the next three years.
   a. If the interest rate were 12 percent, what is the present value of each of the future returns that Whitewater Raft expects to receive?

   _____

   _____

b. If the interest rate were 12 percent, should Whitewater Raft invest in the rafts? Explain.

_____

_____

c. If the interest rate were 7 percent, should Whitewater Raft invest in the rafts? Explain.

_____

_____

d. Compare your answers to parts *b* and *c* above. What general principle about the relationship between investment and the interest rate is demonstrated?

_____

_____

2. Use the *rule of 70* to answer the following questions. Suppose that real GDP/person in Fastcountry grows at an annual rate of 2 percent and that real GDP/person in Slowcountry grows at an annual rate of 1 percent.

a. How many years does it take for real GDP/person to double in Fastcountry?

_____

_____

b. If real GDP per person in Fastcountry is $2,000 in 1930, how much will it be in the year 2000?

_____

_____

c. How many years does it take for real GDP/person to double in Slowcountry?

_____

_____

d. If real GDP per person in Slowcountry is $2,000 in 1930, how much will it be in the year 2000?

_____

_____

e. Use the numbers you calculated above to help explain the concept of compound growth.

_____

_____

f. If Fastcountry stopped growing in the year 2000, how many years would it take for the standard of living in Slowcountry to catch that of Fastcountry?

_____

_____

3. For each of the following, determine the type of problem from which the insurance market suffers (adverse selection or moral hazard) and explain.
    a. Susan buys health insurance at the nonsmoker rate. After she obtains the insurance, she begins smoking again.

    _____

    _____

    b. Bryce discovers that he has a liver condition that will shorten his life. He seeks life insurance to help pay for his children's college expenses.

    _____

    _____

    c. Fred gets a new job and will have to commute to Chicago. Fearing that he will get into an auto accident in the heavy traffic, he increases his auto coverage.

    _____

    _____

    d. After Lisa gets fire insurance on her house, she burns fires in the fireplace without closing the fireplace doors.

    _____

    _____

4. Rachel is an extremely picky eater. When choosing a restaurant, she always chooses to eat at a buffet. At a buffet, she doesn't have to order off a menu so she doesn't have to risk ordering something she may not like. Rachel knows that buffet food is very ordinary, and because she avoids nice restaurants, she misses the chance to eat some exceptional foods that she would enjoy very much. On the other hand, she never has a meal that she is unwilling to eat.
    a. Does Rachel gain as much utility from a truly great meal as she loses from eating a meal she dislikes? Explain.

    _____

    _____

    b. What can you say about Rachel's utility function with regard to her preferences toward risk? Explain.

    _____

    _____

    c. How does the availability of a buffet help Rachel reduce her risk? Explain.

    _____

    _____

Short-Answer Questions

1. Suppose that the interest rate is 6 percent. Which would you prefer to receive: $100 today or $110 one year from today? Why?

_____

_____

_____

2. Suppose you put $100 in your savings account at your bank. If your account earns 8 percent interest and it is compounded annually, how much will be in your account after one year? after two years? How much more interest did you earn in the second year? Why?

_____

_____

_____

3. You just won a lottery that pays you $100,000 at the end of each of the next three years. Alternatively, the lottery is willing to pay you a lesser amount in one lump sum today. What is the least you should accept in a lump sum payment today if the interest rate is 9 percent? Explain.

_____

_____

_____

4. According to the *rule of 70*, how long will it take for your income to double if you get a 5 percent raise every year? If you start work at the age of 23 earning $40,000 per year and get a 5 percent raise every year, how much will you be earning if you retire at 65?

_____

_____

_____

5. What property of an individual's utility function is necessary for that individual to be risk averse? Explain.

_____

_____

_____

6. Suppose that people wreck their autos once every ten years and the autos are a total loss. People can buy insurance with annual premiums of 1/10 of the value of a car. Would a risk-averse person buy collision insurance for his auto? Why?

_____

_____

_____

7. What are the two types of problems from which insurance markets suffer? Explain. What problem does this cause for low-risk people?

    _____

    _____

    _____

8. What are the two types of risk someone faces when they buy stock? Which type of risk can be reduced with diversification and which type cannot? Explain.

    _____

    _____

    _____

9. Which are riskier, stocks or government bonds? Why? How can people use this information to adjust the amount of risk they face? If people reduce risk in this way, what happens to their return? Explain.

    _____

    _____

    _____

10. What are three ways that people can reduce the risk they face in their investment portfolios?

    _____

    _____

    _____

11. What three features of health insurance distinguish it from other kinds of insurance, leading to excessive healthcare spending?

    _____

    _____

    _____

12. What is fundamental analysis, and what are three ways to perform fundamental analysis?

    _____

    _____

    _____

SELF-TEST

True/False Questions

_____ 1. If the prevailing interest rate is 10 percent, a rational person should be indifferent between receiving $1,000 today and $1,000 one year from today.

_____ 2. You are going to receive a $100,000 inheritance in ten years. If the prevailing interest rate is 6 percent, the present value of your inheritance is $55,839.48.

_____ 3. The *rule of 70* suggests that, on average, people's incomes double every 70 years.

_____ 4. If interest is compounded annually, $100 placed in a bank account earning 10 percent interest should generate $30 interest after three years.

_____ 5. According to the *rule of 70*, if your income grows at 7 percent per year, it will double in ten years.

_____ 6. The present value of a future sum is the amount of money today that would be needed, at prevailing interest rates, to produce that future sum.

_____ 7. If people are risk averse, the utility gained from winning $1,000 is equal to the utility lost from losing a $1,000 bet.

_____ 8. If someone's utility function exhibits diminishing marginal utility of wealth, this person is risk averse.

_____ 9. The insurance market demonstrates the problem of adverse selection when those that are sicker than average seek health insurance.

_____ 10. People can reduce what is known as *market risk* by diversifying their portfolios.

_____ 11. Increasing the diversification of a portfolio from 1 stock to 10 stocks reduces the portfolio's risk by the same amount as increasing the diversification from 10 to 20 stocks.

_____ 12. As a person allocates more of his savings to stocks and less to government bonds, he will earn a higher rate of return but he must accept additional risk.

_____ 13. The efficient markets hypothesis suggests that since markets are efficient, it is easy to engage in fundamental analysis to purchase undervalued stock and then earn greater than average market returns.

_____ 14. If the efficient markets hypothesis is true, stock prices follow a random walk. Therefore, buying a diversified portfolio, by purchasing an index fund or by throwing darts at the stock page, is probably the best that you can do.

_____ 15. The value of a stock is based on the present value of the future stream of dividend payments and the final sales price.

Multiple-Choice Questions

1. The amount today that would be needed, at prevailing interest rates, to produce a particular sum in the future is known as
   a. compound value.
   b. future value.
   c. present value.
   d. fair value.
   e. beginning value.

2. If a depositor puts $100 in a bank account that earns 4 percent interest compounded annually, how much will be in the account after five years?
   a. $104.00
   b. $120.00
   c. $121.67
   d. $123.98
   e. $400.00

3. General Electric has the opportunity to purchase a new factory today that will provide them with a $50 million return four years from now. If prevailing interest rates are 6 percent, what is the maximum that the project can cost for General Electric to be willing to undertake the project?
   a. $34,583,902
   b. $39,604,682
   c. $43,456,838
   d. $50,000,000
   e. $53,406,002

4. An increase in the prevailing interest rate
   a. decreases the present value of future returns from investment and decreases investment.
   b. decreases the present value of future returns from investment and increases investment.
   c. increases the present value of future returns from investment and decreases investment.
   d. increases the present value of future returns from investment and increases investment.

5. If two countries start with the same real GDP per person, and one country grows at 2 percent while the other grows at 4 percent,
   a. one country will always have 2 percent more real GDP per person than the other.
   b. the standard of living in the country growing at 4 percent will start to accelerate away from the slower growing country due to compound growth.
   c. the standard of living in the two countries will converge.
   d. next year the country growing at 4 percent will have twice the GDP per person as the country growing at 2 percent.

6. Using the *rule of 70*, if your income grows at 10 percent per year, your income will double in approximately
   a. 700 years.
   b. 70 years.
   c. 10 years.
   d. 7 years.
   e. There is not enough information to answer this question.

7. Using the *rule of 70*, if your parents place $10,000 in a deposit for you on the day you are born, approximately how much will be in the account when you retire at 70 years old if the deposit earns 3 percent per year?
   a. $300
   b. $3,000
   c. $20,000
   d. $70,000
   e. $80,000

8. If people are risk averse, then
   a. they dislike bad things more than they like comparable good things.
   b. their utility functions exhibit the property of diminishing marginal utility of wealth.
   c. the utility they would lose from losing a $50 bet would exceed the utility they would gain from winning a $50 bet.
   d. all of the above are true.
   e. none of the above is true.

9. Which of the following does *not* help reduce the risk that people face?
   a. buying insurance
   b. diversifying their portfolio
   c. increasing the rate of return within their portfolio
   d. All of the above help reduce risk.

10. Which of the following is an example of moral hazard?
    a. After Joe buys fire insurance, he begins to smoke cigarettes in bed.
    b. Doug has been feeling poorly lately so he seeks health insurance.
    c. Both of Susan's parents lost their teeth due to gum disease, so Susan buys dental insurance.
    d. All of the above demonstrate moral hazard.
    e. None of the above demonstrates moral hazard.

11. Firm-specific risk is the
    a. uncertainty associated with the entire economy.
    b. uncertainty associated with specific companies.
    c. risk associated with moral hazard.
    d. risk associated with adverse selection.

12. Diversification of a portfolio can
    a. reduce market risk.
    b. reduce firm-specific risk.
    c. eliminate all risk.
    d. increase the standard deviation of the portfolio's return.

13. Compared to a portfolio composed entirely of stock, a portfolio that is 50 percent government bonds and 50 percent stock will have a
    a. higher return and a higher level of risk.
    b. higher return and a lower level of risk.
    c. lower return and a lower level of risk.
    d. lower return and a higher level of risk.

14. The study of a company's accounting statements and future prospects to determine its value is known as
    a. diversification.
    b. risk management.
    c. information analysis.
    d. fundamental analysis.

15. If the efficient markets hypothesis is true, then
    a. stocks tend to be overvalued.
    b. the stock market is informationally efficient so stock prices should follow a random walk.
    c. fundamental analysis is a valuable tool for increasing one's stock returns.
    d. an index fund is a poor investment.
    e. all of the above are true.

16. Which of the following reduces risk in a portfolio the greatest?
     a. increasing the number of stocks in the portfolio from 1 to 10
     b. increasing the number of stocks from 10 to 20
     c. increasing the number of stocks from 20 to 30
     d. All of the above provide the same amount of risk reduction.

17. Which of the following should cause the price of a share of stock to rise?
     a. a reduction in market risk
     b. an increase in expected dividends
     c. a reduction in the interest rate
     d. All of the above should cause the price to rise.
     e. None of the above should cause the price to rise.

18. Speculative bubbles may occur in the stock market
     a. when stocks are fairly valued.
     b. only when people are irrational.
     c. because rational people may buy an overvalued stock if they think they can sell it to someone for even more at a later date.
     d. during periods of extreme pessimism because so many stocks become undervalued.

19. Stock prices will follow a random walk if
     a. people behave irrationally when choosing stock.
     b. markets reflect all available information in a rational way.
     c. stocks are undervalued.
     d. stocks are overvalued.

20. It is difficult for an actively managed mutual fund to outperform an index fund because
     a. index funds generally do better fundamental analysis.
     b. stock markets tend to be inefficient.
     c. actively managed funds trade more often and charge fees for their alleged expertise.
     d. index funds are able to buy undervalued stocks.
     e. all of the above are true.

ADVANCED CRITICAL THINKING

You are a student in the business college at an exclusive private university. The tuition is extremely expensive. Near the end of your senior year, your parents come to visit you in your dorm room. As they enter the room, they see you throwing darts at the stock pages on your bulletin board. You inform them that you received an enormous signing bonus from the company for which you agreed to work after graduation. You are now in the process of picking the stocks in which you plan to invest. Your parents are horrified and they want their money back for your expensive education. Your father says, "There's got to be a better way to choose stocks. I can give you the phone number of my stock analyst or you could at least buy a well-known, well-managed mutual fund."

1. What is the stock valuation method to which your father is referring, and what is its goal?

_____

_____

_____

2. Explain the efficient markets hypothesis to your parents. If the efficient markets hypothesis is true, can your father's method for picking stocks achieve its goal?

_____

_____

_____

_____

_____

_____

3. If the efficient markets hypothesis is true, what is the only goal of your dart-throwing exercise? Explain.

_____

_____

_____

4. If the efficient markets hypothesis is true, which will likely provide the greater return in the long run: your dart-throwing exercise or an actively managed mutual fund? Why?

_____

_____

_____

SOLUTIONS

Terms and Definitions

_4_ Finance

_2_ Present value

_9_ Future value

_7_ Compounding

12 Risk averse

10 Diversification

_6_ Firm-specific risk

11 Market risk

_3_ Fundamental analysis

_8_ Efficient markets hypothesis

_1_ Informationally efficient

_5_ Random walk

Practice Problems

1. a. $40,000/1.12 = $35,714.29; $40,000/(1.12)^2 = $31,887.76; $40,000/(1.12)^3 = $28,471.21

   b. No, the cost is $100,000 but the present value of the return is only $96,073.26.

   c. Yes. Although the cost is still $100,000, the present value of the return is now the sum of $[$40,000/1.07] + [$40,000/(1.07)^2] + [$40,000/(1.07)^3] = $104,972.65.

   d. Investment is inversely related to the interest rate—lower interest rates stimulate investment.

2. a. 70/2 = 35 years.

   b. $8,000

   c. 70/1 = 70 years.

   d. $4,000

   e. Fastcountry adds $2,000 to its GDP/person in the first 35 years. Growing at the same percent, it adds $4,000 to its GDP over the next 35 years because the same growth rate is now applied to a larger base.

   f. Another 70 years.

3. a. Moral hazard, because after she obtains the insurance, she is less careful with her health.

   b. Adverse selection, because after he knows that his probability of death is higher than average, he seeks life insurance.

   c. Adverse selection, because after he knows that his probability of an accident is higher than average, he seeks more auto insurance.

   d. Moral hazard, because after she obtains the insurance, she becomes less careful with fire.

4. a. No. She dislikes bad food more than she likes good food.

   b. Rachel is risk averse because she exhibits diminishing marginal utility of wealth (she dislikes spending, say, $30 on a meal she dislikes more than she enjoys spending $30 on a meal she loves).

   c. She can diversify her risk at a buffet—she does not "put all of her eggs in one basket" at a buffet. This reduces her standard deviation of meals because her meals are always adequate but never terrible or great. A buffet is like a mutual fund of food.

Short-Answer Questions

1. You should prefer $110 one year from today because the _PV_ of $110 one year from today is $110/1.06 = $103.77 and this is greater than $100.

2. After one year: $100(1.08) = $108. After two years: $100(1.08)^2 = $100(1.1664) = $116.64. The account earned $0.64 more interest in the second year because the account earned interest on the first year's interest payment: 0.08($8) = $0.64.

3. The least you should accept is the present value of the future stream of payments which is: $100,000/1.09 + $100,000/(1.09)^2 + $100,000/(1.09)^3 = $91,743.12 + $84,168.00 + $77,218.35 = $253,129.47.

4. 70/5 = 14 years. Your income would double three times in the 42-year period or $40,000(2)^3 = $320,000 per year.

5. Diminishing marginal utility of wealth. Therefore, the increase in utility from a $1 gain is less than the decrease in utility from a $1 loss.

6. Yes. Due to diminishing marginal utility of wealth, the reduction in utility from a lump sum payment to replace a car exceeds the reduction in utility from the payment of 10 premiums of 1/10 of the value of a car.

7. Adverse selection: A high-risk person is more likely to apply for insurance than a low-risk person. Moral hazard: After people buy insurance, they have less incentive to be careful. As a result, the price of insurance is often too high for low-risk people so they don't buy it.

8. Firm-specific risk—the uncertainty associated with specific companies, and market risk—the uncertainty associated with the entire economy that affects all companies in the stock market. Firm-specific risk can be eliminated with diversification because when one firm does poorly, another unrelated firm may do well reducing

the volatility in returns. Market risk cannot be reduced because when the entire economy does poorly, the market portfolio does poorly.

9. Stocks, because the standard deviation in the returns to government bonds is zero while the standard deviation in stock returns is significantly higher. People can vary the proportion they invest in stocks versus risk-free government bonds. Low-risk assets generate low returns, so putting a larger portion of the portfolio in government bonds lowers the return of the portfolio.

10. Buy insurance, diversify a portfolio, and accept a lower return on the portfolio.

11. Health insurance covers routine expenses, small random expenses, and is connected with employment.

12. Determining a company's value by analyzing its accounting statements and future prospects. You can do it yourself, rely on Wall Street analysts, or buy a mutual fund that is actively managed.

True/False Questions

1. F; the present value of $1,000 one year from today is $1,000/1.10 = $909.09.
2. T
3. F; if people's incomes grow at x percent, they double in $70/x$ years.
4. F; $10 the first year, $11 the second year, $12.10 the third year for a total of $33.10.
5. T
6. T
7. F; the utility lost from losing $1,000 is greater.
8. T
9. T
10. F; diversification reduces firm-specific risk.
11. F; diversification of a portfolio from 1 stock to 10 stocks reduces the portfolio's risk to a greater degree.
12. T
13. F; if markets are efficient, stocks are always fairly valued.
14. T
15. T

Multiple-Choice Questions

1. c
2. c
3. b
4. a
5. b
6. d
7. e
8. d
9. c
10. a
11. b
12. b
13. c
14. d
15. b
16. a
17. d
18. c
19. b
20. c

Advanced Critical Thinking

1. Fundamental analysis is the detailed analysis of a firm's accounting statements and future prospects to determine its value. The goal is to choose stocks that are undervalued—those whose stock prices are less than their values.

2. The efficient markets hypothesis argues that the stock market is informationally efficient in that it reflects all available information about the value of the traded stocks. That is, market participants monitor news that affects the value of a stock. Since at any given time the number of buyers of a stock equals the number of sellers, an equal number of people think a stock is undervalued as overvalued. Thus, stock is fairly valued all the time and its price should follow a random walk. If true, it is not possible to consistently buy undervalued stock.

3. The only thing a person can do is diversify their portfolio to reduce firm-specific risk.

4. If you throw enough darts to remove most of the firm-specific risk (your portfolio starts to resemble the entire market like an index fund) and if you bought and held the stock (you didn't trade often), then it is likely that throwing darts would give you the greater return. This is because active managers of mutual funds tend to trade frequently incurring trading costs, and they charge fees as compensation for their alleged expertise, yet they cannot reduce market risk.

Unemployment

GOALS

In this chapter you will

- Learn about the data used to measure the amount of unemployment

- Consider how unemployment arises from the process of job search

- Consider how unemployment can result from minimum-wage laws

- See how unemployment can arise from bargaining between firms and unions

- Examine how unemployment results when firms choose to pay efficiency wages

OUTCOMES

After accomplishing these goals, you should be able to

- Use data on the number of employed, unemployed, and not in the labor force to calculate the unemployment rate and the labor-force participation rate

- Explain why some job search unemployment is inevitable

- Diagram the impact of the minimum wage on high-wage and low-wage sectors

- List the reasons why unions cause unemployment, and alternatively, why unions might increase efficiency in some cases

- Describe the four reasons why firms may choose to pay wages in excess of the competitive wage

CHAPTER OVERVIEW

Context and Purpose

Chapter 28 is the fourth chapter in a four-chapter sequence on the level and growth of output in the long run. In Chapter 25, we learned that capital and labor are among the primary determinants of output and growth. In Chapter 26, we addressed how saving and investment in capital goods affect the production of output. In Chapter 27, we learned about some of the tools people and firms use when choosing capital projects in which to invest. In Chapter 28, we see how full utilization of our labor resources improves the level of production and our standard of living.

The purpose of Chapter 28 is to introduce you to the labor market. We will see how economists measure the performance of the labor market using unemployment statistics. We will also address a number of sources of unemployment and some policies that the government might use to lower certain types of unemployment.

Chapter Review

Introduction If a country keeps its workers fully employed, it achieves a higher level of GDP than if it leaves many workers idle. In this chapter, we are concerned largely with the **natural rate of unemployment**, which is the amount of unemployment that the economy normally experiences. "Natural" does not mean constant or impervious to economic policy. It means that it is the unemployment that doesn't go away on its own. This chapter addresses the measurement and interpretation of unemployment statistics and some causes and cures for unemployment.

Identifying Unemployment

The Bureau of Labor Statistics (BLS) uses the Current Population Survey to categorize all surveyed adults (16 and older) as employed, unemployed, or not in the labor force.

- Employed: worked as paid employees, worked in their own business, or had a job but didn't work due to temporary absence.

- Unemployed: not employed but were available for work and looked for work in the last four weeks, or on temporary layoff.

- Not in the labor force: not in previous two categories (student, homemaker, retiree).

BLS then computes:

- Labor force = number of employed + number of unemployed

- Unemployment rate = (number of unemployed/labor force) × 100

- Labor-force participation rate = (labor force/adult pop.) × 100

The **labor force** is the total number of workers who have made themselves available for work. The **unemployment rate** is the percent of the labor force that is unemployed. The **labor-force participation** rate is the percent of the total adult population who are in the labor force. The unemployment rate and the labor-force participation rate vary widely across demographic groups—men, women, black, white, young, old. Women ages 20 and over have lower labor-force participation rates than men, but once in the labor force, they have similar unemployment rates. Blacks and teenagers have higher unemployment rates than whites and older workers. Female labor-force participation is rising while male participation is falling.

The normal rate of unemployment around which the unemployment rate fluctuates is the *natural rate of unemployment.* The deviation in unemployment from the natural rate is known as **cyclical unemployment.** In 2004, the natural rate of unemployment in the United States was estimated at 5.2 percent. This chapter is concerned with explaining the characteristics and causes of the natural rate.

Because people move into and out of the labor force so often, unemployment is difficult to measure and interpret. For example, over one-third of the unemployed are recent entrants to the labor force, and almost half of all spells of unemployment end when the unemployed person leaves the labor force. In addition, unemployment may be inaccurately measured because:

- Some people are counted in the labor force but unemployed even though they are only pretending to look for work so that they can collect government assistance or because they are being paid "under the table." This behavior biases the unemployment statistics upward.

- Some people have had an unsuccessful search for a job and have given up looking for work so they are not counted in the labor force. These individuals are called **discouraged workers.** This behavior biases the unemployment statistics downward.

Because of these and other problems, the BLS calculates alternative measures of labor underutilization, known as U1 through U6. These statistics attempt to measure the impact on the labor market of long-term unemployment, temporary jobs, discouraged workers, part-time workers, and marginally attached workers.

Knowledge about the duration of unemployment spells may help us design corrective policies for unemployment. Evidence suggests that *most spells are short term, but most unemployment at any given time is long term.* This means that many people are unemployed for short periods, but a few people are unemployed for very long periods. Economists think short-term unemployment is much less of a social problem than long-term unemployment.

In most markets, prices adjust to balance supply and demand. In the ideal labor market, wages would adjust so that there would be no unemployment. However, even when the economy is doing well, the unemployment rate never falls to zero. The following sections address four reasons why the labor market falls short of the ideal market. The first source of unemployment we discuss is due to job search. **Frictional unemployment** is the unemployment that results from the time it takes for workers to search for the jobs that best suit their tastes and skills. The next three sources of unemployment fall within the category of structural unemployment. **Structural unemployment** is the unemployment that results because the number of jobs available in some labor markets is insufficient for everyone who wants a job to get one. Structural unemployment occurs because the wage is held above the equilibrium wage. Three possible sources of an excessive wage are minimum-wage laws, unions, and efficiency wages. Frictional unemployment tends to explain shorter spells of unemployment while structural unemployment tends to explain longer spells of unemployment.

Job Search

Job search is the process of matching workers and jobs. Just as workers differ in their skills and tastes, jobs differ in their attributes. Moreover, information about jobs disseminates slowly. Therefore, it takes time for job candidates and job vacancies to match. *Frictional unemployment* is due to this search time.

Frictional unemployment is inevitable in a dynamic economy. As the demand for products changes, some industries and regions will experience growth while others will contract. These changes in the composition of demand among industries or regions are called *sectoral shifts*. Sectoral shifts cause temporary frictional unemployment as workers in contracting sectors lose their jobs and search for work in the growing sectors.

Frictional unemployment may be reduced by improved information about job openings provided by the Internet. Government may be able to lower frictional unemployment by engaging in activities that shorten the job search time. Two such programs are (1) government-run employment agencies to help match workers and jobs and (2) worker-training programs to retrain workers laid off from contracting sectors. Critics argue that government is ill-suited to do these things and that the market does a more efficient job at matching and retraining.

Unemployment insurance pays laid-off workers a portion of their original salaries for a period of time. Unemployment insurance increases frictional unemployment because unemployed workers are more likely to (1) devote less effort to their job search, (2) turn down unattractive job offers, and (3) be less concerned with job security. This does not mean unemployment insurance is bad. Unemployment insurance does provide the worker partial protection against job loss, and it may improve the efficiency of the job market by allowing workers to search longer for the best job match.

German unemployment benefits have been so generous that many unemployed workers have little incentive to find work. Social insurance spending is so burdensome that Germany now plans to reduce unemployment benefits.

Minimum-Wage Laws

Structural unemployment results when the number of jobs is insufficient for the number of workers. Minimum-wage laws are one source of structural unemployment. Recall that minimum-wage laws force the wage to remain above the equilibrium wage. This causes the quantity of labor supplied to exceed the quantity of labor demanded. There is a surplus of labor or unemployment. Since the equilibrium wage for most workers exceeds the minimum wage, the minimum wage tends to cause unemployment only for the least skilled and least experienced, such as teenagers. Minimum-wage workers tend to be young, less-educated, part-time workers in food services and drinking places. Tips supplement their wages.

Although only a small portion of total unemployment is due to the minimum wage, an analysis of the minimum wage points out a general rule: *If a wage is held above the equilibrium level, the result is unemployment.* The next two sections develop two additional reasons why the wage may be held above the equilibrium level. That is, the next two sections provide two additional sources for structural unemployment.

Note that with frictional unemployment, workers are *searching* for the right job even if the wage is at the competitive equilibrium. In contrast, structural unemployment exists because the wage exceeds the competitive equilibrium wage and workers are *waiting* for jobs to open up.

Unions and Collective Bargaining

A **union** is a worker association that engages in **collective bargaining** with employers over wages, benefits, and working conditions. A union is a cartel because it is a group of sellers organized to exert market power. If the union and firm fail to reach an agreement, the union can **strike**—that is, withdraw its labor services from the firm. Because of the threat of a strike, workers in unions earn about 10 to 20 percent more than nonunion workers. Less-educated workers gain a greater financial advantage from union membership than do better-educated workers.

Unions benefit *insiders* (members) at the expense of *outsiders* (nonmembers). When the union raises the wage above the equilibrium wage, unemployment results. Insiders earn higher wages, and outsiders are either unemployed or must take jobs with nonunion firms. This increases the supply of labor in the nonunion sector and lowers the wage further for nonunion workers.

Most cartels are illegal, but unions are exempt from antitrust legislation. Indeed legislation, such as the Wagner Act of 1935, promotes the establishment of labor unions. Alternatively, state *right-to-work laws* discourage union membership by making it illegal to require union membership for employment.

There is little agreement about whether unions are good or bad for the economy. Critics argue that unions are cartels that raise the price of labor above the competitive equilibrium. This is inefficient (causes unemployment) and inequitable (insiders gain at the expense of outsiders). Supporters of unions argue that firms have market power and are able to depress the wage, so unions are just a counterbalance to the firm's power. This is most likely to be true in a *company town* where one firm hires most of the workers in the region. Supporters also argue that unions are efficient because firms don't have to bargain with individual workers about salary and benefits. That is, unions may reduce transactions costs.

The Theory of Efficiency Wages

The theory of **efficiency wages** suggests that firms may intentionally hold wages above the competitive equilibrium because it is efficient for them to do so. Efficiency wages are similar to minimum-wage laws and unions because, in all three cases, unemployment results from wages being held above the equilibrium wage. However, an efficiency wage is unusual in that it is paid voluntarily by the firm. Below, we address four reasons why firms may find it efficient (or profitable) to pay a wage in excess of the competitive equilibrium:

- *Worker health* may be improved by paying a higher wage. Better-paid workers eat a better diet and are more productive. This is more applicable to firms in developing nations and is probably not relevant for firms in the United States.

- *Worker turnover* may be reduced by paying a higher wage because workers will find it difficult to find alternative jobs at the higher wage. Firms may find it profitable to reduce worker turnover because there is a cost associated with hiring and training new workers and because new workers are not as experienced.

- *Worker quality* can be improved by paying a higher wage. Firms cannot perfectly gauge the quality of their job applicants. By paying a wage above the competitive equilibrium, firms have a higher probability of attracting a better pool of high-quality applicants for a job opening.

- *Worker effort* may be increased by paying a higher wage. When a worker's effort cannot be easily monitored, workers may shirk their responsibilities. If caught and fired, a worker earning the competitive equilibrium wage can easily find another job at the same wage. Higher wages make workers eager to keep their jobs and work hard.

Helpful Hints

1. Job search takes time even at the competitive equilibrium wage. Minimum-wage laws, unions, and efficiency wages all create an excess supply of labor (unemployment) by holding the wage above the competitive equilibrium wage. Frictional unemployment, however, exists even at the competitive equilibrium wage because it is inevitable that it takes time for workers and firms to match regardless of the wage. For this reason, structural unemployment resulting from the wage being held above the equilibrium wage can often be thought of as additional unemployment beyond the inherent frictional unemployment.

2. The natural rate of unemployment is persistent, not constant. Changes in minimum-wage laws, unions, and efficiency wages and changes in the job-search process due to the information revolution all have an impact on the natural rate of unemployment. Therefore, the natural rate will change as government policies, institutions, and behaviors change. But since policies, institutions, and behaviors change slowly, so does the natural rate of unemployment.

Terms and Definitions

Choose a definition for each key term.

Key Terms

____ Labor force

____ Unemployment rate

____ Labor-force participation rate

____ Natural rate of unemployment

____ Cyclical unemployment

____ Discouraged workers

____ Frictional unemployment

____ Structural unemployment

____ Job search

____ Sectoral shifts

____ Unemployment insurance

____ Union

____ Collective bargaining

____ Strike

____ Insiders

____ Outsiders

____ Right-to-work laws

____ Efficiency wages

Definitions

1. Workers who stop looking for work due to an unsuccessful search

2. The deviation of the unemployment rate from its natural rate

3. Wages voluntarily paid in excess of the competitive equilibrium wage to increase worker productivity

4. Changes in the composition of demand across industries or regions

5. The process by which workers find appropriate jobs given their tastes and skills

6. Unemployment due to the time it takes for workers to search for the jobs that best suit their tastes and skills

7. Normal rate of unemployment about which the unemployment rate fluctuates

8. Percentage of the adult population in the labor force

9. Legislation that makes it illegal to require union membership for employment

10. An organized withdrawal of labor from the firm

11. Worker association that bargains with employers over wages, benefits, and working conditions

12. Those employed in union jobs

13. A government program that pays laid-off workers a portion of their original salaries

14. The total number of workers, which is the sum of the unemployed and the employed

15. Unemployment that results because the number of jobs available in some labor markets is insufficient for everyone who wants a job to get one

16. Percentage of the labor force that is unemployed

17. The process by which unions and firms agree on labor contracts

18. Those not employed in union jobs

PROBLEMS AND SHORT-ANSWER QUESTIONS

Practice Problems

1. Use the following information about Employment Country to answer question 1. Numbers are in millions.

	2004	2005
Population	223.6	226.5
Adult population	168.2	169.5
Number of unemployed	7.4	8.1
Number of employed	105.2	104.2

   a. What is the labor force in 2004 and 2005?

   _____

   _____

   b. What is the labor force participation rate in 2004 and 2005?

   _____

   _____

   c. What is the unemployment rate in 2004 and 2005?

   _____

   _____

   d. From 2004 to 2005, the adult population went up while the labor force went down. Provide a number of explanations why this might have occurred.

   _____

   _____

   _____

   _____

   e. If the natural rate of unemployment in Employment Country is 6.6 percent, how much is cyclical unemployment in 2004 and 2005? Is Employment Country likely to be experiencing a recession in either of these years?

   _____

   _____

   _____

   _____

2. Suppose the labor market is segmented into two distinct markets: the market for low-skill workers and the market for high-skill workers. Further, suppose the competitive equilibrium wage in the low-skill market is $3.00/hour while the competitive equilibrium wage in the high-skill market is $15.00/hour.

1 EXHIBIT

Wage | | Wage | |

LOW-SKILL MARKET — Quantity of Labor

HIGH-SKILL MARKET — Quantity of Labor

a. If the minimum wage is set at $5.00/hour, which market will exhibit the greatest amount of unemployment? Demonstrate it graphically in Exhibit 1.

_____

_____

b. Does the minimum wage have any impact on the high-skill market? Why?

_____

_____

c. Do your results seem consistent with labor market statistics? Explain.

_____

_____

d. Suppose the high-skill market becomes unionized and the new negotiated wage is $18.00/hour. Will this have any effect on the low-skill market? Explain.

_____

_____

_____

3. Answer the following questions about the composition of unemployment.
    a. What are some of the sources of unemployment?

_____

_____

b. Which type of unemployment is initiated by the firm?

_____

_____

c. Why might a firm pay wages in excess of the competitive equilibrium?

_____

_____

d. Which type of efficiency wage is unlikely to be relevant in the United States? Why?

_____

_____

e. How does frictional unemployment differ from the other sources of unemployment?

_____

_____

Short-Answer Questions

1. Name two reasons why the unemployment rate is an imperfect measure of joblessness.

_____

_____

_____

2. Explain the statement, "Most spells of unemployment are short, and most unemployment observed at any given time is long term."

_____

_____

_____

3. Where would a labor union be more likely to increase efficiency rather than reduce it: a small remote town with one large employer or a major city with many employers? Why?

_____

_____

_____

4. Name two ways that a union increases the disparity in wages between members and nonmembers.

_____

_____

5. Which alternative measure of unemployment attempts to include the impact of discouraged workers in the unemployment statistics? Explain. Is it higher or lower than the official unemployment rate? Explain.

_____

_____

_____

6. Does the minimum wage cause much unemployment in the market for accountants? Why?

_____

_____

_____

7. Which type of unemployment will occur even if the wage is at the competitive equilibrium? Why?

_____

_____

_____

_____

8. How does unemployment insurance increase frictional unemployment?

_____

_____

_____

9. How might the government help reduce frictional unemployment?

_____

_____

_____

10. Which of the following individuals is most likely to be unemployed for the long term: a buggy whip maker who loses his job when automobiles become popular or a waitress who is laid off when a new cafe opens in town? Why?

_____

_____

_____

SELF-TEST

True/False Questions

_____ 1. The natural rate of unemployment is the amount of unemployment that won't go away on its own, even in the long run.

_____ 2. If the unemployment rate falls, we can be certain that more workers have jobs.

_____ 3. In post–World War II United States, the labor-force participation rate has been rising for women and has been falling for men.

_____ 4. The unemployment rate is about the same for the various demographic groups: men, women, black, white, young, old.

_____ 5. A minimum wage is likely to have a greater impact on the market for skilled workers than on the market for unskilled workers.

_____ 6. The presence of a union tends to raise the wage for insiders and lower the wage for outsiders.

_____ 7. A union is a labor cartel.

_____ 8. Unions may increase efficiency in some circumstances because they decrease the cost of bargaining between labor and management.

_____ 9. An efficiency wage is like a minimum wage in that firms are required by legislation to pay it.

_____ 10. Paying efficiency wages tends to increase worker turnover because workers can get continually higher wages if they "job hop."

_____ 11. Firms may voluntarily pay wages above the level that balances the supply and demand for workers because the higher wage improves the average quality of workers that apply for employment.

_____ 12. If wages were always at the competitive equilibrium, there would be absolutely no unemployment.

_____ 13. Due to the existence of "discouraged workers," the official unemployment rate may overstate true unemployment.

_____ 14. The presence of unemployment insurance tends to decrease the unemployment rate because recipients of unemployment benefits are not counted in the labor force.

_____ 15. Whenever the wage rises above the competitive equilibrium, regardless of the source, the result is additional unemployment.

Multiple-Choice Questions

1. The amount of unemployment that the economy normally experiences is known as
   a. efficiency wage unemployment.
   b. frictional unemployment.
   c. cyclical unemployment.
   d. the natural rate of unemployment.

2. According to the Bureau of Labor Statistics, a husband who chooses to stay home and take care of the household is
    a. unemployed.
    b. employed.
    c. not in the labor force.
    d. a discouraged worker.

Use the following table to answer questions 3 through 5. Numbers are in millions.

Total population	195.4
Adult population	139.7
Number of unemployed	5.7
Number of employed	92.3

3. The labor force is
    a. 92.3 million.
    b. 98.0 million.
    c. 134.0 million.
    d. 139.7 million.
    e. none of the above.

4. The unemployment rate is
    a. 3.2 percent.
    b. 5.7 percent.
    c. 5.8 percent.
    d. 6.2 percent.
    e. Not enough information is available to answer this question.

5. The labor-force participation rate is
    a. 47.1 percent.
    b. 50.2 percent.
    c. 65.9 percent.
    d. 70.2 percent.
    e. none of the above.

6. An accountant with a CPA designation that has been unable to find work for so long that she has stopped looking for work is considered to be
    a. employed.
    b. unemployed.
    c. not in the labor force.
    d. not in the adult population.

7. Which of the following statements is true?
    a. Women tend to have similar unemployment rates as men.
    b. The labor-force participation rate of men is rising.
    c. Blacks have a lower unemployment rate than whites.
    d. Most spells of unemployment are long term, but most unemployment observed at any given time is short term.
    e. All of the above are true.

8. A minimum-wage law tends to
    a. create more unemployment in high-skill job markets than in low-skill job markets.
    b. create more unemployment in low-skill job markets than in high-skill job markets.
    c. have no impact on unemployment as long as it is set above the competitive equilibrium wage.
    d. help all teenagers because they receive a higher wage than they would otherwise.

9. Which one of the following types of unemployment results from the wage being held above the competitive equilibrium wage?
    a. structural unemployment
    b. cyclical unemployment
    c. frictional unemployment
    d. sectoral unemployment
    e. None of the above is correct.

10. If, for any reason, the wage is held above the competitive equilibrium wage,
    a. unions will likely strike and the wage will fall to equilibrium.
    b. the quality of workers in the applicant pool will tend to fall.
    c. the quantity of labor supplied will exceed the quantity of labor demanded and there will be unemployment.
    d. the quantity of labor demanded will exceed the quantity of labor supplied and there will be a labor shortage.

11. Which of the following is not a characteristic of minimum-wage workers? They tend to be
    a. young.
    b. less educated.
    c. full time.
    d. in the food service and drinking place industry.

12. Which of the following government policies would fail to lower the unemployment rate?
    a. reduce unemployment benefits
    b. establish employment agencies
    c. establish worker training programs
    d. raise the minimum wage
    e. establish right-to-work laws

13. Sectoral shifts tend to raise which type of unemployment?
    a. frictional unemployment
    b. structural unemployment
    c. unemployment due to unions
    d. unemployment due to efficiency wages

14. Which of the following is an example of a reason why firms might pay efficiency wages?
    a. At equilibrium wages, workers often quit to find better jobs.
    b. At equilibrium wages, workers sleep when the boss is not looking because workers are not deeply concerned about being fired.
    c. At equilibrium wages, only minimally qualified workers apply for the job.
    d. At equilibrium wages, workers cannot afford a healthy diet so they fall asleep at work due to a lack of energy.
    e. All of the above are true.

15. Some frictional unemployment is inevitable because
    a. efficiency wages may hold the wage above the equilibrium wage.
    b. of minimum-wage laws.
    c. there are changes in the demand for labor among different firms.
    d. of unions.
    e. of all of the above.

16. Unions might increase efficiency in the case where they
    a. raise the wage for insiders above the competitive equilibrium.
    b. offset the market power of a large firm in a "company town."
    c. lower the wage of local outsiders.
    d. threaten a strike but don't actually follow through, so there are no lost hours of work.

17. Which of the following statements about efficiency wage theory is true?
    a. Firms do not have a choice about whether they pay efficiency wages or not because these wages are determined by law.
    b. Paying the lowest possible wage is always the most efficient (profitable).
    c. Paying above the competitive equilibrium wage tends to cause workers to shirk their responsibilities.
    d. Paying above the competitive equilibrium wage may improve worker health, lower worker turnover, improve worker quality, and increase worker effort.

18. Unions tend to increase the disparity in pay between insiders and outsiders by
    a. increasing the wage in the unionized sector, which may create an increase in the supply of workers in the nonunionized sector.
    b. increasing the wage in the unionized sector, which may create a decrease in the supply of workers in the nonunionized sector.
    c. decreasing the demand for workers in the unionized sector.
    d. increasing the demand for workers in the unionized sector.

19. Which of the following types of unemployment will exist even if the wage is at the competitive equilibrium?
    a. unemployment due to minimum-wage laws
    b. unemployment due to unions
    c. unemployment due to efficiency wages
    d. frictional unemployment

20. If unemployment insurance were so generous that it paid laid-off workers 95 percent of their regular salary,
    a. the official unemployment rate would probably understate true unemployment.
    b. the official unemployment rate would probably overstate true unemployment.
    c. there would be no impact on the official unemployment rate.
    d. frictional unemployment would fall.
    e. none of the above is true.

ADVANCED CRITICAL THINKING

You are watching the national news with your roommate. The news anchor says, "Unemployment statistics released by the Department of Labor today show an increase in unemployment from 6.1 percent to 6.2 percent. This is the third month in a row where the unemployment rate has increased." Your roommate says, "Every month there are fewer and fewer people with jobs. I don't know how much longer the country can continue like this."

1. Can your roommate's statement be deduced from the unemployment rate statistic? Why?

   _____

   _____

   _____

2. What information would you need to determine whether there are really fewer people with jobs?

   _____

   _____

   _____

SOLUTIONS

Terms and Definitions

<u>14</u> Labor force

<u>16</u> Unemployment rate

<u>8</u> Labor-force participation rate

<u>7</u> Natural rate of unemployment

<u>2</u> Cyclical unemployment

<u>1</u> Discouraged workers

<u>6</u> Frictional unemployment

<u>15</u> Structural unemployment

<u>5</u> Job search

<u>4</u> Sectoral shifts

<u>13</u> Unemployment insurance

<u>11</u> Union

<u>17</u> Collective bargaining

<u>10</u> Strike

<u>12</u> Insiders

<u>18</u> Outsiders

<u>9</u> Right-to-work laws

<u>3</u> Efficiency wages

Practice Problems

1. a. 2004: 7.4 + 105.2 = 112.6 million
        2005: 8.1 + 104.2 = 112.3 million
    b. 2004: (112.6/168.2) × 100 = 66.9%
        2005: (112.3/169.5) × 100 = 66.3%
    c. 2004: (7.4/112.6) × 100 = 6.6%
        2005: (8.1/112.3) × 100 = 7.2%
    d. Earlier retirements, students staying in college longer, more parents staying at home with children, discouraged workers discontinuing their job search.
    e. 2004: 6.6% − 6.6% = 0%
        2005: 7.2% − 6.6% = 0.6%
        In 2004, unemployment is "normal" for Employment Country; therefore, there is no recession. However, in 2005, unemployment is above normal (positive cyclical unemployment), so Employment Country may be in a recession.

2. a. The low-skill market will experience unemployment because there will be an excess supply of labor. (See Exhibit 2.)

b. No, because the competitive equilibrium wage is above the wage floor.

c. Yes. We observe a greater amount of unemployment among low-skill workers who are often young and inexperienced.

d. Yes. The excess supply of skilled workers may cause some skilled workers to move to the unskilled market increasing the supply of labor in the unskilled market, further reducing the competitive equilibrium wage and causing even more unemployment there.

3. a. Job search, minimum wage, unions, efficiency wages.

    b. Efficiency wages.

    c. To improve worker health, lower worker turnover, improve worker quality, increase worker effort.

    d. Worker health, because in the U.S. workers' wages are significantly above subsistence.

    e. Frictional unemployment exists even when the wage is at a competitive equilibrium.

Short-Answer Questions

1. Some people claim to be looking for work just to collect unemployment benefits or they are being paid "under the table." Others are discouraged workers and have stopped looking for work due to an unsuccessful search.

2. Many people are unemployed for short periods. A few people are unemployed for very long periods.

3. In a small "company" town where a single company has market power that may depress the wage below the competitive equilibrium. This may need to be offset by organized labor.

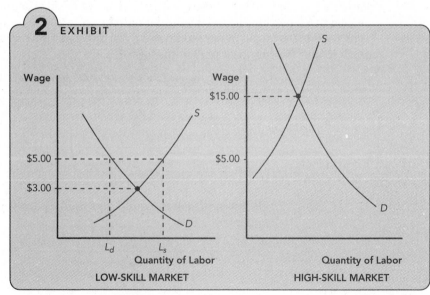

2 EXHIBIT

LOW-SKILL MARKET

HIGH-SKILL MARKET

4. It raises the wage above the competitive equilibrium in the unionized sector. Some of those unemployed in the unionized sector move to the nonunionized sector increasing the supply of labor and lowering the wage in the nonunion sector.

5. U4. It is total unemployed plus discouraged workers as a percent of the civilian labor force plus discouraged workers. It is a little higher than the official unemployment rate because it includes some nonworking people that have given up looking for work and have fallen out of the labor force.

6. No, because the competitive equilibrium wage for accountants exceeds the minimum wage, and hence, the minimum wage is not a binding constraint for accountants.

7. Frictional unemployment, because job matching takes time even when the wage is at the competitive equilibrium. Also, continuous sectoral shifts and new entrants into the job market make some frictional unemployment inevitable.

8. Unemployed workers devote less effort to their job search, turn down unattractive job offers, and are less concerned with job security.

9. By establishing employment agencies and worker training programs to retrain workers laid off in the contracting sectors.

10. The buggy whip maker. He will have to retrain because the contraction of the buggy whip business is permanent, while the waitress may just have to relocate, possibly just down the street.

True/False Questions

1. T
2. F; the unemployment rate falls when unemployed workers leave the labor force.
3. T
4. F; unemployment differs across demographic groups.
5. F; a minimum wage has a greater impact on low-wage workers.
6. T
7. T
8. T
9. F; efficiency wages are paid voluntarily by firms.
10. F; efficiency wages reduce turnover.
11. T
12. F; there would still be frictional unemployment.

13. F; the official unemployment rate may understate true unemployment.
14. F; unemployment insurance increases the unemployment rate because it increases frictional unemployment.
15. T

Multiple-Choice Questions

1. d
2. c
3. b
4. c
5. d
6. c
7. a
8. b
9. a
10. c
11. c
12. d
13. a
14. e
15. c
16. b
17. d
18. a
19. d
20. b

Advanced Critical Thinking

1. No. The unemployment rate is the ratio of the number of unemployed to the labor force. If the labor force grows (new graduates, housewives and househusbands entering the labor force) and if few of the new members of the labor force find work, then the unemployment rate will rise but the number of employed could stay the same or rise.

2. The number of employed is a component of the labor force and you can get information on that number directly.

The Monetary System

GOALS

In this chapter you will

- Consider what money is and what functions money has in the economy

- Learn what the Federal Reserve System is

- Examine how the banking system helps determine the supply of money

- See what tools the Federal Reserve uses to alter the supply of money

OUTCOMES

After accomplishing these goals, you should be able to

- Define money and list the three functions of money

- Explain the role of the Fed in money creation

- Explain the money multiplier in a fractional reserve banking system

- List and explain the three tools the Fed uses to change the money supply

CHAPTER OVERVIEW

Context and Purpose

Chapter 29 is the first chapter in a two-chapter sequence dealing with money and prices in the long run. Chapter 29 describes what money is and develops how the Federal Reserve controls the quantity of money. Since the quantity of money influences the rate of inflation in the long run, the following chapter concentrates on the causes and costs of inflation.

The purpose of Chapter 29 is to help you develop an understanding of what money is, what forms money takes, how the banking system helps create money, and how the Federal Reserve controls the quantity of money. An understanding of money is important because the quantity of money affects inflation and interest rates in the long run and production and employment in the short run.

Chapter Review

Introduction If there were no such thing as money, people would have to rely on barter. *Barter* is when people trade goods and services directly for other goods and services. Barter requires that there be a *double coincidence of wants*. For a trade to take place, each trader has to have what the other one wants—an unlikely event. The existence of money facilitates production and trade, which allow people to specialize in what they do best and raise the standard of living.

The Meaning of Money

Money is the set of assets commonly used to buy goods and services. That is, money is the portion of someone's wealth that is directly spendable or exchangeable for goods and services.

There are three functions of money:

- Money serves as a **medium of exchange** because money is the most commonly accepted asset when a buyer purchases goods and services from a seller.

- Money serves as a **unit of account** because money is the yardstick with which people post prices and record debts.

- Money serves as a **store of value** because people can use money to transfer purchasing power from the present to the future. Other types of wealth—stocks, bonds, rare art—may be a better store of value, but they are not as good at providing liquidity. **Liquidity** is the ease with which an asset can be converted into a medium of exchange. Money is liquid but loses value when prices rise. The value of rare art tends to rise with inflation, but it is much less liquid.

Money can be divided into two fundamental types—commodity money and fiat money.

- **Commodity money** is money that has "intrinsic value." That is, it has value independent of its use as money. Gold, silver, and cigarettes in a prisoner-of-war camp are all examples of commodity money. When a country uses gold as money, it is operating under a gold standard.

- **Fiat money** is money without intrinsic value. It is money by government fiat or declaration. Paper dollars are an example of fiat money.

When we measure the quantity of money, sometimes called the money stock, we should clearly include **currency** (paper bills and coins in the hands of the public) and **demand deposits** (balances in bank accounts that can be accessed on demand by check) because these assets are a medium of exchange. Savings balances, however, can easily be transferred into checking; other more restrictive checking accounts, such as money market mutual funds, offer some degree of spendability. In an economy with a complex financial system, it is difficult to draw the line between assets that are money and assets that are not. For this reason, in the United States, we calculate multiple measures of the money stock, two of which are shown below:

- M1: Currency, demand deposits, traveler's checks, other checkable deposits

- M2: M1, savings deposits, small time deposits, money market mutual funds, a few minor categories

For our purposes, consider money in the United States to be currency and spendable deposits.

Credit cards are not counted in the stock of money because they are not a method of payment but are instead a method of deferring payment. Debit cards are like an electronic check in that money from the buyer's account is directly transferred to the seller's account. Thus, the value is already captured by the account balance.

In comparison to the size of the U.S. population, there is an unusually large amount of currency in circulation. It is likely that a large portion of this currency is circulating overseas or used by criminal enterprises.

The Federal Reserve System

The **Federal Reserve (Fed)** is the **central bank** of the United States. It is designed to oversee the banking system and regulate the quantity of money in the economy.

The Fed was created in 1914 in response to a series of bank failures in 1907. The Fed is run by the Board of Governors, which has seven members appointed by the president and approved by the Senate. The members of the Board of Governors have fourteen-year terms to insulate them from political pressures. One of the seven members of the Board of Governors is appointed by the president to serve as chairman for a four-year term. The Federal Reserve System is composed of the Federal Reserve Board in Washington, D.C., and twelve regional Federal Reserve Banks.

The Fed has two main jobs:

- To regulate the banks and ensure the health of the banking system. The Fed monitors each bank's financial condition and helps clear checks. In a crisis, when banks find themselves short of cash, the Fed may act as the *lender of last resort* to the banks.

- To control the quantity of money in the economy, called the **money supply**. The Fed's decisions about the money supply are called **monetary policy**.

The monetary policy branch of the Fed is the *Federal Open Market Committee* (FOMC). There are twelve voting members on the FOMC—the seven members of the Board of Governors plus five of the twelve regional bank presidents. The voting among the regional bank presidents is rotated. The FOMC meets about every six weeks to discuss the condition of the economy and to vote on changes in monetary policy.

The Fed primarily changes the money supply with **open-market operations,** which are the purchase and sale of U.S. government bonds by the Fed in the open market for debt (thus, the name Federal Open Market Committee).

- To increase the money supply, the Fed creates dollars and uses them to purchase government bonds. After the transaction, additional dollars are in the hands of the public, so the money supply is larger.

- To decrease the money supply, the Fed sells government bonds to the public. After the transaction, fewer dollars are in the hands of the public, so the money supply is smaller.

Changing the money supply changes inflation in the long run and may change employment and output in the short run.

Banks and the Money Supply

Recall that the public can hold its money as currency or demand deposits. Since these deposits are in banks, the behavior of banks affects the money supply. This complicates the Fed's task of controlling the money supply.

The impact that banks have on the money supply can be seen by going through the following three cases:

- Suppose there are *no banks.* Then currency is the only money. If there is $1,000 of currency, there is $1,000 of money.

- Suppose there is *100-percent-reserve banking.* Deposits that are received by a bank but are not loaned out are called **reserves.** With 100-percent-reserve banking, banks are safe places to store money, but they are not lenders. If the public deposits all $1,000 of its currency in Bank 1, Bank 1's T-account, which records changes in the bank's assets and liabilities, would be the following:

Bank 1

assets	liabilities
reserves $1,000	deposits $1,000

Bank 1 has liabilities of $1,000 because it owes the $1,000 deposit back to the depositor. It has assets of $1,000 because it has cash reserves of $1,000 in its vault. Since currency held by the public has gone down by $1,000 and deposits held by the public have increased by $1,000, the money supply is unaffected. *If banks hold all deposits on reserve, banks do not influence the money supply.*

- Suppose there is **fractional-reserve banking.** Since few people request the return of their deposit on any given day, Bank 1 need not hold all $1,000 of the deposit as cash reserves. It could lend some of the $1,000 and keep only the remainder on reserve. This is called fractional-reserve banking. The fraction of deposits held as reserves is the **reserve ratio.** The Fed sets the minimum reserve ratio with a reserve requirement. Suppose Bank 1 has a *reserve ratio* of 10 percent, which means that it keeps 10 percent of its deposits on reserve and lends out the rest. Its T-account becomes:

Bank 1

assets	liabilities
reserves $100	deposits $1,000
loans $900	

Bank 1 has created money because it still holds a $1,000 deposit, but now a borrower has $900 in currency. *When banks hold only a fraction of deposits as reserves, banks create money.*

This story is not complete. Suppose the borrower of the $900 spends it and the receiver of the $900 deposits it in Bank 2. If Bank 2 also has a reserve ratio of 10 percent, its T-account becomes:

Bank 2

assets		liabilities	
reserves	$ 90	deposits	$900
loans	$810		

Bank 2 has created another $810 by its lending activity. Each time money is deposited and a portion of it loaned, more money is created.

If this process continues forever, the total amount of money created by the banking system from the original deposit of $1,000 is $1,000 + $900 + $810 + $729 + . . . = $10,000 (in this case, each loan is 90 percent of the previous loan).

The amount of money the banking system creates from each dollar of reserves is called the **money multiplier.** The money multiplier is the reciprocal of the reserve ratio. If R is the reserve ratio, then the money multiplier is $1/R$. In the case described above, the money multiplier is $1/.10$ or 10. Thus, $1,000 of new reserves created from the original $1,000 deposit can create a total of $10,000 in deposits. The smaller the reserve ratio, the greater the amount of lending from the same amount of reserves and, hence, the larger the money multiplier. The larger the reserve ratio, the smaller the multiplier.

Fractional-reserve banking does not create net wealth because when a bank loans reserves, which creates money (someone's asset), it also creates an equal value debt contract (someone's liability).

The Fed has three main tools it uses to alter the money supply:

- *Open-market operations:* Recall, when the Fed buys government bonds from the public, the dollars it uses to pay for them increase the dollars in the economy. Each new dollar held as currency increases the money supply one dollar. Each dollar deposited with banks increases bank reserves and, thus, increases the money supply by some multiple. When the Fed sells government securities, dollars are removed from circulation and reserves are reduced at banks. This reduces lending and further reduces the money supply. Open-market operations can easily be used for small or large changes in the money supply. Hence, it is the day-to-day tool of the Fed.

- *Reserve requirements:* **Reserve requirements** set the minimum reserve ratio for a bank. An increase in the reserve requirement reduces the money multiplier and decreases the money supply. A decrease in the reserve requirement increases the money multiplier and increases the money supply. The Fed rarely changes reserve requirements because changes in reserve requirements disrupt the business of banking. For example, an increase in reserve requirements immediately restricts bank loans.

- *Discount rate:* The **discount rate** is the interest rate the Fed charges on loans to banks. When the Fed raises the discount rate, banks tend to borrow fewer reserves from the Fed and the money supply decreases. When the Fed decreases the discount rate, banks tend to borrow more reserves from the Fed and the money supply increases. The Fed also acts as a lender of last resort to banks during a crisis when depositors withdraw unusually large amounts of their deposits from banks.

The Fed's control of the money supply is not precise because:

- The Fed does not control the amount of money people choose to hold as deposits versus currency. When the public deposits a greater amount of their currency, bank reserves increase and the money supply increases.

- The Fed does not control the amount of reserves that the banks lend. The reserve requirement sets the minimum reserve ratio, but banks can hold *excess reserves*—reserves in excess of those required. If banks increase their excess reserves, lending decreases and the money supply decreases.

In times prior to the existence of deposit insurance, if depositors feared that a bank had made unsound loans with their deposits and that the bank might become bankrupt, they would "run" to the bank to remove their deposit. This is known as a "bank run." With fractional reserves, only a few depositors can immediately get their money back. This behavior causes a decrease in the money supply for two reasons. First, people increase their holdings of currency by withdrawing deposits from banks. This reduces reserves, bank lending, and the money supply. Second, banks, fearing deposit withdrawal, hold excess reserves and further decrease lending and the money supply. This is no longer a problem due to the Federal Deposit Insurance Corporation (FDIC). Also, the Fed collects weekly data on reserves and deposits so it can detect changes in depositor and bank behavior.

The federal funds rate is the interest rate banks charge each other for short-term loans. When the Fed lowers the target for the federal funds rate, it buys bonds with open-market operations supplying more bank reserves, and the money supply increases. When the Fed raises the federal funds target, the money supply decreases.

Helpful Hints

1. Fiat money maintains value due to artificial scarcity. Gold has value because people desire it for its intrinsic value and because it is naturally scarce (alchemists have never been able to create gold). However, fiat money is cheap and easy to produce. Therefore, fiat money maintains its value only because of self-restraint on the part of the producer. If U.S. dollars are a quality store of value, it is because the dollar is difficult to counterfeit and the Fed shows self-restraint in the production of dollars.

2. Paper dollars are considered "currency" only when in the hands of the non-bank public. When economists use the word currency, we mean "currency in the hands of the non-bank public." When you deposit currency in the bank, you now own a deposit and your paper dollars are now the "reserves" of the bank. Currency in the hands of the non-bank public has decreased while deposits have increased by an equal amount. At this point, the money supply is unaltered because money is the sum of currency (in the hands of the non-bank public) and deposits.

3. The money multiplier is most easily understood in words. If we state the relationship between reserves, deposits, and the multiplier in words, it clarifies the relationship. Since a fractional reserve system implies that "reserves are some percent of deposits," it follows that "deposits are some multiple of reserves." For example, if reserves are 1/5 (or 20 percent) of deposits, then deposits are five times (or 1/.20) reserves. Since deposit expansion actually takes place due to banks' lending some of their reserves, it is most useful to us to think in terms of "deposits are some multiple of reserves."

4. It is easy to remember the impact of open-market operations by asking yourself, "Who pays?" When the Fed buys a government bond from the public, the Fed pays with "new dollars" and the money supply expands. When the Fed sells government bonds, the public pays with dollars and the Fed "retires" the dollars. That is, the dollars cease to exist when the Fed receives payment. Note that when the Fed sells bonds, it is not "issuing" bonds. It is selling existing bonds that were previously issued by the U.S. government.

Terms and Definitions

Choose a definition for each key term.

Key Terms

____ Barter

____ Double coincidence of wants

____ Money

____ Medium of exchange

____ Unit of account

____ Store of value

____ Liquidity

____ Commodity money

____ Fiat money

____ Currency

____ Demand deposits

____ Federal Reserve (Fed)

____ Central bank

____ Money supply

____ Monetary policy

____ Federal Open Market Committee

____ Open-market operations

____ Reserves

____ Fractional-reserve banking

____ Reserve ratio

____ Money multiplier

____ Reserve requirements

____ Discount rate

____ Excess reserves

Definitions

1. A banking system in which banks hold only a fraction of deposits as reserves

2. Paper bills and coins in the hands of the public

3. The function of money when used to transfer purchasing power to the future

4. The interest rate the Fed charges on loans to banks

5. Trading goods and services directly for goods and services

6. The function of money when used as a yardstick to post prices and record debts

7. Money in the form of a commodity with intrinsic value

8. The central bank of the United States

9. The set of assets generally accepted in trade for goods and services

10. The fraction of deposits held as reserves

11. Reserves held beyond the minimum reserve requirement

12. The quantity of money in the economy

13. Money without intrinsic value

14. The function of money when used to purchase goods and services

15. The purchase and sale of U.S. government bonds by the Fed

16. The accident that two people bartering have what the other wants

17. The minimum legal percent of deposits that banks must hold as reserves

18. Decisions by the central bank concerning the money supply

19. Balances in bank accounts that can be accessed on demand by check

20. The amount of money the banking system generates from each dollar of reserves

21. The monetary policy committee within the Federal Reserve

22. An institution designed to regulate the banking system and money supply

23. The ease with which an asset can be converted into the economy's medium of exchange

24. Deposits that banks have received but have not lent out

PROBLEMS AND SHORT-ANSWER QUESTIONS

Practice Problems

1. Suppose the Federal Reserve purchases a U.S. government bond from you for $10,000.

   a. What is the name of the Fed's action?

   _____

   b. Suppose you deposit the $10,000 in First Student Bank. Show this transaction on First Student Bank's T-account.

   First Student Bank

assets	liabilities

   c. Suppose the reserve requirement is 20 percent. Show First Student Bank's T-account if they loan out as much as they can.

   First Student Bank

assets	liabilities

   d. At this point, how much money has been created from the Fed's policy action?

   _____

   e. What is the value of the money multiplier?

   _____

   f. After infinite rounds of depositing and lending, how much money could be created from the Fed's policy action?

   _____

   g. If during the rounds of depositing and lending some people keep extra currency and fail to deposit all of their receipts, will there be more or less money created from the Fed's policy action than you found in part f? Why?

   _____

   _____

   h. If during the rounds of depositing and lending, some banks fail to loan the maximum amount of reserves allowed but instead keep excess reserves, will there be more or less money created from the Fed's policy action than you found in part *f*? Why?

_____

_____

_____

2. Suppose the entire economy contains $1,000 worth of one dollar bills.
   a. If people fail to deposit any of the dollars but instead hold all $1,000 as currency, how large is the money supply? Explain.

   _____

   _____

   b. If people deposit the entire $1,000 worth of bills in banks that are required to observe a 100 percent reserve requirement, how large is the money supply? Explain.

   _____

   _____

   c. If people deposit the entire $1,000 worth of bills in banks that are required to observe a 20 percent reserve requirement, how large could the money supply become? Explain.

   _____

   _____

   d. In part *c*, what portion of the money supply was created due to the banks? (Hint: $1,000 of bills already existed.)

   _____

   _____

   _____

   e. If people deposit the entire $1,000 worth of bills in banks that are required to observe a 10 percent reserve requirement, how large could the money supply become?

   _____

   _____

   f. Compare your answer in part *e* to part *c*. Explain why they are different.

   _____

   _____

   _____

   g. If people deposit the entire $1,000 worth of bills in banks that are required to observe a 10 percent reserve requirement, but they choose to hold another 10 percent as excess reserves, how large could the money supply become?

   _____

   _____

h. Compare your answer in part *c* to part *g*. Are these answers the same? Why?

_____

_____

_____

Short-Answer Questions

1. What is barter and why does it limit trade?

   _____

   _____

2. What are the three functions of money?

   _____

   _____

3. What are the two basic kinds of money?

   _____

   _____

4. What two main assets are clearly money in the United States, and how do they differ from all other assets? (i.e., define money)

   _____

   _____

   _____

5. What are the two main jobs of the Federal Reserve?

   _____

   _____

6. What are the three monetary policy tools of the Fed?

   _____

   _____

7. If the Fed wished to expand the money supply, how should they adjust each of the three policy instruments described in question 6 above?

   _____

   _____

   _____

8. If the Fed buys $1,000 of government bonds from you and you hold all of the payment as currency at home, by how much does the money supply rise?

_____

9. If the Fed buys $1,000 of government bonds from you, you deposit the entire $1,000 in a demand deposit at your bank, and banks observe a 10 percent reserve requirement, by how much could the money supply increase?

_____

_____

10. Suppose the reserve requirement is 20 percent. If you write a check on your account at Bank 1 to buy a $1,000 government bond from your roommate, and your roommate deposits the $1,000 in her account at Bank 2, by how much will the money supply change?

_____

_____

11. Suppose there is no deposit insurance. Suppose rumors circulate that banks have made many bad loans and may be unable to repay their depositors. What would you expect depositors and banks to do, and what would their behavior do to the money supply?

_____

_____

_____

SELF-TEST

True/False Questions

_____ 1. Money and wealth are the same thing.

_____ 2. Fiat money is money that is used in Italy.

_____ 3. Commodity money has value independent of its use as money.

_____ 4. The M1 money supply is composed of currency, demand deposits, traveler's checks, and other checkable deposits.

_____ 5. When you are willing to go to sleep tonight with $100 in your wallet and you have complete confidence that you can spend it tomorrow and receive the same amount of goods as you would have received had you spent it today, money has demonstrated its function as a medium of exchange.

_____ 6. Money has three functions: It acts as a medium of exchange, a unit of account, and a hedge against inflation.

_____ 7. Credit cards are part of the M2 money supply and are valued at the maximum credit limit of the cardholder.

_____ 8. The Federal Reserve is the central bank of the United States and is run by the seven members of the Board of Governors.

_____ 9. The Federal Open Market Committee (FOMC) meets about every six weeks and discusses the condition of the economy and votes on changes in monetary policy.

_____ 10. If there is 100 percent reserve banking, the money supply is unaffected by the proportion of the dollars that the public chooses to hold as currency versus deposits.

_____ 11. If the Fed purchases $100,000 of government bonds, and the reserve requirement is 10 percent, the maximum increase in the money supply is $10,000.

_____ 12. If the Fed desires to contract the money supply, it could do any of the following: sell government bonds, raise the reserve requirement, and raise the discount rate.

_____ 13. If the Fed sells $1,000 of government bonds, and the reserve requirement is 10 percent, deposits could fall by as much as $10,000.

_____ 14. An increase in the reserve requirement increases the money multiplier and increases the money supply.

_____ 15. If banks choose to hold excess reserves, lending decreases and the money supply decreases.

Multiple-Choice Questions

1. Which of the following is not a function of money?
   a. unit of account
   b. store of value
   c. hedge against inflation
   d. medium of exchange

2. The M1 money supply is composed of
   a. currency, demand deposits, traveler's checks, and other checkable accounts.
   b. currency, demand deposits, savings deposits, money market mutual funds, and small time deposits.
   c. currency, government bonds, gold certificates, and coins.
   d. currency, NOW accounts, savings accounts, and government bonds.
   e. none of the above.

3. An example of fiat money is
   a. gold.
   b. paper dollars.
   c. coins.
   d. cigarettes in a prisoner-of-war camp.

4. The Board of Governors of the Federal Reserve System consists of
   a. 7 members appointed by Congress and 7 appointed by the president.
   b. 7 members elected by the Federal Reserve Banks.
   c. 12 members appointed by Congress.
   d. 7 members appointed by the president.
   e. 5 members appointed by the president and 7 rotating presidents of the Federal Reserve Banks.

5. Commodity money
   a. has no intrinsic value.
   b. has intrinsic value.
   c. is used exclusively in the United States.
   d. is used as reserves to back fiat money.

6. To insulate the Federal Reserve from political pressure,
   a. the Board of Governors are elected by the public.
   b. the Board of Governors have lifetime tenure.
   c. the Board of Governors are supervised by the House Banking Committee.
   d. the Board of Governors are appointed to 14-year terms.

7. Which of the following statements is true?
   a. The FOMC meets once per year to discuss monetary policy.
   b. The Federal Reserve was created in 1871 in response to the Civil War.
   c. When the Fed sells government bonds, the money supply decreases.
   d. The primary tool of monetary policy is the reserve requirement.

8. Required reserves of banks are a fixed percentage of their
   a. loans.
   b. assets.
   c. deposits.
   d. government bonds.

9. If the reserve requirement is 25 percent, the value of the money multiplier is
   a. 0.25.
   b. 4.
   c. 5.
   d. 25.
   e. none of the above.

10. Which of the following policy actions by the Fed is likely to increase the money supply?
    a. reducing reserve requirements
    b. selling government bonds
    c. increasing the discount rate
    d. All of these will increase the money supply.

11. Suppose Joe changes his $1,000 demand deposit from Bank A to Bank B. If the reserve requirement is 10 percent, what is the potential change in demand deposits as a result of Joe's action?
    a. $1,000
    b. $9,000
    c. $10,000
    d. $0

12. A decrease in the reserve requirement causes
    a. reserves to rise.
    b. reserves to fall.
    c. the money multiplier to rise.
    d. the money multiplier to fall.
    e. none of the above.

13. The discount rate is
    a. the interest rate the Fed pays on reserves.
    b. the interest rate the Fed charges on loans to banks.
    c. the interest rate banks pay on the public's deposits.
    d. the interest rate the public pays when borrowing from banks.

14. Which of the following policy combinations would consistently work to increase the money supply?
    a. sell government bonds, decrease reserve requirements, decrease the discount rate
    b. sell government bonds, increase reserve requirements, increase the discount rate
    c. buy government bonds, increase reserve requirements, decrease the discount rate
    d. buy government bonds, decrease reserve requirements, decrease the discount rate
    e. none of the above

15. Suppose the Fed purchases a $1,000 government bond from you. If you deposit the entire $1,000 in your bank, what is the total potential change in the money supply as a result of the Fed's action if reserve requirements are 20 percent?
    a. $1,000
    b. $4,000
    c. $5,000
    d. $0

16. Suppose all banks maintain a 100 percent reserve ratio. If an individual deposits $1,000 of currency in a bank,
    a. the money supply is unaffected.
    b. the money supply increases by more than $1,000.
    c. the money supply increases by less than $1,000.
    d. the money supply decreases by more than $1,000.
    e. the money supply decreases by less than $1,000.

17. If the Fed engages in an open-market purchase, and at the same time, it raises reserve requirements,
    a. the money supply should rise.
    b. the money supply should fall.
    c. the money supply should remain unchanged.
    d. we cannot be certain what will happen to the money supply.

18. Given the following T-account, what is the largest new loan this bank can prudently make if the reserve requirement is 10 percent?

Test Bank

assets		liabilities	
reserves	$150	deposits	$1000
loans	$850		

    a. $0
    b. $50
    c. $150
    d. $1,000
    e. None of the above is correct.

19. The three main tools of monetary policy are
    a. government expenditures, taxation, and reserve requirements.
    b. the money supply, government purchases, and taxation.
    c. coin, currency, and demand deposits.
    d. open-market operations, reserve requirements, and the discount rate.
    e. fiat, commodity, and deposit money.

20. Suppose the Fed purchases a government bond from a person who deposits the entire amount from the sale in her bank. If the bank holds some of the deposit as excess reserves, the money supply will
   a. rise less than the money multiplier would suggest.
   b. rise more than the money multiplier would suggest.
   c. fall less than the money multiplier would suggest.
   d. fall more than the money multiplier would suggest.

ADVANCED CRITICAL THINKING

Suppose you are a personal friend of Ben Bernanke (the chairman of the Board of Governors of the Federal Reserve System on the date of publication of this Study Guide). He comes over to your house for lunch and notices your couch. Mr. Bernanke is so struck by the beauty of your couch that he simply must have it for his office. Mr. Bernanke buys it from you for $1,000 and, since it is for his office, pays you with a check drawn on the Federal Reserve Bank of New York.

1. Are there more dollars in the economy than before? Why?

   _____

   _____

2. Why do you suppose that the Fed doesn't buy and sell couches, real estate, and so on, instead of government bonds when they desire to change the money supply?

   _____

   _____

   _____

   _____

3. If the Fed doesn't want the money supply to rise when it purchases new furniture, what might it do to offset the purchase?

   _____

   _____

   _____

SOLUTIONS

Terms and Definitions

_5_ Barter

_16_ Double coincidence of wants

_9_ Money

_14_ Medium of exchange

_6_ Unit of account

_3_ Store of value

_23_ Liquidity

_7_ Commodity money

_13_ Fiat money

_2_ Currency

_19_ Demand deposits

_8_ Federal Reserve (Fed)

_22_ Central bank

_12_ Money supply

_18_ Monetary policy

_21_ Federal Open Market Committee

_15_ Open-market operations

_24_ Reserves

_1_ Fractional-reserve banking

_10_ Reserve ratio

_20_ Money multiplier

_17_ Reserve requirements

_4_ Discount rate

_11_ Excess reserves

Practice Problems

1. a. Open-market operations

   b.

   First Student Bank

assets		liabilities	
reserves	$10,000	deposits	$10,000

   c.

   First Student Bank

assets		liabilities	
reserves	$2,000	deposits	$10,000
loans	$8,000		

   d. $10,000 + $8,000 = $18,000

   e. $1/.20 = 5$

   f. $10,000 \times 5 = $50,000

   g. Less, because a smaller amount of each loan gets redeposited to be available to be loaned again.

   h. Less, because a smaller amount of each deposit gets loaned out to be available to be deposited again.

2. a. $1,000, because there is $1,000 of currency and $0 of deposits.

   b. $1,000, because there is now $0 of currency and $1,000 of deposits.

   c. $1,000 \times (1/.20) = $5,000$, because $1,000 of new reserves can support $5,000 worth of deposits.

   d. The total potential increase is $5,000, but $1,000 was currency already in the system. Thus, an additional $4,000 was created by the banks.

   e. $1,000 \times (1/.10) = $10,000$.

   f. Banks can create more money from the same amount of new reserves when reserve requirements are lower because they can lend a larger portion of each new deposit.

   g. $1,000 \times 1/(.10 + .10) = $5,000$.

   h. Yes, they are the same. With regard to deposit creation, it doesn't matter why banks hold reserves. It only matters how much they hold.

Short-Answer Questions

1. Barter is trading goods and services directly for other goods and services. It requires a double coincidence of wants.

2. Medium of exchange, unit of account, store of value.

3. Commodity money, fiat money.

4. Currency and demand deposits. They are the assets that are directly spendable or are commonly accepted in trade for goods and services.

5. To regulate banks and ensure the health of the banking system and to control the quantity of money in the economy.

6. Open-market operations, reserve requirements, and the discount rate.

7. Buy U.S. government bonds, lower the reserve requirement, and lower the discount rate.

8. $1,000

9. $1,000 \times (1/.10) = $10,000$

10. The money supply will not change at all. In this case, reserves are only moved from one bank to another.

11. Depositors will withdraw their deposits reducing bank reserves. Banks will try to hold excess reserves to prepare for the deposit withdrawal. Both will reduce bank lending and the money supply.

True/False Questions

1. F; money is the spendable portion of one's wealth.
2. F; fiat money is money without intrinsic value.
3. T
4. T
5. F; money demonstrated its function as a store of value.
6. F; store of value, not a hedge against inflation.
7. F; credit cards are not included in the money supply.
8. T
9. T
10. T
11. F; the maximum increase in the money supply is $100,000 \times (1/0.10) = \$1,000,000$.
12. T
13. T
14. F; an increase in the reserve requirement decreases the money multiplier, which decreases the money supply.
15. T

Multiple-Choice Questions

1. c
2. a
3. b
4. d
5. b
6. d
7. c
8. c
9. b
10. a
11. d
12. c
13. b
14. d
15. c
16. a
17. d
18. b
19. d
20. a

Advanced Critical Thinking

1. Yes. When the Fed purchases anything, it pays with newly created dollars, and there are more dollars in the economy.
2. The transaction costs and storage costs would be staggering. Also, the value of the inventory of "items" would never be certain. The open market for government bonds is much more efficient.
3. The Fed could sell government bonds of equal value to offset other purchases.

Money Growth and Inflation

CHAPTER OVERVIEW

Context and Purpose

Chapter 30 is the second chapter in a two-chapter sequence dealing with money and prices in the long run. Chapter 29 explained what money is and how the Federal Reserve controls the quantity of money. Chapter 30 establishes the relationship between the rate of growth of money and the inflation rate.

The purpose of this chapter is to acquaint you with the causes and costs of inflation. You will find that, in the long run, there is a strong relationship between the growth rate of money and inflation. You will also find that there are numerous costs to the economy from high inflation but that there is not a consensus on the importance of these costs when inflation is moderate.

Chapter Review

Introduction *Inflation* is an increase in the overall level of prices. *Deflation* is a decrease in the overall level of prices. *Hyperinflation* is extraordinarily high inflation. There is great variation in inflation over time and across countries. In this chapter, we address two questions: What causes inflation, and why is inflation a problem? The answer to the first question is that inflation is caused when the government prints too much money. The answer to the second question requires more thought and will be the focus of the second half of this chapter.

The Classical Theory of Inflation

This section develops and employs the **quantity theory of money** as an explanation of the price level and inflation.

When prices rise, it is rarely because products are more valuable but rather because the money used to buy them is less valuable. Thus, *inflation is more about the value of money than about the value of goods.* An increase in the overall price level is equivalent to a proportionate fall in the value of money. If P is the price level (the value of goods and services measured in money), then $1/P$ is the value of money measured in terms of goods and services. If prices double, the value of money has fallen to $1/2$ its prior value.

GOALS

In this chapter you will

- See why inflation results from rapid growth in the money supply

- Learn the meaning of the classical dichotomy and monetary neutrality

- See why some countries print so much money that they experience hyperinflation

- Examine how the nominal interest rate responds to the inflation rate

- Consider the various costs that inflation imposes on society

OUTCOMES

After accomplishing these goals, you should be able to

- Demonstrate the link between money and prices with the quantity equation

- Explain why money has no impact on real variables in the long run

- Explain the concept of an inflation tax

- Show the relationship between the nominal interest rate, the real interest rate, and the inflation rate

- Explain who gains and who loses on a loan contract when inflation rises unexpectedly

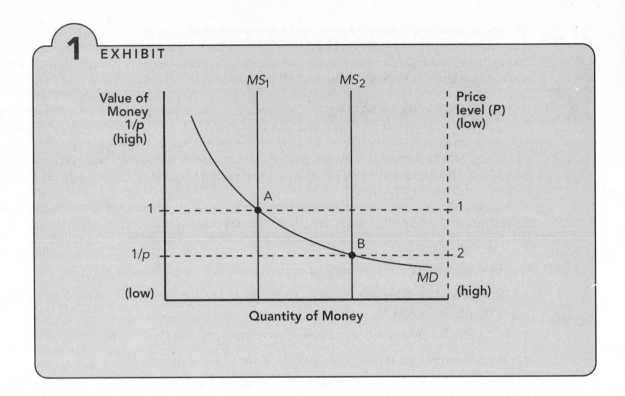

1 EXHIBIT

The value of money is determined by the supply and demand for money. If we ignore the banking system, the Fed controls the money supply. Money demand reflects how much wealth people want to hold in liquid form. While money demand has many determinants, in the long run, one is dominant—the price level. People hold money because it is a medium of exchange. If prices are higher, more money is needed for the same transaction, and the quantity of money demanded is higher.

Money supply and money demand need to balance for there to be monetary equilibrium. Monetary equilibrium is shown in Exhibit 1 for money supply MS_1 at point A. Recall that the value of money measured in goods and services is $1/P$. When the value of money is high, the price level is low and the quantity of money demanded is low. Therefore, the money demand curve slopes negatively in the graph. Since the Fed fixes the quantity of money, the money supply curve is vertical. In the long run, the overall level of prices adjusts to equate the quantity of money demanded to the quantity of money supplied.

Suppose the Fed doubles the quantity of money in the economy from MS_1 to MS_2. There is now an excess supply of money at the original price level. Since people now are holding more money than they desire, they will rid themselves of the excess supply of money by buying things—goods and services or bonds. Even if people buy bonds (lend money), the bond issuer (borrower) will take the money and buy goods and services. Either way, an injection of money increases the demand for goods and services. Since the ability of the economy to produce goods and services has not changed, an increase in the demand for goods and services raises the price level. The price level will continue to rise (and the value of money will fall) until the quantity of money demanded is raised to the level of the quantity of money supplied (point B). That is, the price level adjusts to equate money supply and money demand. Thus, the conclusions of the *quantity theory of money* are: (1) The quantity of money in the economy determines the price level (and the value of money), and (2) an increase in the money supply increases the price level, which means that growth in the money supply causes inflation.

The **classical dichotomy** suggests that economic variables can be divided into two groups—**nominal variables** (those measured in monetary units) and **real variables** (those measured in physical units). Although prices are nominal variables, relative prices are real variables. For example, the ratio of your earnings per hour to the price of candy bars is a real variable measured in candy bars per hour. Changes in the money supply affect nominal variables but not real variables. Real output is determined by productivity and factor supplies, and not by the quantity of money. However, the value of nominal variables is determined by and is *proportional* to the quantity of money. For example, if the money supply doubles, prices double, wages double, and all dollar values double but real output, employment, real interest rates, and real wages remain unchanged. This result is known as **monetary neutrality.** Money is unlikely to be neutral in the short run, but it is likely to be neutral in the long run.

The classical dichotomy and monetary neutrality can be demonstrated with the quantity equation. To begin, we define velocity as the speed of circulation of money. Then $V = (P \times Y)/M$ where V is the **velocity of money,** P is the price of output, and Y is the amount of real output (and $P \times Y$ = nominal GDP), and M is the quantity of money. If nominal output is \$500 (500 items at \$1 each) and M is \$100, then $V = 5$. That is, in order for \$100 to accommodate \$500 of purchases and sales, each dollar must be spent, on average, five times.

Rearranged, we get the **quantity equation:** $M \times V = P \times Y$. If the quantity of money increases, P or Y must rise, or V must fall. Our theory of inflation takes five steps:

- V is relatively stable in the long run.

- Therefore, changes in M cause proportional changes in nominal output ($P \times Y$).

- Real output (Y) is determined by productivity and factor supplies in the long run and is not affected by changes in M.

- If Y is fixed, an increase in M causes *proportional* changes in P.

- Thus, inflation results from rapid growth in the money supply.

Hyperinflation is sometimes defined as inflation that exceeds 50 percent per month. In those cases, the data show that there is a close link between money growth and inflation. This supports the conclusions of the quantity theory.

Why do countries print too much money if they know it causes inflation? Governments do it to pay for expenditures. When governments spend, they get the money by taxing, borrowing, or printing more money. Countries that have high spending, inadequate tax revenue, and limited ability to borrow may turn to printing money. When a government raises revenue by printing money, it has engaged in an **inflation tax.** When the government prints money and prices rise, the value of the existing money held by people falls. An inflation tax is a tax on people who hold money. The German hyperinflation between the two world wars was the largest hyperinflation ever recorded for any advanced country. For a number of reasons, the German government spent far more than it collected in taxes and printed money to cover the difference. Some argue that the German hyperinflation led to World War II.

If money is neutral, changes in money will have no effect on the *real interest rate*. Recall the relationship between the real interest rate, *nominal interest rate*, and inflation:

$$\text{real interest rate} = \text{nominal interest rate} - \text{inflation rate}$$

Solving for the nominal interest rate:

$$\text{nominal interest rate} = \text{real interest rate} + \text{inflation rate}$$

The real interest rate depends on the supply and demand for loanable funds. In the long run, money is neutral and only affects nominal variables, not real variables. Thus, when the Fed increases the growth rate of money, there is an increase in the inflation rate and a one-for-one increase in the nominal interest rate while the real interest rate remains unchanged. The one-for-one adjustment of the nominal interest rate to inflation is called the **Fisher effect.** Note that the nominal interest rate is set when the loan is first made, and thus, the Fisher effect actually says that the nominal interest rate adjusts one-for-one with *expected inflation*.

The Costs of Inflation

People often argue that inflation is a serious economic problem because when prices rise, their incomes can't buy as many goods and services. Thus, they believe that inflation directly lowers their standard of living. This argument, however, has a fallacy. Since people earn incomes by selling services, such as labor, inflation in nominal incomes goes hand in hand with inflation in prices. Therefore, inflation generally does not directly affect people's real purchasing power.

There are, however, a number of more subtle costs of inflation:

- *Shoeleather costs:* Recall, inflation is a tax on people who hold money. To avoid the tax, people hold less money and keep more invested in interest-bearing assets when inflation is high than they do when inflation is low. As a result, people have to go to the bank and withdraw money more often than they would if there were no inflation. These costs are sometimes metaphorically called **shoeleather costs** (since your shoes are worn out from all those trips to the bank). The actual cost of holding less cash is wasted time and inconvenience. At high rates of inflation, this cost is more than trivial.

- **Menu costs:** There are numerous costs associated with changing prices—the cost of printing new menus, price lists, and catalogs; mailing costs to distribute them; the cost of advertising new prices; and the cost of deciding the new prices themselves.

- *Relative-price variability and the misallocation of resources:* Since it is costly to change prices, firms change prices as rarely as possible. When there is inflation, the relative price of goods whose price is held constant for a period of time is falling with respect to the average price level. This misallocates resources because economic decisions are based on relative prices. A good whose price is changed only once per year is artificially expensive at the beginning of the year and artificially inexpensive by the end of the year.

- *Inflation-induced tax distortions:* Inflation raises the tax burden on income earned from saving and, thus, discourages saving and growth. Inflation affects two types of taxes on saving:

  (1) *Capital gains* are the profits made from selling an asset for more than its purchase price. Nominal capital gains are subject to taxation. Suppose you buy a stock for $20 and sell it for $50. Also suppose the price level doubles while you owned the stock. You only have a $10 real gain (because you would need to sell the stock for $40 just to break even), yet you must pay taxes on the $30 nominal capital gain because the tax code does not account for inflation.

  (2) *Nominal interest* is taxed even though part of the nominal interest rate is to compensate for inflation. When government takes a fixed percent of the nominal interest rate as taxes, the after-tax real return grows smaller as inflation increases. This is because the nominal interest rate rises one-for-one with inflation and taxes increase with the nominal interest rate, yet the pretax real return is unaffected by inflation. Therefore, the after-tax real return falls.

Because there are taxes on nominal capital gains and nominal interest, inflation lowers the after-tax real return on saving, and thus, inflation discourages saving and growth. This problem can be solved by eliminating inflation or by indexing the tax system so that taxes are assessed only on real gains.

- *Confusion and inconvenience:* Money serves as the unit of account, which means that the dollar is the yardstick by which we measure economic values. When the Fed increases the money supply and causes inflation, it decreases the value of money and shrinks the size of the economic measuring stick. This makes accounting for firms' profits more difficult and, thus, makes choosing investments more complicated. It also makes daily transactions more confusing.

- *A special cost of unexpected inflation—arbitrary redistribution of wealth:* The costs of inflation described above exist even if inflation is stable and predictable. Inflation has an additional cost to the economy, however, if it is unexpected because it arbitrarily redistributes wealth. For example, the terms of a loan are generally expressed in nominal values based on a certain amount of expected inflation (see the Fisher effect equation). However, if inflation becomes higher than expected, borrowers are allowed to repay the loan with dollars that purchase less than expected. Borrowers gain at the expense of lenders. The opposite is true when inflation is less than expected. If inflation were perfectly predictable, regardless of its size, this redistribution would not take place. However, high inflation is never stable. Therefore, low inflation is preferred because it is more stable and predictable.

The U.S. Treasury has just begun to issue bonds that automatically adjust the interest payment based on inflation thereby maintaining a stable real return. These bonds cannot accidentally redistribute wealth. "Inflation-indexed bonds" have been sold in other countries for a number of years.

Helpful Hints

1. The price of money is $1/P$. Since we measure the price of goods and services in terms of money, we measure the price of money in terms of the quantity of goods and services for which money can be exchanged. For example, if a basket of goods and services costs $5, then $P = \$5$. The price of a dollar is then $1/P$ or $1/5$ of the basket of goods. That is, one dollar exchanges for $1/5$ of the basket of goods. If the price of the basket of goods doubles so that it now sells for $10, the price of money has fallen to one-half its original value. Numerically, since the price of the basket is now $10, or $P = \$10$, the price of money has fallen to $1/P$ or $1/10$ of the basket of goods. To summarize, when the price of a basket of goods and services doubles from $5 to $10, the price of money falls by half from $1/5$ to $1/10$ of the basket of goods.

2. When dealing with the quantity theory, imagine you are at an auction. At the end of the auction, we can calculate the number of items sold and the average price of each item sold. Suppose we repeat the auction, only now the doorman doubles the money each buyer takes into the auction—if you had $20, you now have $40, and so on. If all participants spend the same percent of their money as at the prior auction (equivalent to a constant velocity) and if the items available to buy are unchanged (equivalent to a constant real output), what must happen to the average price of goods sold at the auction? Prices at the auction will precisely double, showing that prices are proportional to the quantity of money.

3. Unexpected inflation works like a tax on future receipts. We know that unexpected inflation redistributes wealth. Although it can be difficult to remember who wins and who loses on nominal contracts through time, you can always keep things straight if you remember that *unexpected inflation works like a tax on future receipts and a subsidy to future payments.* Therefore, when inflation turns out to be higher than we thought it would be when a loan contract was written, the recipient of the future payments is worse off because they receive dollars with less purchasing power than they had bargained for. The person who borrowed is better off because they were able to use the money when it had greater value, yet they were allowed to repay the loan with money of lower value. Therefore, when inflation is higher than expected, wealth is redistributed from lenders to borrowers. Alternatively, when inflation is less than expected, winners and losers are reversed.

    This concept can be applied to any contract that extends through time. Consider a labor contract. Recall, when inflation is greater than we expected, those who receive money in the future are harmed and those who pay are helped. Therefore, firms gain at the expense of workers when inflation is greater than anticipated. When inflation is less than expected, winners and losers are reversed.

Terms and Definitions

Choose a definition for each key term.

Key Terms

____ Inflation

____ Deflation

____ Hyperinflation

____ Quantity theory of money

____ Nominal variables

____ Real variables

____ Classical dichotomy

____ Monetary neutrality

____ Velocity of money

____ Quantity equation

____ Inflation tax

____ Nominal interest rate

____ Real interest rate

____ Fisher effect

____ Shoeleather costs

____ Menu costs

____ Capital gains

Definitions

1. Resources wasted when inflation causes people to economize on money holdings

2. The practice of a government raising revenue by printing money

3. The theory that the quantity of money determines prices and the growth rate of money determines inflation

4. Variables measured in physical units

5. The costs associated with changing prices

6. Interest rate uncorrected for inflation

7. Profits made from selling an asset for greater than the purchase price

8. The one-to-one adjustment of the nominal interest rate to inflation

9. An increase in the overall level of prices

10. Extraordinarily high inflation

11. $M \times V = P \times Y$

12. The theoretical separation of nominal and real variables

13. Interest rate corrected for inflation

14. Variables measured in monetary units

15. Rate at which money circulates

16. A decrease in the overall level of prices

17. The property that changes in the money supply affect nominal variables but not real variables

PROBLEMS AND SHORT-ANSWER QUESTIONS

Practice Problems

1. Use the quantity equation for this problem. Suppose the money supply is $200, real output is 1,000 units, and the price per unit of output is $1.
    a. What is the value of velocity?

    _____

    b. If velocity is fixed at the value you solved for in part *a*, what does the quantity theory of money suggest will happen if the money supply is increased to $400?

    _____

    _____

    c. Is your answer in part *b* consistent with the classical dichotomy? Explain.

    _____

    _____

    _____

    d. Suppose that when the money supply is doubled from $200 to $400, real output grows a small amount (say 2 percent). Now what will happen to prices? Do prices more than double, less than double, or exactly double? Why?

    _____

    _____

    _____

    e. When inflation gets very high, people do not like to hold money because it is losing value quickly. Therefore, they spend it faster. If when the money supply is doubled, people spend money more quickly, what happens to prices? Do prices more than double, less than double, or exactly double? Why?

    _____

    _____

    _____

    f. Suppose the money supply at the beginning of this problem refers to M1. That is, the M1 money supply is $200. What would the M2 quantity equation look like if the M2 money supply were $500 (and all other values were as stated at the beginning of the problem)?

    _____

    _____

2. The following questions are related to the Fisher effect.
   a. To demonstrate your understanding of the Fisher effect, complete the following table.

Real interest rate	Nominal interest rate	Inflation rate
3%	10%	
	6	2%
5		3

The following questions about the Fisher effect are unrelated to the table above.

   b. Suppose people expect inflation to be 3 percent, and suppose the desired real interest rate is 4 percent. What is the nominal rate?

   _____

   _____

   c. Suppose inflation turns out to be 6 percent. What is the actual real interest rate on loans that were signed based on the expectations in part *b*?

   _____

   _____

   d. Was wealth redistributed to the lender from the borrower or to the borrower from the lender when inflation was expected to be 3 percent but, in fact, turned out to be 6 percent?

   _____

   _____

   _____

   e. What would have happened had inflation turned out to be only 1 percent?

   _____

   _____

   _____

3. Income taxes treat nominal interest earned on savings as income even though much of the nominal interest is simply to compensate for inflation.
   a. To see what this does to the incentive to save, complete the following table for both the low inflation and high inflation country.

	Low-inflation Country	High-inflation Country
Real interest rate	5%	5%
Inflation rate	3	11
Nominal interest rate		
Reduced interest rate due to a 25% tax		
After-tax nominal interest rate		
After-tax real interest rate		

b. In which country is there a greater incentive to save? Why?

_____

_____

c. What could the government do to eliminate this problem?

_____

_____

Short-Answer Questions

1. If the money supply doubles, what must happen in the long run to the quantity of money demanded and the price level?

_____

_____

_____

2. Explain the classical dichotomy.

_____

_____

_____

3. Within the framework of the classical dichotomy, which type of variables are affected by changes in money and which type are not? What phrase do we use to capture this effect?

_____

_____

4. Is money more likely to be neutral in the long run or the short run? Why?

_____

_____

_____

5. Suppose the money supply were to increase by 10 percent. Explain what would happen to each variable in the quantity equation.

_____

_____

6. What are the three sources of revenue a government can use to support its expenditures? Which method causes inflation, and who bears the burden of this method of raising revenue?

_____

_____

7. In the long run, what does an increase in the growth rate of the money supply do to real and nominal interest rates?

    _____

    _____

    _____

8. Does inflation erode the value of our income and, thereby, lower our standard of living? Explain.

    _____

    _____

9. What are the costs of inflation when inflation is perfectly anticipated?

    _____

    _____

    _____

10. Suppose inflation turns out to be lower than we had expected. Who is likely to gain: borrowers or lenders? union workers or firms? Why?

    _____

    _____

    _____

11. What is the inconsistency in the following statement? "When inflation is high but stable and predictable, inflation does not redistribute wealth."

    _____

    _____

12. Does inflation (if correctly anticipated) make borrowers worse off and lenders better off when it raises nominal interest rates? Why?

    _____

    _____

    _____

SELF-TEST

True/False Questions

_____ 1. An increase in the price level is the same as a decrease in the value of money.

_____ 2. The quantity theory of money suggests that an increase in the money supply increases real output proportionately.

_____ 3. If the price level were to double, the quantity of money demanded would double because people would need twice as much money to cover the same transactions.

_____ 4. In the long run, an increase in the money supply tends to have an effect on real variables but no effect on nominal variables.

_____ 5. If the money supply is $500, real output is 2,500 units, and the average price of a unit of real output is $2, the velocity of money is 10.

_____ 6. The Fisher effect suggests that, in the long run, if the rate of inflation rises from 3 percent to 7 percent, the nominal interest rate should increase 4 percentage points, and the real interest rate should remain unchanged.

_____ 7. An inflation tax is "paid" by those that hold money because inflation reduces the value of their money holdings.

_____ 8. Monetary neutrality means that a change in the money supply doesn't cause a change in anything at all.

_____ 9. Inflation erodes the value of people's wages and reduces their standard of living.

_____ 10. Inflation reduces the relative price of goods whose prices have been temporarily held constant to avoid the costs associated with changing prices.

_____ 11. The shoeleather costs of inflation should be approximately the same for a medical doctor and for an unemployed worker.

_____ 12. Inflation tends to stimulate saving because it raises the after-tax real return to saving.

_____ 13. Countries that spend more money than they can collect from taxing or borrowing tend to print too much money which causes inflation.

_____ 14. If inflation turns out to be higher than people expected, wealth is redistributed to lenders from borrowers.

_____ 15. If the nominal interest rate is 7 percent and the inflation rate is 5 percent, the real interest rate is 12 percent.

Multiple-Choice Questions

1. In the long run, inflation is caused by
   a. banks that have market power and refuse to lend money.
   b. governments that raise taxes so high that it increases the cost of doing business and, hence, raises prices.
   c. governments that print too much money.
   d. increases in the price of inputs, such as labor and oil.
   e. none of the above.

2. When prices rise at an extraordinarily high rate, it is called
   a. inflation.
   b. hyperinflation.
   c. deflation.
   d. hypoinflation.
   e. disinflation.

3. If the price level doubles,
   a. the quantity demanded of money falls by half.
   b. the money supply has been cut by half.
   c. nominal income is unaffected.
   d. the value of money has been cut by half.
   e. none of the above is true.

4. In the long run, the demand for money is most dependent upon
   a. the level of prices.
   b. the availability of credit cards.
   c. the availability of banking outlets.
   d. the interest rate.

5. The quantity theory of money concludes that an increase in the money supply causes
   a. a proportional increase in velocity.
   b. a proportional increase in prices.
   c. a proportional increase in real output.
   d. a proportional decrease in velocity.
   e. a proportional decrease in prices.

6. An example of a real variable is
   a. the nominal interest rate.
   b. the ratio of the value of wages to the price of soda.
   c. the price of corn.
   d. the dollar wage.
   e. none of the above.

7. The quantity equation states that
   a. money × price level = velocity × real output.
   b. money × real output = velocity × price level.
   c. money × velocity = price level × real output.
   d. none of the above is true.

8. If money is neutral,
   a. an increase in the money supply does nothing.
   b. the money supply cannot be changed because it is tied to a commodity such as gold.
   c. a change in the money supply only affects real variables such as real output.
   d. a change in the money supply only affects nominal variables such as prices and dollar wages.
   e. a change in the money supply reduces velocity proportionately; therefore, there is no effect on either prices or real output.

9. If the money supply grows 5 percent, and real output grows 2 percent, prices should rise by
   a. 5 percent.
   b. less than 5 percent.
   c. more than 5 percent.
   d. none of the above.

10. Velocity is
    a. the annual rate of turnover of the money supply.
    b. the annual rate of turnover of output.
    c. the annual rate of turnover of business inventories.
    d. highly unstable.
    e. impossible to measure.

11. Countries that employ an inflation tax do so because
    a. the government doesn't understand the causes and consequences of inflation.
    b. the government has a balanced budget.
    c. government expenditures are high and the government has inadequate tax collections and difficulty borrowing.
    d. an inflation tax is the most equitable of all taxes.
    e. an inflation tax is the most progressive (paid by the rich) of all taxes.

12. An inflation tax is
    a. an explicit tax paid quarterly by businesses based on the amount of increase in the prices of their products.
    b. a tax on people who hold money.
    c. a tax on people who hold interest-bearing savings accounts.
    d. usually employed by governments with balanced budgets.
    e. none of the above.

13. Suppose the nominal interest rate is 7 percent while the money supply is growing at a rate of 5 percent per year. Assuming real output remains fixed, if the government increases the growth rate of the money supply from 5 percent to 9 percent, the Fisher effect suggests that, in the long run, the nominal interest rate should become
    a. 4 percent.
    b. 9 percent.
    c. 11 percent.
    d. 12 percent.
    e. 16 percent.

14. If the nominal interest rate is 6 percent and the inflation rate is 3 percent, the real interest rate is
    a. 3 percent.
    b. 6 percent.
    c. 9 percent.
    d. 18 percent.
    e. none of the above.

15. If actual inflation turns out to be greater than people had expected, then
    a. wealth was redistributed to lenders from borrowers.
    b. wealth was redistributed to borrowers from lenders.
    c. no redistribution occurred.
    d. the real interest rate is unaffected.

16. Which of the following costs of inflation does not occur when inflation is constant and predictable?
    a. shoeleather costs
    b. menu costs
    c. costs due to inflation-induced tax distortions
    d. arbitrary redistributions of wealth
    e. costs due to confusion and inconvenience

17. Suppose that, because of inflation, a business in Russia must calculate, print, and mail a new price list to its customers each month. This is an example of
    a. shoeleather costs.
    b. menu costs.
    c. costs due to inflation-induced tax distortions.
    d. arbitrary redistributions of wealth.
    e. costs due to confusion and inconvenience.

18. Suppose that, because of inflation, people in Brazil economize on currency and go to the bank each day to withdraw their daily currency needs. This is an example of
   a. shoeleather costs.
   b. menu costs.
   c. costs due to inflation-induced tax distortions.
   d. costs due to inflation-induced relative price variability, which misallocates resources.
   e. costs due to confusion and inconvenience.

19. If the real interest rate is 4 percent, the inflation rate is 6 percent, and the tax rate is 20 percent, what is the after-tax real interest rate?
   a. 1 percent
   b. 2 percent
   c. 3 percent
   d. 4 percent
   e. 5 percent

20. Which of the following statements is true about a situation where real incomes are rising at 3 percent per year?
   a. If inflation were 5 percent, people should receive raises of about 8 percent per year.
   b. If inflation were 0 percent, people should receive raises of about 3 percent.
   c. If money is neutral, an increase in the money supply will not alter the rate of growth of real income.
   d. All of the above are true.
   e. None of the above is true.

ADVANCED CRITICAL THINKING

Suppose you explain the concept of an "inflation tax" to a friend. You correctly tell them, "When a government prints money to cover its expenditures instead of taxing or borrowing, it causes inflation. An inflation tax is simply the erosion of the value of money from this inflation. Therefore, the burden of the tax lands on those who hold money." Your friend responds, "What's so bad about that? Rich people have all the money, so an inflation tax seems fair to me. Maybe the government should finance all of its expenditures by printing money."

1. Is it true that rich people hold more money than poor people?

   _____

   _____

2. Do rich people hold a higher percent of their income as money than poor people?

   _____

   _____

   _____

3. Compared to an income tax, does an inflation tax place a greater or lesser burden on the poor? Explain.

_____

_____

_____

_____

_____

4. Are there any other reasons why engaging in an inflation tax is not good policy?

_____

_____

_____

SOLUTIONS

Terms and Definitions

_9_ Inflation

_16_ Deflation

_10_ Hyperinflation

_3_ Quantity theory of money

_14_ Nominal variables

_4_ Real variables

_12_ Classical dichotomy

_17_ Monetary neutrality

_15_ Velocity of money

_11_ Quantity equation

_2_ Inflation tax

_6_ Nominal interest rate

_13_ Real interest rate

_8_ Fisher effect

_1_ Shoeleather costs

_5_ Menu costs

_7_ Capital gains

Practice Problems

1. a. $(1,000 \times \$1)/\$200 = 5$

    b. $\$400 \times 5 = \$2 \times 1,000$, prices will double from $1 to $2

    c. Yes. The classical dichotomy divides economic variables into real and nominal. Money affects nominal variables proportionately and has no impact on real variables. In part *b*, prices double, but real output remains constant.

    d. The quantity equation says that nominal output must change in proportion to money. Prices will still rise, but since real output is larger, prices will less than double.

    e. Money has a proportional impact on nominal output if V is constant. If V grows, a doubling of M will cause P to more than double.

    f. $\$500 \times 2 = \$1 \times 1,000$, M2 velocity is 2.

2. a.

Real interest rate	Nominal interest rate	Inflation rate
3%	10%	7%
4	6	2
5	8	3

    b. $3\% + 4\% = 7\%$

    c. People would have signed loan contracts for 7 percent nominal interest. Therefore, $7\% - 6\% = 1\%$.

    d. People expected a real interest rate of 4 percent, but the actual real interest rate turned out to be 1 percent. Wealth was redistributed to the borrower from the lender.

    e. The original loan contract would be the same. Thus $7\% - 1\% = 6\%$. The actual real rate is 6 percent instead of 4 percent, so wealth is redistributed to lenders from borrowers.

3. a.

	Low-Inflation Country	High-Inflation Country
Real interest rate	5%	5%
Inflation rate	3	11
Nominal interest rate	8	16
Reduced interest rate due to a 25% tax	2	4
After-tax nominal interest rate	6	12
After-tax real interest rate	3	1

    b. In the low-inflation country, because the after-tax real interest rate is larger.

    c. They could eliminate inflation or tax only real interest income.

Short-Answer Questions

1. The quantity of money demanded must double to maintain monetary equilibrium because spending will double on the same amount of goods causing prices to double and the value of money to fall by half.

2. The view that macroeconomic variables can be divided into two groups: real (measured in physical units) and nominal (measured in monetary units).

3. Nominal are affected. Real are not. Monetary neutrality.

4. In the long run, because it takes time for people and markets to adjust prices in response to a change in the money supply. In the short run, mistakes are likely to be made.

5. V remains constant. Y remains constant. M rises by 10 percent, and P rises by 10 percent.

6. Taxes, borrowing, and printing money. Printing money. Those that hold money because its value decreases.

7. No impact on the real interest rate. Raises the nominal interest rate one-to-one with the increase in the growth rate of money and prices.

8. No. Income is a result of selling labor services, the value of which rises along with other prices during an inflation.

9. Shoeleather costs; menu costs; costs due to relative-price variability, which misallocates resources; tax distortions; confusion; and inconvenience.

10. Lenders and workers. Those that receive dollars in the future on contract receive dollars of greater value than they bargained for.

11. When inflation is high, it is always unstable and difficult to predict.

12. No. The nominal interest rate adjusts one-to-one with the rise in inflation so that the real rate is unaffected. Neither the borrower nor lender gains.

True/False Questions

1. T
2. F; it increases price proportionately.
3. T
4. F; the money supply tends to have an effect on nominal variables but not real variables.
5. T
6. T
7. T
8. F; it doesn't cause a change in real variables.
9. F; inflation in incomes goes hand in hand with inflation in prices.
10. T
11. F; the opportunity costs of trips to the bank are greater for a medical doctor.
12. F; inflation tends to reduce the after-tax return to saving.
13. T
14. F; wealth is redistributed to borrowers from lenders.
15. F; the real interest rate is 2 percent because 7% − 5% = 2%.

Multiple-Choice Questions

1. c
2. b
3. d
4. a
5. b
6. b
7. c
8. d
9. b
10. a
11. c
12. b
13. c
14. a
15. b
16. d
17. b
18. a
19. b
20. d

Advanced Critical Thinking

1. Yes, rich people probably hold more dollars than poor people.

2. No, by a wide margin, poor hold a larger percent of their income as money. In fact, the poor may have no other financial asset at all.

3. An inflation tax places a far greater burden on the poor than on the rich. The rich are able to keep most of their assets in inflation-adjusted, interest-bearing assets. We observed this in Brazil and Argentina during periods of high inflation.

4. Inflation imposes many other costs on the economy besides the inflation tax: shoeleather costs, menu costs, tax distortions, confusion, etc.

Open-Economy Macroeconomics: Basic Concepts

CHAPTER OVERVIEW

Context and Purpose

Chapter 31 is the first chapter in a two-chapter sequence dealing with open-economy macroeconomics. Chapter 31 develops the basic concepts and vocabulary associated with macroeconomics in an international setting: net exports, net capital outflow, real and nominal exchange rates, and purchasing-power parity. The next chapter, Chapter 32, builds an open-economy macroeconomic model that shows how these variables are determined simultaneously.

The purpose of Chapter 31 is to develop the basic concepts macroeconomists use to study open economies. We address why a nation's net exports must equal its net capital outflow. We also address the concepts of the real and nominal exchange rate and develop a theory of exchange rate determination known as purchasing-power parity.

Chapter Review

Introduction Earlier in the text, we learned that people gain from trade because they can specialize in the production of goods for which they have a comparative advantage and trade for other people's production. However, until now, most of our study of macroeconomics has been based on a **closed economy:** one which does not interact with other countries. We now begin the study of macroeconomics in an **open economy:** an economy that interacts with other economies.

The International Flows of Goods and Capital

An open economy interacts with other economies in two ways: It buys and sells goods and services in world product markets, and it buys and sells capital assets in world financial markets.

The Flow of Goods and Services: Exports, Imports, and Net Exports **Exports** are domestically produced goods and services sold abroad while **imports** are foreign-produced goods and services sold domestically. **Net exports** are the value of a country's exports minus the value of its imports. Net exports are also called the **trade balance.** If exports exceed imports, net exports are positive and the country is said to have a **trade surplus.** If imports exceed exports, net

GOALS

In this chapter you will

- Learn how net exports measure the international flow of goods and services

- Learn how net capital outflow measures the international flow of capital

- Consider why net exports must always equal net capital outflow

- See how saving, domestic investment, and net capital outflow are related

- Learn the meaning of the nominal exchange rate and the real exchange rate

- Examine purchasing-power parity as a theory of how exchange rates are determined

OUTCOMES

After accomplishing these goals, you should be able to

- Define net exports

- Define net capital outflow

- Explain why net exports and net capital outflow are two sides of the same coin

- Explain why a trade deficit and a negative net capital outflow can be beneficial to a country if that country has a small savings rate

- Show the relationship between the real and nominal exchange rate

- Show why the nominal exchange rate between two countries' currencies should equal their relative price levels exports are negative and the country is said to have a **trade deficit.** If imports equal exports, net exports are zero and there is **balanced trade.**

Net exports are influenced by the tastes of consumers for domestic versus foreign goods, the relative prices of foreign and domestic goods, exchange rates, foreign and domestic incomes, international transportation costs, and government policies toward trade. These factors will be addressed in the following chapter.

Since 1950, the U.S. economy has engaged in an increasing amount of international trade for the following reasons: (1) improved transportation such as larger cargo ships, (2) advances in telecommunications that allow for better overseas communication, (3) technologically advanced goods are more valuable per pound and easier to transport, and (4) governments look more favorably on trade as evidenced by their support of the North American Free Trade Agreement (NAFTA) and the General Agreement on Tariffs and Trade (GATT).

The Flow of Financial Resources: Net Capital Outflow   **Net capital outflow** (also called net foreign investment) is the purchase of foreign assets by domestic residents minus the purchase of domestic assets by foreigners. When a domestic resident buys and controls capital in a foreign country, it is known as foreign direct investment. When a domestic resident buys stock in a foreign corporation but has no direct control of the company, it is known as foreign portfolio investment.

Net capital outflow is influenced by the relative real interest rates paid on foreign versus domestic assets, the relative economic and political risks, and government policies that affect foreign ownership of domestic assets. These factors will be addressed in the following chapter.

The Equality of Net Exports and Net Capital Outflow   Net exports measure the imbalance of a country's imports and exports. Net capital outflow is the imbalance of a country's purchase and sale of assets. These two imbalances offset each other. That is, net capital outflow (NCO) equals net exports (NX):

$$NCO = NX$$

This is an identity because every international transaction is an exchange. When Ford sells a car to a Mexican resident, Ford receives pesos. NX and NCO have increased. Any subsequent transaction undertaken by Ford preserves the equality of NX and NCO. (1) If Ford holds the pesos, NCO increases because Ford is now holding additional foreign assets (pesos). (2) If Ford uses the pesos to buy other Mexican assets (stocks, etc.), it maintains the increase in NX and NCO. (3) If Ford uses the pesos to purchase Mexican goods of equal value, it reverses the transaction so that NX and NCO return to their original values. (4) If Ford exchanges the pesos for dollars, the new owners of the pesos could buy Mexican assets, maintaining the increase in NX and NCO, or they could buy Mexican goods, reducing NX and NCO to their original levels. Simply put, when someone exports goods and receives foreign currency, the foreign currency will either be held, used to buy assets from the importing country, or used to buy goods from the importing country. In each case, $NX = NCO$ is maintained. Alternatively, if a country runs a trade deficit ($NX < 0$), then it must finance this by selling assets abroad ($NCO < 0$).

Saving and Investment in an Open Economy Saving and investment are important for growth. Saving is the income of a nation that is left over after paying for consumption and government purchases. Recall, gross domestic product (Y) is the sum of consumption (C), investment (I), government purchases (G), and net exports (NX). Therefore,

$$Y = C + I + G + NX$$

and saving is

$$Y - C - G = I + NX$$

or,

$$S = I + NX.$$

Since $NX = NCO$, we can write

$$S = I + NCO.$$

Thus, in an open economy, when the U.S. economy saves a dollar, it can invest in domestic capital (I) or foreign capital (NCO). It does not have to invest only in domestic capital (I). When $S > I$, $NCO > 0$

and a nation is investing in foreign assets. When $I > S$, $NCO < 0$ and foreigners are helping finance a country's investment.

In summary, if a country runs a trade surplus, net exports (NX) are positive, domestic saving is greater than domestic investment, and net capital outflow (NCO) is positive. If a country runs a trade deficit, net exports (NX) are negative, domestic saving is less than domestic investment, and net capital outflow (NCO) is negative, indicating that the country is financing some investment by selling assets abroad. If a country has balanced trade, net exports (NX) are zero, domestic saving is equal to domestic investment, and net capital outflow (NCO) is zero.

When the U.S. trade deficit increased from 1980 to 1987, the accompanying decrease in net capital outflow (foreigners invested more in the United States) was largely due to a decrease in U.S. saving. While this is not the preferred method to finance investment, it is better to have foreigners than no one invest in the United States. When the U.S. trade deficit increased from 1991 to 2000, the accompanying decrease in net capital outflow (foreigners invested more in the United States) was largely due to an increase in U.S. investment. This type of trade deficit induced capital inflow in a country is not necessarily bad as long as the investment projects yield the desired returns. After 2000, government budget deficits have again reduced national saving and decreased net capital outflow.

The Prices for International Transactions: Real and Nominal Exchange Rates

The **nominal exchange rate** is the rate at which people can trade one currency for another currency. An exchange rate between dollars and any foreign currency can be expressed in two ways: foreign currency per dollar or dollars per unit of foreign currency. For example, if 80 yen are equal to 1 dollar, the nominal exchange rate is 80 yen per dollar or .0125 (which is 1/80) dollar per yen. We will always express exchange rates as foreign currency per dollar. When the dollar buys more foreign currency, there has been an **appreciation** of the dollar. When the dollar buys less foreign currency, there has been a **depreciation** of the dollar. Because there are so many currencies in the world, the dollar exchange rate is often expressed by an exchange rate index that compares a group of currencies to the dollar.

The **real exchange rate** is the rate at which people can trade the goods and services of one country for the goods and services of another. Two things are considered when we directly compare the value of goods in one country to those in another: the relative values of the currencies (nominal exchange rate) and the relative prices of the goods to be traded. The real exchange rate is defined as:

$$\text{real exchange rate} = \frac{\text{nominal exchange rate} \times \text{domestic price}}{\text{foreign price}}$$

Just as the nominal exchange rate is expressed as units of foreign currency per unit of domestic currency, the real exchange rate is expressed as units of foreign goods per unit of domestic goods. For example, suppose that a case of Mexican beer is 20 pesos while a case of U.S. beer is $10 and that the nominal exchange rate is 4 pesos per dollar. The real exchange rate of Mexican beer to U.S. beer is

$$\text{real exchange rate} = \frac{(4 \text{ pesos}/1 \text{ dollar}) \times (\$10/\text{case U.S. beer})}{20 \text{ pesos}/\text{case Mexican beer}}$$

$$= \frac{40 \text{ pesos}/\text{case U.S. beer}}{20 \text{ pesos}/\text{case Mexican beer}}$$

$$= \frac{40 \text{ pesos}}{\text{case U.S. beer}} \times \frac{\text{case Mexican beer}}{20 \text{ pesos}}$$

$$= \frac{2 \text{ cases Mexican beer}}{1 \text{ case U.S. beer}}$$

The real exchange rate is the true relative cost of goods across borders.

Since macroeconomists are concerned with the economy as a whole, they are concerned with overall prices rather than individual prices. Therefore, instead of using the price of beer to compute the real exchange rate, macroeconomists use each country's price index:

$$\text{real exchange rate} = (e \times P)/P^*$$

where e is the nominal exchange rate, P is a domestic price index, and P^* is a foreign price index.

When this measure of the real exchange rate rises, U.S. goods are more expensive relative to foreign goods and net exports fall. When this measure of the real exchange rate falls, U.S. goods are cheaper relative to foreign goods and net exports rise.

Many European countries now share a common currency called the *euro*. It has replaced the French franc, German mark, Italian lira, and so on. The euro is controlled by the European Central Bank (ECB). A single currency makes trade easier, is more convenient, and helps reduce nationalistic feelings in Europe.

A First Theory of Exchange-Rate Determination: Purchasing-Power Parity

The simplest explanation of why an exchange rate takes on a particular value is called **purchasing-power parity.** This theory says that a unit of any given currency should buy the same quantity of goods in all countries. The logic of this theory is based on the *law of one price*. The law of one price says that a good must sell for the same price in all locations because, if there were different prices for the same good, people would buy the good where it is cheap and sell it where it is expensive. This behavior will continue to drive up the price where it was low and drive down the price where it was high until the prices are equalized. This process is called *arbitrage*. Thus, a dollar should buy the same amount of beer in Mexico as it buys in the United States. If it did not, there would be opportunities for profit and traders would buy where it is cheap and sell where it is expensive.

If purchasing-power parity is true, the nominal exchange rate between two countries' currencies depends on the price levels in those two countries. For example, if beer in Mexico is 20 pesos per case while beer in the United States is $10 per case, then the exchange rate should be 20 pesos per $10, or 2 pesos/dollar so that one dollar buys the same amount of beer in both countries. Notice, *the nominal exchange rate of 2 pesos/dollar is simply the ratio of the prices in the two countries*.

To put this concept into a formula, suppose P is the U.S. price level, P^* is the foreign price level, and e is the exchange rate in terms of foreign currency per dollar. A dollar can buy $1/P$ units in the United States and e/P^* units in the foreign country. Purchasing-power parity suggests that a dollar should buy the same amount in each country.

$$1/P = e^*/P$$

Solving for e,

$$e = P^*/P.$$

Thus, if purchasing-power parity holds, the nominal exchange rate is the ratio of the foreign price level to the domestic price level.

Recall, a country's price level depends on how much money its central bank creates. If a central bank creates more money, its currency will buy fewer goods and services and fewer units of other currencies. That is, its currency will depreciate.

Purchasing-power parity is most likely to hold in the long run. However, even in the long run, the theory of purchasing-power parity is not completely accurate because (1) some goods are not easily traded (such as services) and (2) even tradable goods are not always perfect substitutes.

Helpful Hints

1. Negative net capital outflow augments domestic investment. National saving is used to support domestic investment and net capital outflow:

   $$S = I + NCO.$$

   If *NCO* is negative, as it is for the United States, it means that foreigners invest more in the United States than Americans invest abroad. This allows domestic investment to remain adequate in spite of very small saving on the part of Americans. For example, suppose saving is $700 billion and net capital outflow is –$200 billion. Domestic investment is $I = \$700 + \$200$ or $900 billion.

2. Always express nominal and real exchange rates in terms of foreign units to domestic units. Expressing exchange rates in terms of foreign units relative to domestic units helps avoid confusion because a rise in this exchange rate is associated with a rise in the value of the domestic unit. For example, suppose the nominal exchange rate between the yen and the dollar is expressed as 200 yen/dollar. If the exchange rate rises to 210 yen/dollar, the value of the dollar has risen.

3. When generating nominal or real exchange rates, always identify the units of measurement. A common mistake committed by students when calculating exchange rates (particularly real exchange rates) is to fail to identify the units of measurement throughout the problem and to try to attach the units of measurement at the end of the problem after a numerical solution has been found. This leaves much room for error and confusion. Notice in the real exchange rate example about Mexican and American beer that the units are attached to the numbers throughout. This is not just for your convenience. It is necessary to avoid making mistakes even if you have done it numerous times.

4. Purchasing-power parity should hold for goods of high value and low transportation costs. The law of one price applies to goods for which arbitrage is most likely. Hence, we might expect the dollar price of diamonds to be the same in all countries because small deviations in the price of diamonds create substantial profit opportunities. However, large deviations in prices of shoe shines between London and New York are unlikely to create profit opportunities and a movement of goods or services. While many goods and services are not currently traded across borders, growth in the production and trade of light, high-technology, high-value commodities should increase the applicability of the purchasing-power parity theory.

Terms and Definitions

Choose a definition for each key term.

Key Terms

____ Closed economy

____ Open economy

____ Exports

____ Imports

____ Net exports

____ Trade surplus

____ Trade deficit

____ Balanced trade

____ Net capital outflow

____ Nominal exchange rate

____ Appreciation

____ Depreciation

____ Real exchange rate

____ Purchasing-power parity

____ Arbitrage

Definitions

1. The amount by which exports exceed imports
2. Goods and services produced domestically and sold abroad
3. The rate at which people can trade the goods and services of one country for those of another country
4. Taking advantage of two prices for the same commodity by buying where it is cheap and selling where it is expensive
5. The rate at which people can trade one currency for another currency
6. A decrease in the value of a currency measured in terms of other currencies
7. An economy that does not interact with other economies
8. The value of exports minus the value of imports or the trade balance
9. The theory that a unit of a country's currency should buy the same quantity of goods in all countries
10. An increase in the value of a currency measured in terms of other currencies
11. An economy that interacts with other economies
12. The amount by which imports exceed exports
13. Goods and services produced in foreign countries and sold domestically
14. The purchase of foreign assets by domestic residents minus the purchase of domestic assets by foreigners
15. A situation in which exports equal imports

PROBLEMS AND SHORT-ANSWER QUESTIONS

Practice Problems

1. How would each of the following transactions affect U.S. *NCO*? Does the transaction affect direct investment or portfolio investment?
   a. Ford buys stock in Mazda.

   _____

   _____

   b. Ford buys steel from a Japanese manufacturer to use in the production of its cars.

   _____

   _____

   _____

   c. Mazda expands its plant in Tennessee.

   _____

   _____

   d. A Japanese mutual fund buys shares of stock in Ford.

   _____

   _____

   e. Dow Chemical builds a plant in Germany.

   _____

   _____

2. Suppose a resident of Great Britain buys a computer from a U.S. manufacturer using British pounds.
   a. If the U.S. manufacturer holds on to the British pounds, does $NX = NCO$ in this case? Explain.

   _____

   _____

   _____

   b. Suppose the U.S. manufacturer uses the pounds to help build a factory in Great Britain. Does $NX = NCO$ in this case? Explain. What kind of foreign investment is this?

   _____

   _____

c. Suppose the U.S. manufacturer uses the pounds to buy stock in a British corporation. Does $NX = NCO$ in this case? Explain. What kind of foreign investment is this?

_____

_____

_____

d. Suppose the U.S. manufacturer uses the pounds to buy computer chips manufactured in Great Britain. Does $NX = NCO$ in this case? Explain.

_____

_____

_____

3. Suppose the nominal exchange rate is 100 yen per dollar. Further, suppose the price of a bushel of American corn is $5 per bushel and the price of a bushel of Japanese corn is 750 yen.

a. What is the real exchange rate between Japan and the United States in terms of corn?

_____

_____

b. Does a dollar have purchasing-power parity in the United States and Japan? Explain.

_____

_____

_____

c. Is there a profit opportunity that you could exploit with arbitrage? Where would you buy and where would you sell?

_____

_____

d. If the nominal exchange rate stayed the same, what should happen to the price of corn in the United States and Japan? Explain.

_____

_____

_____

e. Suppose prices move as you have suggested in part *d*. What has happened to the real exchange rate?

_____

_____

_____

4. Suppose the price of a pair of Lee jeans is $40 in the United States and 400 pesos in Mexico.

a. What is the nominal peso/dollar exchange rate if purchasing-power parity holds?

_____

_____

b. Suppose Mexico's central bank is politically pressured to double its money supply, which doubles its price level. If purchasing-power parity holds, what is the new peso/dollar exchange rate? Did the peso appreciate or depreciate?

_____

_____

c. Suppose the Fed now doubles the U.S. money supply, which doubles the U.S. price level. If purchasing-power parity holds, what is the value of the peso/dollar exchange rate? Did the dollar appreciate or depreciate?

_____

_____

_____

d. Compare your answers to parts *a* and *c*. What has happened to the exchange rate? Why?

_____

_____

_____

Short-Answer Questions

1. Identify four reasons why the U.S. economy has engaged in an increasing amount of trade over the last 40 years.

_____

_____

_____

2. Define net capital outflow. When foreigners invest in the United States, what happens to the value of U.S. *NCO*?

_____

_____

3. What are the two mutually exclusive locations where national saving can be invested?

_____

_____

4. If national saving is held constant, what happens to domestic investment if *NCO* decreases? Why?

    _____

    _____

    _____

5. Suppose the U.S. dollar appreciates relative to world currencies. Would Pier One Imports (a domestic chain selling "exotic" foreign goods) be pleased or upset?

    _____

    _____

    _____

6. In terms of the real exchange rate, what three variables could change to make the United States more competitive internationally?

    _____

    _____

    _____

7. Suppose a Ford Escort sells for 10,000 U.S. dollars in the United States and 12,000 Canadian dollars in Canada. If purchasing-power parity holds, what is the Canadian dollar/American dollar exchange rate? How many U.S. dollars will a Canadian dollar buy?

    _____

    _____

8. Suppose trade increases between countries. Would this increase or decrease the predictive accuracy of the purchasing-power parity theory of exchange rate determination?

    _____

    _____

9. If the money supply grows at an average annual rate of 5 percent in the United States and at an average annual rate of 35 percent in Mexico, what should happen over time to the peso/dollar exchange rate if purchasing-power parity holds? Why?

    _____

    _____

    _____

10. Why might purchasing-power parity fail to be completely accurate?

    _____

    _____

SELF-TEST

True/False Questions

_____ 1. Net exports are defined as imports minus exports.

_____ 2. U.S. net capital outflow falls when Toyota buys stock in Hilton Hotels, an American corporation.

_____ 3. For any country, net exports are always equal to net capital outflow because every international transaction involves an exchange of an equal value of some combination of goods and assets.

_____ 4. For a given amount of U.S. national saving, an increase in U.S. net capital outflow decreases U.S. domestic investment.

_____ 5. Valuable technologically advanced goods are less likely to be traded internationally because shipping costs absorb too much of the potential profit.

_____ 6. A country that exports more than it imports is said to have a trade deficit.

_____ 7. If the yen/dollar exchange rate rises, the dollar has appreciated.

_____ 8. If a case of Pepsi costs $8 in the United States and 720 yen in Japan, then according to the purchasing-power parity theory of exchange rates, the yen/dollar exchange rate should be 5,760 yen/dollar.

_____ 9. If purchasing-power parity holds, the real exchange rate is always equal to 1.

_____ 10. If Great Britain's money supply grows faster than Mexico's, the value of the British pound should rise relative to the value of the peso.

_____ 11. If the nominal exchange rate is 2 British pounds to the dollar, and if the price of a Big Mac is $2 in the United States and 6 pounds in Great Britain, then the real exchange rate is 2/3 British Big Mac per American Big Mac.

_____ 12. In order to increase domestic investment, a country must either increase its saving or decrease its net foreign investment.

_____ 13. Arbitrage is the process of taking advantage of differences in prices of the same good by buying where the good is cheap and selling where it is expensive.

_____ 14. Arbitrage tends to cause prices for the same good to diverge from one another.

_____ 15. If a company based in the United States prefers a strong dollar (a dollar with a high exchange value), then the company likely exports more than it imports.

Multiple-Choice Questions

1. An economy that interacts with other economies is known as
   a. a balanced trade economy.
   b. an export economy.
   c. an import economy.
   d. a closed economy.
   e. an open economy.

2. Each of the following is a reason why the U.S. economy continues to engage in greater amounts of international trade *except* which one?
    a. There are larger cargo ships and airplanes.
    b. High-technology goods are more valuable per pound and, thus, more likely to be traded.
    c. NAFTA imposes requirements for increased trade between countries in North America.
    d. There have been improvements in technology that have improved telecommunications between countries.
    e. All of the above are reasons for increased trade by the United States.

3. Which of the following statements is true about a country with a trade deficit?
    a. Net capital outflow must be positive.
    b. Net exports are negative.
    c. Net exports are positive.
    d. Exports exceed imports.
    e. None of the above is true.

4. Which of the following would directly increase U.S. net capital outflow?
    a. General Electric sells an aircraft engine to Airbus in Great Britain.
    b. Microsoft builds a new distribution facility in Sweden.
    c. Honda builds a new plant in Ohio.
    d. Toyota buys stock in AT&T.

5. Which of the following is an example of foreign direct investment?
    a. McDonald's builds a restaurant in Moscow.
    b. Columbia Pictures sells the rights to a movie to a Russian movie studio.
    c. General Motors buys stock in Volvo.
    d. General Motors buys steel from Japan.

6. If Japan exports more than it imports,
    a. Japan's net exports are negative.
    b. Japan's net capital outflow must be negative.
    c. Japan's net capital outflow must be positive.
    d. Japan is running a trade deficit.

7. If the United States saves $1,000 billion and U.S. net capital outflow is –$200 billion, U.S. domestic investment is
    a. –$200 billion.
    b. $200 billion.
    c. $800 billion.
    d. $1,000 billion.
    e. $1,200 billion.

8. If the exchange rate changes from 3 Brazilian reals per dollar to 4 reals per dollar,
    a. the dollar has depreciated.
    b. the dollar has appreciated.
    c. the dollar could have appreciated or depreciated depending on what happened to relative prices in Brazil and the United States.
    d. none of the above is true.

9. Suppose the real exchange rate between Russia and the United States is defined in terms of bottles of Russian vodka per bottle of U.S. vodka. Which of the following will increase the *real* exchange rate (that is, increase the number of bottles of Russian vodka per bottle of U.S. vodka)?
   a. a decrease in the ruble price of Russian vodka
   b. an increase in the dollar price of U.S. vodka
   c. an increase in the number of rubles for which the dollar can be exchanged
   d. All of the above will increase the real exchange rate.
   e. None of the above will increase the real exchange rate.

10. The most accurate measure of the international value of the dollar is
    a. the yen/dollar exchange rate.
    b. the Brazilian real/dollar exchange rate.
    c. the peso/dollar exchange rate.
    d. the British pound/dollar exchange rate.
    e. an exchange rate index that accounts for many exchange rates.

11. If the nominal exchange rate between British pounds and dollars is 0.5 pound per dollar, how many dollars can you get for a British pound?
    a. 2 dollars
    b. 1.5 dollars
    c. 1 dollar
    d. 0.5 of a dollar
    e. None of the above is correct.

12. Suppose the nominal exchange rate between the Japanese yen and the U.S. dollar is 100 yen per dollar. Further, suppose that a pound of hamburger costs $2 in the United States and 250 yen in Japan. What is the real exchange rate between Japan and the United States?
    a. 0.5 pound of Japanese hamburger/pound of American hamburger
    b. 0.8 pound of Japanese hamburger/pound of American hamburger
    c. 1.25 pounds of Japanese hamburger/pound of American hamburger
    d. 2.5 pounds of Japanese hamburger/pound of American hamburger
    e. none of the above

13. Which of the following people or firms would be pleased by a depreciation of the dollar?
    a. a U.S. tourist traveling in Europe
    b. a U.S. importer of Russian vodka
    c. a French exporter of wine to the United States
    d. an Italian importer of U.S. steel
    e. a Saudi Arabian prince exporting oil to the United States

14. Suppose a cup of coffee is 1.5 euros in Germany and $0.50 in the United States. If purchasing-power parity holds, what is the nominal exchange rate between euros and dollars?
    a. 1/3 euro per dollar
    b. 3 euros per dollar
    c. 1.5 euros per dollar
    d. 0.75 euro per dollar

15. Which of the following products would likely be the least accurate if used to calculate purchasing-power parity?
    a. gold
    b. automobiles
    c. diamonds
    d. dental services

16. Suppose the money supply in Mexico grows more quickly than the money supply in the United States. We would expect that
    a. the peso should depreciate relative to the dollar.
    b. the peso should appreciate relative to the dollar.
    c. the peso should maintain a constant exchange rate with the dollar because of purchasing-power parity.
    d. none of the above is true.

17. When people take advantage of differences in prices for the same good by buying it where it is cheap and selling it where it is expensive, it is known as
    a. purchasing-power parity.
    b. net capital outflow.
    c. arbitrage.
    d. net exports.
    e. currency appreciation.

18. Suppose a U.S. resident buys a Jaguar automobile from Great Britain and the British exporter uses the receipts to buy stock in General Electric. Which of the following statements is true from the perspective of the United States?
    a. Net exports fall, and net capital outflow falls.
    b. Net exports rise, and net capital outflow rises.
    c. Net exports fall, and net capital outflow rises.
    d. Net exports rise, and net capital outflow falls.
    e. None of the above is true.

19. Which of the following statements is *not* true about the relationship between national saving, investment, and net capital outflow?
    a. Saving is the sum of investment and net capital outflow.
    b. For a given amount of saving, an increase in net capital outflow must decrease domestic investment.
    c. For a given amount of saving, a decrease in net capital outflow must decrease domestic investment.
    d. An increase in saving associated with an equal increase in net capital outflow leaves domestic investment unchanged.

20. Suppose the inflation rate over the last 20 years has been 10 percent in Great Britain, 7 percent in Japan, and 3 percent in the United States. If purchasing-power parity holds, which of the following statements is true? Over this period,
    a. the value of the dollar should have fallen compared to the value of the pound and the yen.
    b. the yen should have risen in value compared to the pound and fallen compared to the dollar.
    c. the yen should have fallen in value compared to the pound and risen compared to the dollar.
    d. the value of the pound should have risen compared to the value of the yen and the dollar.
    e. None of the above is true.

ADVANCED CRITICAL THINKING

You are watching a national news broadcast with your parents. The news anchor explains that the exchange rate for the dollar just hit its lowest value in a decade. The on-the-spot report shifts to a spokesman for Caterpillar, a heavy equipment manufacturer. The spokesman reports that sales of their earthmoving equipment have hit an all-time high and so has the value of their stock. Your parents are shocked by the report's positive view of the low value of the dollar. They just cancelled their European vacation because of the dollar's low value.

1. Why do Caterpillar and your parents have different opinions about the value of the dollar?

   _____

   _____

   _____

   _____

2. Caterpillar imports many parts and raw materials for their manufacturing processes and they sell many finished products abroad. Since they are happy about a low dollar, what must be true about the proportions of Caterpillar's imports and exports?

   _____

   _____

3. If someone argues that a strong dollar is "good for America" because Americans are able to exchange some of their GDP for a greater amount of foreign GDP, is it true that a strong dollar is good for *every* American? Why?

   _____

   _____

   _____

SOLUTIONS

Terms and Definitions

_7_ Closed economy

_11_ Open economy

_2_ Exports

_13_ Imports

_8_ Net exports

_1_ Trade surplus

_12_ Trade deficit

_15_ Balanced trade

_14_ Net capital outflow

_5_ Nominal exchange rate

_10_ Appreciation

_6_ Depreciation

_3_ Real exchange rate

_9_ Purchasing-power parity

_4_ Arbitrage

Practice Problems

1. a. *NCO* rises. Foreign portfolio investment.
   b. U.S. *NX* falls and a Japanese manufacturer is holding U.S. dollars, therefore, *NCO* falls. Foreign portfolio investment.
   c. *NCO* falls. Foreign direct investment.
   d. *NCO* falls. Foreign portfolio investment.
   e. *NCO* rises. Foreign direct investment.

2. a. Yes, *NX* has risen by the size of the sale, and *NCO* has risen an equal amount and is the size of the company's holdings of foreign currency.
   b. Yes, *NX* has risen by the size of the sale, and *NCO* has risen an equal amount and is the size of the company's purchase of foreign capital. Foreign direct investment.
   c. Yes, *NX* has risen by the size of the sale, and *NCO* has risen an equal amount and is the size of the company's purchase of foreign capital. Foreign portfolio investment.
   d. Yes, *NX* and *NCO* are both unchanged because exports rise by the same amount as imports, leaving *NX* unchanged. *NCO* was not involved.

3. a. $$\frac{(100 \text{ yen}/\$3) \times (\$5/\text{American bushel})}{750 \text{ yen}/\text{Japanese bushel}}$$
   = 0.67 Japanese bushel per American bushel
   b. No, $1 buys $1/$5 bushel or 0.20 of a bushel of American corn. $1 buys 100 yen and 100 yen buys 100/750 or 0.13 of a bushel of

Japanese corn. (Or 1 bushel costs $5 in the United States and $7.50 in Japan.)
   c. Yes. Buy corn in the United States and sell it in Japan.
   d. The price should rise in the United States due to an increase in demand and fall in Japan due to an increase in supply.
   e. The real exchange rate will rise until it is equal to one (1 Japanese bushel to 1 American bushel).

4. a. 400 pesos/40 dollars = 10 pesos/dollar
   b. 800 pesos/40 dollars = 20 pesos/dollar, depreciate
   c. 800 pesos/80 dollars = 10 pesos/dollar, depreciate
   d. It is unchanged. When prices rise symmetrically, it has no effect on the nominal exchange rate if purchasing-power parity holds.

Short-Answer Questions

1. improved transportation, advances in telecommunications, more valuable technologically advanced products, favorable government policies

2. Purchase of foreign assets by domestic residents minus purchase of domestic assets by foreigners. *NCO* decreases or becomes negative.

3. Domestically (*I*) or foreign countries (*NCO*) because $S = I + NCO$.

4. Domestic investment grows because less national saving is allocated abroad, and/or more foreign saving is allocated here.

5. Pleased, because a strong dollar means they can buy imports cheaply and offer lower prices to their customers.

6. If U.S. prices fall, the foreign currency/dollar exchange rate falls, or the foreign price level rises, U.S. goods are less expensive to foreigners.

7. 1.2 Canadian dollars/U.S. dollar. 1 U.S. dollar/1.2 Canadian dollars = 0.83 or 83 cents U.S.

8. Increase the accuracy because the greater the number of traded goods, the more accurate is purchasing-power parity.

9. It should rise because, in the long run, a higher rate of growth of money causes a higher rate of growth in prices. Lower inflation in the United States increases the relative value of its currency.

10. Some goods are not easily traded, and traded goods are not always perfect substitutes.

True/False Questions

1. F; net exports are exports minus imports.
2. T
3. T
4. T
5. F; they are more likely to be traded because shipping costs are a small portion of the total cost of the good.
6. F; if exports exceed imports, the country has a trade surplus.
7. T
8. F; the exchange rate should be 90 yen/dollar.
9. T
10. F; the value of the British pound should fall relative to the peso.
11. T
12. T
13. T
14. F; arbitrage causes prices to converge.
15. F; companies preferring a strong dollar import more than they export.

Multiple-Choice Questions

1. e
2. c
3. b
4. b
5. a
6. c
7. e
8. b
9. d
10. e
11. a
12. b
13. d
14. b
15. d
16. a
17. c
18. a
19. c
20. b

Advanced Critical Thinking

1. Caterpillar sells much of its equipment to foreigners, and the low value of the dollar makes Caterpillar's products inexpensive to foreigners. Your parents were going to buy foreign goods and services and the dollar cost became higher.

2. Caterpillar must sell a greater amount of products abroad than they purchase. That is, they are a net exporter.

3. No. A strong dollar benefits Americans who are net importers and harms Americans who are net exporters.

A Macroeconomic Theory of the Open Economy

CHAPTER OVERVIEW

Context and Purpose

Chapter 32 is the second chapter in a two-chapter sequence on open-economy macroeconomics. Chapter 31 explained the basic concepts and vocabulary associated with an open economy. Chapter 32 ties these concepts together into a theory of the open economy.

The purpose of Chapter 32 is to establish the interdependence of a number of economic variables in an open economy. In particular, Chapter 32 demonstrates the relationships between the prices and quantities in the market for loanable funds and the prices and quantities in the market for foreign-currency exchange. Using these markets, we can analyze the impact of a variety of government policies on an economy's exchange rate and trade balance.

Chapter Review

Introduction This chapter constructs a model of the open economy that allows us to analyze the impact of government policies on net exports, net capital outflow, and exchange rates. This model is based on our previous long-run analysis in two ways: (1) We assume that output is determined by technology and factor supplies so output is fixed or given, and (2) prices are determined by the quantity of money so prices are fixed or given. The model constructed in this chapter is composed of two markets—the market for loanable funds and the market for foreign-currency exchange. These markets simultaneously determine the interest rate and the exchange rate (and also the level of overall investment and the trade balance).

Supply and Demand for Loanable Funds and for Foreign-Currency Exchange

In this section, we address two markets—the market for loanable funds and the market for foreign-currency exchange.

The market for loanable funds in an open economy is just an extension of the domestic loanable-funds market. Loanable funds are the domestically generated flow of resources available for capital accumulation. We assume that there is one financial market where savers lend and investors borrow. However, in an open economy,

GOALS

In this chapter you will

- Build a model to explain an open economy's trade balance and exchange rate

- Use the model to analyze the effects of government budget deficits

- Use the model to analyze the macroeconomic effects of trade policies

- Use the model to analyze political instability and capital flight

OUTCOMES

After accomplishing these goals, you should be able to

- Explain the slope of supply and demand in the market for foreign-currency exchange

- Show why a budget deficit tends to cause a trade deficit

- Demonstrate that a quota on imports fails to have an effect on net exports

- Show why capital flight causes a currency to depreciate

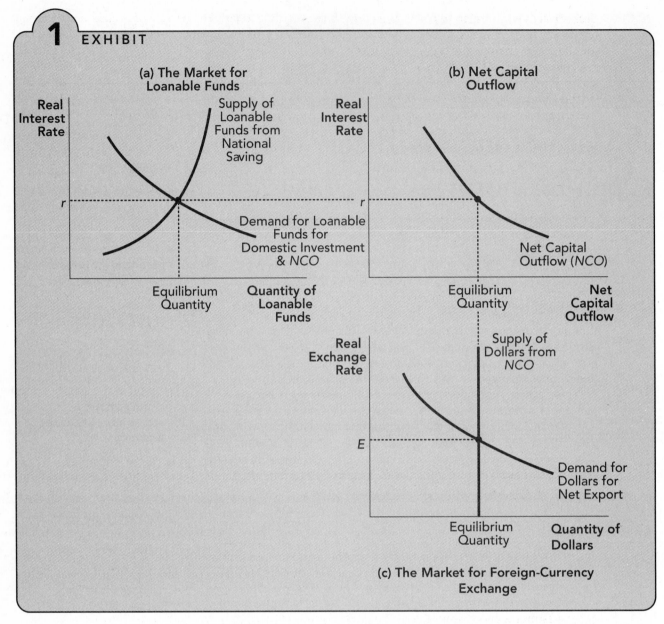

1 EXHIBIT

(a) The Market for Loanable Funds

Real Interest Rate

Supply of Loanable Funds from National Saving

r

Demand for Loanable Funds for Domestic Investment & NCO

Equilibrium Quantity

Quantity of Loanable Funds

(b) Net Capital Outflow

Real Interest Rate

r

Net Capital Outflow (NCO)

Equilibrium Quantity

Net Capital Outflow

Real Exchange Rate

Supply of Dollars from NCO

E

Demand for Dollars for Net Export

Equilibrium Quantity

Quantity of Dollars

(c) The Market for Foreign-Currency Exchange

$S = I + NCO$. Therefore, as before, the supply of loanable funds comes from national saving (S). The supply of loanable funds (desire to lend) is positively related to the real interest rate. The demand for loanable funds, however, now comes from two sources—domestic investment (I) and net capital outflow (NCO). The demand for capital assets, both domestic and foreign, is negatively related to the real interest rate. That is, a higher real interest rate reduces the desire of domestic residents to borrow to buy U.S. capital assets, and a higher domestic real interest rate reduces the desire of U.S. residents to buy foreign assets (and increases foreigners' desire to buy U.S. assets) thus reducing NCO. If NCO is positive, it adds to the demand for funds. If NCO is negative, it subtracts from it. Both the supply and demand for loanable funds are shown in panel (a) of Exhibit 1. At equilibrium, the amount people save is balanced by the amount people want to invest in domestic and foreign assets.

The second market in our model is the market for foreign-currency exchange. Recall, net capital outflow = net exports, or $NCO = NX$ because if NX are positive, Americans must be using the dollars earned from net exports to increase their holdings of foreign assets, which makes NCO positive by the same amount. In the market for foreign-currency exchange, NCO represents the quantity of dollars supplied to buy net foreign assets. NX represents the quantity of dollars demanded for the purpose of buying U.S. net exports. The demand for dollars is negatively related to the real exchange rate because a rise in the real exchange rate means that U.S. goods are relatively more expensive and less attractive to foreign and domestic buyers causing NX to fall. The supply of dollars on the foreign-exchange market is vertical because NCO (the source of the supply of dollars) does not depend on the real exchange rate but instead depends on the real interest rate. We assume that the real interest rate is given while addressing the foreign-exchange market. The supply and demand for dollars in the foreign-exchange market is shown in panel (c) of Exhibit 1. The supply and demand for dollars in this market determine the exchange rate. At equilibrium, the quantity of dollars demanded to buy net exports is balanced by the quantity of dollars supplied to buy net foreign assets.

Equilibrium in the Open Economy

The market for loanable funds is linked to the market for foreign-currency exchange by net capital outflow (NCO). In the market for loanable funds, NCO is a portion of demand along with private investment. In the market for foreign-currency exchange, NCO is the source of supply. The quantity of net capital outflow is negatively related to the real interest rate because when the U.S. real interest rate is high, U.S. assets are more attractive and U.S. NCO is low. This is shown in panel (b) of the previous graph.

Rather than viewing each panel in Exhibit 1 individually, we can view them as a group and see how these two markets determine simultaneously the equilibrium values of the real interest rate, the real exchange rate, NCO, NX (the trade balance), saving, and domestic investment.

The supply and demand for loanable funds in panel (a) determine the real interest rate. The real interest rate from panel (a) determines the quantity of NCO in panel (b). The quantity of NCO is the supply of dollars in the foreign-currency exchange market in panel (c). This supply curve in conjunction with the demand for dollars (determined by NX) in the foreign-currency exchange market determines the real exchange rate in panel (c). It is arbitrary whether we consider an increase in NCO as an addition to the demand for loanable funds or a reduction in the supply of loanable funds. Similarly, it is arbitrary whether we consider a decrease in NX (an increase in imports) as a decrease in the demand for dollars on the foreign-exchange market or as an increase in the supply of dollars on the foreign-exchange market.

How Policies and Events Affect an Open Economy

We can use this model to see how various government policies and other events affect the equilibrium values of the variables in the model.

- *Government budget deficits:* An increase in the government's budget deficit reduces national saving and, thus, shifts the supply of loanable funds to the left in panel (a) of Exhibit 1. The decrease in the supply of loanable funds increases the domestic real interest rate and crowds out domestic investment. This is no different from the closed economy case. However, in an open economy, the rise in the domestic real interest rate makes foreign investments less attractive (and domestic investments more attractive to foreigners), so the quantity of net capital outflow decreases in panel (b). This reduces the supply of dollars in the foreign-currency exchange market in panel (c) because fewer people are supplying dollars to buy foreign assets. This raises the real exchange rate of the dollar and reduces net exports (to equal the reduction in NCO). Hence, an increase in the budget deficit reduces national saving, raises the real interest rate, crowds out investment, reduces NCO, raises the real exchange rate, and moves the trade balance toward deficit.

Note that our model suggests that government budget deficits cause trade deficits. Thus, budget and trade deficits are often referred to as the *twin deficits* because they are closely related.

- *Trade policy:* A **trade policy** is a government policy that directly affects the quantity of a country's imports or exports. A *tariff* is a tax on imported goods. An *import quota* is a limit on the quantity of a good which is produced abroad that can be sold domestically.

Suppose the government places an import quota on autos produced in Japan for the purpose of moving the U.S. trade balance toward surplus. The import restriction reduces imports at each exchange rate and, thus, increases net exports at each exchange rate. It follows that foreigners need more dollars at each exchange rate, so the demand for dollars in the foreign-currency exchange market shifts to the right in panel (c) of Exhibit 1 and raises the real exchange rate for the dollar. Since there has been no change in the loanable-funds market in panel (a) and no change in NCO in panel (b), the final net exports must remain unchanged because $S - I = NCO = NX$. Thus, the import quota reduces imports, but the rise in the exchange value of the dollar offsets this effect by reducing exports, leaving the trade balance unchanged. As a result, the United States imports fewer autos (which benefits U.S. auto manufacturers) but sells fewer airplanes abroad (which harms U.S. aircraft producers), but there are no significant macroeconomic effects beyond the increase in the exchange rate. The impact of trade policy is more microeconomic than macroeconomic.

- *Political instability and capital flight:* **Capital flight** is a sudden reduction in the demand for domestic assets coupled with a sudden increase in the demand for foreign assets. It may occur due to domestic political instability.

  Suppose the United States becomes politically unstable. Investors might decide to sell U.S. assets and buy foreign assets. This act increases net capital outflow and shifts the demand for loanable funds to be used for foreign investment at each real interest rate to the right in panel (a) of Exhibit 1. It simultaneously shifts the NCO curve to the right in panel (b). The increase in net capital outflow increases the supply of dollars in the foreign-currency exchange market in panel (c), reducing the real exchange rate. Thus, capital flight increases the domestic real interest rate, increases net capital outflow and net exports, and reduces the value of the dollar in the foreign-currency exchange market. Note that the increase in the interest rate reduces domestic investment, which slows capital accumulation and growth. It has the opposite effect on the country to which the capital is flowing.

  The U.S. economy has an enormous negative net capital outflow and has, thus, become the world's largest debtor. This is due to a low U.S. saving rate. U.S. citizens save little, and the U.S. government runs a fiscal deficit.

  Although capital flight usually occurs in developing countries, the U.S. economy is not immune to potential capital flight.

Helpful Hints

1. A change in national saving generates the same result regardless of whether the change was from private saving or public saving. In your text, there is a demonstration of the impact of an increase in a government budget deficit on an open economy. It is shown that a budget deficit causes a reduction in the public saving component of national saving and shifts the supply of loanable funds to the left. Note that a reduction in the private saving component of national saving also shifts the supply of loanable funds to the left. Thus, the example given in your text can be utilized for cases when there is a change in private saving. (The source of the change in saving will generate differences in the amount of output purchased by consumers versus government, but it will not alter any of the international analysis.)

2. To find the change in NX (net exports), remember that $NX = NCO$ (net capital outflow). When we use our model to discover the impact of a government policy or an economic event on the economic variables in an open economy, there is no way to directly read net exports (the trade balance) from any of the graphs. However, the quantity of NCO is always directly measurable from panel (b) of Exhibit 1. Since $NCO = NX$, whenever there is an increase in NCO, there is an equivalent increase in NX (which is an improvement in the trade balance). Whenever NCO declines, there is an equivalent decline in NX.

3. Capital flight reduces domestic investment. The discussion of capital flight in the text and in the chapter review above notes that capital flight increases net capital outflow and the supply of the domestic currency on the foreign-currency exchange market, which lowers the exchange value of the domestic currency. Since these activities raise net exports (improve the trade balance), why is capital flight considered bad for the economy rather than good? Look at panel (a) of Figure 7 of your text. The increase in net capital outflow within the demand for loanable funds absorbs a greater amount of national saving than the tiny increase in national saving induced by the rise in the real interest rate. Thus, domestic investment is reduced an amount similar to the increase in net exports. As a result, the prospect for long-term growth in a country exhibiting capital flight is reduced due to the reduction in domestic investment.

4. Work the examples in the text backward. The three policy problems demonstrated in your text require a significant degree of concentration to understand. Once you have mastered them, you should feel comfortable that you can follow someone else's demonstration. The next step is to work those same problems backward, alone. That is, address the effect of a reduction in the budget deficit, the lowering of a trade restriction, and the effect of capital inflow. So that you may check your work, the first practice problem below is composed of the chapter examples where the source of the change has been reversed.

Terms and Definitions

Choose a definition for each key term.

Key Terms

____ Twin deficits

____ Trade policy

____ Tariff

____ Import quota

____ Capital flight

Definitions

1. A limit on the quantity of a good that is produced abroad that can be sold domestically

2. A government policy that directly affects the quantity of a country's imports or exports

3. A sudden reduction in the demand for domestic assets coupled with a sudden increase in the demand for foreign assets

4. The government budget deficit and the trade deficit

5. A tax on imported goods

PROBLEMS AND SHORT-ANSWER QUESTIONS

Practice Problems

1. This problem is composed of the examples in the chapter except the source of the change has been reversed. Use the model described by Exhibit 1 to answer the following questions.

   a. Suppose the government reduces its budget deficit. Describe the sequence of events in the model by describing the shifts in the curves in Exhibit 1 and discuss the movements in the relevant macroeconomic variables.

   _____

   _____

   _____

   b. Suppose the government eliminates a quota on the importing of Japanese automobiles. Describe the sequence of events in the model by describing the shifts in the curves in Exhibit 1 and discuss the movements in the relevant macroeconomic variables.

   _____

   _____

   _____

c. Suppose there is a sudden inflow of capital into the United States because we are believed to be more politically stable than the rest of the world. Describe the sequence of events in the model by describing the shifts in the curves in Exhibit 1 and discuss the movements in the relevant macroeconomic variables.

_____

_____

_____

_____

2. a. Suppose private saving increased at each real interest rate. What would happen to the important macroeconomic variables in our model of an open economy?

_____

_____

_____

_____

  b. Is there any difference between your answer above and the answer you would write if the government had reduced its deficit? Why?

_____

_____

_____

  c. Suppose the government passes an investment tax credit that increases domestic investment at each real interest rate. How would this change the important economic variables in the model?

_____

_____

_____

_____

  d. Compare your answer in part _a_ (an increase in saving at each real interest rate) to your answer in part _c_ (an increase in domestic investment at each real interest rate). Are there any differences?

_____

_____

_____

3. Suppose the American taste for Japanese automobiles increases. (Answer this question using the open-economy model from the Japanese perspective.)
  a. What happens to the demand for yen in the foreign-currency exchange market?

_____

_____

b. What happens to the value of yen in the foreign-currency exchange market?

_____

_____

c. What happens to Japanese net exports? Why?

_____

_____

d. If the Japanese are selling more cars, what must be true about Japanese imports and exports of other items?

_____

_____

e. Keeping in mind your answers to *a* through *c*, do you think Japan runs an overall trade surplus with the rest of the world because its autos are better built or because of its domestic saving and *NCO*? Explain.

_____

_____

4. Suppose Canada is perceived to be politically unstable, which induces capital flight to the United States.
    a. Describe what happens in the foreign-currency exchange market from the perspective of Canada.

_____

_____

_____

b. Describe what happens in the foreign-currency exchange market from the perspective of the United States.

_____

_____

_____

c. Are your answers to parts *a* and *b* above consistent with one another? Why?

_____

_____

_____

_____

d. If the economy of Canada is small when compared to the economy of the United States, what should this event do to each country's balance of trade?

_____

_____

_____

e. Which country will tend to grow faster in the future? Why?

_____

_____

_____

Short-Answer Questions

1. Explain the slope of the demand for loanable funds in an open economy.

    _____

    _____

    _____

    _____

2. Does net capital outflow add to or subtract from domestic investment when we create the demand for loanable funds? Explain.

    _____

    _____

    _____

3. Explain the source of the supply of dollars in the market for foreign-currency exchange.

    _____

    _____

    _____

4. Explain the source of the demand for dollars in the market for foreign-currency exchange.

    _____

    _____

5. Why might certain companies and unions support tariffs and import quotas even if they know that these restrictions cannot alter the trade balance?

    _____

    _____

    _____

6. Suppose the quality of U.S. goods and services falls and, as a result, foreigners choose to buy fewer U.S. goods. Does this affect the U.S. balance of trade? Why?

    _____

    _____

7. What happens to the value of a country's currency if there is capital flight from that country? Explain.

_____

_____

_____

8. What would an increase in the saving of U.S. residents do to the U.S. trade balance and the dollar exchange rate? Explain.

_____

_____

_____

_____

9. Why are the budget and trade deficits referred to as the "twin deficits"?

_____

_____

_____

10. Do trade restrictions (such as tariffs and import quotas) alter NX?

_____

_____

_____

SELF-TEST

True/False Questions

_____ 1. Net capital outflow is the purchase of domestic assets by foreigners minus the purchase of foreign assets by domestic residents.

_____ 2. A country's net capital outflow (NCO) is always equal to its net exports (NX).

_____ 3. Other things being the same, an increase in a country's real interest rate reduces net capital outflow.

_____ 4. An increase in U.S. net capital outflow increases the supply of dollars in the market for foreign-currency exchange and decreases the real exchange rate of the dollar.

_____ 5. If labor unions convince Americans to "buy American," it will improve (move toward surplus) the U.S. trade balance.

_____ 6. If a country's net capital outflow (NCO) is positive, it is an addition to its demand for loanable funds.

_____ 7. An increase in the government's budget deficit shifts the supply of loanable funds to the right.

_____ 8. An increase in the government's budget deficit tends to cause the real exchange rate of the dollar to depreciate.

_____ 9. The term "twin deficits" refers to a country's trade deficit and its government budget deficit.

_____ 10. If the United States raises its tariff on imported sugar, it will reduce imports and improve the trade balance.

_____ 11. If the United States raises its tariff on imported sugar, domestic sugar growers will benefit, but the dollar will appreciate and domestic producers of export goods will be harmed.

_____ 12. An increase in the government budget deficit reduces net exports.

_____ 13. A country experiencing capital flight will experience a reduction in its net capital outflow and its net exports.

_____ 14. If Americans increase their saving, the dollar will appreciate in the market for foreign-currency exchange.

_____ 15. A rise in Mexico's net exports (NX) will increase the demand for pesos in the market for foreign-currency exchange and the peso will appreciate in value.

Multiple-Choice Questions

1. Which of the following statements regarding the loanable-funds market is _not_ true?
   a. An increase in a country's net capital outflow raises its real interest rate.
   b. An increase in a country's net capital outflow shifts the supply of loanable funds to the left.
   c. An increase in domestic investment shifts the demand for loanable funds to the right.
   d. A decrease in a country's net capital outflow shifts the demand for loanable funds to the left.

2. An increase in the government budget deficit
   a. increases the real interest rate and crowds out investment.
   b. decreases the real interest rate and crowds out investment.
   c. has no impact on the real interest rate and fails to crowd out investment because foreigners buy assets in the deficit country.
   d. does none of the above.

3. Which of the following statements regarding the loanable-funds market is true?
   a. An increase in private saving shifts the supply of loanable funds to the left.
   b. A decrease in the government budget deficit increases the real interest rate.
   c. An increase in the government budget deficit shifts the supply of loanable funds to the right.
   d. An increase in the government budget deficit shifts the supply of loanable funds to the left.

4. Other things unchanging, a higher U.S. real interest rate
   a. increases U.S. net capital outflow because U.S. residents and foreigners prefer to invest in the United States.
   b. decreases U.S. net capital outflow because U.S. residents and foreigners prefer to invest in the United States.
   c. decreases U.S. net capital outflow because U.S. residents and foreigners prefer to invest abroad.
   d. does none of the above.

5. An increase in Europe's taste for U.S.-produced Fords would cause the dollar to
   a. depreciate and would increase U.S. net exports.
   b. depreciate and would decrease U.S. net exports.
   c. appreciate and would increase U.S. net exports.
   d. appreciate and would decrease U.S. net exports.
   e. appreciate, but the total value of U.S. net exports stays the same.

6. An increase in the U.S. government budget deficit
   a. increases U.S. net exports and decreases U.S. net capital outflow.
   b. decreases U.S. net exports and increases U.S. net capital outflow.
   c. decreases U.S. net exports and U.S. net capital outflow the same amount.
   d. increases U.S. net exports and U.S. net capital outflow the same amount.

7. The phrase "twin deficits" refers to
   a. a country's trade deficit and its government budget deficit.
   b. a country's trade deficit and its net capital outflow deficit.
   c. the equality of a country's saving deficit and its investment deficit.
   d. the fact that if a country has a trade deficit, its trading partners must also have trade deficits.

8. Which of the following statements regarding the market for foreign-currency exchange is true?
   a. An increase in U.S. net exports increases the supply of dollars and the dollar depreciates.
   b. An increase in U.S. net exports decreases the supply of dollars and the dollar depreciates.
   c. An increase in U.S. net exports decreases the demand for dollars and the dollar appreciates.
   d. An increase in U.S. net exports increases the demand for dollars and the dollar appreciates.

9. Which of the following statements regarding the market for foreign-currency exchange is true?
   a. An increase in U.S. net capital outflow increases the supply of dollars and the dollar appreciates.
   b. An increase in U.S. net capital outflow increases the supply of dollars and the dollar depreciates.
   c. An increase in U.S. net capital outflow increases the demand for dollars and the dollar appreciates.
   d. An increase in U.S. net capital outflow increases the demand for dollars and the dollar depreciates.

10. If the United States imposes a quota on the importing of apparel produced in China, which of the following is true regarding the market for foreign-currency exchange?
    a. The supply of dollars increases and the dollar depreciates.
    b. The supply of dollars decreases and the dollar appreciates.
    c. The demand for dollars increases and the dollar appreciates.
    d. The demand for dollars decreases and the dollar depreciates.

11. If the United States imposes a quota on the importing of apparel produced in China, which of the following is true regarding U.S. net exports?
    a. Net exports will rise.
    b. Net exports will fall.
    c. Net exports will remain unchanged.
    d. None of the above is true.

12. Suppose, due to political instability, Mexicans suddenly choose to invest in U.S. assets as opposed to Mexican assets. Which of the following statements is true regarding U.S. net foreign investment?
    a. U.S. net foreign investment rises.
    b. U.S. net foreign investment falls.
    c. U.S. net foreign investment is unchanged because only U.S. residents can alter U.S. net foreign investment.
    d. None of the above is true.

13. Suppose, due to political instability, Mexicans suddenly choose to purchase U.S. assets as opposed to Mexican assets. Which of the following statements is true regarding the value of the dollar and U.S. net exports?
    a. The dollar appreciates, and U.S. net exports fall.
    b. The dollar depreciates, and U.S. net exports fall.
    c. The dollar appreciates, and U.S. net exports rise.
    d. The dollar depreciates, and U.S. net exports rise.

14. An increase in U.S. private saving
    a. increases U.S. net exports and decreases U.S. net capital outflow.
    b. decreases U.S. net exports and increases U.S. net capital outflow.
    c. decreases U.S. net exports and U.S. net capital outflow the same amount.
    d. increases U.S. net exports and U.S. net capital outflow the same amount.

15. Which of the following statements about trade policy is true?
    a. A restrictive import quota increases a country's net exports.
    b. A restrictive import quota decreases a country's net exports.
    c. A country's trade policy has no impact on the size of its trade balance.
    d. None of the above is true.

16. Which of the following groups would *not* benefit from a U.S. import quota on Japanese autos?
    a. stockholders of Ford Motor Company
    b. U.S. farmers who export grain
    c. members of the United Auto Workers union
    d. U.S. consumers who buy electronics from Japan

17. An example of a trade policy is
    a. an increase in the government budget deficit because it reduces a country's net exports.
    b. capital flight because it increases a country's net exports.
    c. a tariff on sugar.
    d. All are examples of trade policy.

18. An export subsidy should have the opposite effect of
    a. a tariff.
    b. capital flight.
    c. a government budget deficit.
    d. an increase in private saving.

19. Which of the following groups would be most harmed by a U.S. government budget deficit?
    a. U.S. residents wishing to buy foreign-produced autos
    b. lenders of loanable funds
    c. foreigners who wish to buy assets in the United States
    d. Boeing Aircraft Manufacturing wishing to sell jets to Saudi Arabia

20. Capital flight
    a. decreases a country's net exports and increases its long-run growth path.
    b. decreases a country's net exports and decreases its long-run growth path.
    c. increases a country's net exports and decreases its long-run growth path.
    d. increases a country's net exports and increases its long-run growth path.

ADVANCED CRITICAL THINKING

Hong Kong has a capitalistic economic system. It was leased from China by Great Britain for 100 years. In 1997, it was returned to China, a socialist republic.

1. What do you think this event should do to the net capital outflow of Hong Kong? Why?

    _____

    _____

    _____

    _____

2. If the residents of Hong Kong choose Canada as a place to move some of their business activity, what impact do you suppose this will have on the value of the Canadian interest rate and exchange rate? Why?

    _____

    _____

    _____

    _____

3. Which Canadian industries, those engaged in importing or exporting, are likely to be pleased with Hong Kong's investment in Canada? Why?

    _____

    _____

    _____

    _____

4. What impact will Hong Kong's return to China have on the growth rate of Canada?

    _____

    _____

SOLUTIONS

Terms and Definitions

_4_ Twin deficits

_2_ Trade policy

_5_ Tariff

_1_ Import quota

_3_ Capital flight

Practice Problems

1. a. Panel (a), supply of loanable funds shifts right, real interest rate decreases. NCO increases, increasing the supply of dollars in the foreign-currency exchange market and causing the real exchange rate to depreciate. Saving and domestic investment have increased, and the trade balance has moved toward surplus.

   b. Panel (c), NX fall at each exchange rate as imports increase causing the demand for dollars in the foreign-currency exchange market to shift left; the real exchange rate falls increasing NX to their original level. No change in trade balance, but a higher volume of trade (more imports and more exports).

   c. NCO falls as U.S. residents and foreigners buy U.S. assets. In panel (a), demand for loanable funds shifts left. Panel (b), NCO shifts left because of a decrease in NCO at each interest rate causing the supply of dollars in the foreign-currency exchange market to shift left and the exchange rate to rise. Result, real interest rate down, NCO and NX down, value of the dollar up, increase in domestic investment.

2. a. Panel (a), supply of loanable funds shifts right, real interest rate decreases. NCO increases, increasing the supply of dollars in the foreign-currency exchange market and causing the real exchange rate to depreciate. Saving and domestic investment have increased and the trade balance has moved toward surplus.

   b. No, because it doesn't matter why national saving increased. Either one will shift the supply of loanable funds to the right.

   c. Increase in the demand for loanable funds, raises real interest rate, lowers NCO and NX, decreases the supply of dollars in the foreign-currency exchange market, which raises the value of the dollar. Domestic saving and investment have increased.

   d. Both increase domestic saving and investment, but an increase in saving moves the trade balance toward surplus while an increase in investment demand moves it toward deficit.

3. a. Shifts right.

   b. Real exchange rate rises so value of yen rises.

   c. NCO is unchanged, therefore, NX as a total is unchanged.

   d. If NX are constant, they must be importing more or exporting less of other items.

   e. NX as a total are determined by NCO, so Japan's overall level of trade surplus is based on its saving behavior. However, the composition of its exports may be based on its relative quality of production.

4. a. The supply of Canadian dollars shifts right and the value of the Canadian dollar falls.

   b. The supply of U.S. dollars shifts left and the value of the U.S. dollar rises.

   c. Yes. A rise in the value of the U.S. dollar relative to the Canadian dollar should correspond to the fall in the value of the Canadian dollar relative to the U.S. dollar.

   d. The fall in the value of the Canadian dollar should improve its NX by a greater percentage than the fall in NX by the United States.

   e. Canada is increasing its NCO in the United States, and the United States is decreasing its NCO in Canada, so the United States will likely grow faster.

Short-Answer Questions

1. It is negatively sloped because a higher real interest rate reduces the desire to borrow funds to purchase capital domestically, and it discourages U.S. residents from buying foreign assets and encourages foreign residents to buy U.S. assets.

2. If NCO is positive, it adds to the demand for loanable funds. If NCO is negative, it subtracts.

3. It comes from dollars U.S. residents used for NCO.

4. It comes from the need for dollars from foreigners purchasing U.S. NX.

5. Because trade restrictions can improve the sales of some domestic companies facing competition from imports, but largely at the expense of other domestic companies producing for export.

6. No, it reduces the demand for dollars in the market for foreign-currency exchange and lowers the value of the dollar to keep *NX* unchanged.

7. It increases the supply of their currency in the market for foreign-currency exchange and lowers the exchange rate.

8. It decreases the U.S. real interest rate, increases *NCO* and *NX*, increases the supply of dollars on the foreign-currency exchange market, and lowers the dollar exchange rate.

9. Because a budget deficit tends to cause a trade deficit when it raises the domestic real interest rate, reducing *NCO* and *NX*.

10. Trade restrictions don't alter the total value of *NX* because *NX* = *NCO*. An increase in trade restrictions reduces both imports and exports by the same amount.

True/False Questions

1. F; *NCO* is the purchase of foreign assets by domestic residents minus the purchase of domestic assets by foreigners.
2. T
3. T
4. T
5. F; net exports are unchanged because *NCO* is unchanged.
6. T
7. F; an increase in the government's budget deficit shifts the supply of loanable funds to the left.
8. F; an increase in the government's budget deficit raises the real exchange rate.
9. T
10. F; net exports are unchanged because *NCO* is unchanged.
11. T
12. T
13. F; a country experiencing capital flight will experience an increase in its *NCO* and its net exports.
14. F; the dollar will depreciate.
15. T

Multiple-Choice Questions

1. b
2. a
3. d
4. b
5. e
6. c
7. a
8. d
9. b
10. c
11. c
12. b
13. a
14. d
15. c
16. b
17. c
18. a
19. d
20. c

Advanced Critical Thinking

1. It should increase the *NCO* of Hong Kong because foreigners are not buying assets in Hong Kong and Hong Kong residents are buying assets abroad—capital flight. Investors fear that China may nationalize much of Hong Kong's industry.

2. This will decrease Canada's *NCO*. This shifts the demand for loanable funds left and lowers the real interest rate. The reduced *NCO* reduces the supply of Canadian dollars in the foreign-currency exchange market, raises the exchange rate, and moves *NX* toward deficit.

3. The increase in the value of the Canadian dollar will make Canadian producers less competitive abroad but will make imports cheaper.

4. The reduction in Canada's *NCO* (due to Hong Kong's increased *NCO*) increases the capital stock of Canada, causing it to grow.

Aggregate Demand and Aggregate Supply

CHAPTER OVERVIEW

Context and Purpose

To this point, our study of macroeconomic theory has concentrated on the behavior of the economy in the long run. Chapters 33 through 35 now focus on short-run fluctuations in the economy around its long-term trend. Chapter 33 introduces aggregate demand and aggregate supply and shows how shifts in these curves can cause recessions. Chapter 34 focuses on how policymakers use the tools of monetary and fiscal policy to influence aggregate demand. Chapter 35 addresses the relationship between inflation and unemployment.

The purpose of Chapter 33 is to develop the model economists use to analyze the economy's short-run fluctuations—the model of aggregate demand and aggregate supply. We will learn about some of the sources for shifts in the aggregate-demand curve and the aggregate-supply curve and how these shifts can cause recessions. We will also introduce actions policymakers might undertake to offset recessions.

Chapter Review

Introduction Over the last 50 years, U.S. real GDP has grown about 3 percent per year. However, in some years, GDP has not grown at this normal rate. A period when output and incomes fall, and unemployment rises, is known as a **recession** when it is mild and a **depression** when it is severe. This chapter focuses on the economy's short-run fluctuations around its long-term trend. To do this, we employ the model of aggregate demand and aggregate supply.

Three Key Facts about Economic Fluctuations

- *Economic fluctuations are irregular and unpredictable:* Although economic fluctuations are often termed *the business cycle*, the term "business cycle" is misleading because it suggests that economic fluctuations follow a regular, predictable pattern. In reality, economic fluctuations are irregular and unpredictable.

- *Most macroeconomic quantities fluctuate together:* Although real GDP is usually used to monitor short-run changes in the economy, it really doesn't matter which measure of economic activity is used

GOALS

In this chapter you will

- Learn three key facts about short-run fluctuations

- Consider how the economy in the short run differs from the economy in the long run

- Use the model of aggregate demand and aggregate supply to explain economic fluctuations

- See how shifts in either aggregate demand or aggregate supply can cause booms and recessions

OUTCOMES

After accomplishing these goals, you should be able to

- Explain why the term "business cycle" is misleading

- Explain why money is unlikely to be neutral in the short run

- List three reasons why the aggregate-demand curve is downward sloping

- Demonstrate the short-run and long-run effects of an oil price shock on the economy because most macroeconomic variables that measure income, spending, or production move in the same direction, though by different amounts. Investment is one type of expenditure that is particularly volatile across the business cycle.

- *As output falls, unemployment rises:* When real GDP declines, the rate of unemployment rises because when firms produce fewer goods and services, they lay off workers.

Explaining Short-Run Economic Fluctuations

Classical theory is based on the classical dichotomy and monetary neutrality. Recall, the classical dichotomy is the separation of economic variables into real and nominal while monetary neutrality is the property that changes in the money supply only affect nominal variables, not real variables. Most economists believe these classical assumptions are an accurate description of the economy in the long run but not in the short run. That is, over a period of a number of years, changes in the money supply should affect prices but should have no impact on real variables such as real GDP, unemployment, real wages, and so on. However, in the short run, from year to year, changes in nominal variables such as money and prices are likely to have an impact on real variables. That is, in the short run, nominal and real variables are not independent. As a result, in the short run, increases in money can temporarily move real GDP above its long-run trend.

We use the **model of aggregate supply and aggregate demand** to explain economic fluctuations. This model can be graphed with the price level, measured by the CPI or the GDP deflator on the vertical axis and real GDP on the horizontal axis. The **aggregate-demand curve** shows the quantity of goods and services households, firms, the government, and customers abroad wish to buy at each price level. It slopes negatively. The **aggregate-supply curve** shows the quantity of goods and services that firms produce and sell at each price level. It slopes positively (in the short run). The price level and output adjust to balance aggregate supply and demand. This model looks like an ordinary microeconomic supply-and-demand model. However, the reasons for the slopes and the sources of the shifts in the aggregate-supply and -demand curves differ from those for the microeconomic model.

The Aggregate-Demand Curve

Exhibit 1 illustrates the model of aggregate supply and aggregate demand.

The aggregate-demand curve shows the quantity of goods and services demanded at each price level. Recall, GDP = $C + I + G + NX$. To address why aggregate demand slopes downward, we

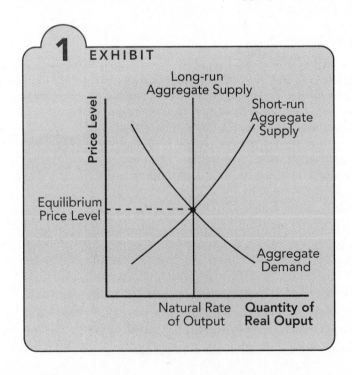

1 EXHIBIT

address the impact of the price level on consumption (C), investment (I), and net exports (NX). (We ignore government spending (G) because it is a fixed policy variable.) A decrease in the price level increases consumption, investment, and net exports for the following reasons:

- The price level and consumption: *the wealth effect.* At a lower price level, the fixed amount of nominal money in consumers' pockets increases in value. Consumers feel wealthier and spend more, increasing the consumption component of aggregate demand.

- The price level and investment: *the interest-rate effect.* At a lower price level, households need to hold less money to buy the same products. They lend some money by buying bonds or depositing in banks, either of which lowers interest rates and stimulates the investment component of aggregate demand. (Lower interest rates may also stimulate spending on consumer durables.)

- The price level and net exports: *the exchange-rate effect.* Since, as described above, a lower price level causes lower interest rates, some U.S. investors will invest abroad, increasing the supply of dollars in the foreign-currency exchange market. This act causes the real exchange rate of the dollar to depreciate, reduces the relative price of domestic goods compared to foreign goods, and increases the net exports component of aggregate demand.

The three effects described above also work in reverse. All three explanations of the downward slope of the aggregate-demand curve assume that the money supply is fixed.

When something causes a change in the quantity of output demanded at each price level, it causes a shift in the aggregate-demand curve. The following events and policies cause shifts in aggregate demand:

- *Shifts arising from changes in consumption:* If consumers save more, if stock prices fall so that consumers feel poorer, or if taxes are increased, consumers spend less and aggregate demand shifts left.

- *Shifts arising from changes in investment:* If firms become optimistic about the future and decide to buy new equipment, if an investment tax credit increases investment, or if the Fed increases the money supply, which reduces interest rates and increases investment, aggregate demand shifts right.

- *Shifts arising from changes in government purchases:* If federal, state, or local governments increase purchases, aggregate demand shifts right.

- *Shifts arising from changes in net exports:* If foreign countries have a recession and buy fewer goods from the United States or if the value of the dollar rises on foreign exchange markets, net exports are reduced and aggregate demand shifts left.

The Aggregate-Supply Curve

The aggregate-supply curve shows the quantity of goods and services firms produce and sell at each price level. In the long run, the aggregate-supply curve is vertical while in the short run, it is upward (positively) sloping. Both can be seen in Exhibit 1.

The *long-run aggregate-supply curve* is vertical because, in the long run, the supply of goods and services depends on the supply of capital, labor, and natural resources, and on production technology. In the long run, the supply of goods and services is independent of the level of prices. It is the graphical representation of the classical dichotomy and monetary neutrality. That is, if the price level rises and all prices rise together, there should be no impact on output or any other real variable.

The long-run aggregate-supply curve shows the level of production that is sometimes called *potential output* or *full-employment output.* Since in the short run output can be temporarily above or below this level, a better name is the **natural rate of output** because it is the amount of output produced when unemployment is at its natural, or normal, rate. Anything that alters the natural rate of output shifts the long-run aggregate-supply curve to the right or left. Since in the long run, output depends on labor, capital, natural resources, and technological knowledge, we group the sources of the shifts in long-run aggregate supply into these categories:

- *Shifts arising from changes in labor:* If there is immigration from abroad or a reduction in the natural rate of unemployment from a reduction in the minimum wage, long-run aggregate supply shifts right.

- *Shifts arising from changes in capital:* If there is an increase in physical or human capital, productivity rises and long-run aggregate supply shifts right.

- *Shifts arising from changes in natural resources:* If there is a discovery of new resources, or a favorable change in weather patterns, long-run aggregate supply shifts right.

- *Shifts arising from changes in technical knowledge:* If new inventions are employed, or international trade opens up, long-run aggregate supply shifts right.

Long-run growth and inflation may be depicted as a rightward shift in the long-run aggregate-supply curve (from the events described above) and an even larger rightward shift in the aggregate-demand curve due to increases in the money supply. Thus, over time, output grows and prices rise.

The short-run aggregate-supply curve slopes upward (positively) because a change in the price level causes output to deviate from its long-run level for a short period of time, say, a year or two. There are three theories that explain why the short-run aggregate-supply curve slopes upward, and they all share a common theme: Output rises above the natural rate when the actual price level exceeds the expected price level. The three theories are:

- *The sticky-wage theory:* Suppose firms and workers agree on a nominal wage contract based on what they expect the price level to be. If the price level falls below what was expected, firms pay the same wage but receive lower prices for their output. This reduces profits, causing the firm to hire less labor and reduce the quantity of goods and services supplied.

- *The sticky-price theory:* Because there is a cost to firms for changing prices, termed *menu costs*, some firms will resist reducing their prices when the price level unexpectedly falls. Thus, their prices are "too high" and their sales decline, causing the quantity of goods and services supplied to fall.

- *The misperceptions theory:* When the price level unexpectedly falls, suppliers only notice that the price of their particular product has fallen. Hence, they mistakenly believe that there has been a fall in the *relative price* of their product, causing them to reduce the quantity of goods and services supplied.

The three effects described above also work in reverse.

Note two features of the explanations above: (1) In each case, the quantity of output supplied changed because actual prices deviated from expected prices, and (2) the effect will be temporary because people will adjust their expectations over time. We can express aggregate supply mathematically with the following equation:

$$\text{Quantity of Output Supplied} = \text{Natural Rate of Output} + a\left(\text{Actual Price Level} - \text{Expected Price Level}\right)$$

where a is a number that determines how much output responds to unexpected changes in the price level.

Events that shift the long-run aggregate-supply curve also tend to shift the short-run aggregate-supply curve in the same direction. However, the short-run aggregate-supply curve can shift while the long-run aggregate-supply curve remains stationary. In the short run, the quantity of goods and services supplied depends on perceptions, wages, and prices, all of which were set based on the expected price level. If people and firms expect higher prices, they set wages higher, reducing the profitability of production and reducing the quantity supplied of goods and services at each price level. Thus, the short-run aggregate-supply curve shifts left. A lower expected price level shifts the short-run aggregate-supply curve to the right. In general, things that cause an increase in the cost of production (an increase in wages or oil prices) cause the short-run aggregate-supply curve to shift left while a decrease in the cost of production causes the short-run aggregate-supply curve to shift right.

Two Causes of Economic Fluctuations

Exhibit 1 shows the model of aggregate supply and aggregate demand in long-run equilibrium. That is, the level of output is at the long-run natural rate where aggregate demand and long-run aggregate supply intersect, and perceptions, wages, and prices have fully adjusted to the actual price level as demonstrated by short-run aggregate supply intersecting at the same point.

There are two basic causes of a recession: a leftward shift in aggregate demand and a leftward shift in aggregate supply.

A Shift in Aggregate Demand   We use a four-step approach: (1) Determine which curve the event affects. (2) Determine which way the curve moves. (3) Determine the new short-run equilibrium. (4) Determine the transition from the short-run equilibrium to the long-run equilibrium.

Suppose households cut back on their spending because they are pessimistic or nervous about the future. Consumers spend less at each price level so aggregate demand shifts left in Exhibit 2. In the short run, the economy moves to point B because the drop in the price level was unexpected. When prices fall below expectations, sticky wages, sticky prices, and misperceptions about relative prices cause firms to cut back on production. We can see that the economy is in a recession at P_2, Y_2 because output is below the natural rate. The recession will remedy itself or self-correct over time. Since actual prices are below prior expectations, price expectations will be reduced over time and wages and prices will fall to levels commensurate with P_3. In particular, the sticky-wage theory suggests that once workers and firms expect lower prices, they will negotiate lower wages. This encourages production, the short-run aggregate-supply curve shifts right, and the economy arrives at point C. Policymakers could try to eliminate the recession by increasing aggregate demand with an increase in government spending or an increase in the money supply. If properly done, the government moves the economy back to point A. To summarize, in the short run, shifts in aggregate demand cause fluctuations in output. In the long run, shifts in aggregate demand only cause changes in prices. Policymakers can potentially mitigate the severity of economic fluctuations.

Exhibit 2 can be used to demonstrate that money matters in the short run, but money is neutral in the long run. Starting at point A, if the Fed reduces the money supply, the economy moves to point B

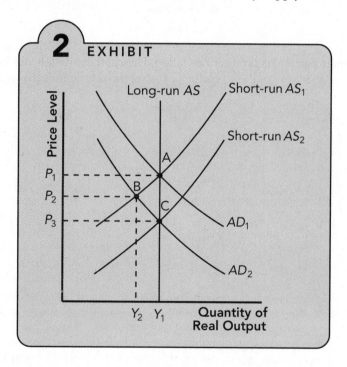

2 EXHIBIT

Long-run *AS*   Short-run *AS*₁

Short-run *AS*₂

Price Level

P_1
P_2
P_3

A
B
C

*AD*₁

*AD*₂

Y_2 Y_1 **Quantity of Real Output**

and experiences a recession. Since output falls, we say that money matters. In the long run, price expectations and wages are reduced, and the economy moves to point C. Output returns to the natural rate and prices have fallen; therefore, money is neutral in the long run.

The two biggest shocks to aggregate demand in the United States were the leftward shift during the Great Depression and the rightward shift during World War II. During the recession in 2001, aggregate demand shifted left for three reasons: (1) the dot.com bubble in the stock market burst, reducing both consumer and investment spending; (2) the terrorist attacks on September 11, 2001, caused uncertainty and reduced spending; and (3) a further reduction in the stock market due to the corporate accounting scandal further reduced aggregated demand. Policymakers responded by lowering taxes, increasing money growth, and reducing interest rates.

A Shift in Aggregate Supply Use the same four-step method described above. Suppose OPEC raises the price of oil, which raises the cost of production for many firms. This reduces profitability, firms produce less at each price level, and short-run aggregate supply shifts to the left in Exhibit 3. In the short run, prices rise, reducing the quantity demanded along the aggregate-demand curve and the economy arrives at point B. Since output has fallen (stagnation) and the price level has risen (inflation), the economy has experienced **stagflation.** Higher prices may temporarily cause workers to demand higher wages, further shifting short-run aggregate supply to the left and temporarily causing a *wage-price spiral*. However, in the long run, the unemployment at Y_2 will, in time, put downward pressure on workers' wages, will increase profitability, and will shift aggregate supply back to its original position, and the economy returns to point A. Alternatively, policymakers could increase aggregate demand and move the economy to point C, avoiding point B altogether. Here, policymakers *accommodate* the shift in aggregate supply by allowing the increase in costs to raise prices permanently. Output is returned to long-run equilibrium, but prices are higher. To summarize, a reduction in short-run aggregate supply causes stagflation. If policymakers shift aggregate demand in a manner to increase output, it causes more inflation.

Helpful Hints

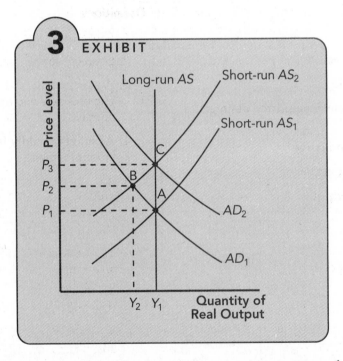

3 EXHIBIT

1. There are no changes in real variables along the long-run aggregate-supply curve. When all prices change equally, no real variables have changed. A vertical long-run aggregate-supply curve simply demonstrates this classical lesson. Pick any point on the long-run aggregate-supply curve. Now double the price level and all nominal values such as wages. Although the price level has doubled, relative prices have remained constant including the real wage, W/P. There has been no change in anyone's incentive to produce and, thus, no change in output. It follows that if the economy is temporarily producing a level of output other than the long-run natural rate, then at least some wages or prices have failed to adjust to the long-run equilibrium price level. This causes at least some relative prices to change, which stimulates or discourages production. This is, in fact, what is happening along a short-run aggregate-supply curve.

2. Output can fluctuate to levels both above and below the natural rate of output. The examples of economic fluctuations in the text tend to focus on recessions. That is, the examples deal with periods when output is less than the natural level. Note, however, that output can be above the natural rate temporarily because unemployment can be below its natural rate. This economic condition is known as a boom. A boom will occur when there is a positive aggregate demand

shock—for example, if there is an increase in the money supply, an increase in domestic investment, or an increase in government purchases. A boom will also occur if there is a positive aggregate-supply shock—for example, if the price of oil were to fall or union wage demands were to decrease. To help you, these cases are addressed in the problems that follow.

3. You may shift the short-run aggregate-supply curve left and right or up and down. Suppose there is an increase in the wage of workers. We have suggested that the rise in the wage will increase the cost of production, decrease profitability at each price level, and decrease production at each price level. That is, it will shift the short-run aggregate-supply curve to the left. However, we could have suggested that the increase in the wage will increase the cost of production, requiring firms to charge a higher price in order to continue the same level of production. That is, it shifts the short-run aggregate-supply curve upward on the graph. In the first case, we lowered the quantity supplied at each price. In the second case, we raised the price at each quantity supplied. The resulting shift is the same.

Terms and Definitions

Choose a definition for each key term.

Key Terms

____ Recession

____ Depression

____ The business cycle

____ Model of aggregate demand and aggregate supply

____ Aggregate-demand curve

____ Aggregate-supply curve

____ Natural rate of output

____ Menu costs

____ Stagflation

____ Accommodative policy

Definitions

1. Costs associated with changing prices

2. Short-run economic fluctuations

3. A policy of increasing aggregate demand in response to a decrease in short-run aggregate supply

4. A period of mildly falling incomes and rising unemployment

5. A curve that shows the quantity of goods and services that households, firms, the government, and customers abroad are willing to buy at each price level

6. The production of goods and services that an economy achieves in the long run when unemployment is at its natural or normal rate

7. A period of falling output and rising prices

8. A period of unusually severe falling incomes and rising unemployment

9. A curve that shows the quantity of goods and services that firms are willing to produce at each price level

10. The model most economists use to explain short-run fluctuations in the economy around its long-run trend

PROBLEMS AND SHORT-ANSWER QUESTIONS

When necessary, draw a graph of the model of aggregate demand and aggregate supply on scratch paper to help you answer the following problems and questions.

Practice Problems

1. For the following four cases, trace the impact of each shock in the aggregate-demand and aggregate-supply model by answering the following three questions for each: What happens to prices and output in the short run? What happens to prices and output in the long run if the economy is allowed to adjust to long-run equilibrium on its own? If policymakers had intervened to move output back to the natural rate instead of allowing the economy to self-correct, in which direction should they have moved aggregate demand?

    a. aggregate demand shifts left

    _____

    _____

    b. aggregate demand shifts right

    _____

    _____

    c. short-run aggregate supply shifts left

    _____

    _____

    d. short-run aggregate supply shifts right

    _____

    _____

2. The following events have their *initial impact* on which of the following: aggregate demand, short-run aggregate supply, long-run aggregate supply, or both short-run and long-run aggregate supply? Do the curves shift to the right or left?

    a. The government repairs aging roads and bridges.

    _____

    b. OPEC raises oil prices.

    _____

    c. The government raises unemployment benefits, which raises the natural rate of unemployment.

    _____

    d. Americans feel more secure in their jobs and become more optimistic.

    _____

e. A technological advance takes place in the application of computers to the manufacturing of steel.

_____

f. The government increases the minimum wage.

_____

g. Because price expectations are reduced, wage demands of new college graduates fall.

_____

h. The Federal Reserve decreases the money supply.

_____

i. A drought destroys much of the Midwest corn crop.

_____

3. Suppose the economy is in long-run equilibrium. Then, suppose the Federal Reserve suddenly increases the money supply.
   a. Describe the initial impact of this event in the model of aggregate demand and aggregate supply by explaining which curve shifts which way.

   _____

   _____

   _____

   b. What happens to the price level and real output in the short run?

   _____

   _____

   c. If the economy is allowed to adjust to the increase in the money supply, what happens to the price level and real output in the long run when compared to their original levels? What name do economists attach to the long-run impact of a change in the money supply on the economy?

   _____

   _____

   _____

   d. Does an increase in the money supply move output above the natural rate indefinitely? Why?

   _____

   _____

   _____

4. Suppose the economy is in long-run equilibrium. Then, suppose workers and firms suddenly expect higher prices in the future and agree to an increase in wages.

   a. Describe the initial impact of this event in the model of aggregate demand and aggregate supply by explaining which curve shifts which way.

   _____

   _____

   b. What happens to the price level and real output in the short run?

   _____

   _____

   c. What name do we have for this combination of movements in output and prices?

   _____

   d. If policymakers wanted to move output back to the natural rate of output, what should they do?

   _____

   _____

   e. If policymakers were able to move output back to the natural rate of output, what would the policy do to prices?

   _____

   _____

   f. If policymakers had done nothing at all, what would have happened to the wage rate as the economy self-corrected or adjusted back to the natural rate of output on its own?

   _____

   _____

   g. Is it likely that an increase in price expectations and wages *alone* can cause a permanent increase in the price level? Why?

   _____

   _____

   _____

5. Suppose the economy is at a point such as point B in Exhibit 2. That is, aggregate demand has decreased and the economy is in a recession. Describe the adjustment process necessary for the economy to adjust on its own to point C for each of the three theoretical short-run aggregate-supply curves.

   a. the sticky-wage theory

   _____

   _____

   _____

   _____

   _____

   b. the sticky-price theory

   _____

   _____

   _____

   _____

   c. the misperceptions theory

   _____

   _____

   _____

   d. Do you think the type of adjustments described above would take place more quickly from a recession or from a period when output was above the long-run natural rate? Why?

   _____

   _____

   _____

Short-Answer Questions

1. Name the three key facts about economic fluctuations.

   _____

   _____

2. What are the three reasons the aggregate-demand curve slopes downward? Explain them.

   _____

   _____

   _____

   _____

3. Explain the slope of the short-run aggregate-supply curve using the sticky-wage theory.

    _____

    _____

4. Does a shift in aggregate demand alter output in the short run? Why?

    _____

    _____

    _____

5. Does a shift in aggregate demand alter output in the long run? Why?

    _____

    _____

    _____

6. If the economy is in a recession, why might policymakers choose to adjust aggregate demand to eliminate the recession rather than let the economy adjust, or self-correct, on its own?

    _____

    _____

    _____

7. Which component of aggregate demand is most volatile over the business cycle?

    _____

8. Why is a decrease in the money supply unlikely to be neutral in the short run?

    _____

    _____

9. Suppose OPEC breaks apart and oil prices fall substantially. Initially, which curve shifts in the aggregate-supply and aggregate-demand model? In what direction does it shift? What happens to the price level and real output?

    _____

    _____

10. What causes both short-run and long-run aggregate supply to shift together? What causes only the short-run aggregate supply to shift while the long-run aggregate supply remains stationary?

    _____

    _____

    _____

SELF-TEST

True/False Questions

_____ 1.   Over the last 50 years, U.S. real GDP has grown at about 5 percent per year.

_____ 2.   Investment is a particularly volatile component of spending across the business cycle.

_____ 3.   An increase in price expectations shifts the long-run aggregate-supply curve to the left.

_____ 4.   If the classical dichotomy and monetary neutrality hold in the long run, then the long-run aggregate-supply curve should be vertical.

_____ 5.   Economists refer to fluctuations in output as the "business cycle" because movements in output are regular and predictable.

_____ 6.   One reason aggregate demand slopes downward is the wealth effect: A decrease in the price level increases the value of money holdings and consumer spending rises.

_____ 7.   If the Federal Reserve increases the money supply, the aggregate-demand curve shifts to the left.

_____ 8.   The misperceptions theory explains why the long-run aggregate-supply curve is downward sloping.

_____ 9.   A rise in price expectations that causes wages to rise causes the short-run aggregate-supply curve to shift left.

_____ 10.   If the economy is in a recession, the economy will adjust to long-run equilibrium on its own as wages and price expectations rise.

_____ 11.   In the short run, if the government cuts back spending to balance its budget, it will likely cause a recession.

_____ 12.   The short-run effect of an increase in aggregate demand is an increase in output and an increase in the price level.

_____ 13.   A rise in the price of oil tends to cause stagflation.

_____ 14.   In the long run, an increase in government spending tends to increase output and prices.

_____ 15.   If policymakers choose to try to move the economy out of a recession, they should use their policy tools to decrease aggregate demand.

Multiple-Choice Questions

1.   Which of the following statements about economic fluctuations is true?
   a.   A recession is when output rises above the natural rate of output.
   b.   A depression is a mild recession.
   c.   Economic fluctuations have been termed the "business cycle" because the movements in output are regular and predictable.
   d.   A variety of spending, income, and output measures can be used to measure economic fluctuations because most macroeconomic quantities tend to fluctuate together.
   e.   None of the above is true.

2. According to the interest-rate effect, aggregate demand slopes downward (negatively) because
    a. lower prices increase the value of money holdings and consumer spending increases.
    b. lower prices decrease the value of money holdings and consumer spending decreases.
    c. lower prices reduce money holdings, increase lending, interest rates fall, and investment spending increases.
    d. lower prices increase money holdings, decrease lending, interest rates rise, and investment spending falls.

3. Which of the following would *not* cause a shift in the long-run aggregate-supply curve?
    a. an increase in the available labor
    b. an increase in the available capital
    c. an increase in the available technology
    d. an increase in price expectations
    e. All of the above shift the long-run aggregate-supply curve.

4. Which of the following is *not* a reason why the aggregate-demand curve slopes downward?
    a. the wealth effect
    b. the interest-rate effect
    c. the classical dichotomy/monetary neutrality effects
    d. the exchange-rate effect
    e. All of the above are reasons why the aggregate-demand curve slopes downward.

5. In the model of aggregate demand and aggregate supply, the initial impact of an increase in consumer optimism is to
    a. shift short-run aggregate supply to the right.
    b. shift short-run aggregate supply to the left.
    c. shift aggregate demand to the right.
    d. shift aggregate demand to the left.
    e. shift long-run aggregate supply to the left.

6. Which of the following statements is true regarding the long-run aggregate-supply curve? The long-run aggregate-supply curve
    a. shifts left when the natural rate of unemployment falls.
    b. is vertical because an equal change in all prices and wages leaves output unaffected.
    c. is positively sloped because price expectations and wages tend to be fixed in the long run.
    d. shifts right when the government raises the minimum wage.

7. According to the wealth effect, aggregate demand slopes downward (negatively) because
    a. lower prices increase the value of money holdings and consumer spending increases.
    b. lower prices decrease the value of money holdings and consumer spending decreases.
    c. lower prices reduce money holdings, increase lending, interest rates fall, and investment spending increases.
    d. lower prices increase money holdings, decrease lending, interest rates rise, and investment spending falls.

8. The natural rate of output is the amount of real GDP produced
   a. when there is no unemployment.
   b. when the economy is at the natural rate of investment.
   c. when the economy is at the natural rate of aggregate demand.
   d. when the economy is at the natural rate of unemployment.

9. Suppose the price level falls. Because of fixed nominal wage contracts, firms become less profitable and they cut back on production. This is a demonstration of the
   a. sticky-wage theory of the short-run aggregate-supply curve.
   b. sticky-price theory of the short-run aggregate-supply curve.
   c. misperceptions theory of the short-run aggregate-supply curve.
   d. classical dichotomy theory of the short-run aggregate-supply curve.

10. Suppose the price level falls but suppliers only notice that the price of their particular product has fallen. Thinking there has been a fall in the relative price of their product, they cut back on production. This is a demonstration of the
    a. sticky-wage theory of the short-run aggregate-supply curve.
    b. sticky-price theory of the short-run aggregate-supply curve.
    c. misperceptions theory of the short-run aggregate-supply curve.
    d. classical dichotomy theory of the short-run aggregate-supply curve.

11. Suppose the economy is initially in long-run equilibrium. Then suppose there is a reduction in military spending due to the end of the Cold War. According to the model of aggregate demand and aggregate supply, what happens to prices and output in the *short run*?
    a. Prices rise; output rises.
    b. Prices rise; output falls.
    c. Prices fall; output falls.
    d. Prices fall; output rises.

12. Suppose the economy is initially in long-run equilibrium. Then suppose there is a reduction in military spending due to the end of the Cold War. According to the model of aggregate demand and aggregate supply, what happens to prices and output in the *long run*?
    a. Prices rise; output is unchanged from its initial value.
    b. Prices fall; output is unchanged from its initial value.
    c. Output rises; prices are unchanged from the initial value.
    d. Output falls; prices are unchanged from the initial value.
    e. Output and the price level are unchanged from their initial values.

13. Suppose the economy is initially in long-run equilibrium. Then suppose there is a drought that destroys much of the wheat crop. According to the model of aggregate demand and aggregate supply, what happens to prices and output in the *short run*?
    a. Prices rise; output rises.
    b. Prices rise; output falls.
    c. Prices fall; output falls.
    d. Prices fall; output rises.

14. Suppose the economy is initially in long-run equilibrium. Then suppose there is a drought that destroys much of the wheat crop. If policymakers allow the economy to adjust to long-run equilibrium on its own, according to the model of aggregate demand and aggregate supply, what happens to prices and output in the *long run*?
    a. Prices rise; output is unchanged from its initial value.
    b. Prices fall; output is unchanged from its initial value.
    c. Output rises; prices are unchanged from the initial value.
    d. Output falls; prices are unchanged from the initial value.
    e. Output and the price level are unchanged from their initial values.

15. Stagflation occurs when the economy experiences
    a. falling prices and falling output.
    b. falling prices and rising output.
    c. rising prices and rising output.
    d. rising prices and falling output.

16. Which of the following events shifts the short-run aggregate-supply curve to the right?
    a. an increase in government spending on military equipment
    b. an increase in price expectations
    c. a drop in oil prices
    d. a decrease in the money supply
    e. none of the above

Use Exhibit 4 to answer questions 17 and 18.

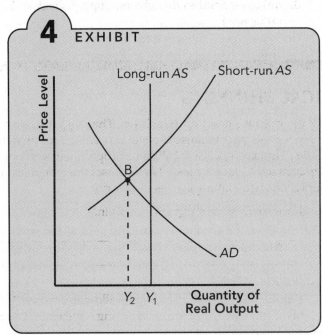

17. Suppose the economy is operating in a recession such as point B in Exhibit 4. If policymakers wished to move output to its long-run natural rate, they should attempt to
    a. shift aggregate demand to the right.
    b. shift aggregate demand to the left.
    c. shift short-run aggregate supply to the right.
    d. shift short-run aggregate supply to the left.

18. Suppose the economy is operating in a recession such as point B in Exhibit 4. If policymakers allow the economy to adjust to the long-run natural rate on its own,
    a. people will raise their price expectations and the short-run aggregate supply will shift left.
    b. people will reduce their price expectations and the short-run aggregate supply will shift right.
    c. people will raise their price expectations and aggregate demand will shift left.
    d. people will reduce their price expectations and aggregate demand will shift right.

19.   According to the model of aggregate supply and aggregate demand, in the long run, an increase in the money supply should cause
   a.   prices to rise and output to rise.
   b.   prices to fall and output to fall.
   c.   prices to rise and output to remain unchanged.
   d.   prices to fall and output to remain unchanged.

20.   Policymakers are said to "accommodate" an adverse supply shock if they
   a.   respond to the adverse supply shock by increasing aggregate demand, which further raises prices.
   b.   respond to the adverse supply shock by decreasing aggregate demand, which lowers prices.
   c.   respond to the adverse supply shock by decreasing short-run aggregate supply.
   d.   fail to respond to the adverse supply shock and allow the economy to adjust on its own.

ADVANCED CRITICAL THINKING

You are watching the evening news on television. The news anchor reports that union wage demands are much higher this year because the workers anticipate an increase in the rate of inflation. Your roommate says, "Inflation is a self-fulfilling prophecy. If workers think there are going to be higher prices, they demand higher wages. This increases the cost of production and firms raise their prices. Expecting higher prices simply causes higher prices."

1.   Is this true in the short run? Explain.

   _____

   _____

2.   If policymakers do nothing and allow the economy to adjust to the natural rate of output on its own, does expecting higher prices cause higher prices in the long run? Explain.

   _____

   _____

3.   If policymakers accommodate the adverse supply shock, does the expectation of higher prices cause higher prices in the long run? Explain.

   _____

   _____

   _____

   _____

   _____

SOLUTIONS

Terms and Definitions

<u>4</u> Recession

<u>8</u> Depression

<u>2</u> The business cycle

<u>10</u> Model of aggregate supply and demand

<u>5</u> Aggregate-demand curve

<u>9</u> Aggregate-supply curve

<u>6</u> Natural rate of output

<u>1</u> Menu costs

<u>7</u> Stagflation

<u>3</u> Accommodative policy

Practice Problems

1. a. Prices fall, output falls. Prices fall, output returns to the natural rate. Shift aggregate demand to the right.

    b. Prices rise, output rises. Prices rise, output returns to the natural rate. Shift aggregate demand to the left.

    c. Prices rise, output falls. Price level returns to original value, output returns to the natural rate. Shift aggregate demand to the right.

    d. Prices fall, output rises. Price level returns to original value, output returns to the natural rate. Shift aggregate demand to the left.

2. a. aggregate demand, right

    b. short-run aggregate supply, left

    c. both short-run and long-run aggregate supply, left

    d. aggregate demand, right

    e. both short-run and long-run aggregate supply, right

    f. both short-run and long-run aggregate supply, left

    g. short-run aggregate supply, right

    h. aggregate demand, left

    i. both short-run and long-run aggregate supply, left

3. a. Aggregate demand shifts to the right.

    b. Price level rises and real output rises.

    c. Price level rises and real output stays the same. Money neutrality.

    d. No. Over time, people and firms adjust to the new higher amount of spending by raising their prices and wages.

4. a. Short-run aggregate supply shifts left.

    b. Prices rise and output falls.

    c. Stagflation.

    d. Shift aggregate demand to the right.

    e. Prices would rise more and remain there.

    f. The high unemployment at the low level of output would put pressure on the wage to fall back to its original value shifting short-run aggregate supply back to its original position.

    g. No. Increases in the cost of production need to be "accommodated" by government policy to permanently raise prices.

5. a. At point B, prices have fallen, but nominal wages are stuck at a high level based on a higher price expectation. Firms are less profitable and they cut back on production. As workers and firms recognize the fall in the price level (learn to expect P_3), new contracts will have a lower nominal wage. The reduction in labor costs causes firms to increase production at each price level shifting the short-run aggregate supply to the right.

    b. At point B, some firms have not reduced their prices because of menu costs. Their products are relatively more expensive and sales fall. When they realize the lower price level is permanent (learn to expect P_3), they lower their prices and output rises at each price level, shifting the short-run aggregate supply to the right.

    c. At point B, some firms mistakenly believe that only the price of their product has fallen and they have cut back on production. As they realize that all prices are falling (learn to expect P_3), they will increase production at each price, which will shift short-run aggregate supply to the right.

    d. More slowly from a recession because it requires prices to be reduced, and prices are usually more sticky downward. The adjustment when output is above normal requires prices and wages to rise.

Short-Answer Questions

1. Economic fluctuations are irregular and unpredictable; most macroeconomic quantities fluctuate together; and when output falls, unemployment rises.

2. Wealth effect: Lower prices increase the value of money holdings and consumer spending increases. Interest-rate effect: Lower prices reduce the quantity of money held, some is loaned, interest rates fall, and investment spending increases. Exchange-rate effect: Lower prices decrease interest rates, the dollar depreciates, and net exports increase.

3. In the short run, nominal wages are fixed based on fixed-price expectations. If actual prices unexpectedly fall while nominal wages remain fixed, firms are less profitable and they cut back on production.

4. Yes. Changes in aggregate demand cause actual prices to deviate from expected prices. Due to sticky wages, sticky prices, and misperceptions about relative prices, firms respond by changing output.

5. No. In the long run, output is determined by factor supplies and technology (long-run aggregate supply). Changes in aggregate demand only affect prices in the long run.

6. Because they think they can get the economy back to the long-run natural rate of output more quickly or, in the case of a negative supply shock, because they are more concerned with output than inflation.

7. Investment.

8. Because a decrease in aggregate demand from a decrease in the money supply may reduce the price level unexpectedly. In the short run, some prices and wages are stuck, and some producers have misperceptions regarding relative prices causing output to fall.

9. Short-run aggregate supply shifts right. Prices fall and output rises.

10. Changes in the available factors (labor, capital, natural resources) and technology shift both long-run and short-run aggregate supply. Changes in price expectations that may be associated with wage demands and oil prices only shift short-run aggregate supply.

True/False Questions

1. F; the U.S. economy has grown at about 3 percent per year.
2. T
3. F; changes in price expectations shift the short-run aggregate-supply curve.
4. T
5. F; fluctuations in output are irregular.
6. T
7. F; aggregate demand shifts to the right.
8. F; it explains why the short-run aggregate-supply curve is upward sloping.
9. T
10. F; in a recession, the economy adjusts to long-run equilibrium as wages and prices fall.
11. T
12. T
13. T
14. F; in the long run, it tends to increase prices, but it has no impact on output.
15. F; policymakers should increase aggregate demand.

Multiple-Choice Questions

1. d
2. c
3. d
4. c
5. c
6. b
7. a
8. d
9. a
10. c
11. c
12. b
13. b
14. e
15. d
16. c
17. a
18. b
19. c
20. a

Advanced Critical Thinking

1. Yes. An increase in price expectations shifts the short-run aggregate-supply curve to the left and prices rise.

2. No. In the long run, the increase in unemployment will cause wages and price expectations to fall back to their prior levels.

3. Yes. If policymakers accommodate the adverse supply shock with an increase in aggregate demand, the price level will rise permanently.

The Influence of Monetary and Fiscal Policy on Aggregate Demand

GOALS

In this chapter you will

- Learn the theory of liquidity preference as a short-run theory of the interest rate

- Analyze how monetary policy affects interest rates and aggregate demand

- Analyze how fiscal policy affects interest rates and aggregate demand

- Discuss the debate over whether policymakers should try to stabilize the economy

OUTCOMES

After accomplishing these goals, you should be able to

- Show what an increase in the money supply does to the interest rate in the short run

- Illustrate what an increase in the money supply does to aggregate demand

- Explain crowding out

- Describe the lags in fiscal and monetary policy

CHAPTER OVERVIEW

Context and Purpose

Chapter 34 is the second chapter in a three-chapter sequence that concentrates on short-run fluctuations in the economy around its long-term trend. In Chapter 33, we introduced the model of aggregate supply and aggregate demand. In Chapter 34, we see how the government's monetary and fiscal policies affect aggregate demand. In Chapter 35, we will see some of the trade-offs between short-run and long-run objectives when we address the relationship between inflation and unemployment.

The purpose of Chapter 34 is to address the short-run effects of monetary and fiscal policies. In Chapter 33, we found that when aggregate demand or short-run aggregate supply shifts, it causes fluctuations in output. As a result, policymakers sometimes try to offset these shifts by shifting aggregate demand with monetary and fiscal policy. Chapter 34 addresses the theory behind these policies and some of the shortcomings of *stabilization policy*.

Chapter Review

Introduction Chapters 25 through 30 demonstrated the impact of fiscal and monetary policy on saving, investment, and long-term growth. Chapter 33 demonstrated that shifts in aggregate demand and short-run aggregate supply cause short-run fluctuations in the economy around its long-term trend and how monetary and fiscal policymakers might shift aggregate demand to stabilize the economy. In this chapter, we address the theory behind stabilization policies and some of the shortcomings of stabilization policy.

How Monetary Policy Influences Aggregate Demand

The aggregate-demand curve shows the quantity of goods and services demanded at each price level. Recall from Chapter 33, aggregate demand slopes downward due to the wealth effect, the interest-rate effect, and the exchange-rate effect. Since money is a small part of total wealth and since the international sector is a small part of the U.S. economy, the most important reason for the downward slope of U.S. aggregate demand is the interest-rate effect.

The interest rate is a key determinant of aggregate demand. To see how monetary policy affects aggregate demand, we develop Keynes's theory of interest rate determination called the **theory of liquidity preference.** This theory suggests that the interest rate is determined by the supply and demand for money. Note that the interest rate being determined is both the nominal and the real interest rate because, in the short run, expected inflation is unchanging so changes in the nominal rate equal changes in the real rate.

Recall, the money supply is determined by the Fed and can be fixed at whatever level the Fed chooses. Therefore, the money supply is unaffected by the interest rate and is a vertical line in Exhibit 1. People have a demand for money because money, as the economy's most liquid asset, is a medium of exchange. Hence, people have a demand for it even though it has no rate of return because it can be used to buy things. The interest rate is the opportunity cost of holding money. When the interest rate is high, people hold more wealth in interest-bearing bonds and economize on their money holdings. Thus, the quantity of money demanded is reduced. This is shown in Exhibit 1. The equilibrium interest rate is determined by the intersection of money supply and money demand.

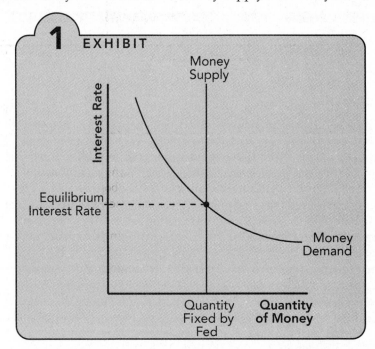

Note that, in the long run, the interest rate is determined by the supply and demand for loanable funds. In the short run, the interest rate is determined by the supply and demand for money. This poses no conflict.

- In the long run, output is fixed by factor supplies and technology, the interest rate adjusts to balance the supply and demand for loanable funds, and the price level adjusts to balance the supply and demand for money.

- In the short run, the price level is sticky and cannot adjust. For any given price level, the interest rate adjusts to balance the supply and demand for money. The interest rate influences aggregate demand and thus output.

Each theory highlights the behavior of interest rates over a different time horizon.

We can use the theory of liquidity preference to add precision to our explanation of the negative slope of the aggregate-demand curve. Recall from previous chapters, the demand for money is positively related to the price level because at higher prices, people need more money to buy the same quantity of goods. Thus, a higher price level shifts money demand to the right, as shown in Exhibit 2, panel (a). With a fixed money supply, a larger money demand raises the interest rate. A higher interest rate reduces investment expenditures and causes the quantity demanded of goods and services to fall in Exhibit 2, panel (b).

2 EXHIBIT

Panel (a)

Panel (b)

Returning to the point of this section: How does monetary policy influence aggregate demand? Suppose the Fed buys government bonds shifting the money supply to the right, as in Exhibit 3, panel (a). The interest rate falls, reducing the cost of borrowing for investment. Hence, the quantity of goods and services demanded at each price level increases, shifting aggregate demand to the right in Exhibit 3, panel (b).

The Fed can implement monetary policy by targeting the money supply or interest rates. In recent years, the Fed has targeted the interest rate because the money supply is hard to measure. In particular, the Fed has targeted the *federal funds rate*—the interest rate banks charge each other for short-term

3 EXHIBIT

Panel (a)

Panel (b)

loans. Whether the Fed targets the money supply or interest rates has little effect on our analysis because every monetary policy can be described in terms of the money supply or the interest rate. For example, the monetary policy expansion used to increase aggregate demand in the example above could be described as an increase in the money supply or a decrease in the interest rate target.

How Fiscal Policy Influences Aggregate Demand

Fiscal policy refers to the government's choices of the levels of government purchases and taxes. While fiscal policy can influence growth in the long run, its primary impact in the short run is on aggregate demand.

An increase in government purchases of $20 billion to buy military aircraft is reflected in a rightward shift in the aggregate-demand curve. There are two reasons why the actual rightward shift may be greater than or less than $20 billion:

- *The multiplier effect:* When the government spends $20 billion on aircraft, incomes rise in the form of wages and profits of the aircraft manufacturer. The recipients of the new income raise their spending on consumer goods, which raises the incomes of people in other firms, which raises their consumption spending, and so on for many rounds. Since aggregate demand may rise by much more than the increase in government purchases, government purchases are said to have a multiplier effect on aggregate demand. There is a formula for the size of the multiplier effect. It says that for every dollar the government spends, aggregate demand shifts to the right by $1/(1 - MPC)$, where MPC stands for the *marginal propensity to consume*—the fraction of extra income that a household spends on consumption. For example, if the MPC is 0.75, the multiplier is $1/(1 - 0.75) = 1/0.25 = 4$, which means that $1 of government spending shifts aggregate demand to the right by a total of $4. An increase in the MPC increases the multiplier.

  In addition to the multiplier, the increase in purchases may cause firms to increase their investment expenditures on new equipment, further increasing the response of aggregate demand to the initial increase in government purchases. This is known as the *investment accelerator*.

  Thus, the aggregate demand curve may shift by more than the change in government purchases.

  The logic of the multiplier effect applies to other changes in spending besides government purchases. For example, shocks to consumption, investment, and net exports may have a multiplier effect on aggregate demand.

- *The crowding-out effect:* The **crowding-out effect** works in the opposite direction of the multiplier. An increase in government purchases (as in the case above) raises incomes, which shifts the demand for money to the right. This raises the interest rate, which lowers investment. Thus, an increase in government purchases increases the interest rate and reduces, or crowds out, private investment. Due to crowding out, the aggregate demand curve may shift right by less than the increase in government purchases.

Whether the final shift in the aggregate-demand curve is greater than or less than the original change in government spending depends on which is larger: the multiplier effect or the crowding-out effect.

The other half of fiscal policy is taxation. A reduction in taxes increases households' take-home pay and, hence, increases their consumption. Thus, a decrease in taxes shifts aggregate demand to the right while an increase shifts aggregate demand to the left. The size of the shift in aggregate demand depends on the relative size of the multiplier and crowding-out effects described above. In addition, a reduction in taxes that is perceived by households to be permanent improves the financial condition of the household a great amount and increases aggregate demand substantially. A change in taxes that is perceived to be temporary has a much smaller effect on aggregate demand.

Finally, fiscal policy might have an effect on aggregate supply for two reasons. First, a reduction in taxes might increase the incentive to work and cause aggregate supply to shift right. *Supply-siders* believe this effect could be so large that tax revenue could increase. Most economists do not believe this is the normal case. Second, government purchases of capital, such as roads and bridges, may increase the amount of goods supplied at each price level and shift the aggregate supply curve to the right. This effect is more likely to be important in the long run.

Using Policy to Stabilize the Economy

Keynes (and his followers) argued that the government should actively use monetary and fiscal policies to stabilize aggregate demand and, as a result, output and employment.

The Employment Act of 1946 holds the federal government responsible for promoting full employment and production. The act has two implications: (1) The government should not be the cause of fluctuations, so it should avoid sudden changes in fiscal and monetary policy, and (2) the government should respond to changes in the private economy in order to stabilize it. For example, if consumer pessimism reduces aggregate demand, the proper amount of expansionary monetary or fiscal policy could stimulate aggregate demand to its original level, thereby avoiding a recession. Alternatively, if excessive optimism increases aggregate demand, contractionary monetary or fiscal policy could dampen aggregate demand to its original level, thereby avoiding inflationary pressures. Failure to actively stabilize the economy may allow for unnecessary fluctuations in output and employment.

Some economists argue that the government should not use monetary and fiscal policy to try to stabilize short-run fluctuations in the economy. While they agree that, in theory, activist policy can stabilize the economy, they feel that, in practice, monetary and fiscal policy affect the economy with a substantial lag. The lag for monetary policy is at least six months, so it may be hard for the Fed to "fine-tune" the economy. Fiscal policy has a long political lag because it takes months or years to pass spending and taxation legislation. These lags mean that activist policy could be destabilizing because expansionary policy could accidentally increase aggregate demand during periods of excessive private aggregate demand, and contractionary policy could accidentally decrease aggregate demand during periods of deficient private aggregate demand.

Automatic stabilizers are changes in fiscal policy that automatically stimulate aggregate demand in a recession so that policymakers do not have to take deliberate action. The tax system automatically lowers tax collections during a recession when incomes and profits fall. Government spending automatically rises during a recession because unemployment benefits and welfare payments rise. Hence, both the tax and government spending systems increase aggregate demand during a recession. A strict balanced budget rule would eliminate automatic stabilizers because the government would have to raise taxes or lower expenditures during a recession.

Helpful Hints

1. The multiplier can be derived in a variety of different ways. Your text shows you that the value of the multiplier is $1/(1 - MPC)$. However, it doesn't show you how this number is generated. Below, you will find one of the many different ways that the value of the multiplier can be derived for the case of an increase in government spending:

    $$\Delta \text{output demanded} = \Delta \text{spending on output},$$

    which says that the change in output demanded equals the change in spending on output. Denoting Y as output demanded, G as government spending, and noting that output equals income, then

    $$\Delta Y = \Delta G + [(MPC) \times \Delta Y],$$

    which says that the change in output demanded is equal to the change in total spending where total spending is composed of the change in government spending plus the change in consumption spending induced by the increase in income (say 0.75 of the change in income).

    Solving for ΔY, we get

    $$\Delta Y - [(MPC) \times \Delta Y] = \Delta G$$
    $$\Delta Y \times (1 - MPC) = \Delta G$$
    $$\Delta Y = 1/(1 - MPC) \times \Delta G,$$

    which says that a \$1 increase in government spending causes an increase in aggregate demand of $1/(1 - MPC) \times \$1$. If the MPC equals 0.75, then $1/(1 - 0.75) = 4$ and a \$1 increase in government spending shifts aggregate demand to the right by \$4.

2. An increase in the *MPC* increases the multiplier. If the *MPC* were 0.80, suggesting that people spend 80 percent of an increase in income on consumption goods, the multiplier would become $1/(1 - 0.80) = 5$. This is larger than the multiplier generated above from an *MPC* of 0.75. There is an intuitive appeal to this result. If people spend a higher percentage of an increase in income on consumption goods, any new government purchase will have an even larger multiplier effect and shift the aggregate-demand curve further to the right.

3. The multiplier works in both directions. If the government reduces purchases, the multiplier effect suggests that the aggregate-demand curve will shift to the left by a greater amount than the initial reduction in government purchases. When the government reduces purchases, wages and profits of people are reduced and they reduce their consumption expenditures, and so on, creating a multiple contraction in aggregate demand.

4. Activist stabilization policy has many descriptive names. Activist stabilization policy is the use of discretionary monetary and fiscal policies to manage aggregate demand in such a way as to minimize the fluctuations in output and to maintain output at the long-run natural rate. As such, activist stabilization policy is sometimes called *discretionary policy* to distinguish it from automatic stabilizers. It is also called *aggregate demand management* because monetary and fiscal policies are used to adjust or manage total spending in the economy. Finally, since policymakers attempt to counter the business cycle by reducing aggregate demand when it is too high and by increasing aggregate demand when it is too low, stabilization policy is sometimes referred to as *countercyclical policy*.

5. Activist stabilization policy can be used to move output toward the long-run natural rate from levels of output that are either above or below the natural rate of output. As in the previous chapter, most of the examples of stabilization policy in the text assume the economy is in a recession—a period when output is below the long-run natural rate. However, activist stabilization policy can be used to reduce aggregate demand and output in periods when output exceeds the long-run natural rate. When output exceeds the natural rate, we sometimes say that the economy is in a boom, an expansion, or that the economy is overheating. When the economy's output is above the natural rate, the economy is said to be overheating because, left alone, the economy will adjust to a higher level of expected prices and wages and output will fall to the natural rate (short-run aggregate supply shifts left). Most economists believe that the Federal Reserve needs political independence to combat an overheating economy. This is because the activist policy prescription for an overheating economy is a reduction in aggregate demand, which usually faces political opposition. That is, "taking away the punch bowl just as the party gets going" is not likely to be politically popular.

Terms and Definitions

Choose a definition for each key term.

Key Terms

_____ Theory of liquidity preference

_____ Liquidity

_____ Federal funds rate

_____ Fiscal policy

_____ Multiplier effect

_____ Investment accelerator

_____ Marginal propensity to consume, or *MPC*

_____ Crowding-out effect

_____ Stabilization policy

_____ Automatic stabilizers

Definitions

1. The dampening of the shift in aggregate demand from expansionary fiscal policy, which raises the interest rate and reduces investment spending

2. The interest rate banks charge one another for short-term loans

3. The amplification of the shift in aggregate demand from expansionary fiscal policy, which raises investment expenditures

4. Keynes's theory that the interest rate is determined by the supply and demand for money in the short run

5. Changes in fiscal policy that do not require deliberate action on the part of policymakers

6. The use of fiscal and monetary policies to reduce fluctuations in the economy

7. The amplification of the shift in aggregate demand from expansionary fiscal policy, which raises incomes and further increases consumption expenditures

8. The ease with which an asset is converted into a medium of exchange

9. The fraction of extra income that a household spends on consumption

10. The setting of the level of government spending and taxation by government policymakers

PROBLEMS AND SHORT-ANSWER QUESTIONS

Practice Problems

1. If the Federal Reserve were to engage in activist stabilization policy, in which direction should they move the *money supply* in response to the following events?
   a. A wave of optimism boosts business investment and household consumption.

   _____

   b. To balance its budget, the federal government raises taxes and reduces expenditures.

   _____

    c. OPEC raises the price of crude oil.

_____

    d. Foreigners experience a reduction in their taste for U.S.-produced Ford automobiles.

_____

    e. The stock market falls.

_____

2. If the Federal Reserve were to engage in activist stabilization policy, in which direction should they move *interest rates* in response to the same events listed in the previous question?
    a. A wave of optimism boosts business investment and household consumption.

_____

    b. To balance its budget, the federal government raises taxes and reduces expenditures.

_____

    c. OPEC raises the price of crude oil.

_____

    d. Foreigners experience a reduction in their taste for U.S.-produced Ford automobiles.

_____

    e. The stock market falls.

_____

    f. Explain the relationship between Fed policy in terms of the money supply and policy in terms of the interest rate.

_____

_____

_____

3. If policymakers were to use fiscal policy to actively stabilize the economy, in which direction should they move government spending and taxes?
    a. A wave of pessimism reduces business investment and household consumption.

_____

    b. An increase in price expectations causes unions to demand higher wages.

_____

    c. Foreigners increase their taste for domestically produced Ford automobiles.

_____

d. OPEC raises the price of crude oil.

_____

4. Suppose the economy is in a recession. Policymakers estimate that aggregate demand is $100 billion short of the amount necessary to generate the long-run natural rate of output. That is, if aggregate demand were shifted to the right by $100 billion, the economy would be in long-run equilibrium.

a. If the federal government chooses to use fiscal policy to stabilize the economy, by how much should they increase government spending if the marginal propensity to consume (*MPC*) is 0.75 and there is no crowding out?

_____

_____

b. If the federal government chooses to use fiscal policy to stabilize the economy, by how much should they increase government spending if the marginal propensity to consume (*MPC*) is 0.80 and there is no crowding out?

_____

_____

c. If there is crowding out, will the government need to spend more or less than the amounts you found in *a* and *b* above? Why?

_____

_____

_____

d. If investment is very sensitive to changes in the interest rate, is crowding out more of a problem or less of a problem? Why?

_____

_____

_____

e. If policymakers discover that the lag for fiscal policy is two years, should that make them more likely to employ fiscal policy as a stabilization tool or more likely to allow the economy to adjust on its own? Why?

_____

_____

_____

5. a. What does an increase in the money supply do to interest rates in the short run? Explain.

_____

_____

_____

_____

_____

b. What does an increase in the money supply do to interest rates in the long run? Explain.

_____

_____

_____

c. Are these results inconsistent? Explain.

_____

_____

_____

Short-Answer Questions

1. Why is the money supply curve vertical when it is drawn on a graph with the interest rate on the vertical axis and the quantity of money on the horizontal axis?

    _____

    _____

    _____

2. Why does the money demand curve slope negatively when it is drawn on a graph with the interest rate on the vertical axis and the quantity of money on the horizontal axis?

    _____

    _____

    _____

3. Why does an increase in the price level reduce the quantity demanded of real output? (Use the interest-rate effect to explain the slope of the aggregate-demand curve.)

    _____

    _____

    _____

    _____

4. Explain how an increase in the money supply shifts the aggregate-demand curve.

    _____

    _____

    _____

    _____

5. Explain the intuition of the multiplier effect resulting from an increase in government spending. Why should a bigger *MPC* make the multiplier effect larger?

_____

_____

_____

_____

6. Explain how an increase in government spending may lead to crowding out.

_____

_____

_____

7. Suppose the government spends $10 billion on a public works program, which is intended to stimulate aggregate demand. If the crowding-out effect exceeds the multiplier effect, will the aggregate-demand curve shift to the right by more or less than $10 billion? Why?

_____

_____

_____

8. How does a cut in taxes affect aggregate supply?

_____

_____

9. Which is likely to have a greater impact on aggregate demand: a temporary reduction in taxes or a permanent reduction in taxes? Why?

_____

_____

10. Explain why taxes and government spending may act as automatic stabilizers. What would a strict balanced-budget rule cause policymakers to do during a recession? Would this make the recession more or less severe?

_____

_____

_____

_____

_____

SELF-TEST

True/False Questions

_____ 1. An increase in the interest rate increases the quantity demanded of money because it increases the rate of return on money.

_____ 2. When money demand is drawn on a graph with the interest rate on the vertical axis and the quantity of money on the horizontal axis, an increase in the price level shifts money demand to the right.

_____ 3. Keynes's theory of liquidity preference suggests that the interest rate is determined by the supply and demand for money.

_____ 4. The interest-rate effect suggests that aggregate demand slopes downward because an increase in the price level shifts money demand to the right, increases the interest rate, and reduces investment.

_____ 5. An increase in the money supply shifts the money supply curve to the right, increases the interest rate, decreases investment, and shifts the aggregate-demand curve to the left.

_____ 6. Suppose investors and consumers become pessimistic about the future and cut back on expenditures. If the Fed engages in activist stabilization policy, the policy response should be to decrease the money supply.

_____ 7. In the short run, a decision by the Fed to increase the money supply is essentially the same as a decision to decrease the interest rate target.

_____ 8. Because of the multiplier effect, an increase in government spending of $40 billion will shift the aggregate-demand curve to the right by more than $40 billion (assuming there is no crowding out).

_____ 9. If the MPC (marginal propensity to consume) is 0.80, then the value of the multiplier is 8.

_____ 10. Crowding out occurs when an increase in government spending increases incomes, shifts money demand to the right, raises the interest rate, and reduces private investment.

_____ 11. Suppose the government increases its expenditure by $10 billion. If the crowding-out effect exceeds the multiplier effect, then the aggregate-demand curve shifts to the right by more than $10 billion.

_____ 12. Suppose investors and consumers become pessimistic about the future and cut back on expenditures. If fiscal policymakers engage in activist stabilization policy, the policy response should be to decrease government spending and increase taxes.

_____ 13. Many economists prefer automatic stabilizers because they affect the economy with a shorter lag than activist stabilization policies.

_____ 14. In the short run, the interest rate is determined by the loanable-funds market, while in the long run, the interest rate is determined by money demand and money supply.

_____ 15. Unemployment benefits are an example of an automatic stabilizer because when incomes fall, unemployment benefits rise.

Multiple-Choice Questions

1. Keynes's liquidity preference theory of the interest rate suggests that the interest rate is determined by
    a. the supply and demand for loanable funds.
    b. the supply and demand for money.
    c. the supply and demand for labor.
    d. aggregate supply and aggregate demand.

2. When money demand is expressed in a graph with the interest rate on the vertical axis and the quantity of money on the horizontal axis, an increase in the interest rate
    a. increases the quantity demanded of money.
    b. increases the demand for money.
    c. decreases the quantity demanded of money.
    d. decreases the demand for money.
    e. does none of the above.

3. When the supply and demand for money are expressed in a graph with the interest rate on the vertical axis and the quantity of money on the horizontal axis, an increase in the price level
    a. shifts money demand to the right and increases the interest rate.
    b. shifts money demand to the left and increases the interest rate.
    c. shifts money demand to the right and decreases the interest rate.
    d. shifts money demand to the left and decreases the interest rate.
    e. does none of the above.

4. For the United States, the most important source of the downward slope of the aggregate-demand curve is
    a. the exchange-rate effect.
    b. the wealth effect.
    c. the fiscal effect.
    d. the interest-rate effect.
    e. none of the above.

5. In the market for real output, the initial effect of an increase in the money supply is to
    a. shift aggregate demand to the right.
    b. shift aggregate demand to the left.
    c. shift aggregate supply to the right.
    d. shift aggregate supply to the left.

6. The initial effect of an increase in the money supply is to
    a. increase the price level.
    b. decrease the price level.
    c. increase the interest rate.
    d. decrease the interest rate.

7. The long-run effect of an increase in the money supply is to
    a. increase the price level.
    b. decrease the price level.
    c. increase the interest rate.
    d. decrease the interest rate.

8. Suppose a wave of investor and consumer pessimism causes a reduction in spending. If the Federal Reserve chooses to engage in activist stabilization policy, it should
   a. increase government spending and decrease taxes.
   b. decrease government spending and increase taxes.
   c. increase the money supply and decrease interest rates.
   d. decrease the money supply and increase interest rates.

9. The initial impact of an increase in government spending is to shift
   a. aggregate supply to the right.
   b. aggregate supply to the left.
   c. aggregate demand to the right.
   d. aggregate demand to the left.

10. If the marginal propensity to consume (*MPC*) is 0.75, the value of the multiplier is
    a. 0.75.
    b. 4.
    c. 5.
    d. 7.5.
    e. none of the above.

11. An increase in the marginal propensity to consume (*MPC*)
    a. raises the value of the multiplier.
    b. lowers the value of the multiplier.
    c. has no impact on the value of the multiplier.
    d. rarely occurs because the *MPC* is set by congressional legislation.

12. Suppose a wave of investor and consumer optimism has increased spending so that the current level of output exceeds the long-run natural rate. If policymakers choose to engage in activist stabilization policy, they should
    a. decrease taxes, which shifts aggregate demand to the right.
    b. decrease taxes, which shifts aggregate demand to the left.
    c. decrease government spending, which shifts aggregate demand to the right.
    d. decrease government spending, which shifts aggregate demand to the left.

13. When an increase in government purchases raises incomes, shifts money demand to the right, raises the interest rate, and lowers investment, we have seen a demonstration of
    a. the multiplier effect.
    b. the investment accelerator.
    c. the crowding-out effect.
    d. supply-side economics.
    e. none of the above.

14. Which of the following statements regarding taxes is correct?
    a. Most economists believe that, in the short run, the greatest impact of a change in taxes is on aggregate supply, not aggregate demand.
    b. A permanent change in taxes has a greater effect on aggregate demand than a temporary change in taxes.
    c. An increase in taxes shifts the aggregate-demand curve to the right.
    d. A decrease in taxes shifts the aggregate-supply curve to the left.

15. Suppose the government increases its purchases by $16 billion. If the multiplier effect exceeds the crowding-out effect, then
    a. the aggregate-supply curve shifts to the right by more than $16 billion.
    b. the aggregate-supply curve shifts to the left by more than $16 billion.
    c. the aggregate-demand curve shifts to the right by more than $16 billion.
    d. the aggregate-demand curve shifts to the left by more than $16 billion.

16. When an increase in government purchases increases the income of some people, and those people spend some of that increase in income on additional consumer goods, we have seen a demonstration of
    a. the multiplier effect.
    b. the investment accelerator.
    c. the crowding-out effect.
    d. supply-side economics.
    e. none of the above.

17. When an increase in government purchases causes firms to purchase additional plant and equipment, we have seen a demonstration of
    a. the multiplier effect.
    b. the investment accelerator.
    c. the crowding-out effect.
    d. supply-side economics.
    e. none of the above.

18. Which of the following is an automatic stabilizer?
    a. military spending
    b. spending on public schools
    c. unemployment benefits
    d. spending on the space shuttle
    e. All of the above are automatic stabilizers.

19. Which of the following statements about stabilization policy is true?
    a. In the short run, a decision by the Fed to increase the targeted money supply is essentially the same as a decision to increase the targeted interest rate.
    b. Congress has veto power over the monetary policy decisions of the Fed.
    c. Long lags enhance the ability of policymakers to "fine-tune" the economy.
    d. Many economists prefer automatic stabilizers because they affect the economy with a shorter lag than activist stabilization policy.
    e. All of the above are true.

20. Which of the following best describes how an increase in the money supply shifts aggregate demand?
    a. The money supply shifts right, the interest rate rises, investment decreases, and aggregate demand shifts left.
    b. The money supply shifts right, the interest rate falls, investment increases, and aggregate demand shifts right.
    c. The money supply shifts right, prices rise, spending falls, and aggregate demand shifts left.
    d. The money supply shifts right, prices fall, spending increases, and aggregate demand shifts right.

ADVANCED CRITICAL THINKING

You are watching a nightly network news broadcast. The opening report is a story about today's meeting of the Fed's Federal Open Market Committee. The business correspondent reports that the Fed raised interest rates by a quarter of a percent today to head off future inflation. The report then moves to interviews with prominent politicians. The response of a member of Congress to the Fed's move is negative. She says, "The Consumer Price Index has not increased, yet the Fed is restricting growth in the economy, supposedly to fight inflation. My constituents will want to know why they are going to have to pay more when they get a loan, and I don't have a good answer. I think this is an outrage and I think Congress should have hearings on the Fed's policy-making powers."

1. What interest rate did the Fed raise?

   _____

2. State the Fed's policy in terms of the money supply.

   _____

   _____

3. Why might the Fed raise interest rates before the CPI starts to rise?

   _____

   _____

   _____

   _____

4. Many economists believe that the Fed needs to be independent of politics. Use the congresswoman's statement to explain why so many economists argue for Fed independence.

   _____

   _____

   _____

   _____

SOLUTIONS

Terms and Definitions

_4_ Theory of liquidity preference

_8_ Liquidity

_2_ Federal funds rate

_10_ Fiscal policy

_7_ Multiplier effect

_3_ Investment accelerator

_9_ Marginal propensity to consume, or _MPC_

_1_ Crowding-out effect

_6_ Stabilization policy

_5_ Automatic stabilizers

Practice Problems

1. a. Decrease the money supply
   b. Increase the money supply
   c. Increase the money supply
   d. Increase the money supply
   e. Increase the money supply
2. a. Increase interest rates
   b. Decrease interest rates
   c. Decrease interest rates
   d. Decrease interest rates
   e. Decrease interest rates
   f. In the short run, with prices sticky or fixed, an increase in the money supply implies a reduction in interest rates and a decrease in the money supply implies an increase in interest rates.
3. a. Increase spending, decrease taxes
   b. Increase spending, decrease taxes
   c. Decrease spending, increase taxes
   d. Increase spending, decrease taxes
4. a. Multiplier = 1/(1 − 0.75) = 4; 100/4 = $25 billion.
   b. Multiplier = 1/(1 − 0.80) = 5; 100/5 = $20 billion.
   c. More, because as the government spends more, investors spend less so aggregate demand won't increase by as much as the multiplier suggests.
   d. More of a problem. Government spending raises interest rates. The more sensitive investment is to the interest rate, the more it is reduced or crowded out by government spending.
   e. More likely to allow the economy to adjust on its own because if the economy adjusts

before the impact of the fiscal policy is felt, the fiscal policy will be destabilizing.

5. a. It lowers interest rates because, in the short run, with prices sticky or fixed, money demand is unchanging. Thus, an increase in the money supply requires a decrease in interest rates to induce people to hold the additional money.
   b. It has no effect because, in the long run, the increase in spending causes a proportional increase in prices, output is fixed at the natural rate, money is neutral, and interest rates are determined by the supply and demand for loanable funds, which have not changed.
   c. No. Prices are likely to be sticky in the short run and flexible in the long run.

Short-Answer Questions

1. Because the quantity of money is fixed at whatever value the Fed chooses and this quantity is not dependent on the interest rate.
2. The interest rate is the opportunity cost of money since money earns no rate of return. Thus, an increase in the interest rate causes people to economize on cash balances and hold more wealth in interest-bearing bonds.
3. An increase in the price level shifts money demand to the right, increases the interest rate, and decreases investment.
4. The money supply shifts right, the interest rate decreases, investment increases at each price level, which is a rightward shift in the aggregate-demand curve.
5. When the government purchases goods, it causes an increase in the incomes of the sellers. They spend some percent of their new higher income on goods and services, raising others' incomes, and so on. The higher the _MPC_, the greater the percent of new income spent in each round.
6. An increase in government spending raises incomes, shifts money demand right, raises the interest rate, and reduces investment.
7. By less than $10 billion because the crowding-out effect, which reduces the shift in aggregate demand, more than offsets the multiplier effect, which amplifies the shift.
8. It causes an increase in aggregate supply by increasing the incentive to work.
9. Permanent, because it improves the financial condition of the household more, and thus, they spend more.

10. Income tax collections fall during a recession, and government spending on welfare and unemployment benefits rises. It would cause the government to raise other taxes and lower other spending. More severe.

True/False Questions

1. F; an increase in the interest rate decreases the quantity demanded of money because it raises the opportunity cost of holding money.
2. T
3. T
4. T
5. F; an increase in the money supply decreases the interest rate, increases investment, and shifts aggregate demand to the right.
6. F; the Fed should increase the money supply.
7. T
8. T
9. F; the value of the multiplier is 5.
10. T
11. F; the aggregate-demand curve shifts to the right by less than $10 billion.
12. F; policymakers should increase government spending and decrease taxes.
13. T
14. F; in the short run, the interest rate is determined by money demand and money supply, while in the long run, it is determined by the loanable-funds market.
15. T

Multiple-Choice Questions

1. b
2. c
3. a
4. d
5. a
6. d
7. a
8. c
9. c
10. b
11. a
12. d
13. c
14. b
15. c
16. a
17. b
18. c
19. d
20. b

Advanced Critical Thinking

1. The federal funds rate.
2. They decreased the money supply (or lowered its growth rate).
3. Because monetary policy acts on the economy with a lag. If the Fed waits until inflation has arrived, the effect of its policy will arrive too late. Thus, the Fed may wish to respond to its forecast of inflation.
4. Politicians must be responsive to the short-term needs of voters. Monetary policy must take a long-term view and make politically painful decisions when the economy is overheating (when output is above the long-run natural rate). In this case, there is pressure for prices to rise in the future so the standard policy response is to contract aggregate demand now. It is unpopular to "take the punch bowl away just as the party gets going."

35

The Short-Run Trade-off between Inflation and Unemployment

GOALS

In this chapter you will

- Learn why policymakers face a short-run trade-off between inflation and unemployment

- Consider why the inflation-unemployment trade-off disappears in the long run

- See how supply shocks can shift the inflation-unemployment trade-off

- Consider the short-run cost of reducing the rate of inflation

- See how policymakers' credibility affects the cost of reducing inflation

CHAPTER OVERVIEW

Context and Purpose

Chapter 35 is the final chapter in a three-chapter sequence on the economy's short-run fluctuations around its long-term trend. Chapter 33 introduced aggregate supply and aggregate demand. Chapter 34 developed how monetary and fiscal policy affect aggregate demand. Both Chapters 33 and 34 addressed the relationship between the price level and output. Chapter 35 will concentrate on a similar relationship between inflation and unemployment.

The purpose of Chapter 35 is to trace the history of economists' thinking about the relationship between inflation and unemployment. You will see why there is a temporary trade-off between inflation and unemployment and why there is no permanent trade-off. This result is an extension of the results produced by the model of aggregate supply and aggregate demand where a change in the price level induced by a change in aggregate demand temporarily alters output but has no permanent impact on output.

Chapter Review

Introduction   Since both inflation and unemployment are undesirable, the sum of inflation and unemployment has been termed the *misery index*. Inflation and unemployment are independent in the long run because unemployment is determined by features of the labor market while inflation is determined by money growth. However, in the short run, inflation and unemployment are related because an increase in aggregate demand temporarily increases inflation and output while it lowers unemployment. In this chapter, we trace the history of our understanding of the relationship between unemployment and inflation.

The Phillips Curve

In 1958, a British economist named A. W. Phillips found a negative relationship between inflation and unemployment. That is, years of high inflation are associated with low unemployment. This negative relationship has been found for other countries, including the United States, and has been termed the **Phillips curve.** The Phillips curve

OUTCOMES

After accomplishing these goals, you should be able to

- Draw a graph of a short-run Phillips curve

- Draw a graph of a long-run Phillips curve

- Show the relationship between a shift in the short-run aggregate-supply curve and a shift in the short-run Phillips curve

- Explain the sacrifice ratio

- Explain why more than rational expectations are needed to reduce inflation costlessly appears to offer policymakers a menu of inflation and unemployment choices. To have lower unemployment, one need only choose a higher rate of inflation.

The model of aggregate supply and aggregate demand can explain the relationship described by the Phillips curve. The Phillips curve shows the combinations of inflation and unemployment that arise in the short run as shifts in the aggregate-demand curve move along a short-run aggregate-supply curve. For example, an increase in aggregate demand moves the economy along a short-run aggregate-supply curve to a higher price level, a higher level of output, and a lower level of unemployment. Since prices in the previous period are now fixed, a higher price level in the current period implies a higher rate of inflation, which is now associated with a lower rate of unemployment. This can be seen in Exhibit 1. An increase in aggregate demand, which moves the economy from point A to point B in panel (a), is associated with a movement along the short-run Phillips curve from point A to point B.

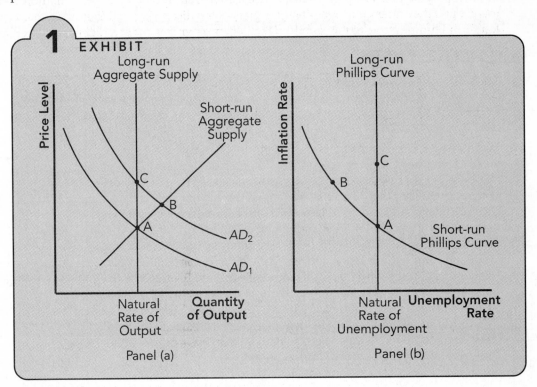

1 EXHIBIT

Panel (a)

Panel (b)

Shifts in the Phillips Curve: The Role of Expectations

In 1968, U.S. economists Friedman and Phelps argued that the Phillips curve is not a menu policymakers can exploit. This is because, in the long run, money is neutral and has no real effects. Money growth just causes proportional changes in prices and incomes and should have no impact on unemployment. Therefore, the long-run Phillips curve should be vertical at the *natural rate of unemployment*—the rate of unemployment to which the economy naturally gravitates.

A vertical long-run Phillips curve corresponds to a vertical long-run aggregate-supply curve. As Exhibit 1 illustrates, in the long run, an increase in the money supply shifts aggregate demand to the right and moves the economy from point A to point C in panel (a). The corresponding Phillips curve is found in panel (b) where an increase in money growth increases inflation, but because money is neutral in the long run, prices and incomes move together and inflation fails to affect unemployment. Thus, the economy moves from point A to point C in panel (b) and traces out the long-run Phillips curve.

Friedman and Phelps used the phrase "natural" rate of unemployment, not because it is either desirable or constant, but because it is beyond the influence of monetary policy. Changes in labor market policies such as changes in minimum-wage laws and unemployment insurance that lower the natural rate of unemployment shift the long-run Phillips curve to the left and the long-run aggregate-supply curve to the right.

Even though Friedman and Phelps argued that the long-run Phillips curve is vertical, they argued that, in the short run, inflation could have a substantial impact on unemployment. Their reasoning is similar to that surrounding the short-run aggregate-supply curve in that they assume, in the short run, *price expectations* are fixed. If price expectations are fixed in the short run, an increase in aggregate demand causes inflation, temporarily increases output, and lowers unemployment below the natural rate. For example, according to the sticky-price theory of short-run aggregate supply, nominal wages are set based on fixed price expectations. When actual prices exceed expected prices, firms are more profitable, they expand output and employment, and unemployment is reduced. In Exhibit 2, this is a movement from point A to point B. However, *in the long run, people adjust to the higher rate of inflation by raising their expectations of inflation (and demanding higher wages) and the short-run Phillips curve shifts upward*. The economy moves from point B to point C with higher inflation but no change in unemployment. Thus, policymakers face a short-run trade-off between inflation and unemployment, but if they attempt to exploit it, the relationship disappears and they arrive back on the vertical long-run Phillips curve at the natural rate of unemployment but at a higher rate of inflation.

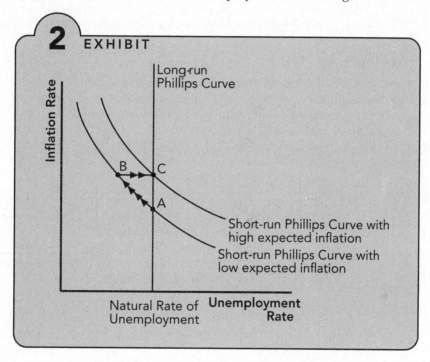

The analysis of Friedman and Phelps can be summarized by the following equation:

$$\text{Unemployment Rate} = \text{Natural Rate of Unemployment} - a\left(\text{Actual Inflation} - \text{Expected Inflation}\right)$$

This says that for any given expected inflation rate, if actual inflation exceeds expected inflation, unemployment will fall below the natural rate by an amount that depends on the parameter a. However, in the long run, people learn to expect the inflation that actually exists, and the unemployment rate will equal the natural rate.

Friedman and Phelps proposed the **natural-rate hypothesis,** which states that unemployment eventually returns to its natural rate, regardless of inflation. While controversial, it proved to be true. During the 1960s, expansionary monetary and fiscal policies steadily increased the rate of inflation and unemployment fell. However, in the early 1970s, people raised their expectations of inflation and the unemployment rate returned to the natural rate—about 5 or 6 percent.

Shifts in the Phillips Curve: The Role of Supply Shocks

The short-run Phillips curve can also shift due to a supply shock. A **supply shock** is an event that directly alters firms' costs and prices, shifting the economy's aggregate-supply curve and Phillips curve. A supply shock occurred in 1974 when OPEC raised oil prices. This act raised the cost of production and shifted the U.S. short-run aggregate-supply curve to the left, causing prices to rise and output to fall, or *stagflation*. Since inflation has increased and unemployment has increased, this corresponds to a rightward (upward) shift in the short-run Phillips curve. Policymakers now face a less favorable trade-off between inflation and unemployment. That is, policymakers must accept a higher inflation rate for each unemployment rate, or a higher unemployment rate for each inflation rate. Also, policymakers now have a difficult choice because if they reduce aggregate demand to fight inflation, they will further increase unemployment. If they increase aggregate demand to reduce unemployment, they further increase inflation.

If the supply shock raises expected inflation, the Phillips-curve shift is "permanent." If it does not raise expected inflation, the shift is temporary. In the United States during the 1970s, the Fed accommodated two adverse aggregate supply shocks by increasing aggregate demand to keep output from falling. This caused expected inflation to rise, and the rightward (upward) shift in the Phillips curve was "permanent." By 1980, inflation was 9 percent and unemployment was 7 percent.

Independent central banks are less likely than politicians to be tempted to exploit a short-run Phillips curve. Therefore, independent central banks help keep inflationary expectations low and provide a more favorable inflation-unemployment combination.

The Cost of Reducing Inflation

In October 1979, Fed Chairman Paul Volcker chose to pursue a policy of *disinflation*—a reduction in the rate of inflation. A reduction in the money supply reduces aggregate demand, reduces production, and increases unemployment. This is shown in Exhibit 3 as a movement from point A to point B. Over time, expected inflation falls and the short-run Phillips curve shifts downward and the economy moves from point B to point C.

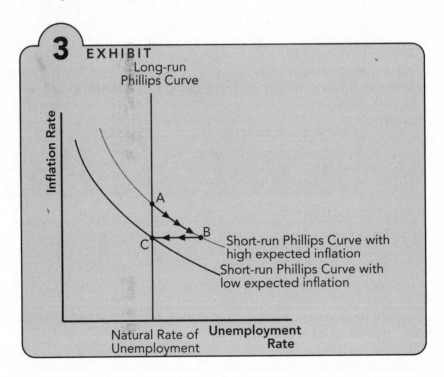

3 EXHIBIT

Long-run Phillips Curve

Inflation Rate

A

B — Short-run Phillips Curve with high expected inflation

C

Short-run Phillips Curve with low expected inflation

Natural Rate of Unemployment

Unemployment Rate

The cost of reducing inflation is a period of unemployment and lost output. The **sacrifice ratio** is the number of percentage points of annual output that is lost to reduce inflation one percentage point. The amount of output lost depends on the slope of the Phillips curve and how fast people lower their expectations of inflation.

Some economists estimated the sacrifice ratio to be about five, which is very large. Supporters of a theory called **rational expectations** suggested that the cost of disinflation could be much smaller and may be zero. Rational expectations suggest that people optimally use all available information, including information about government policies, when forecasting the future. Thus, an announced policy of disinflation *that is credible* could move the economy from point A to point C without traveling through point B. Volcker announced a disinflationary policy in late 1979 and reduced inflation from 10 percent to 4 percent by 1984 but at the cost of a substantial increase in unemployment. Note, however, that the increase in unemployment was less than that predicted by the estimated sacrifice ratio. The rational expectations theory may not be accurate, or people may not have believed the policy announcement.

Monetary policy under Alan Greenspan did not repeat the mistakes of the 1960s when excessive aggregate demand pushed unemployment below the natural rate.

There are a variety of explanations regarding why the United States experienced low unemployment and low inflation in the 1990s (i.e., explanations of why the Phillips curve has shifted left):

- Tight monetary policy reduced inflation expectations

- Commodity prices declined (including oil prices)

- Labor markets included more older workers with lower unemployment rates

- Technological advances increased productivity

Some economists argue that the Fed should publicly commit to an inflation target of about 2 percent. This policy would (1) institutionalize the successful anti-inflationary preferences of Volcker and Greenspan; (2) focus monetary policy on price stability—something it can influence; (3) reduce uncertainty about future Fed policy; and (4) prevent deflation.

Helpful Hints

1. Short-run and long-run Phillips curves are almost a mirror image of short-run and long-run aggregate-supply curves. Look at the supply curves that appear in Exhibit 1. Notice the aggregate-supply curves in panel (a). Compare them to the Phillips curves in panel (b). They appear to be mirror images of each other. The long-run aggregate-supply curve is vertical because, in the long run, an increase in the price level is met by a proportionate increase in all prices and incomes so there is no incentive to alter production. Since an increase in prices has no effect on output in the long run, it has no effect on unemployment, and the long-run Phillips curve is vertical in panel (b). In the short run with price expectations fixed, an increase in the price level provides an incentive for firms to increase production, causing the short-run aggregate-supply curve to be positively sloped in panel (a). When output rises, unemployment tends to fall, so the short-run Phillips curve is negatively sloped in panel (b). In summary, since both graphs employ some measure of prices on the vertical axis, and since each graph uses real measures of economic activity that are negatively correlated on their respective horizontal axes (an increase in output is associated with a decrease in unemployment), then aggregate-supply curves and Phillips curves should "mirror" each other.

2. To understand the short-run Phillips curve, review short-run aggregate supply. To gain confidence deriving and shifting short-run Phillips curves, review the sources to the positive slope of the short-run aggregate-supply curve in Chapter 33. There you will be reminded that there are a number of reasons why a short-run aggregate-supply curve slopes positively—misperceptions about relative price, sticky wages, and sticky prices. Since short-run aggregate-supply curves and Phillips curves are mirror images of each other, the very same reasons that produce a positive slope in aggregate supply produce a negative slope in the Phillips curve. Also, recall that all three theories of the short-run aggregate-supply curve are based on the assumption of fixed price expectations. When price expectations rise, the short-run aggregate-supply curve shifts left. Correspondingly, since the short-run aggregate-supply curve and the Phillips curve are mirror images, a rise in price expectations shifts the Phillips curve to the right.

3. The Phillips curve establishes a relationship between inflation and unemployment, but it does not establish causation. Reading the Phillips curve from the unemployment axis to the inflation axis suggests that when unemployment is unusually low, the labor market is tight and wages and prices start to rise more quickly.

4. Estimates of the natural rate of unemployment vary widely, causing policymakers to disagree on the appropriate monetary and fiscal policies. When looking at a Phillips curve graph or the

model of aggregate supply and aggregate demand, it appears as if policymakers should always know whether to expand or contract aggregate demand or whether to leave aggregate demand alone. This is because we can see whether the economy is operating above or below the long-run natural rate that we have chosen on the graph. In reality, however, the natural rate is very difficult to measure and policymakers are uncertain whether the economy is actually operating above or below the natural rate. For example, if the economy is currently operating at 6 percent unemployment, the economy is operating below capacity if the natural rate of unemployment is 5 percent, at capacity if the natural rate is 6 percent, and above capacity if the natural rate is 7 percent. Each situation might suggest a different stabilization policy, even though the actual rate of unemployment is unchanged at 6 percent.

Terms and Definitions

Choose a definition for each key term.

Key Terms

_____ Misery index

_____ Phillips curve

_____ Natural rate of unemployment

_____ Natural-rate hypothesis

_____ Disinflation

_____ Supply shock

_____ Sacrifice ratio

_____ Rational expectations

Definitions

1. A reduction in the rate of inflation

2. The normal rate of unemployment toward which the economy gravitates

3. The theory that suggests that people optimally use all available information, including about government policies, when forecasting the future

4. The sum of inflation and unemployment

5. The theory that unemployment returns to its natural rate, regardless of inflation

6. The short-run trade-off between inflation and unemployment

7. The number of percentage points of annual output that is lost in order to reduce inflation one percentage point

8. An event that directly alters firms' costs and prices, shifting the economy's aggregate-supply curve and, thus, the Phillips curve

PROBLEMS AND SHORT-ANSWER QUESTIONS

Practice Problems

1. Describe the initial effect of the following events on the short-run and long-run Phillips curve. That is, describe the movements along a given curve or the direction of the shift in the curve.

   a. An increase in expected inflation

   _____

   _____

   b. An increase in the price of imported oil

   _____

   _____

c. An increase in the money supply

_____

_____

d. A decrease in government spending

_____

_____

e. A decrease in the minimum wage, which lowers the natural rate

_____

_____

2. Use the Phillips curves in Exhibit 4 to answer the following questions.

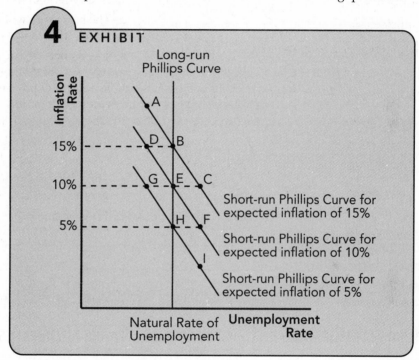

a. At what point is the economy located if people expect 10 percent inflation and inflation actually is 10 percent?

_____

b. Referring to *a* above, is unemployment above, below, or equal to the natural rate?

_____

c. At what point is the economy located if people expect 10 percent inflation and the actual rate of inflation is 15 percent?

_____

d. Suppose the economy is operating at point D. Over time, in which direction will people revise their expectations of inflation—up or down?

_____

e. Suppose the economy is operating at point D. As people revise their expectations of inflation, in which direction will the short-run Phillips curve shift—right or left?

_____

f. Suppose the economy is operating at point E. In the short run, a sudden decrease in aggregate demand will move the economy toward which point?

_____

g. Suppose the economy is operating at point E. In the long run, a decrease in government spending will tend to move the economy toward which point?

_____

h. Suppose people expect 5 percent inflation. If inflation actually ends up being 10 percent, in which direction will unemployment move—above or below the natural rate?

_____

3. Use a Phillips curve graph to answer the following questions. Assume the economy is initially in long-run equilibrium.
   a. What happens to unemployment and inflation in the short run if the Fed increases the growth rate of the money supply?

   _____

   _____

   b. What happens to unemployment and inflation in the long run if the Fed increases the growth rate of the money supply?

   _____

   _____

   c. Can printing money keep unemployment below the natural rate? Explain.

   _____

   _____

   d. What is the end result of a central bank repeatedly attempting to hold unemployment below the natural rate with expansionary monetary policy? Explain.

   _____

   _____

4. Suppose the economy is operating at the natural rate of unemployment with a high rate of inflation (point A in Exhibit 5). Suppose the Federal Reserve announces a sudden monetary contraction to reduce inflation. Shown below are two possible paths the economy might take to adjust to the new lower rate of money growth. Choose the path that best depicts what might happen in each of the following cases and explain your reasoning.

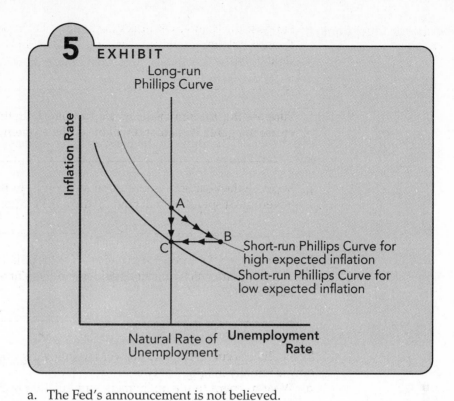

5 EXHIBIT

Long-run
Phillips Curve

Inflation Rate

A

C

B

Short-run Phillips Curve for
high expected inflation

Short-run Phillips Curve for
low expected inflation

Natural Rate of
Unemployment

**Unemployment
Rate**

a. The Fed's announcement is not believed.

_____

_____

b. The Fed's announcement is believed and expectations of inflation are adjust-
    ed quickly.

_____

_____

c. The Fed's announcement is believed but all workers have long-term wage
    contracts that cannot be renegotiated.

_____

_____

d. Which of the above cases (*a*, *b*, or *c*) best describes what would happen if, in
    the past, the Fed had repeatedly announced that inflation is its number one
    priority, but it failed to actually engage in the threatened monetary contrac-
    tion? Why?

_____

_____

_____

_____

Short-Answer Questions

1. If unemployment is 6 percent and inflation is 5 percent, what is the value of the so-called misery index?

   _____

2. Use the model of aggregate demand and aggregate supply to describe why the short-run Phillips curve is negatively sloped.

   _____

   _____

   _____

3. Use the model of aggregate demand and aggregate supply to describe why the long-run Phillips curve is vertical.

   _____

   _____

   _____

4. Is the short-run Phillips curve actually a menu of inflation and unemployment combinations permanently available to the policymaker? Why or why not?

   _____

   _____

   _____

   _____

5. What is the natural-rate hypothesis?

   _____

   _____

6. If actual inflation exceeds expected inflation, is the unemployment rate above or below the natural rate? Why?

   _____

   _____

7. Which way does the short-run Phillips curve shift when there is an adverse aggregate supply shock such as an increase in the price of imported oil? Why?

   _____

   _____

   _____

   _____

8. Referring to question 7 above, are the trade-offs between unemployment and in-flation that the economy now faces more favorable or less favorable than before the adverse supply shock? Explain.

_____

_____

_____

_____

9. Referring to question 8 above, if the Fed accommodates the adverse supply shock, what have they revealed about the weights they attach to the goals of low infla-tion and low unemployment?

_____

_____

10. If the sacrifice ratio is five, how much will output be reduced in order for inflation to be reduced four percentage points? If people have rational expectations, is the sacrifice ratio likely to be larger or smaller than five? Why?

_____

_____

_____

SELF-TEST

True/False Questions

_____ 1. The Phillips curve illustrates the positive relationship between inflation and unemployment.

_____ 2. If inflation is 4 percent and unemployment is 6 percent, the misery index is 2 percent.

_____ 3. In the short run, an increase in aggregate demand increases prices and output and decreases unemployment.

_____ 4. When unemployment is below the natural rate, the labor market is unusually tight, putting pressure on wages and prices to rise.

_____ 5. An increase in price expectations shifts the Phillips curve upward and makes the inflation-unemployment trade-off less favorable.

_____ 6. An increase in the money supply increases inflation and permanently decreases unemployment.

_____ 7. In the long run, the unemployment rate is independent of inflation and the Phil-lips curve is vertical at the natural rate of unemployment.

_____ 8. When actual inflation exceeds expected inflation, unemployment exceeds the natural rate.

_____ 9. The natural-rate hypothesis suggests that, in the long run, unemployment returns to its natural rate, regardless of inflation.

_____ 10. An adverse supply shock, such as an increase in the price of imported oil, shifts the Phillips curve upward and makes the inflation-unemployment trade-off less favorable.

_____ 11. A decrease in unemployment benefits reduces the natural rate of unemployment and shifts the long-run Phillips curve to the right.

_____ 12. An increase in aggregate demand temporarily reduces unemployment, but after people raise their expectations of inflation, unemployment returns to the natural rate.

_____ 13. A sudden monetary contraction moves the economy up a short-run Phillips curve, reducing unemployment and increasing inflation.

_____ 14. If people have rational expectations, an announced monetary contraction by the Fed that is credible could reduce inflation with little or no increase in unemployment.

_____ 15. If the sacrifice ratio is four, a reduction of inflation from 9 percent to 5 percent requires a reduction in output of 8 percent.

Multiple-Choice Questions

1. The misery index, which some commentators suggest measures the health of the economy, is
   a. the sum of the growth rate of output and the inflation rate.
   b. the sum of the unemployment rate and the inflation rate.
   c. the sum of the Dow Jones Industrial Average and the federal funds rate.
   d. the sum of the natural rate of unemployment and the actual rate of unemployment.

2. The original Phillips curve illustrates
   a. the trade-off between inflation and unemployment.
   b. the positive relationship between inflation and unemployment.
   c. the trade-off between output and unemployment.
   d. the positive relationship between output and unemployment.

3. The Phillips curve is an extension of the model of aggregate supply and aggregate demand because, in the short run, an increase in aggregate demand increases prices and
   a. decreases growth.
   b. decreases inflation.
   c. increases unemployment.
   d. decreases unemployment.

4. Along a short-run Phillips curve,
   a. a higher rate of growth in output is associated with a lower unemployment rate.
   b. a higher rate of growth in output is associated with a higher unemployment rate.
   c. a higher rate of inflation is associated with a lower unemployment rate.
   d. a higher rate of inflation is associated with a higher unemployment rate.

5. If, in the long run, people adjust their price expectations so that all prices and incomes move proportionately to an increase in the price level, then the long-run Phillips curve
   a. is positively sloped.
   b. is negatively sloped.
   c. is vertical.
   d. has a slope that is determined by how fast people adjust their price expectations.

6. According to the Phillips curve, in the short run, if policymakers choose an expansionary policy to lower the rate of unemployment,
   a. the economy will experience a decrease in inflation.
   b. the economy will experience an increase in inflation.
   c. inflation will be unaffected if price expectations are unchanging.
   d. none of the above is true.

7. An increase in expected inflation
   a. shifts the short-run Phillips curve upward, and the unemployment-inflation trade-off is less favorable.
   b. shifts the short-run Phillips curve downward, and the unemployment-inflation trade-off is more favorable.
   c. shifts the short-run Phillips curve upward, and the unemployment-inflation trade-off is more favorable.
   d. shifts the short-run Phillips curve downward, and the unemployment-inflation trade-off is less favorable.

8. Which of the following would shift the long-run Phillips curve to the right?
   a. an increase in the price of foreign oil
   b. an increase in expected inflation
   c. an increase in aggregate demand
   d. an increase in the minimum wage

9. When actual inflation exceeds expected inflation,
   a. unemployment is greater than the natural rate of unemployment.
   b. unemployment is less than the natural rate of unemployment.
   c. unemployment is equal to the natural rate of unemployment.
   d. people will reduce their expectations of inflation in the future.

10. A decrease in the price of foreign oil
    a. shifts the short-run Phillips curve upward, and the unemployment-inflation trade-off is more favorable.
    b. shifts the short-run Phillips curve upward, and the unemployment-inflation trade-off is less favorable.
    c. shifts the short-run Phillips curve downward, and the unemployment-inflation trade-off is more favorable.
    d. shifts the short-run Phillips curve downward, and the unemployment-inflation trade-off is less favorable.

11. The natural-rate hypothesis argues that
    a. unemployment is always above the natural rate.
    b. unemployment is always below the natural rate.
    c. unemployment is always equal to the natural rate.
    d. in the long run, the unemployment rate returns to the natural rate, regardless of inflation.

Use Exhibit 6 to answer questions 12 through 17.

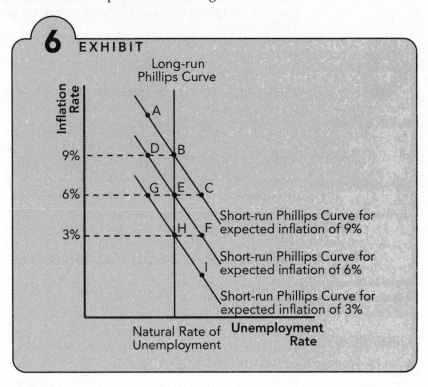

12. If people in the economy expect inflation to be 3 percent and inflation is 3 percent, the economy is operating at point
    a. A.
    b. B.
    c. C.
    d. D.
    e. E.
    f. F.
    g. G.
    h. H.
    i. I.

13. If people in the economy expect inflation to be 6 percent but inflation turns out to be 3 percent, the economy is operating at point
    a. A.
    b. B.
    c. C.
    d. D.
    e. E.
    f. F.
    g. G.
    h. H.
    i. I.

14. Suppose the economy is in long-run equilibrium at point E. A sudden increase in government spending should move the economy in the direction of point
    a. A.
    b. B.
    c. C.
    d. D.
    e. E.
    f. F.
    g. G.
    h. H.
    i. I.

15. Suppose the economy is operating at point D. As people revise their price expectations,
    a. the short-run Phillips curve will shift in the direction of the short-run Phillips curve associated with an expectation of 3 percent inflation.
    b. the short-run Phillips curve will shift in the direction of the short-run Phillips curve associated with an expectation of 6 percent inflation.
    c. the short-run Phillips curve will shift in the direction of the short-run Phillips curve associated with an expectation of 9 percent inflation.
    d. the long-run Phillips curve will shift to the left.

16. Suppose the economy is operating in long-run equilibrium at point E. An unexpected monetary contraction will move the economy in the direction of point
    a. A.
    b. B.
    c. C.
    d. D.
    e. E.
    f. F.
    g. G.
    h. H.
    i. I.

17. Suppose the economy is operating in long-run equilibrium at point E. *In the long run,* a monetary contraction will move the economy in the direction of point
    a. A.
    b. B.
    c. C.
    d. D.
    e. E.
    f. F.
    g. G.
    h. H.
    i. I.

18. If people have rational expectations, a monetary policy contraction that is announced and is credible could
    a. reduce inflation but it would increase unemployment by an unusually large amount.
    b. reduce inflation with little or no increase in unemployment.
    c. increase inflation but it would decrease unemployment by an unusually large amount.
    d. increase inflation with little or no decrease in unemployment.

19. If the sacrifice ratio is five, a reduction in inflation from 7 percent to 3 percent would require
     a. a reduction in output of 5 percent.
     b. a reduction in output of 15 percent.
     c. a reduction in output of 20 percent.
     d. a reduction in output of 35 percent.

20. If the Fed were to continuously use expansionary monetary policy in an attempt to hold unemployment below the natural rate, the long-run result would be
     a. an increase in the level of output.
     b. a decrease in the unemployment rate.
     c. an increase in the rate of inflation.
     d. all of the above.

ADVANCED CRITICAL THINKING

A worldwide drought has reduced food production. Inflation has increased; unemployment has risen above the natural rate. Americans are frustrated with their government. Your roommate says, "This economic mess has got to be somebody's fault—probably the president or Congress. A year ago, both inflation and unemployment were lower. We need to vote in some policymakers that know how to get rid of this inflation and unemployment."

1. Whose fault is the stagflation that is present in the economy?

     _____

2. Are the current inflation and unemployment choices facing the economy better or worse than before the supply shock? What has happened to the short-run Phillips curve?

     _____

     _____

3. If policymakers *increase* aggregate demand in response to the supply shock, in what direction will the economy move along the new short-run Phillips curve? What will happen to inflation and unemployment?

     _____

     _____

4. If policymakers *decrease* aggregate demand in response to the supply shock, in what direction will the economy move along the new short-run Phillips curve? What will happen to inflation and unemployment?

     _____

     _____

5. Is there a policy that can immediately reduce both inflation and unemployment? Explain.

     _____

     _____

SOLUTIONS

Terms and Definitions

_4_ Misery index

_6_ Phillips curve

_2_ Natural-rate of unemployment

_5_ Natural rate hypothesis

_1_ Disinflation

_8_ Supply shock

_7_ Sacrifice ratio

_3_ Rational expectations

Practice Problems

1. a. Shifts short-run Phillips curve to the right (upward).
   b. Shifts short-run Phillips curve to the right (upward).
   c. Move up the short-run Phillips curve.
   d. Move down the short-run Phillips curve.
   e. Long-run and short-run Phillips curves shift left (downward).

2. a. E.
   b. Equal to the natural rate.
   c. D.
   d. Up.
   e. Right.
   f. F.
   g. H.
   h. Below the natural rate.

3. a. Inflation increases, unemployment decreases.
   b. Inflation increases, unemployment stays at the natural rate.
   c. No. Unemployment temporarily decreases, but as people grow to expect the higher inflation, unemployment returns to the natural rate.
   d. Continued attempts to move unemployment below the natural rate simply cause inflation.

4. a. Economy moves from A to B because people fail to reduce their price expectations and wage demands, so unemployment rises as inflation falls.
   b. Economy moves from A to C because people reduce their prices and wages proportionately.
   c. Economy moves from A to B because people are unable to actually reduce some of their wages and prices, so unemployment rises as inflation falls.

   d. Case _a_, because people are rational to distrust a policymaker that has previously been untruthful.

Short-Answer Questions

1. 11 percent.
2. An increase in aggregate demand increases prices and output along the short-run aggregate-supply curve, which reduces unemployment. Prices have increased and unemployment has decreased.
3. An increase in aggregate demand increases prices, but output remains at the natural rate due to a vertical long-run aggregate-supply curve. Prices have increased but unemployment remains at the natural rate.
4. No. When inflation increases above expected inflation, unemployment temporarily decreases. However, after people revise their price expectations upward and ask for higher wages, the Phillips curve shifts upward (to the right).
5. Unemployment returns to the natural rate in the long run, regardless of inflation.
6. Below, because if prices are higher than expected, additional output is produced and additional people are employed, reducing unemployment.
7. Aggregate supply shifts left showing lower production at each price. Thus, the Phillips curve shifts right (upward) showing more unemployment at each rate of inflation.
8. Less favorable. Now, at each level of unemployment, inflation is higher, or at each rate of inflation, unemployment is higher.
9. The Fed is more concerned with low unemployment.
10. 20 percent. Smaller because they will reduce their price expectations more quickly, shifting the Phillips curve to the left.

True/False Questions

1. F; the Phillips curve illustrates the negative relationship between inflation and unemployment.
2. F; the misery index is 10 percent.
3. T
4. T
5. T
6. F; an increase in the money supply may temporarily decrease unemployment.
7. T
8. F; when actual inflation exceeds expected inflation, unemployment is below the natural rate.
9. T

10. T
11. F; it shifts the long-run Phillips curve to the left.
12. T
13. F; a sudden monetary contraction moves the economy down a short-run Phillips curve, increasing unemployment and reducing inflation.
14. T
15. F; output must be reduced by $4 \times 4\% = 16\%$.

Multiple-Choice Questions

1. b
2. a
3. d
4. c
5. c
6. b
7. a
8. d
9. b
10. c
11. d
12. h
13. f
14. d
15. c
16. f
17. h
18. b
19. c
20. c

Advanced Critical Thinking

1. No one's. It was an act of nature.
2. Worse because the short-run Phillips curve has shifted upward.
3. The economy moves upward along the new short-run Phillips curve. Unemployment will be reduced, but inflation will be increased.
4. The economy moves downward along the new short-run Phillips curve. Inflation will be reduced, but unemployment will be increased.
5. No, the economy faces trade-offs in the short run. A policy that reduces inflation increases unemployment. A policy that reduces unemployment increases inflation.

Five Debates over Macroeconomic Policy

GOALS

In this chapter you will

- Consider whether policymakers should try to stabilize the economy

- Consider whether monetary policy should be made by rule rather than by discretion

- Consider whether the central bank should aim for zero inflation

- Consider whether the government should balance its budget

- Consider whether the tax laws should be reformed to encourage saving

OUTCOMES

After accomplishing these goals, you should be able to

- Give an example of a macroeconomic policy response that "leans against the wind"

- Explain what is meant by the "time inconsistency of policy"

- List the costs of inflation

- Explain the benefits of reducing the budget deficit

- Explain why a consumption tax encourages saving but enhances economic inequality

CHAPTER OVERVIEW

Context and Purpose

Chapter 36 is the final chapter in the text. It addresses five unresolved issues in macroeconomics, each of which is central to current political debates. The chapter can be studied all at once, or portions of the chapter can be studied in conjunction with prior chapters that deal with the related material.

The purpose of Chapter 36 is to provide both sides of five leading debates over macroeconomic policy. It employs information and tools that you have accumulated in your study of this text. This chapter may help you take a position on the issues addressed, or at least, it may help you understand the reasoning of others who have taken a position.

Chapter Review

Introduction This chapter presents both sides of five leading debates over macroeconomic policy. These issues are central to current political debates.

Should Monetary and Fiscal Policymakers Try to Stabilize the Economy?

Pro: Policymakers Should Try to Stabilize the Economy. Pessimism on the part of households and firms reduces aggregate demand and causes a recession. The resulting reduction in output and the increase in unemployment are a waste of resources. This waste of resources is unnecessary because the government has the power to *"lean against the wind"* and stabilize aggregate demand by, in this case, increasing government spending, reducing taxes, and increasing the money supply. If aggregate demand is excessive, these policies can be reversed.

Con: Policymakers Should Not Try to Stabilize the Economy. Monetary and fiscal policy affect the economy with a substantial lag. Monetary policy affects interest rates, which may take six months or more to affect residential and business investment spending. A change in fiscal policy involves a long political process. Because forecasting is difficult and because many shocks are unpredictable, stabilization policy must be based on educated guesses about future economic conditions. Mistakes can make activist policy destabilizing. The first rule of policy should be to "do no harm" so policymakers should refrain from intervening often in the economy.

Should Monetary Policy Be Made by Rule Rather than by Discretion?

Recall, every six weeks the Federal Open Market Committee sets monetary policy by choosing an interest rate target and adjusting the money supply to reach that target. At present, the FOMC sets monetary policy with almost complete discretion.

Pro: Monetary Policy Should Be Made by Rule.   There are two problems with *discretionary policy*.

- First, discretionary policy does not limit incompetence and abuse of power. A central bank abuses its power when it manipulates monetary policy to favor a particular political candidate. It can increase the money supply prior to an election to benefit the incumbent and the resulting inflation doesn't show up until after the election. This creates what is known as the *political business cycle*.

- Second, discretionary policy might lead to more inflation than is desirable due to the *time inconsistency of policy*. This occurs because policymakers are tempted to announce a low inflation target, but once people have formed their inflation expectations, policymakers can raise inflation to lower unemployment by exploiting the short-run trade-off between inflation and unemployment. As a result, people expect more inflation than policymakers say they are targeting, which shifts the Phillips curve upward to a less favorable position.

These problems can be avoided by committing the central bank to a policy rule. Congress could require the Fed to increase the money supply by a certain percent each year, say 3 percent, which is just enough to accommodate growth in real output. Alternatively, Congress could require a more active rule whereby the Fed would respond with a specific increase in the money supply if unemployment rose a certain percent above the natural rate.

Con: Monetary Policy Should Not Be Made by Rule.   Discretionary monetary policy is needed because monetary policy must be flexible enough to respond to unforeseen events such as a significant reduction in aggregate demand or a negative supply shock. Further, political business cycles may not exist and time inconsistency problems may be avoided if a central bank's announcements are credible. Finally, if monetary policy were to be guided by a rule, it is unclear what type of rule Congress should impose.

Should the Central Bank Aim for Zero Inflation?

Pro: The Central Bank Should Aim for Zero Inflation.   Inflation imposes the following costs on society:

- shoeleather costs associated with reduced money holdings,

- menu costs associated with frequent adjustment of prices,

- increased variability of relative prices,

- unintended changes in tax liabilities due to non-indexation of the tax code,

- confusion and inconvenience resulting from a changing unit of account,

- arbitrary redistributions of wealth associated with dollar-denominated debts.

The costs associated with reducing inflation to zero are temporary while the benefits of zero inflation are permanent. The costs can be reduced further if an announced policy of zero inflation is credible. The policy would be more credible if Congress made price stability the Fed's primary goal. Finally, zero inflation is the only nonarbitrary target for inflation. All other target levels can be incrementally revised upward.

Con: The Central Bank Should Not Aim for Zero Inflation. There are a number of reasons why the central bank should not aim for zero inflation:

- The benefits of zero inflation are small and uncertain while the costs of achieving it are large. Recall, estimates of the sacrifice ratio are 5 percent of one year's output for a 1 percent reduction in inflation.

- The unemployment and social costs associated with the reduction in inflation are borne by the unskilled and inexperienced—those least able to afford it.

- People tend to dislike inflation because they mistakenly think it erodes their living standards but incomes tend to rise with inflation.

- Many of the costs of inflation can be eliminated without reducing inflation by indexing the tax system and issuing inflation-indexed bonds.

- Reducing inflation costlessly is unlikely to be possible.

- Disinflation leaves permanent scars on the economy because the capital stock is smaller and the unemployed workers have diminished skills.

Should the Government Balance Its Budget?

Pro: The Government Should Balance Its Budget. Government debt places a burden on future generations of taxpayers who must choose to pay higher taxes, cut government spending, or both. Current taxpayers pass the bill for current spending to future taxpayers. Moreover, the macroeconomic effect of a deficit is to reduce national saving by making public saving negative. This increases interest rates, reduces capital investment, reduces productivity and real wages, and thus, reduces future output and income. As a result, deficits raise future taxes and lower future incomes. While deficits are justified during wars and recessions, the increase in the deficit from 1980 through 1995 occurred during peace and prosperity. The most recent deficits may be due to the recession of 2001 and the war on terrorism.

Con: The Government Should Not Balance Its Budget. The problem of government debt is exaggerated. The $16,000 of national debt per person is small compared to expected lifetime earnings of $1.2 million. Also, since some of government spending is on education, reducing the budget deficit by reducing spending on education may not improve the welfare of the next generation. Other government policies redistribute income across generations such as Social Security benefits. If people wish to reverse the intergenerational redistribution of income caused by budget deficits, they need only save more during their lifetime (due to their lower taxes) and leave bequests to their children so they can pay the higher taxes. Finally, government debt can continue to grow forever yet not grow as a percent of GDP as long as the debt fails to grow more quickly than the nation's nominal income. In the United States, that would be a rate of about 5 percent, which equates to about a $235 billion sustainable deficit.

Should the Tax Laws Be Reformed to Encourage Saving?

Pro: The Tax Laws Should Be Reformed to Encourage Saving. A nation's standard of living depends on its productive capability, which in turn, depends on how much it saves and invests. Since people respond to incentives, the government could encourage saving (or stop discouraging saving) by:

- Reducing taxes on the return to saving (interest income).

- Removing the double taxation of capital income from stocks. At present, corporations pay a corporate income tax. Then profits paid to stockholders in the form of dividends are subject to individual income tax.

- Reducing inheritance taxes so people will save and create bequests to the next generation.

- Reducing means-tested government benefits such as welfare and Medicaid. These benefits are currently reduced for those that have been prudent enough to save, which creates a disincentive to save.

- Increasing the availability of tax-advantaged savings accounts such as the Individual Retirement Account (IRA). In these accounts, income that is saved is not taxed until it is withdrawn at retirement.

- Replacing the income tax with a consumption tax. Income that is saved would not be taxed, making all saving equivalent to an IRA.

Con: The Tax Laws Should Not Be Reformed to Encourage Saving. One goal of taxation is to distribute the tax burden fairly. All of the proposals above will increase the incentive to save by reducing taxes on saving. Since high-income people save more than low-income people, this will increase the tax burden on the poor. Also, saving may not be sensitive to changes in the return to saving, so reducing taxes on saving will just enrich the wealthy. This is because a higher return to saving has both a substitution effect and an income effect. An increase in the return to saving will increase saving as people substitute saving for current consumption. However, the income effect suggests that an increase in the return to saving lowers the amount of saving needed to achieve any targeted level of future consumption.

A reduction in the deficit increases public saving and, thus, national saving. This could be accomplished by raising taxes on the wealthy. Indeed, reductions in taxes on saving might backfire by increasing the deficit and reducing national saving.

Helpful Hints

1. A policy that destabilizes the economy moves the economy away from the natural rate of output. Stabilization policy is the use of monetary and fiscal policy to help move the economy toward the natural rate of output. However, if policy lags are long and unpredictable, the economy may have adjusted back to the natural rate (from an aggregate demand or aggregate supply shock) before the impact of the stabilization policy is felt. In this case, the stabilization policy would then move the economy away from the long-run natural rate, and we would consider the policy to be destabilizing.

2. A political business cycle tends to involve both a monetary expansion prior to an election and a monetary contraction after an election. Political business cycles are discussed in the text with regard to the policymaker's behavior prior to elections. That is, prior to an election, a monetary expansion could increase output and decrease unemployment, enhancing the probability of the incumbent's re-election. Since this will tend to cause inflation after the election, however, this type of abuse of power usually involves a monetary contraction after the election to reduce inflationary pressures. Thus, the economy would tend to fluctuate between good economic performance prior to an election and poor economic performance after an election.

3. Zero money growth does not cause zero inflation if real output is growing. Recall, the quantity equation states that $M \times V = P \times Y$, which says that money times velocity equals the price level times real output. If velocity is fixed, and if real output grows at about 3 percent per year, then the money supply would have to grow at 3 percent for prices to remain constant. Therefore, a monetary policy rule requiring the Fed to increase the money supply at 3 percent should generate zero inflation. If output is growing at 3 percent, money growth of 0 percent would actually create deflation.

Terms and Definitions

Choose a definition for each key term.

Key Terms

____ "Leaning against the wind"

____ Destabilizing policy

____ Discretionary policy

____ Political business cycle

____ Time inconsistency of policy

Definitions

1. Economic fluctuations caused by policymakers allying themselves with elected politicians

2. Policy that moves output away from the long-run natural rate

3. Engaging in a policy that stabilizes aggregate demand

4. The discrepancy between policy announcements and policy actions

5. A policy chosen by policymakers who have few guidelines

PROBLEMS AND SHORT-ANSWER QUESTIONS

Practice Problems

1. Suppose a wave of pessimism engulfs consumers and firms, causing them to reduce their expenditures.
   a. Demonstrate this event in Exhibit 1 using the model of aggregate demand and aggregate supply and assuming that the economy was originally in long-run equilibrium.

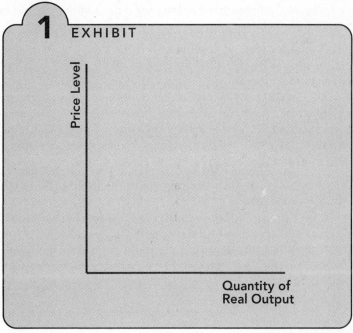

1 EXHIBIT

Price Level

Quantity of Real Output

   b. What is the appropriate activist policy response for monetary and fiscal policy? In which direction would the activist policy shift aggregate demand?

_____

_____

c. Suppose the economy can adjust on its own in two years from the recession described in part *a*. Suppose policymakers choose to use fiscal policy to stabilize the economy but the political battle over taxes and spending takes more than two years. Demonstrate these events in Exhibit 2 using the model of aggregate demand and aggregate supply.

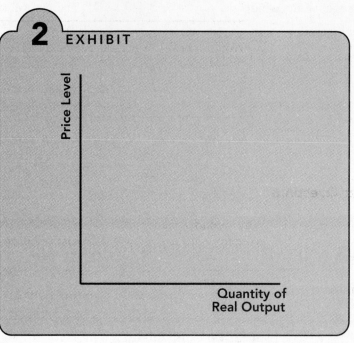

2 EXHIBIT

Price Level

Quantity of Real Output

d. Describe the sequence of events shown in the graph you created in part *c* above.

_____

_____

e. Did the activist fiscal policy stabilize or destabilize the economy? Explain.

_____

_____

_____

2. Suppose the Fed repeatedly announces that it desires price stability and that it is aiming for 0 percent inflation. However, it consistently generates 3 percent inflation.
   a. Will this type of behavior on the part of the Fed reduce unemployment below the natural rate in the long run? Why?

_____

_____

_____

_____

b. Once people have formed expectations of 3 percent inflation, what would happen in the short-run if the Fed actually did target zero inflation?

_____

_____

_____

c. Would it help if Congress passed a law requiring the Fed to target zero inflation? Explain your answer.

_____

_____

_____

Short-Answer Questions

1. Why would an improvement in our ability to forecast shocks to the macro-economy improve our use of activist stabilization policy?

   _____

   _____

   _____

2. What three reasons are given in support of a monetary policy rule?

   _____

   _____

   _____

3. Why are the costs of inflation permanent but the costs of reducing inflation temporary?

   _____

   _____

   _____

4. What could the government do to reduce the cost of continuous inflation?

   _____

   _____

5. In what two ways does a government budget deficit harm future generations?

   _____

   _____

   _____

   _____

6. Does a balanced government budget guarantee the elimination of all redistributions of wealth across generations? Explain.

_____

_____

_____

7. For an increase in the after-tax return to saving to cause an increase in saving, which effect must outweigh the other—the substitution effect or the income effect? Why?

_____

_____

_____

_____

_____

8. Why will reforming our tax laws to encourage saving tend to increase the tax burden on the poor?

_____

_____

_____

SELF-TEST

True/False Questions

_____ 1. Monetary policy affects the economy with a lag, but fiscal policy has no lag.

_____ 2. Discretionary monetary policy suffers from time inconsistency because policymakers have an incentive to engage in a policy that differs from their policy announcements.

_____ 3. The political business cycle refers to a situation where corporate executives also hold political office.

_____ 4. Opponents of a monetary policy rule argue that a rule would make it more difficult for the Fed to respond to an unusual crisis.

_____ 5. Supporters of a zero inflation target for monetary policy argue that the cost of reducing inflation is temporary while the benefits of reducing inflation are permanent.

_____ 6. Those opposed to a zero inflation target for monetary policy argue that many of the costs of inflation can be eliminated by inflation-indexed taxes and bonds.

_____ 7. Government budget deficits tend to redistribute wealth from the current generation to future generations.

_____ 8. The United States has only incurred government budget deficits during wars and recessions.

_____ 9. Replacing the income tax with a consumption tax may increase saving, but it will tend to benefit the rich more than the poor.

_____ 10. A reduction in taxes on interest income will increase saving if the substitution effect from the increase in after-tax interest outweighs the income effect.

Multiple-Choice Questions

1. Suppose that the economy is suffering from pessimism on the part of consumers and firms. Which of the following is an activist stabilization policy that "leans against the wind"?
   a. Policymakers should decrease the money supply.
   b. Policymakers should increase taxes.
   c. Policymakers should decrease government spending.
   d. Policymakers should decrease interest rates.
   e. None of the above is true.

2. Economists who argue that policymakers should *not* try to stabilize the economy make all of the following arguments *except:*
   a. Since stabilization policy affects the economy with a lag, well-intended policy could be destabilizing.
   b. Since forecasting shocks to the economy is difficult, well-intended policy could be destabilizing.
   c. Stabilization policy has no effect on the economy in the short run or the long run.
   d. The first rule of policymaking should be "do no harm."

3. Fluctuations in the economy caused by policymakers' manipulation of the economy for the purpose of affecting electoral outcomes is known as the
   a. political business cycle.
   b. time inconsistency of policy.
   c. discretionary effect.
   d. substitution effect.
   e. income effect.

4. The discrepancy between policy announcements and policy actions is known as the
   a. political business cycle.
   b. time inconsistency of policy.
   c. discretionary effect.
   d. substitution effect.
   e. income effect.

5. Economists who argue that monetary policy should be made by a rule make all of the following arguments *except:*
   a. A policy rule limits the incompetence of policymakers.
   b. A policy rule limits the abuse of power of policymakers.
   c. A policy rule is more flexible than discretionary policy.
   d. A policy rule eliminates the time inconsistency problem.

6. Which of the following is an example of a discretionary policy action that further destabilizes the economy?
   a. Investors become pessimistic, and the Fed responds with a reduction in interest rates.
   b. Consumers become pessimistic, and fiscal policymakers respond with a reduction in taxes.
   c. Investors become excessively optimistic, and the Fed responds with a reduction in the money supply.
   d. Consumers become pessimistic, and fiscal policymakers respond with a reduction in government spending.

592 **PART 13**   FINAL THOUGHTS

7. Economists who support a zero inflation target for monetary policy make all of the following arguments *except:*
   a. Even small levels of inflation impose permanent costs on the economy such as shoeleather costs and menu costs.
   b. Inflation erodes peoples' incomes and zero inflation eliminates this problem.
   c. The cost of reducing inflation to zero is temporary while the benefits are permanent.
   d. The cost of reducing inflation to zero could be nearly eliminated if a zero inflation policy were credible.

8. A government budget deficit tends to
   a. redistribute wealth from future generations to the current generation.
   b. redistribute wealth from the current generation to future generations.
   c. have no redistributive effects.
   d. do none of the above.

9. Which of the following is *not* true with regard to government budget deficits?
   a. Budget deficits place the burden of current spending on future taxpayers.
   b. Budget deficits reduce national saving.
   c. Budget deficits should be scrutinized because they are the only way to transfer wealth across generations of taxpayers.
   d. Budget deficits reduce capital investment, future productivity, and therefore, future incomes.

10. Which of the following is a cost of inflation?
    a. shoeleather costs associated with reduced money holdings
    b. menu costs associated with frequent adjustment of prices
    c. confusion and inconvenience resulting from a changing unit of account
    d. all of the above

11. Economists who argue that the government need not balance its budget make all of the following arguments *except:*
    a. The national debt per person is actually quite small compared to a person's lifetime earnings.
    b. The effects of budget deficits can be somewhat offset if the current generation saves more and leaves bequests to the next generation.
    c. Budget deficits will not become an increasing burden as long as they do not grow more quickly than a nation's nominal income.
    d. Budget deficits increase future growth because they transfer wealth from the present generation to future generations.

12. Which of the following changes to tax laws would encourage more saving but also increase the tax burden on low-income people?
    a. reduce taxes on the return to saving
    b. remove the double taxation on capital income from stocks
    c. reduce inheritance taxes
    d. replace the income tax with a consumption tax
    e. all of the above

13. A reduction in taxes that increases the after-tax return to saving will increase the quantity of saving in the economy if the
    a. substitution effect from the increase in after-tax return to saving exceeds the income effect.
    b. income effect from the increase in after-tax return to saving exceeds the substitution effect.
    c. income effect from the increase in after-tax return to saving equals the substitution effect.
    d. policy is time inconsistent.

14. Tax reform that encourages saving tends to
    a. shift the tax burden toward high-income people away from low-income people.
    b. shift the tax burden toward low-income people away from high-income people.
    c. reduce the rate of growth of output.
    d. reduce the deficit.

15. If discretionary monetary policy is time inconsistent,
    a. the long-run Phillips curve shifts to the right.
    b. the long-run Phillips curve shifts to the left.
    c. the short-run Phillips curve shifts upward.
    d. the short-run Phillips curve shifts downward.

ADVANCED CRITICAL THINKING

Those opposed to government budget deficits argue, among other things, that budget deficits redistribute wealth across generations by allowing the current generation to enjoy the benefits of government spending while future generations must pay for it.

1. Under which of the following cases would you argue that there is a greater intergenerational transfer of wealth? Why?

   a. The government increases spending on social programs by buying apples and oranges for the poor but refuses to raise taxes and instead increases the budget deficit.
   b. The government increases spending on bridges, roads, and buildings but refuses to raise taxes and instead increases the budget deficit.

   _____

   _____

   _____

   _____

   _____

2. Does the preceding example provide a method by which we might judge when a government budget deficit is fair to each generation and when it is not? Explain.

   _____

   _____

   _____

3. Why might this method be difficult to enforce in practice?

   _____

   _____

   _____

SOLUTIONS

Terms and Definitions

_3_ "Leaning against the wind"

_2_ Destabilizing policy

_5_ Discretionary policy

_1_ Political business cycle

_4_ Time inconsistency of policy

Practice Problems

1. a. See Exhibit 3.

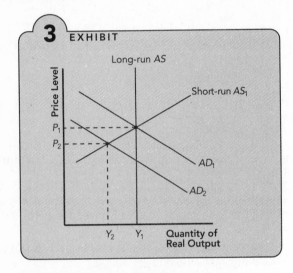

3 EXHIBIT

b. Increase the money supply, increase government spending, decrease taxes. Shift aggregate demand to the right.

c. See Exhibit 4.

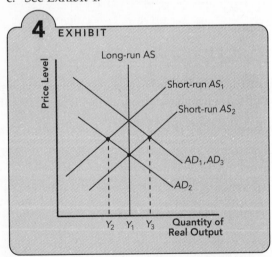

4 EXHIBIT

d. As short-run aggregate supply shifts downward, the economy adjusts to the intersection of short-run AS_2 and AD_2. Then the expansionary aggregate demand policy shifts aggregate demand to AD_3 and the economy moves to the intersection of short-run AS_2 and AD_3.

   e. Destabilize, because the economy had already adjusted back to the long-run natural rate so the increase in aggregate demand caused output to rise above the natural rate.

2. a. No. In the long run, people will grow to expect 3 percent inflation and wages and prices will rise accordingly.

   b. We would move down a short-run Phillips curve and inflation would fall while unemployment would rise above the natural rate.

   c. Yes. The Fed's announcement of a zero inflation target would be more credible, and the movement toward zero inflation would create a smaller increase in unemployment.

Short-Answer Questions

1. Macroeconomic shocks need to be forecast months or years into the future because there are lags in the implementation of activist stabilization policy.

2. A rule limits incompetence, abuse of power, and time inconsistency.

3. Inflation imposes continuous costs on the economy such as shoeleather costs and menu costs. Reducing inflation to zero will increase unemployment only temporarily, but it will eliminate the continuous costs of inflation.

4. Index the tax system and issue inflation-indexed bonds.

5. It increases future taxes and lowers future incomes because it reduces the capital stock.

6. No. An increase in Social Security benefits paid for by an increase in the payroll tax moves income from working people to retired people, yet the budget deficit is unaffected.

7. The substitution effect must outweigh the income effect. An increase in after-tax interest causes people to save more as people substitute saving for current consumption. However, the income effect of an increase in after-tax interest causes people to reduce the amount of saving necessary to reach a targeted amount of saving.

8. High-income people save more than low-income people, so the tax relief would go disproportionately to the rich. Also, to maintain tax revenue, consumption taxes might have to be raised causing an additional burden on the poor.

True/False Questions

1. F; fiscal policy has a long decision lag due to the political process.
2. T
3. F; a political business cycle results when policymakers manipulate the economy to improve the incumbent's chance of re-election.
4. T
5. T
6. T
7. F; government budget deficits redistribute wealth to the current generation from future generations.
8. F; from 1980 through 1995, the United States has incurred budget deficits during peace and prosperity.
9. T
10. T

Multiple-Choice Questions

1. d
2. c
3. a
4. b
5. c
6. d
7. b
8. a
9. c
10. d
11. d
12. e
13. a
14. b
15. c

Advanced Critical Thinking

1. Case *a*, because the government purchased consumption goods that cannot be enjoyed by later generations, while in case *b* the government purchased capital, which is durable and can be enjoyed by later generations.
2. It is more reasonable for the government to run a budget deficit and force future generations to pay for current expenditures if the expenditures are for capital goods.
3. Nearly every interest group can defend their spending as if it has a positive impact on future generations—military, education, etc.